# CAMBRIDGE LATIN AMERICAN STUDIES

GENERAL EDITOR
SIMON COLLIER

ADVISORY COMMITTEE
MARVIN BERNSTEIN, MALCOLM DEAS
CLARK W. REYNOLDS, ARTURO VALENZUELA

63

THE POLITICAL ECONOMY OF
CENTRAL AMERICA SINCE 1920

# THE POLITICAL ECONOMY OF CENTRAL AMERICA SINCE 1920

## VICTOR BULMER-THOMAS
*Queen Mary College, London University*

DISCARD

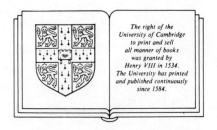

The right of the
University of Cambridge
to print and sell
all manner of books
was granted by
Henry VIII in 1534.
The University has printed
and published continuously
since 1584.

## CAMBRIDGE UNIVERSITY PRESS

*Cambridge*
*New York   New Rochelle   Melbourne   Sydney*

Published by the Press Syndicate of the University of Cambridge
The Pitt Building, Trumpington Street, Cambridge CB2 1RP
32 East 57th Street, New York, NY 10022, USA
10 Stamford Road, Oakleigh, Melbourne 3166, Australia

First published 1987

Printed in Great Britain at The Bath Press, Avon

*British Library cataloguing in publication data*
Bulmer-Thomas, V.
The political economy of Central America
since 1920. —— (Cambridge Latin American
studies; 63).
1. Central America —— Economic conditions
2. Central America —— Politics and government
I. Title
330.9728'05 HC141

*Library of Congress cataloguing in publication data*
Bulmer-Thomas, V.
The political economy of Central America since 1920.
(Cambridge Latin American studies; 63)
Bibliography.
Includes index.
1. Central America —— Economic policy. I. Title.
II. Series.
HC141.B78 1987    338.9728    87–11779

ISBN 0 521 34284 8 hard covers
ISBN 0 521 34839 0 paperback

# Contents

|  |  | page |
|---|---|---|
| *List of figures* |  | viii |
| *List of tables* |  | ix |
| *Preface* |  | xiii |
| *List of acronyms* |  | xvi |
| *Table of official exchange rate parities to US dollar* |  | xxiii |
| *Map: Central America* |  | xxiv |

**1 A century of independence: foundations of export-led growth** — 1
Integration into the world economy — 2
Pitfalls of export-led growth — 10
The political context — 16
The social structure — 20

**2 Central America in the 1920s: reform and consolidation** — 25
The 1920–1 depression and the export-led model — 26
Monetary and financial reform — 28
Consolidation of the export-led model — 33
Economic development outside the export economy — 38
Political repercussions — 43

**3 The 1929 depression** — 48
Onset of the depression — 49
Impact of the depression outside the external sector — 55
Social unrest — 58
Political change – the rise of *caudillismo* — 61

**4 Economic recovery and political reaction in the 1930s** — 68
Policy responses in the 1930s — 69
Export promotion and export diversification — 74
Import substitution and economic recovery — 79
Economic recovery and the new political model — 82

5   Central America and the Second World War                      87
    Hemispheric defence and US strategic interests               88
    Exports, imports and the balance of payments                 91
    Money, finance and inflation                                 95
    The challenge to *caudillismo*                               100

6   Post-war economic recovery                                  105
    The boom in traditional exports                             107
    Agricultural diversification                                110
    Private sector development outside agriculture              116
    Policy and performance in the public sector                 121
    Capitalist modernisation                                    125

7   The struggle for democracy, the Cold War and the Labour
    movement in the first post-war decade                       130
    The rebirth of the Labour movement                          131
    The years of reaction, 1947–50                              133
    The crisis of 1954                                          140
    External actors in the first post-war decade                144
    Conclusions                                                 148

8   The foundations of modern export-led growth, 1954–60        150
    The crisis in traditional exports                           151
    Export diversification and agro-industrial development      156
    Agriculture for internal consumption                        160
    From foreign exchange abundance to balance of payments
    crisis                                                      165
    The formation of the Central American Common Market         171

9   The illusion of a golden age, 1960–70                       175
    The Central American Common Market (CACM) and the
    strategy of industrialisation                               177
    The fiscal crisis                                           180
    The agricultural response to the CACM and the hybrid model  185
    Industrialisation and the CACM                              190
    Crisis in the hybrid model                                  195

10  External shocks and the challenge to the social order, 1970–9  200
    Agriculture and the marginalisation of the peasantry        201
    The decline of the CACM and industrial strategy             207
    Inflation, debt and the public sector                       212
    The state, the Labour movement and real wages               218
    The fall of Somoza and the challenge to US hegemony         225

11  The descent into regional crisis                                    230
    The challenge of *Sandinismo*                                       232
    The balance of payments crisis                                      237
    Stabilisation programmes and the burden of adjustment              244
    Growth and adjustment in Nicaragua                                  252
    National and international responses to the crisis                  258

12  Conclusions                                                         267
    Macroeconomic performance over the long-run                         268
    The export-led model                                                275
    Reform and the labour movement                                      279
    External influence, economic policy and political change            284
    The 1979 crisis in historical perspective                           291

    *Methodological Appendix*                                           295
    *Statistical Appendix*                                              307
    *Notes*                                                             338
    *Bibliography*                                                      387
    *Index*                                                             403

# Figures

|  |  | *page* |
|---|---|---|
| 3.1 | Central America: imports and exports ($ million), 1927–36 | 52 |
| 3.2 | Barter terms of trade (1928 = 100), 1921–39 | 53 |
| 5.1 | Central America: gold and foreign exchange holdings at year-end ($ million), 1939–45 | 96 |
| 5.2 | Central America: money-supply at year-end ($ million), 1939–45 | 98 |
| 6.1 | Central America: coffee exports by value ($ million), 1944–54 | 111 |
| 10.1 | Public external debt at year-end ($ million), 1970–9 | 217 |

# Tables

|     |                                                                                                 | page |
|-----|-------------------------------------------------------------------------------------------------|------|
| 1.1 | Bank origins in Central America                                                                  | 4    |
| 1.2 | Railway origins in Central America                                                               | 6    |
| 1.3 | Central America: exports by value, 1913, in US dollars                                           | 8    |
| 1.4 | Central America: destination of trade (%), 1913 and 1920                                         | 9    |
| 1.5 | Public external debts (1920/1)                                                                   | 14   |
| 1.6 | Urban population centres c. 1920                                                                 | 23   |
| 2.1 | Central America's exports, 1929 (% of total)                                                     | 34   |
| 2.2 | Required and actual rates of growth of domestic use agriculture, 1921–8. Annual geometric rates of change (%) | 39   |
| 3.1 | Central America: coffee exports, 1929–39 (million lb)                                            | 50   |
| 3.2 | Central America: banana exports, 1929–39 (million bunches)                                       | 51   |
| 3.3 | Summary of budget accounts, 1928–36                                                              | 55   |
| 3.4 | Central America: total public debt, 1928–36                                                      | 56   |
| 3.5 | Real GDP per head in the depression                                                              | 58   |
| 4.1 | Central America: Germany's share of imports and exports (%), 1932–9                              | 79   |
| 4.2 | Annual average rates of growth (%) for domestic use agriculture and manufacturing value added at constant (1970) prices, 1921–38 | 80   |
| 5.1 | Central America: external trade shares (%) by main countries, 1939, 1940 and 1945               | 92   |
| 5.2 | Central America: coffee exports (thousand lb), 1939–45                                           | 93   |
| 5.3 | Central America: volume of banana exports (thousand quintals), 1939–45                           | 93   |
| 5.4 | Central America: cost of living index, 1939–45 (1937 = 100)                                      | 100  |
| 6.1 | Central America: banana exports (millions of boxes), 1944–54                                     | 107  |
| 6.2 | Direct foreign investment (million dollars), 1947–54                                             | 108  |
| 6.3 | Annual average rates of growth (%) for domestic use agriculture and export agriculture value added per head at constant 1970 prices, 1944–54 | 115  |
| 6.4 | Central America: profile of the industrial sector, 1950–3                                        | 119  |

6.5   Private investment, 1944–54 120

6.6   Changes in private foreign exchange holdings abroad
(thousand dollars), 1947–54 128

8.1   Coffee yields (kg per hectare) 1950, 1958/9 and 1961/2 154

8.2   Central America: value of traditional exports, 1954–60,
(million dollars) 155

8.3   Volume and value of cotton exports, 1954–60 157

8.4   Beef exports ($ million) 158

8.5   Agricultural landless workers (early 1960s) 162

8.6   Land tenure and land cultivation, 1950–2 and 1961–6 163

8.7   Net trade in cereals (thousand metric tons) 164

8.8   Central America: net output per person in domestic use
agriculture (constant 1970 dollars), 1954 and 1960 165

9.1   The structure of taxation (as percentage of government
revenue), 1960, 1965 and 1970 182

9.2   Central government current revenue (as percentage of GDP),
1960, 1965 and 1970 184

9.3   Commercial bank credit to agriculture (including livestock)
at year-end ($ million), 1961, 1965 and 1970 186

9.4   Net output at 1970 prices ($ million) for cotton, beef and
sugar, 1960, 1965 and 1970 187

9.5   Exports of traditional products as percentage of total extra-
regional exports in 1970 188

9.6   Import intensity in industry in Central America in 1970 ($
million) 193

9.7   Income distribution: wage shares (%), 1960 and 1971 197

10.1  Annual average inflation rates (%) in Central America, 1950–
79 202

10.2  Basic grains net output per person (1970 dollars), 1970–9 206

10.3  Modern industrial sector concentration, 1961–5 and
1975–9 210

10.4  Sectoral distribution of industrial value added (%), 1969 and
1978–9 211

10.5  Tax revenue as percentage of national GDP, 1970, 1975 and
1979 213

10.6  Real public expenditure per person (1970 dollars) on health
and education, 1970, 1975 and 1979 215

10.7  Real wages in Central America (1970 = 100) 219

11.1  Balance of payments contributions to cumulative reserve
losses, 1978–82 238

11.2  Contributions to deterioration in current account deficit,
1978–81 240

11.3  Responses to balance of payments crisis 241

11.4 Disbursed public external debt: increase from end-1978 to
     end-1981 ($ million)                                         243
11.5 Imports in nominal and real terms ($ million), 1978–83       248
11.6 Indicators of burden of adjustment, 1980–3                   251
12.1 Central America: trade coefficients (%), 1920–84             269
12.2 Agriculture's share of GDP (%), 1920–84                      271
12.3 Manufacturing share of GDP (%), 1920–84                      273

*For my parents*

# Preface

Central America since 1979 has been in the grip of a regional crisis with many dimensions. There have been civil wars in three countries (El Salvador, Guatemala and Nicaragua) producing substantial loss of life and a massive refugee problem. The consolidation of a Marxist régime in Nicaragua and the revolutionary challenge from Marxist guerrilla movements in El Salvador and Guatemala has turned Central America into an area of East–West conflict with the Sandinista government in Nicaragua increasingly reliant on support from Cuba and the Soviet Union, and the other Central American republics (Costa Rica, El Salvador, Guatemala and Honduras) in receipt of unprecedented aid flows from the United States of America. Efforts by Latin American countries in the Contadora group (Colombia, Mexico, Panama and Venezuela) have since 1983 been aimed at reducing regional tension in Central America, but the crisis has not diminished and living standards in all five republics have fallen sharply.

The current crisis has been widely studied and there is general recognition that economic factors help to account for its origins. There is, however, a certain amount of confusion about the nature of these economic factors, which is very understandable. First, for several decades prior to the current crisis economic performance in Central America on the basis of conventional indicators (e.g. growth rates, inflation rates) looked satisfactory. Secondly, all five republics followed roughly the same economic model before 1979, but social and political upheaval in Costa Rica and Honduras has been much less severe since 1979 than in the other three republics. The role of economic factors in the generation of the current crisis is therefore not immediately obvious.

The purpose of this book is to examine the nature of economic development in Central America and to resolve the confusion over the part played by economic factors in the current crisis. This is a matter of some urgency since the internationalisation of the Central American crisis has provoked a series of 'blueprints' for the future, which show little understanding of the role of economic factors and run the risk of recreating in the future the conditions which contributed to the current crisis in the first place. Much can be learnt from the way the economic model functioned (or failed to function) in each republic before 1979, and this information needs to be incorporated in future plans.

I have chosen 1920 as the starting point of this book for several reasons. First, the 1920s marked the consolidation of the export-led model (based on coffee and bananas) inherited from the second half of the nineteenth century, which had an overwhelming influence on social and political relations in each republic. Secondly, the 1920s represented a decade in which – despite a brief depression in 1920–1 – the export-led model operated under relatively optimal external conditions, so that it is possible to explore how in practice the model worked in each republic when the external stimulus was favourable. By contrast, a study of the 1930s allows us to observe the impact on the home economy and social and political relations under extremely adverse external conditions.

In order to provide a quantitative basis for many of the judgements in this book, I have extended the official national accounts for each republic back to 1920. I began this work in 1981 as part of a project on Latin America in the 1930s (see Thorp (ed.), 1984) and the series (see the Statistical Appendix) runs from 1920 to 1984, although the book itself covers the period 1920 to 1986. Reference is frequently made in the text to the Statistical Appendix to avoid excessive use of tables. The Statistical Appendix consists of fifteen tables each marked by the prefix 'A' (e.g. Gross Domestic Product is given as Table A.1 in the Statistical Appendix).

The book carries the phrase 'political economy' in the title rather than 'economic development' or 'economic history'. At its most basic, the label 'political economy' simply permits the author to stray beyond economics into one or several related disciplines – a licence which is clearly essential in the case of Central America. At a more sophisticated level, it permits the author to try and forge the links between economic development and political change without resorting to vulgar historical materialism. This has been my purpose in this book, which accounts for the chronological treatment of the material.

Although Central America has had no political unity in the period covered by this book, it has had a certain 'economic unity' as a result of its subjection to common external influences; these influences have filtered through domestic institutions to affect each economy in slightly different ways. Thus, the region exhibits both conformity and diversity and the problem facing an author is to see the one without losing sight of the other. Many books on Central America have fallen into this trap, so that the number of outstanding books on Central America since independence (e.g. Munro (1918), Kepner and Southill (1935), Torres Rivas (1973)) is quite small. Needless to say, I hope that this book will be included among the latter, but that is something which readers will have to decide for themselves.

I began writing this book in 1981, although I have been concerned with Central American questions for some twenty years in various capacities. During that time, I have received exceptional support, advice and kindness from individuals in all five republics. In particular, I would like to thank Edelberto Torres Rivas in Costa Rica, Francisco Serrano in El Salvador, Enrique Delgado in Guatemala, Mario Posas in Honduras and Xavier Gorostiaga in Nicaragua for their patience and understanding in dealing with innumerable requests for information and opinions. I have also been given access to unpublished information in each republic, which would be difficult to obtain even in my own country (United Kingdom). I am immensely grateful for this support, which I hope has made the book a better one. I am also grateful for the financial assistance I have received in support of this book from the British Academy and London University

In writing this book, I owe a special debt to Rosemary Thorp. Since 1981 she has organised two workshops (on Latin America in the 1930s and the contemporary Latin American debt crisis), which gave me the opportunity not only to work on Central America during those periods, but also to develop my ideas in a stimulating and critical environment of international scholars, which included Charles Kindleberger and Carlos Díaz-Alejandro. The latter's premature death was a great shock to all members of the workshop for Carlos' contribution to all our researches, including this book, was enormous.

# Acronyms

| | |
|---|---|
| AFL-CIO | American Federation of Labor – Congress of Industrial Organisations |
| AIFLD | American Institute for Free Labor Development |
| ANACH | Asociación Nacional de Campesinos Hondureños (National Association of Honduran Peasants) |
| ANDES | Asociación Nacional de Educadores Salvadoreños (National Association of Salvadorean Teachers) |
| ANEP | Asociación Nacional de la Empresa Privada (National Private Enterprise Association – El Salvador) |
| APP | Area Propiedad del Pueblo (Area of Public Ownership – Nicaragua) |
| APROH | Asociación para el Progreso de Honduras (Association for Honduran Advancement) |
| ATC | Asociación de Trabajadores del Campo (Association of Rural Workers – Nicaragua) |
| ATLAS | Agrupación de Trabajadores Latino-Americanos Sindicalizados (Federation of Latin American Trade Unionists) |
| BANAMER | Grupo Banco de America (Bank of America Conglomeration – Nicaragua) |
| BANIC | Grupo Banco Nicaragüense (Bank of Nicaragua Conglomeration) |
| BCCR | Banco Central de Costa Rica (Central Bank of Costa Rica) |
| BCIE | Banco Centroamericano de Integración Económica (Central American Bank of Economic Integration) |
| BOP | Balance of Payments |
| BPAU | Bulletin of the Pan-American Union |
| CABEI | Central American Bank for Economic Integration |
| CACIF | Cámara de Agricultura, Comercio, Industria y Finanza (Chamber of Agriculture, Trade, Industry and Finance – Guatemala) |

xvi

| | |
|---|---|
| CACM | Central American Common Market |
| CAN | Comité de Alto Nivel (High Level Committee – set up to revive CACM) |
| CAT | Certificado de Abonos Tributarios (Tax Credit Certificate) |
| CBI | Caribbean Basin Initiative |
| CCO | Comité Coordinador Obrero (Workers' Coordinating Committee – Honduras) |
| CCTD | Confederación Costarricense de Trabajadores Democráticos (Costa Rican Confederation of Democratic Workers) |
| CCTRN | Confederación Católica de Trabajadores Rerum Novarum (Catholic Workers' Confederation Rerum Novarum – Costa Rica) |
| CD | Christian Democrat |
| CEDOH | Centro de Documentación de Honduras (Honduran Documentation Centre) |
| CEPAL | Comisión Económica para América Latina (Economic Commission for Latin America) |
| CET | Common External Tariff |
| CFTU | International Confederation of Free Trade Unions |
| CGS | Confederación General de Sindicatos (General Confederation of Trade Unions – El Salvador) |
| CGT | Confederación General de Trabajadores (General Workers' Confederation – Costa Rica) |
| CGTC | Confederación General de Trabajadores Costarricenses (General Confederation of Costa Rican Workers) |
| CGTG | Confederación General de Trabajadores de Guatemala (General Confederation of Guatemalan Workers) |
| CIA | Central Intelligence Agency |
| CLAT | Confederación Latinoamericano de Trabajadores (Latin American Workers' Confederation) |
| CNCG | Confederación Nacional Campesina de Guatemala (Guatemalan National Peasants' Confederation) |
| CNUS | Comité Nacional de Unidad Sindical (National Committee for Labour Unity – Guatemala) |
| COCTN | Comité Organizador de la Confederación de Trabajadores Nicaragüense (Nicaraguan Organising Committee for the Workers' Confederation) |
| CODESA | Corporación Costarricense de Desarrollo (Costa Rican Development Corporation) |
| CONADI | Corporación Nacional de Inversiones (National Investment Corporation – Honduras) |

| | |
|---|---|
| CONDECA | Consejo de Defensa Centroamericano (Central American Defence Council) |
| CORFINA | Corporación Financiera Nacional (National Finance Corporation – Guatemala) |
| COSEP | Consejo Superior de la Empresa Privada (Private Enterprise Council – Nicaragua) |
| CROS | Comité de Reorganización Obrero Sindical (Trade Unionists' Reorganising Committee – El Salvador) |
| CST | Central Sandinista de Trabajadores (Sandinista Workers' Federation – Nicaragua) |
| CSUCA | Consejo Superior Universitario Centroamericano (University Council of Central America) |
| CTAL | Confederación de Trabajadores de América Latina (Latin American Workers' Confederation) |
| CTCR | Confederación de Trabajadores de Costa Rica (Costa Rican Workers' Confederation) |
| CTG | Confederación de Trabajadores de Guatemala (Guatemalan Workers' Confederation) |
| CTN | Confederación de Trabajadores de Nicaragua (Nicaraguan Workers' Confederation) |
| CUC | Comité de Unidad Campesina (Committee for Peasant Unity – Guatemala) |
| CUS | Comité de Unidad Sindical (Committee for Labour Unity – Honduras) |
| CUTS | Confederación Unificada de Trabajadores Salvadoreños (United Confederation of Salvadorean Workers) |
| DCE | Domestic Credit Expansion |
| DFI | Direct Foreign Investment |
| DGEC | Dirección General de Estadísticas y Censos (Office of Statistics and Censuses – Costa Rica) |
| DUA | Domestic Use Agriculture |
| ECLA | Economic Commission for Latin America |
| EEC | European Economic Community |
| EFF | Extended Fund Facility |
| ENABAS | Empresa Nicaragüense de Alimentos Basicos (National Foodstuffs Enterprise – Nicaragua) |
| ERP | Effective Rate of Protection |
| EXA | Export Agriculture |
| FAO | Food and Agriculture Organisation |
| FAPU | Frente de Acción Popular Unificada (United Popular Action Front – El Salvador) |
| FARO | Frente de Agricultores de la Región Oriental (Eastern Farmers' Front – El Salvador) |

| | |
|---|---|
| FASGUA | Federación Autónoma Sindical de Guatemala (Guatemalan Independent Labour Federation) |
| FDR | Frente Democrático Revolucionario (Democratic Revolutionary Front) |
| FECCAS | Federación Cristiana de Campesinos Salvadoreños (Christian Federation of Salvadorean Rural Workers) |
| FECORAH | Federación de Cooperativas de la Reforma Agraria de Honduras (Honduran Federation of Land Reform Cooperatives) |
| FENACH | Federación Nacional de Campesinos de Honduras (Honduran National Peasant Federation) |
| FENAGH | Federación Nacional de Agricultores y Ganaderos de Honduras (National Federation of Honduran Farmers and Ranchers) |
| FMLN | Frente Farabundo Martí para la Liberación Nacional (Farabundo Martí National Liberation Front – El Salvador) |
| FSG | Federación Sindical de Guatemala (Guatemalan Labour Federation) |
| FSLN | Frente Sandinista de Liberación Nacional (Sandinista National Liberation Front – Nicaragua) |
| FUNC | Frente de Unidad Campesina (Front for Peasant Unity – Honduras) |
| FUR | Frente Unido de la Revolución (United Revolutionary Front – Guatemala) |
| GDP | Gross Domestic Product |
| IBRD | International Bank for Reconstruction and Development |
| IIC | Integration Industries' Convention |
| IMF | International Monetary Fund |
| INA | Instituto Nacional de Aprendizaje (National Apprenticeship Institute – Costa Rica) |
| INCEI | Instituto Nacional de Comercio Exterior y Interior (National Institute for Domestic and Foreign Commerce – Nicaragua) |
| INFONAL | Instituto de Fomento Nacional (National Development Institute – Nicaragua) |
| INFOP | Instituto Hondureño de Formación Profesional (Salvadorean Institute for Professional Training) |
| INSAFI | Instituto Salvadoreño de Fomento Industrial (Salvadorean Institute for Industrial Development) |
| INTA | Instituto Nacional de Transformación Agraria (National Institute for Agrarian Transformation – El Salvador) |

| | |
|---|---|
| INTAL | Instituto par la Integración de America Latina (Institute for Latin American Integration) |
| INVU | Instituto Nacional de Vivienda y Urbanismo (National Institute for Housing and Urbanisation – Costa Rica) |
| IRA | Instituto Regulador de Abastecimientos (Institute for Regulating Food Supply – El Salvador) |
| IRCA | International Railways of Central America |
| ISA | Import Substitution in Agriculture |
| ISI | Import Substitution in Industry |
| ISTA | Instituto Salvadoreño de Transformación Agraria (Salvadorean Institute for Agrarian Transformation) |
| ITCO | Instituto de Tierras y Colonización (Institute for Lands and Colonisation – Costa Rica) |
| JGRN | Junta de Gobierno de Reconstrucción Nacional (Governing Junta for National Reconstruction – Nicaragua) |
| LDC | Less Developed Country |
| MNE | Multinational Enterprise |
| MT | Multilateral Treaty on Free Trade and Central American Economic Integration |
| NACLA | North American Congress on Latin America |
| NAUCA | Nomenclatura Arancelaria Uniforme Centroamericana (Central American Uniform Tariff Nomenclature) |
| OAS | Organisation of American States |
| ODECA | Organización de Estados Centroamericanos (Organisation of Central American States) |
| OPEC | Organisation of Petroleum Exporting Countries |
| ORDEN | Organización Democrática Nacionalista (Democratic National Organisation – El Salvador) |
| ORIT | Organización Regional Interamericana de Trabajadores (Interamerican Regional Labour Organisation) |
| PAR | Partido Acción Revolucionaria (Revolutionary Action Party – Guatemala) |
| PCH | Partido Comunista de Honduras (Communist Party of Honduras) |
| PDRH | Partido Democrático Revolucionario Hondureño (Democratic Revolutionary Party of Honduras) |
| PGT | Partido Guatemalteco de Trabajadores (Guatemalan Workers' Party) |
| PL | Partido Liberal (Liberal Party – Honduras) |
| PLI | Partido Liberal Independiente (Independent Liberal Party – Nicaragua) |
| PLN | Partido Liberación Nacional (National Liberation Party – Costa Rica) |

| | |
|---|---|
| PN | Partido Nacional (National Party – Honduras) |
| PRAM | Partido Revolucionario Abril y Mayo (April and May Revolutionary Party – El Salvador) |
| PREALC | Programa Regional Del Empleo para América Latina y El Caribe (Regional Employment Programme for Latin America and the Caribbean) |
| PRUD | Partido Revolucionario de Unificación Democrático (Revolutionary Party of Democratic Unity – El Salvador) |
| PSBR | Public Sector Borrowing Requirement |
| PSC | Partido Socialcristiano (Social Christian Party – Nicaragua) |
| PSD | Partido Social Demócrata (Social Democratic Party – Costa Rica) |
| PSN | Partido Socialista Nicaragüense (Nicaraguan Socialist Party) |
| PTN | Partido Trabajador Nicaragüense (Nicaraguan Workers' Party) |
| PUD | Partido Unión Democrática (Democratic Union Party – El Salvador) |
| PUN | Partido Unión Nacional (National Union Party – Costa Rica) |
| RN | Revolución Nacional (National Revolution Party – Guatemala) |
| SIECA | Secretaria de Integración Económica Centroamericana (Secretariat for Central American Economic Integration) |
| SITRATERCO | Sindicato de Trabajadores de la Tela Railroad Co. (Trade Union for Tela Railroad Co. Workers – Honduras) |
| SUTRASFCO | Sindicato Unificado de Trabajadores de la Standard Fruit Co. (Trade Union for Standard Fruit Co. Workers – Honduras) |
| TEC | Tariff Equalization Convention |
| TOT | Terms of Trade |
| TT | Tripartite Treaty |
| UDEL | Unión Democrática de Liberación (Democratic Liberation Union – Nicaragua) |
| UFCO | United Fruit Co. |
| UNO | Unión Nacional Opositora (National Opposition Union – El Salvador) |
| UNT | Unión Nacional de Trabajadores (National Workers' Union – El Salvador) |
| UPEB | Unión de Países Exportadores de Banano (Union of Banana Exporting Countries) |
| USAID | United States Agency for International Development |

| | |
|---|---|
| VD | Vanguardia Democrática (Democratic Vanguard Party – Guatemala) |
| VP | Vanguardia Popular (Popular Vanguard Party – Costa Rica) |
| WFTU | World Federation of Trade Unions |

# Table of official exchange rate parities to US dollar

| Currency | Costa Rica Colón | El Salvador Colón | Guatemala Quetzal | Honduras Lempira | Nicaragua Córdoba |
|---|---|---|---|---|---|
| *Year* | | | | | |
| 1920 | 3.34 | 2.0 | 30.56[1] | 2.0[2] | 1.0 |
| 1921 | 4.43 | | 50.56[1] | | |
| 1922 | 4.35 | | 55.30[1] | | |
| 1923 | 4.55 | | 60.2[1] | | |
| 1924 | 4.06 | | 60.0[1] | | |
| 1925 | 4.0 | | 1.0 | | |
| 1932 | 4.4 | 2.54 | | | |
| 1933 | 4.55 | 2.95 | | | |
| 1934 | 4.25 | 2.59 | | | 1.1 |
| 1935 | 5.94 | 2.5 | | | |
| 1936 | 6.13 | | | | |
| 1937 | 5.61 | | | | 2.0 |
| 1938 | | | | | 4.58 |
| 1939 | | | | | 5.0 |
| 1955 | | | | | 7.0 |
| 1961 | 6.625 | | | | |
| 1974 | 8.57 | | | | |
| 1979 | | | | | 10.0 |
| 1981 | 36.09 | | | | |
| 1982 | 40.25 | | | | |
| 1983 | 43.40 | | | | |
| 1984 | 47.75 | | | | |
| 1985 | 53.70 | | | | 28.0 |
| 1986 | 55.75 | 5.0 | 2.5 | | 70.0 |

*Note*: after 1920, only changes in the official parity are recorded.
[1] From 1920 to January 1925, the Guatemalan currency was the peso. It was replaced by the quetzal at the rate of 60 pesos per quetzal.
[2] From 1920 to March 1931, the Honduran currency was the peso. It was replaced at par by the lempira.

*Map*: Central America

# 1

# A century of independence: foundations of export-led growth

To much of the outside world, Central America in 1920 was a source of amusement. O. Henry's unflattering description of 'banana republics' in *Cabbages and Kings* (Henry, 1917) had caught the foreigners' imagination and even those who had travelled widely in the region (e.g. Cunningham, 1922) could not resist the lure of characters like Lee Christmas, the former United States railway engineer, who was widely credited with making and breaking governments in the northern republics of Central America. The US occupation of Nicaragua since 1912 did little to encourage the outside world to associate the region with progress and development and the fact that a Nicaraguan President had invited the US marines in the first place probably only made matters worse.

Central Americans, however, viewing the progress of the region in the century since independence,[1] had reasons for feeling a sense of satisfaction. The turmoil of the first fifty years had given way to a half-century (1870–1920) of steady, if not unbroken, economic progress. This was based above all on the solid foundations of two export crops (coffee and bananas), which appeared to be well suited to climatic conditions in Central America and which were absorbed in increasing quantities by the world market. The introduction of crops to Central America of permanent utility to the world market ended a search which had been going on fruitlessly since colonial times (McLeod, 1973). It also solved the problem of how to integrate the region into the world economy (a goal considered desirable by all Central American leaders in the nineteenth century). To facilitate the establishment of coffee and banana production, almost no sacrifice was considered too great and the liberal revolutions of the 1870s were followed by a series of reforms and concessions involving considerable political and social upheaval.

The increase in economic prosperity contributed towards a decline in political turmoil and led to occasional periods of stability based on authoritarian rule. The problem of order began to be solved, although not much progress was made in the direction of political liberty outside of Costa Rica. The Costa Rican example might have been followed elsewhere, if Central America had been left free to work out its own solutions to its peculiar

1

political problems. This was not to be, however, as the rivalry between the European powers before 1914 and the construction of the Panama Canal compelled the United States to take a more active interest in the region's development than it had previously felt necessary.

The rise of a dynamic export sector in the half-century before 1920 transformed the region's social relations. The traditional élite, consisting of a small merchant class and landowners with extensive cattle interests, began to be replaced by a powerful group associated with the export sector either as growers, traders or financiers. This new élite, based fundamentally on coffee, had been activity promoted by the state during the liberal reforms; the effort had been so successful, however, that the new interests came to form a virtual oligarchy exercising economic, social and political influence out of all proportion to their numbers. The new élite absorbed foreigners into its midst without losing its national character and demanded from the state changes in legislation to guarantee an adequate supply of land and labour for the expansion of the export sector. This produced a conflict between the export sector's need for modernisation and traditional forms of land tenure, labour relations, etc., which was generally resolved in favour of the former. In turn, much resentment was created in traditional (mainly Indian) communities, while the labour legislation enacted during this period of liberal rule had a distinctly illiberal flavour.

## Integration into the world economy

Although coffee had been brought to Central America in the latter half of the eighteenth century, the first exports were not attempted until the 1830s, when a German merchant despatched a few sacks from Costa Rica to Chile (Facio, 1972, p. 39). At this time, the obstacles against coffee exports from Central America were almost insurmountable. Grown in the highlands, coffee exports had to be transported to the Pacific along 'roads' which even ox-drawn carts could barely pass (the connection with the Atlantic was even more tenuous). From ports on the Pacific, the coffee then had to pass by way of Cape Horn before gaining access to the lucrative European market or the eastern seaboard of the United States. Despite these obstacles, Costa Rica did in fact begin regular exports of coffee in the 1840s and steps were taken to improve the connections between the Highlands and the Pacific coast; the trade with Europe, furthermore, was made considerably easier by the opening of the railroad across Panama in 1854.

The entry of the rest of Central America into the coffee trade was somewhat later,[2] but by the 1880s it was established throughout the isthmus. From then until the 1920s it enjoyed spectacular growth in El Salvador, Guatemala and Nicaragua. Growth in Costa Rica was more modest, because the period of rapid expansion occurred before the 1880s, while progress in Honduras was impeded by a shortage of labour and the location of the most suitable land in areas where communal ownership was widespread (see Molina, 1982, p. 52). The establishment of the coffee trade was so successful that by 1890 all the republics except Honduras had come to rely heavily on it as a source of foreign exchange earnings. The export trade inherited from the colonial period – involving products such as Peruvian balsam, indigo, hides and skins – was confined to a minor role in both relative and absolute terms. Coffee was king and accounted for 96% of export earnings from Guatemala (1889), 91% from Costa Rica (1890), 71% from Nicaragua (1890) and 66% from El Salvador (1892).

The growth of the coffee trade necessitated an improvement in the inadequate financial system inherited from colonial days. The first commercial bank opened in Costa Rica in 1864 (see Table 1.1) in deference to that republic's early lead in coffee production, but several banks opened their doors in Guatemala in the 1870s and the other republics saw the introduction of modern banking in the 1880s. It is customary to link the spread of modern banking in Central America with the liberal revolutions of the 1870s. A glance at Table 1.1, however, shows that it is perhaps better explained by the spread of coffee production; the most important coffee producers before the First World War (Costa Rica, El Salvador and Guatemala) had by far the best banking facilities, while Honduras (a minor coffee producer) had the worst. The fact that Costa Rica's first bank predates the liberal revolutions in the 1870s should also not be overlooked.

Like coffee production, modern banking was firmly controlled by nationals in the nineteenth century. By 1914, German nationals had acquired an important position in the coffee trade of Guatemala[3] and to a lesser extent of Nicaragua, but they were in general resident in Central America and often married into Central American families. British banks acquired their first foothold in the early twentieth century, but they remained of relatively minor importance. US banks were forbidden from owning affiliates abroad until the administration of Woodrow Wilson and played no role in Central American banking until 1912, when US banking firms acquired a 51% stake in the Banco Nacional de Nicaragua.[4]

The growth of coffee production required improvements in the internal transportation system. From the 1870s onwards, each republic dedicated itself to the construction of a national railway system. The objective was not only to promote trade, but also to achieve national integration; the small Atlantic coast populations, particularly of Honduras and Nicaragua, were virtually a nation within a nation in the nineteenth century[5] and republican governments were deeply concerned that they might fall prey to the ambitions of imperialist countries (see Rossbach and Wunderich, 1985). Early efforts to complete the railway network soon ran into difficulties. The Honduran government issued bonds between 1867 and 1871 for com-

Table 1.1 *Bank origins in Central America*

| | Date | Comments |
|---|---|---|
| *(A) Costa Rica* | | |
| 1. Banco Anglo-Costarricense | 1864 | |
| 2. Banco de Costa Rica | 1877 | Known as Banco de la Unión until 1891 and given a monopoly of note issue from 1884 to 1896 |
| 3. Banco Comercial | 1904 | Failed in 1914. Its assets and liabilities taken over by A(5) in 1915 |
| 4. Banco Mercantil de Costa Rica | 1908 | Affiliated with the Bank of Central and South America |
| 5. Banco Internacional | 1914 | Government-owned |
| 6. Royal Bank of Canada | 1915 | |
| *(B) El Salvador* | | |
| 1. Banco Internacional | 1880 | Monopoly of note issue until 1885 |
| 2. Banco Salvadoreño | 1885 | Known as Banco Particular until 1892. Absorbed B(1) in 1898 |
| 3. Banco Occidental | 1889 | Founded in the city of Santa Ana |
| 4. Banco Agricola Comercial | 1895 | Partly owned by the Anglo-South American Bank Ltd from 1906 |
| 5. Banco de Nicaragua | 1893 | The name was later changed to London Bank of Central America Ltd and the branch in El Salvador was taken over in 1902 by B(2) |
| 6. Banco Nacional | 1907 | Failed in November 1913 |
| *(C) Guatemala* | | |
| 1. Banco Nacional de Guatemala | 1874 | Formed by the government out of property confiscated from the Church in 1873. The bank was liquidated in 1876 |
| 2. Banco Internacional | 1877 | Initially shared monopoly of note issue with C(3) |
| 3. Banco Colombiano | 1878 | |
| 4. Banco de Occidente | 1881 | Founded at Quezaltenango |
| 5. Banco Agrícola-Hipotecario | 1894 | |
| 6. Banco de Guatemala | 1895 | |
| 7. Banco Americano | 1895 | |
| *(D) Honduras* | | |
| 1. Banco de Honduras | 1889 | Monopoly of note issue until creation of D(2) |
| 2. Banco Atlántida | 1913 | Owned and established by Standard Fruit |
| *(E) Nicaragua* | | |
| 1. Banco de Nicaragua | 1887 | Merged with E(3) in 1904. Given monopoly of note issue |

Table 1.1 *(cont.)*

|  | Date | Comments |
|---|---|---|
| 2. Banco Nacional de Nicaragua | 1912 | Set up under the Monetary Law of 1912, 49% of the shares belonged to the government until 1924, when it bought the remainder from US banking firms. Monopoly of note issue |
| 3. Commercial Bank of Spanish America Ltd | 1904 | Formed by a merger of E(1) with the Colombian firm of Enrique Cortés and Co. Taken over by British interests in 1911 |

pletion of a line from Puerto Cortés on the Atlantic coast to the capital, Tegucigalpa, but was the victim of massive fraud by the contractors, and only 57 miles of track were completed, which left the highland capital without a coastal connection (see León Gómez, 1978). In Nicaragua, a line connecting the Pacific port of Corinto with the principal cities of León, Granada and Managua was built in the 1880s, but it never reached the important coffee-growing district of Matagalpa nor the Atlantic coast.

Despite these difficulties, ownership of the Honduran and Nicaraguan lines remained in government hands in the nineteenth century. Elsewhere, financial difficulties led to the granting of concessions to foreign companies, as a result of which ownership of most of the rail network had fallen into foreign hands by 1920 (see Table 1.2). One of the most important concessions granted to foreigners was in Costa Rica, where Minor Keith (nephew of Henry Meggs – the contractor for the Peruvian railways) was given a contract to complete a railroad from San José to the Atlantic coast in 1884, a task that was completed in 1890. Work began at the Atlantic end and Keith, to help defray the considerable costs, started to export bananas grown at the side of the track on concessionary lands. These humble beginnings, which have been fully documented elsewhere (see, for example, Wilson, 1947), led to the spectacular growth of the banana industry in Costa Rica. Similar projects were soon attempted in other Central American republics with an Atlantic seaboard[6] and by 1920 the industry was firmly established in Costa Rica, Guatemala and Honduras, with developments in Nicaragua lagging somewhat behind.

From the start, there were important differences in the impact of the coffee and banana industries in Central America and these help to explain some of the divergences between the five republics in the twentieth century. The differential impact of the two industries on the national economy took many years to manifest itself, but already by 1920 several contrasts were clear.

Table 1.2 _Railway origins in Central America_

| | Area | Mileage | Comments |
|---|---|---|---|
| **(A) Costa Rica** | | | |
| 1. Costa Rica Railway Co. Ltd | Puerto Limón to San José | 189 | The Company was formed in 1886. The complete line was opened in 1890. The Co. leased the line to the Northern Railway Co. of Costa Rica, a subsidiary of United Fruit |
| 2. Ferrocarril del Pacífico (Pacific Railway Co.) | Puntarenas to San José | 80 | The Company is owned and operated by the government. The line was opened in 1909 |
| **(B) El Salvador** | | | |
| 1. The Salvador Railway Co. Ltd | San Salvador to Acajutla and Santa Ana | 100 | Formed and owned by the government in 1882, but later sold to a British company. The complete line was opened in 1909 |
| 2. International Railways of Central America (IRCA) | La Unión to Guatemala via San Salvador | 200 | A subsidiary of the United Fruit Co. The line through El Salvador was not completed until 1927 |
| **(C) Guatemala** | | | |
| 1. International Railways of Central America (IRCA) | From Puerto Barrios to San José via Guatemala City Also lines to El Salvador, Champerico and Ocos | 427 | The Pacific line was completed in 1884; the Atlantic connection in 1908; the connection to El Salvador in 1929. IRCA was formed in 1912 from foreign- and Guatemalan-owned companies |
| 2. Ferrocarril Verapaz | Verapaz | 28 | Used to ship coffee to point of export. Privately owned |
| **(D) Honduras** | | | |
| 1. National Railway | South from Puerto Cortés | 57 | Between 1867 and 1871, the government issued bonds in an effort to construct a railway from the coast to the capital. The government was cheated by the contractors and the line was never completed |

Table 1.2 (*cont.*)

| | Area | Mileage | Comments |
|---|---|---|---|
| *(E) Nicaragua* | | | |
| Ferrocarril del Pacífico de Nicaragua | Corinto to León, Managua and Granada | 165 | Government owned until 1913, when US bankers bought a 51% stake. It connected the capital with the Pacific only and did not reach the important coffee growing area of Matagalpa. Constructed in the 1880s |

Note: In addition to the above lines, the fruit companies in Costa Rica, Guatemala and Honduras owned a network of branch lines used exclusively for transporting bananas.

Although the banana companies responsible for shipping the fruit from Central America to North America or Europe always purchased a certain proportion of their exports from local growers, the industry remained firmly under foreign control. Vertical integration, furthermore, was the rule rather than the exception (in contrast to coffee production) and the fruit companies tended to own or control all aspects of the industry from production to marketing, including internal transportation, loading and shipping. Monopolistic and monopsonistic tendencies became prevalent soon after the foundation of the banana industry, unlike the case of coffee where such tendencies developed slowly and were counteracted to some extent by other forces. The United Fruit Company (UFCO) was formed in 1899 from a series of smaller companies throughout the Caribbean and acquired a monopoly in Costa Rica and Guatemala.[7] In Honduras, UFCO competed with Vaccaro Brothers (later the Standard Fruit and Steamship Co.) and Sam Zemurray's Cuyamel Fruit Co. These three, however, were responsible for virtually all Honduran exports by 1914.

In the case of the coffee industry, the stimulus to railway construction postdates the establishment of exports. With bananas, however, it either predates it (Costa Rica) or is contemporaneous. Since, furthermore, the railroads linked to banana production were owned or run by the fruit companies themselves, they tended to serve no purpose other than the banana trade itself.

Because the banana trade was vertically integrated, export sales led to a demand for banking facilities in North rather than Central America. Local currency was required to meet local expenditures only, most of which consisted of wages and salaries; few workers were in a position to open bank accounts and a high proportion of expenditure returned to the company in the form of payment in company stores. Only one bank in Central America

Table 1.3 *Central America: exports by value, 1913, in US dollars*

| Commodity | Costa Rica | El Salvador | Guatemala | Honduras | Nicaragua |
|---|---|---|---|---|---|
| Coffee | 3,605,029 | 7,495,214 | 12,254,724 | 116,302 | 5,004,449 |
| Bananas | 5,194,428 | | 825,670 | 1,714,398 | 429,802 |
| Precious metals | 1,021,473 | 1,495,805 | | 886,591 | 1,063,077 |
| Hides | 132,883 | 95,870 | 455,476 | 159,820 | 326,599 |
| Timber | 141,361 | | 247,759 | 12,617 | 321,869 |
| Rubber | 44,482 | 18,092 | 100,323 | 14,289 | 278,763 |
| Sugar | | 72,852 | 349,052 | | 31,805 |
| Chicle | | | 142,108 | | |
| Balsam of Peru | | 89,476 | | | |
| Coconuts | | | | 219,968 | |
| Indigo | | 52,984 | | | |
| Cacao | 105,034 | | | | 39,828 |
| Live cattle | | | | 251,361 | 288,009 |
| Total | 10,324,149 | 9,411,112 | 14,449,926 | 3,421,000 | 7,712,047 |
| Bananas and coffee as % of total | 85.2% | 79.6% | 90.5% | 53.5% | 70.5% |

Source: Munro (1918), pp. 266 and 274

owed its origin to the banana trade and that was the Banco Atlántida, founded by the Vaccaro brothers in Honduras in 1913.

The rapid development of the banana industry in the decade leading up to the First World War completed Central America's integration into the world market and brought to maturity the export-led model on which it had been based. By 1913, coffee and bananas (see Table 1.3) had come to dominate the value of exports, with precious metals (gold and silver) the only other exports of any real significance. The export of precious metals, however, was a legacy from the colonial period and had long ago ceased to be a source of much dynamism. The growth of exports had for many years been intimately associated with the growth in production of coffee and bananas.

The outbreak of hostilities in 1914 between the major European powers sent shockwaves through the Central American economy, although the long-run impact (unlike in other parts of Latin America) was to be negligible. The first reaction of European banks was to call in credits extended to coffee farmers on the one hand, and importers on the other. At the same time, the export of commodities to Europe – despite an early declaration of neutrality by Central American republics – became more difficult as a result of a shortage of shipping and the closing of certain markets. The result was a sharp depreciation of the currency, which restricted the demand for imports and brought them closer into line with available supply.

Table 1.4 *Central America: destination of trade (%), 1913 and 1920*

|  | Costa Rica | El Salvador | Guatemala | Honduras | Nicaragua |
|---|---|---|---|---|---|
| **1. Exports 1913** | | | | | |
| (a) USA | 50.4 | 28.4 | 27.2 | 86.9 | 35.3 |
| (b) UK | 41.8 | 7.1 | 12.9 | 0.5 | 12.9 |
| (c) Germany | 4.9 | 17.1 | 53.0 | 4.8 | 24.5 |
| **2. Exports 1920** | | | | | |
| (a) USA | 71.1 | 64.8 | 83.4 | 96.0 | 86.2 |
| (b) UK | 20.8 | 4.2 | 2.5 | 0.1 | 2.8 |
| (c) Germany | 0.2 | 0.8 | 0.6 | 0 | 0.2 |
| **3. Imports 1913** | | | | | |
| (a) USA | 50.4 | 40.4 | 50.2 | 79.4 | 56.2 |
| (b) UK | 14.5 | 26.0 | 16.4 | 6.9 | 19.9 |
| (c) Germany | 15.1 | 11.6 | 20.3 | 7.9 | 10.7 |
| **4. Imports 1920** | | | | | |
| (a) USA | 52.1 | 61.6 | 64.9 | 87.5 | 81.1 |
| (b) UK | 14.2 | 15.4 | 21.5 | 6.2 | 11.8 |
| (c) Germany | 13.4 | 2.9 | 4.2 | 0.1 | 1.1 |

Sources: for 1913, Munro (1918), p. 277; for 1920, League of Nations, *International Trade Statistics*

The United States, however, was not at first affected by the hostilities, and soon exports of coffee were being diverted to the USA, whose dominant role in the supply of imports to Central America was increased still further. Coffee had to be sold in North America, however, at prices lower than those obtainable in European markets, and trade remained stagnant in value terms for most of the war period. In economic terms, therefore, the impact of the First World War was felt in the geographical redirection of trade rather than a reallocation of resources towards new activities. Whereas in 1913 the United States accounted for 55% of all imports into Central America and nearly 40% of all exports from Central America (see Table 1.4), by 1920 the figures were 70% and 80% respectively. In both cases, the adjustment was made principally at the expense of Germany.

By 1920, the beginning of the period that will form the focus of this book, the Central American economies had acquired a structure which will look familiar to students of developing countries. Agriculture was dominant as a proportion of Gross Domestic Product (GDP) throughout the isthmus, with agriculture for export (EXA) more important than domestic use agriculture (DUA) in several republics (see Tables A.1, A.4, A.5 and A.6 in the Statistical Appendix). Mining was still of some importance in Honduras and Nicaragua (see Table A.7). The development of manufacturing was virtually confined to activities where international transport costs were prohibitive and remained very small-scale. Even bags for the export of coffee were imported from outside the region, although a rudimentary textile industry had come into existence in several republics. Direct foreign investment (DFI) outside of the banana industry was important only in railways and mining. The small size of the urban market meant that even public utilities (favoured by foreign investors elsewhere in Latin America) had failed to attract much interest.[8]

The position of the Central American republics relative to each other can be studied using the concept of Gross Domestic Product (GDP) per head. Costa Rica was already by 1920 the richest (surely a reverse of the position at the time of independence), while El Salvador and Nicaragua were the poorest (see Table A.3). The lowly position of El Salvador in 1920 is something of a surprise. It was due, however, to two factors: first, El Salvador (like Honduras) was restricted to an export monoculture (see Table 1.3) and was unable to advance on two export fronts (as in Guatemala, Nicaragua and Costa Rica); secondly, El Salvador (unlike Honduras) had a high population density and a scarcity of land for development of DUA. The relative affluence of Costa Rica, on the other hand, can be explained by its head start in developing the export sector. Not only did it establish coffee exports before the rest of Central America, it was also the first in the field of commercial banking, Atlantic railways and banana exports. It was also the first to stabilise its currency (see next section) and was the only republic where opposition parties stood a realistic chance of forming the government peacefully through the electoral process.

### Pitfalls of export-led growth

By 1920, the development of the export sector in Central America on the basis primarily of coffee and bananas had established the region's links with the world market on a permanent basis; many books began to appear on the 'Conquest of the Tropics' theme (e.g. Adams, 1914) and the more informed foreign observers (e.g. Thompson, 1926) were on the whole sanguine about the future. The period up to 1920 in which export-led growth was established, however, witnessed the emergence of several intractable problems, some of which have not yet been solved. To a large extent, these problems arose out of the way in which export-led growth was operated in Central America, so that their solution could be said to lie in Central American hands. On the other hand, historical accident – over which the region exercised little or no control – also played a part, as we shall see.

By 1920, if not before, signs of saturation were already present in the coffee and banana sectors. Coffee exports in volume terms had peaked in Costa Rica as early as 1898 and the levels reached in Guatemala and Nicaragua in 1906/7 were not surpassed in this period either. Even in the newer banana industry, exports from Costa Rica had peaked as early as 1913 and developments in Nicaragua had run into apparently insoluble problems. Worse still, disease on banana plantations had raised its ugly head shortly before the First World War and no known antidote then existed other than to abandon affected lands and develop new ones. While there was clearly scope for increased exports of coffee from El Salvador and Honduras and increased exports of bananas from Guatemala and Honduras, the need for diversification was also apparent. This was true both for export agriculture and for activities directed towards the home market. Unfortunately, a bias against diversification in both directions had already by 1920 been built into the model of export-led growth.

The problem of introducing new crops into export agriculture arose from the monoculture bias of the social infrastructure system. The banking system, which had developed to serve the needs of coffee production, was reluctant to adapt, and the state, which had marshalled all its resources to encourage coffee production, was now controlled or dominated by coffee interests (except in Honduras). In the case of bananas, the monoculture bias of the social infrastructure system was even more marked. The one bank (Banco Atlántida in Honduras) whose origins can be traced to the banana trade had no interest in encouraging a diversified export agriculture, and much of the railway system promoted by the development of the industry, because of its geographical location, could be used only for the carriage of bananas. Furthermore, the state initiatives to establish the trade in bananas, which had resulted in generous concessions to foreign companies and a web of political intrigue, made it fairly certain that neither side had an interest in developing alternative exports by similar means.

A monoculture bias does not imply that alternative export crops could not develop, but it did put obstacles in their path in addition to those which would have had to be met anyway. Much the same can be said about diversification into activities serving the home market, whether in agriculture or industry, although the reasons are different. Since the earliest colonial days, the development of an export sector had been plagued by problems of labour supply. Low population density implied ease of access to land, and it became an article of faith among both colonial and republican administrations that no one would work for wages as hired labour unless he or she was compelled; the clear implication was that the development of an export sector depended on restricting access to land and the use of force in controlling the labour supply.

Both these methods were used in the republican period and were most marked after the period of liberal revolutions in which coffee developments began in earnest. Communal lands were alienated and antivagrancy laws were strengthened.[9] These methods of securing an adequate supply of labour varied in detail between the republics and were least necessary where either the average farm size was small (Costa Rica) or population pressure obliged a portion of the rural labour force to seek outside work (El Salvador). Irrespective of the methods employed, the idea that the supply of labour was an increasing function of money wage rates was never seriously considered. The methods by which the coffee industry obtained its labour supply did little, therefore, to encourage the development of activities for the home market. The restrictions on access to land discouraged domestic use agriculture, while cheap labour did nothing to help overcome the limitations on market size against which embryonic manufacturing establishments struggled.

The problem of labour supply was posed very acutely after the opening of the banana trade. The population of Central America had always been concentrated in the highlands, regarding living conditions in the coastal regions (particularly on the Atlantic) as unhealthy and dangerous. Since the growing of bananas had to be confined at first to the Atlantic coast, its development seemed to impose insuperable problems. Securing an adequate supply of labour for the development of coffee production in the highlands had proved difficult enough and the political élite clearly felt that not even coercion would be sufficient to induce labour to move from the highlands to the coastal region. The proposal, therefore, put forward by the fruit companies for importing black labour from the West Indies was readily accepted. Virtually the only exception to the use of black labour was the presence of Salvadorean immigrants on the north coast banana plantations in Honduras.

Black labour, being free, was better remunerated than highland labour on coffee fincas.[10] Any impact this might have had on national wage rates, however, was neutralised by a fairly rigid segmentation of the two labour markets; highland labour was reluctant to migrate to the coast and black labour was often forbidden from migrating to the highlands.[11] Furthermore, the enclave nature of banana plantations meant that the higher wages paid were a stimulus to increased imports (purchased through company stores) rather than to additional domestic production.

A further bias against the development of activities geared to the home market was provided by currency instability. With the domestic price of traded goods determined above all by the exchange rate, currency instability increased the risk attached to domestically orientated industry. Even import merchants found their business seriously complicated by exchange rate instability since a purchase of goods at a high 'peso' price could lead to disaster if the exchange rate later appreciated.

Fluctuations in export earnings were not the only cause of exchange rate instability. By an historical accident, Central America entered the republican period with silver as the principal circulating medium. As a consequence, two republics (Honduras and El Salvador) found themselves on the silver standard throughout the period after 1873, when the gold price of silver began its long decline.[12] The fall in the gold price of silver meant that more 'pesos' were required in Honduras and El Salvador to buy a unit's worth of imports from gold standard countries. Since virtually all their imports came from such countries, there began a long period of exchange rate depreciation leading to domestic inflation.

The same combination of exchange rate depreciation and domestic inflation was also experienced in Guatemala and Nicaragua, although this time the causal mechanism was reversed. Following the issue of banknotes after the 1870s, the administrations in both republics found the attractions of printing money irresistible. The result was a huge increase in the note issue,[13] which drove silver coinage out of circulation and forced a break with the silver standard. The two régimes were therefore based on inconvertible paper and the increase in the note issue drove up domestic prices and forced down the exchange rate. Nicaragua, under the US occupation, adopted the gold exchange standard in 1912, but this move to stabilise the currency will be discussed more fully in the next chapter.

Costa Rica, like El Salvador and Honduras, was at first on the silver standard, but made a skilful switch to the gold standard in 1896 which became fully operational in 1900.[14] From then until 1914 Costa Rica enjoyed exchange rate stability, although the loss of export markets at the start of the First World War forced her to abandon the gold standard and adopt a system of inconvertible paper.

Although efforts were made to reduce currency instability and exchange rate depreciation, they were (with the exception of Costa Rica in 1896) somewhat half-hearted.[15] One reason for this was the identity of interests between coffee exporters and exchange rate depreciation. Coffee growers sold in a gold market, but their expenses arose in 'peso' terms. Provided the fall in the exchange rate preceded the corresponding rise in their 'peso' costs, they stood to gain windfall profits. This was certainly true in the silver standard countries; even in the inconvertible paper republics, however, they stood to gain, because wage costs responded with a considerable lag to the rise in domestic prices. Thus, the coffee growers had little interest in reforming a system which worked in their favour, while the fruit companies were largely unconcerned because they both bought and sold heavily in gold markets.[16]

The establishment and development of the coffee trade would not have been possible without strong state support. Government expenditure was needed to provide incentives and establish essential infrastructure; at the same time, a rising level of trade could generate the increase in government revenue needed both to finance the increase in government expenditure and to overcome the political instability which always afflicts revenue-starved governments. All this suggested the need for a revenue structure which would

Table 1.5 *Public external debts (1920/1)*

|  | Costa Rica | El Salvador | Guatemala | Honduras | Nicaragua |
|---|---|---|---|---|---|
| External debt (£ million) | 3.13 | 0.96 | 1.9 | 28.65 | 0.9 |
| External debt per head | £6.13s.7d | 12s.9d | £1.3s.10d | £44.19s.5d | £1.8s.6d |
| Debt/revenue ratio | 3.88 | 3.2 | 2.8 | 31.5 | 1.94 |
| External debt/revenue ratio | 1.67 | 1.29 | 2.2 | 31.0 | 1.06 |

Source: derived from Council of Foreign Bondholders, *Annual Report*, London, 1921

be highly elastic with respect to foreign trade. Unfortunately, this was not the case and revenue did not rise as fast as the value of external trade. The pressures to increase government expenditure remained acute, however, and public sector deficits were not uncommon. In Guatemala and Nicaragua, inconvertible paper was issued and the internal public debt rose rapidly, while in all republics deficits were from time to time financed by external borrowing.

By modern standards, the public external debt before 1920 seems incredibly low (see Table 1.5).[17] This was not, however, how it was seen by contemporary observers; furthermore, debt repayments and servicing were taken very seriously by foreign bondholders, who could usually rely on their governments for diplomatic, if not military, support. The history of Central America's public external debt in the century to 1920 is not a happy one and it caused problems out of all proportion to its size. Because it was contracted in gold standard countries, its repayment and servicing in the period after 1870 necessitated, cet. par., increased quantities of domestic currency. When export earnings boomed no problems were experienced, but when earnings fell the pressure on falling revenues often caused governments to default.

The reaction of the foreign bondholders was to insist on the establishment of a formal link between taxes on external trade and the service of the debt, often with a creditor country appointee taking charge of customs. In the event of a fall in exports, the foreign bondholders would then have a prior claim on declining government revenue. From the point of view of Central American development, this system was fairly disastrous. It earmarked a high proportion of scarce revenue to meet external commitments often of dubious legality. At the same time, it discouraged governments from raising taxes on trade and increasing the buoyancy of the tax system.

The fluctuation in export earnings is a marked feature of export-led growth based on primary commodities, and some of the problems caused by these fluctuations have already been mentioned. The problems are most acute when only one commodity is exported, and can be reduced by the export of other commodities provided that shifts in the relevant supply and demand schedules are uncorrelated. The development of the banana industry might have offered some comfort in this respect. The market for sales was geographically distinct from that facing coffee exports, so that a shift in the demand curve for one would not necessarily affect the other.[18] At the same time, weather conditions in Central America were not likely to shift supply curves in the same direction, as the regions specialising in coffee were far from the Atlantic coast.

This potential advantage from introducing a seemingly uncorrelated export was largely lost when the banana industry fell under foreign control. Because of vertical integration within the fruit companies, the price paid to Central American growers was an administered and not a free market price, which changed only slowly. This, it is true, isolated the growers to some extent from price instability and meant that the fruit companies carried the risks of export fluctuations. At the same time, the exporting country lost the chance that a fall in coffee prices might be compensated by a rise in the price of bananas. A further consequence of foreign control was the virtual exemption of the industry from taxes on trade, both exports and imports. This was particularly serious in the early years and led to a long struggle for rental shares between companies and governments, which is still not fully resolved. This struggle will surface at various points in this book, but its origins should be noted now.

Export-led growth before 1920 therefore failed to resolve the problem of public revenue, which had contributed so much to political instability before 1870. The problem was most acute in Honduras, because taxes on trade generated by coffee exports were negligible and the banana trade was virtually exempt. In the absence of a profitable nationally owned export sector, the upper classes continued to gravitate towards politics; stable, or even strong, government was virtually impossible in a country where public employees often had to be paid in postage stamps and election time invariably saw the involvement of different fruit companies in support of rival candidates.

Despite all the criticisms subsequently levelled against the fruit companies (e.g. Kepner and Soothill, 1935), it is difficult to see how they could have resisted the temptation to meddle in internal politics. The pressure to become involved and safeguard a potential interest must have been enormous. What is not so clear, however, is why the industry should have fallen under foreign control in the first place. The usual explanations of foreign domination in the banana industry refer to the need for finance to build railways, ports, wharves etc. or to problems of marketing. What tends to be forgotten in these explanations, however, is that very similar problems were faced by the coffee industry, where considerable efforts had been made to maintain national control.

Outside of Costa Rica, the banana industry was run by nationals until the early 1900s. Ships from North America called at Atlantic ports in Guatemala, Honduras and Nicaragua and bought what they were offered by Central American growers. Development was slow, however, because the lack of infrastructure was a serious impediment and because the population was so scarce. Such impediments had been overcome by Central American governments in the case of coffee, but no enthusiasm for similar efforts was displayed in the case of bananas. The reason, one suspects, was as follows: banana production was confined to the unhealthy Atlantic coast and national control would have meant the migration of both owners and workers to the area. Owners of coffee fincas had no interest in such a move and potential capitalists found highland coffee a much more attractive proposition. The experience with coffee, furthermore, convinced owners and governments alike that the problem of labour supply on the Atlantic coast would be insuperable. When, therefore, the fruit companies offered to build the infrastructure and provide the labour in an area where the opportunity cost of land appeared to be zero, the temptation to accept seemed too great to resist. In cost-benefit terms the benefits might be small, but they could hardly be negative. Furthermore, there was always the prospect of withdrawing the concession on tax exemption at a later date.

The integration of Central America into the world market was therefore accompanied by some very serious problems. The need for diversification had become apparent, but the bias against it was considerable. The means for securing the labour supply in export agriculture often involved coercive measures and worked against the development of the internal market. Currency instability hindered the development of new activities and undermined government efforts to solve the problem of the external debt. Government revenue remained inadequate to meet public sector responsibilities and this contributed to political instability. Finally, the banana industry and much of the railway system had fallen under foreign control, while foreign penetration of the coffee industry had reached serious levels in Guatemala. In the years after 1920 each of these problems was to be tackled with varying degrees of success. The main features of export-led growth were now apparent, although the connection between the problems outlined above and export-led growth were not always noted.

### The political context

Central America's 'banana republic' image was derived primarily from the instability of its political system. There is some evidence to suggest that the development and expansion of export-led growth in the half-century before 1920 might have gone some way, cet. par., to reducing this instability. Unfortunately, other things were not equal and the change in the international context at the start of the twentieth century meant that Central America would never again be able to develop its internal political system without reference to the external dimension.

The struggle for power and the spoils of office assumes particular ferocity in countries where the opportunities for enrichment through economic activities are seriously limited. This was true of all Central America in the period from Independence to the 1870s with the partial exception of Costa Rica, where coffee growing was already important. Professional politics was the monopoly of the upper classes, who as early as the 1820s divided into liberals and conservatives. Liberals were distinguished from their rivals by their anti-clericalism and strong preference for Central American union, but the labels ceased to have much meaning after the liberal revolutions of the 1870s.

After the 1870s, if not before, politics ceased to have an ideological base and centred round personalities. Although liberals dominated the presidency throughout the isthmus, the brief period of conservative rule never challenged the assumptions of the export-led model, and all were united in the belief that Central America's competitive advantage lay in the export of primary commodities for the world market in exchange for manufactured goods.[19]

The influence of the US Constitution was strong on the fledgling republics, although the concept of the separation of powers was either ignored or little understood. The franchise was extended to cover a high proportion of the population, often without a literacy test, and elections were held with great frequency. With very few exceptions, however, these elections were manipulated to secure the victory of a man favourable to the outgoing president. With the electoral process firmly controlled by the government, individuals and groups excluded from power had to resort to violent methods to secure their ambitions. These revolutions were frequent, but often involved only a small number of people, with the great mass of the population largely unconcerned and even unaffected. With government revenue so weak, national armies were small, poorly paid and based on conscript labour. A determined opponent of the president did not find it difficult to raise the men and weapons to mount a serious challenge to the government in power.

This dismal state of affairs was seen at its worst in Honduras, where the absence of an important nationally owned export sector provided no diversion for the upper classes from their traditional interest in politics. With economic opportunities severely limited, control of the presidency was the one sure route to fame and fortune, and the ambitions of the competing groups led to the involvement of the principal fruit companies in the byzantine intrigues of Honduran politics. The companies had both financial and material (means of transportation) resources for backing a revolution, and politicians had the carrot of concessions to dangle in front of them.[20]

The growth of the coffee sector elsewhere in Central America, however, made the situation in Honduras the exception rather than the rule. There were three main reasons for this: first, the expansion of exports gave members of the upper classes a new route for enhancing their wealth and social prestige; secondly, it gave a growing portion of the upper classes a real interest in political stability, since revolutions tended to play havoc with coffee's labour supply and means of transportation; thirdly, it provided (through increases in public revenue) the means by which law and order could be preserved.

The expansion of coffee therefore introduced an element of order and stability into Central American politics outside Honduras.[21] This was most noticeable in Guatemala, where two *caudillos* ruled for thirty-six of the fifty years between 1870 and 1920. It was also true of Costa Rica, where the benevolent dictatorship of Tomás Guardia lasted from 1870 to 1882, and Nicaragua, where José Santos Zelaya ruled with an iron fist from 1893 to 1909. In El Salvador, Rafael Zaldívar ruled for nine years from 1876 as a virtual appointee of the Guatemalan *caudillo* Justo Rufino Barrios, but political stability was put on a more secure footing only after the Meléndez family took control in 1913.

All these *caudillos* called themselves liberals, but there was nothing liberal about the régimes over which they presided. Despite the extended franchise and the use of elections, voting was firmly controlled and popular participation was minimal; press censorship was strict and independent labour organisations were not tolerated. The political system outside Honduras began to provide order without liberty, but this was generally regarded as an improvement on the previous system of no order and no liberty.

The claim has frequently been made that Costa Rica was an exception, its political system allegedly providing both order and liberty. It is true that from 1889 to 1917 power changed hands peacefully in relatively free elections, but the political difference between Costa Rica and the rest of Central America in this period can easily be exaggerated. Until the resignation of Guardia in 1882, Costa Rican politics was not much different from elsewhere on the isthmus and popular participation in elections after 1889 developed only slowly. The political system remained highly personalistic and efforts to manipulate the results of elections were considerable. Where Costa Rica did distinguish itself from its sister republics was in the field of education. Schools developed rapidly after the 1880s and contributed substantially to the increase in popular participation in elections in later years. The emphasis on education is still a marked feature of Costa Rican life and perhaps owes its origins to the country's peculiar social composition; in Guatemala, for example, even the great reformer Justo Rufino Barrios doubted the wisdom of educating the Indians who at that time constituted at least two-thirds of the population.

It is conceivable that, left to their own devices, the republics of Central America would have developed their political systems along the lines taken by Costa Rica. They had, after all, followed her example in establishing coffee, banking, railways and bananas. Circumstances, however, conspired to produce a situation where external interests would also have to be considered. The fact that each republic in Central America had once been part of the same administrative unit meant that Presidents in one country felt at liberty to meddle in the affairs of another. This interference was made all the more probable through ties of marriage within the upper classes of the region and by the fact that Central American exiles usually took up residence in neighbouring republics. This meddling in each other's affairs was not so serious when governments were weak, because such an administration usually could not afford the risk of foreign adventurism. For the liberal *caudillos* after 1870, however, whose domestic authority was almost absolute, the position was different.

At the beginning of the twentieth century, the Guatemalan dictator Estrada Cabrera and his Nicaraguan counterpart José Santos Zelaya both intrigued against the governments in Honduras and El Salvador. The result was a state of turmoil in Central America between 1905 and 1907, which forced itself on the attention of the United States. Ostensibly, the USA was concerned that the chaos in certain Central American republics with foreign debts would compel the European powers to intervene in the region, thereby challenging the Monroe Doctrine. The real reason, however, appears to be the change in US interests dictated by the building of the Panama Canal, which had begun in 1903.

The construction of the Canal gave the United States an even greater strategic interest in the stability of Central America and the absence of foreign powers than it had previously had. Although the USA had become Central America's major trading partner and although US companies had invested in the fruit trade, railways and mining, these economic interests did not loom so large in the consideration of the State Department, and relations with the fruit companies were often strained.[22] Strategic interests, however, were quite another matter, and US concern over Central American developments increased sharply under the presidency of Theodore Roosevelt. This led to the proclamation of the Roosevelt Corollary, in which the USA committed itself towards the maintenance of peace and order in the region in order to reduce the risk of European intervention; the USA also tried to reschedule Central American debt so that it would be owed to US rather than European bondholders.[23]

The turmoil of 1905 to 1907 led to the Washington Peace Conference of 1907, in the organisation of which the USA played a large part and which was attended by all the Central American republics together with Mexico. Each republic committed itself to a policy of non-interference in the affairs of others and agreed to resolve any disputes among themselves through a Central American Court of Justice. Even more ambitious was the provision for non-recognition of a government which came to power by force. The Conference decisions were not respected either by the Central American republics or by the USA, but it did serve as a symbol of the new US commitment to the region and the resulting Treaty's main articles were reaffirmed in the 1922 Treaty of Peace and Amity (see Chapter 2).

The rules of the game laid down by the Washington Conference were openly flaunted during the last years of the Zelaya dictatorship in Nicaragua. Zelaya continued to meddle in the affairs of other republics, but was eventually deposed in 1909 in a civil war in which the US navy played a key role. Zelaya was hostile to successive US administrations, but it was an accident of geography rather than this hostility which persuaded the US to help in his overthrow. Nicaragua throughout the nineteenth century had been widely recognised as the best site for a proposed inter-oceanic canal, and both British and US diplomacy in the region had been based on that premise. With the Panama Canal now under construction, it was imperative for the US to control any prospective rival canal; such control, however, was not possible to achieve while Zelaya remained in power.

The removal of Zelaya set in motion a train of events leading to the occupation of Nicaragua by US marines in 1912; this period has been well documented elsewhere,[24] and it marked the beginning of a new era of US domination in Central America. Thus, by 1920 the USA was deeply concerned over political developments in the region and the Central American political élites were obliged to consider US interests in all their major decisions.

## The social structure

In the half-century before 1920 the export-led model, based primarily on coffee and bananas, was pursued with such vigour that inevitably it had major repercussions on social relations and the social structure. The outstanding feature of Central America in 1920 was its rural character; the vast majority of the labour force was employed in agriculture, and migration was more rural–rural than rural–urban. In Guatemala, for example, the 1921 census recorded an *increase* in the rural population from 60·6% of the total in 1893 to 73·4% in 1921 with a slight decline in the absolute urban population, despite the fact that the total population of Guatemala had risen by nearly 80 per cent.

The rural labour force divided its working time between export agriculture (EXA) and domestic use agriculture (DUA). A small part of the labour force was specialised exclusively in EXA and this part was mainly constituted by banana workers on the Atlantic coast (many of whom were migrants from outside the region) and permanent workers on the coffee estates; some efforts had been made by banana workers to organise, but trade unions remained illegal and only in Honduras could their efforts be said to have met with any success.[25] There was also a small mining proletariat in rural areas, with the most important concentrations in Honduras.[26]

A part of the rural labour force remained untouched by the expansion of EXA and was specialised in DUA. By 1920, however, this group had shrunk in importance and was confined on the whole to the most remote areas in each republic. The remainder of the rural labour force, a majority probably in Costa Rica, El Salvador and Guatemala, was obliged to provide labour services on a seasonal basis to EXA while retaining access to small plots of land for purposes of DUA (partly for subsistence, partly for sale to local markets).

The success of the export crops (particularly coffee, but also sugar) depended on this supply of seasonal labour, which was obtained in each republic through a mixture of coercion and market forces. The worst case of coercion was Guatemala, where the racial separation of owners (*ladinos*) and workers (Indians) added to the tension; coffee owners in Guatemala, and the liberal governments from 1871 onwards, had little success in suppressing communal ownership of land in the Indian highlands, so that coercion through *mandamientos* (a form of forced recruitment), vagrancy laws and legalised debt peonage was used instead intensively.[27] By contrast, governments in El Salvador from the 1870s onwards, under pressure from the coffee élite, granted or sold public lands to private individuals and alienated communal and church lands with such vigour that access to land on the part of the mass of the rural labour force was severely restricted and 'market forces' could be used more than coercion to obtain the necessary seasonal labour inputs.[28] Nicaraguan governments, following the restoration of the conservative aristocracy in 1858, tried to adopt both methods (labour coercion and restrictions on access to land), but the policies were not pursued with the same ruthlessness as in Guatemala and El Salvador until the presidency was seized by the liberal José Santos Zelaya in 1893.[29] Costa Rica, on the other hand, was unable to resolve the problem of a shortage of labour supply for coffee either through coercion[30] or market forces;[31] the coffee oligarchy, in consequence, shifted its interests from coffee production (which was dominated by small-scale producers) to coffee processing (in *beneficios*) and coffee exporting. In both activities, the opportunities for expansion were less restricted by labour shortages, and a single firm could purchase coffee from a multitude of growers.[32] In Honduras, the problem of labour shortages was not felt in such acute form because of the low level of development of export crops requiring seasonal labour.

In view of the fact that the profitability of coffee depended critically on the control of labour costs, all manifestations of rural labour unrest were ruthlessly crushed. Rural labour organisations were banned and the main problem faced by the authorities was revolts by Indian communities (particularly in El Salvador, Guatemala and Nicaragua) in protest against the alienation of communal lands. There was little danger of highland labour making common cause with the rural proletariat in the banana zones for reasons of both language and geography and even rural labour in the highlands was fragmented by race, language and physical barriers outside of Costa Rica. A small military presence was therefore usually sufficient to enable the growers to secure their labour requirements in the manner they felt most appropriate.

The export-led model required small urban concentrations as centres for distribution, finance and marketing. These included the capital cities, but the urban population (see Table 1.6) remained tiny in both absolute and relative terms. Not one city in 1920 could claim a population in excess of 100,000 and less than ten per cent of the total population (except in Costa Rica) lived in the capital of each republic. A few modern factories had begun operations,[33] but labour organisations were generally confined to the artisan sector; labour federations were established shortly before 1920 in Costa Rica, El Salvador and Guatemala, and these three republics each sent one delegate to the Pan-American Federation of Labour conference in 1919,[34] but urban labour was still very weak and played a supportive role only in political upheavals such as the overthrow of Estrada Cabrera in Guatemala in 1920.[35]

The acceleration of the export-led model after the liberal revolutions had two consequences for the social élite in each republic. First, it led to a partial eclipse of the traditional oligarchy whose wealth and social position was derived from activities originating in the colonial period. Secondly, it catapulted coffee interests, many of whose families had only recently migrated to Central America, into a position of economic, social and political prominence. Only in Honduras was the influence of the traditional oligarchy not seriously challenged by the rise of coffee, although the dominance of the fruit companies put a severe limitation on their authority.

The influence of the coffee oligarchy was at its most extreme in El Salvador and Guatemala. The Meléndez-Quiñónez dynasty had ruled El Salvador in the interests of the coffee growers since 1913 and the idea that the nation's wealth was owned by a mere fourteen families, all of whom had powerful coffee interests, was firmly established;[36] the interests of growers, processors and exporters to some extent overlapped, and much of the banking capital was owned by the same groups. The coffee oligarchy in both El Salvador and Guatemala felt so confident of the support of their respective governments that neither had yet developed a formal association to defend its interests.

In the other republics, the dominance of the coffee oligarchy was much

Table 1.6 *Urban population centres c. 1920*

| | Costa Rica | | El Salvador | | Guatemala | | Honduras | | Nicaragua | |
|---|---|---|---|---|---|---|---|---|---|---|
| | Name | Size | Name | Size | Name | Size | Name | Size | Name | Size |
| Capital | San José | 54,000 | San Salvador | 80,900 | Guatemala | 91,300 | Tegucigalpa | 35,000 | Managua | 60,342[2] |
| %age of population | | 12.9% | | 6.9% | | 7.2% | | 4.9% | | 9.4% |
| Second city | Cartago | 19,000 | Santa Ana | 59,815 | Quezaltenango | 35,000 | Choluteca | 18,000 | León | 47,243[2] |
| Third city | Heredia | 13,000 | San Miguel | 30,406 | Totonicapán | 30,000[1] | Juticalpa | 17,800 | Matagalpa | 32,271[2] |
| Fourth city | Alajuela | 13,000 | San Vicente | 30,080 | Cobán | 27,000[1] | Comayagua | 10,000 | Granada | 21,925[2] |

Sources: *South American Handbook* (1924) unless otherwise stated
(1) Pan-American Union (1927), p. 13
(2) Thompson (1926), p. 44

more qualified. Although coffee remained of overwhelming importance to the economy of Costa Rica, governments in that republic since the late 1880s had begun to distance themselves from coffee interests and acquire a separate identity. President Ricardo Jiménez Oreamuno, for example, although a member of the coffee oligarchy, recognised the distortions introduced to the Costa Rican economy by a monoculture based on coffee[37] and a modest export tax on coffee had been in force since the 1890s.[38] Both Presidents Jiménez and Cleto González Víquez, who dominated Costa Rican politics from 1905 to 1936, were open to outside influence (notably positivism)[39] and had sufficient vision and idealism to govern in more than just sectarian (coffee) interests; as a result, conflicts between coffee and other national interests were not always resolved in favour of the former, and the political life of Costa Rica (based on an all male suffrage) began to acquire a certain independence of the groups linked to the export sector.

The authority of the coffee oligarchy in Nicaragua was undermined first by the rivalry between conservatives and liberals and, secondly, by the US intervention. In addition, the main coffee-growing area around Matagalpa was difficult to reach from the traditional Liberal (León) and Conservative (Granada) centres, and the traditional oligarchy based on those two cities was reluctant to abandon its former pursuits. Coffee production never reached such intense levels as in El Salvador, Guatemala or Costa Rica, and much of the expansion was due to immigrants from Europe. The US intervention after the fall of Zelaya forced the small social élite to share political influence with North Americans, so that the élite lacked the strong sense of nationalism manifest in other republics.

In Honduras, coffee interests remained minor and the economic base of the local élite was derived mainly from cattle and commerce. Foreign interests dominated bananas, mining and banking, and control of the presidency was the one sure way to achieve wealth and prestige. Political factions were weak, however, and Honduran governments lacked sufficient resources to achieve independence from fruit company influence. The period leading up to 1920 was marked by a long struggle for the presidency which produced civil wars, frequent changes of government and charges of corruption. It was one of the bleakest periods in Honduran history and destroyed the hopes of the generation which had pushed through political and social reforms in the 1870s.

# 2

## Central America in the 1920s: reform and consolidation

The decade of the 1920s did not begin well for Central America. Despite the euphoria associated with the end of the World War and the increase in business confidence which was felt throughout the world economy in 1919, the first year of the decade ushered in the beginning of a mild depression which had serious repercussions on several Central American republics.

On the political front, the period of relative peace in the region begun with the entry of US marines into Nicaragua in 1912 proved to be more apparent than real. US attempts to apply non-recognition clauses from the 1907 Washington Treaty, which had eventually proved successful against Federico Tinoco in Costa Rica,[1] failed badly in Guatemala at the time of the overthrow of Estrada Cabrera (April 1920);[2] in Honduras, General López Gutiérrez forced recognition in 1920 from the USA for his government which had come to power through a successful revolt against the duly elected Francisco Bertrand.[3]

Relations between Central and North America were strained still further when Nicaragua thwarted efforts to form a Central American Federation in 1920/1. With Nicaragua still occupied by marines, it was generally believed that her opposition reflected US policy.[4] Although a Treaty of Union was signed by the remaining republics,[5] the fact that Nicaragua was so centrally located gave the Federation little chance of success and it collapsed soon after.

The failure (yet again) of union prompted the USA to put its relations with Central America on a better footing and the result was the 1923 Treaty of Peace and Amity, which aimed to strengthen the 1907 Washington Treaty. Although the US was not a signatory, it committed itself to determining policy towards the region on the basis of the Treaty. The non-recognition clauses,[6] reaffirmed in the 1923 Treaty, were applied successfully in Nicaragua against Emiliano Chamorro in 1926; they were to prove a stumbling block and source of embarrassment, however, to the USA after 1929.

The financial and monetary weakness of Central America had been recognised by many as an area requiring urgent reform; the need for urgency was made even more apparent after the onset of the 1920 depression, and monetary reform, already applied in El Salvador and Nicaragua, was adopted throughout Central America. The result was a period of remarkable exchange rate stability, which survived, in several cases, the worst years of the post-1929 depression and which still exists in part to this day.

With financial and monetary reform completed, the opportunities for economic diversification increased (see Chapter 1, pp. 11–13). These opportunities were not exploited, however, and instead the export-led model based on coffee and bananas was enthusiastically promoted; the result was an intense degree of export specialisation by the end of the 1920s in Central America, and the costs of this specialisation were to prove considerable.

Developments in the rest of the economy were largely overshadowed by the promotion of exports. The railway network and communications were further strengthened, but other activities geared to the home market exhibited little progress. The growth of external trade, however, coupled with exchange rate stability put both government revenue and the public external debt on a firmer foundation.

The growth of the economy, based on favourable prices and volumes for exports, contributed to a certain relaxation of the political climate. Labour organisations began to emerge in both town and country, and elections, although in general far from free, were regularly used to permit a peaceful transfer of power with only a few exceptions. The US attempt to withdraw its marines from Nicaragua in 1925, however, proved disastrous and the civil war which launched Sandino on his revolutionary career began in 1926.

### The 1920–1 depression and the export-led model

By 1919, the world economy had begun to recover from the impact of the First World War and Central America experienced the benefits in several areas: the return of European markets, temporarily lost during hostilities; the greater availability of international shipping services, now that registered banana boats had been restored to the fruit companies, and a spectacular rise in commodity prices, particularly coffee and sugar.

The boom in exports quickly fed through to a rise in imports, customs duties and government revenue. Prosperity was short-lived, however, and by mid-1920 world commodity prices had begun to tumble. The price of raw sugar per pound, which touched 22.5 US cents (c.i.f.) in New York in May, had fallen to 3.625 cents by the end of the year.[7] The fall in coffee prices was not so precipitate, but the average for 1921 was less than half that recorded in 1919 and below the levels recorded even in the First World War.

The impact of the fall in commodity prices on Central America's export earnings in foreign currency terms depended on several factors. First republics with a high proportion of bananas in the total were largely unaffected; the banana price received by producing countries, being an administered price, was largely unaffected by short-run movements in supply or demand, and prices received actually rose between 1919/20 and 1921/2 during the worst of the depression. Thus, the exports of the two main banana producers (Costa Rica and Honduras) were much less affected by the depression than the rest of Central America, as the risks attached to flexible commodity prices were borne by the fruit companies.

Secondly, the fall in the value of coffee exports depended on the quality and timing of sales. In general, low-quality coffee sold in spot markets did much worse than high-quality coffee sold in forward markets. The unit value[8] of the high-quality Costa Rican beans, for example, fell by as little as 10% between 1920 and 1921, while the unit value of the low-quality Nicaraguan beans fell by some 60% in the same period.[9]

Thirdly, mineral prices were not exempt from the general trend, and the price of silver in particular plummeted from its high level in New York of $1.339 per fine ounce in January 1920 to $0.567 in March 1921. This offset the impact of higher banana prices on the exports of Honduras and had an adverse influence on the exports of Nicaragua as well.

The impact of the decline in exports – most severe in El Salvador and Guatemala – on the rest of the economy depended on the flexibility of the exchange rate. In countries where the rate varied little (El Salvador, Honduras, Nicaragua), the decline in exports provoked a decline in imports reducing both customs and government revenue.[10] The decline in government revenue in these stable currency countries then led to a quick adjustment in non-debt government expenditure, although not all classes of expenditure were affected equally. (In El Salvador, for example, the departments whose budgets were reduced most sharply between 1920 and 1921 were Government, Internal Development and War.) The service of the public external debt now assumed a greater proportion of public revenue, but only El Salvador (in 1921) went into default.

The adjustment of government expenditure to the reduced level of government revenues in the stable currency countries meant that the deflationary impact of the reduction in external trade was not offset by a rise in public sector deficits and the money supply tended to fall; this pushed down prices and made the reduction in money costs (including money wages) within the public sector more palatable. Adjustment to an external imbalance was therefore almost automatic, with the burden shifted to the home economy and shared by all sectors more or less equally. As long as the externally induced depression did not last too long, there was no need for a change in policy, and political stability was not threatened. There were no popular uprisings or revolutions in the stable currency countries in the 1920/1 depression.

In the flexible currency countries (Costa Rica and Guatemala), the dollar value of imports fell, but the 'peso' (i.e. local currency) value was much less affected. Customs duties in 'peso' terms did not necessarily fall, and government revenue rose in both countries. The inflationary impact of exchange rate depreciation, however, affected expenditure more severely than revenue in Guatemala and the budget deficit widened between 1920 and 1921 from 27.2 million pesos to 131.1 million pesos. In both countries, the 'peso' cost of servicing the public external debt rose and reached over 25% of revenue.

The world economy recovered quickly from the 1920/1 depression. Commodity prices rose steadily; the unit value of coffee exports from Central America in 1922 exceeded those in 1921 by 25% to 50%,[11] while sugar and mineral prices also increased. Recovery in the flexible currency countries, however, was made more difficult by the rise in domestic inflation. In Costa Rica, still adjusting to the fall of the military dictatorship of Federico Tinoco (1917–19), public disturbances were avoided only by prompt social initiatives on the part of the government of Julio Acosta García,[12] while the transfer of power in Guatemala following the fall of Estrada Cabrera (April 1920) was far from smooth. The 'unionist' Carlos Herrera was forced to resign from the presidency in December 1921 and his place was taken by the 'localist' General José M. Orellana.

The need for monetary and financial reform predated the 1920/1 depression, but the latter re-emphasised the need for change in those republics which had not yet attempted it. In the next few years, all Central America adopted exchange rate régimes designed to minimise the impact on the home economy of external shocks. The latter, it was recognised, was a fact of life for small, open economies; although no one could have predicted the ferocity of the shock unleashed at the end of the 1920s, the reforms adopted in that decade went some way to prevent the complete breakdown of the economic and social order.

## Monetary and financial reform

The coffee interests in Central America, as pointed out in Chapter 1, tended to gain from currency instability and exchange rate depreciation; the losers were those whose revenue was fixed in depreciated currency. This included the government, so that a certain clash of interests developed between the politically dominant class and the export oligarchy despite the overlap between the two groups.

A symptom of the government's problem under a régime of unstable currency was the burden of external public debt service. With payment required in gold currency terms, the burden tended to increase with currency and exchange rate depreciation. Default then brought the risk of foreign intervention and a challenge to the Monroe Doctrine. The United States, therefore, acquired a considerable interest in the reform of Central America's financial system and this became one of the key elements in dollar diplomacy.[13]

Dollar diplomacy was certainly responsible for the reform of Nicaragua's currency system in the period after the fall of Zelaya. Under the latter, the issue of inconvertible paper money had pushed the value of the Nicaraguan peso from 48 US cents in 1900 to 11 cents in 1909 (it fell to 5 cents in 1911). A treaty between the USA and Nicaragua in 1911 paved the way for currency reform by proposing a US loan of over $13 million, which was designed *inter alia* to take over Nicaragua's debt owed to Europe and make it payable to North America instead, with payment guaranteed by US appointment of a Collector-General of Customs.

The Collector-General was duly appointed, but the US Senate did not ratify the treaty. Nevertheless, a much smaller loan ($1.5 million) was obtained in September 1911 for the purposes of currency stability, and additional funds were secured in the following year. In March 1912, Nicaragua's National Assembly passed a Currency Law which introduced a new monetary unit (the córdoba) and put Nicaragua on the gold exchange standard.[14]

The Currency Law established the Banco Nacional de Nicaragua with a monopoly of the new note issue, its notes to be exchangeable on demand against drafts on an Exchange Fund to be set up in New York. As usual, therefore, the problem was to ensure that the new notes (backed by gold) did not go out of circulation, while the old notes (inconvertible paper) were still in use. The business of retiring the old notes was effected swiftly and efficiently, however, and by the end of 1912 a fixed rate had been established of 12.5 pesos (old notes) to one córdoba equivalent to one US dollar.

It was fortunate, indeed, that the transition to the new currency was made so swiftly, because the outbreak of hostilities in Europe in 1914 put a severe strain on the currency system. The Banco Nacional in October 1914 was forced to suspend the sale of bills of exchange (contrary to the Currency Law) and the Exchange Fund in New York was closed. For a period the córdoba went to a 30% discount against the dollar.

Nicaragua therefore came off the gold exchange standard at the end of 1914, but the Banco Nacional eventually resumed its practice of selling drafts on New York against córdobas at par. Thus, Nicaragua from 1916 enjoyed a stable exchange rate against the dollar and *de facto* membership of the gold standard. This system survived the 1920/1 depression and did not break down until the late 1930s.

In Honduras, currency reform was also motivated by dollar diplomacy, although the circumstances were somewhat different. From the turn of the century, Honduras for currency purposes had been split in two parts; on the northern coast, where the banana companies operated, the US dollar circulated freely, while in the rest of the country silver currency was in use. When the First World War began, silver began to leave the country and its export was banned in April 1916. Between 1916 and 1920, however, high prices for silver (as a metal) led to its disappearance from circulation as a means of payment and US gold and paper currency was increasingly in use.

The Honduran government was therefore presented with something of a *fait accompli*; in May 1918 it authorised the Banco Atlántida (owned by Vaccaro Bros.) to redeem its notes in dollars and in the following year it obliged the bank to keep its reserves in gold or US currency. These provisions, however, did not apply to the Banco de Honduras, where redemption continued in silver. Thus it could be said with some fairness that Honduras was on both the gold and silver standards.

The existence of US dollars and silver currency in circulation at the same time forced the government in 1918 to make US currency legal tender with a legal rate of exchange of one dollar for two pesos. From that time on, however, the market rate of exchange came very close to the legal rate, although this was by accident rather than design. Even during the 1920/1 depression, the peso stood at a discount to the dollar of only a few per cent.

If the price of silver as a metal had remained high, Honduras might have drifted into a *de facto* gold standard since silver coins would have remained out of circulation – a situation with which both the government and the USA would have been content. The fall in the price of silver after January 1920, however, brought the silver coins back into circulation and the dollar started to disappear from the North.

Honduras now found itself drifting back onto the silver standard and emergency measures were called for. Arthur Young, a US currency expert, was appointed Financial Adviser to the Government of Honduras and in February, 1921, he presented a plan to Congress for monetary reform based on the gold exchange standard.[15] Although it was not acted on, the government did try to maintain the circulation of US currency by prohibiting, in March 1921, the import of silver coins other than US ones and by decreeing that 50% of customs duty be paid in US currency.

The government's efforts to keep the dollar in circulation were successful, but Honduras did not succeed in carrying out a thorough-going monetary reform in the 1920s and both gold and silver continued as circulating mediums; when the price of silver rose, the coins were hoarded or exported and silver as a circulating medium declined; when it fell, the government had some difficulty in maintaining the legal rate of two pesos to the gold dollar and the banks demanded a premium for gold drafts payable in silver (in May 1923, it reached 12.5%, i.e. 2.25 pesos to the dollar).

Despite the absence of the discipline of the gold standard (in effect Honduras continued on a gold and silver standard), the fact that the government was prepared to support the legal rate of two pesos to the dollar kept exchange rate movements within acceptable limits. When a new unit of currency (the Lempira) was finally introduced in 1931,[16] it was also made equal to 50 cents US currency, which has remained its official value to this day. Thus the Honduran rate of exchange to the dollar has been effectively unchanged since 1918.

El Salvador had made an unsuccessful attempt to switch from the silver to the gold standard in 1892, but her second attempt in 1919 could not have been more fortunate. By a happy coincidence, the law of 11 September, which introduced a new monetary unit (the colón) and put the country on the gold standard, coincided with the peak of the gold price of silver.

During the First World War, the banks in El Salvador had been relieved of their obligation to redeem notes in silver. By 1919, therefore, they were in possession of a large metallic reserve whose gold equivalent had appreciated considerably. Following the monetary law in September, this reserve was sold in North America for gold coins, which achieved two objectives: it saved the government from the need to mint its own coins and it meant that by January 1920 the banks could redeem their own notes in gold on demand. El Salvador was now on the gold standard.

By the end of 1920, the fall in the price of silver and the decline in exports had pushed the exchange rate to the gold export point and the newly imported US gold began to leave the country. The gold reserve, which had looked so generous in January 1920 at 10½ million colones, had fallen to 3 million colones by the middle of 1921. Soon afterwards, however, business conditions began to improve and El Salvador survived its first crisis on the gold standard.

The currency law of September 1919 established a legal rate of exchange of 2 colones to the US dollar (¢2 = $1). Although the market rate fluctuated around this after January 1920, going to a maximum discount of 13% (i.e. ¢2.26 per dollar) in November 1920, it did keep within the gold points. By 1922, furthermore, the maximum discount was only 5% and the rate of two colones to the dollar survived until 1932.

Dollar diplomacy was not responsible for El Salvador's currency reform, where the desire to stabilise the currency was dictated by the needs of government and the risk-aversion of the merchant class. Much the same was true of Costa Rica, which had enjoyed currency stability under the gold standard from 1896 to 1914, but which had suffered badly from the Tinoco dictatorship's issue of inconvertible paper money.[17]

The inauguration as President of Julio Acosta García paved the way for currency reform, but action was delayed by the 1920/1 depression. The first step was taken in April 1921, when private banks were obliged to redeem their notes in gold; this did not apply to the state-run Banco Internacional, where redemption was made impossible because of Tinoco's use of this bank's notes to pay his debts.

In July of the same year, the Banco Internacional was made the bank of sole issue, giving it (like the Banco Nacional in Nicaragua) the character, if not the name, of a Central Bank. By 1922, its notes had become the only legal money and other notes were retired. The tricky question of building up a gold reserve to provide a metallic backing to the note issue now had to be faced. In October 1922, a Caja de Conversión was set up with funds earmarked from various taxes (including the $0.01 tax per bunch of bananas exported). When the Caja's reserve reached $1.5 million in March 1924, the Banco Internacional's notes were made redeemable in gold and Costa Rica had joined the gold standard. When the Caja was set up in 1922, it began by stabilising the colón at four to the dollar. This rate was later adopted as the legal basis and by 1925 exchange rate stability was complete. This rate survived, as in El Salvador, until 1932.

Costa Rica's experience was to prove useful in Guatemala's monetary reform, which was completed only in 1926 after several frustrated attempts. In 1919, E. W. Kemmerer was invited to present a proposal for monetary reform after pressure had been applied by the United States.[18] The latter was seriously concerned about the implications of the Guatemalan external debt owed to European powers, the service of which was becoming more and more burdensome with currency depreciation.

The fall of Estrada Cabrera in 1920 prevented Kemmerer's proposals for adoption of a gold standard from being put into effect. The administration of Carlos Herrera showed an interest in monetary reform, but was over-thrown in December 1921 before any positive action could be taken. By this time, public demonstrations against the falling value of the peso were becoming common. In September 1923, the administration of General Orel-lana followed Costa Rica's example by setting up a Caja Reguladora to stabilise the exchange rate with funds earmarked from the tax on coffee. In 1924, Kemmerer was invited back and in November a currency reform was initiated. The new monetary unit was to be the quetzal (Q) and was to be issued at par with the US dollar.

The Caja was charged with supervision of the total monetary circulation and in 1925 began to substitute new quetzal notes for the old (depreciated) paper pesos, which were burnt at the rate of 12 million per month. The banks and the government took responsibility for building up a gold reserve to back the new notes and by 1926 Guatemala was on the gold standard. The Caja was reorganised into the Banco Central de Guatemala with a monopoly of note issue. The currency reform provided for a rate of exchange of 60 pesos to the quetzal or dollar (the peso had been at par with the dollar in 1870). The new currency was therefore at par with the dollar, which eased problems in the banana zones. The official rate of exchange of one quetzal to the dollar has never varied to this day, although *de facto* devaluation was finally forced on Guatemala in 1986.

Currency reform with exchange rate stability may have been slow in coming to Central America, but when it came it was thorough and on the whole efficiently executed; it also set a tradition for currency stability which survived until very recently and converted an area noted for its currency instability into one famed for the rareness of its exchange rate changes. The financial reforms also weeded out some of the weaknesses in the export-led model mentioned in Chapter 1 – the bias against diversification through production for the home market.[19] Yet one of the tragedies of Central America is that the opportunities presented by financial and currency stability in the 1920s were wasted; the region marched on towards a pitch of export specialisation which made the economy particularly vulnerable to external shocks. Currency reform and exchange rate stability turned out to be necessary, but not sufficient, conditions for diversification.

## Consolidation of the export-led model

By the First World War, the growth of coffee and banana production had produced a situation where earnings from these two commodities dominated exports (see Table 1.3). By the end of the 1920s, this domination was to be further extended with coffee and bananas accounting for over 70% of export earnings in all republics, nearly 90% in Costa Rica and Honduras and over 90% in El Salvador and Guatemala (see Table 2.1). The expansion of the banana industry was particularly spectacular. Between 1920 and 1929, exports from Guatemala, Honduras and Nicaragua trebled, although in Costa Rica they remained virtually stagnant until 1926, declining thereafter as Panama disease swept through the Atlantic coast plantations.

The expansion of banana exports from Honduras took that country to the leading position in terms of world supply.[20] It was based primarily on the efforts of four US-owned fruit companies, two of which (Tela and Truxillo Railroad Co.) were subsidiaries of the United Fruit Company (UFCO). By the end of 1929, however, Sam Zemurray's Cuyamel Co. had been sold to UFCO, so that competition was effectively reduced to UFCO and Standard Fruit (Vaccaro Bros.). UFCO alone increased its banana cultivations in Honduras from 14,081 acres in 1918 to 87,808 acres in 1924, although the uncultivated area under its control was several times larger. For all companies, the main method of expansion in the 1920s was not so much railway concessions (although these were still used), but leasing and purchase from private owners.

Under Honduras' agricultural law of 1895, land was supposed to be sold in alternate lots in order to prevent foreign companies from obtaining

Table 2.1 *Central America's exports, 1929 (% of total)*

| Commodity | Costa Rica | El Salvador | Guatemala | Honduras[1] | Nicaragua |
|---|---|---|---|---|---|
| Coffee | 67.2 | 92.6 | 76.6 | 2.1 | 54.3 |
| Bananas | 25.2 | | 12.9 | 84.9 | 18.3 |
| Precious metals | 0.4 | | 0.7 | 6.1 | 4.2 |
| Hides | 0.3 | | 0.7 | | 1.3 |
| Timber | 0.6 | | 3.5 | | 12.3 |
| Raw cotton | | 0.1 | | | |
| Sugar | | 4.9 | 1.3 | 2.3 | 2.2 |
| Chicle | | | 1.3 | | |
| Balsam of Peru | | 0.6 | | | |
| Coconuts | | | 0.6 | | 0.3 |
| Indigo | | 0.2 | | | |
| Cacao | 4.9 | | | | 0.5 |
| Live cattle | | | | 0.9 | |
| Henequen | | 1.1 | | | |
| Honey | | | 0.5 | | |
| | | | | | |
| Bananas and coffee as % of total | 92.4 | 92.6 | 89.5 | 87.0 | 72.6 |

Source: Derived from League of Nations, *International Trade Statistics*, Geneva, 1930
[1] 1928/9

complete control of a region; in 1930, however, Congress found that serious illegalities had occurred during the administration (1920–4) of General López Gutiérrez and that the fruit companies had acquired nearly 300,000 acres to which they did not have legal title. The clear implication was that the rapid expansion of the early 1920s had bypassed the 1895 law through the use of nominees, bribes, etc.[21]

In Nicaragua, the expansion of the banana industry in the 1920s was also due to several foreign-owned companies. Standard Fruit (still Vaccaro Bros.) entered in 1921 by purchasing Bragman's Bluff Lumber Co. and signed a new contract with the government in 1922; by the end of the decade it accounted for 50% of exports. UFCO had huge holdings in Nicaragua, but never developed much of them and played a very minor role. Both Cuyamel and Atlantic Fruit Co. had plantations in excess of 100,000 acres and all companies bought from private planters as well as growing their own.

Railway concessions and railroad construction were much less important in the development of the Nicaraguan banana industry than elsewhere in Central America and access to plantations was often by river. This was one reason why the industry never acquired much importance, and it was also affected by the civil war in Nicaragua after 1926. Indeed, Sandino's army frequently raided the properties of Standard Fruit and other US banana companies on the Atlantic coast.[22]

In Guatemala, where UFCO had a virtual monopoly of banana exports, a new concession was sought from Congress in 1924, which was granted in 1927.[23] This land was in the region south of the Motagua river close to the disputed border with Honduras. At the same time that UFCO was pushing into this region from Guatemala, Sam Zemurray's Cuyamel Co. was building a railroad into it from Honduras. The dispute between the two companies brought Guatemala and Honduras close to war in 1928, although their merger in December 1929 reduced the tension and the border question was finally settled by arbitration in the 1930s.[24] In the 1920s, UFCO also began to develop the banana industry on the Pacific coast, although to start with it contented itself by buying from private planters.

The stagnation of the banana industry in Costa Rica was a reflection of the falling yield to be expected from 'old' banana lands.[25] As a consequence of this, UFCO switched its strategy in the 1920s from one of growing its own bananas to one of buying from private planters under five year contracts. Many of the planters were descendants of the Jamaican negroes whose labours had proved so decisive in building the Atlantic railroad in the 1870s and 1880s. By the 1920s, however, the health hazard of the Atlantic coast had been sharply reduced and a number of Costa Ricans from the Meseta Central had also begun to be attracted by the high wages and/or profits expected from the banana trade.

Some of the planters formed themselves into a cooperative (the Co-operativa Bananera Costariccense) and by 1928 had formed a tentative agreement with the Cuyamel Fruit Co. The prospective entry of the Cuyamel Co. challenged the monopoly of UFCO and the company reacted accordingly. UFCO had also fought off a challenge by the Atlantic Fruit Co. to its hegemony in Costa Rica in 1912 and was prepared to resort to all sorts of tricks, including raising freight rates on its railway subsidiary and filling all available space in its ships (The Great White Fleet).[26] In response to this pressure the Cuyamel withdrew from Costa Rica. It is still not clear how serious the company's intentions were, but at face value the terms and conditions it offered were revolutionary. Not only did the company offer to pay a banana export tax with the rate to be adjusted at the pleasure of the government, it also offered to share with the planters the net profits on the sale of the fruit overseas.

Both proposals challenged the traditional practices established by the fruit companies themselves (including the Cuyamel). In the 1920s, the banana export tax in Central America varied from 1 to 2 cents US gold per stem which represented between one and two per cent of the f.o.b. valuation[27] and a negligible amount of government revenue; even this was an advance on the rate of tax (often zero) applied before the 1920s. Furthermore, the fruit companies were accustomed to signing long-term contracts with the relevant governments, which could not be altered in the intervening period. UFCO's 1910 contract in Costa Rica did not expire until 1930, while its 1929 contract with Guatemala was expected to last until 1949. The proposal to share the profits, however, which would have given Central Americans a stake in the banana industry comparable to that they enjoyed in coffee, was even more revolutionary and has never been applied to this day. Where the fruit companies bought from private planters, it was the custom to pay a fixed price as agreed in the contract. This price varied from one country to another, although it seems to have been set so that the gross return per acre was much the same.[28]

This price, being fixed by contract, did not vary with conditions in wholesale or retail markets and was altered only rarely. In Costa Rica, for example, it was doubled between 1919 and 1920 to compensate for the rise in inflation provoked by exchange rate depreciation, but did not alter again until 1931. The private planter was therefore insulated from the risks associated with export crops, although he also lost out on the benefits and was not insured against the risks of rising costs and crop failure.

The banana price recorded at the point of export (i.e. the f.o.b. value) reflected the price paid to private planters, together with a charge for inland freight, loading charges and export duties. It was therefore an official or administered price and hardly varied at all. In Costa Rica, for example, the unit value from 1910 to 1920 was one colón ($\phi$) per stem, made up of $\phi 0.67$ to the planter, $\phi 0.21$ for inland freight, $\phi 0.10$ for loading charges and $\phi 0.02$ for export duty. This system of pricing became even more arbitrary, when the foreign company did not rely on private planters, but instead produced its own bananas.[29] In the latter case, the f.o.b. 'price' was virtually an internal book-keeping value applied by a vertically integrated company to the transfer of a product from one branch of the company's operations (production) to another (international shipping).

As virgin banana lands became less accessible, the companies preferred to buy from private planters. While wholesale prices were rising in the 1920s, private planters did not benefit, but when prices started falling at the end of the decade they found their contract prices revised downwards. It was an asymmetry which was to be the cause of much bitterness.

In the 1920s, the banana industry enjoyed perhaps its most spectacular decade of expansion. Monopolistic tendencies increased and the benefits to the exporting countries were correspondingly reduced. Wages remained high for banana workers, however, particularly in comparison with unskilled work elsewhere, and improvements in health conditions also encouraged the migration of workers to the banana zones, while currency stability made fixed price contracts more attractive for private planters. These were not the only routes by which banana developments affected the rest of the economy. The operation of price-discrimination by company-controlled railways in Costa Rica and Guatemala pulled resources away from the Pacific towards the Atlantic banana ports.[30] The new policy in Honduras of leasing or purchasing land from private owners also affected the allocation of resources and brought to an end the period when the opportunity cost of banana land was zero. Finally, the onslaught of disease, particularly in Costa Rica, faced the producing countries with a new challenge: possible decline of a 'growth' industry, in which the mobility of resources was very low.

Coffee production and exports also expanded significantly in the 1920s, although their growth tended to be overshadowed by the spectacular rise of the banana industry. The decade did not begin auspiciously; the collapse of coffee prices in the 1920/1 depression was quite severe and the monetary reforms deprived coffee growers of the advantages of selling in gold and buying in paper during a period of rising inflation. World developments for coffee, however, were very favourable. The Brazilian valorisation scheme in 1921[31] contributed substantially to the recovery of coffee prices and per caput consumption increased in all major importing areas. Between 1920 and 1929, world imports grew by 30%, while exports of countries other than Brazil rose by 46%. As 'mature' producers, neither El Salvador nor Guatemala were able to match that rate of increase, but exports rose by nearly 50% in Costa Rica and Nicaragua and trebled from Honduras. Even in El Salvador and Guatemala, however, production and exports increased, although the world market share of both declined slightly. Towards the end of the decade, Central American production accounted for some 7% of the world's total.

The increase in coffee prices after the 1920/1 depression contributed to the expansion of the industry. Unit values almost doubled from the low point recorded in 1921 to the peak in the late 1920s and nearly surpassed the high levels achieved in 1920. These unit values, unlike equivalent prices for bananas, reflected market conditions in consuming countries and the increase represented a genuine rise in national income.[32] Money wages paid to coffee workers in the 1920s appear to have risen modestly, although the evidence is not conclusive, and a part of the proceeds from increased coffee exports found its way into government hands through the coffee tax. In Costa Rica, a law of 1923 introduced a tax of $1.50 per quintal (46 kg) on coffee with the proviso that if the price should fall below $15 per quintal, the tax would become an *ad valorem* one at 8%.[33] In Guatemala, the export tax on coffee was twice increased in the 1920s and in 1925 was even made progressive, but this was reversed in 1926 when the tax was cut in half.[34]

Coffee through the export tax therefore contributed a reasonable share of government revenue in the 1920s[35] (at least compared with the export tax on bananas), but it tended to be a declining share because of the regressive nature of the tax. In none of the republics could it be said that coffee interests directly controlled the government, but at the same time their interests were always considered and there were few leading politicians without at least a small coffee finca.

Developments in the remainder of the export sector throughout the 1920s were of little significance. Gold and silver exports from Nicaragua declined steadily (at least for customs purposes) and gold exports from Costa Rica dwindled to a trickle as seams were exhausted. The only favourable trend was an increase in the value of silver exports from Honduras, which rose from $976,000 in 1920 to $1,433,000 in 1929. Sugar exports recovered in value terms after prices recovered from the low levels recorded in 1921, but production and export in volume terms did not respond except in Honduras and the industry declined in relative importance as a source of foreign exchange earnings. The only export other than coffee and bananas which prospered was timber from Nicaragua's Atlantic coast region, which accounted for some 10% of exports by the end of the 1920s.

By 1929 (see Table 2.1), the dominance of coffee and bananas as sources of foreign exchange earnings had been pushed to the limit. In real terms, value added in export agriculture (EXA) accounted for at least 15% of GDP in all countries except Guatemala (see Tables A.1 and A.5, pp. 308, 316). Its impact on the economy, however, was even greater than this, because of the close relationship between export earnings on the one hand and imports, commerce, transport and government revenue on the other.

### Economic development outside the export economy

The expansion of the export sector in the 1920s increased export earnings and permitted a higher volume of imports; this stimulated commerce, particularly in the urban areas, and also had a favourable impact on the transport system, which in many cases (e.g. railways) earned most of its income from the carriage of freight. Some agricultural commodities (e.g. coffee and sugar) also required processing before export and this increased value added in certain branches of industry.

Those sectors complementary to export agriculture (EXA) therefore gained from its expansion in the 1920s. Not all sectors were so favoured, however, and the competition between EXA and other branches of the economy began to be a source of concern; this competition has been much under-estimated in research on Central America and accounts for the dangerous tendency to equate an increase in exports with an increase in aggregate performance.[36]

The sector competing most closely with EXA for resources was (and is) domestic use agriculture (DUA). Coffee and sugar lands, for example, could be used for alternative crops, while the expansion of banana lands in the 1920s began for the first time to take place through the acquisition of private

Table 2.2 *Required and actual rates of growth of domestic use agriculture (DUA), 1921–8.[1] Annual geometric rates of change (%)*

|  | Costa Rica | El Salvador | Guatemala | Honduras | Nicaragua |
|---|---|---|---|---|---|
| Population growth rate | 1.7 | 2.1 | 3.3 | 2.9 | 0.7 |
| Real demand for food per person[2] | 0.1 | 0.9 | 0.5 | 1.8 | 2.3 |
| Required rate of growth of DUA | 1.8 | 3.0 | 3.8 | 4.7 | 3.0 |
| Actual rate of growth of DUA | 0.9 | 1.5 | 2.1 | 0.6 | 5.2 |

[1] Annual data based on three-year averages
[2] This is the product of real income per head and the income elasticity of demand for food (assumed to be 0.8)

farms previously producing crops for the home market.

In the case of labour, the expansion of coffee required either *colonos* or *jornaleros*, permanent and temporary workers respectively.[37] In both cases, additional employment meant that the resources available for growing domestic crops were reduced. In the banana zones, the importation of foreign labour did not at first make any demands on the workforce devoted to DUA,[38] but by the 1920s high wages on the banana plantations and improvements in health conditions on the Atlantic coast had encouraged the migration of native labour towards the banana zones. Some of the labour came in search of higher wages; a few, however, came in search of profits as private banana planters selling to the fruit companies. In both cases, the expansion of EXA tended to be achieved at the expense of DUA.

For DUA to grow at a rate consistent with no changes in prices and imports, its rate of growth must be approximately equal to the rate of growth of population plus the rate of growth of GDP per head times the income elasticity for food.[39] Assuming the latter to be 0.8, the required rates of growth of DUA are given in Table 2.2. As can be seen, in only one case (Nicaragua) did the actual rate of growth of DUA exceed the required rate. The weakness of DUA therefore resulted in a huge increase in imports of foodstuffs.[40] This helped to prevent a large rise in prices, although in Guatemala (where imports did not rise as rapidly as elsewhere) food price inflation was substantial.[41] The competition between DUA and EXA was not purely economic; the social status attached to coffee production in particular was much greater than any other form of agricultural production (except possibly cattle raising), and it provided, through producers' associations, a springboard for the politically ambitious.[42] The economic impact, however, of an expansion of EXA on DUA should never be forgotten.

Although the growth of EXA had a favourable impact on parts of the food processing industry,[43] developments in manufacturing activity in general in the 1920s were minimal. There remained very considerable obstacles in the way of industrial expansion; the failure to develop the country's hydro-electric potential[44] and the absence of indigenous fuels other than wood kept the average industrial establishment to a very small size. In addition, the banking system (which had developed in response to the needs of EXA and which was heavily involved in the coffee trade as both buyer and seller)[45] was not interested in stimulating industrial development and was under no obligation to do so.

The absence of bank credit for productive activities outside EXA meant that potential entrepreneurs had to have access to their own sources of funds. It is no accident therefore that new industrial developments in the 1920s, such as there were, tended to be funded by immigrants using their own capital. This continued the pattern of the past, where the milling of sugar cane in *ingenios* and the drying of coffee in *beneficios* had both been activities with a high level of foreign participation. Outside of food-processing, the most important developments in the 1920s were the emergence of a small textile industry in El Salvador and Quetzaltenango.[46] Cement was manufactured near Guatemala City, and San Salvador also boasted two small iron foundries. Throughout the region, native fibres were used to make hammocks, shawls, straw hats, baskets and nets, and there were several breweries in operation.

Despite all the problems it faced, the low level of industrial development in the 1920s is surprising. The effective market for many goods, it is true, was very small, because of the low levels of real wages and cash incomes in rural areas, but even the poorest have to consume articles of basic necessity and often even these were imported. The barriers against industrial expansion, furthermore, were reduced significantly in the 1920s. The railway system was improved in several countries; the state Ferrocarril al Pacífico in Costa Rica was electrified and in Honduras the national railway line was managed by the Cuyamel Fruit Co. with a gain in its efficiency. Minor Keith's International Railways of Central America (ICRA) continued its building plans and the lines connecting Guatemala with El Salvador in the South and Mexico were completed.[47]

The urban economy was also big enough to attract US foreign investment into public utilities. In Guatemala, the Electric Bond and Share Co. gained control of an existing German enterprise,[48] which had been expropriated in the First World War, and new developments started elsewhere. By 1929, US direct foreign investment in public utilities in Central America had reached $22.5 million compared with $0.5 million in 1919,[49] with telecommunications dominated by subsidiaries of UFCO.

The expansion of the export sector in the 1920s had a favourable impact on imports (see Table A.11, p. 328) and the value of external trade in general rose rapidly, particularly after the 1920/1 depression. The most serious exceptions to this were in Honduras and Nicaragua; in the former case, revolutionary conditions in the middle 1920s following the disputed election of 1923 took their toll on the *declared* value of imports, since for much of the period the government was not in control of the customs house; in Nicaragua, the oscillation in the value of coffee earnings after 1925 prevented imports from exhibiting the steady increase experienced elsewhere. The increase in imports (in both volume and value terms) gave a boost to commercial activities, and the urban merchant class thrived. At the same time, the increase in the value of external trade made possible a substantial increase in customs revenue and put government revenue on a firmer footing. The rise in revenue was due not to the introduction of new taxes,[50] but to the increase in prosperity and a change in the level of certain export duties and import tariffs.

The expenditure of the additional revenue in theory gave Central American governments a variety of choices, but in practice the main priority was servicing the public debt. New loans were contracted in order to consolidate and simplify the public debt, both external and internal. Costa Rica issued bonds on the New York market with a face value of $8 million, which were used in the main to retire part of the huge internal debt built up under the Tinoco dictatorship. El Salvador in 1923 issued three new bonds in an effort to resolve its accumulated debts to bankers, foreign bondholders and Minor Keith's IRCA, while Honduras in 1926 finally came to an arrangement for repaying the £5.4 million principal owed to British bondholders from the time of the railway scandal (1867–71), the bondholders abandoning their claim for £25 million arrears of interest.

Not all the new loans contracted in the 1920s were for the purpose of retiring the old public debt. Costa Rica and Guatemala both contracted additional debts as part of their rail network programmes; the former issued bonds to a German company in 1923 as payment for electrification of the Pacific Railway, while the latter issued bonds in 1924 and 1927 for construction of the electric Los Altos railway from Guatemala City to Quetzaltenango. It proved to be a disaster, however, and fell into disuse three years after its inauguration in March 1930.

The new loans were in general secured against customs revenues and consular fees, and the service of the public debt was met promptly in the second half of the 1920s. Indeed, such was the priority given to the public debt that towards the end of the decade 20% to 30% of government revenue was given over to servicing and amortization. By 1929, the external debt in *per caput* terms was approximately one pound sterling in Guatemala, El Salvador and Nicaragua; although it was higher in Honduras (£6) and Costa Rica (£7.5), this was not a cause for concern. In the former case it represented a sharp reduction because of the cancellation of arrears of interest and in the latter case it represented a switch from internal to external debt.

The consolidation of the export-led model in the 1920s produced increases in GDP, which were in general in excess of population growth (see Table A.3, p. 312). Except for Honduras in the period 1924–9, however, when new banana lands were brought into cultivation, growth was by no means spectacular and the model was beginning to show distinct signs of fatigue by the end of the decade in Costa Rica and El Salvador.[51] Furthermore, the growth of GDP in the 1920s took place against a favourable external environment, in which both the net barter terms of trade and the purchasing power of exports increased rapidly after 1921 (see Tables A.14 and A.15, pp. 334 and 336). Because of the deficit in net factor payments (interest on the public external debt, profit remittances, etc.), the trade balance was generally in surplus, unless there was a sudden shortfall in export earnings (as in 1920/1). Under the gold standard, however, a deficit in the trade balance tended to be automatically corrected, so that it was not at first a source of concern when in 1929 three countries registered an excess of imports over exports (see Tables A.10 and A.11, pp. 326 and 328).

Successful export-led growth depended not only on a rapid expansion of the export sector, but also on the ability to convert the latter into a stimulus for the transformation and growth of the non-export economy. The temptation to identify successful export-led growth merely with growth of the export sector must be resisted.

Judged in these terms, the export-led model followed by Central America in the 1920s left much to be desired. It is true that favourable world market conditions contributed to a marked increase in traditional exports (bananas and coffee), but there is very little evidence to suggest that this led to the tranformation and growth of the non-export economy. On the contrary, given the exceptional conditions facing the export sector, the growth of real GDP per head in the 1920s was poor. Furthermore, the outlook for traditional exports was beginning to look much less favourable by the late 1920s (e.g. the spread of disease on banana plantations) so that it was not realistic to expect the exceptional conditions of the 1920s to continue indefinitely; thus the model performed relatively poorly under good conditions and this provided little optimism for its expected performance under adverse conditions.

The major weakness of the export-led model was the tendency towards export specialisation in two senses: first, the growing proportion of exports accounted for by coffee and bananas; secondly, the rise in the ratio of export agriculture (mainly coffee and bananas) to real GDP. The capitalist surplus in traditional exports tended to be invested in traditional exports or not invested at all. This problem was compounded by foreign control of the banana sector, since reinvestment in the latter was very import-intensive.

The reluctance of coffee interests to reinvest the capitalist surplus outside the coffee sector was due less to an absence of entrepreneurship than to the existence of formidable barriers. Direct investment in the non-export economy was discouraged by a combination of unfavourable internal terms of trade, a lack of suitable social infrastructure and a shortage of energy supplies. Indirect investment through financial intermediation was discouraged by a banking system which appeared content to serve only the interests of the export sector itself.

Many of these barriers to the investment of the capitalist surplus outside the traditional export sector could be removed only through state intervention. The state, however, was generally too weak to undertake these tasks and failed to take advantage of the boom in exports to strengthen its position through fiscal reforms. Government revenue rose, but the government's share of real GDP (compare Tables A.1 and A.9, pp. 308 and 324) remained very modest outside of Guatemala through the 1920s, and in all republics debt servicing was made a higher priority than expenditure on social infrastructure.

## Consolidation of the export-led model: political repercussions

With the exceptions of Honduras (1923/4) and Nicaragua (after 1926), consolidation of the export-led model in the 1920s coincided with a period of comparative peace and stability in Central America; this stability, combined with the improvement in economic conditions, permitted a certain relaxation of the political climate and made possible a strengthening of the incipient labour movement. These trends were to be short-lived, however, and were reversed soon after the 1929 depression had begun.

Political stability was most apparent in Costa Rica, where the two great figures of the liberal state – Don Ricardo Jiménez and Don Cleto González – succeeded each other in the 1920s. Military expenditure was kept to a minimum and the fear of another dictatorship, such as the Tinoco régime, gradually subsided. The elections leading to the administrations of Julio Acosta García (1920–4), Ricardo Jiménez Oreamuno (1924–8) and Cleto González Víquez (1928–32) were free and fair and the level of popular participation steadily increased; the campaigns, however, were centred round personalities rather than issues and both Don Ricardo and Don Cleto clung to the ideals of the liberal state.[52]

The power of the Costa Rican state, however, was extended in one important direction with the founding of the Instituto Nacional de Seguros, a national insurance monopoly.[53] This state-run company gradually took over all insurance activities in the country and continues to this day to enjoy a monopoly. In other respects, however, the state confined itself to its traditional activities and met with little challenge from organised labour, once the general strike of February 1920 had been resolved (see Rojas Bolaños, 1978).

In El Salvador, the Meléndez dynasty strengthened its grip on the country with manipulated elections which kept the presidency in the family throughout the 1920s. The 'election' of Pío Romero Bosque in 1927, however, proved to be a mistake for the dynasty, as Don Pío – a friend and fellow townsman of the previous President Alfonso Quiñónez – refused to be controlled and he organised in 1930 the freest elections in El Salvador's history.

Even the president before Don Pío had permitted a certain relaxation of the political climate, and in 1924 the Regional Federation of Workers of El Salvador (FRTS) came into existence. According to Miguel Marmol, later a founder member of the Communist Party, the FRTS had 70,000 members in the 1920s, consisting mainly of craft workers in the towns. There were some rural members, among coffee workers and fishermen, but union activity in the countryside was on the whole ruthlessly suppressed.[54]

In Guatemala, events moved fast after the fall of Estrada Cabrera and a Communist Party (CP) was founded in 1922/3. This was also the period when the Federación Regional Obrera de Guatemala was founded, joining both the Central American Federation of Labour and the Pan-American Federation of Labour.[55] The anti-imperialist propaganda of the CP caught the attention of President Orellana, who had successfully deposed Carlos Herrera at the end of 1921, and the leaders were arrested. They were interviewed personally by Orellana, however, who seems to have decided that they posed no threat.[56]

Despite this, both political and labour activity were tightly controlled in Guatemala under General Orellana. When he died in office in December 1926, no disturbances followed and he was succeeded by the first designate, General Lázaro Chacón, who was later 'elected'. Chacón did not deviate from the policies of the Orellana administration, but his control was much weaker and his régime was characterised by indecision and corruption.[57]

In Honduras, General López Gutíerrez came to power in February 1920 following a successful revolt against Francisco Bertrand and soon extracted recognition from a reluctant US administration to whom he presented a *fait accompli*. In the election campaign of October 1919, which put the seal of respectability on his revolt, the General had promised higher wages to banana workers; soon after taking office he was forced to sow what he had reaped.

The banana strike of 1920 was not the first in Honduras,[58] but it was the most violent and achieved most of the strikers' demands. The dispute concerned the employees of Vaccaro Bros., but – as so often in Honduras – the legitimate demands of the workers were used by disgruntled politicians to further their own claims.[59] The López administration declared a state of siege, but was too weak to impose a solution, and the workers obtained an increase in wages to $1.75 per day with double pay for overtime.

The presidential election of 1923 was a three-cornered contest to choose a successor to López. No candidate obtained a clear majority, although Tiburcio Carías Andino of the newly founded National Party secured the largest number of votes. When Congress was unable to resolve the deadlock, General López declared his intention of staying in office; this provoked Carías into beginning a civil war.

The major banana towns on the North coast were soon caught up in hostilities and US marines were sent in to protect US interests. By April, General Vicente Tosta controlled the North in the name of Carías, while the latter controlled the capital; Carías was now in a position to negotiate and the United States was invited to mediate. The result was the Pact of Amapala, under which General Tosta would serve as president until new elections were called.

The elections of 1924 resulted in a clear majority for Miguel Paz Baraona, an ally of Carías. President Paz ruled from 1925 until 1929 when he was succeeded peacefully by Vicente Mejía Colindres, who had defeated Carías in a fair electoral fight in 1928. By the end of the 1920s, therefore, Honduras had succeeded almost for the first time in the twentieth century in securing a peaceful transition of power.

The first months of Paz's administration, however, were anything but peaceful. A strike in the sugar refinery at La Lima, property of the Cuyamel Fruit Co., soon spread to the whole of the North coast and affected the fruit companies. Once again, the work of political agitators gave the strike the character of a confrontation with the government, but this time the strikers' demands were not met.[60] In 1926, nevertheless, the Railroad Union of Honduras received government recognition and from then on labour activity in Honduras became more syndicalist in character.

In Nicaragua, a virtual US protectorate was operated throughout the 1920s; US domination of the country's finances was exercised through collection of the customs revenue, control of the National Bank,[61] refunding of the public debts and appointments to various Claims Commissions.[62] There were, however, several challenges to US authority within Nicaragua. The first came from General Emiliano Chamorro, who had succeeded the pliant Adolfo Díaz to the presidency in undisputed elections in 1917. Chamorro was able to secure his own replacement in 1921 by his uncle, but the latter died in 1923. His constitutional successor, Bartolomé Martínez, ruled until elections brought Carlos Solórzano to the presidency in 1925.

Solórzano was a conservative, but his vice-president (Juan Bautista Sacasa) was a liberal. This apparent display of bipartisan leadership convinced the US that this was an opportune moment for the withdrawal of the marines. Within weeks Chamorro had revolted, and engineered himself back into the presidency by 1926. The US administration could not tolerate Chamorro's abuse of constitutional procedures and refused him recognition. He was replaced, however, not by Sacasa (the constitutional successor), but by Adolfo Díaz who had full US support. This sparked off a liberal revolt and initiated a civil war which brought back the US marines in 1927. An effort to resolve the civil war was made by former US Secretary of State Henry Stimson,[63] and elections were called for 1928 which brought the liberal José María Moncada to power in January 1929. One of the leaders of the Liberal revolt, Augusto C. Sandino, refused to accept the Stimson plan and resolved to carry on armed struggle until all US marines were withdrawn. His struggle won him an international reputation and was to provide the inspiration for a later generation of rebels in Nicaragua.

This overview of political events in Central America in the 1920s provides us with the following conclusions. The liberal oligarchic state had been successfully consolidated in Costa Rica, El Salvador and Guatemala with the observance of constitutional forms and the elimination of monetary and financial instability. The threat to the liberal state through labour unrest was still very minor and did not require very repressive measures for its control. Nevertheless, the 'liberalism' of the oligarchic state did not extend in general to personal liberties, and political activity remained tightly controlled.

In Honduras, the absence of a nationally owned coffee sector had delayed the emergence of a liberal oligarchic state and the republic continued the nineteenth-century tradition of revolt and revolution. Although it is difficult to establish what role the fruit companies played in the perpetuation of political instability, it seems clear that they stood to gain from a continuation of weak government. Political unrest, fiscal poverty and massive external indebtedness left Honduras at the mercy of foreign interests and it is perhaps surprising that the United States never chose to exercise its dominance more directly.

In Nicaragua, consolidation of the liberal oligarchic state was arrested by the US occupation after 1912, although financial stability was achieved. The presence of the marines, however, undermined US relations with other Latin American countries, including those in Central America,[64] and became a source of embarrassment by the early 1920s. The first attempt to withdraw was a failure and by the time of the second (1933), the opportunity for consolidating the liberal oligarchic state had passed.

The liberal oligarchic state did not survive the aftermath of the 1929 depression, being replaced by authoritarian *caudillismo* and an extension of state powers. The main features of the liberal oligarchic state were its narrow definition of government responsibilities, its emphasis on the desirability of export-led growth and its search for national integration through improvements in transport and communications (often under foreign control

The state regarded export-led growth as a desirable objective and was willing to aid it in every way possible, but the interests of the state were not identical with those of export agriculture and tensions could arise (e.g. exchange rate policy).

# 3

## The 1929 depression

Although the world economic crisis which developed at the end of the 1920s is known as the 1929 depression, the decline in economic activity occurred in different years in the Central America republics; the first country to experience a downturn in the value of exports was Nicaragua in 1926, while in Honduras the fall in exports was delayed until 1930/1; the phrase '1929 depression' is therefore a convenient, if slightly inaccurate, description for the events which unfolded in Central America in the period after 1926.

The impact of the world depression was transmitted to Central America in the first instance through a fall in commodity prices. The peculiar nature of banana prices received by Central America, however, meant that earnings from this commodity (see Chapter 2, pp. 35–6) did not follow the pattern set by other primary exports, and the performance of those republics mainly dependent on banana exports (the banana republics) differed accordingly from those mainly dependent on coffee earnings (the coffee republics).

The decline in commodity prices, particularly for coffee, could not be offset by increases in volume, and export earnings fell. This reduction put a severe strain on the newly established currency stability, but the exchange rate at first held its ground and imports were savagely reduced through a combination of demand-reducing falls in real income and non-price rationing. By 1932, however, Costa Rica and El Salvador were obliged to break the link with gold, and their exchange rates began to depreciate against the US dollar.

The sharp fall in the value of external trade reduced public sector revenues and provoked in all republics a fiscal crisis. The first victim of the crisis was investment expenditure, but it soon proved necessary to reduce or 'defer' the salaries of public employees. Service on the public external debt was at first met promptly, but defaults occurred, as in the rest of Latin America, after 1931.

Although import prices fell, bringing down with them the domestic cost of living,[1] this could not prevent a sharp initial decline in real incomes, which contributed to a significant increase in social unrest and represented a challenge to the liberal oligarchic state. Within the small urban economy, unemployment became serious in the private sector, while the public sector suffered a decline in real wages as well as some unemployment. In the rural economy, open unemployment became serious in the banana zones, provoking a series of strikes, while in the coffee sector the real wages of employees fell and a labour surplus began to appear. A further challenge to the government came from the coffee growers, who were threatened by foreclosure and bankruptcy in the wake of falling coffee prices. At the same time, the wealthier group within the coffee sector pressured the state to withdraw the timid reforms which had been extended to labour organisations in the 1920s.

These competing pressures on the liberal oligarchic state proved too great and it collapsed throughout the region after 1930. In each republic, even Costa Rica, the state came to the rescue of coffee growers, large and small, and brought an end to the division of labour between the two groups which had become most noticeable in the 1920s. The new state, marked by authoritarian *caudillismo*, ruled much more directly on behalf of the coffee interests and the export sector, and rolled back many of the modest social and political reforms of the 1920s. The challenge from groups other than the export sector was therefore met by force, and the state lost all pretence of arbitrating between competing class interests.

## Onset of the depression – the external sector

Throughout the inter-war period coffee prices (and the unit values received by Central America) were determined above all by the behaviour of Brazil. The latter's valorisation scheme at the beginning of the 1920s had contributed to the speedy recovery of coffee prices after the 1920/1 depression, and the enormous rise in Brazilian production in 1927/8[2] heralded a decline in prices as stocks began to rise.

The fall in coffee prices after 1928 was indeed severe; the same, however, had occurred in 1920/1, and at first there was no reason to believe that the recovery would not be equally swift. In this respect, coffee growers were to be disappointed; prices fell in the early 1930s to one-third of peak levels achieved in the 1920s and remained there throughout most of the decade. Even at these low prices, coffee exports from Central America continued at pre-depression levels, although there were sharp year to year fluctuations (see Table 3.1). The maintenance of the quantum of exports was made possible by government support for the coffee industry (see Chapter 4, pp. 74–5) together with the ability of growers to reduce marginal cost below price. The huge rental income associated with coffee production in 'good' years was, however, wiped out and the demand for imports was consequently reduced.

While Brazil was the single biggest influence on coffee prices, the behaviour

Table 3.1  Central America: coffee exports, 1929–39 (million lb)

| Year | Costa Rica | El Salvador | Guatemala | Honduras | Nicaragua |
|------|-----------|-------------|-----------|----------|-----------|
| 1929 | 43.4 | 103.2 | 97.4 | 3.5 | 29.1 |
| 1930 | 51.8 | 129.2 | 125.7 | 3.1 | 33.7 |
| 1931 | 50.7 | 120.4 | 80.0 | 2.4 | 34.8 |
| 1932 | 40.8 | 87.5 | 100.5 | 3.5 | 17.9 |
| 1933 | 61.3 | 123.9 | 78.5 | 4.2 | 30.2 |
| 1934 | 42.1 | 110.0 | 106.9 | 4.2 | 32.4 |
| 1935 | 53.4 | 110.5 | 89.9 | 2.4 | 40.8 |
| 1936 | 47.0 | 108.9 | 112.0 | 3.3 | 28.9 |
| 1937 | 58.4 | 149.0 | 103.8 | 5.5 | 34.8 |
| 1938 | 55.1 | 118.6 | 108.2 | 2.6 | 31.5 |
| 1939 | 44.5 | 123.0 | 96.3 | 4.2 | 38.4 |

Source: Torres Rivas, 1973, table 2, pp. 286–7

of the United Fruit Company (UFCO) had a great impact on banana prices.[3] By purchasing Sam Zemurray's Cuyamel Fruit Company at the end of 1929, UFCO acquired a 60% share of the banana market and was in a position to influence end-use prices through its global production decisions. UFCO's strategy was to engineer a sharp fall in production; banana prices in North America as a result fell by much less than other commodities.[4] A policy of raising efficiency in its various divisions helped to reduce unit costs, and UFCO found itself able to pay its shareholders a dividend even in the worst years of the depression.[5]

The impact of these policies on Central America was somewhat varied. Costa Rica was the worst affected; production had already begun to decline after 1926 as a result of the spread of disease and this trend was not reversed until new plantations were opened on the Pacific in the mid-1930s (see Table 3.2). UFCO's 1910 contract with the Costa Rican government fell due for renewal in 1930 and the administration of Ricardo Jiménez was obliged to negotiate under very unfavourable circumstances.[6] With the purchase of the Cuyamel, Honduras became the jewel in UFCO's crown and banana exports increased until 1930/1. The decline that followed, however, was not due to a policy decision, but to the spread of disease which affected the plantations of Standard Fruit as well. In Guatemala, production continued at pre-depression levels, but in Nicaragua export levels declined as Sandino's guerrilla war and, more importantly, disease both took their toll (see Table 3.2).

The decline in production brought with it a sharp rise in unemployment in the banana zones with little or no alternative sources of work available.[7] Even those who continued in employment, however, or who had contracts for the sale of fruit to the banana companies were not unaffected. The fruit

Table 3.2 *Central America: banana exports, 1929–39 (million bunches)*

| Year | Costa Rica | Guatemala | Honduras[1] | Nicaragua |
|------|-----------|-----------|-------------|-----------|
| 1929 | 6.1 | 6.4 | 26.9 | 4.1 |
| 1930 | 5.8 | 4.9 | 29.1 | 3.9 |
| 1931 | 5.1 | 5.8 | 29.0 | 3.0 |
| 1932 | 4.3 | 5.2 | 27.9 | 3.4 |
| 1933 | 4.3 | 5.6 | 23.5 | 3.7 |
| 1934 | 3.2 | 5.2 | 19.5 | 2.7 |
| 1935 | 2.9 | 5.6 | 15.8 | 3.0 |
| 1936 | 3.9 | 7.5 | 12.2 | 1.9 |
| 1937 | 5.5 | 8.6 | 12.7 | 2.5 |
| 1938 | 5.0 | 9.5 | 8.5 | 2.0 |
| 1939 | 3.4 | 10.6 | 12.5 | 1.7 |

Source: International Institute of Agriculture, *International Yearbook of Agricultural Statistics*, Rome, various years
[1] Fiscal year (i.e. 1929 is 1928/9) up to 1938; thereafter calendar year

companies honoured their old contracts,[8] but offered new contracts to private planters at sharply reduced prices. In Costa Rica, UFCO lowered the nine-hand count-bunch price[9] in two stages from 60 cents in 1929 to 24 cents in 1932. In Honduras, the price offered fell from 50 cents in 1929 to 30 cents by 1932. There was therefore a deliberate attempt by the fruit companies to shift the burden of adjustment to the world depression on to its tropical divisions. The attempt, however, was less successful where the bulk of the fruit was produced on company plantations, because the only effective way to reduce unit costs was by lowering money wages. This strategy was adopted, but resistance was high and company policy in this sphere provoked several violent strikes (see below, p. 59).

Other commodity prices also tumbled in the wake of the 1929 depression. The price of raw sugar per pound, for example, which had soared to 22.5 cents in New York in May 1920, had fallen to 0.59 cents in May 1932. Exporters' problems were further compounded by the Chadbourne Committee's 'carve-up' of the US market, which gave preferential treatment to US producers, Cuba, Hawaii, Puerto Rico and the Philippines;[10] Central American exports of sugar virtually collapsed after 1930 as a result of this agreement.[11]

The fall in commodity prices after 1929 brought a precipitate decline in export earnings. Exports had already peaked before 1929 (see Figure 3.1) as a result of the earlier drop in coffee prices and the spread in some countries of banana disease (e.g. Costa Rica). The initial decline in export values, however, was not considered very serious in Central America. The cyclical nature of export earnings was accepted and reserves built up in

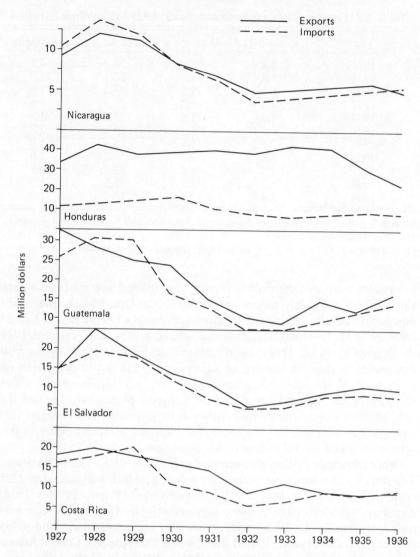

*Figure 3.1* Central America: imports and exports ($ million), 1927–36
(Source: Tables A.10 and A.11)

good years were used to support imports in bad years; thus, in all the republics except El Salvador and Honduras[12] a visible trade deficit was at first tolerated (see Figure 3.1). By 1930, however, the severity of the depression had become apparent and imports by value fell even more rapidly than the value of exports; thus, all Central American countries ran surpluses on visible trade in the worst years of the depression.

The sharp decline in the value of imports during the depression (to about one quarter of peak levels) was not all due to volume changes. Import prices in dollar terms did fall, although the evidence is rather indirect.[13] The barter terms of trade, however, initially rose or fell depending on whether a republic specialised in bananas or coffee (see Figure 3.2).[14] Thus, in the case of Hon-

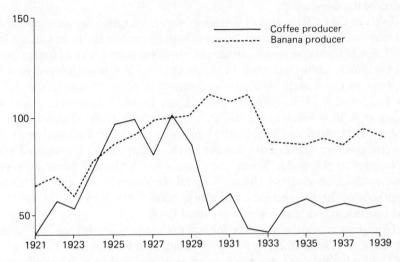

*Figure 3.2* Barter terms of trade (1928 = 100), 1921–39

*Note:* import prices have been derived from data on real and money values of imports for Honduras (see Banco Central de Honduras, 1956). Coffee prices are unit values for El Salvador and banana prices are unit values for Costa Rica

duras (where the bulk of exports was accounted for by bananas) the terms of trade index rose steadily until 1933 (see Table A.14). Coffee producers were not so fortunate. The steep fall in coffee prices brought a sharp decline in the barter terms of trade after 1928 which was reversed only in 1934 (see Figure 3.2). El Salvador, for example, whose export earnings came almost entirely from coffee, was the worst affected, although the other coffee producing countries also experienced a deterioration in the barter terms of trade.

The collapse of export earnings at the end of the 1920s put a severe strain on the monetary and fiscal reforms, which in several cases had only just been completed. Gold began to flow out of the region, putting pressure on the republics' banking reserves,[15] and one by one the Central American governments were obliged to abandon the gold standard and prohibit the export of gold.[16] The first to do so was El Salvador in October 1931, while the last was Guatemala in July 1933. With the abandonment of the gold standard, the management of the exchange rate became a critical policy decision. Despite the falls in real income associated with the collapse of export earnings, demand for foreign exchange (particularly dollars) tended to outstrip supply and a choice had to be made between price and non-price rationing. With the exception of Costa Rica and El Salvador, non-price rationing was adopted and the quetzal, the lempira and the córdoba all maintained their pre-depression parity with the US dollar during the worst years of the depression.

Even in Costa Rica and El Salvador, non-price rationing was important, so that exchange rate depreciation was kept to modest levels. In Costa Rica, the Caja de Conversión maintained the pre-depression parity of four colones to the dollar until December 1931. At that point it was changed to 4.25 colones to the dollar, before being lowered to 4.50 colones to the dollar in 1932 and 4.75 in February 1933. Later in 1933, however, it was set again at 4.50 colones to the dollar.[17] In El Salvador, the abandonment of the gold standard in October 1931 provoked a sharp depreciation of the currency, which fell to 2.95 colones to the dollar in 1933 compared with 2 colones to the dollar before the depression. A Central Bank, however, was established in 1934 (Banco Central de Reserva) and this led to the appreciation of the currency and a new official parity to the US dollar of 2.5 colones, which was not changed until 1986.

Non-price rationing of scarce foreign exchange was achieved in a variety of ways. In Costa Rica, a Board of Control was established in January 1932 to which those requiring foreign exchange had to make application. In the following year, the Board's powers were strengthened by a decree which stated that 80% of the funds it received should be used for the importation of merchandise, of which 60% was to be used for articles of necessity, 30% for 'useful' articles and 10% for luxuries. In Nicaragua, a similar control board was established with the US-appointed Collector General of Customs as one of its three members. Elsewhere, however, foreign exchange was sold through the banks to their favoured customers according to availability. It seems safe to assume that, under these circumstances, a black market developed in foreign currency, although no reliable information is available.

The decision to maintain the parity with the US dollar after the collapse of the gold standard (with the partial exception of Costa Rica and El Salvador) can be attributed to several factors. First, the memory of currency instability before the monetary reforms was still fresh; secondly, the burden of debt service to non-US bondholders would become less severe insofar as their currencies (e.g. the pound sterling) were depreciating against the US dollar; thirdly, the idea that import-substituting industrialisation (ISI) could be achieved through currency depreciation was not considered realistic; and, fourthly, the support which currency depreciation might give to the export sector was not considered necessary in view of the other measures taken (see Chapter 4, pp. 74–9).

Table 3.3 *Summary of budget accounts (Receipts in million of units of domestic currency; expenditure in brackets)*

| Year | Costa Rica | El Salvador | Nicaragua | Honduras | Guatemala | Year |
|------|-----------|-------------|-----------|----------|-----------|------|
| 1928 | 33.3 (26.9) | 27.0 (27.2) | N.A. | 13.7 (13.1) | 15.4 (16.4) | 1928/9 |
| 1929 | 35.4 (36.2) | 24.6 (25.8) | 5.9 (3.8) | 14.3 (15.0) | 13.4 (14.3) | 1929/30 |
| 1930 | 27.5 (32.5) | 20.5 (N.A.) | 5.4 (4.9) | 11.8 (13.9) | 10.7 (13.2) | 1930/1 |
| 1931 | 24.8 (27.6) | 14.4 (17.9) | 4.7 (4.8) | 10.9 (10.1) | 9.2 (9.9) | 1931/2 |
| 1932 | 23.1 (25.0) | 17.4 (16.6) | 3.8 (4.2) | 9.0 (12.3) | 8.3 (8.3) | 1932/3 |
| 1933 | 23.9 (24.2) | 14.6 (15.6) | 4.2 (4.7) | 10.1 (12.7) | 8.6 (8.2) | 1933/4 |
| 1934 | 26.4 (25.9) | 19.4 (16.1) | 5.0 (4.9) | 10.8 (12.5) | 9.6 (8.8) | 1934/5 |
| 1935 | 27.2 (30.8) | 17.7 (19.9) | 5.3 (5.5) | 10.0 (14.1) | 10.5 (10.0) | 1935/6 |
| 1936 | 34.5 (32.5) | 19.9 (19.4) | 7.5 (6.9) | 11.7 (11.7) | 11.6 (10.4) | 1936/7 |

Source: League of Nations, 1938

**Impact of the depression outside the external sector**

The decline in the value of external trade, both imports and exports, brought with it a sharp fall in customs revenues and provoked a severe budget crisis. Government attempts to reduce expenditure to match the fall in revenue were not successful and budget deficits (see Table 3.3) were common in the first years of the depression.

The crisis was tackled by governments from both the revenue and expenditure sides. Import tariffs were raised and new taxes were introduced; Costa Rica, for example, introduced a personal income tax in 1931 on a sliding scale from 0.6% to 6.0%, but the yields from this and other new taxes were very small indeed. On the expenditure side, governments' freedom of manoeuvre was very limited. Outgoings were dominated by wages and salaries on the one hand and public debt service on the other. For various reasons, it was felt essential to maintain the service at least on the *foreign* debt; in several cases, these payments were already secured by a first lien on the customs revenue and, in any case, default would rob the offending government of the opportunity for additional borrowing from abroad. A failure to pay the wage and salary bill, however, or a cut in rates of pay threatened the survival of the government in power.

Despite these difficulties, salaries were reduced in some cases, although more often than not they were simply 'deferred'. The unpaid salary bills were added to the internal public debt (along with loans from the banking system to help cover the budget deficit) and this contributed to a sharp rise in domestic indebtedness (see Table 3.4). Efforts to obtain additional funding from abroad, however, were not entirely unsuccessful; Costa Rica in 1931 obtained a loan from the National City Bank of New York and Guatemala secured in 1930 a $2.5 million loan from the Swedish Match

Table 3.4 *Central America: total public debt, 1928–36 (Internal debt in brackets; in millions of units of domestic currency)*

| Year | Costa Rica[3] | El Salvador[3] | Nicaragua[1] | Honduras[2] | Guatemala[3] |
|------|---------------|----------------|--------------|-------------|--------------|
| 1928 | 83.6 (15.0) | 45.8 (4.7) | 23.5 (20.2) | 28.4 (17.2) | 17.6 (2.9) |
| 1929 | 87.8 (17.9) | 42.7 (3.7) | 23.2 (20.1) | 29.4 (18.6) | 15.6 (2.1) |
| 1930 | 94.1 (25.8) | 43.6 (7.6) | 22.5 (19.7) | 27.0 (16.6) | 20.0 (4.6) |
| 1931 | 101.8 (27.4) | 46.6 (11.8) | 21.9 (19.3) | 25.5 (17.0) | 20.9 (6.4) |
| 1932 | 108.4 (30.9) | 49.0 (12.3) | 21.6 (19.2) | 25.6 (16.2) | 21.3 (7.1) |
| 1933 | 114.5 (30.6) | 46.9 (9.8) | 17.9 (15.5) | 28.0 (19.1) | 22.2 (7.6) |
| 1934 | 115.5 (31.8) | 45.3 (8.6) | 10.0 (7.7) | 28.7 (21.1) | 22.1 (7.6) |
| 1935 | 119.7 (36.7) | 45.7 (6.2) | 8.2 (5.9) | 27.8 (20.8) | 22.2 (7.2) |
| 1936 | 141.9 (37.7) | 42.1 (6.2) | 9.0 (6.7) | 28.3 (21.8) | 20.2 (6.0) |

Source: League of Nations, 1938
[1] 1928–32, 31 March; 1932–6, 28 February
[2] 31 July
[3] 31 December

Company in return for a monopoly on match sales. El Salvador also obtained a $1 million loan in 1931.

The problems of maintaining debt payments in the face of declining revenues raised the burden of debt service in relative terms. In Costa Rica, for example, external debt service (interest and amortization payments) jumped from 14.1% of government revenue in 1929 to 30.3% in 1932. The incentive to shoulder this sort of financial burden steadily receded as the prospects dimmed for significant inflows of new foreign capital. Not surprisingly, therefore, most of the Central American republics (all except Honduras) defaulted on their external debt obligations from 1932 onwards.[18] These defaults gave some relief not only to the pressures on the balance of payments, but also to the weak fiscal position; debt service payments as a proportion of (declining) government revenue fell by around 50% in the defaulting countries, so that the latter were running a modest budget surplus by 1934/5 (see Table 3.3).

The budget deficits run by Central American governments in the worst years of the depression were not due to any attempt at counter-cyclical spending with the possible exception of Costa Rica. Indeed, one may safely conclude that the 'full employment' budget was substantially in surplus and the deficit arose from the inability of administrations to cut expenditure as quickly as revenue was falling. In any case, the government's contribution to real GDP in this period was very small (see Tables A.1 and A.9) and this contribution actually fell in relative terms during the depression despite the budget deficits.

In Costa Rica, there was a half-hearted attempt at employment-generating public works expenditure in the worst years of the depression, and government borrowing from the banking system (and with it internal debt) increased substantially. The road-building programme continued and an effort was made to form agricultural colonies on disused UFCO land, but these efforts did not amount to much, the governments' contribution to real GDP actually declined, and the principal cause of the rise in internal debt was the need for emergency borrowing to cover the current rather than capital account.

The private sector outside the export zones was also not exempt from the impact of the depression. Indeed, the heavy dependence of so many branches of the private economy on the fortunes of the export sector was brought into sharp focus after 1929 and provided much ammunition for the critics of monoculture and export-led growth. Commerce, particularly in urban areas, was badly hit by the shortage of imports and those branches of transport, such as railways, tied to the movement of external trade were seriously affected.[19] The decline in urban real incomes also affected the demand for the products of 'mature' industries, such as footwear, tobacco and furniture, while the 'immature' industries (e.g. clothing) were unable to exploit the shortage of competing imports because of a lack of foreign exchange for raw materials, spare parts and machinery.

The risks inherent in extreme export specialisation were now apparent. In the absence of a significant import competing sector, whose output could increase in response to import restrictions, adjustment to external equilibrium required huge falls in real income to lower demand for imports. Furthermore, the collapse of the export sector threatened the whole social and political basis of the export-led model. The depression was therefore a major challenge not just for export-led growth, but also for the liberal oligarchic state.

Although the weak industrial sector could not be expected to derive much advantage from the shortage of imports, domestic use agriculture (DUA) was better placed to increase production at the expense of food imports. DUA did not, in general, require foreign exchange for its expansion, although it did require land and labour; as will be shown in the next chapter, however, the release of land and labour from the export sector to promote DUA proved easier to achieve in the 'coffee republics' (Costa Rica, El Salvador and Guatemala) than elsewhere.

The shift of resources into DUA took some time to achieve and the immediate impact of the external crisis was a sharp fall in real GDP per head (see Table 3.5). These declines in real income were aggravated by terms of trade losses and the hardship was experienced with particular severity by three groups: public sector employees, the urban proletariat and the export sector. The latter's interests took precedence over all other groups,

*The 1929 depression*

Table 3.5 *Real GDP per head in the depression*

|  | Costa Rica | El Salvador | Guatemala | Honduras | Nicaragua |
|---|---|---|---|---|---|
| Peak | 1926 | 1926 | 1930 | 1931 | 1929 |
| Trough | 1932 | 1932 | 1933 | 1937 | 1936 |
| Decline (%) | 21.3 | 23.2 | 23.9 | 31.7 | 43.0 |

Source: Table A.3

so that policy both during and after the depression continued to be heavily influenced by the short-term needs of the export sector. Thus, it proved just as difficult to escape from the pressures in favour of the export-led model as it had in the 1920s, although the motivation was now different.

### Social unrest

The collapse of export-led growth in the wake of the 1929 depression left some groups in the Central American economies more exposed than others. The most affected were those who gained their living from the export sector – workers, tenant farmers and landowners. Public sector employees, however, suffered from the crisis in government finance, while the private urban sector was also hit by the decline in real incomes.

The crisis in the coffee industry was particularly serious, as it called into question the whole export-led model; the mechanisms previously relied on for safeguarding the interests of the coffee sector in a period of depression (as in 1920/1) proved inadequate after the 1929 depression. The weak state built up under the period of the liberal oligarchy was subject to pressure from several angles and the interests of the coffee industry were no longer secure.

The collapse of coffee prices was not the only problem which growers faced. Under the gold standard, gold flowed out of the commercial banking system in response to a payments deficit, thereby reducing the banks' reserve base. This forced a reduction in new lending and a demand for the recovery of old loans by the banks, which fell particularly heavily on coffee growers. The banking system, after all, had grown up in response to their needs and they were the prime beneficiary from the expansion of bank lending; inevitably, they were the main victims when lending declined. The initial response of the growers to the decline in price and the threat of foreclosure by the banks was two-fold. First, an attempt was made to reduce unit costs by lowering money wages and laying off part of their labour force; secondly, coffee growers tried to improve their effectiveness as a pressure group through the formation of more powerful national associations.

Unemployment was also important in the banana zones, where employment conditions were determined more by the spread of banana diseases than by the impact of the depression itself. In Costa Rica, banana exports had begun to decline after 1926 and the position was not made any easier by the fall (albeit modest) in banana auction prices. The United Fruit Company (UFCO) responded by lowering the price to private planters with new contracts, from 60 to 30 cents per count-bunch.

This reduction put downward pressure on the money wages of banana workers. More serious for the workers, however, was the steady reduction in employment prospects on the Atlantic coast, as production fell, and the possibility that migration restrictions might prevent the black workers among them from moving to the new plantations on the Pacific coast. By 1934, these fears – coupled with skilful agitation by the newly formed Communist Party (see pp. 64–5) – resulted in a major strike against both UFCO and the private planters. When the latter capitulated, the strike was renewed against UFCO alone, resulting in some of the workers' demands being met.[20]

In Honduras, banana production at first increased after 1929 despite low world prices, as both UFCO and Standard Fruit capitalised on new investments in the banana zones. Exports peaked, however, in 1930/1 and the subsequent drop in production affected employment conditions and the prices paid to private planters. The latter were of relatively minor importance in Honduras, however, as most bananas were grown on fruit company lands.

In addition to lay-offs, the fruit companies tried to reduce money wages. The Tela Railroad Co. (subsidiary of UFCO) tried to lower the wages of port workers, for example, from 25 US cents per hour, while the Truxillo Railroad Co. (another UFCO subsidiary) tried to do the same. Both actions sparked off strikes early in 1932, which ended in some satisfaction for the workers.[21] In the same year, the employees of Standard Fruit went on strike in pursuit of higher wages; this, however, was not successful, although the workers' non-wage demands were met.[22]

Before 1929, the interests of the coffee sector had been served informally without either powerful producers' associations or government interference. As a group, coffee growers had been able to rely on government support and a sympathetic ear, whenever needed, and there had been no need to formalise the relationship. After 1929, however, producers' associations sprang up in response to the crisis. In El Salvador, a society for the defence of coffee was founded in 1929 which became in 1930 the Asociación Cafetalera de El Salvador;[23] in Costa Rica, the Asociación Nacional de Productores de Café was founded in 1930 with the purpose of pressuring the government into regulating the relationship between producers and exporters,[24] while in Guatemala a similar association was also formed. Within a few years, these organisations would exert a profound influence on the relationship between government and the coffee industry (see Chapter 4); indirectly, they contributed substantially to the transition from liberal oligarchy to authoritarian *caudillismo* (see pp. 61–4).

Money wages for coffee workers before the depression averaged 25–30 US cents per day in cases where subsistence was also supplied. Efforts were made to reduce these wages after 1929 to around 15 US cents per day, which met with considerable opposition and resulted in frequent clashes between workers and representatives of the armed forces.[25] It is impossible to establish whether the *real* wages of coffee workers declined in the first years of the depression; a more serious threat to their standard of living probably came from the rise in unemployment, as workers were laid off, rather than the reduction in money wages.[26]

Although the social unrest in the banana zones and on the coffee estates was serious and represented a challenge to both employers and government, the latter were more immediately threatened by the deteriorating situation in the public sector. The collapse of state revenue made it increasingly difficult for public sector employees to be paid on time and efforts to reduce expenditure by cutting wages and salaries called into question the government's survival.

The situation was particularly serious in El Salvador, where the three-month delay in paying the army is generally thought to have contributed to the military coup in 1931.[27] In Costa Rica, the deterioration in the fortunes of public sector employees was temporarily arrested in 1931 through a series of bank loans to bring their salaries up to date,[28] but in Guatemala deferred salary payments at the end of 1930 were one factor accounting for the military coup in December 1930.[29]

The deterioration of employment conditions in the wake of the depression prompted the Costa Rican government to conduct an unemployment census in 1932.[30] This estimated the number of unemployed at 8,863, equivalent to 6% of the labour force.[31] Over 70% of the unemployed were landless labourers in agriculture, mainly from the coffee rather than banana regions, while only seven workers are described as public employees. The most important urban professions affected by unemployment are listed as carpenters, bricklayers and shoemakers.

These figures for unemployment are not high, but then (as now) open unemployment was something of a luxury in the absence of social security payments, and one must assume that the responses to the depression took the form of an increase in under-employment and second-choice jobs. Certainly there was social unrest in the urban areas, which resulted in confrontations with the police on several occasions. In addition, one must remember that the organisational strength of the urban labour movement had been considerably increased in the 1920s and solid gains made, so that the decline of real income at the start of the 1930s appeared much worse by comparison.

## Political change – the rise of *caudillismo*

The liberal oligarchic states had developed after 1870 in response to the needs of export-led growth. The model had reached its finest expression in Costa Rica, particularly under the liberals Ricardo Jiménez and Cleto González Víquez. In Nicaragua, its consolidation had been thwarted by the US occupation, while in Honduras its development had been delayed by the absence of a large coffee export sector. Nevertheless, throughout the region, the elements of a political model common to all the republics were readily apparent by the end of the 1920s.

The 1929 depression cruelly exposed the weaknesses of the liberal oligarchic state and the related model of export-led growth. Faced with a collapse of state revenues and pressure for state action by the most affected groups, the governments of the republics responded in ways which were wholly inadequate. It was a time for decisive action, but the liberal oligarchic state seemed to have run out of ideas.

Within each republic, the most powerful interest groups experienced a convergence of ideas. First, it was necessary to safeguard the interests of the export sector, to which such groups were tied; secondly, all manifestations of social and labour unrest must be crushed while, thirdly, public finance must be restored to a sound position through a balanced budget. Only a strongman, a *caudillo*, could be relied upon to exercise such a programme of government, but there was no shortage of candidates.

The rise of the *caudillos* throughout the region, with the partial exception of Costa Rica, posed a threat to the relationship with the United States. According to the 1923 Washington Treaty, the normal routes through which *caudillos* came to power (*golpes de estado*) and retained power (*continuismo*) were supposed to lead to non-recognition. US opposition, however, was eventually overcome and the 1930s became politically the decade of the *caudillos*. The authoritarian rule established in this period was to have a profound effect on Central America for several decades.

The first *caudillo* to emerge from the ashes of the depression was General Jorge Ubico in Guatemala. The government of General Lazaro Chacón proved increasingly incompetent as the depression deepened and it might well have been overthrown before elections were due (in 1932), if Chacón had not resigned in December 1930, when he suffered a stroke. The Cabinet and Assembly selected Second Designate Baudilla Palma as Provisional President on the grounds that the First Designate, General Mauro de León, was ineligible.[32] As Baudillo Palma was a relative of Chacón, the latter's opponents were provided with a convenient excuse for intervention and a military coup led by General Manuel Orellana toppled the régime before the end of 1930.

The Orellana régime soon learnt, however, that it would not receive US recognition and the General resigned. A new provisional president was appointed by the Assembly on 31 December and elections were called for February 1931. General Ubico immediately announced his candidacy. Ubico's early entry into the electoral ring combined with the fact that he had his own long-established political party (a splinter group from the liberals) gave him a marked advantage. Indeed, he was unopposed, as neither the conservatives nor the liberal groups felt able to field a candidate against him.

Because his ascent to power was constitutional, Ubico received US recognition soon after his inauguration as president on 14 February 1931. He rapidly made clear that in the struggle between liberty and order, he preferred the latter; Ubiquistas gained control of the Assembly, the Supreme Court and the bureaucracy, and several newspapers closed during his first year in office. He did, however, insist on honesty in the public sector, and the Law of Probity was passed in May 1931, requiring a declaration of personal wealth by all public employees earning more than $200 per month or who administered public funds. Ubico lost no time in repressing any manifestation of labour unrest and by the end of 1931 several hundred political prisoners had been incarcerated in the central penitentiary. The uprising in El Salvador in January 1932 provoked repressions in Guatemala and soon the better known labour leaders in the country had either been imprisoned or shot.[33]

The transition from liberal oligarchic rule to authoritarian *caudillismo* in El Salvador was complicated by the brief reformist interlude during the presidency of Pío Romero Bosque (1927–31). Although Don Pío suppressed ruthlessly various manifestations of social unrest in the last months of his presidency and exiled the communist leader Augustín Farabundo Martí,[34] he did permit free elections in January 1931 and did not try to handpick his successor.

The fairness of the elections (generally conceded to have been the most free in the country's history) permitted the Partido Laborista Salvadoreño of Arturo Araujo to make a late entry on the electoral scene. Don Arturo was a *finquero* who had studied engineering in Great Britain at the turn of the century and whose political ideas had been influenced by the British Labour Party. Within El Salvador, however, his election campaign was supported vigorously by Alberto Masferrer, a professor and social reformer whose political programme was captured by the slogan 'Mínimum Vital'.[35]

The year before the elections in El Salvador had been marked by severe labour unrest leading to confrontations with the police and National Guard and a ban in August 1930 on workers' meetings and political agitation. These circumstances gave Araujo a plurality of votes in the presidential elections and his victory was cemented by congressional approval in February 1931.[36]

Don Arturo's presidency began in March 1931, but it was destined to be short-lived. Although he had not campaigned on a programme of land reform, his administration was expected by rural labourers to be sympathetic to their demands. Faced with a fiscal crisis, however, as elsewhere in Central America, the Araujo régime appeared incapable of decisive action and public sector salaries, including those of the military, fell several months into arrears. By November 1931, the pressure on the régime had become intense and a military coup overthrew Araujo.

It was made clear to the junta which carried out the coup that it would not receive US recognition. The presidency therefore reverted to Araujo's vice-president, General Maximiliano Hernández Martínez, whose presidential ambitions went back to the early 1920s. The role of General Martínez in the coup itself is still uncertain, but there can be no doubt that he was acceptable to the ruling classes of El Salvador, despite his brief association with Araujo's social reformist ideas.[37]

Just how acceptable was made clear following the unsuccessful peasant revolt of January 1932. This remarkable uprising, which combined racial antagonisms with communist ideology,[38] was doomed to failure before it had begun because of the state of alertness of the security forces, who had received prior warning. The uprising, however, has secured its place in history because of the bloodthirsty revenge (*la matanza*) exacted by General Martínez in which between 10,000 and 30,000 people lost their lives. All manifestations of rural trade unionism and labour activity were crushed after the uprising and coffee growers were once again faced with a pliant labour force.

The Martínez régime may have represented the *caudillismo* sought by the ruling classes, but it was not acceptable to the US State Department. This policy of non-recognition was not due to *la matanza*, but to the unconstitutional nature of General Martínez's ascent to power which offended the 1923 Washington Treaty. The latter had been invoked against General Orellana in Guatemala and it seemed inconsistent to the Hoover administration not to apply it against General Martínez.

Martínez, however, made it clear that he had no intention of quitting and campaigned for recognition throughout Central America. By the end of 1932, Costa Rica had succumbed and denounced the Washington treaty. Recognition was then obtained from the rest of Central America in January 1934 and the United States immediately followed suit. The US had been thwarted, the Washington Treaty was in shreds and the path had been cleared for the renewal of *caudillismo* through the policy of *continuismo*.

The transition to *caudillismo* in Honduras was affected by the timing of the depression, which did not reach the republic until 1931. Indeed, the liberal government of President Vicente Mejía Colindres (1929–33) felt confident enough to present Congress in 1931 with a labour code recognising the right to strike, abolishing 'truck shops' (company stores) and payment in kind, and similar reforms. The Code did not receive Congressional support, however, as Congress was controlled by the conservative National Party.[39]

The leader of the Nationalists, Tiburcio Carías Andino, had been frustrated in his political ambitions throughout the 1920s (see pp. 44–5 above). In the 1932 elections, he was again a candidate and his campaign benefited from the serious fiscal crisis through which the government was by now passing. Carías defeated his Liberal opponent in a comparatively fair election, but a part of the Liberal Party did not accept the result and resorted to arms.

Carías had been denied the Presidency in 1924 through a similar tactic, but this time he made no mistake, ruthlessly crushing the revolt and assuming power in February 1933. Although the elections which brought him to power were reasonably free, they were to be the last until 1948 as Carías retained himself in power beyond his allotted term through *continuismo*.

Costa Rica suffered as much as any republic from the ravages of the depression, but the response at the political level was somewhat different owing to its unusual democratic traditions.[40] Nevertheless, a *Tico* version of *caudillismo* operated during part of the 1930s and 1940s, although the tradition of presidential elections every four years was not broken. The solution is a good example of how problems are resolved in Costa Rica *a la Tica*.[41]

In 1930 there were several manifestations of labour unrest. Meetings of farmworkers on the Meseta Central were broken up violently[42] and four hundred shoemakers went on strike in San José when their salaries were reduced.[43] The deteriorating situation proved fertile ground for left-wing activism and the Communist Party was founded in June 1931, having developed out of the Asociación Revolucionaria Cultura Obrera (ARCO) set up in 1929.[44] ARCO had set up a Unión General de Trabajadores in 1930, which campaigned for and among the unemployed, but the Communist Party was not ready to field a presidential candidate in the 1932 elections and confined itself at first to propaganda and agitation, particularly among the banana workers on the Atlantic coast.

The presidential elections resulted in a victory for Ricardo Jiménez, who succeeded to the presidency for the third time. Don Ricardo was a classic representative of the liberal oligarchy and there were voices among Costa Rica's ruling classes who felt that the crisis through which the country was passing demanded stronger measures than could be expected from the president-elect. The opposition of these sections of the ruling class to the continuation of the liberal oligarchy led to a revolt, which received the backing of soldiers from one of the barracks in San José, but which was soon put down.

Don Ricardo owed his victory more to his extraordinary reputation among Costa Ricans than to his programme of political action. Nevertheless, one of his first acts was to introduce a minimum wage law, which was extended to rural workers in 1935.[45] This helped to reduce the popularity of the Communist Party, which had been forced for electoral purposes to change its name to Bloque de Obreros y Campesinos and which had elected two deputies to Congress in 1934.

The reforms of the Jiménez régime may have helped to keep labour unrest in check, but they were not acceptable to the still powerful coffee interests. Their candidate in the 1936 presidential elections was León Cortés, who had been Jiménez's minister of development, but to whom Don Ricardo was only lukewarm. Cortés represented a break with the liberal oligarchic tradition and his victory marked a turning-point in Costa Rican politics, a turning-point which was reached earlier elsewhere in Central America. Although he was not an army man, Cortés while president was described as *caudillo*. The reform programme of Don Ricardo was halted, although not reversed, and the president harassed the Communist Party, refusing to allow the deputy from San José, Manuel Mora Valverde, to take his seat.[46] In the best traditions of *caudillismo*, Cortés tried to retain his influence after 1940 by handpicking his successor, but as in El Salvador in 1927, this attempt at *continuismo* (see Chapter 4, p. 84) turned out differently to what was intended.

Political developments in Nicaragua during the depression were conditioned more by the consequences of the US occupation than by the deterioration in economic and social conditions. Despite this, events were to lead to the establishment of *caudillismo* in the 1930s in a particularly ruthless form. Sandino's refusal to accept the Stimson Plan (see p. 46 above) led to his launching a guerrilla war against the US marines and the National Guard. The latter had been created through US influence in the late 1920s in an effort to establish a professional, non-political army, and in an attempt to ensure this objective the leading positions were occupied by US marines, although the rank-and-file were Nicaraguans.

Sandino adopted his tactics so skilfully to the needs of bush warfare that he was never defeated. At the political level, his struggle was conducted on a nationalistic, patriotic and anti-imperialist platform, which struck a chord in many Nicaraguans and provided valuable civilian assistance for his guerrilla army. All efforts by international communists, such as Farabundo Martí, to turn the war into a class struggle failed.[47]

By 1931, the Hoover administration had accepted that peace would never come to Nicaragua so long as it was occupied by US marines and a decision was taken to withdraw all troops after the 1932 presidential elections. This plan was adhered to and the last marines withdrew in January 1933, although Sandino continued to harass them until the day they left.[48] The withdrawal of the marines accelerated plans for replacing US officials at the head of the National Guard by Nicaraguans. By mid-1932, it was announced that the new director of the Guard would be Anastasio 'Tacho' Somoza, a liberal who had filled various posts in the Moncada régime.[49] Even before the last marines left, it was clear from the nature of the senior appointments that the Guard would not be non-political.

The elections in November 1932, supervised by US marines, resulted in a victory for the liberal Juan Bautista Sacasa over his conservative opponent, Adolfo Díaz. Within months of the US withdrawal, Sandino had laid down his arms and made an honourable peace with the Sacasa government, but his mere presence was a threat to the burning ambitions of Somoza, and Sandino was assassinated in February 1934. The death of Sandino cleared the path to the presidency for 'Tacho' Somoza.[50] He pressured his uncle, President Sacasa, into resigning in June 1936; having resigned from the National Guard, he was then able to stand for the presidency in December (his only opponent being in exile). Before the end of the year he had resumed his position as Director of the National Guard and was inaugurated as president on 1 January 1937.

With the ascent to power of Somoza in Nicaragua, the transition to authoritarian *caudillismo* in Central America was completed. As with the liberal oligarchic state, the new political model varied from republic to republic; Costa Rica, under León Cortés, preserved its democratic traditions, although the nature of the Costa Rican state had changed; indeed, in the following decade, even the democratic traditions of Costa Rica came under threat. In Guatemala, the power of the president was virtually absolute, while in El Salvador General Martínez was obliged to consider the interests of various pressure groups (above all the coffee oligarchy) in policy-making.

The new state rolled back most of the modest social and political reforms of the 1920s, but remained wedded to the export-led model. Given the difficulties of external trade in the 1930s, such a policy meant little more than safeguarding the interests of the export sector in the hope that more favourable external conditions would soon return. It did have the undesirable side-effect, however, of stifling efforts to develop an alternative economic model and it discouraged the emergence of new pressure groups, which might have challenged the hegemony of the export interests. In a very real sense, therefore, authoritarian *caudillismo* achieved the worst of both worlds: it clung to the export-led model without achieving export-led growth and it eliminated many of the positive features of the export-led model, which had slowly begun to emerge in the 1920s.

The rise of authoritarian *caudillismo* marked a critical turning-point in the political economy of Central America. Its demise took many years to achieve and its legacy is still apparent in several republics. It is important, therefore, to account for its origins and to consider whether any alternatives were available.

The export-led model of growth in the 1920s had proved that it could be combined with modest social and political reform, but progress was in general painfully slow. Thus, when the model moved into crisis at the end of the 1920s, the dominant pressure groups (representing the export sector) did not face any serious challenge in their search for alternative political solutions which would safeguard their interests. It was inevitable, therefore, that the political shift favoured authoritarianism rather than populism (as happened in some Latin American republics in the 1930s), but the responsibility lies with the slow pace at which social and political reform was introduced during the earlier period of export-led growth.

The main cause of the rise of authoritarian *caudillismo* was therefore the depression itself. The drop in real incomes (see Table 3.5) was very sharp and political upheaval in consequence (as in the rest of Latin America) was inevitable. This upheaval took the form of a shift towards authoritarianism, because the social and economic base for a more populist alternative was very underdeveloped. This was true even for Costa Rica, despite its longer and more serious tradition of introducing reforms.

The United States has frequently been blamed for the long survival of authoritarian *caudillismo*, a charge we shall consider in later chapters, but the USA played little part in the creation of the new authoritarian states. Indeed, the dictatorship of General Hernández Martínez was consolidated in the face of US opposition and even General Ubico faced initial US hostility to his policy of *continuismo*. The critics of US policy are on stronger ground in Nicaragua, where successive US administrations did nothing to stop the irresistible rise of 'Tacho' Somoza despite frequent warnings of his intentions from US embassy staff in Managua. Even in Nicaragua, however, it cannot be said that the United States engineered the ascent of Somoza; the harshest criticism is that nothing was done to prevent or deter his rise, but this absence of active intervention was consistent with the tenets of the Good Neighbor Policy adopted by President Roosevelt after 1933. Nor should it be forgotten that over twenty years of almost unbroken active intervention in the affairs of Nicaragua by the USA had failed miserably to achieve its stated objectives.

# 4

# Economic recovery and political reaction in the 1930s

Most of Central America reached its economic nadir in 1932, although in Honduras and Nicaragua economic decline continued until 1936/7. The fall in economic activity during the 1929 depression was severe and proved too great a challenge for the liberal oligarchic state, which was replaced throughout the region by authoritarian *caudillismo*. The new régimes, mostly sympathetic to the rise of fascism in Europe,[1] brought to a swift end the *apertura* in the political process which had been apparent in the second half of the 1920s. Even in Costa Rica, Communist deputies – democratically elected – were banned from taking their seats during the presidency of León Cortés (1936–40).[2] Trade union activity was sharply curtailed and many rural labour organisations were banned. This political reaction was mirrored by a commitment to the export-led model, in which the state intervened more directly on behalf of the traditional export interests. The export sector, however, in Central America was largely stagnant in the 1930s despite state intervention on its behalf.

With political repression on a massive scale, stagnation in the traditional export sector and an unwillingness on the part of the authorities to countenance an alternative to the export-led model, the decade of the 1930s has not surprisingly earned a reputation as the dark age of Central American history.[3] Yet, in several countries, economic recovery was rapid after 1932. The mechanism of recovery was in part similar to that which occurred in other Latin American countries. The collapse of the gold standard brought to the fore the question of exchange rate management. Although exchange rate depreciation was adopted by some republics primarily as a defence against falling world prices for traditional exports, it also increased the profitability of import-competing production. Debt default, as in most of Latin America, also increased the region's room for manoeuvre and served a double function in terms of economic recovery. It released scarce foreign exchange for the purchase of much-needed imports and it permitted a reallocation of government expenditure towards output-increasing activities.

The recovery, however, also differed in important respects from that

68

observed in the rest of Latin America. Import-substitution took place in agricultural more than industrial commodities. This was a reflection of the extraordinary heights to which export specialisation had been carried out in the 1920s, when Central America found itself exporting bananas and coffee, while importing maize, beans, rice, etc.

Economic recovery was most apparent in Guatemala, El Salvador and Costa Rica; output oscillated violently in Nicaragua and declined sharply in Honduras until 1937. This difference in performance reflected to a large extent differences in policy, although it was also due to the spread of disease among banana plantations in Honduras and Nicaragua over which the authorities had little or no control.

Sympathy towards the rise of fascism did not indicate a weakening of the ties with the United States. The unwritten rule, as always, was the acceptance of US hegemony among the external powers. In return, the United States under President Roosevelt's Good Neighbor Policy turned a blind eye to the manifold abuses of the 1923 Washington Treaty, as the *caudillos* outside of Costa Rica institutionalised dictatorship; the United States also observed with apparent impotence the manipulation of the 'non-political' Nicaraguan National Guard by General Somoza to further his own political and business career.

Despite the rapid economic recovery in three of the five republics, it is not incorrect to regard the 1930s as a dark age. The recovery did not provide a real alternative to the export-led model and could not provide the basis for long-term self-sustained growth. Although a dark age, the decade was not, however, one of lost opportunities. The advances of the 1920s on the political, social and economic front had been too timid to enable new political groups to mount a serious challenge to the economic and political hegemony of the traditional oligarchy. Where they tried to do so, as in El Salvador in 1932, the result was wholly counter-productive.

### Policy responses in the 1930s: balance of payments, budgets and banking

Throughout the 1930s, the balance of payments and government budget remained harsh constraints on the operation of economic policy. In both cases, the prime cause of difficulty was the collapse of foreign exchange earnings from exports: in the case of the balance of payments, the decline of exports forced governments to seek methods of suppressing imports; in the case of the budget, the fall in exports coupled with import suppression reduced government revenue from taxes on external trade (the major source) and obliged the authorities to cut public expenditure as best they could.

The fall in the dollar value of exports was not halted in the early 1930s. On the contrary (see Table A.10), the value of exports did not bottom out in Costa Rica and Nicaragua until the period 1935/6 ( 1938 in Honduras). By the early 1930s, however, import suppression had already imposed severe economic and social costs and there were strict limits to how much further imports could be cut.

During the depression, imports had been cut more sharply than exports and a trade surplus had emerged (see Figure 3.1). which was needed above all to service the public external debt. The decision to default in whole or in part on external obligations after 1932 therefore created an opportunity for imports to expand despite declining export receipts (see Table A.11). The rise in imports after debt default looks modest when imports are expressed in current dollars. The 1930s, however, were a decade of falling import, not just export, prices. In constant prices (see Table A.13), imports throughout the region fell to their lowest level by 1932 (1933 in Honduras) and recovered fairly swiftly thereafter.

Not all the recovery in imports in the 1930s can be attributed to the debt default. In Costa Rica and Guatemala, for example, where the recovery went furthest, a huge stimulus to imports was provided in the late 1930s through the development of Pacific coast banana plantations by the United Fruit Company. Yet it must surely be relevant that import recovery was least effective in those countries where default was avoided altogether (Honduras) or where only amortization payments were suspended (Nicaragua). Furthermore, the cost of default was very low in the 1930s; new sources of foreign credit were generally unavailable even for non-defaulting countries and revolving trade credits had not acquired their current importance. Thus, a country in default had little to fear by way of retaliation, while the release of foreign exchange for imports brought some relief for the hard-pressed urban economy.[4]

Debt default also eased the government budget constraint. Unlike the balance of payments, however, the budget constraint was eased by internal as well as external debt default. Thus, Honduras gained a certain breathing space in 1932 when it suspended interest and amortization payments on most of the internal debt.[5] The 'peso'[6] resources released by debt default offered a number of different opportunities.[7] They could be used to reduce the budget deficit; they could be reallocated to some other item of expenditure or, most imaginitively, they could be used to purchase the foreign bonds (on which defaults had occurred) at very attractive prices.

All three options were employed in Central America in the 1930s. Budget deficits had been replaced by modest surpluses in all republics other than Honduras by 1934/5. The internal public debt was kept roughly constant in Costa Rica and Guatemala, although it rose in Honduras quite sharply between 1932 and 1934 when repayment was suspended and unpaid interest was added to the total. In El Salvador and Nicaragua, the level of internal debt actually fell, although in the latter case it was due mainly to a massive scaling down of claims arising out of past civil wars.[8]

Costa Rica, with the largest external public debt,[9] was the only one to repurchase its own bonds in default. In 1932, the incoming government of President Ricardo Jiménez found itself paying out nearly one-third of government revenue in public debt service, representing some 20% of exports.[10] A three-year moratorium on sterling and dollar bonds came into force at the end of 1932 and new bonds were issued to cover the unpaid interest. At the end of the three-year period, the moratorium was again extended and at the end of 1936 service payments on even the new bonds were suspended. Despite these suspensions, the amount dedicated to public debt service rose steadily in the budget after 1934. By 1938, it had exceeded its 1932 level and much of the money was used by the government to buy its own bonds. By the end of 1939, the principal on the sterling debt had been reduced from £1.6 million to £1.2 million, the principal on the dollar debt had fallen from $7.6 million to $5.4 million and the face value of outstanding Pacific Railway Electrification bonds had fallen from $1.8 million to $1.2 million.

The third option available was compensating increases in other items of government expenditure. Given the rise to power of generals throughout the republics other than Costa Rica, one might be forgiven for assuming that military expenditure would expand as debt service shrank. This was not generally the case, however,[11] although increased expenditure on secret police, informants etc. would not in any case appear as part of the War Ministry Budget. The main beneficiary from reduced debt service provisions was in fact the road-building programme. By 1930, railway construction had virtually ceased and the main priority had become the construction of a road network. Road construction served many purposes, which made it attractive to Central American governments in the 1930s. It was labour-intensive and provided jobs without demanding much, if any, complementary imports. It cemented the alliance between the government and the traditional oligarchy based on export interests and it served a useful military purpose. Furthermore, unlike the railway network, it was not under foreign domination.

Between 1932 and 1939, public works expenditure rose by 320% in Costa Rica compared with a more modest increase of 43% in the education budget.[12] In El Salvador, some 1,600 miles of national roads were in operation by the end of the decade, while in Nicaragua the mileage had reached 1,100. Even in Honduras, some 500 miles of road were in existence by the end of the 1930s, most of which were passable all the year round. The most spectacular case of road-building was in Guatemala, where the road network increased from 1,375 miles in 1932 to 4,775 miles in 1940 (this had risen to 6,375 miles by 1943). Expenditure on public works in the same period, however, rose only modestly, as General Ubico resorted to a tax in kind to secure the labour services he needed. Under Ubico's *Ley Vialidad*, every adult was liable to two weeks' unpaid work on the roads, a burden which could be escaped only through payment of two quetzales. This was equivalent to about two weeks' wages for day labourers on coffee plantations and a very large number of Guatemalans were obliged to pay off the tax in the form of unpaid labour services.[13]

The collapse of the gold standard obliged each Central American government to add exchange rate management to its list of functions (see above, pp. 53–4). The response, however, was very varied: two republics (Costa Rica and El Salvador) allowed their currencies to depreciate against the dollar and other major trading partners immediately; Nicaragua permitted a rapid depreciation of the córdoba against the dollar after 1936, while Guatemala and Honduras maintained a constant peg to the dollar throughout this period. These differences in response require some comment. From a purely abstract perspective, exchange rate depreciation in the 1930s favoured import-substitution as well as exports, while raising the 'peso' cost of external debt service. There is little evidence, however, that governments in the 1930s deliberately sought to foster import-substitution (see pp. 79–82). Thus, depreciation can be seen as an instrument which favoured the traditional oligarchy through its impact on the 'peso' price of world exports, while discriminating against the merchant class in each city tied to imports and aggravating the budgetary problems of external debt servicing.

In this context, the decision taken in Costa Rica and El Salvador to depreciate is hardly surprising. In both countries, the traditional oligarchy (see pp. 59–60 above) had formed powerful associations to defend its export interests (mainly coffee). In El Salvador, the exchange rate against the dollar began to depreciate as the country went off the gold standard in October 1931, and the Martínez administration, after coming to power in December 1931 without having yet established its credentials in the eyes of the coffee élite, permitted the colón to depreciate over the next two years by nearly 50%. By 1934, however, Martínez was firmly installed and the inauguration of a Central Bank (see below) coincided with a mild appreciation of the currency and a fixed rate to the dollar (the official rate until 1986) of 2.5 colones. In Costa Rica, a Board of Control was established in January 1932. Between that date and February 1935, the Board engineered a modest depreciation of the currency, reaching a maximum of 20% during part of 1934. After February 1935, exchange control was relaxed (although not abolished),[14] and the colón depreciated sharply throughout 1935 and 1936, reaching an average of 6.13 colones to the dollar in the latter year compared with 4.0 in 1931. In January 1937, under a new banking law, the currency was pegged at 5.61 colones to the dollar, a rate which was considered very satisfactory by coffee interests, which had been pressing for a rate of 5.5 colones to the dollar.[15]

The circumstances surrounding exchange rate stability in the remaining three republics differ in each case. In Nicaragua, the decision not to depreciate until after 1936 (when Somoza consolidated his rise to power with the assumption of the presidency) is best explained by the country's semi-colonial status: the management of the exchange rate was placed in the hands of a Board of Control in November 1931, consisting of the Minister of Finance, the manager of the Bank of Nicaragua and the US Collector General of Customs. Somoza, however, realised that devaluation was the easiest way to earn himself the goodwill of his potential rivals among the traditional bourgeoisie as well as those foreign companies engaged in the extraction of minerals and natural resources. Somoza therefore defied 'sound' financial advice[16] and earned the gratitude of the traditional export interests through a depreciation of the córdoba from parity to the dollar in 1936 to a fixed rate of five córdobas to the dollar by 1939.[17]

There were two rather different reasons behind the Honduran exchange rate stability. First, the republic lacked a national bourgeoisie tied to export interests: exports (both bananas and silver) were entirely in the hands of foreign companies, who conducted their day to day operations in dollars, not lempiras. Depreciation would neither help nor harm such companies, but it would have hindered the government in its successful effort to meet external debt service payments. Secondly, the republic – with US paper and gold money circulating freely and legally – was scarcely in a position to operate an independent exchange rate policy; much of the country, particularly the Northern provinces, was in effect in the dollar area.

The most surprising case of exchange rate stability was Guatemala. Ubico, however, had won an uncontested election in early 1931 and was firmly in power by July 1933, when Guatemala left the gold standard and imposed a gold export embargo. Ubico was not therefore beholden to the coffee oligarchy, who in any case lacked a powerful organisation to defend their interests.[18] At the same time, the memory of currency instability was all too recent in Guatemala (see above, pp. 32–3) and this proved a powerful incentive for linking the quetzal to the dollar.

Throughout Central America, the money supply fell rapidly during the depression and the problems facing banks were compounded by the decision to impose a moratorium on loan repayments (see next section). Despite this, however, the banking system survived almost intact, and there were in fact several important advances in the 1930s. These included the establishment of a Central Bank in El Salvador and the conversion of the Banco Internacional in Costa Rica into the state-owned Banco Nacional.

The survival of the banking system can be attributed to two causes in particular. First, even before 1929 the banks had followed a cautious lending policy and remained far more liquid than was demanded by legal reserve ratios;[19] when the depression deepened, the liquidity of the banks increased, rather than decreased, as it became increasingly difficult to find safe investments. This situation proved most efficacious for governments seeking to borrow funds to cover budget deficits; the Costa Rican government, for example, issued bonds in 1933 for 8 million colones which were to be bought by the banks with depositors' funds.

Secondly, the state through the monetary authority was always prepared to intervene to safeguard the interests of private commercial banks. Thus, in Costa Rica, the Crédito Hipotecario was taken over in March 1933 by the Banco Internacional[20] when it ran into difficulties occasioned by the sharp fall in land prices after 1929. In El Salvador, where the note issue was in the hands of three private banks until the establishment of the Central Bank in 1934, Congress authorised in June 1933 the issue of 5 million colones in silver coins – just sufficient to cover the decline in monetary circulation since 1928.

By the end of the 1930s, *de facto* Central Banks had been established throughout Central America except for Honduras. At the same time, indirect leverage over private banks also increased, as a result of bond issues and debt moratoria. The financial system was therefore subject to government influence in a number of ways which had not been possible before 1929, but it was only towards the end of the 1930s that this influence was used to affect resource allocation other than through the promotion of traditional exports.

## Export promotion and export diversification

The 1930s marked a change in the character of the state in Central America. The replacement of the liberal oligarchic state by authoritarian *caudillismo* did not, however, mark a change in *policy* towards the traditional export sector; although the *relationship* between the state and the export sector changed, the objective remained the same: consolidation and expansion of the export-led model leading to the modernisation of Central America.

In the context of the 1930s, rapid expansion of the export sector was unrealistic, but its survival was considered all-important. In this respect, the state tended to focus on the coffee sector, because – being in national hands – it was more responsive to policy initiatives than bananas, the other traditional export. This policy had some success, and the volume of coffee exports was maintained at pre-depression levels despite the huge fall in world coffee prices.

Some of the instruments used to promote coffee exports have already been discussed. Exchange rate depreciation, for example, in Costa Rica, El Salvador and (after 1936) Nicaragua was of some assistance to coffee producers and exporters in the face of falling world prices. Export duties were also varied in order to lower the burden on exporters; this was most important in Guatemala, where the rate was lowered in May 1931 (soon after Ubico had taken power) from 2.0 to 1.50 quetzales per quintal. In El Salvador, the export duty on coffee was not reduced until the fiscal year 1935/6,[21] but from 1931/2 onwards a portion of the tax yield was paid into a state Mortgage Bank which was created to help coffee growers. In return, the coffee oligarchy purchased shares issued by the government to establish the Central Bank in 1934. The strong alliance between the military, represented by Martínez, and the coffee growers, represented by the Comisión de Defensa del Café Salvadoreño, was therefore established at an early stage of military rule.[22]

The use of debt moratoria to safeguard the interests of coffee producers (at the expense of banks and, to some extent, coffee exporters) was confined to Costa Rica and El Salvador. In each case the moratorium (applied in 1931/2) suspended amortization payments on bank loans and reduced the interest rate payable from 8% to 6%. Although the law applied to all loans, the main beneficiaries were coffee growers because coffee loans formed such a large part of the structure of bank lending. In addition, the moratoria applied to loans of all sizes, so that small-scale coffee holdings were also exempt from foreclosure.[23]

The state was able to affect the profitability of coffee production directly through exchange rate depreciation, export duty variations, debt moratoria and interest rate changes. It could affect labour costs only indirectly, however, either through minimum wage laws (as in Costa Rica) or through the control of rural labour organisations. Certainly, there was downward pressure on wage rates,[24] although this was sometimes counteracted by other forces,[25] but the easiest way for growers to reduce labour costs was through hiring fewer workers.

The measures adopted were undoubtedly helpful for coffee producers and exporters, although they could not compensate fully for the massive fall in world prices. Coffee production, however, was still profitable in the 1930s; in a careful study of El Salvador, Monfils (1938) estimated the gross profit (including interest and depreciation) in 1937 at between $2.25 and $3.50 per quintal of exported coffee, giving a gross rate of return on capital between 5.6% and 8.8%. Thus the instruments at the disposal of the state were sufficient to produce a positive rate of return, where otherwise a negative one could have confidently been expected.

The relationship between the state and coffee interests was in complete contrast to that between the state and the banana industry. In the latter case, exports were monopolised by two foreign companies and their relationship with the state was governed by means of long-term contracts. Both sides sought favours from each other in the short term, but the state could not influence the profitability, and therefore level, of current production other than marginally. The only exception, and it proved to be an important one, was the state's leverage over future production through the granting of new contracts.

In many ways, the 1930s could hardly have been more favourable for the fruit companies. For example, with the election to the presidency in Honduras of General Tiburcio Carías in 1932, the United Fruit Company (UFCO) found itself dealing with a man considered favourable to UFCO's interests, while the purchase of Zemurray's Cuyamel Co. in 1929 had left UFCO in a dominant position in Honduras. An UFCO lawyer, Plutarco Muñoz P., was president of the national Congress in the 1930s, and UFCO subsidiaries in Honduras acted as guarantors of a $300,000 loan contracted by Carías with the Central Bank and Trust Co. of New Orleans; in return, UFCO received tax exemptions and a guarantee against further taxes.[26]

None of these advantages, however, could offset the impact of the spread of disease. The fruit companies were familiar with Panama disease, which had already affected production by the late 1920s in Costa Rica, but the arrival of the Sigatoka disease[27] in the mid-1930s in Central America caused massive destruction and was not brought under control until the end of the decade. The result was a sharp fall in banana exports from Central America throughout much of the 1930s (see Table 3.2).

The obvious response to the spread of disease was relocation of production on virgin lands. This was still possible in Honduras on the Atlantic coastal plains, but elsewhere the Atlantic plantations were exhausted and disease-ridden. In Nicaragua, where UFCO had no major interests, Standard Fruit responded by running down its operations (see Karnes, 1978, ch. 7); in Costa Rica and Guatemala, however, where UFCO was dominant, the expansion of production could be achieved only through the opening of Pacific coast plantations.

The original contracts under which UFCO operated made no provision for Pacific coast production. Thus, new contracts had to be negotiated, but the circumstances in the 1930s favoured the fruit companies much more than the governments. Already by 1930, UFCO had established in Costa Rica its right in principle to develop Pacific plantations[28] and in 1934 a new contract was signed which permitted UFCO to develop 3,000 hectares on the Pacific coast. In 1938, a further contract was signed permitting the Pacific coast development of an additional 4,000 hectares, which reproduced the privileged conditions UFCO had previously enjoyed on the Atlantic coast.

In Guatemala UFCO had signed a contract in 1930, permitting the development of banana plantations on the Pacific side. In return for the customary tax concessions, however, the Company was obliged to build a Pacific port (none existed up to that time) within five years of the contract entering into force. The development of a Pacific port was a long-standing ambition of successive Guatemalan governments. At first it also made good sense for UFCO, for whom the alternative was the shipment of bananas by rail from the Pacific coast to Puerto Barrios on the Atlantic. The railway company concerned, however, International Railways of Central America (IRCA), was partly owned by UFCO and was virtually bankrupt by 1933. Cross-country haulage of bananas was therefore seen as a way of rescuing IRCA from collapse, but first UFCO had to withdraw from its commitment to build a Pacific port.

Negotiations with the government on this delicate issue were begun in 1935 and completed by 1936. In return for suspension of its obligation to construct a Pacific port,[29] UFCO extended a $1 million loan to the government and the banana export tax was raised from 1.0 to 1.5 US cents per bunch. At the same time, UFCO contributed $2.5 million towards settlement of IRCA's debts and increased its stake in the Company from 17% to 42.6%. UFCO had therefore wriggled out of its contractual obligations at a comparatively low cost, but worse was yet to come. Under the new arrangements, IRCA adopted a pricing policy which discriminated blatantly in favour of UFCO's bananas against other goods. While UFCO was charged $60 per banana car moved, competitors were charged $130.[30] This differential pricing policy was to be a major cause of hostility towards UFCO under later governments.

The relocation of production towards the Pacific produced a sharp increase in banana exports after the mid-1930s in Costa Rica and Guatemala (see Table 3.2). In Honduras, the decline in exports which had taken place every year from 1931 to 1936 was finally arrested in 1937, although the level of exports then remained stagnant. In Nicaragua, production and exports steadily declined so that by 1943 the export figure was no longer reported by the government.[31]

Efforts at export diversification during the 1930s were rather disappointing. Even in the 1920s, the dominance of traditional (coffee and banana) exports was not absolute; in several republics, sugar had become a minor export crop and timber was a useful source of foreign exchange in Nicaragua and Guatemala. Cacao exports grew rapidly in Costa Rica in the 1920s, largely because of experiments by United Fruit on idle banana lands, and chicle remained a vital source of income for the Petén region in northern Guatemala. The major non-traditional exports, however, remained gold and silver, which were shipped in significant quantities from Nicaragua and Honduras and in much smaller quantities from Costa Rica and El Salvador.

The onset of the depression virtually killed the promising sugar industry, as the United States in 1931 built a protective wall around its own sugar activities. Much the same was true of the cattle trade, both live and slaughtered, which was not important in Central America in the 1920s (except for Nicaragua which exported to Costa Rica), but which was effectively prevented from establishing itself in the 1930s by world-wide protectionist policies.

The major scope for diversification for the region was into mining activities, and both Honduras and Nicaragua intensified their production and export of precious metals.[32] In Nicaragua, the output of the gold mines grew fairly steadily so that by 1938 production at 1522 kg was twice the level achieved in 1928; the 1938 figure, however, was more than doubled the following year and by 1940 was seven times greater than in 1928. Gold exports also grew steadily in Honduras in the 1930s, although silver exports were fairly static, but El Salvador emerged from the depression as an important producer of gold for the first time, with exports rising from 910,000 colones in 1930 to 4.42 million colones in 1940.

There were also some attempts to introduce new products: cotton from Nicaragua, now a mainstay of that country's economy, appeared on the export list in the 1930s and by 1937 had reached 7.5% by value of total exports. Timber exports also steadily increased in importance from Nicaragua after a collapse in 1931/2. In Costa Rica, the cacao experiment grew in importance as more and more idle banana lands on the Atlantic coast were turned over to cacao production by the United Fruit Company, and tobacco began to appear for the first time among the export statistics in Honduras.

The measures adopted to promote and diversify exports were sufficient to prevent a decline in their real value (outside of Honduras), but exports were not a source of dynamism in the 1930s (see Table A.10). There were, however, sharp changes in the destination of exports (and origin of imports), which arose above all from the commercial policy adopted by the Third Reich. Germany had always been an important market for Guatemala's exports as a consequence of German penetration of the coffee industry, particularly in Guatemala's Alta Verapaz. It was also an important market for El Salvador's coffee exports. Both republics had traditionally run a large export surplus on trade with Germany, while the rest of Central America had run a small surplus. The decision by Hitler's government to issue Aski-marks in exchange for Central America's exports had profound repercussions on the trade of all countries in the region (see Table 4.1.) Aski-marks could be used only for the purchase of German goods, and this encouraged (if not forced) Central America to reduce its imports from other countries in favour of Germany.[33]

Between 1932 and the late 1930s, Germany trebled its market share of imports in Guatemala, El Salvador, Honduras and Nicaragua and doubled it in Costa Rica (see Table 4.1). The main loser was the United States, although the United Kingdom share also declined sharply in Costa Rica

Table 4.1  *Central America: Germany's share of imports (M) and exports (X) (%), 1932–9*

| Year | Costa Rica | | El Salvador | | Guatemala | | Honduras | | Nicaragua | |
|------|------|------|------|------|------|------|------|------|------|------|
|      | X    | M    | X    | M    | X    | M    | X    | M    | X    | M    |
| 1932 | 7.8  | 11.8 | 33.2 | 9.9  | 28.3 | 12.2 | 9.7  | 3.6  | 9.3  | 8.6  |
| 1933 | 15.7 | 12.5 | 28.9 | 5.7  | 34.4 | 12.5 | 13.0 | 4.5  | 14.1 | 7.1  |
| 1934 | 12.1 | 12.1 | 30.5 | 8.8  | 36.9 | 11.5 | 10.4 | 3.3  | 13.5 | 8.2  |
| 1935 | 14.7 | 23.1 | 13.0 | 24.6 | 22.2 | 22.5 | 2.2  | 3.4  | 12.4 | 16.9 |
| 1936 | 16.3 | 23.6 | 14.3 | 33.6 | 18.5 | 31.0 | 2.1  | 11.1 | 16.0 | 24.0 |
| 1937 | 19.5 | 23.1 | 11.2 | 31.7 | 17.4 | 32.4 | 1.3  | 9.5  | 21.4 | 15.2 |
| 1938 | 19.2 | 19.8 | 9.9  | 21.1 | 14.1 | 35.1 | 2.8  | 6.3  | 14.7 | 10.0 |
| 1939 | 25.1 | 17.7 | 9.0  | 17.5 | 11.5 | 27.0 | 1.8  | 11.4 | 10.9 | 12.2 |

Source: League of Nations, *International Trade Statistics*, Geneva

and Guatemala. The impact of Germany's commercial policy on Central America's exports was, however, much less uniform. El Salvador and Guatemala, because of the large surpluses both had run with Germany in the early 1930s, found themselves accumulating Aski-marks which could be disposed of only at a heavy discount[34] and, as a result, from 1935 onwards alternative markets were sought and found. Costa Rica and Nicaragua, however, were content to increase their sales to Germany under the stimulus of the relatively attractive prices paid by Nazi Germany for their exports. Germany's share of these two countries' exports had climbed to around twenty per cent by 1937 and in Costa Rica it rose to twenty-five per cent on the eve of the Second World War.

## Import substitution and economic recovery

Although external debt default permitted a modest recovery in the volume of imports (see Table A.13), the foreign exchange constraint remained severe throughout the 1930s and provided at least some of the pre-conditions for increasing production through import substitution. This was a similar position to that faced elsewhere in Latin America, but there were important differences. The level of manufacturing output was extremely low in the 1920s and the capacity to increase production without importing additional equipment was very modest; on the other hand, half a century's reliance on the traditional export-led model had left the region heavily dependent on imported foodstuffs.

Import substitution therefore occurred in two quite separate activities in Central America: import-substituting agriculture (ISA) and import-substituting industrialisation (ISI). The performance of domestic use agriculture (DUA) and manufacturing value added in each republic in the 1920s and 1930s is summarised in Table 4.2, and a number of patterns can be discerned.

Table 4.2  *Annual average rates of growth (%) for domestic use agriculture (DUA) and manufacturing (MAN) value added at constant (1970) prices, 1921–38*

| Period[1] | Costa Rica DUA | MAN | El Salvador DUA | MAN | Guatemala DUA | MAN | Honduras DUA | MAN | Nicaragua DUA | MAN |
|---|---|---|---|---|---|---|---|---|---|---|
| 1921–28 | 0.9 | 3.2 | 1.5 | 2.8 | 2.1 | 4.6 | 0.6 | 2.3 | 5.2 | −3.5 |
| 1928–32 | 1.5 | 3.8 | −1.8 | −6.4 | 4.6 | −0.5 | 1.3 | −2.5 | −3.4 | −5.3 |
| 1932–38 | 5.7 | 8.8 | 4.4 | 3.6 | 16.8[2] | 4.3 | 4.6 | 5.0 | −2.9 | 6.9 |

Source: Tables A.6 and A.8
[1] Three-year average
[2] This is biased upwards by a distortion in the underlying statistics (see Methodological Appendix)

First, in the case of DUA there is a marked contrast (except in Nicaragua) between the stagnation of the 1920s and the expansion of the 1930s;[35] secondly, the rate of growth of manufacturing accelerated in all republics in the 1930s, except in Guatemala where it remained the same as in the 1920s.

No deliberate attempt to promote ISI was made by governments in Central America,[36] but incentives nonetheless were available. Tariffs on imported goods were increasing;[37] although this was conceived as a revenue-raising measure, it clearly operated as a protective device as well. Exchange rate changes (at least in Costa Rica, El Salvador and – after 1936 – in Nicaragua) offered some incentive to ISI activities, and the difficulty of obtaining foreign exchange for imports of consumer goods may have permitted the domestic price of the latter to rise above world prices plus tariffs (a further stimulus to domestic production).

As a result, some industrial development did take place. In El Salvador, one factory with a monopoly concession produced bags from local henequen suitable for use in the coffee trade, and three mills were producing cotton textiles in San Salvador by the end of the 1930s, while a further four factories used locally grown cotton to produce yarn for the cotton mills. A small iron foundry was also in operation, producing spare parts for imported coffee and sugar machinery, as well as for motor-cars. Cotton mills were also established in Nicaragua in the 1930s, while flour milling, shoe and beer production expanded throughout the region and cement production rose in Guatemala.

This industrial expansion did not, however, amount to much. By the end of the decade, the share of non-food consumer goods imports in the total import bill was much the same as it had been ten years before. Despite the price advantages conferred by tariff and exchange rate changes, the obstacles in the way of rapid industrial growth remained considerable.

Energy supplies were woefully inadequate and development of the region's hydro-electric potential had scarcely begun. Virtually no credit was available from the organised financial market, and foreign exchange for essential capital equipment was hard to obtain. On the demand side, although income per head began to rise in the late 1930s, the market remained too small for the production of many goods and efforts at regional integration in this period came to nothing.[38]

The obstacles to the expansion of DUA in the 1930s were much less severe; the stagnation of the 1920s in production for the home market reflected the profitability of the traditional export sector, as resources switched into the latter. The replacement of imports of maize, beans, rice, wheat and cattle did not depend greatly on the availability of foreign exchange and credit was not so necessary as with ISI. Although capital may not have been a serious problem, ISA clearly required land and labour. The latter was provided by those made redundant or required less intensively by the export sector. In the case of the coffee-producing zones, migrant workers could often return full-time to their own farms or, in the case of the *colonos*, they could rent a bigger plot on the unoccupied part of the estate; in the banana zones, however, the labour force in general had no access to land of its own and the presence of a large, depressed banana zone was a serious impediment to economic recovery.

Other factors were also at work in promoting ISA. In Guatemala, for example, which experienced a particularly sharp rise in domestic use agriculture in the 1930s, production for the home market was affected by changes in the labour laws in 1934, when the legalised system of debt peonage was replaced by an anti-vagrancy law. The latter was intended to ensure a regular supply of labour into the export sector, but it also had the effect of increasing the labour-time supplied by a given workforce (see Jones, 1940, p. 164); with the weakness of the traditional export sector, much of the increase in labour-time supplied went into domestic use agriculture.[39] A second influence in Guatemala was the massive road-building programme initiated by Ubico in the 1930s, which brought an almost five-fold increase in the road network in a decade (see above, pp. 71–2). As the programme relied essentially on forced labour, it gave Ubico a highly unsavoury reputation in liberal circles, particularly when coupled with his wholehearted admiration for European fascism; the new roads, however, did open up parts of the country which had previously been isolated and gave remote villages the opportunity to market a surplus where none had existed before. The expansion of the road network was an important stimulant for ISA in other parts of Central America as well.

It would be an exaggeration to claim that governments in the 1930s deliberately set out to promote ISA. Indeed, there were complaints in Costa Rica at the end of the decade that government-authorised food imports were undermining the country's efforts to become more self-sufficient (see Facio, 1972, pp. 113–19). By the end of the decade, however, Costa Rica, El Salvador and Nicaragua had organised modest lines of credit to small farmers which were used to promote ISA. El Salvador also created a Social Improvement Fund in 1932/3 which was used to acquire land for landless rural workers and was the closest El Salvador came to land reform until 1980.

Although import substitution was not promoted aggressively through government policy, the replacement of previously imported goods by domestic production was an important element in recovery. Within the agricultural sector, the proportion of value added accounted for by domestic use agriculture rose steadily throughout the 1930s with a corresponding decrease in the proportion accounted for by export agriculture. As a result, the long-term trend towards export specialisation went temporarily into reverse and an increase in the real value of exports was no longer a pre-condition for an increase in real GDP.

This change in the dynamics of the Central American economy passed largely unheeded, so that the model of export-led growth was not seriously challenged.[40] In the rest of Latin America, the success of the import substitution strategy (much of it spontaneous) eventually led to a profound revision of public policy towards import-competing sectors. That this did not happen in Central America can be attributed to various factors: first, the traditional export sector (despite adverse external conditions) remained profitable and, although it could not secure very high returns under such circumstances, it was assumed that the prospects would again be good once the external environment improved; secondly, there were strict limits to the possible extent of import substitution in foodstuffs, and a large increase in supply could be self-defeating through its impact on prices.

### Economic recovery and the new political model

By 1932, real Gross Domestic Product (GDP) had fallen to its lowest level everywhere except in Honduras and Nicaragua and the following years witnessed a significant increase in Costa Rica, El Salvador and Guatemala (see Table A.1). By 1935/6, each of these three countries had surpassed the pre-depression peak in real GDP and within the next two years, even real GDP per head was at its highest recorded level. The economic performance of Honduras and Nicaragua, on the other hand, was in harsh contrast. In Honduras, real GDP reached its nadir in 1937 and by 1939 real GDP per head was still nearly thirty per cent below its peak recorded in 1930/1. In Nicaragua, real GDP at first recovered well after 1932, but declined sharply in 1936, falling to its global minimum. In the years 1936–8, Nicaragua enjoyed the unwelcome distinction of having the lowest figure for real

GDP per head in Central America; by 1942, however, this unenviable position was claimed by Honduras, a position she has yet to vacate.

The reasons for the poor economic performance in Honduras are different from those applicable in Nicaragua. Honduras was essentially a victim of its dependence on banana exports; with the latter crippled by disease, the engine of growth of the Honduran economy went into reverse, bringing down with it a whole series of related activities (e.g. government expenditure, imports, commerce). ISA performed quite well in Honduras in the 1930s, but it could not offset the dramatic impact of export decline. In Nicaragua, the real value of exports fluctuated wildly in the 1930s, but the trend was neither upwards nor downwards. Nicaragua, however, for most of the 1930s was forced to adopt a very orthodox approach to fiscal, monetary and exchange rate policy. Import recovery was very slow and, despite the foreign exchange constraint, ISA registered the weakest performance of all the Central American countries.

The poor performances of Honduras and Nicaragua did have one factor in common. Policy was largely 'passive' in contrast to the rest of Central America, where policy could be generally described as 'active'.[41] Debt default, debt moratoria and exchange rate depreciation were all applied aggressively in Costa Rica and El Salvador, while in Guatemala the road-building programme and labour coercion were applied more extensively than elsewhere.

Why was policy more active in some republics than others? In the Nicaraguan case, a passive policy appears to have been a consequence of its semi-colonial status. The withdrawal of the US marines did not at first end this status; the US Collector General of Customs remained at his post and the High Commission established under the 1917 financial plan continued in force.[42] By 1937, however, with the consolidation of Somoza's rule, policy became more active; the córdoba was massively devalued and the external debt was unilaterally rescheduled.[43] Between 1936 and 1939, it should also be noted, real GDP recovered by nearly 40% (see Table A.1).

In the first half of the 1930s, Nicaragua was little more than a client state, an outpost of informal empire. It would be wrong, however, to describe Honduras in the same terms. The influence of the fruit companies was, of course, immense, but the relationship between them and the Honduran state was one of mutual dependence. With the rise to power of Tiburcio Carías, the period of civil wars (in which the fruit companies had often supported rival factions) came to an end. During the years of Carías' presidency, he and the fruit companies would do each other favours, but neither dictated to the other.[44] Other Central American countries also faced powerful fruit companies, but unlike them Honduras could not boast of a national bourgeoisie tied to its export interests. The active nature of policy in Costa Rica, El Salvador, Guatemala and (after 1936) in Nicaragua is best explained by the presence of such interests, particularly those linked to coffee. By contrast, the state in Honduras was subject to no such pressures and policy, as a result, remained passive. Honduras therefore paid dearly in the 1930s for its failure to establish a dynamic coffee sector in the nineteenth century.[45]

The rise of authoritarian *caudillismo* in the 1930s marked a sharp political break with the 1920s. It also led to a new, more assertive relationship between the state and the traditional oligarchy; it did not, however, mark a break with the model of export-led growth nor is it appropriate to imagine that it could have. The diversification of the economy in the 1920s had been far too timid to provide a solid foundation for inward-looking policies. In the context of the 1930s in Central America, neglect of the export sector would have simply led to economic decline – as happened in Honduras.

The break with the past represented by authoritarian *caudillismo* was most apparent in the political arena. The *apertura* policies of the 1920s went sharply into reverse as *continuismo* was practised everywhere outside Costa Rica. Even in Costa Rica, President León Cortés succeeded in hand-picking Rafael Angel Calderón as his successor in 1940, although Calderón (like Pío Romero Bosque in El Salvador in 1927) turned out very differently from what his patron had intended. Party politics virtually came to an end in the 1930s, as *caudillo* rule was consolidated. In Guatemala, Ubico's Progressive Liberal Party held a monopoly of seats in the National Assembly. In El Salvador, Martínez permitted elections for the Legislative Assembly and local government to proceed in January 1932 (just ten days before the peasant uprising) according to the plans of his deposed predecessor Arturo Araujo. In these elections, even the Communist Party was allowed to participate freely, although this move is generally conceded to have been motivated by Martínez's need for international support. Within a few weeks of the 1932 uprising, however, all political opposition (including trade unions) was banned and Martínez's *Pro-Patria* party enjoyed a virtual monopoly. Yet in both El Salvador and Guatemala, the traditional oligarchy had little reason to complain at the suppression of political activity. A marriage of convenience took place between themselves and the military, with the latter occupying the presidency and other key posts, while the civilian élite continued to exercise an important influence over economic affairs.

In Nicaragua and Honduras, neither Somoza nor Carías could dispose of political opposition in such a summary fashion as occurred in El Salvador and Guatemala. Carías, a member of the National Party, had to tolerate the continued existence of the much older Liberal Party, although after 1932 the latter had no opportunity to contest anything other than municipal elections until 1948. Somoza, on the other hand, whose election victory in 1936 had been carried under the banner of the Liberal Party, saw no reason to ban the Conservative Party, which had also supported his virtually uncontested election.[46]

The traditional, oligarchic parties therefore survived in Honduras and Nicaragua (as well as in Costa Rica) but throughout the region the organisations representing the new social forces which had emerged in the 1920s were almost totally eclipsed. These organisations were essentially of two kinds: reformist organisations such as the Partido Laborista in El Salvador, which had been created in response to the rise of an urban middle class, and revolutionary organisations (such as the Guatemalan Communist Party) which were directed towards the rural and urban working class. The banning of the revolutionary organisations eliminated only their legal activities. Miguel Marmol has given a vivid account of their work in El Salvador in the 1930s (see Dalton, 1972), which culminated in the formation of the Alianza Nacional de Zapateros.[47] The Nicaraguan Communist Party was formed in exile in 1939.[48] In Costa Rica, on the other hand, Manuel Mora's Communist Party organised legally under the title Bloque de Obreros y Campesinos.

Illegal activity was expected in revolutionary circles, but the impact of proscription on middle-class organisations led to a cessation of all their activities. The 1930s, however, witnessed a further rise in the economic importance of the middle classes in much of Central America and this conflict between relatively strong economic and weak political representation was to be a major factor behind the struggle to overthrow *caudillismo* in 1944 (see Chapter 5, pp. 100–4).

While the 1930s witnessed the consolidation of *caudillo* rule within each republic, no government was immune from the growing international tensions. The similarity between *caudillismo* in Central America and fascism in Europe was not lost on many observers, least of all the *caudillos* themselves. León Cortés in Costa Rica displayed marked pro-Nazi sentiments[49] and chose a German, Max Effinger, as one of his principal advisers.[50] Somoza's *Camisas Azules* (blueshirts) were a conscious copy of Mussolini's blackshirts, while the governments of Ubico, Somoza and Martínez were among the very first to recognise Franco in Spain.

This sympathy for fascism, which was not shared by Carías in Honduras,[51] did not imply anti-US sentiment, but it did present a challenge to President Roosevelt. The Good Neighbor Policy, following the failure of the Nicaraguan intervention, obliged the US administration to give *caudillismo* in Central America a fairly free hand. Once the Martínez administration had been finally recognised in 1934, it was clear that the United States would not, indeed could not, oppose the consolidation of *caudillo* rule through *continuismo*. The spread of German influence throughout Central America, however, was another matter. This was a direct threat to US hegemony and a threat to her strategic interests. Provided no Central American government aided German territorial ambitions directly, the United States was prepared to turn a blind eye; when, however, as in Panama in 1941, the US felt directly threatened by actions which could be interpreted as pro-Axis, she was prepared to act swiftly and ruthlessly.[52] This lesson was not lost on Central American leaders, some of whom remained both pro-US and pro-Axis until the final moment that a choice between the two had to be made.

# 5

## Central America and the Second World War

The outbreak of hostilities in Europe in September 1939 had a major impact on Central America not just during the war years, but also over the longer term. The immediate impact was felt through a loss of European markets for exports, particularly coffee, while the efforts to replace imports from Europe with imports from the United States were to some extent thwarted by the war-related priorities of US production and the shortage of shipping.

Central America's efforts to find alternative markets for its exports, aided to a very large degree by the cooperation achieved within the inter-American system, were quite successful. At the same time, capital inflows surged as capital was channelled towards Central America in an effort to meet the production targets and strategic requirements of the war effort. As a result, international reserves and the money supply boomed and, with imports scarce and rising steeply in price, Central America found itself in the middle of a sharp inflation in complete contrast to the falling prices of the 1930s.

The rise in the cost of living dug deep into the living standards of the urban middle and working classes. Their discontent provided a major challenge to *caudillo* rule, which was compounded by the rhetoric of the Allied war effort and the struggle against totalitarianism. Yet *caudillismo* survived the challenge in Honduras and Nicaragua, and even Costa Rica practised its own brand of *continuismo*. In El Salvador, Martínez fell in the face of urban discontent, but the political system he had erected survived intact; only in Guatemala was *caudillismo* defeated and even there it took a military revolt to provide substance to the middle-class challenge.

*Caudillismo* in Central America placed the United States in an awkward position. The region's strategic position, so close to the Panama Canal and the shipping routes of the Caribbean, obliged the United States on the outbreak of war to work closely with whatever governments were in power provided they were friendly to the United States. Each *caudillo* in Central America recognised this and, unlike Arias in Panama, bent over backwards to accomodate the US economic and strategic needs.

As a result of the close co-operation between the United States and Central

American governments in the war years, the system of *caudillo* rule gained a certain international legitimacy in spite of some obvious parallels between *caudillismo* in Central America and fascism in Europe. At the same time, through the war effort, the United States furnished *caudillismo* with the material means to increase its chances of survival. Thus, indirectly, the United States contributed to defeat the middle-class challenge to *caudillismo* which reached its peak in 1944, although the US administration did not raise a finger directly to defeat the challenge. The failure to overthrow *caudillismo* other than in Guatemala was, however, a missed opportunity of enormous long-run importance. Within a few years, the rise of the Cold War would make it much more difficult for reformists to gain power in Central America, because of the ambivalence – if not hostility – of successive US administrations to the inevitable presence of Marxists and Marxist parties in any reform movement. In 1944 there was no such hostility and, if the middle-class challenge to *caudillo* rule had proved successful, the recent history of Central America might have been very different.

The rise of authoritarian *caudillismo* in the 1930s was a Central American response to the deep economic crisis which began at the end of the 1920s. By 1944, *caudillo* rule had outlived its purpose, but it survived virtually intact in Honduras and Nicaragua and in modified form in El Salvador and Costa Rica (until 1948). In the early 1930s, the social base to mount an effective challenge to *caudillismo* was too weak; this was no longer true in 1944, but the broad democratic movement still could not match the monopoly of force held by the *caudillos*. Under these circumstances, discreet US pressure might have tilted the balance against dictatorship, but the Roosevelt administration remained strictly neutral in what was in reality an unequal struggle.

### Hemispheric defence and US strategic interests

When war was declared between Great Britain and Germany in September 1939, the inter-American system faced its greatest challenge. The declaration of neutrality by the foreign ministers of the American republics, meeting in Panama immediately after the announcement of hostilities,[1] was all very well, but it had to be supported by actions; this meant that the concept of a hemispheric neutrality zone had to be given teeth. In the waters around Central America, there was never any question but that such a zone would have to be policed by the United States. The Central American countries could provide facilities, however, and this they were very ready to do; it was a small price to pay for gaining a large measure of international goodwill.[2] The offer of bases and facilities by all the Central American countries laid to rest any fears the US may have had that Axis influence in the region posed a threat to US strategic interests. Nevertheless, between 1939 and

1941 US military missions were sent to all Central America, other than Honduras, and by the end of 1941 a Lend-Lease Agreement for the supply of arms had been signed with Nicaragua.[3]

Following Pearl Harbor, all Central American countries immediately broke off diplomatic relations with Japan, Germany and Italy and declared war. Restrictions were placed on the property and persons of Axis nationals resident in Central America and the Salvadorean Congress voted as early as 8 December 1941 to authorise its president to permit the forces of any American nation to occupy part of the national territory and to take whatever measures were felt appropriate as a contribution to the defence of the continent.[4] These measures destroyed the residual Axis influence in Central America and left Axis property-owners prey to the greed and venality of government officials. Somoza, in particular, was quick to exploit the opportunity provided by expropriation of German-owned assets,[5] while in Guatemala the takeover of the German coffee fincas was to bring into public ownership some of the country's most prized assets.[6]

The removal of the internal Axis threat did not, however, remove the external threat, and the United States was particularly concerned with the defence of the Panama Canal. Central America's contribution to the defence of the canal principally took three forms: naval bases, air bases and the Inter-American Highway.

The idea of a Pan-American Highway had been first introduced at the Fifth International Conference of American States in Santiago, Chile, in 1923. In 1930, the first Inter-American (i.e. Mexico to Panama) Highway Conference was held in Panama and a decision was taken to carry out reconnaissance surveys for a continuous road. Progress in construction of the Inter-American Highway before Pearl Harbor was fairly modest. In December 1941, however, the US Congress voted $20 million to help Central America and Panama to construct their sections of the road with the United States paying two-thirds of the cost and each isthmian government the remaining third. As a result, progress on the Highway's construction speeded up and by the end of the war was virtually complete, with only 17% of the distance from the US border to Panama consisting of trails.[7]

The Inter-American Highway system was one of many ways in which Central American governments could contribute to the Allied war effort at very little cost to themselves. The provision of bases was another, because there was little or no danger in Central America of a nationalist backlash arising against the stationing of foreign troops on Central American soil. This absence of a backlash, in contrast to other parts of Latin America,[8] is perhaps surprising in view of the Sandino episode. The latter, however, had occurred before the Good Neighbor Policy was introduced and it was clear that in the Second World War US troops did not represent an interference in internal affairs. The absence of opposition by Communists and

Communist sympathisers in Central America was assured through the wartime alliance which brought the USSR and the USA together and, finally, Central America manifestly lacked the air and naval resources to co-operate in the defence of the Panama Canal.

The air and naval bases established by the United States in Costa Rica, El Salvador, Nicaragua and Guatemala[9] provided vital links in the defence of the Panama Canal. Bombers flew from bases near Guatemala City and naval patrols radiated out of both Atlantic and Pacific ports in Nicaragua. Essential supplies could be channelled to Panama by road, and the United States had much for which to thank the wartime governments in Central America.

The co-operation between the United States and Central America was not confined to the military sphere. Following Pearl Harbor, the United States lost access to Pacific supplies of vital raw materials and was anxious to develop replacements within the American hemisphere. Some of these materials could not, of course, be produced in Central America, but the region was considered suitable for growing rubber, cinchona bark (from which quinine is obtained) and abacá (Manila hemp). The development of these products took place within the framework of the Inter-American system. The meeting of foreign ministers in Panama in September 1939 had provided for the creation of an Inter-American Financial and Economic Advisory Committee (FEAC) and in June 1940 the Inter-American Development Commission was set up with the aim of developing new primary products needed by the United States and capable of production in Latin America. In August 1940, following the Havana Conference of foreign ministers, the office of the co-ordinator of Inter-American Affairs was created to investigate long-term projects involving Latin American exports to the United States, and various procurement agencies, such as the Rubber Reserve Co., were set up to purchase strategic raw materials. The impact of these projects on the Central American economies in the war years was somewhat slight. Only abacá, grown by the United Fruit Co. (UFCO) in Guatemala, Honduras and Costa Rica, came to figure significantly in the export statistics and even that was not achieved until 1944. Most of the cinchona bark exported from Guatemala was unsuitable for medicinal purposes and was used instead in metallurgical operations.[10]

None of the new products was to have a lasting impact on the Central American economies, but they did stimulate an interest in export diversification. This interest was increased by the creation of two important institutions; in October 1942 Turrialba in Costa Rica was chosen as the field headquarters of the Inter-American Institute of Agricultural Sciences and in 1941 UFCO provided the funds for the establishment of a School of Pan-American Agriculture in Honduras. The benefits from this interest in agricultural diversification were not, however, fully realised until after the war.

In the economic sphere, a more significant contribution to the war effort was made by Central America in the provision of an agricultural surplus for export to US troops and workers in the Panama Canal Zone. These exports took place under cooperative food programmes between the USA on the one hand and Costa Rica, Nicaragua and Honduras on the other. Individual contracts were signed with growers who were guaranteed minimum prices. By May 1943, Costa Rica had shipped nearly 8 million lb of fruits and vegetables to the Canal Zone and a further 3 million lb to companies constructing the Inter-American Highway in Costa Rica. By 1945, these sales accounted for over 5% of Costa Rica's exports.

The war years brought the United States and Central America closer together in strategic and economic terms and US direct foreign investment, much of it by UFCO, rose significantly.[11] The Central American *caudillos* lost no opportunity, large or small, to demonstrate their commitment to the US war effort; Guatemala, for example, responded immediately to a US request for 4 million cubic feet of mahogany required in ship construction, and Somoza offered Nicaragua's scrap metal to Roosevelt as a gesture of solidarity. These gestures cost the *caudillos* little in either economic or political terms, but they served as a constant reminder to the Roosevelt administration of the goodwill of the Central American dictators.

### Exports, imports and the balance of payments

The declaration of war in September 1939 effectively isolated the European market and was very damaging for those Central American republics which had come to depend heavily on Great Britain and Germany as sources of imports or markets for exports (see Table 5.1). Costa Rica was particularly vulnerable, shipping 49.1% of her exports to those two markets in 1939. The principal commodity shipped to Europe was, of course, coffee, and the declaration of war provoked a fall in coffee prices. Several republics responded to this threat to the profitability of production by lowering export duties. The newly elected government in Costa Rica of President Rafael Angel Calderón, for example, abolished all national and municipal taxes on the production and export of coffee in July 1940.[12]

Prices, however, were only one dimension of the problem; a more important dimension was markets, and it was clear to all producing countries that only the United States was capable of absorbing most of the production previously shipped to Europe. This idea was first floated at the Third Pan-American Coffee Conference in May 1940[13] and resulted in the Inter-American Coffee Agreement of November 1940.[14] The Agreement went into effect in April 1941 and was unique in the history of commodity agreements in including as a signatory a leading consuming country, the USA. It was also

Table 5.1 *Central America: external trade shares (%) by main countries, 1939, 1940 and 1945*

|  | Costa Rica | El Salvador | Guatemala | Honduras | Nicaragua |
|---|---|---|---|---|---|
| *(A) Exports* | | | | | |
| (1) 1939 (a) USA | 45.6 | 59.9 | 70.7 | 90.7 | 77.5 |
| (b) UK | 16.9 | 0.2 | 0.4 | 1.8 | 1.3 |
| (c) Germany | 25.0 | 9.0 | 11.5 | 1.9 | 10.9 |
| (2) 1940 (a) USA | 58.8 | 75.2 | 91.0 | 95.6 | 94.2 |
| (b) UK | 25.1 | 0.2 | 1.3 | 0.1 | 0.4 |
| (c) Germany | — | — | * | 0.5 | — |
| (3) 1945 (a) USA | 84.4 | 84.6 | 90.7 | 83.2 | 90.0 |
| (b) UK | * | 0.4 | 0.5 | * | 0.9 |
| (c) Germany | — | — | — | — | — |
| *(B) Imports* | | | | | |
| (1) 1939 (a) USA | 58.8 | 53.0 | 54.5 | 65.2 | 68.4 |
| (b) UK | 4.0 | 6.9 | 3.7 | 2.0 | 5.2 |
| (c) Germany | 17.7 | 17.5 | 27.0 | 11.4 | 12.2 |
| (2) 1940 (a) USA | 75.0 | 67.4 | 73.8 | 62.7 | 84.0 |
| (b) UK | 4.5 | 7.6 | 1.6 | 2.9 | 3.0 |
| (c) Germany | 3.5 | 1.3 | 2.9 | 6.5 | 0.8 |
| (3) 1945 (a) USA | 69.5 | 67.8 | 67.4 | 70.8 | 70.6 |
| (b) UK | 1.5 | 2.3 | 1.7 | 0.9 | * |
| (c) Germany | — | — | — | — | — |

Source: *Bulletin* of the Pan-American Union (various issues)
* Insignificant

exceptionally generous to producing countries in Central America by providing quotas to the US market well in excess of exports previously shipped to North America. Even Honduras, a very minor producer, was given a basic quota, which had nearly doubled by 1945 and which contributed to the post-war emergence of Honduras as an important coffee exporter.[15]

The Inter-American Coffee Agreement assured Central America of a market for virtually all its exportable surplus in the United States and as a result the volume of exports in the war years was very similar to the average of the previous five years (see Table 5.2). Furthermore the drafting and later signing of the Agreement was the signal for heavy speculative buying in the New York coffee market, and the unit value of Central American coffee exports rose by some 50% between 1941 and 1945. This rise in prices, coupled with unchanged volumes, was good news for republics heavily dependent on coffee exports.[16] For those republics relying on bananas to generate foreign exchange, however, the prospects were much more chequered. No matter what influence the fruit companies may have had in Central America, bananas could not be classified by the United States as essential imports; furthermore, even the possibility of shipping the fruit

Table 5.2  *Central America: coffee exports (thousand lb), 1939–45*

| Year | Costa Rica | El Salvador | Guatemala | Honduras[1] | Nicaragua |
|------|-----------|-------------|-----------|-------------|-----------|
| 1939 | 44,534 | 123,018 | 96,342 | 4,189 | 38,361 |
| 1940 | 41,227 | 124,569 | 91,492 | 3,086 | 33,731 |
| 1941 | 47,400 | 82,154 | 92,159 | 1,984 | 27,999 |
| 1942 | 45,636 | 117,066 | 109,570 | 4,850 | 27,999 |
| 1943 | 53,352 | 124,341 | 108,468 | 4,409 | 26,456 |
| 1944 | 41,447 | 139,112 | 102,515 | 4,189 | 28,881 |
| 1945 | 48,061 | 127,207 | 118,389 | 5,953 | 27,117 |
| Average 1939/43 | 46,430 | 116,228 | 99,605 | 3,704 | 30,909 |
| Average 1934/8 | 51,192 | 119,403 | 104,191 | 3,616 | 33,687 |

Source: Torres Rivas, 1973, table 2
[1] Fiscal year, i.e., 1939 = 1 August 1938 to 31 July 1939

Table 5.3  *Central America: volume of banana exports (thousand quintals), 1939–45*

| Year | Costa Rica | Guatemala | Honduras | Nicaragua |
|------|-----------|-----------|----------|-----------|
| 1939 | 832.6 | 2,362.5 | 2,845.6 | 330.7 |
| 1940 | 715.4 | 1,883.9 | 2,877.3 | 231.2 |
| 1941 | 1,096.6 | 1,577.7 | 3,053.8 | 146.4 |
| 1942 | 514.1 | 1,138.6 | 2,658.0 | 16.5 |
| 1943 | 541.2 | 577.6 | 881.6 | 0 |
| 1944 | 427.3 | 1,115.7 | 2,083.1 | 2.3 |
| 1945 | 562.2 | 1,938.7 | 2,949.5 | 24.2 |

Source: International Institute of Agriculture, *International Yearbook of Agricultural Statistics 1941/2 to 1945/6, Vol. II, International Trade*, Rome 1947. Missing data for Guatemala have been obtained from *Revista de Economía*, April–September, Guatemala, 1949, table 12

shrank severely, when the fleets of both the United Fruit Co. and the Standard Fruit and Steamship Co. were taken over by the US navy.

Before Pearl Harbor, the problems facing banana exports were not too serious. Costa Rica even managed to increase the quantum exported by 50% between 1939 and 1941, as United Fruit's Pacific coast plantations began to come on stream. The entry of the United States into the war in December 1941, however, completely altered the situation. Banana ships were requisitioned and the companies found their purchases of insecticides, fuel, etc. cut down by rationing, thereby increasing the risk of disease on banana plantations.[17] The fall in exports after 1941 was in consequence very severe (see Table 5.3). By 1943, Nicaragua had ceased to export altogether, but the reduction between 1940 and 1943 of nearly 60% in Honduran banana exports was the most serious because of the republic's reliance on bananas to generate foreign exchange. Towards the end of the war, however, shipping shortages and the danger of attack became much less acute, so that Honduran and Guatemalan banana exports were able to recover to near their previous peak by 1945.

Throughout the war, both Standard and United Fruit continued to make profits and declare a dividend,[18] and one reason was their involvement in the production and export of strategic materials from Central America. The most important of these was abacá (Manila hemp), which first entered the export list in Costa Rica and Guatemala in 1944, but which had grown to considerable importance by 1945. These new ventures helped to offset the decline in banana exports and to maintain company profitability.

Not all examples of export diversification were induced by the requirements of the Allied war effort. Cotton and sugar production, for example, rose rapidly in El Salvador, although coffee continued to dominate the value of exports;[19] in Nicaragua, production and export of sesame increased sharply in the war years, but the most spectacular change was in mining, with gold accounting for 56% of merchandise exports (including gold) by the end of the war.[20] Despite these efforts at diversification, the main determinant of the value of exports remained in general the performance of traditional exports (bananas and coffee).[21] Thus Honduras – the country most reliant on banana exports – saw its export earnings collapse after Pearl Harbor, while El Salvador enjoyed a boom following the signing of the Inter-American Coffee Agreement (see Table A.10). By the end of the war, however, export earnings were substantially higher than they had been at the beginning in all republics.

This rise in export earnings did not result in an import boom. On the contrary, shipping shortages, the war in Europe and US rationing all combined to exert a downward pressure on the quantum of imports entering Central America (see Table A.13). Only El Salvador escaped a sharp contraction between 1939 and 1942/3, although the easing of shipping problems after 1943 helped to produce a recovery throughout the region in the quantum of imports to roughly pre-war levels. The shortage of imports was reflected in a price rise, which surpassed that for exports in most republics. The unit value of imports virtually doubled between 1939 and 1945 in Costa Rica and Nicaragua, while the rise was nearer 50% in El Salvador and Honduras.[22] Thus, the terms of trade (see Table A.14) and the purchasing power of exports (see Table A.15) tended to decline during the war in Central America in contrast to the modest rise experienced by Latin America as a whole.[23]

Inflation in import prices did not provoke a substantial advance in import substitution either in agriculture or in industry. The 'easy' stage in import substitution in agriculture (ISA) was complete by 1939 and priority was given instead to agricultural export diversification. Some progress was made in organising credit for small-scale farming, particularly in Costa Rica[24] and El Salvador,[25] and the Calderón government also established the Consejo Nacional de Producción (CNP) for regulating the price of staples in the home economy,[26] but regulation in an inflationary environment tended to reduce real farm prices and throughout the region price control for staples was one factor accounting for the stagnation, if not decline, of agricultural production for the home market (see Table A.6).

Industry, including import-substituting industrialisation (ISI), achieved some progress in the war years. A cement factory was established in Nicaragua in 1941, with Somoza as the main shareholder, and a whole series of small-scale industrial enterprises appeared in Guatemala. In general, however, new industrial development was held back by the shortage of machinery, spare parts and raw materials with which to start operations, not to mention the continuing drought of bank credit available for industrial activities.

The difficulty of obtaining imports in the war years was so great that, despite their rise in price, all republics other than Costa Rica ran a trade surplus.[27] In more 'normal' pre-war years, a trade surplus was the counterpart to a modest amount of interest payment on debt service and returns on direct investment; with new capital inflows at negligible levels (other than for banana expansion) the current account balance was close to zero and international reserves largely unchanged. The war period, however, was not one of normal years. The demands of the Allied war effort were such that debt defaults in the 1930s were not allowed to block additional lending to Central America where strategic considerations required it. Thus, funds poured in through Lend-Lease, through the US Export-Import Bank and through the Inter-American Highway System, in addition to direct foreign investment by the United Fruit Co. and others in war-related production plans.

The result was an unprecedented boom in gold and foreign exchange reserves, which increased four-fold between 1940 and 1945 (see Figure 5.1). Indeed, the increase was so great that some republics (notably Nicaragua) were able to pay off a substantial part of the pre-war external public debt. Both Nicaragua and Honduras reduced the old debt faster than they contracted new debt for much of the war so that the total value actually fell even in nominal terms. The other three republics continued to default on the foreign debt until after the Second World War, but by that time the rise in world prices (and the value of Central American exports) had made a settlement of the debt problem a relatively simple matter.

## Money, finance, inflation

The difficulties facing foreign trade at the beginning of the war period produced a predictable fiscal crisis. Customs revenue came under pressure and

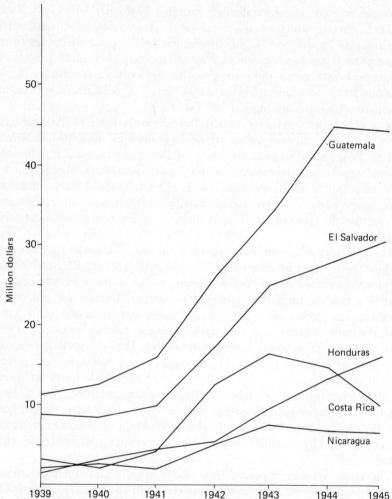

*Figure 5.1* Central America, gold and foreign exchange holdings at year-end
($ million), 1939–45

(Source: International Monetary Fund, 1950)

government revenue was virtually stagnant between 1939 and 1942, except in Nicaragua where the revenue from internal taxes proved very buoyant.[28] Yet, despite the revenue crisis between 1939 and 1942, most republics ran a fiscal surplus or a small deficit during this period as a result of expenditure constraint. This was achieved by keeping public sector nominal wage increases below the rate of inflation, although there were a few exceptions.[29]

This panorama of fiscal purity was marred, not for the first time, by Costa Rica. The outgoing administration of León Cortés had left the public finances in good order and had achieved in 1939 a fiscal surplus equivalent to ten per cent of government revenue. The new administration of Rafael Calderón, elected by a massive majority in February 1940, changed this position in a very short time.

Calderón, a medical doctor hand-picked by Cortés as his successor, was clearly in the *caudillo* tradition by now firmly established in Central America. Yet he was also a populist with advanced social ideas, which he had learnt in Belgium before the war and in which he was encouraged by the remarkable Costa Rican Archbishop, Victor Manuel Sanabria.[30] This unusual combination of *caudillismo*, populism and social Christianity earned Calderón the title of founder of Costa Rica's welfare state, about which much more will be said in the next section. By the end of 1941 Calderón had established a social security programme in Costa Rica; in 1942 he reformed the constitution to include a chapter on social guarantees and in 1943 introduced an advanced labour code.[31] The fiscal consequences of this programme were serious. While revenue stagnated between 1939 and 1942, expenditure increased by nearly one-third and both the internal and external debt increased rapidly. The government's problems were increased by an opposition campaign encouraging non-payment of taxes, but were also exacerbated by corruption and sharp practices within the administration itself.[32]

After 1942, government revenue rose rapidly throughout Central America. The increase in import and export prices produced increases in customs revenues, although not in the same proportion, and the yield from government monopolies (liquor, tobacco, etc.) rose sharply. A fiscal surplus was achieved in 1943 and 1944 everywhere except in Costa Rica; public sector salaries were raised, but at a much more modest rate than inflation, and the fiscal surplus was essentially achieved through cuts in real public sector wages and salaries. In Costa Rica, on the other hand, the fiscal crisis deepened still further. While revenue started to rise after 1942, expenditure started to soar and the fiscal deficit reached 42 per cent of revenue in 1943. The government resorted to borrowing from the banking system, and the internal public debt doubled between 1940 and 1945.[33]

The fiscal restraint exercised in Central America, outside Costa Rica, produced a decline in bank credit outstanding to the government; even in Costa Rica, lending by the National Bank (the sole bank of issue) declined as fiscal expansion was financed by the rest of the banking system. Despite this, the money supply exploded in Central America in the war years (see Figure 5.2). The monetary explosion was due, of course, to the rise in international reserves (money of external origin). Fiscal restraint was incapable of sterilising the impact of rising reserves on the money supply, which rose by a factor of three to four between 1939 and 1945.

In Costa Rica, Honduras and Nicaragua, the increase in the money supply produced a commensurate increase in bank lending in the private sector.

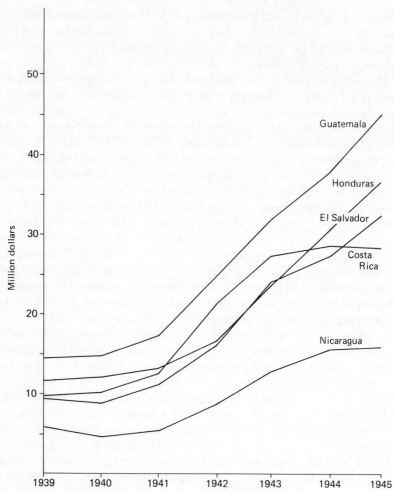

*Figure 5.2* Central America, money supply at year-end ($ million), 1939–45
(Source: International Monetary Fund, 1950)

In El Salvador and Guatemala, however, the increase in bank lending was very modest despite the fact that real interest rates were strongly negative. The modest rise was due to the ultra-cautious policies favoured by those two republics, and bank reserves rose far above the legal requirements.

The impact of the rise in international reserves on the money supply and inflation (see below) produced a novel situation for the financial system with which in many ways it was not able to cope. This provoked attempts at financial reform, although the results were not in general very satisfactory. Honduras, without a Central Bank, was the least able to cope with the new situation. The early years of the war provoked a drain of currency from Honduras, and the Carías administration was forced to import $1.5 million in US currency in the fiscal year 1942/3 to make good the loss. A US mission, including Robert Triffin as a member, visited Honduras in 1943 to advise on establishing a Central Bank, but no action was taken until much later.[34] In Nicaragua, the National Bank was organised into a Central Bank in 1941, following the recommendation of the Chilean Herman Max.[35] The latter had also organised the National Bank of Costa Rica in 1937 as a Central Bank, but the 'Max Banks' were established on the assumption that flexible exchange rates would operate. As they did not, and as Dr Max also did not provide for flexible reserve requirements, the scope for monetary management was virtually non-existent.[36] Costa Rica increased its scope for monetary management by raising reserve requirements in October 1943. This was also the year in which a US technocrat, Kekrich, carried out a study on the feasibility of reorganising Costa Rica's public finances, although the findings of the report were not carried out.

Given the huge increases in gold and foreign exchange holdings, it was not to be expected that even flexible reserve requirements could do much to stabilise the monetary impact of the foreign inflows. What was needed was the creation of a market in negotiable government securities as a prelude to open-market operations, which would mean overcoming the public's reluctance to hold government debt. El Salvador went some way in this direction in April 1940, when the Central Bank (Banco de Reserva) was permitted to buy and sell cedulas of the Mortgage Bank guaranteed by the government and to deal in government bonds quoted on the New York and London markets.[37]

None of these measures to stabilise the impact of foreign inflows proved sufficient, and the cost of living soared in Central America (see Table 5.4). Imported inflation, acting through a rise in the unit value of imports, contributed to the problem, but was by no means the only cause. The main problem was the excess supply of money which could not be fully absorbed by imports even at their new higher prices.

In every country some efforts were made at price control, but (as Table 5.4 shows all too clearly) these were largely ineffective. A Board of Price and Trade Control was established in Nicaragua and granted jurisdiction over imports in 1944; Costa Rica passed laws to curb speculation and used the Consejo Nacional de Producción (established in 1943) to regulate the price of basic grains and other essential foodstuffs, while Honduras imposed price ceilings and restrictions on imports in order to increase supply for the home market. Guatemala imposed a quota system for imports to prevent speculation and direct the goods where most needed.

Given the buoyancy of international reserves, it is perhaps surprising that no republics resorted to exchange rate appreciation as an anti-inflationary

Table 5.4  *Central America: cost of living index (1937 = 100\*)*

| Year | Costa Rica | El Salvador (1) | (2) | Guatemala (3) | (4) | Honduras (1) | Nicaragua (1) |
|------|-----------|-----------------|-----|---------------|-----|--------------|---------------|
| 1939 | 101 | 74 | 100 | 92 | 93 | 100 | 224 |
| 1940 | 99 | 77 | 88 | 91 | 90 | 138 | 274 |
| 1941 | 102 | 78 | 110 | 87 | 81 | NA | 269 |
| 1942 | 123 | 78 | 130 | 94 | 96 | NA | 363 |
| 1943 | 158 | 103 | 156 | 111 | 122 | 183 | 478 |
| 1944 | 167 | 150 | 176 | 130 | 140 | 295 | 813 |
| 1945 | 177 | 174 | 203 | 163 | 174 | 305 | 954 |

Source: International Monetary Fund (1950)
* Except for Honduras, where 1939 = 100
(1) Retail food prices
(2) Wholesale prices (1939 = 100)
(3) Index for Guatemala City only
(4) Food wholesale prices

device. After 1940/1, there was a modest appreciation of the exchange rate in Costa Rica and Nicaragua, bringing it very close to the official rate by 1943,[38] yet this did not amount to an anti-inflation device, because merchandise imports were in general obtained at the official rate.

The main argument against appreciation was the damage it would do to export interests, particularly coffee; the coffee oligarchy remained immensely powerful, even in Calderón's Costa Rica,[39] although in Nicaragua their interests did not always coincide with those of the Somoza family.[40] A further argument was provided by the psychological pull of fixed exchange rates. By 1944, Honduras had enjoyed twenty-five years of exchange rate stability, Guatemala twenty years and El Salvador ten years. It had worked well and the governments concerned were reluctant to abandon it, while the future looked so uncertain.

## The challenge to *caudillismo*

During much of the 1930s, Central America had achieved under *caudillo* rule an increase in material prosperity, but the benefits had flowed disproportionately to the small urban sector. The latter, although accounting for less than a quarter of total population in 1940,[41] was growing rapidly through a combination of natural increase in population[42] and rural–urban migration. The result was a quiet transformation of the urban sector, which made it very different from the Great Depression. In particular, in the two decades leading up to the Second World War, there had been a notable change in the composition of employment, resulting in a substantial increase in the numerical importance of the middle classes. In Nicaragua, for example, the number of office-workers had grown thirteen-fold between 1920 and 1940, while the labour force had grown by only 52%.[43] Similarly, the number of teachers in Guatemala City had grown five-fold over the same period.[44]

This urban and middle-class growth had come too late to affect the outcome of the political struggles at the start of the 1930s, when the liberal oligarchies collapsed. By the beginning of the 1940s, however, the numerical importance of the urban middle classes had changed, although they still lacked any form of political representation. Even Rafael Calderón, a medical doctor by training, and his newly formed Partido Republicano Nacional could not be seen as a representative of these groups, who had in any case turned firmly against him by 1944.

Lack of political representation may have been tolerable while real living standards for the urban middle classes continued to rise. The war years, however, witnessed a decline in the expansion of real GDP in several republics, while real GDP per head between 1940 and 1944 actually fell in Costa Rica, Guatemala and Honduras (see Table A.3). What growth there was occurred mainly in the export sector, which helped to underpin living standards in rural areas.[45] The urban economy, however, was adversely affected by restrictions on imports (hurting commerce in particular) and by fiscal restraint, which caused problems because public sector pay increases almost invariably fell behind inflation, and real living standards for such employees dropped accordingly. Urban areas were better served than rural areas in terms of access to health and education facilities, but progress in these departments had not been rapid under *caudillo* rule. Priority had been given to public works expenditure, particularly roads, and illiteracy and death rates (outside of Costa Rica) were still high even in urban areas.

The final factor contributing to political unrest was the war itself. The espousal of the Atlantic Charter and Roosevelt's four freedoms[46] by Central America's *caudillos* appeared at odds with the policies of domestic political repression. It is doubtful if this argument on its own could have accounted for the events which unfolded in Central America in 1944, but combined with the other arguments it added up to a powerful case for political change.

Discontent began to surface in 1943 with unsuccessful military revolts in Honduras[47] and El Salvador.[48] In April 1944, another military coup was attempted in El Salvador and failed, but the repression which followed unleashed a strike by students which was taken up by the whole of San Salvador. By mid-May, Martínez had resigned, following the advice of the US ambassador, and his resignation sent a tremor through the neighbouring republics. In the next four months, there were student strikes and urban protests throughout Central America. In Honduras[49] and Nicaragua,[50] the protests were crushed, but the movements did produce new political parties;[51] in Guatemala, however, a general strike achieved the resignation of Ubico, following a protest by students and teachers.[52]

Similar events occurred in Costa Rica, but the situation was vastly complicated by Calderón's populism. By 1942, Calderón's social programme and
his actions against Axis residents had earned him the enmity of the traditional
oligarchy and his former mentor, León Cortés, had broken away to form
the Democratic Party. Members of the oligarchy began to plot Calderón's
overthrow and even approached Manuel Mora, the charismatic leader of
the Costa Rican Communist Party (CP). Mora had gained ten per cent of
the popular vote in the 1940 presidential elections (Calderón securing 85%),
but his Communist Party had increased its share of the vote to sixteen per
cent in elections for deputies in February 1942. The CP was clearly a force
to be reckoned with, but Mora did not throw in his lot with the conspirators;
instead, he warned Calderón, whose social programme appealed strongly
to the CP leader. Mora's warning convinced Calderón of the need to do
a deal with the CP in order to underpin his social programme and provide
a counterweight to oligarchic reaction. In his presidential message for May
1942, Calderón announced plans for an informal alliance with the CP at
the same time as preparing to reform the constitution to include a chapter
on social guarantees.

In the war years, an alliance with the Communists did not present international complications,[53] but there could have been a problem with the Catholic
church. This potential conflict, however, was resolved in 1943, following
the dissolution of the Communist International. Mora changed the name
of his party to Vanguardia Popular and, in a public exchange of letters,
Archbishop Sanabria declared that the new party did not represent a conflict
of conscience for Catholics.[54]

The fact that the old oligarch, León Cortés, and many export interests
were lined up against the informal alliance between Calderón's Partido
Republicano Nacional (PRN) and Mora's Vanguardia Popular (VP) gave
the superficial impression that the 'Calderón-communistas' represented the
new social forces in Costa Rica, the same social forces that were seeking
ascendancy throughout Central America. The position was complicated,
however, by the inclusion of a social democratic movement in the opposition,
which owed much to the work of the Centre for the Study of National
Problems, established in 1940. The Centre, which comprised some of the
best intellectuals in Costa Rica,[55] opposed Calderón not because of his social
programme (which by and large they supported), but because of his authoritarian and anti-democratic tendencies.

It was these same alleged authoritarian tendencies which launched José
Figueres on his controversial political career. Don Pepe, as he is universally
known in Costa Rica, was outraged by the acts of violence committed in
July 1942 in San José against the properties of Germans and Italians follow-
ing the sinking of an UFCO ship in Limón harbor by a German submarine.
He purchased radio time to denounce the Calderón government, but was

arrested before the broadcast was complete and went into self-imposed exile.

Calderón's social programme continued in 1943. An advanced labour code was introduced and in October 1943 the Communist-dominated Confederación de Trabajadores Costarricenses (CTCR) was formed, replacing the Comité Sindical de Enlace founded by the CP in 1938. In the next two years, 125 unions joined the CTCR.[56] Yet, despite the social programme, opposition to Calderón continued to mount. The informal alliance with the CP was not well received by the middle classes, and Calderón began to manoeuvre to secure an electoral victory for his chosen successor, Teodoro Picado, without the need for Mora's support. He tried to do this by changing the law in a way which would have permitted electoral fraud. The opposition to this mobilised the middle classes (especially the students)[57] in a wave of street protests. The government withdrew the plan, but was therefore obliged to continue the alliance with the Communists. Teodoro Picado, as the candidate of this alliance (Bloque de la Victoria), handsomely defeated León Cortés, candidate of the Democratic Party, in the presidential elections of 1944, but charges of fraud and violence were widespread (on both sides) and the election did little to calm the fears of those who believed that Calderón and/or Mora were intent on institutionalising a Tico brand of *caudillismo*.

In Costa Rica, it could therefore be argued that *caudillismo* survived the challenge of 1944 through electoral fraud. Elsewhere in Central America, a mixture of repression and concession was employed to try and achieve the same end. In Honduras, the government of Tiburcio Carías launched a literacy campaign and, more significantly, started to meet the unpaid salary bill of civil servants, so that the internal floating debt fell by one-third between the end of 1943 and the end of 1944. In Nicaragua, Somoza faced a strong challenge from students and the middle classes, but his tactical skill thwarted an alliance between these groups and the emerging labour movement. The latter refused to support a threatened general strike in 1944 and a grateful Somoza introduced a rent control law, opened four 'people's stores', where articles of prime necessity could be bought cheaply, and in the following year drew up a Labour Code, which on paper was the most advanced piece of social legislation in Latin America at the time. Within a short period, however, Somoza turned on his erstwhile allies in the labour movement after they had served their purpose of undermining the possibility of a united opposition against him (see Chapter 7, pp. 133–5).[58]

In El Salvador, the resignation of Martínez paved the way for anticipated free elections by the end of 1944. The expected winner was Arturo Romero, a doctor, who had played a leading part in the revolts of April and May, and who clearly represented the new Salvadorean social forces aspiring for political office. Their aspirations were crushed in October, however, when a coup was carried out (with the possible support of the provisional president) by the Chief of Police, Colonel Osmin Aguirre y Salinas. The latter, a hard-line supporter of Martínez,[59] expelled Romero and threw his weight behind General Salvador Castañeda Castro, who easily won the elections at the end of the year.

The news of the fall of Martínez was a serious blow to the Ubico administration in Guatemala and enormous efforts were made to prevent the information reaching the Guatemalan people. These efforts were unsuccessful, however, and by June 1944 the University Students Association began to press for educational reform. At first, the government made concessions, but this simply increased the scale of demands, and repression was used. This provoked a general strike in Guatemala City, and Ubico resigned in favour of a junta composed of three generals.

In July, a compliant Congress elected General Federico Ponce, strongman of the junta, as Provisional President, and for a time it looked as if Ubiquismo would continue without Ubico. The opposition, however, moved fast and secured the support of junior officers in the army. On 20 October, these officers revolted and the Ponce régime fell. Ubico and the Ubiquistas fled the country and Juan Jose Arévalo, a pedagogue around whom the opposition had united, won a handsome victory in the December presidental elections.[60]

By the end of 1944, therefore, *caudillismo* had been defeated in Guatemala, but had survived elsewhere. In El Salvador, Castañeda Castro had replaced Martínez and in Costa Rica populist rule was represented by Picado rather than Calderón, but in both countries the political system survived largely intact. The challenge to *caudillismo* continued after 1944, and eventually triumphed in Costa Rica in 1948. Yet the opportunities provided in 1944 were never to be matched again. The opposition enjoyed the sympathy, if not actual support, of the United States despite the fact that it included significant numbers of communists. Within a few years, the Cold War had made the US administration much more ambivalent about supporting the opposition to *caudillismo*, and Costa Rica is the exception which proves the rule. In Costa Rica, the revolutionary opposition in 1948 was fighting against the communists, who continued to support Calderón.

# 6

## Post-war economic recovery

The first decade after the Second World War was a period of economic, social and political upheaval for Central America. Some of the political events, particularly the Guatemalan revolutionary experience and the Costa Rican civil war of 1948, are well known; yet the economic background against which these developments unfolded has not been so well explored. This chapter will therefore concentrate on the economic changes in the decade up to 1954, the year in which the Guatemalan revolution ended, while the following chapter will be concerned with social and political developments in the same period.

Central America came out of the Second World War with an economy which exhibited many of the classic signs of under-development. Exports continued to be dominated by earnings from coffee and bananas, both of which were non-essential as far as the Allied war effort was concerned, and output had suffered accordingly. Although foreign exchange reserves had expanded during the war, there had been no possibility of translating this into imports of machinery to start new industrial activities because of wartime shortages of such goods. Production of goods for the home market, whether agricultural or industrial, was held back by inadequate infrastructure, a weak financial system and low effective demand, and the state's ability to correct these deficiencies was retarded by a regressive fiscal system, which remained over-dependent on import duties, and a political system which was in some cases overtly hostile to capitalist modernisation.

The first decade after the war provided an unprecedented opportunity for Central America to correct some of these deficiencies in the economic system. The value of exports surged as never before, bringing unheard-of wealth to both individuals and governments. Foreign exchange receipts soared, freeing each republic from a constraint which had been effectively binding since 1929, and this increased the degrees of freedom of each republic enormously. An additional factor contributing to the unprecedented nature of the post-war opportunity was the continued existence of a land frontier. While the central highlands in each republic were devoted to coffee and domestic crops and the Atlantic lowlands were used for bananas, timber, cacao and other export crops, the Pacific littoral was virtually untouched; in the 1930s, some banana production in Costa Rica and Guatemala had been transferred to the Pacific lowlands, but most of the area (even in El Salvador) was still uncultivated or given over to cattle-raising of the most land-extensive kind. Tropical diseases, such as malaria, were a factor accounting for the low population density on the Pacific littoral, but by the end of the war there had been major advances in disease control.

With land and capital (through foreign exchange) available in abundance, the only serious obstacle to agricultural growth and diversification was thought to be shortages of labour.[1] Emphasis was therefore given to the introduction of crops with possibilities for mechanisation and to labour-saving technical progress on existing cropland. With the benefit of hindsight, one can see that this use of the agricultural frontier was a serious error. Far from permitting Central America to escape some of the pitfalls of export-led growth, the land frontier was used to introduce new export crops on the pre-war pattern so that the benefits of export diversification and capitalist modernisation were as narrowly distributed as before.

The most important example of export diversification was the expansion of cotton production. The latter, from its humble beginnings in the 1930s, came to occupy a place of major importance in the economies of El Salvador, Guatemala and Nicaragua (and minor importance elsewhere). The industry was highly concentrated from its earliest days, and cotton growers began to form a distinct social class and pressure group comparable to coffee growers (both coffee and cotton were largely in national hands). Their combined influence was sufficient to distort the fiscal system in their favour (see below, p. 123) and to rob the state of an equitable share in the two industries' expansion.

The profitability of the agricultural export sector in the decade after 1944 generated a capitalist surplus which could not be absorbed by the sector itself through increased investment and/or consumption. The existence of this surplus therefore gave a stimulus to capitalist modernisation outside the export sector, which affected all five republics to a certain extent. Capitalist modernisation — increasing the opportunities and incentives for private investment outside the export sector – did not necessarily imply a shift in favour of political liberalisation, although in Guatemala (at least during the presidency of Juan José Arévalo), in Costa Rica (after 1948) and in Honduras (after 1954) the two were linked. El Salvador and Nicaragua, however, were characterised throughout the period by a conception of capitalist modernisation which retained harsh social controls and restrictions on individual liberty.

By 1954, the exceptionally favourable conditions facing the agricultural sector had come to an end. The decade had been used with relative efficiency to promote a narrow conception of capitalist modernisation throughout

Table 6.1. *Central America: banana exports (millions of boxes), 1944–54*

| Year | Costa Rica | Guatemala | Honduras | Nicaragua[1] |
|---|---|---|---|---|
| 1944 | 3.5 | 7.7 | 14.1 | 11.3 |
| 1945 | 4.6 | 13.4 | 20.0 | 121.0 |
| 1946 | 9.0 | 15.3 | 19.0 | 313.7 |
| 1947 | 11.5 | 20.1 | 24.7 | 467.6 |
| 1948 | 15.4 | 18.4 | 24.9 | 678.6 |
| 1949 | 17.6 | 10.3 | 21.7 | 769.5 |
| 1950 | 16.3 | 10.4 | 21.1 | 661.6 |
| 1951 | 15.9 | 7.9 | 21.4 | 587.0 |
| 1952 | 18.5 | 5.9 | 20.1 | 492.8 |
| 1953 | 16.2 | 10.7 | 19.8 | 459.3 |
| 1954 | 16.2 | 9.5 | 14.7 | 576.8 |
| 1944–9 percentage change | +403 | +34 | +54 | +6170 |
| 1949–54 percentage change | −8 | −8 | −32 | −25 |

Sources: For 1947–54 Costa Rica, Guatemala and Honduras, see Ellis, 1983, p. 400. Figures for 1944–7 were derived from the export volume index in the IMF's *International Financial Statistics*. For Nicaragua, see Dirección General de Estadísticas, *Memoria de Aduanas*, 1955
[1] In 1,000 bunches (each bunch is roughly equivalent to 1.5 boxes)

the region, but progress towards political modernisation had been painfully slow. By the end of the first post-war decade, Guatemalan political life had returned to the dark ages and only Costa Rica had made genuine progress towards political and social democracy, although events in Honduras in 1954 (see Chapter 7, pp. 143–4) offered some prospects for peaceful social reform. Just as in the 1920s, therefore, the opportunities provided by favourable external conditions had been exploited too timidly so that the chances of social and political progress receded with the adverse external conditions which prevailed after 1954.

## The boom in traditional exports

The end of hostilities in Europe brought high hopes for the recovery of traditional exports (bananas and coffee), both of which had suffered grievously in the war. In the case of the banana industry, these hopes were initially fulfilled; the volume of banana exports (see Table 6.1) bounced back swiftly to reach or pass pre-war levels by 1948. Even in Nicaragua, where production had virtually ceased during the war, exports ran to nearly 800,000 bunches by 1949. Panama disease, however, continued to strike at banana plantations in the late 1940s and the only known antidote was the technique of flood-fallow.[2] This method proved extremely expensive

Table 6.2. *Direct foreign investment ($ million), 1947–54*
(Figures in brackets are income payments on direct foreign investment
($ Millions))

| Year | Costa Rica | El Salvador[2] | Guatemala | Honduras | Nicaragua[3] |
|------|-----------|---------------|-----------|----------|-------------|
| 1947 | +6.6 (4.7) | +0.1 (0.6) | −0.6 (2.2) | +9.4 (22.4) | +0.9 (4.3) |
| 1948 | +2.1 (7.9) | − (0.8) | +1.0 (7.1) | +4.6 (22.6) | +0.9 (4.5) |
| 1949 | −0.6 (15.0) | − (0.9) | +3.3 (7.2) | +5.2 (18.4) | +1.1 (4.5) |
| 1950 | +0.6 (13.2) | − (1.4) | +1.5 (2.8) | +0.1 (20.7) | +2.1 (5.9) |
| 1951 | +2.5 (11.9) | −0.1 (1.4) | −0.5 (−0.2)[1] | +12.1 (18.9) | +1.1 (6.3) |
| 1952 | +1.5 (14.7) | −0.1 (1.4) | −1.6 (−6.7)[1] | +15.7 (13.5) | +2.3 (5.4) |
| 1953 | +0.3 (12.0) | − (2.0) | −2.1 (−4.2)[1] | +8.8 (14.3) | +2.0 (6.7) |
| 1954 | −0.4 (11.4) | − (2.0) | −1.5 (2.7) | +2.6 (−3.6)[1] | +2.0 (5.6) |
| Totals | +12.6 (90.8) | −0.1 (10.5) | −0.5 (10.9) | +58.5 (127.2) | +12.4 (43.2) |

Source: International Monetary Fund, *Balance of Payments Yearbook*, various years
[1] Minus sign indicates loss
[2] The figures refer mainly to the operations of public utilities, in which foreign direct investment in El Salvador was concentrated
[3] The figures are dominated by the operations of foreign-owned mining companies. A small amount of direct investment was carried out in this period by the Cukra Development Corporation, a subsidiary of UFCO, but this was concerned with the development of African palm trees, not bananas

and much of the increase in the book value of direct foreign investment in Central America in this period[3] can be attributed to expenditure by the two main fruit companies on infrastructure works. It was to prove a losing battle, however, and both production and yields fell after 1948 in many of the major divisions. Only in Costa Rica, where the United Fruit Co.'s Golfito division was taking over from the disease-ridden Quepos division (both on the Pacific coast), did yields achieve a modest increase at the start of the 1950s.[4] Despite the problems with production and yields, earnings from banana exports were buoyant for much of the period due to improved prices aided by post-war recovery.[5] The price increases were not spectacular, however, and the vertically integrated fruit companies continued to operate effectively with transfer prices; in addition, the profit outflow on direct foreign investment (DFI) far exceeded inflows of DFI (both flows being mainly accounted for by the fruit companies) in most of the decade (see Table 6.2).[6]

Although the fruit companies improved their earnings from the Central American divisions far above wartime levels, the first decade after the war was a stormy one which ended with a significant shift in the balance of power in favour of the host governments. Such an observation may seem strange in view of the role of the United Fruit Co. (UFCO) in the fall of the Arbenz government in Guatemala (see Chapter 7); there can be little doubt, however, that after 1954 the share of the benefits accruing to Central America from banana operations was much higher, while at the same time the companies adopted a much lower political profile.

The change in the share of benefits was due to the adoption of new contracts. While the Arbenz government was involved in a head-on clash with UFCO over land reform and financial compensation for expropriated land, José Figueres Ferrer in Costa Rica and Manuel Galvez in Honduras were pressing for new contracts to increase the company's tax liability. By 1949, these two governments had amended the existing contracts to impose a 15% profits tax, and by the end of 1954 (1955 in Honduras),[7] the tax had been raised to 30% with UFCO also agreeing to hand over most of its schools, hospitals, etc. in Costa Rica to the government.[8] The new arrangements were mirrored in the contract signed by UFCO in 1954 with the counter-revolutionary government of Castillo Armas in Guatemala.[9]

The year 1954 not only marked the culmination of the conflict between UFCO and the Arbenz government, but also the dramatic banana strike in Honduras. Both events had major political repercussions, which will be discussed in the next chapter, and one can observe a distinct change in the political profile of the fruit companies after 1954. The overt political presence gave way to a much more subtle, discreet influence, only occasionally threatening to become a party political issue,[10] and the relative economic importance of the companies steadily declined after 1954 in accordance with the pace of agricultural and industrial diversification. This change in profile came about because the governments in each republic where the fruit companies had operations were no longer dependent on short-term financial support from the multinationals, as they had been (particularly Honduras) in the pre-war period.

Coffee exports had not suffered as badly as bananas during the war, as a result of the operation of the Pan-American Coffee Agreement. Prices under the Agreement, however, had not kept pace with the rise in costs, and exporters were anxious to remove some of the restrictions surrounding coffee sales now that more favourable prospects were in view.[11] Few producers, however, anticipated the surge in prices when the demise of the Pan-American Coffee Agreement[12] brought price controls to an end. After 1945, prices rose steadily and the unit value of coffee exports had doubled by 1949; the outbreak of the Korean war in 1950 produced a further sharp increase and by 1954 prices had reached an all-time peak at a level some four times higher than the previous peak in the late 1920s.

Producers did not at first respond to higher prices by increasing the area planted nor were any efforts made initially to increase the yield per hectare, which (with the exception of El Salvador) was abysmally low. The persistence of high and rising prices, however, eventually produced a predictable response; new plantings (which bear fruit in three years and reach maturity in five years) were undertaken in Nicaragua and Honduras, the latter recording a three-fold increase in area planted between 1944 and 1953 and surpassing the area devoted to coffee production in Nicaragua and even Costa Rica.

In the three 'senior' coffee republics (Costa Rica, El Salvador and Guatemala), the most suitable lands had long ago been planted to coffee and the best prospects for increasing production (particularly in Costa Rica and Guatemala) were through improvements in yield. This could be achieved through replantings,[13] more careful husbandry and irrigation; above all, however, yields responded to applications of chemicals, both fertilisers and insecticides.[14] Of the five republics only Costa Rica made a serious effort to improve yields. After the civil war in 1948, this task was given a high priority by the Ministry of Agriculture and the nationalised banking system, which financed nearly all the crop in the first half of the 1950s;[15] some 80% of imported fertilisers were estimated to be destined to coffee in this period[16] and even the area planted to coffee increased by roughly 15% between the two census years of 1950 and 1955.[17]

With prices received increasing in all republics and the volume of exports also rising in Costa Rica, Honduras and Nicaragua, earnings from coffee recorded a majestic advance throughout Central America (see Figure 6.1). The most spectacular case was Honduras, where the value of exports increased by a factor of thirty-five in the decade after 1944, reaching 26% of total export earnings by 1954. Even in El Salvador, however, where production was stagnant, earnings rose from $19 million in 1944 to $92 million in 1954.

The coffee industry in Central America had become highly concentrated by 1950.[18] Even in Costa Rica, it has been estimated that the large farms (those with more than 100 mazanas (=69 hectares)) represented only 6% of all farm units, but controlled 40% of production.[19] In addition, in each republic the preparation of coffee for sale in *beneficios* and its subsequent export were both processes even more highly concentrated than production.[20] While deplorable on social and, indeed, economic grounds, this concentration within the coffee sector did create opportunities for maximising the size of the capitalist surplus. The bonanza in export earnings tended to accrue in the form of profits, which were far greater than required within the coffee sector itself for investment, renovation etc. A surplus was therefore available to finance activities outside the coffee sector, which gave a huge stimulus to capitalist modernisation.

### Agricultural diversification

The improvement in the fortunes of traditional exports (bananas and coffee) meant that their share of total exports remained close to peak levels in the decade after the Second World War. By 1954, these two crops were

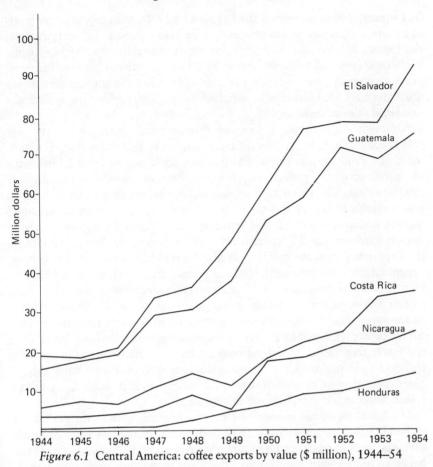

*Figure 6.1* Central America: coffee exports by value ($ million), 1944–54

still responsible for nearly 90% of total foreign exchange earnings in Costa Rica, El Salvador and Guatemala, while only in Nicaragua (where gold exports were still important) was the share less than 50%.[21] This apparent commodity concentration of exports, however, was distorted by the exceptionally high prices for coffee in the early 1950s and concealed the fact that in the decade up to 1954, some progress was made in agricultural diversification in terms of both exports and output for the home market.

The progress towards diversification was all the more surprising, given that the decade began badly. During the war (see Chapter 5) production of strategic raw materials (e.g. rubber, abacá) had been stepped up to help meet the needs of the Allied war effort. This task was carried out through long-term contracts between US government agencies and various multinational companies (particularly UFCO and the Goodyear Rubber Co.).[22]

By the early 1950s, however, the Far East had returned to its pre-war levels of production, with costs of production far below those in Central America; the export of abacá in particular fell off dramatically after 1952,[23] while rubber exports had virtually ceased by 1950.[24] A further blow to the prospects for export diversification came in 1946 when the contracts by which the Panama Canal Zone was supplied from Central America with fruits and vegetables came to an end.[25]

Although the potential for export diversification at the end of the war was readily apparent,[26] many obstacles had to be overcome first. The existence of a land frontier on the Pacific coast could not be denied, but access to that land was impeded in several republics by disease and inadequate infrastructure. The conviction among policy-makers that Central America was a region of labour shortage[27] meant that export diversification would involve mechanisation, but the latter in turn required foreign exchange to import machinery and long-term credit to finance its purchase. In addition, the experience with the coffee crop in each republic suggested that farmers depended on short-term bank credit to finance their working capital requirements.[28] This dependence could be expected to increase in the case of new export crops, where land rent might prove to be an important addition to annual outlays.[29] There was a further lesson to be learnt from the successful coffee experience. The powerful institutions, which had developed since the Great Depression to defend coffee interests,[30] had secured preferential treatment for coffee in the factor markets and in access to bank capital. No export diversification efforts could be expected to achieve significant results without comparable institutional support.

The most important example of export diversification in the period was provided by cotton, which by 1954 had become a major source of export earnings in Nicaragua and a minor source elsewhere.[31] In addition, cotton began to fulfil a significant proportion of the textile industry's raw material requirements, and cotton imports had virtually ceased by 1954 throughout the region. In each republic, one may note the importance of the preconditions for successful export diversification mentioned above. In El Salvador, a key role was played by the growers' association (Co-operativa Algodonera Salvadoreña), founded in 1940 with government support;[32] in addition, the construction of the Pacific littoral highway proved to be a crucial element in the expansion of the cotton industry.[33] In Nicaragua, rapid expansion (particularly after 1950) was achieved despite the absence of a powerful growers' association, but the crop was heavily supported by the Banco Nacional de Nicaragua from the early 1950s.[34] Diversification in Nicaragua was further assisted by cotton-seed exports, which reached 32 million kg in 1954 with a value of $1.5 million.[35] In Guatemala, an important part was played by the Instituto de Fomento de Producción, a state development bank founded in 1948.[36]

There were other examples of export diversification, but none which affected all republics as powerfully as cotton. In Costa Rica, UFCO's experiment on the Atlantic coast in turning idle banana lands over to cacao production continued, and output rose steadily up to 1954, when exports reached 10.1% of total foreign exchange earnings. The subsequent fall in prices, however, provoked a collapse of production in the remainder of the decade. In Nicaragua, the Pacific frontier in Chinandega province provided lands for sesame production, as well as cotton, and the crop received strong support from the banking system; sesame exports were valued at $4 million in 1952 (7.9% of total exports), although this value had been nearly halved by 1954. Finally, this period saw Guatemala turn itself into the world's largest producer of citronella oil and the second largest supplier of lemongrass oil, an achievement which the IBRD credited to a co-operative linking the seventy leading producers.[37]

While export agriculture was dominated at the start of the period by coffee and bananas, production for the home market was dominated by cereals. This gave rise to an unsatisfactory diet, which was somewhat unvaried and deficient in proteins and fats, although the intake of carbohydrates was often excessive.[38] The consumption of meat and dairy products was particularly low and even in Costa Rica[39] in the early 1950s the proportion of daily calorie intake obtained from proteins barely exceeded 10%. The inadequacies of production were to some extent made up by food imports. These, however, tended to be dominated by flour and cereals, reinforcing the carbohydrate bias in the diet rather than reducing it through food imports rich in proteins and fats.[40] The structure of food imports, of course, reflected the low purchasing power of most of the population for whom meat and dairy products remained a luxury good.

The expansion of production for the home market was constrained by factors in addition to those facing export diversification. First, price movements in the small, home market tended to be extremely erratic, and this militated against a steady increase in production; secondly, while a bumper crop in the export sector would not affect the world price, the same phenomenon in the home market could lead to a fall in earnings, and this created a bias in favour of export crops; thirdly, the social status attached to the production of export crops (particularly coffee) was undoubtedly much higher than that attached to production for the home market.

Some republics took seriously the problems posed by erratic prices in this period. In Costa Rica, for example, the Consejo Nacional de Producción (CNP), founded in 1943 as a subsidiary of the Banco Nacional, was given greater status by the revolutionary junta in 1949 as a semi-autonomous agency. Throughout the period, it fixed the minimum price to be received by growers for a variety of crops, buying and selling in the market in order to establish market prices close to the minimum level. Elsewhere, however,

small producers were often at the mercy of middlemen whose stronger bargaining position resulted in their receiving a disproportionate share of the
net benefits from production and distribution.

The 1950 agricultural census for each republic (1952 in Nicaragua)
revealed clearly that domestic use production (DUA) tended to be equated
with the small-farm sector, with the important exception of cattle-raising.
As such, DUA faced particularly severe problems of access to credit in view
of the unwillingness of the financial system to lend to smallholders, whether
farmers or peasants, because of their lack of collateral. This problem had
been recognised before 1944 by Costa Rica and El Salvador, both of which
had set up facilities for small-scale rural credit within their banking systems
(see above, p. 82). After the 1944 revolution, Guatemala also sought to
promote DUA through the formation of the Crédito Hipotecario Nacional
and the banking department of the Instituto de Fomento de Producción.
Only in Costa Rica, however, where the small farmer frequently owned
his own land,[41] could it be said that the small-scale peasantry was given
access to credit on a significant scale. The much higher literacy rate in Costa
Rica among the rural population was an additional reason why that republic
found it easier to incorporate small-scale producers within the financial
network.

Population growth, which accelerated throughout Central America in this
period,[42] also created special problems for DUA. First, it imposed a minimum
rate of expansion on this sector of at least three per cent per year in order
to keep pace with demographic changes, the rise in income per head and
the need for food security through import substitution in agriculture.
Secondly, past population expansion put pressure on the *minifundistas* (who
were responsible for the bulk of DUA's production) through its impact on
the subdivision of holdings.

With the possible exception of El Salvador, there is even now no absolute
shortage of land suitable for cultivation in Central America. There has always
been, however, a problem of access to land, because the ownership of land
had been highly concentrated in private hands and large landowners have
tended to restrict access in order to secure an adequate labour supply for
the harvesting of export crops. In the period 1929–44, the expansion of
DUA was not in general hampered by access to land; on the contrary, the
stagnation of export agriculture (EXA) meant that labour supply for export
crops was not a serious problem and the peasantry were able to increase
production of crops for the home market. As far as one can tell, however,
this was achieved through the cultivation of more land[43] rather than an
increase in yields, which remained very low by world or even Latin American
standards. The recovery of EXA after 1944, therefore, and its expansion
to include cotton, was bound to have an impact on DUA. Given EXA's
demand for additional land and labour, how could DUA achieve the mini-

Table 6.3. *Annual average rates of growth (%) for domestic use agriculture (DUA) and export agriculture (EXA), value added per head at constant 1970 prices, 1944–54*

| | Costa Rica | | El Salvador | | Guatemala | | Honduras | | Nicaragua | |
|---|---|---|---|---|---|---|---|---|---|---|
| Period[1] | DUA | EXA | DUA | EXA | DUA | EXA | DUA | EXA | DUA | EXA |
| 1944–49 | +5.9 | +11.2 | +6.7 | +3.2 | +3.6 | +0.3 | +0.8 | +4.6 | −2.0 | +4.3 |
| 1949–54 | +1.0 | −1.4 | −1.2 | +0.2 | −1.8 | +0.1 | −0.5 | −7.5 | −1.0 | +18.0 |

Source: Tables A.2, A.5 and A.6
[1] Three-year averages

mum required rate of expansion of three per cent per annum? The first possibility was through an increase in yields per hectare, the second was the participation of DUA in the exploitation of the Pacific land frontier and the third was an increase in access to already cultivated land through land reform.

All studies in the decade after 1944 recognised both the need for and the possibility of increasing yields in DUA, particularly basic grains.[44] Nothing was achieved, however, and indeed a study by the Economic Commission for Latin America (ECLA) showed that by 1955/6 maize yields had·actually fallen in each republic.[45] This failure was not particularly surprising; first, access to land in this period (see below) was not unduly restricted and, secondly, the task of providing the peasantry with access to the resources needed to raise yields proved to be beyond the administrative and political capabilities of most of the region's governments.

The initial steps taken to exploit the Pacific land frontier did benefit DUA. Indeed, as Table 6.3 shows, in the five years after 1944 the expansion of DUA exceeded population growth in all republics except Nicaragua (where political uncertainty was a major cause of slow growth in all branches of the economy). The main products to benefit from this expansion of the land frontier were rice and cattle, both of which were well suited to the Pacific lowlands. In the next period (1949–54), however, there was a marked reduction in the rate of expansion of DUA. The growth of DUA appeared to be suffering from the lack of access to suitable land and from the competition with EXA for scarce resources (particularly credit).

Under the circumstances, it is not surprising that the question of land reform should have raised its head. The two countries where the small peasantry faced the most serious problems of access to land were El Salvador and Guatemala and both addressed the question of land redistribution, although in radically different ways. In El Salvador, the Martínez government had established in 1932 the Junta Nacional de la Defensa Nacional to administer the Fondo de Mejoramiento Social in an effort to promote a very mild form of land reform. In 1942, the Junta was renamed the Instituto de Mejoramiento Social, but by 1950 only 73,655 acres had been redistributed in nearly two decades of effort and a new government agency formed in 1950, Instituto de Colonización Rural, was not to prove any more successful.[46] The revolutionary government in Guatemala, formed after the fall of Ubico in 1944, paid lip-service to land reform from the earliest days, and the Constitution of 1945 provided for the expropriation of land with compensation.[47] Given the political importance of land reform in Guatemala, it will be discussed in more detail in the next chapter. Here, one may mention that relatively little was done by way of land distribution until the Law of Agrarian Reform was passed in June 1952. Expropriation of large estates then proceeded rapidly (UFCO being a prime target) and land redistribution followed, but little effort was made to give the beneficiaries access to complementary inputs; as a result, the two years in which the programme was in force were marked by administrative chaos and the output of DUA actually fell (see Table A.6).

The case for or against land reform in Central America was therefore clearly not proven: the Salvadorean experience too mild, the Guatemalan one too short-lived. In the absence of land reform, however, the expansion of DUA required either increments in yields or access to new lands. Both strategies involved changes in traditional attitudes towards the peasantry and competition with EXA for scarce resources. Where the state continued to be dominated by export interests, such a competition was never likely to favour DUA. On the contrary, the expansion of EXA to include cotton increased the pressure on scarce resources (land, credit, foreign exchange etc.) while disrupting labour markets in an effort to ensure that the export crops never suffered from a shortage of workers.

### Private sector development outside agriculture

Although the first steps were taken towards agricultural diversification in the decade after 1944, investment in agriculture was not on a scale sufficient to absorb the massive surpluses generated by high world prices in the export sector. This left the agricultural sector in possession of a net financial surplus (i.e. over and above its own investment finance requirements) which could in principle be invested directly in non-agricultural activities or lent to financial institutions and therefore invested indirectly in the same pursuits. The alternative, of course, was the dissipation of the surplus in non-productive investment, increased consumption or capital exports.

Textbooks on development economics often refer to a link between the increased value of agricultural exports and the diversification of an economy through above proportional expansion of non-agricultural activities. Economic history has given us concrete examples of such links,[48] but the causal mechanisms prove to be much more complex than the textbooks allow for and economic history also provides examples where the links fail to materialise.[49] The Central American experience before the world war had provided mixed results: prosperity in EXA in the 1920s had brought the first steps towards diversification, but the foreign-owned branches of agriculture operated as enclaves which robbed the rest of the economy from deriving much benefit from an improvement in their fortunes.

Undoubtedly, there were various obstacles in the way of reinvestment of the agricultural surplus in Central America after the world war. The most commonly cited factors were the small size of the market in each country and the inadequacy of social infrastructure facilities. One can also mention the almost complete absence at the start of the period of financial institutions geared towards lending to non-agricultural activities.

Private investment in industry (particularly manufacturing) was subject to special problems in addition to those mentioned above. First, its ability to transform raw materials into a range of industrial produce suitable for domestic consumption was hampered at the start of the period by the low level of agricultural diversification, so that many basic raw materials could only be obtained through imports; secondly, the legal framework within which industry had to operate was in some cases frankly hostile to modern manufacturing methods and had been designed to safeguard craft and artisan production.[50] Thirdly, although each government relied on import duties for the bulk of its revenues, in no case had the tariff system been adopted for protectionist purposes and the resulting tariff structure did not always favour those industries which were suitable for introduction to Central America. Fourthly, the commercial supply of energy (heavily dependent on imported fuels) was in general insufficient, and industrial firms were often obliged to generate their own electricity.

The size of the market also presented special problems for industrial development in Central America. With world prices given, the profitability of EXA depended to a large extent on the control of labour costs; this ruled out a wage structure which might threaten the availability of labour to EXA at a low real wage and led to a highly unequal distribution of income.[51] As a result, the effective market was even smaller than implied by population figures, and Central American industrialisation at the end of the Second World War was below the level which might be expected in countries with comparable living standards.

Despite all these obstacles, industrial net output increased in each republic in the decade up to 1954 (see Table A.8) and in some cases industry even acted as a leading sector. The most successful republic was El Salvador, where the industrial share of GDP rose from 11.7% in 1944 to 14.4% in 1954. In Guatemala, on the other hand, this ratio declined after 1948 as the revolution entered its most radical phase. Industrial expansion was helped in several republics by the adoption of a legal framework which was more conducive to its growth. El Salvador lifted its restrictions on industrial investment after 1948[52] and passed a Ley de Fomento de Industrias de Transformación in 1952 giving tariff and tax exemptions for certain activities,[53] while Guatemala passed a similar law in 1947.[54] Costa Rica, on the other hand, continued to operate with its unhelpful Law of New Industries, adopted in 1940,[55] although in 1954 a new tariff structure was adopted which was overtly protectionist.[56]

State support for industry was shown in other ways. First, the deficiency of sources of medium- and long-term finance for industry was partially corrected through the creation of suitable government institutions. In Guatemala, for example, the Instituto de Fomento de Producción was founded in 1948 (the year in which the Economic Commission for Latin America – ECLA – was also formed) and similar institutions were created elsewhere for channelling long-term finance to industry. The state also promoted the supply of short-term lending to industry through its intervention in commercial banking either through the formation or reform of Central Banks (Costa Rica, Honduras, Guatemala) or through nationalisation of the commercial banking system (Costa Rica).

The second form of state support involved widening of the market. By the early 1950s ECLA ideas on economic development were already making their presence felt and governments nominally committed to a 'developmentalist' approach had taken power in Costa Rica, El Salvador, Guatemala and even Honduras. None of these governments, however, with the possible exception of Guatemala, were willing to put at risk their export sectors through a big increase in rural wages so that the widening of the market had to be achieved in other ways. For this reason, the first steps were taken in the early 1950s towards regional economic integration through a series of bilateral trade treaties.[57] The increase in trade flows resulting from these treaties was in general experienced later in the decade, although by 1954 exports to Central America were already equal to nearly 9% of total exports in Honduras and 4.2% in El Salvador.

Although industrial expansion was rapid after 1944, the sector remained very small in absolute terms. Each republic carried out its first industrial census in this period and the information is summarised in Table 6.4. The outstanding feature is the low level of employment and the dominance of small-scale firms; only a minority of industrial workers belonged to unions and in any case conditions of work, pay, etc. were usually covered by the Labour Codes which each government (except Honduras) had introduced in the 1940s.[58]

While the industrial sector remained dominated by the 'traditional' sector (food, drink and tobacco), some 'non-traditional' industries began to

Table 6.4. *Central America: profile of the industrial sector, 1950–3*

|  | Costa Rica | El Salvador | Guatemala[1] | Honduras | Nicaragua[2] |
|---|---|---|---|---|---|
| Year | 1951 | 1951 | 1953 | 1950 | 1953 |
| No. of establishments | 3,381 | 8,266 | 1,070 | 3,750 | 1,575 |
| Persons employed | 19,434 | 51,738 | 20,478 | 19,556 | 21,124 |
| Average size | 5.7 | 6.3 | 19.1 | 5.2 | 13 |
| Value added per worker ($) | 1,293 | 1,004 | 1,276 | 961 | 1,258 |
| Wages per worker ($) | 311 | 187 | 625 | 392 | 511 |

Source: Derived from United Nations, 1957, pp. 37–40
[1] 3 or more workers
[2] Establishments with monthly sales of at least 1,000 córdobas

increase in importance; these included textiles, rubber products and cement, while lead mining grew in importance in Guatemala. These 'non-traditional' industries, however, continued to rely on domestic raw materials and for all countries dependence on imported inputs was quite modest. Indeed, in several cases industrial developments in this period appear to have been in response to the availability in sufficient quantities of domestically produced raw materials such as cotton and rubber.[59]

The expansion of the industrial sector, with the exception of mining, was achieved without any significant direct foreign investment (DFI). Outside agriculture and mining, DFI remained concentrated in public utilities and transport (railways and civil aviation), but there was little increase in foreign investment in these sectors after 1944. On the contrary, the state (see pp. 121–5 below) began to increase public investment significantly in these activities, reducing the relative importance of DFI as elsewhere in Latin America.

Outside the agricultural and industrial sectors, good opportunities for domestic private investment were found in construction, commerce and transport. The former was helped by the fact that commercial banks were willing to lend to finance the purchase of real estate;[60] commerce, on the other hand, was stimulated by the relaxation of the foreign exchange constraint, which enabled each republic to import a vast range of goods which had previously been virtually unobtainable.[61] In addition, high world prices for commodities encouraged the formation of new export firms, such as Exportadora Comercial Internacional (CISA) in Nicaragua.

Private investment in financial services proved much more controversial. In Costa Rica, the revolutionary junta led by José Figueres nationalised the commercial banks in 1948, while in Guatemala under Arbenz private financial institutions were tolerated rather than encouraged. In El Salvador

Table 6.5. *Private investment, 1944–54*

| | Costa Rica | El Salvador | Guatemala | Honduras |
|---|---|---|---|---|
| *(A) Private Investment (PI)*<br>as % of GDP | | | | |
| 1. 1944 | NA | 3.7[1] | 3.8 | 4.8 |
| 2. 1950 | 14.0 | 5.2 | 8.0 | 9.7 |
| 3. 1954 | 12.4 | 7.5 | 7.0 | 12.5[2] |
| *(B) Ratio of Increase in PI*<br>to increase in exports (%) | | | | |
| 1. 1944–50 | NA | 25.8 | 72.1 | 32.0 |
| 2. 1950–4 | 26.1 | 49.9 | 9.6 | 140[3] |

Sources: Private investment in Costa Rica is given in Saenz, 1969, while GDP and exports were taken from IMF, *International Financial Statistics*. The source for El Salvador was Mooney, 1968, for Guatemala the source was Banco Central de Guatemala, 1955, and for Honduras it was Banco Central de Honduras, 1956. There are no figures for private investment in Nicaragua in this period
NA = Not available
[1] 1945
[2] 1953
[3] 1950–3

and Nicaragua, there was a major extension of private investment in financial institutions. In both cases, the stimulus appears to have been provided by the huge surpluses accruing to agro-exporters as a result of high world prices for cotton and coffee. In El Salvador, the Banco de Comercio was formed in 1950 and the Banco Agrícola Comercial in 1954. In Nicaragua, the Banco de América (BANAMER) was formed in 1952 and the Banco Nicaragüense (BANIC) in 1953. Both banks provided an important route for capital accumulation for that part of the Nicaraguan bourgeoisie not tied to the Somoza family, and their formation was in response to the 1950 truce between Somoza and his Liberal and Conservative opponents (see Chapter 7). By the 1970s, both groups had become formidable conglomerates with investments in virtually all sectors of the economy.[62]

The opportunities for private investment in the decade after the world war were considerable and helped to absorb the net financial surplus in agriculture. As a result, the ratio of private investment to GDP (see Table 6.5) rose rapidly from its very low level in 1944 to a more respectable figure by 1950. By 1954, however, this ratio had risen over its 1950 level only in El Salvador and Honduras despite the unprecedented increase in export earnings. The performance of private investment can be gauged by comparing the increase in exports in a given period ($\Delta E$) with the corresponding increase in private investment ($\Delta PI$). The ratio ($\Delta PI/\Delta E$) is shown in Table 6.5 for two periods and the results are very illuminating. In the first period (1944–50) only Guatemala reinvested a high proportion of incremental export earnings, while in the second period (1950–4) only Honduras (with large investments in banana plantations) recorded a dynamic performance.

Several factors explained the relative weakness of private investment. First, political uncertainty hampered private investment in some periods (e.g. Guatemala, 1950–4, and El Salvador, 1944–50). Secondly, the rise of the 'developmentalist' state produced a massive rise in public sector investment, in some cases 'crowding out' the private sector (e.g. Costa Rica, 1950–4). Thirdly, the financial institutions needed to translate agriculture's net financial surplus into capital formation outside the agricultural sector were still weak and poorly developed. The most important explanation, however, is provided by the lack of 'animal spirits' among the small capitalist class. In the years after 1954 this deficiency began to change, but in the immediate post-war period a rise in export prices was very often seen as an opportunity for increased consumption rather than investment or savings. Business pressure groups outside the coffee, cotton and cattle sectors were still of minor importance and the political situation in several republics imparted a bias in favour of short-term investments. Growth and development were still defined in very narrow terms by the dominant export interests, who identified 'progress' with export expansion, so that the exceptional conditions for private investment in the period 1944–54 were only partially exploited and the investment rate remained low.

### Policy and performance in the public sector

Economic recovery in the 1930s owed much to state intervention, particularly on behalf of coffee growers. The resources of the state, however, remained pitifully weak and its ability to influence the allocation of resources along other than traditional lines was very modest. The post-war environment offered enormous potential opportunities for capitalist modernisation, but initially the weakness of the state was a barrier to their exploitation.

The first problem faced by the state was the low level of government revenue together with an inelastic and inequitable tax structure. Nearly all revenue came from indirect taxes (import, export and excise duties) and many of these taxes were of a regressive nature, falling particularly heavily on the consumption of the poor.[63] Within indirect taxes there was a very heavy reliance on import duties and the yield from these had been adversely affected by the problems of the external sector from 1929 until the end of the Second World War. Despite an extremely high pre-tax inequality in the distribution of income, the rich paid virtually no direct taxes and post-tax inequality was probably at least as great.

The boom in external trade, particularly imports, changed the fortunes of the public sector dramatically after 1944. Despite the fact that many tariffs were specific and that the tariff code in use in some cases went back to the nineteenth century,[64] the revenue collected from customs duties rose rapidly. The stimulus to internal trade also pushed up the yield from excise duties and initially at least the impact of rising revenue from existing taxes was sufficient to postpone or avoid the need for fiscal reform.

This state of affairs could not last long, however, for several reasons. First, there arose in each Central American republic in the years after 1944 a government committed to capitalist modernisation, which in turn required increased state expenditure, particularly on social infrastructure. Governments of this type reached power in 1948 in El Salvador, Honduras and Costa Rica, while in Guatemala the Arévalo government paid lip-service to capitalist modernisation from the time it came to power in 1945, but did little to foster it until 1947. In Nicaragua, Somoza was preoccupied with political survival in the late 1940s, but by the early 1950s his government was also committed to capitalist modernisation. Secondly, even before capitalist modernisation, the growth of public expenditure tended to outstrip the increase in revenue leading to budget deficits. In the period 1944–8, budget deficits were more common than surpluses; such deficits tended to be funded through the bank system and brought with them inflationary consequences.

In each republic, therefore, an effort was eventually made to supplement existing sources of revenue through new or increased taxes, and a prime candidate was direct income tax. By 1944, only El Salvador and Costa Rica had a direct tax on personal income (although Guatemala had a tax on business profits), but in any case the yields were negligible. By 1954, however, all countries had a direct income tax, although Guatemala continued to resist a tax on personal income until 1963.[65]

With the marginal tax rate as high as 44% in El Salvador (1951), 30% in Nicaragua (1952) and Costa Rica (1954) and 15% in Honduras (1949),[66] the yield from income tax held great promise; the main problem, however, was whether it would apply to the export sector (particularly the banana companies). Both Costa Rica and Honduras did succeed in bringing the fruit companies within the tax net through contract revision, although in Guatemala this was not achieved until after the fall of Arbenz.[67] This proved to be the key to the success of the tax; by 1950, direct taxes reached 23% of all revenue in Costa Rica, while in Honduras it reached 17% with foreign companies contributing 91% of all income taxes.[68] In El Salvador the influence of the coffee and cotton growers was sufficient to exempt them from the 1951 income tax law. In its place, the growers were subject to export taxes on a sliding scale; exceptionally high world commodity prices pushed the yield from export taxes to 28% of all government revenue by 1954,[69] while the income tax (paid by only 0.4% of the population) yielded a mere 6.6% of revenue.[70]

Outside El Salvador, only Costa Rica made a serious attempt to exploit the opportunities for increased government revenue represented by high world commodity prices.[71] By 1954, coffee exporters in Costa Rica were subject to three taxes, although the banana export tax (as elsewhere in the region) remained unchanged. Nicaragua, by contrast, left the structure of its export taxes untouched, with the gold export duty unchanged since 1898, the silver duty since 1904 and the coffee duty since 1939. The coffee export tax was raised in Guatemala in 1950 from 1.65 cents to 6 cents per lb, but this was still only a small fraction of the value of coffee exports in the early 1950s.[72]

The new taxes, combined with higher yields from the old ones, did not eliminate the fundamentally regressive nature of the fiscal system, but they did contribute to a huge rise in government revenue. By the end of the 1940s, the republics were in a strong position to undertake development expenditures in support of capitalist modernisation; by the early 1950s, furthermore, the state's resources could be supplemented with foreign borrowing through the international agencies which were being formed for this purpose. The main beneficiaries in the early 1950s from new foreign borrowing were El Salvador and Nicaragua; in the former case, the increased liabilities referred to an IBRD (World Bank) loan for construction of the Guayabo dam and the Rio Lempa hydroelectric plant. Much smaller amounts were received by Honduras, part of which was a loan to the Honduran National Railway.

Expenditure on capitalist modernisation took many forms. The most important was the steep rise in the importance of public investment in social infrastructure projects, particularly roads, dams and airports. By the early 1950s, public investment was responsible for roughly one-third of total investment in Guatemala and El Salvador and one-fifth in Honduras and Costa Rica.[73] In absolute terms, there was a huge increase everywhere. The state's contribution to capitalist modernisation also took the form of an improvement in financial institutions. This took place in two ways: first, central banking institutions were brought firmly within the public sector, wherever this had not already happened. Thus, in Guatemala the state-run Banco de Guatemala acquired all central banking functions in 1946 and in Costa Rica the Banco Central was founded in 1950 taking over the duties of the Banco Nacional. Honduras, in belated response to the 1943 Bernstein mission and prodded by an IMF mission in 1949,[74] set up a Central Bank for the first time in 1950. The second feature of state intervention in financial institutions was the creation of development banks. These banks were designed to fill the gap left by commercial banks, which in general lent only short-term to the four 'c's' (coffee, cotton, cattle and commerce). The development banks, on the other hand, were encouraged to lend long-term to non-traditional activities.

Alone among the republics, Costa Rica did not set up a development bank. Instead, the revolutionary junta, led by Figueres, nationalised the commercial banks in 1949: the reasons given, however, were very similar to those used elsewhere in support of development banks,[75] so that Costa Rica achieved the same end by different means. The choice of means, it is widely believed, was conditioned by political factors, since the private banks had supported the Calderonistas right up to the civil war, while the bank employees had played a leading part in the general strike against the Picado régime in 1947.[76]

The huge increase in government revenue permitted the republics to make considerable progress in resolving the problem of the external public debt. War-time inflation had, in any case, reduced the burden, since the debt service was fixed in nominal terms. As early as July 1944, the post-Ubico government in Guatemala took steps to resolve the external debt problem by offering to purchase at full face value all outstanding sterling bonds. The offer was closed in 1945 and the government passed a decree in September of that year 'erasing' the outstanding balance. In 1951, the last of the outstanding dollar bonds (Los Altos Railways) were also redeemed. El Salvador reached agreement with its foreign bondholders in 1946 and Costa Rica in 1952, both on terms which could be considered satisfactory for the governments concerned.[77] By 1954, public debt service had fallen to a negligible share of total government revenue in all republics.

The rise in government revenue was so large that, despite the increase in development and other expenditures, budget deficits had in general given way to surpluses by the early 1950s. Only Guatemala consistently recorded deficits in this period and was obliged to borrow heavily from the banking system; by 1954, the year in which the Arbenz government was overthrown, bank lending (commercial and central) to the government was nearly 25% of total bank assets. By contrast, this ratio was close to 10% in Costa Rica and Honduras and a miserly 3% in El Salvador and Nicaragua. The switch from budget deficits to surpluses contributed to a slowdown in the growth of money of internal origin. The money supply, however, rose much more rapidly in the period 1949–54 than in the period 1944–9, except in Guatemala. The reason was the rapid growth in money of external origin as a result of the accumulation of foreign exchange reserves through trade surpluses.

This acceleration of money supply creation did not result in an acceleration of inflation. On the contrary, inflation rates throughout Central America started to decline towards the end of the 1940s and by 1952 the cost of living index itself was actually falling in three republics (Costa Rica, El Salvador, Guatemala), while the increase was insignificant in Honduras and Nicaragua. From this period until the early 1970s, inflation ceased to be of any consequence in Central America. The apparent insensitivity of the inflation rate to changes in the money supply confirmed the special character of the inflation process in the region. Money creation in excess of what the public wanted to hold simply spilled over into imports, leaving the inflation rate to be determined by dollar prices adjusted for tariffs and exchange rates. By 1948, dollar prices (as measured by the unit value of imports) had stopped rising; the reform of the tariff was not carried out until 1954 or later and considerable progress towards exchange rate stability had been made by the early 1950s. Only Nicaragua devalued its official exchange rate in the decade after 1944,[78] although both Nicaragua and Costa Rica operated a free market in foreign exchange throughout the period. By 1954, however, the official and free rates differed by less than 15% in these two republics,[79] while elsewhere on the isthmus exchange rate stability at pre-war parities continued to be the rule.

## Capitalist modernisation

At the end of the Second World War, the economies of Central America faced the task of capitalist modernisation. The initial efforts made in this direction in the 1920s had been crushed during the Great Depression with its traumatic consequences; although there was economic recovery in the 1930s, capital accumulation contributed in only a minor way towards it, and the export sector – the traditional engine of growth and one of the few sources from which a capitalist surplus could be extracted – was either stagnant or in decline.

The task of capitalist modernisation involved the creation of an environment in which capital accumulation could take place outside the traditional export sector. This meant breaking down the obstacles created by a weak financial system, a highly unequal pattern of income distribution and a poorly integrated internal market. Capitalist modernisation did not imply a bias against the traditional export sector. On the contrary, profitable conditions in the traditional export sector could ease the task of capitalist modernisation by providing the resources with which the domestic economic environment could be changed; the traditional export sector, however, was incapable on its own of generating all the capital accumulation and growth required in the region; ensuring that the sector played its part in the transformation of the rest of the economy was therefore one of the tasks of capitalist modernisation itself.

The external environment in the decade after 1944 could not have been more favourable for the task at hand, and in some respects performance was satisfactory. In the first quinquennium, real GDP per person rose impressively (see Table A.3) everywhere except Nicaragua, where the traditional export sector continued to stagnate. In the second quinquennium (1949–54), however, only Nicaragua registered a significant increase in real GDP per head and two republics (Guatemala and Honduras) recorded declines, although the fall in Honduras was the result of exceptional factors in 1954.[80]

By 1954, the Central American economies had undergone a series of transformations which left them in a much stronger position to withstand the adverse external conditions which prevailed after 1954 than had happened after 1929. This transformation, however, involved only a partial completion of the task of capitalist modernisation, with the result that the allocation of resources after 1954 was seriously distorted, a distortion that was to bring with it major long-term implications. The most striking transformation was provided by the increase in the state's share of net benefits from banana production. Throughout this period, the profits from banana production accrued in the main to the two US multinationals, UFCO and Standard Fruit; without an increase in the state's share, the bulk of these profits were lost to the region, for reinvestment in the industry even in 'normal' years tended to average only 20% of gross profits. By 1949, however, the fruit companies had been brought within the direct tax net in Honduras and Costa Rica, while by the end of 1954 their total revenue contribution was roughly equivalent to half their gross profits in all the major banana producing countries.

The huge increase in tax contributions had major political repercussions. The Honduran government, for example, which had frequently been reduced to dependence on a fruit company loan for its very survival, never again made an official request for funds, while the bitter struggle between UFCO and the government in Guatemala from 1948 onwards was avoided under later administrations, as a result of the increased tax contributions achieved through the 1954 contract with President Castillo Armas.

The state was much less successful in bringing other foreign-owned companies within the tax net. The framework used for foreign investors was typically that of the 'contrato ley'; this involved a contract between the host government and foreign companies which was unaffected by national laws. Thus, a change in the taxation of foreign companies involved a revision of the contract, and outside of banana production most foreign-owned companies remained largely untaxed. The most important cases were the railway companies, the public utilities and the gold and silver mining companies in Honduras and Nicaragua.

Although the banana sector began to contribute (through increased taxation) towards economic transformation, the contribution of the coffee sector was less significant. Only El Salvador and Costa Rica introduced progressive export taxes and in El Salvador government receipts from coffee (and cotton) were depressed by exempting growers from income tax. In Guatemala, despite the alleged left-wing bias of the Arbenz government, coffee growers paid no income tax[81] and only a modest export tax.

The state therefore lost to a certain extent the excellent opportunity provided by high world prices for increasing the fiscal contribution of the export sector; on the contrary, exporters continued to be feather-bedded in many ways. This was understandable in the case of new exports (e.g., cotton, and coffee from Honduras), but had no justification in the case of traditional exports. Nicaragua, for example, offered coffee growers in 1950 a particularly favourable exchange rate at a time when export prices were exceptionally high. When export prices started to fall after 1954, it would prove much more difficult for the state to increase the export sector's fiscal contribution.

Government revenues rose despite this lost opportunity, and, aided by foreign grants and loans, the transformation of the region's social infrastructure proceeded rapidly. The greatest gains were in road construction and energy supply, where the state took over from the private sector the task of adding to existing capacity. Control of most of the rail network, communications and some ports (e.g., Puerto Barrios in Guatemala) remained in foreign hands, however, and this provided a continuing source of irritation in future years. The improvement of the social infrastructure was complemented by changes in the financial system, which contributed to greater monetary stability and strengthened the economy's ability to transfer financial resources from 'surplus' to 'deficit' sectors.[82]

Capitalist modernisation, however, faced its greatest challenge in the field of national economic integration. The bulk of the labour force in 1944 was employed in agriculture at very low wages; as such, its purchasing power remained abysmally low, and this represented a serious obstacle to capital accumulation in the non-export economy in the medium term. In addition, the low levels of literacy outside Costa Rica (particularly in the rural economy) provided a serious obstacle to self-improvement and the raising of productivity by the peasantry. Yet some progress was made. The Guatemalan revolution, in one of its first acts, abolished Ubico's vagrancy laws and instituted a free market in rural labour for the first time in Guatemala's history. Increased health expenditure by the state made it possible for large numbers to settle on the fertile Pacific lowlands, which had previously been rendered a death-trap by the prevalence of various tropical diseases. Labour codes provided for minimum wages (even in rural areas in some cases), a social security system with widely differing coverage was developed and trade unions began to spring up again after the repression of the 1930s.

The impact of these changes, however, was felt mainly in the small urban economy. The social security system hardly affected any rural workers and this was also true, outside Costa Rica, of the minimum wage provisions of the Labour Codes. Trade unions for rural labour were rigorously suppressed in Honduras, Nicaragua and El Salvador, while even in revolutionary Guatemala rural labour never carried anything like the influence of the Communist-dominated urban labour movement (see Chapter 7). Revolutionary

Table 6.6.  Changes in private foreign exchange holdings abroad
(thousand $), 1947–54

| Year | Costa Rica | El Salvador | Guatemala | Honduras | Nicaragua |
|------|-----------|-------------|-----------|----------|-----------|
| 1947 | −2,600 | +3,400 | +1,700 | — | +580 |
| 1948 | +600 | +1,120 | +500 | — | +1,206 |
| 1949 | −700 | +2,600 | +14,500 | — | −142 |
| 1950 | +300 | +120 | +1,300 | — | +1,128 |
| 1951 | −2,600 | +1,960 | −100 | — | −3,079 |
| 1952 | +2,000 | +3,360 | +13,800 | +600 | +2,178 |
| 1953 | −900 | +5,080 | +200 | +600 | +896 |
| 1954 | +2,500 | +7,160 | +200 | +1,100 | −3,174 |
| Total | −1,400 | +24,800 | +32,100 | +3,300 | −707 |

Source: IMF, *Balance of Payments Yearbook*
Note: Figures refer to changes in Central American private holdings in US banks.
A plus (+) means an increase in these holdings (i.e. capital outflow from Central
America)

Guatemala did try land reform, but the programme launched by Arbenz
in 1952 was ill-conceived and disastrously executed. Indeed, the chaotic
way in which it was administered almost certainly set back the cause of
land reform by many years elsewhere in Central America and was, of course,
a major reason for its suppression under Castillo Armas in Guatemala itself.

The problem of access to land was already serious in post-war Central
America and was exacerbated by demographic pressures. The opening up
of the Pacific littoral, made possible through disease control on the one
hand and highway construction on the other, provided an outstanding
opportunity for resolving the land problem through an increase in the small-
farm sector, an increase that could easily have been justified on short-term
economic grounds by the need to reduce dependence on imported foodstuffs.
That opportunity was lost, even in Costa Rica, and this inevitably meant
that efforts to resolve the land question in later years would involve the
redistribution of lands already owned or occupied privately.

The failure to make much progress in national economic integration meant
that the export sector continued to represent some of the best opportunities
for profitable investments. This involved more than just coffee and bananas,
however, and several new products were added to the export list; the financial system played a major part in this export diversification, as did public
investments in social infrastructure. It would be difficult to exaggerate the
importance of export diversification. In addition to all the conventional
arguments against monoculture, dependence on coffee in particular posed
a major obstacle to economic integration. Coffee is not only a crop with
a highly seasonal demand for labour, but it is also a very labour-intensive
product. With given world prices, higher money wages for hired labour

squeeze profits, given the difficulty of adopting labour-saving techniques;[83] thus, a high wage policy was unlikely to be feasible while coffee was a major source of export earnings.

Despite the limitations of the market, there were some profitable investment opportunities in the non-export sector as well. The exploitation of these opportunities was reflected in the growth of capital goods imports (much of which was destined to the non-export sector). By 1954, the machinery share of imports was at least 19% in all republics and an impressive 34% in Nicaragua. Furthermore, nearly all these opportunities were exploited by Central Americans rather than by foreign investors. The absorptive capacity of the region, however, was limited and investment was very sensitive to the political climate. In Table 6.6, the changes in the private sector holdings of foreign assets (short- and long-term) have been recorded. El Salvador and Guatemala both experienced very serious capital outflow[84] over the period, although for rather different reasons. In the former case, profits from coffee were almost certainly in excess of absorptive capacity given the weakness of the internal market, while in Guatemala the political climate seems to have been the major determinant.[85]

# 7

## The struggle for democracy, the Cold War and the Labour movement in the first post-war decade

By the early 1950s many of the preconditions had been met in Central America for capitalist modernisation; the latter in turn generated rapid economic growth, which lasted with only minor interruptions until the end of the 1970s. This high long-run rate of growth was unprecedented in Central America, but like all such secular booms it left unresolved the question of how the benefits would be distributed. Capitalist modernisation could be achieved without necessarily changing the structure of the labour market. Labour's traditionally weak position was therefore not likely to be altered through the operation of market forces; on the contrary, an improvement in the conditions facing labour after the Second World War required either a resurgence in the organised workers' movement (virtually destroyed after the 1920s) and/or a shift towards a more democratic style of government so that labour's interests could carry some electoral weight.

By 1944, the omens for both had become reasonably favourable. *Caudillismo* was on the defensive, under attack in the four northern republics from a broad-based alliance which included the fragmentary workers' movement; only in Costa Rica was the picture complicated (as we shall see) by the alliance of Calderonismo with the Communist wing of the labour movement. Throughout the isthmus, 'democracy' was a catchword with which all but the most recalcitrant identified. Within a year, however, the situation did not look so favourable. *Caudillismo* had crumbled in Guatemala, but elsewhere it had survived through a combination of electoral fraud (Costa Rica), repression (Honduras), external intervention (El Salvador) and opposition factionalism (Nicaragua). By 1948, the pressures of the Cold War had forced the US administration to revise its view of the Somoza dictatorship, and the first misgivings at the influence of the communists in Guatemala were being voiced. By the early 1950s, these concerns had reached hysterical levels and the days of the Guatemalan revolution were numbered.

Despite these setbacks, the organised labour movement scored some successes. The most remarkable was in Honduras, where the banana strike in 1954 – directed initially against UFCO's subsidiary – produced legal

130

recognition for trade unions and the introduction of a labour code later in the decade; in Costa Rica, the communist wing of the labour movement was severely repressed after the 1948 war, but the presence of Father Benjamin Nuñez (founder of the Catholic Rerum Novarum labour confederation) on the winning side helped to give part of the organised labour movement a stake in the new republic. In both republics, the struggle for democracy also bore fruit, although the winner of the 1954 elections in Honduras (Ramon Villeda Morales) had to wait until 1957 before he could finally take office.

It is no accident that in the middle of the 1980s, organised labour is strongest in Costa Rica and Honduras; the foundations for this phenomenon were laid in the first post-war decade, giving the workers' movement an interest in the political future and a share in the benefits of economic growth. Elsewhere, progress on both these fronts was modest to the point of being negligible and the favourable conditions for peaceful social and political change existing at the end of the war were never repeated. In the struggle for democracy only Costa Rica came out of the first post-war decade with *caudillismo* firmly defeated and no threat of military intervention, but Honduras began to tread a reformist path which suggested that naked repression would cease to be the immediate reaction to any threat to the established social order.

## The rebirth of the labour movement

The rise of an organised labour movement among urban workers in the 1920s (see Chapter 2, pp. 43–6) had been brought to an abrupt halt by the crisis at the end of the decade. Organised labour was ruthlessly crushed in the three northern republics; the workers' movement enjoyed sufficient space in Nicaragua in the run-up to the Somoza dictatorship to create the Partido Trabajador Nicaragüense (PTN), but by 1939 the movement had gone into self-liquidation;[1] even in Costa Rica the 1930s was a difficult time for organised labour and trade unionism was not fully accepted, despite the 1934 banana strike, until the alliance between Calderón and Mora in 1942 (see Chapter 5, pp. 102–3).

Towards the end of the Second World War, however, organised labour's revival began and proceeded rapidly, aided by the more favourable internal and external environment. Within a week of Ubico's downfall in Guatemala in 1944, the railway workers had formed a union and by August of the same year a central labour federation – Confederación de Trabajadores de Guatemala (CTG) – had been created.[2] In the brief interlude in El Salvador in 1944 between the fall of Martínez and the coup led by Osmin Aguirre, the Unión Nacional de Trabajadores (UNT) was formed claiming a membership of some 50,000 workers.[3] In Nicaragua, a national labour congress in 1944 founded the Confederación de Trabajadores de Nicaragua (CTN), although it faced competition from the Somocista Comité Organizador de la Confederación de Trabajadores Nicaragüense (COCTN).[4] The Confederación de Trabajadores de Costa Rica (CTCR), founded in 1943, and the Catholic Confederación de Trabajadores Rerum Novarum (CCTRN), founded in 1944, competed for the loyalties of organised labour in Costa Rica, so that only in Honduras was the workers' movement unable to make any impact against the dictatorship.

The organisation of trade unions and labour federations was not the only manifestation of the rebirth of the workers' movement. Several political parties were founded to represent workers directly or with strong labour representation. The Partido Socialista Nicaragüense (PSN), which had operated clandestinely since the late 1930s, was legalised in 1944 and enjoyed close ties with the CTN; the Partido Democrático Revolucionario Hondureño (PDRH) was born in 1947, supported by urban labour groups, with the legal recognition of trade unionism as one of its primary aims.[5] The pro-government Partido Acción Revolucionaria (PAR) and Revolución Nacional (RN) in post-Ubico Guatemala both claimed to represent labour, while a secret group Vanguardia Democrática (VD) was formed within the PAR in 1947 as a prelude to a future Communist Party.[6] Arturo Romero's short-lived Partido Unión Democrática (PUD) was supported by all labour groups in El Salvador before its demise after the October 1944 coup and the Communist Party in Costa Rica enjoyed a new lease of life after 1943, following its change of name to Vanguardia Popular (VP) and its rapprochement with the Catholic Church (see Chapter 5, p. 102).

Inevitably, communists were heavily involved in both the new labour organisations and the new political parties. El Salvador's political élite, deeply scarred by the communist uprising of 1932, viewed their presence with horror and the Communist Party remained illegal; Tiburcio Carías in Honduras took a similar attitude, but Somoza – influenced by a visit to Nicaragua in 1943 of the Mexican Marxist Vicente Lombardo Toledano – recognised the potential advantages to be obtained from a political alliance with a communist-dominated labour movement. The CTN was permitted to join the communist-controlled Confederación de Trabajadores de América Latina (CTAL) led by Toledano, and shared membership of CTAL with CTG and CTCR – both of which were also heavily influenced by communists.

The communist influence, however, in the first post-war years should not be exaggerated. The war-time alliance between the USA and the USSR had created a situation which benefited communists in Central America, but in their alliance with or support for governing parties in Guatemala, Costa Rica and Nicaragua[7] there was no doubting who the junior partners were. Arévalo in Guatemala during his presidency (1945–50) kept communist influence firmly under control through a policy of shrewd overseas appointments[8] and occasional repression.[9] Somoza ruthlessly destroyed his erstwhile PSN partners, and the CTN after 1947 when they had served their purpose,[10] while the Republican Party in Costa Rica (the political expression of Calderonismo) was restrained from breaking with the VP only because of narrow electoral considerations.[11] Furthermore, communist-dominated labour confederations in Costa Rica, Nicaragua and even Guatemala[12] faced rival non-communist labour organisations from an early stage.

The resurgence of the workers' movement in the early post-war years was reflected in a changed attitude on the part of the state towards organised labour. The most spectacular example was the introduction of Labour Codes in Costa Rica (1943), Guatemala (1947) and Nicaragua (1945), although the latter (the most advanced in Latin America) was an example of Somocismo at its most cynical; but the social security programmes in Costa Rica and Guatemala, adopted from 1943 and 1947 onwards respectively, also reflected the change in attitude. Less spectacular, but equally reflective of the new attitude, were the sections on 'social guarantees' added to the Constitution. Even the unsympathetic régime of President Castañeda Castro (1945–8) in El Salvador felt obliged to add sections on labour as a social duty and a social right in the 1945 amendments to the 1886 Constitution.[13]

Labour's gains in this first post-war period were heavily concentrated in urban areas. Trade unions outside the banana zones were rare among rural workers and in Honduras the banana workers' organisation was not legally recognised until 1954; even in revolutionary Guatemala, the provisions of the Labour Code were not extended to all agricultural workers until 1948 and the Confederación Nacional Campesina de Guatemala (CNCG) was not founded until 1950.[14] Rural labour was therefore not in a strong position to take advantage of the sharp rise in earnings from agricultural exports after 1944.

### The years of reaction, 1947–50

While the first period (1944–7) of the post-war decade brought important gains for labour, the second (1947–50) was significantly less favourable for the workers' movement with the exception of Guatemala. The prospects for labour after the 1948 civil war in Costa Rica at first looked bleak, while the replacement of Carías by President Gálvez (1949–54) in Honduras did not initially suggest a softening of government attitudes towards the workers' movement. Labour questions were not a high priority for the military junta which ruled El Salvador from 1948 to 1950, and Somoza's destruction of the communist wing of the Nicaraguan labour movement after 1947 has already been mentioned.

Somoza's flirtation with both the PSN and the CTN in 1944–5 was motivated by his need for popular backing in support of his plans for re-election.

Opposed by the conservative bourgeoisie and not entirely trusted by his own liberals, the arriviste Somoza needed a social base with which to confront his traditional political rivals; at the same time, a successful alliance with labour might suggest to Nicaragua's capitalist class that Somoza was the man to keep labour in check and protect their economic interests. Whatever his motives, Somoza's plans ran foul of the US State Department which could not support his unconstitutional scheme for re-election. Somoza therefore put forward as the candidate of his National Liberal Party the name of Leonardo Argüello; the latter had stood against Somoza in 1936, mustering 100-odd votes, but Argüello's advanced years suggested to the General that he could be manipulated in the presidency. The opposition, including the PSN and CTN, united behind the candidacy of Dr Enoc Aguado despite Somoza's blandishments, but blatant fraud ensured victory for Argüello in April 1947.[15]

Far from being a puppet, Argüello acted swiftly in a brave effort to destroy Somocismo; within five weeks, 'Tacho' Somoza had driven him from the presidential palace and a pliant Congress later in the year chose his uncle, Victor Román y Reyes, as president. These manoeuvres preserved Somocismo in Nicaragua, but earned Somoza the fury of the State Department, which felt it had been cheated.[16] 'Tacho' knew that without US support his days were numbered and proceeded to adopt a series of measures to curry US favour. A new Constituent Assembly was convoked, which offered military bases to the United States on Nicaraguan soil and introduced numerous anti-communist measures; the communist PSN and CTN were victims of these measures and were ruthlessly purged in early 1948.

The US administration, however, was unmoved by these measures and continued to withhold recognition. At this point (March 1948), the civil war in Costa Rica broke out and Somoza played his master stroke: he sent his National Guard across the frontier ostensibly in support of the Picado administration,[17] thus reducing the chances of success for the anti-communist forces led by José Figueres. Pressure from the US State Department, which had no desire to see communism survive in Costa Rica, forced Somoza to withdraw his troops, but in return we may assume that some promise of US recognition was obtained.[18] In any case, four days after the close of the ninth Pan-American Conference in April 1948, the US administration recognised the puppet régime in Nicaragua.[19]

Having destroyed the non-Somocista labour movement and having outmanoeuvred the State Department, the wily 'Tacho' turned his attention to his traditional political rivals led by the Conservative Emiliano Chamorro. A pact signed in 1950 guaranteed the Conservatives a minimum of one-third of the seats in Congress and formal guarantees of free commercial activity; this destroyed any prospect of an anti-Somoza alliance between organised labour and the traditional political groups[20] and paved the way for new presidential elections in May 1950, in which Somoza easily defeated the septuagenarian Chamorro. From his re-election until his assassination in 1956, Somoza had no time for organised labour or democracy. Towards the end of 1948, a new Peronista labour confederation was set up to replace the dissolved CNT, but by 1950 it had split; US labour federations helped to establish in 1953 the Confederación Nacionalista de Trabajadores, but this also split up after 1957. The Nicaraguan labour movement was easily manipulated after its resurgence in the 1940s by the dictator and his sons, so that one of the worst legacies left by Somoza in 1979 was a labour movement with no tradition of independence and little organising ability.

The organised labour movement also suffered a reverse in Costa Rica after the civil war, although the setback was neither so serious nor so permanent as in Nicaragua. The social programme of Calderonismo, the authoritarian and corrupt style of government practised by Presidents Calderón (1940–4) and Picado (1944–8) and the support of the communist party (VP) and labour federation (CTCR) for the régime polarised Costa Rican society in the 1940s, although the class distinctions among the antagonists were not always clearcut. Calderón, the nominee of former president León Cortés, virtually monopolised the presidental vote in 1940, but within two years the coffee oligarchy and the traditional bourgeoisie had turned against him; their standard-bearer was León Cortés himself and their opposition to Calderón was based not only on his social programme and his alliance with the communist VP, but also on his vigorous repression of Axis nationals, who were an important element in the Costa Rican bourgeoisie. Cortés, however, could only muster one-third of the votes in the presidential elections and the anti-Calderonista forces were obliged to rethink their strategy.[21]

Within a year of the 1944 elections, a new anti-Calderonista alliance had been formed. It included the social democrats of the Centro para El Estudio de Los Problemas Nacionales (the Centro) together with José Figueres, whose Acción Democrática faction was originally organised within Cortés' Democratic Party. The new alliance was cemented with the launching of the Partido Social Demócrata (PSD) in 1945. Unlike other social democratic parties in Central America at this time (e.g. PUD in El Salvador and PAR in Guatemala), the PSD was not a broad-based alliance of the middle- and working-classes with a leavening of intellectuals. Certainly, it enjoyed support from Nuñez's Rerum Novarum labour confederation, but the CTCR (the most important labour federation controlled by the communists) was firmly behind Calderón. Many of the intellectuals in the Centro were anti-capitalist (but non-communist), yet they shared a party and programme with Figueres whose political career had begun in Cortés' pro-oligarchic Democratic Party.[22]

The irony of the PSD alliance was compounded further when the PSD

joined forces with the Democratic Party before the 1948 elections in a coalition motivated above all by the desire to defeat Calderonismo.[23] Each faction
reacted to different features of the Calderonista programme while uniting
behind Otilio Ulate, a conservative traditionalist who had defeated Figueres
for the presidential nomination of the new coalition in February 1947.[24]
The electoral prospects for the new coalition, embracing all anti-Calderonista
factions, were looking good by the end of 1947. The general strike of July
1947 (branded a lock-out by Manuel Mora, because of the closure by most
banks and businesses of their offices) had extracted electoral concessions
from President Picado, which gave the opposition substantial control over
voting procedures and offered the prospect of an end to the electoral fraud
which had worked in favour of Calderonismo. These favourable electoral
prospects for the opposition appeared to have been fulfilled, when the National Electoral Tribunal announced that Ulate had won the presidential contest
against Calderón in February 1948 by a substantial margin of 10,000 votes;
this time, however, the Calderonistas denounced electoral fraud and a pliant
Congress annulled the elections. Within a few days, Figueres had launched
the civil war from his *finca* with arms he had been stockpiling for several
years.

The Figueristas emerged victorious from the civil war and Don Pepe (as
Figueres is known in Costa Rica) led a revolutionary junta from May 1948
to November 1949. The Junta is most famous for the nationalisation of
banks, the abolition of the army and the introduction of a (temporary)
ten per cent tax on wealth,[25] but the Junta also outlawed the CTCR and
all its member unions, banned the VP and used the infamous Tribunal de
Probidad to repress individual communists;[26] in addition, UFCO took advantage of the Junta's anti-communist decrees to sack various labour activists.[27]
In its first months the Junta gave no quarter to the Calderonistas and their
communist allies in the labour movement, but it also proved too radical
for the conservative Ulate; the latter's Partido Nacional (PUN) crushed the
PSD (supporting Figueres) in the Constituent assembly elections of December
1948, and Costa Rican politics acquired a less radical flavour in 1949.
Figueres reluctantly made way for Otilio Ulate as president in November
of that year and formed his own Partido Liberación Nacional (PLN) in
1951, which carried him to victory in the presidential elections of 1953.

The presidency of Otilio Ulate (1949–53) was marked by its conservative
character, although neither the social conquests of Calderonismo nor the
main revolutionary acts of the Junta were reversed. It was also a difficult
time for organised labour with the number of trade unions collapsing from
204 in 1948 to 74 in 1953. Even Nuñez's CCTRN faced problems and
1,500 trade unionists abandoned it in 1950 to form a Peronist Confederación
Nacional de Trabajadores.[28] The communists were able to found a new
central in 1953 (Confederación General de Trabajadores Costarricenses –

CGTC), but it did not acquire much importance outside the banana enclaves until the legalisation of Vanguardia Popular in the 1970s.

Although the organised labour movement was on the defensive, the prospects for a genuine democracy increased enormously in Costa Rica. The revolutionary Junta enfranchised women for the first time, an attempted coup (the 'cardonazo')[29] was foiled in 1949 and Figueres' decision to back down in favour of Ulate paved the way for a series of elections which have made Costa Rican democracy a model for Latin America. This democracy has created opportunities for labour's interests to be given an electoral voice; the PLN, in particular, which began life with an anti-labour reputation, has cultivated the urban labour vote[30] and a functioning democracy has gone a long way towards obtaining for the labour movement the advances which superior organisation has achieved in other countries.

While the labour movement in Costa Rica and Nicaragua had built up a favourable position after the Second World War which had come under attack by 1950, the Salvadorean labour movement was largely unaffected by the military coup launched in December 1948. The revolutionary junta, which paved the way for the presidency of Major Oscar Osorio (1950–6), shared Castañeda Castro's distaste for organised labour and hostility towards communism. The new régime – unlike its prececessor – was committed to capitalist modernisation, but the labour movement scarcely entered into its calculations.

Organised labour at first supported the revolutionary junta. A Comité de Reorganización Obrero Sindical (CROS) was formed immediately after the coup and offered its support to the junta in return for recognition of workers' rights. This campaign bore fruit in 1950, when a new constitution was agreed which recognised trade unions and paved the way for a cautious social security programme beginning in 1953. Within a few months of assuming the presidency, however, Osorio outlawed CROS. The government made it clear that the new constitution did not permit the formation of labour federations (only individual trade unions), and organised labour had to operate through a new organisation (Comité Pro-Defensa de Los Derechos Laborales). The latter was in turn declared illegal in 1952, when many labour leaders were exiled,[31] and not even the blandishments of the AFL-CIO in the United States were able to persuade the Osorio régime to tone down its hostility towards organised labour.

There is no doubt that this hostility on the part of the Salvadorean ruling class was conditioned by the communist-inspired uprising of 1932. The same atavistic response coloured their attitude towards free elections; Osorio established the Partido Revolucionario de Unificación Democrático (PRUD) in 1949[32] and set the pattern under which the alliance between the military and the oligarchy would dominate Salvadorean politics (with one brief interlude) until 1979. In this model, democracy was a sophisticated farce in which workers' interests received little or no voice.

As in El Salvador, the organised labour movement had made no progress in Honduras in the first years after the Second World War. When Carías stepped down in 1948 in favour of his former Minister of War, Manuel Gálvez, who secured the presidency in uncontested elections,[33] it was widely assumed that government policies would remain virtually unchanged. Gálvez was no friend of organised labour,[34] but he was no puppet of Carías either. Capitalist modernisation was his highest priority, but he was not opposed to a certain degree of political *apertura*; he allowed the Liberal Party, humiliated during the Carías dictatorship, to reorganise, and promised free elections for 1954, a promise which he kept (see pp. 143–4).

Gálvez's relationship with the PDRH was much more ambivalent. The party remained illegal, but the régime at times tolerated the circulation of its periodical *Vanguardia Revolucionaria*; this organ was finally suppressed in 1953 (it had in any case never been allowed to circulate in the banana zones), but within a few months the PDRH had dissolved; one wing broke away to form the Partido Comunista de Honduras (PCH), while the other joined the Liberal Party, inspired by the reform programme adopted by its leader Villeda Morales. The PDRH's efforts to organise the labour movement, at least in urban areas, gained some success, when a Comité Coordinador Obrero (CCO) was set up in 1950. The CCO was supported by *Voz Obrera*, a periodical established by the Sociedad de Artes Gráficas in 1949, and it embraced a number of skilled urban workers. The CCO later affiliated to the CTAL and the Moscow-dominated World Federation of Trade Unions, earning strong disapproval from the Gálvez régime, which closed down *Voz Obrera* in 1953. The difficulties faced by the CCO under Gálvez led to its dissolution and its reappearance early in 1954 under the guise of the Comité de Unidad Sindical (CUS). The CUS was from the start firmly under the control of the communists in the PDRH, but carried little influence within the labour movement. In the run-up to the banana strike of April 1954, therefore, independent observers could be forgiven for thinking that organised labour had yet to establish any real influence in Honduras.

The one republic where the organised labour movement appeared to be going from strength to strength was Guatemala. This was by no means all due to the successes of the communist-led CTG, which was affiliated to the CTAL. On the contrary, several important unions (including the railway workers) broke with the CTG as early as 1945 to form the non-communist Federación Sindical de Guatemala (FSG). The Arévalo government was sympathetic to labour, introducing a social security programme and a labour code in 1947. Arévalo recognised, however, that capitalist modernisation and workers' demands could produce conflicts, and the Labour Code did not at first extend recognition of trade unions to farms with less than 500 workers; since this was where the bulk of Guatemala's labour force was employed, the Labour Code set clear limits to the influence of organised labour.

In the years after 1948, the situation began to change dramatically. Arévalo, whose régime suffered no less than 23 attempted coups, became more sympathetic to labour's demands; the turning-point came in 1949 following the assassination of Francisco Javier Arana, a possible presidential candidate for 1950 and one of the three leaders of the October 1944 revolution along with Jacobo Arbenz and Jorge Toriello.[35] Arana, as chief of the armed forces, was popular with the military and his death was a prelude to the most serious revolt Arévalo had so far faced. For the first time, the government called for civilian volunteers to defend the régime, and the organised labour movement was the most energetic in responding to the call.

Arévalo was saved and the lessons of the whole episode were not lost on his administration. The peasant union (CNCG), which had been created following the revision of the Labour Code to allow trade unions for all workers, made great strides among rural labour and the Labour Courts (which had been set up to arbitrate in disputes arising from the Labour Code) took a consistently sympathetic line towards the claims of trade unions. The goal of labour unity, however, eluded the workers' movement until after the election of Arbenz as president in 1950. The main Arevalista parties supported the candidacy of Arbenz (although Arévalo himself never publicly endorsed him)[36] and he also enjoyed the support of the organised labour movement and the communists. The traditional oligarchy was in disarray with one of its leaders (Miguel Ydígoras Fuentes) in exile and another (Miguel García Granados) forced into hiding shortly before the election. Not surprisingly, Arbenz won an easy victory and his election marked the high point of the reformist movement in Guatemala.

The unification of the labour movement and its domination by communists came in stages. The first step was the formation in late 1949 of local united labour committees to work for the election of Arbenz: this was followed in January 1950 by a National Workers' Political Committee in which both communists and non-communists participated. All the labour leaders by now recognised the importance of labour unity, given the possibility of further military revolts and the risk of a backlash against organised labour. Early in 1951, the non-communist Federación Sindical de Guatemala (FSG) also joined the CTAL[37] and by January 1952 a new Confederación General de Trabajadores de Guatemala (CGTG) was formed which was joined by the CNCG in the summer; at that point, the goal of labour unity had been achieved with a few very minor exceptions. By 1954 the CGTG claimed 104,000 members, with control over approximately one-third of all urban workers, but much less influence among rural workers.

While the labour movement was uniting, the communists began to emerge into the open despite the constitutional ban on parties identified with foreign interests. In May 1950, José Manuel Fortuny formed a group called 'Octubre Comunistas' (named after the communist weekly *Octubre*) and in the following month Victor Manuel Gutierrez, head of the CTG, announced the formation of a Communist Party.[38] The two groups maintained separate identities until the end of 1951; by the end of 1952, the Communist Party's name had been changed to Partido Guatemalteco de Trabajadores (PGT) and it was registered legally for the congressional elections in December 1952. The PGT put up two candidates (unopposed by the other pro-government parties), but only Carlos Manuel Pellecer in the province of Escuintla won.

The direct appeal of the communists was therefore very limited, but their influence on the united labour movement was substantial. The Secretary-General of the CGTG was Gutierrez, and Pellecer was the Grievance Secretary; the Guatemalan communists were aided in their efforts by the small army of able communists exiled from neighbouring countries, including the Salvadoreans Abel Cuenca and Miguel Marmol, and by the success of their weekly journal *Octubre* (3,000 copies were being sold by the end of 1952). Above all, the influence of the PGT on the labour movement was helped by a sympathetic attitude from Arbenz (who saw labour as the key to his survival) and by non-communist labour leaders who saw labour unity (even under PGT leadership) as the strongest guarantee of the social conquests of the Guatemalan revolution.

## The crisis of 1954

The crisis of 1954 refers to the events in Guatemala and Honduras in the middle of the year, during which the Arbenz régime was overthrown in Guatemala and the banana strike achieved most of its aims in Honduras. Not for the first (or last) time in Central America, the outcome in one republic (Guatemala) had a profound impact on the outcome elsewhere (Honduras) and both events carried major long-term implications for democracy and the labour movement in the two republics.

The numerous unsuccessful revolts against Arévalo bore witness to the discontent of sections of the armed forces and the traditional ruling class to the course of the Guatemalan revolution. These failed attempts produced many exiles, including Colonel Castillo Armas, but their influence and importance in establishing a viable counter-revolutionary movement was negligible until the US administration became seriously concerned at developments in Guatemala. By the end of Arévalo's presidency US diplomatic channels were recording a certain unease over the influence of communists, but despite the Cold War no precipitate action was considered to be necessary; the Soviet Union had not reciprocated Guatemala's recognition of the USSR in 1945 and contact with local communists was maintained through the Soviet embassy in distant Mexico City.[39]

The relationship between Guatemala and the United States began to deteriorate rapidly with the assumption of the presidency by Jacobo Arbenz in 1951. The latter appeared much less concerned than his prececessor over communist influence not only in the labour movement, but also in the media, the judicial system and Congress. His government was very unsympathetic to US companies operating in Guatemala, notably UFCO, its subsidiary International Railways of Central America (IRCA), the Electric Company of Guatemala and the United States Insurance Company. Disputes between the Arbenz government and these US companies were frequent, and the US embassy was invariably dragged in on the side of the latter. The most serious dispute arose following the passage of the Agrarian Reform Law in 1952; agrarian reform had been promised by Arbenz in his election and the law provided, among other things, for confiscation of estates in excess of 664 acres (Article 32) which were not being cultivated by their owners or for the owner's accounts. Compensation was to be paid in three per cent bonds limited to the valuation of the estate for property tax purposes, and implementation of the law was put in the hands of a National Agrarian Department dominated by communists.[40]

Inevitably, much of UFCO's estates were interpreted as falling within Article 32 and UFCO, like virtually all other property owners in Guatemala, had consistently undervalued its plantations for tax purposes. The compensation offered for the expropriation of nearly 400,000 acres of UFCO land was therefore only a fraction of the market value, and it was clear that UFCO would receive little sympathy from the Guatemalan courts. UFCO therefore joined the counter-revolutionary cause in Guatemala and lobbied the US administration intensively for its support. These efforts were successful, but it is now clear (which it was not before) that the US administration had already decided to overthrow the Arbenz régime. The dispute with UFCO may have reinforced this decision, but it did not precipitate it.[41]

US concern at the prospect of a communist Guatemala, loyal to the Soviet Union, looks in retrospect faintly absurd. The communists had no influence in the armed forces and the USSR, at the time busily defending the notion of a Soviet sphere of influence in Eastern Europe, was in no position to help a communist Guatemala if it should come under attack. US sensibilities, however, were heightened by the communist victory in China, by the Korean war and by the hysteria accompanying the Cold War. US attitudes were also affected by the relationship between Guatemala and her sister Central American republics. The Guatemalan revolution shared at least one characteristic with the Ubico régime: a willingness to interfere in the internal affairs of Central American republics and a desire to establish Central American unity under Guatemalan hegemony. The unsuccessful invasion of El Salvador by the hapless Arturo Romero in December 1944 had been launched from Guatemala with the connivance of the authorities, while President Arévalo – as a committed-supporter of the Caribbean Legion (see below pp. 147–8)

– had decided views on *caudillismo* in Nicaragua, Honduras and Costa Rica. Arévalo's intervention with military supplies on behalf of the Figueristas is widely believed to have been crucial in the Costa Rican civil war and there was no love lost after Arbenz came to power between the Guatemalan revolution and the authoritarian governments in El Salvador, Honduras and Nicaragua.

Both Somoza and Miguel Magaña, secretary general of the Salvadorean PRUD, approached the US administration with offers of support for the Guatemalan counter-revolution. In the end, however, the Army of National Liberation was assembled in Honduras with the support of both Gálvez and Somoza: overall guidance was provided by the CIA, flushed with its recent success in overthrowing Prime Minister Mossadegh in Iran.[42] The counter-revolution triumphed when Arbenz lost his nerve by refusing to arm the workers, and the CIA engineered the emergence of Castillo Armas as the leader of a new Guatemalan government in July 1954.

US support for the Castillo Armas government was conditional on the new president weeding out communists from positions of influence and returning property confiscated from US companies. Castillo Armas duly obliged by creating a National Committee of Defence against Communism and passing the Preventive Penal Law against Communism; he repealed Arbenz' Agrarian Reform Law and reached agreement with UFCO on a new contract similar to that signed by the company in Costa Rica and Honduras (see Chapter 6, p. 109), although UFCO voluntarily agreed to relinquish 100,000 acres of land on the Pacific side of Guatemala as a gesture of goodwill towards its Liberator.

Counter-revolutions, however, have a momentum of their own, and Castillo Armas went much further than the relationship with his US mentors strictly demanded. In addition to disbanding the CGTG and the CNCG (as expected), the new government cancelled the registrations of 533 unions and amended the Labour Code in a manner which was exceedingly unfavourable to the workers' movement.[43] Rural labour organisation was virtually destroyed and trade union membership in the first year of the new government fell from over 100,000 to 27,000.[44] Serafino Romualdi of the American Federation of Labor (AFL) was invited to Guatemala to set up a National Committee for Trade Union Reorganisation, which produced in 1955 the Federación Autónoma Sindical de Guatemala (FASGUA),[45] but organised labour never recovered in Guatemala and workers' demands received short shrift from the Labour Courts.

While organised labour was suffering from these setbacks, the prospects for democracy were also shattered. Castillo Armas abolished all political parties, other than his own Movimiento de Liberación Nacional (MLN); illiterates were disenfranchised, only to have their vote restored just in time to participate in the October 1954 plebiscite to confirm Castillo Armas in the presidency. When a measure of democracy was restored to Guatemala after the assassination of Castillo Armas in August 1957, the victor was Ydígoras Fuentes – former aide to General Ubico and implacable enemy of the Guatemalan revolution.[46]

While the counter-revolutionary army was being assembled in Honduras in April 1954, a strike broke out among workers of the Tela Railroad Co., a subsidiary of UFCO. The strike, in favour of trade union recognition as well as better pay and conditions, quickly spread to other workers on the Honduran north coast, including employees of the Standard Fruit Co., and became a general labour stoppage. The Gálvez administration was initially hostile to the workers' demands. It was assumed that the strike was fomented by communists, in league with the Guatemalan government, in order to topple the Gálvez régime and cripple the counter-revolutionary movement. Gálvez therefore arrested the members of the Central Strike Committee and assumed that this would be sufficent to end the dispute.[47]

It was not, however, and the deposed communists on the organising committee were replaced by non-communists, who continued the strike with the same demands. By this time, the Guatemalan counter-revolution had been launched and the days of the Arbenz régime were clearly numbered; the attitude of the Gálvez administration towards the strikers, who were supported by the archbishop of Tegucigalpa and the US Congress of Industrial Organisations (CIO), began to soften and on 9 July a solution was reached. The workers of the Tela Railroad Co. did not achieve all their demands, but in two respects the final agreement marked a watershed in Honduran politics. First, the Central Strike Committee had clearly responded to the government's call for patriotism on the part of the strikers;[48] this may have irritated some workers, but the gesture was not lost on the Honduran traditional political parties nor the armed forces' leadership, both of whom slowly came to recognise organised labour as a potential ally. Secondly, the agreement implicitly awarded recognition by UFCO to the Tela Railroad Co.'s trade union. This meant that the major obstacle to the introduction of a Labour Code and social legislation in favour of labour had disappeared; the Partido Liberal (LP), led by Ramón Villeda Morales, was quick to recognise this and in August 1954, shortly before the presidential elections, promised to introduce a Labour Code.

Villeda Morales won the elections against the aged Carías of the Partido Nacional (PN) and Abraham Williams of the Partido Reformista. He did not gain an outright majority, however, and none of the three candidates could command a two-thirds support in Congress. Gálvez's vice-president, Julio Lozano, therefore assumed the presidency, promising fresh elections in two years and governing with the help of an all-party cabinet in which members of the PL held the key posts. The Lozano administration fulfilled some of the PL's pledges on labour legislation and passed a Fundamental

Charter of Labour Guarantees in 1955, regulating labour contracts, mediation, conciliation and arbitration, collective bargaining and social security.[49] Lozano, however, harboured longer-term political ambitions; he exiled many of his political opponents and organised his own political party, which won the Constituent Assembly elections of October 1956 boycotted by both the PL and PN. Within two weeks Lozano had been ousted by the armed forces and new Constituent Assembly elections were called for September 1957. These were won handsomely by the PL, and Villeda Morales finally assumed the presidency after indirect elections.

Villeda Morales was a social reformer, whose government advanced workers' interests while at the same time resisting communist influence in the organised labour movement. A Social Security Law was passed in 1958 and a Labour Code was introduced guaranteeing unions the right to organise and bargain collectively.[50] The 1957 Constitution allocated an entire chapter to labour and social welfare and the relationship between the organised labour movement and the AFL-CIO in the USA was closer than in any other Central American republic. In terms of Cold War history, it was Honduras rather than Guatemala which was the US success story after 1954.

### External actors in the first post-war decade

The resurgence of the labour movement and the struggle for democracy in Central America after 1944 were not entirely national phenomena. As we have already seen external actors were frequently involved and their intervention could at times be decisive. As the hegemonic power among those countries with an interest in Central America, the United States was the most heavily involved; there were other external actors, however, including Peronist Argentina, Lombardo Toledano's CLAT based in Mexico and the Caribbean dictatorships that were the target of the Caribbean Legion. In addition, all Central American republics continued the time-honoured tradition of interference in each other's internal affairs.

In principle, the first post-war US administration was well disposed towards the revival of organised labour and the struggle for democracy in Central America. The US did not at first feel any need to counter the monopoly enjoyed by CLAT in organising an inter-American labour federation despite the fact that Lombardo Toledano had taken CLAT into the Moscow-dominated World Federation of Trade Unions (WFTU) in 1945. The broad alliances challenging *caudillismo* throughout the region also caused little concern to the US administration despite the active presence of communists in their midst.

The US government, however, frequently faced a conflict of interests even before the start of the Cold War. At the beginning of 1945, for example, it was deeply concerned about the problem of Argentina; the new Argentine government, soon to be led by Juan Perón, was accused by the Roosevelt administration of being under Nazi–Fascist influence and the US wanted a united inter-American movement at the Mexico City Pan-American Conference in February–March 1945 in order to exert pressure on Argentina. For that reason, the US administration moved to a hasty recognition of the Aguirre régime in El Salvador shortly before the assumption of the presidency by Castañeda Castro. Since Aguirre had taken power in a military coup and since the US administration was again committed to a policy of non-recognition of governments instituted by force,[51] it was clear that in this case (even before the Cold War) the conflict between the ideals of democracy and the requirements of inter-American security had been resolved in favour of the latter.

Once the Cold War had started, the chances of a similar resolution of future conflicts of interests were much greater. The policy of non-recognition adopted towards the puppet régime installed by Somoza in Nicaragua in 1947 was certainly genuine, but Somoza's tactical skill in forcing the Truman administration to choose in effect between the survival of communist influence in Costa Rica and acceptance of Somocismo in Nicaragua (see above, p. 134) meant another defeat for the anti-dictatorial struggle. As if to rub salt into the wounds, the US at the Ninth International Conference of American States in 1948 (shortly before the formation of the Organisation of the American States – OAS) pushed through a strongly anti-communist resolution ironically entitled 'The Preservation and Defense of Democracy in America'.[52] These conflicts of interest effectively prevented the US administration from throwing its weight behind the struggle for democracy. Although the US supported the Figueristas in the Costa Rican civil war, it was for their anti-communism rather than their commitment to democracy (which was in any case suspect at first), and the United States played a relatively minor role in the emergence of Costa Rica as a model democracy.

Successive US administrations, on the other hand, took much more seriously the need to develop a non-communist workers' movement in Central America. While communists lacked direct electoral appeal, their influence in the growing labour movement was substantial: this was particularly true in Guatemala and Costa Rica, although their influence in Nicaragua had been destroyed by 1948 when Somoza turned on his erstwhile allies. These concerns culminated in January 1948, when the American Federation of Labor (AFL) joined forces with a number of non-communist labour groups in Latin America to form the Confederación Interamericana de Trabajadores; this was dissolved in January 1951 and a new hemispheric body, Organización Regional Interamericana de Trabajadores (ORIT) was established in its place. ORIT affiliated to the International Confederation of

Free Trade Unions (CFTU) and both organisations were concerned to counter the influence in Latin America of the CTAL and the WFTU.[53]

ORIT's strongest ally in Central America at first was Nuñez's Rerum Novarum labour confederation in Costa Rica, which gained a dominant position in the Costa Rican labour movement after the civil war. ORIT, however, made no impact in Arbenz's Guatemala, where virtually the whole organised labour movement was faithful to CTAL, while its efforts to organise labour in El Salvador and Nicaragua met with little success. ORIT showed little interest in the Honduran labour movement before 1954, but the position was changed dramatically by the banana strike. Both the AFL and ORIT intervened vigorously after the strike to influence the course of the workers' movement and by the end of the decade virtually all organised labour in Honduras was linked to the ORIT. The greatest success for ORIT was winning the allegiance of the two unions formed by employees of UFCO and Standard Fruit.

By the end of 1954, CTAL's influence in Central America had been destroyed, but the vacuum left had not been entirely filled by ORIT. On the contrary, organised labour in Guatemala and Nicaragua suffered a serious reverse with the destruction of CTAL's influence, and ORIT's efforts were no match for the anti-labour policies of the dictatorships in these countries. Even in Costa Rica, organised labour did not fully recover for over two decades following the defeat it suffered in the civil war.

While the United States played a relatively minor role in the destruction of communist influence in Costa Rica and almost no role at all in its destruction in Nicaragua, Honduras and El Salvador, it was clear to policy-makers in the Eisenhower administration that communist influence in Guatemala was going to be crushed only through active US intervention. This presented the US administration with its greatest challenge in Central America since the Sandino episode. The course of the Guatemalan counter-revolution showed clearly the strengths and limitations of US policy in Central America. It demonstrated that, where its perceived security interests were threatened, a US administration could mount a formidable campaign to achieve its goals without committing a single US soldier. On the other hand, its ability to control the social and political policies of its proxies was very limited and Castillo Armas, a handpicked US product if ever there was one, was able to persecute his opponents, crush the labour movement and flaunt democratic ideals despite rumblings of discontent from the State Department.

If democracy in Guatemala after 1954 had been given the same priority as communism before 1954, no doubt even Castillo Armas would have been forced to bow to US pressure. Unfortunately, it is ridiculous to imagine that a superpower will ever demonstrate enormous concern over the internal affairs of a small country unless its wider interests are threatened, and the costs (economic and political) for the United States of mounting a major campaign in Central America were (and are) considerable.[54] The struggle for democracy was therefore treated as largely an internal affair, although political élites supported by successive US administrations in Nicaragua, El Salvador and Guatemala clearly were not going to make any concessions until they came under intense pressure; that pressure would have to come from internal opposition groups, and the greatest failure of post-war US policy in Central America was its inability to identify the right groups at the right time.

While the US administration was becoming concerned over the issue of communism in Guatemala, the democratic left in Central America was focussing on the issue of dictatorship in the Caribbean basin. The prime targets were Somoza in Nicaragua and Trujillo in the Dominican Republic, but Carías in Honduras was also on the list and José Figueres, who met various Nicaraguan exiles in Mexico during his self-imposed sojourn, insisted that the democratic left add Calderonismo in Costa Rica to its list of undesirable régimes. The exiles from all these countries (and a few others) were at first unsuccessful in coordinating their efforts and mounting a serious campaign against any of the dictatorships. A breakthrough came, however, in December 1947 with the signing of a Caribbean Pact in Guatemala by many of the leading members of the democratic left in the region. The pact had the blessing of President Arévalo, who was named as the final arbiter in any case of disputed interpretation.[55]

The Pact formalised the idea of a Caribbean Legion, which would liberate the region from oppressive dictatorships. Due to the powers of persuasion of Figueres, the Legion's first target was chosen as Calderonismo in Costa Rica and the legionaries' chance came in March 1948. By common consent, the military support given by Arévalo and the Caribbean Legion to the Figueristas was crucial for the latter's victory in the Costa Rican Civil war.[56] The defeat of Calderonismo was intended to be a prelude to the overthrow of Somoza in Nicaragua, and the Nicaraguan exiles pressed hard for Figueres' support. Don Pepe owed them a great debt and allowed the legionaries to prepare an invasion from Costa Rica. It proved to be a disastrous decision; Somoza, aware of the group's activities, supported in December 1948 an invasion of Costa Rica from Nicaragua led by Calderón Guardia. Costa Rica, now without a standing army, invoked the Inter-American Treaty of Reciprocal Assistance[57] and called for an emergency meeting of the OAS; together with US pressure on Somoza, these measures were sufficient to defeat the invasion, but the days of the Caribbean Legion in Costa Rica were now numbered and Figueres quickly distanced himself from his former comrades.[58]

The Caribbean Legion's contribution to the establishment of democracy in Central America was therefore confined to Costa Rica (Villeda Morales was a sympathiser of the democratic left, but his assumption of the presidency in Honduras owed nothing to the Legion). The Costa Rican venture, however, was no mean feat and the Legion must therefore be given credit for its part in the struggle for democracy.

The Caribbean Legion paid little attention to organised labour, unlike Perón's Argentina. Perón, flushed by his successful alliance with the labour movement in his own country, created in 1952 a regional labour federation, Agrupación de Trabajadores Latino-Americanos Sindicalizados (ATLAS), which was designed to promote his *Justicialismo* programme; ATLAS was supposed to offer Latin American organised labour a middle ground between the US-dominated ORIT and the Soviet-dominated CTAL and it scored some successes in Costa Rica and Nicaragua (see above, p. 135). ATLAS could not survive the overthrow of Perón in 1955, however, and its influence quickly disappeared in Central America and elsewhere.

The final external actor relevant to the themes of this chapter is the Soviet Union. Before and after the fall of Arbenz, the US administration accused the Soviet Union and Eastern European allies of meddling in Guatemala;[59] while the Guatemalan communist leadership made frequent trips to the Soviet bloc, there is very little evidence that their wholehearted admiration for the Soviet Union was reciprocated. The only tangible proof ever produced was the shipload of arms sent from Czechoslovakia to Arbenz just before his downfall,[60] but by then the US decision to overthrow the régime had already been taken. Moscow may have approved of the difficulties Guatemalan communists were causing the United States, but Moscow was not in a strong position to help the Guatemalan revolution when it came under attack.

### Conclusions

The importance of the first decade after the Second World War in Central America cannot be exaggerated. By the end of 1954, the broad outline of social and political developments for the next twenty-five years (until the Sandinista revolution in Nicaragua) had been determined. El Salvador, Guatemala and Nicaragua were condemned to 'reactionary despotism'[61] with only brief interruptions, but both Costa Rica and Honduras offered their citizens the prospect of a more democratic world with organised labour sharing in the benefits of economic growth; democracy has prospered more in Costa Rica and the workers' movement has perhaps done better in Honduras, but the socio-political situation in both republics stood in marked contrast to the rest of Central America for most of the post-1954 period.

What enabled these two republics to stand apart from the rest of Central America? Part of the answer lies deep in the historical traditions of each republic, but part is due to the course of events after 1944. The struggle for democracy in Costa Rica, for example, was aided by the presence of communists on the side of Calderonismo; this ensured US support for the Figueristas, so that for once US security interests and the cause of democracy coincided rather than clashed. US support was not critical, however, for the democratic cause, and the decision of Figueres to hand power over to Otilio Ulate should not be underestimated. Individuals, too, have their part to play in history.

In Honduras, the struggle for democracy was helped rather than hindered by army intervention in 1956. This was the opposite of what frequently happened in Central America and deserves some comment. The army leadership felt little antagonism towards the reformist Villeda Morales[62] and their removal of him in 1963 was not directed at his social programme, but was designed to prevent a presidential victory for the Liberal firebrand Modesto Rodas Alvarado. The Honduran example also showed that an independent labour movement was not impossible in 'Uncle Sam's Backyard'. Although the banana workers and other labour groups joined ORIT after the banana strike, they were not mere appendages of the AFL-CIO and enjoyed a reputation for independence. At times the Honduran labour movement has faced repression and even assassination of some of its leaders, but it demonstrated in 1954, and again in 1969 (see Chapter 9, p. 199), its willingness to reflect the national interest. For that reason, it has only occasionally been viewed as a security threat by the armed forces and the civilian élite.

Once communists were purged from the leadership of the Central Strike Committee in May 1954, they never regained positions of importance in the Honduran labour movement. In other republics broad-based alliances involving the workers' movement tended to give positions of influence to communists, who were usually the best organised, the most active and had the clearest vision. Inevitably, this led to charges of communist domination and a predictable reaction from the ruling class. In Costa Rica, the experience of the civil war and the ban on VP gave the non-communist labour movement the chance to consolidate its position and achieve greater authority, so that the revival of communist-led unions in the 1970s did not lead to a communist-dominated labour movement.

The solution to this problem outside Costa Rica should not have been suppression of the communists, but the encouragement of a non-communist labour movement and worker-based political parties. Both ORIT and the AFLO-CIO made some efforts in this direction, but (as we shall see) they were easily outmanoeuvred by the local élite; the US administration, fired by its success against Arbenz, never gave these long-term developments a high priority and, when the Central American cauldron came to the boil in 1979, the State Department lacked powerful allies with which to counter the Marxist challenge on the one hand and reactionary despotism on the other.

# 8

# The foundations of modern export-led growth, 1954–60

The expansion of the Central American economies in the first decade after the Second World War represented the final phase of the traditional export-led growth model based on coffee and bananas. Unfavourable developments in the markets for these exports after the end of the Korean war pushed Central America towards a new growth model; this was to be based on the diversification of agricultural exports and the promotion of intra-regional trade in manufactured products, and the bases for the model were firmly laid by the early 1960s. The model had elements common to all five republics, but its distributive impact was affected in each country by a combination of resource endowments and policy initiatives.

Export diversification had begun in the 1940s, but was overshadowed by high prices for coffee. By the end of the 1950s, however, the export list had been expanded to include cotton, sugar and beef and these, together with coffee and bananas, would constitute Central America's future 'traditional' exports. The development of these products, facilitated by strong state support, created new, powerful pressure groups who combined with coffee growers to safeguard the interests of agricultural export-led growth.

Export agriculture (EXA) competed with domestic use agriculture (DUA) for scarce resources. This competition created tensions in which the state usually sided with EXA, although there were exceptions and the relationship between the two branches of agriculture was by no means mechanistic. At its most extreme, however, the intensification of EXA implied a decline in the output of DUA per head, negative import substitution in foodstuffs and a redistribution of agricultural income in favour of greater inequality; these effects could be ameliorated through state intervention or favourable resource endowments (Costa Rica, Guatemala, Honduras) or ignored (El Salvador, Nicaragua), but in all cases the change in the relationship between the two sub-sectors of agriculture posed a social and political challenge.

By the end of the 1950s, the favourable external environment at the start of the decade had given way to foreign exchange scarcity, balance of payments crises and IMF intervention (albeit on a modest scale). The re-emergence of a foreign exchange constraint contributed to the movement in favour

150

of regional economic integration, which had been initiated by the Economic Commission for Latin America (ECLA) and was later supported by the US administration. The resistance of the traditional pressure groups to integration was broken down through generous concessions which safeguarded their interests and the final programme for integration was a compromise among the internal actors on the one hand and between the external actors on the other.

By the beginning of the 1960s, Costa Rica stood out as the republic best able to combine the export-led growth model with agricultural diversification, fiscal and social reform and political democracy. El Salvador, by contrast, identified reform with a threat to the powerful export interests, so that concentration on export-led growth produced no significant social or political progress. Other republics occupied an intermediate position, with Guatemala and Nicaragua closer to the Salvadorean model and Honduras nearer to the Costa Rican example.

## The crisis in traditional exports

The first decade after the Second World War provided Central America with exceptionally favourable circumstances for primary export products and created the conditions for a certain amount of export diversification. The major beneficiaries, however, were the traditional exports of coffee and bananas, whose combined share of total foreign exchange earnings in 1954 was around 80% or more everywhere except Nicaragua (where it was nearly 50%). Thus, by the mid-1950s the economies of Central America were as vulnerable as ever to a deterioration in the fortunes of their traditional exports.

This became embarrassingly clear in the case of bananas, although superficially the industry's prospects looked good. In the decade after the mid-1950s world physical consumption grew at nearly five per cent per annum, while the fiscal reforms in Central America enacted between 1949 and 1954 (see Chapter 6) ensured that a greater share of the benefits would accrue to the region from any expansion. Almost all Central American banana exports in the early 1950s, however, went to the United States, where *per caput* consumption peaked in the late 1950s and declined slowly thereafter;[1] the expansion of consumption therefore took place mainly in 'non-traditional' markets (above all Western Europe) where Central American exports faced certain disadvantages.

These disadvantages referred not only to discriminatory tariffs which the region's exports faced in relation to exports from European colonies,[2] but also to competition from new sources of supply. In the absence of a cheap and effective cure for Panama disease, which continued to spread in Central America, the banana companies' preferred method to increase or maintain production was to locate plantations on virgin lands (which also enjoy higher yields). This accounted for the spectacular rise of Ecuador as a producer after the war; the latter's banana exports had exceeded those of Honduras by 1952 and between 1954 and 1960 nearly 70% of the increase in Latin America's exports came from Ecuador.

Some three-quarters of Ecuador's exports were marketed by the United Fruit Co. (UFCO), which explained the latter's reluctance to increase its operations in Central America. In addition, UFCO found itself in July 1954 dragged into a protracted anti-monopoly suit, which ended in 1958 with a ruling that the Company establish an independent rival by 1966.[3] These were not propitious circumstances for the expansion of the industry in Central America and the situation was not helped by the decline of banana prices even in nominal terms after 1956/7.[4]

Faced with two multinational fruit companies whose production and export decisions were taken on a global basis, there was little that Central American governments could do to reverse the industry's decline. Successive Costa Rican governments were the most active in trying to reverse the trend; when UFCO failed to fulfil its obligations in the 1953 contract to redevelop the Atlantic plantations, the Figueres government introduced a new law[5] extending UFCO's privileges to other companies (including national producers with more than 50 hectares); within a month, the Standard Fruit Co. (until then unrepresented in Costa Rica) had responded with an offer to develop the Atlantic coast region subject to the provision of various additional privileges. Reluctantly, the government and the Legislative Assembly agreed to the changes. Standard Fruit promised to develop its plantations with the Giant Cavendish, a banana type virtually unknown to the trade, but (unlike the dominant Gros Michel) resistant to Panama disease; the Giant Cavendish also produced higher yields, but required more delicate treatment and packaging in boxes before shipment. Standard Fruit's gamble paid off and within a few years UFCO was forced to respond by introducing its own disease-resistant variety (the Valery).

The entry of Standard Fruit to Costa Rica and the introduction to Central America of new banana types had a big impact eventually, but the changes came too late to reverse the industry's decline in the 1950s. UFCO closed its Quepos division in Costa Rica in 1956 and exports from Guatemala declined steadily, as the two giant fruit companies reduced their purchases from independent producers on the Pacific coast.[6] Honduran exports made a modest recovery after the disastrous years of 1954/5 affected by strikes and poor weather, but the levels of the early 1950s were not regained and Nicaragua remained an exporter of negligible importance.[7]

Despite the failure of exports to expand, the industry did not stand still. On the contrary, there was a spectacular rise in labour productivity in the 1950s and a modest increase in yield;[8] the latter was due in particular to the introduction of the Giant Cavendish, but the former implied a huge drop in the labour force because banana output was stagnant or falling. Between 1953 and 1959, employment in Honduras by the two companies fell from 35,000 to 16,000, with similar declines taking place in UFCO's divisions in Guatemala and Costa Rica.[9] The factors behind the sharp decline in labour requirements were various; part of it was due simply to the closing of divisions and the abandonment of high cost plantations in the face of increased competition from Ecuador; another reason, however, was the substitution of capital for labour (e.g. the use of helicopters to fight sigatoka disease rather than the use of manual application), which was in turn a response by the companies to the success of the labour force in securing higher wage rates.[10]

The misfortunes of the banana industry in the second half of the 1950s raised the question of whether earnings from Central America's other traditional export, coffee, could be increased in compensation. The coffee industry remained by and large in national hands, and policy-makers had acquired some experience since 1929 in influencing the level of production and exports. The surge in the coffee price during the Korean war stimulated an increase in production on a global scale, but it was some time before a problem of excess supply was apparent; this was due, of course, to the long lag between the planting of new trees and additions to output.[11] By 1957, however, world coffee stocks had increased rapidly and coffee prices began a precipitate decline; by the end of the 1950s, prices for virtually all grades were down to the level of the late 1940s.

In an effort to reverse the fall in prices, the four 'senior' Central American exporting countries met with Brazil, Colombia and Mexico in late 1957 to sign the Convenio de Mexico; a system of export quotas was adopted for the six-month duration of the pact, but prices fell again on its expiration. This time, other Latin American exporters (including Honduras) joined in the efforts to stabilise prices, and their efforts produced a Latin American Coffee Agreement in 1958 and an International Coffee Agreement (ICA) based on a system of export quotas in September 1959.[12] The ICA did stabilise prices temporarily, but it could not recoup the terms of trade losses incurred in the 1950s.

For most of the 1950s, Central American countries were not bound by export quotas. Thus, the fall in price could in principle be offset by increases in the volume exported. As in the case of bananas, US *per caput* consumption had peaked before the mid-1950s,[13] but in the period 1950–2 *per caput* consumption in Western Europe was only one-fifth of the US level and it grew rapidly thereafter. Furthermore, tariff discrimination in favour of coffee exports from European colonies was less serious than in the case of bananas and Central America had a long experience of supplying the European market.

Table 8.1  *Coffee yields (kg per hectare), 1950, 1958/9 and 1961/2*

|  | c.1950 | c.1958/9 | c.1961/2 |
|---|---|---|---|
| Costa Rica | 373 | 748 | 801 |
| El Salvador | 640 | 787 | 1,002 |
| Guatemala | 364 | 539 | 648 |
| Honduras | 205 | 217 | 274 |
| Nicaragua | 275 | 254 | 351[1] |
| Brazil | 397 | 392 | 406 |

Source: Grunwald and Musgrove, 1970, table 10–9, p. 327
[1] Derived from FAO, *Production Yearbook* 1968, p. 263. Figure refers to 1963

The market prospects for coffee, therefore, were reasonable for producing countries able to increase their exportable surplus. Here, however, Central American republics faced a dilemma; an increase in output based on an improvement in yields required an increase in cash outlays at a time when prices were falling, while an increase based on area planted involved a long lag and in some republics (notably El Salvador) ran up against the difficulty of finding new land.

At the start of the 1950s, yields in Central America were lower than the Latin American average, except in El Salvador where they were the highest in the world. During the decade, yields increased dramatically in Costa Rica and Guatemala and even managed a substantial rise in El Salvador (see Table 8.1). The Costa Rican example, the most spectacular of all, makes clear how this was possible. The nationalised banking system and the Ministry of Agriculture combined to promote and finance new varieties,[14] the installation of drainage systems, the application of fertilisers and the use of fungicides, herbicides, insecticides, etc. The Banco Anglo Costarricense launched its Programa para la Rehabilitación de Cafetales in 1954 with a plan to replant one-seventh of the area devoted to coffee in five years. Such was the success of this and other programmes that the Oficina de Café (representing the growers) pressed the government to make the use of fertilisers compulsory.[15]

In the production of coffee, the main element of cost is not interest charges or material inputs, but wages and salaries.[16] The effort to raise production through an increase in yields required the most rigid control of labour costs by the large estates and was one reason for the extreme hostility demonstrated towards rural trade unions by coffee growers in Guatemala, El Salvador and Nicaragua.[17] There can be no doubt that the increase in yields in Costa Rica, El Salvador and Guatemala would not have been possible without the combined support of the banking system and the relevant ministries; this was also true, however, of an increase in production achieved through an enlargement of area planted. This method of increase was important in Honduras, Nicaragua and Costa Rica,[18] but not in El Salvador and

Table 8.2  *Central America: value of traditional exports, 1954–60*
*($ million)*
*(C = Coffee B = Bananas T = C + B)*

| | Costa Rica | | | El Salvador | | | Guatemala | | | Honduras | | | Nicaragua | | |
|---|---|---|---|---|---|---|---|---|---|---|---|---|---|---|---|
| | C | B | T | C | B | T | C | B | T | C | B | T | C | B | T |
| 1954 | 35.1 | 35.8 | 70.9 | 92.0 | – | 92.0 | 74.2 | 20.3 | 94.5 | 14.0 | 29.3 | 42.3 | 25.1 | 0.1 | 25.2 |
| 1955 | 37.4 | 33.2 | 70.6 | 91.5 | – | 91.5 | 75.5 | 17.0 | 92.5 | 8.5 | 27.4 | 35.9 | 27.9 | 0.1 | 28.0 |
| 1956 | 33.8 | 25.7 | 59.5 | 87.4 | – | 87.4 | 89.2 | 15.0 | 104.2 | 13.3 | 43.9 | 57.2 | 23.2 | – | 23.2 |
| 1957 | 39.1 | 32.3 | 71.4 | 109.8 | – | 109.8 | 82.3 | 14.5 | 96.8 | 12.0 | 33.7 | 45.7 | 28.5 | – | 28.5 |
| 1958 | 49.9 | 26.5 | 76.4 | 78.5 | – | 78.5 | 83.7 | 13.1 | 96.8 | 10.9 | 37.7 | 48.6 | 24.2 | – | 24.2 |
| 1959 | 40.4 | 19.1 | 59.5 | 71.3 | – | 71.3 | 74.4 | 14.7 | 89.1 | 11.7 | 32.1 | 43.8 | 13.9 | – | 13.9 |
| 1960 | 44.7 | 20.3 | 65.0 | 72.6 | – | 72.6 | 70.8 | 17.3 | 88.1 | 11.8 | 28.2 | 40.0 | 19.2 | – | 19.2 |

Source: Grunwald and Musgrove, 1970, tables 10-11 and 13-6

Guatemala where the area suitable for coffee production had reached a local maximum.

Who benefited from this expansion in coffee production? In Costa Rica and Honduras, where production was concentrated in medium-sized farms, the small peasantry stood to gain and in both countries the banking system did not discriminate by size in the supply of credit.[19] In the other republics, the concentration of production on the large estates was reinforced by bank lending policy, leading to increased inequalities within the sector.[20] In all republics, however, there was a big increase in the demand for seasonal labour,[21] although it could not compensate fully for the loss of permanent jobs in the banana sector.

Throughout Central America, the volume of exports rose significantly, with the greatest gain recorded by Costa Rica where production responded to big increases in both yields and acreage. Export earnings, however, could not be raised so easily; only Costa Rica was able to record a modest increase, while El Salvador experienced a drop of 34% in the value of its dominant export between 1957 and 1960 (see Table 8.2). When combined with the fall in banana export earnings the result was dismal indeed. Between 1954 and 1960, the combined earnings from these two key commodities fell in all republics, with the sharpest decline in El Salvador (see Table 8.2). This occurred, of course, against the background of modestly rising import prices.

By the mid-1950s governments in the Central American republics were committed to capitalist modernisation. Despite the best efforts of the state, however, the external crisis provoked by the fall in the terms of trade could not be offset by traditional exports. Other Latin American countries, faced with the same problem, had turned towards their own markets as a way out of the problem; in Central America 'desarrollo hacia dentro' was not as yet considered an option and the state concentrated its efforts instead on export diversification.

## Export diversification and agro-industrial development

Faced with declining foreign exchange earnings from traditional exports, despite all efforts to increase them, Central American republics turned to export diversification in a big way; the results of this transformation were not fully visible until the 1960s, but the groundwork was firmly laid in the 1950s and set the pattern for later developments. Central America therefore increased the openness of its economies at a time when other Latin American republics were reducing their trade coefficients[22] and the justification was provided by the alleged impossibility of a rapid increase in industrial output in such small markets.

Over the years, Central America had acquired a number of minor 'traditional' exports, none of which had seriously challenged the dominance of coffee and bananas;[23] the prospects for export diversification, however, on the basis of these products was poor. In the case of mineral exports (mainly from Nicaragua and Honduras), worked seams were reaching exhaustion which raised costs at a time when world prices were stationary, while other products (e.g. chicle from Guatemala, sesame from Nicaragua) were threatened by cheaper substitutes.[24] Export diversification therefore required a bolder strategy and the obvious candidate was cotton, whose output had increased so spectacularly in the decade after the war. That increase had taken place against a background of rising world prices, but these peaked after 1950/1 and declined steadily thereafter until the early 1960s. Thus, policy-makers faced the challenge of stimulating production in the face of falling prices.

The location of cotton production on the sparsely populated Pacific lowlands meant that increases in area were relatively easy to achieve, provided that financial resources were available in sufficient quantities; these were indeed forthcoming and the area planted to cotton grew steadily until the season 1959/60, when a sharp fall in prices encouraged a switch to other crops. The success of cotton in competing with other activities to obtain new financial resources deserves some comment. From its post-war beginnings, cotton production was very concentrated, with a relatively small number of highly mechanised estates accounting for the bulk of output and exports; these growers constituted a powerful group with close links to financial institutions, which not only guaranteed that cotton's credit needs were met, but also ensured that the lion's share went to the largest estates.[25]

Cotton yields in Central America were already high by world standards in the early 1950s, but still managed to increase steadily for most of the decade. This was achieved through intensive use of imported insecticides, fertilisers etc., and the purchase of cotton-picking and cotton-ginning machinery. By 1957–8, El Salvador had the highest yields in the world[26] and within a few years these had been equalled by the other Central American

Table 8.3 *Volume and value of cotton exports, 1954–60*
*(Vol. = MT(000), Val. = $ million)*

|  | El Salvador | | Guatemala | | Honduras | | Nicaragua | |
|---|---|---|---|---|---|---|---|---|
|  | Vol. | Val. | Vol. | Val. | Vol. | Val. | Vol. | Val. |
| 1954 | 8.4 | 6.5 | 4.9 | 3.7 | 0.6 | 0.1 | 23.2 | 16.8 |
| 1955 | 12.4 | 9.1 | 6.2 | 4.5 | 0.9 | 0.1 | 44.0 | 31.0 |
| 1956 | 27.9 | 17.6 | 7.8 | 5.0 | 3.4 | 0.4 | 36.3 | 23.6 |
| 1957 | 25.2 | 15.8 | 6.7 | 4.2 | 4.1 | 0.4 | 36.0 | 21.8 |
| 1958 | 29.7 | 18.1 | 9.6 | 5.5 | 4.4 | 2.6 | 42.7 | 24.9 |
| 1959 | 44.0 | 23.2 | 9.7 | 4.1 | 4.0 | 2.6 | 61.7 | 29.4 |
| 1960 | 27.2 | 15.8 | 11.5 | 5.8 | 1.2 | 0.7 | 27.4 | 14.7 |

Source: Grunwald and Musgrove, 1970, table 16-5
Note: Costa Rica is excluded from the table, because her exports of cotton remained
at very minor levels throughout the period

republics.[27] Access to cheap credit was a major reason for the ability of
cotton growers to increase production in the face of falling world prices
for most of the decade, but it was not the only one; both Costa Rica and
Nicaragua used their dual exchange rate system to favour cotton exports[28]
and the Nicaraguan government also used the technique of a debt moratorium to help growers.[29] Thus, cotton had joined coffee as a favoured commodity in whose interests the state used the instruments at its disposal to
manipulate the net price. Despite all these efforts, the volume and value
of cotton exports peaked towards the end of the 1950s (see Table 8.3).
Cotton, it would seem, could not on its own carry the burden of export
diversification without which foreign exchange earnings were destined to
decline. The need for new exports was therefore still pressing and encouraged
the development of the cattle and sugar industries.

The raising of cattle in Central America was, of course, as old as the
Spanish conquest, but the industry was monumentally inefficient and production was of very poor quality; live cattle were traded across frontiers (notably
from Nicaragua to Costa Rica), but exports of cattle or its derivatives outside
the region were virtually unknown in the early 1950s. The prospects for
the industry, however, were good; *per caput* consumption continued to rise
steadily in the main consuming regions and exports to the USA (the logical
market for Central America) were unrestricted.[30] The traditional Latin
American suppliers (Argentina, Brazil, Uruguay) faced a problem of shrink-
ing export surpluses, as home consumption soared, and world prices were
rising. In addition, most of Central America appeared to have access to
a suitable land frontier for the development of the industry.

There were, nevertheless, some formidable obstacles to overcome before
cattle-raising in Central America could be turned into a successful export

Table 8.4  *Beef exports ($ million)*

|      | Costa Rica | Guatemala | Honduras | Nicaragua |
| ---- | ---------- | --------- | -------- | --------- |
| 1957 | 0.1        | –         | –        | –         |
| 1958 | 1.1        | –         | 0.1      | –         |
| 1959 | 2.9        | –         | 0.5      | 1.9       |
| 1960 | 4.3        | 0.2       | 1.1      | 3.1       |
| 1961 | 2.8        | 0.8       | 1.6      | 4.4       |
| 1962 | 2.7        | 3.8       | 2.6      | 5.9       |

Source: Grunwald and Musgrove, 1970, table 15-10
Note: El Salvador is excluded from the table, because her exports of beef remained at negligible levels throughout the period

industry. In El Salvador and Honduras, the bulk of the herd was owned by small- and medium-sized proprietors, with unfavourable access to land.[31] The development of the road system since the war had gone some way towards improving marketing opportunities for cattle, but the biggest problem was the poor quality of the herd, the low yield and slow growth of the cattle stock because of the high death rate. Initially, the problem was not so much one of increasing the land in pasture as of improving the quality of the existing pasture, providing an adequate feedstock for cattle during the dry season and importing high quality breeding stock. As in the case of cotton, the key role was provided by the financial system which channelled a growing proportion of bank credit towards cattle-raising;[32] this involved not only commercial banks, but also the newly formed development banks.[33]

If the development of the industry was to involve exports outside the region, investments would also be required in slaughterhouses. Significantly, the biggest investment was undertaken in Nicaragua by the Somoza family in 1958 with the *Matadero Modelo* (an abattoir with capacity for 400 slaughterings per day), although other republics (notably Guatemala and Costa Rica) followed suit on a smaller scale.[34] These new abattoirs provided the basis for exports of chilled beef from Central America for the first time (see Table 8.4). The pace of developments, however, was transformed by the opening in 1960 of a land and sea trucking service run by a US company with sailings from Guatemala every five days. This new method of export led to the decline of the trade in live cattle (except in El Salvador and Honduras, where the industry continued to be run on 'traditional' lines until the 1960s).

The emergence of sugar as a major export from Central America is often dated to the redistribution by the United States of the Cuban sugar quota towards Latin America after 1960. The transformation of the industry began in the 1950s, however, and indeed without such a transformation it is difficult to see how Central America could have qualified for a US import quota after 1960. The sugar industry had developed a small export surplus in the 1920s, but was badly affected by the depression and the retreat into protectionism by the major consuming countries. Honduras' only sugar mill, for example, was forced to close in 1935 and consumption came to depend entirely on *panela*, a crude sugar processed in artisanal form.[35]

The signing of a new International Sugar Agreement (ISA) in 1953 offered the prospect of stable prices (at the high level prevailing at that time) and provided a major stimulus for the development of the industry. The problem was not so much one of acreage planted to cane sugar, but of yields and of milling capacity. Both were transformed in the 1950s. New mills were opened throughout the decade; by the early 1960s, Honduras had four mills with an average capacity almost as high as those in Argentina;[36] milling capacity in Nicaragua was shared between the Somoza family on the one hand and the Pellas-Lacayo group on the other, with the former financed by the Banco Nacional Nicaragüense (BNN) and the latter by BANIC and BANAMER.[37] Although the land area devoted to sugar hardly changed, yields increased sharply both in terms of cane harvested per hectare and in terms of sugar extracted from cane. By the early 1960s, the production of cane sugar was dominated by large-scale producers[38] and yields were among the highest in the world. By the end of the 1950s, a significant export surplus had emerged in Costa Rica, El Salvador and Nicaragua, and these three republics benefited most from the redistribution of the Cuban sugar quota. Guatemala and Honduras did not emerge as net exporters until the early 1960s, but by the middle of the decade sugar had become an important export for all the countries of the region.

The new exports of cotton, beef and sugar represented a transformation of the agricultural sector and led ultimately to a significant degree of export diversification. They also represented a logical answer to the state's quest for capitalist modernisation; unlike bananas, the new products were controlled mainly by nationals; unlike coffee, they all involved heavy capital investments in processing facilities with considerable scope for forward linkages. Thus, not only did the capitalist surplus accrue to nationals, but the opportunities for accumulation within the sector were also substantial.

Although the new products were developed by private enterprise, the role of the state in their development should not be underestimated. State support took many forms; sometimes it was direct (e.g. access to credit from state-owned banks), but more commonly it was indirect. The latter covered such things as exchange rate manipulation, access to imports of complementary and capital goods and development of appropriate infrastructure. The state's role in the distribution of benefits from the new products is more controversial. Sugar and cotton production was highly concentrated in all republics by the early 1960s and the development of beef exports was more rapid in those republics (Costa Rica, Guatemala, Nicaragua) with a high concentration ratio than in those with a low one. Public policy contributed to this trend towards concentration, which was even sharper in the case of processing than production.

Within each farm size class, the distribution of the product between workers and capitalists depended on (a) the capital–labour ratio and (b) the wage rate. Sugar and cotton were highly mechanised (with state support) making labour requirements essentially seasonal; both governments and growers planned on the assumption of seasonal labour shortages, but wages did not in general reflect this excess demand. Policy was geared towards the maximisation of the capitalist surplus in the hope that this would produce a high rate of investment. Export agriculture (EXA) was therefore seen as a complement to work opportunities in the rest of the agricultural sector rather than as a substitute. To the extent that it *was* a complement, development could be considered successful; however, where EXA replaced existing work opportunities the situation was much more serious. In the next section, we shall see how major differences emerged among the republics in this respect in the 1950s; during the following two decades these differences became even more acute.

Export diversification succeeded in reducing significantly the share of total exports taken by coffee and bananas by 1960,[39] and the net output of export agriculture rose quite rapidly (see Table A.5). It could not, however, compensate fully for the terms of trade losses after 1954, and the purchasing power of exports was either unchanged or falling (see Table A.15), except in Honduras where the export sector recovered from the disastrous performance in 1954/5. This failure of export earnings to grow at a rate consistent with import demand provoked a serious balance of payments crisis and suggested the need for alternatives to a model of development based exclusively on agricultural exports.

## Agriculture for internal consumption

The intensification of export agriculture (EXA), supported by the state and involving the most powerful pressure groups in each republic, had a major impact on the rest of the agricultural sector. This Domestic Use Agriculture (DUA), producing for internal consumption, shares a complex relationship with EXA which is revealed through the markets for land, labour and capital. In the absence of state intervention, the intensification of EXA means less (or inferior) resources for DUA, but this implied inverse relationship is not deterministic; indeed, as we shall see, under appropriate conditions (invariably involving active state policy) the relationship can become, if not complementary, at least non-competitive.

The relationship between the two sub-sectors of agriculture is of the utmost importance in understanding the political economy of Central America; in the 1950s, the tension between EXA and DUA became fully apparent, although the dangers of ignoring it were not properly understood. The relationship was made all the more sensitive by two factors: first, the small farm sector tended to be specialised in DUA, while EXA (with the exception of coffee in Costa Rica and Honduras) was largely monopolised by the large farm sector; secondly, the 1950s witnessed a further fall in the crude death rate which (coupled with an acceleration of the birth rate in some republics) pushed the population towards previously inconceivable levels (see Table A.2). With most of the population classified as rural,[40] the demographic factor was an additional source of pressure on DUA and the small farm sector.

The main impact of export intensification on DUA was felt through the labour market. The growth of agricultural exports created new zones of attraction for permanent migration; in Honduras and Guatemala, these zones attracted more migrants than the province where the capital city was located. In terms of the rate of migration, these rural zones were the most important in all republics except Nicaragua and El Salvador. The migration pattern of the latter republic was in marked (and worrying) contrast to the rest of Central America, with even the new export areas formed by cotton becoming zones of expulsion;[41] in both Nicaragua and El Salvador, migration patterns were dominated by the flows towards the capital cities, so that there was an important contrast between those republics (Costa Rica, Guatemala and Honduras) where export intensification produced significant rural–rural migration and the other republics, where migration patterns were dominated by rural–urban migration. Export intensification also created a large demand for seasonal labour. This rural–rural temporary migration has been better documented for the 1960s, but was already important in the 1950s. These migration flows were not fully consistent with the survival of DUA; although the peak demand was at the end of the calendar year (the coffee harvest), the secondary peak in the middle of the calendar year clashed with the peak labour requirements for DUA.[42]

These changes in agriculture contributed to a significant growth in the number of landless workers. Before the 1950s, the rural proletariat was virtually confined to the banana zones, but by the early 1960s this had become an important phenomenon even outside the major banana-producing regions (see Table 8.5) and the figure for Nicaragua (nearly one-third of the agricultural labour force) was particularly high.[43] The average income of landless families and their relative position varied enormously (see Table 8.5). In Costa Rica, such a family received an income over three times higher than in El Salvador and only 20% below the average of a small farm family; in Guatemala, on the other hand, the pay of landless workers (although low in absolute terms) was higher than small farm income and equivalent to 75% of mean farm income. Significantly, El Salvador stands out as the

Table 8.5 Agricultural landless workers (early 1960s)

| | (1) No. of landless workers | (2) % of agricultural labour force | (3) Income per family ($) | (4) Income per family on small farms ($) | (5) (3) as %age of mean farm income |
|---|---|---|---|---|---|
| Costa Rica | 81,675 | 42% | 727 | 908 | 60.6 |
| El Salvador | 75,632 | 15.6% | 229 | 420 | 39.4 |
| Guatemala | 107,309 | 16.5% | 340 | 330 | 75.0 |
| Honduras | 99,099 | 26.1% | NA | NA | NA |
| Nicaragua | 87,796 | 31.4% | 370 | 445 | 41.0 |

Source: Derived from CEPAL et al., 1980

republic with the worst absolute and relative incomes for its landless workers and families.

The changes in agriculture on the market for land were equally profound. By the early 1960s, only Costa Rica and Guatemala had a majority of farms in owner-occupation (see Table 8.6) and renting had replaced access to communal land as the most important form of land tenure in Honduras.[44] In El Salvador, there was a huge drop in the proportion of owner-occupied farms, as various forms of tenancy increased in importance.[45]

The fact that EXA required substantial additional areas of land was not necessarily a threat to DUA. Except for El Salvador, the proportion of land area in farms was very low at the start of the 1950s and even in El Salvador the proportion of farm land area cultivated was still well below 50% by the end of the decade (see Table 8.6). Thus, outside El Salvador all republics still enjoyed a land frontier[46] and everywhere there were substantial opportunities for more intensive use of the existing farm area. Export agriculture, however, tended to take the best lands, which threatened to push DUA towards sub-marginal areas with lower yields. This was most clear in the Salvadorean case, where the area planted to cereals grew by 25% in the 1950s, but yields fell and production was stagnant.[47] It was also apparent in Nicaragua, where the area planted to cereals remained constant between 1952 and 1960, but yields fell by 30%.[48] In Guatemala, the land reform programme of the post-revolutionary governments (although modest by comparison with Arbenz's programme) made a small contribution towards DUA,[49] while in Costa Rica yields were maintained, although the increase in area farmed was achieved mainly through deforestation.[50] Furthermore, active state intervention could not always achieve the desired results; in Costa Rica, there was official support for a policy of agricultural diversification (in favour of DUA) using Italian migrants in one of the banana zones, but the existence of good infrastructure encouraged the migrants to plant coffee instead.

Table 8.6 *Land tenure and land cultivation, 1950–2 and 1961–6*

| | Costa Rica | | El Salvador | | Guatemala | | Honduras | | Nicaragua | |
|---|---|---|---|---|---|---|---|---|---|---|
| | 1950 | 1963 | 1950 | 1961 | 1950 | 1964 | 1952 | 1966 | 1952 | 1963 |
| (1) % of farms owner occupied | 81.0 | 76.4 | 61.9 | 39.6 | 55.6 | 57.9 | 21.3 | 22.4 | NA | 38.6 |
| (2) % of farms rented | 2.1 | 1.4 | 18.9 | 19.1 | 17.0 | 11.3 | 8.6 | 33.7 | NA | 12.6 |
| (3) % of farms under 'colonato'[1] | 0.7 | 0.2 | 19.2 | 24.6 | 12.4 | 11.6 | 4.1 | – | NA | – |
| (4) % of 'ejidal' farms[2] | – | – | – | – | – | – | 33.9 | 24.8 | NA | 8.0 |
| (5) % of land area in farms | 35.8 | 52.7 | 71.5 | 73.9 | 34.2 | 31.7 | 22.4 | 21.5 | 17.1 | 27.5 |
| (6) % of farm area cultivated | NA | 20.9 | NA | 41.3 | NA | 34.5 | NA | 22.0 | NA | 23.1 |
| (7) Share of *microfincas* in total farm area | – | – | 2.3 | 3.9 | 0.7 | 0.9 | 0.4 | – | – | – |
| (8) Share of small farms in total farm area | 2.9 | 2.9 | 16.6 | 18.0 | 13.6 | 17.7 | 15.7 | 12.4 | 2.3 | 3.5 |
| (9) Share of largest farm class in total farm area | 47.5 | 41.5 | 40.4 | 37.7 | 40.8 | 25.9 | 28.3 | 27.5 | 41.8 | 41.2 |
| (10) % of agricultural workers in total employment | 56.5 | 48.9 | 63.1 | 60.0 | 68.2 | 63.5 | 68.0 | 63.3 | 67.7 | 59.4 |

Source: derived from Monteforte Toledo, 1972, Vol. 1
[1] A farm under 'colonato' is one given by the landowner to a *colono* in return for labour services on the estate
[2] An 'ejidal' farm is one cultivated communally

The impact of EXA on DUA via capital (financial) markets was much more modest than was the case via land and labour markets. The reason was simple: very little bank credit was made available to DUA in the early 1950s, so that expansion of credit towards EXA did not affect it.[51] Costa Rica, it is true, had since the 1930s targeted bank credit towards the small farm sector (much of which benefited DUA); this policy continued following bank nationalisation with the National Bank's Sección de Juntas Rurales de Crédito Agrícola being upgraded in 1959 to the Departamento de Crédito Rural, Tierras y Colonias, but by 1960 this department's loans represented only 15% of all bank credit to agriculture (including livestock).[52] There were some important changes, however, in the 1950s. In Honduras the newly formed Banco de Fomento played an important role in channelling credit towards DUA, diffusing new technology towards small farmers and providing a system of sales outlets for agricultural tools;[53] even Nicaragua

Table 8.7  *Net trade in cereals*[1] *(thousand metric tons)*

|  | Costa Rica | El Salvador | Guatemala | Honduras | Nicaragua |
|---|---|---|---|---|---|
| 1948–52 | 0.7 | 7.5 | 1.7 | −3.3 | −14.9 |
| 1957 | 3.9 | 5.8 | 3.6 | −5.8 | 1.0 |
| 1958 | −1.1 | 26.1 | 2.9 | −10.7 | 2.6 |
| 1959 | 7.7 | 41.0 | −1.4 | −24.6 | −1.3 |
| 1960 | −9.9 | 21.0 | −1.7 | −16.5 | −2.4 |

Source: derived from FAO, *Trade Yearbook,* 1961
[1] Defined to include maize, rice, sorghum
N.B. A minus sign denotes net exports

began a system of small-scale rural credits in 1959, although not on the same scale as Costa Rica.[54]

Slowly, therefore, the recognition grew of the need to incorporate DUA within the framework of active state policy, but the latter was sharply divided among the republics on the question of price support. The main commodities in DUA are maize, beans, rice, sorghum and wheat, which are also key components of the cost of reproduction of the labour force;[55] with yields in all these crops low by international standards, supplies could often be obtained more cheaply from abroad. Thus, there was a certain contradiction between the requirements of food self-sufficiency on the one hand and cheap labour policies on the other.

Price support had been adopted in Costa Rica under Calderón Guardia (1940–4) and was organised by the Consejo Nacional de Producción (CNP). It had been adopted in Guatemala during the revolutionary period, where it was organised by the Instituto de Fomento de Producción (INFOP), and it survived the fall of Arbenz in 1954. In Honduras, price support policies for DUA were organised by the Banco de Fomento in the 1950s. Perhaps significantly, these three republics recorded favourable trends in cereals trade during the 1950s (see Table 8.7), with Costa Rica and Honduras in particular achieving substantial net exports of maize. In the other two republics, import penetration increased in importance. Net imports of maize in El Salvador[56] by the late 1950s were massive and Nicaragua had converted a substantial export surplus into a small deficit. These cereals' imports, however, were very cheap and were an important reason for the low cost of labour in these two republics (see Table 8.5). Thus, the conflict between cheap labour and food self-sufficiency was resolved in quite different ways in the two groups of republics.

Not surprisingly, this difference in policy was reflected in the performance of DUA and its contribution to GDP. In the crucial area of maize output, both production and yields slumped in El Salvador and Nicaragua, while

Table 8.8 *Central America: net output per person in domestic use agriculture (constant 1970 dollars), 1954 and 1960*

| Year[1] | Costa Rica | El Salvador | Guatemala | Honduras | Nicaragua |
|---|---|---|---|---|---|
| 1954 | 70.8 | 62.9 | 72.5 | 58.0 | 56.1 |
| 1960 | 87.3 | 61.7 | 73.1 | 53.1 | 54.5 |
| Annual rate of increase (%) | +3.6 | −0.3 | +0.1 | −1.5 | −0.5 |

Source: derived from tables A.2 and A.6
[1] Three-year averages

the harvest elsewhere rose at a satisfactory rate. For DUA as a whole, the picture was not dissimilar (see Table 8.8); net output per person rose rapidly in Costa Rica, modestly in Guatemala and fell elsewhere. The risk of a trade-off between the two branches of agriculture was therefore apparent in several republics.

### From foreign exchange abundance to balance of payments crisis

In the space of a few years in the 1950s, Central America passed from foreign exchange abundance to a balance of payments crisis. The precipitate fall in the external terms of trade[57] exposed in a cruel fashion the limitations of the export-led growth model despite the efforts made in favour of export diversification. The decade was also politically turbulent with 1954 a particularly traumatic year. The counter-revolution triumphed in Guatemala, the labour dispute in the banana zones of Honduras turned into a general strike, while Costa Rica and Nicaragua edged closer to war as Presidents Figueres and Somoza sought to topple each other.[58] Despite this, the commitment towards capitalist modernisation (already apparent by the beginning of the decade) was not reversed, although political conditions in each republic endowed capitalist modernisation with a different emphasis and influenced the means by which it could be achieved.

The victory of Castillo Armas over Arbenz in 1954, confirmed later by a plebiscite giving him a six-year presidential term, has often been interpreted as a return to the pre-1944 situation and a triumph for Ubiquismo. While it is true that the new president relied heavily on former officials from the Ubico period, the shift towards capitalist modernisation during the revolutionary period was not reversed; the uncertainty created by the assassination of Castillo Armas in July 1957, and the narrow victory of Ydígoras Fuentes, a former Ubico official, in the repeat elections of January 1958, were events hardly likely to encourage private sector investment and innovation, but the state's commitment to economic modernisation remained and most of the institutions founded during the revolutionary period to promote it survived.[59]

The social and political reforms of the revolutionary period, however, came under attack in post-1954 Guatemala. Castillo Armas tolerated no political opposition to his own Movimiento de Liberación Nacional (MLN), trade union activity was severely curtailed, and communists were put under heavy restrictions by the changes in the constitution in 1956. The 1952 agrarian law was suspended and most of the expropriated land was returned to its former owners (including UFCO). Despite this, the social programme was not entirely reversed. The Guatemalan Social Security Institute continued to operate and increased its coverage of the labour force in the late 1950s to nearly 25% (almost as high as Costa Rica). A new agrarian law was passed in February 1956 which ruled out expropriation, but provided for a tax on idle land and the settlement of landless workers on government lands in designated zones of agricultural development. Although it was widely attacked as cosmetic, Guatemala was in fact the only Central American republic to pass such a law in the 1950s.

The commitment to capitalist modernisation with no social or political reform was much clearer in El Salvador. While the régime of President Oscar Osorio (1950–6) introduced a number of important changes designed to modernise the economy, the transition to the presidency of Colonel José María Lemus in 1956 was conducted in such a way that all opposition candidates withdrew in protest from the elections. The lack of social and political reform in a republic where the benefits of growth were so narrowly distributed, coupled with the example of the Cuban revolution, provoked a confrontation with the radical left in late 1960 which culminated in a military coup. The junta that came to power, however, was itself thrown out in January 1961, when it became clear that it intended to hold genuinely free elections with the participation of left-wing parties.[60] The collapse of the junta led to the six-year presidency of Colonel Julio Rivera with the support of the newly formed, but misleadingly named, Partido de Conciliación Nacional (PLN).

In Nicaragua, efforts in favour of capitalist modernisation were complicated by the Somoza family's determination to monopolise political power. The 1950 pact with the conservatives broke down within a few years and in 1954 Somoza, flush with arms provided by the United States in the build-up to the fall of Arbenz,[61] survived an invasion attempt by Nicaraguan exiles[62] supported by President Figueres in Costa Rica. Somoza's assassination in September 1956, following his announcement of plans to run for the presidency again, further clouded the situation; Congress, however, quickly chose his eldest son Luis as provisional president[63] and his victory in the 1957 presidential elections was assured when all the serious candidates withdrew in protest. By 1961, Luis Somoza had survived nineteen attempts to overthrow his régime, including one in June 1959 master-minded by Che Guevara and supported by the Honduran President Dr Ramón Villeda Morales.[64]

The commitment of the Honduran president, a sympathiser of the Caribbean Legion,[65] to economic modernisation coupled with social and political progress was not in doubt, and the achievements of his administration (1957–63) were substantial. Villeda Morales' road to the presidency was a hard one, however, with his victory as Liberal Party (LP) candidate in 1954 blocked by constitutional intrigues. The subsequent efforts by former Vice-President Julio Lozano to dominate Honduran politics failed and the LP won a massive 62% of the vote in the Constituent Assembly elections of September 1957; these elections, a rerun of the fraudulent ones organised by Lozano in October 1956, provided the base for Villeda Morales to assume the presidency.[66]

The victory of Villeda Morales was welcome news to José Figueres, who had become President of Costa Rica in November 1953. The conditions for executing the social domestic programme of his Partido Liberación Nacional (PLN) could not have been more favourable, although Figueres came close to disaster in January 1955 when Somoza supported the exiled Calderonistas in their effort to overthrow the Costa Rican government. The Pact of Amity and the Treaty of Conciliation, signed by both Somoza and Figueres in September 1955, put relations between the two countries on a formally correct basis, although the personal enmity between the two leaders persisted.

Figueres' crusade against dictatorship in the Caribbean basin and his involvement in world politics, albeit on a modest scale, are generally thought to have contributed to the PLN defeat in the presidential elections of 1958.[67] With the National Assembly still under PLN control, however,[68] President Mario Echandi's room for manoeuvre was much reduced, although both presidents shared a good deal of the same political and social philosophy.[69] Indeed, the PLN's acceptance of defeat in 1958 bolstered democracy in Costa Rica and prevented the emergence of another Mexican-type Partido Revolucionario Institucional (PRI) with its distorted version of democracy.

While economic modernisation, as we shall see, did not have the same meaning for all governments, it did involve a broad measure of agreement on fundamentals. In addition to the diversification of export agriculture (see above, pp. 156–60) the need to provide incentives for industrial development was widely accepted; this included the promotion of foreign investment, the provision of social infrastructure at state expense and the control of costs through the elimination of inflation. In all republics, even Costa Rica,[70] the emphasis was on private rather than public investment, with the public sector avoiding open competition with private entrepreneurs. Industry was promoted by laws offering fiscal incentives for new activities or the expansion of existing operations. Such laws were passed for the first time in Honduras and Nicaragua in 1958 and 1955 respectively, while Costa Rica and Guatemala revised their 1940s legislation in 1959 and El Salvador relied on its 1952 industrial promotion law until its revision and extension in 1961.[71]

Tariff reform was also carried out in the 1950s with the stated purpose of protecting industry as well as the more general (and traditional) goal of raising revenue. The task of tariff reform was urged on Central America by ECLA's Economic Co-operation Committee for Central America in an effort to promote industrialisation within a regional framework (see below, pp. 172–3), but the Committee's efforts to promote tariff reform were not inconsistent with those seeking to industrialise within national boundaries. The main achievements of the period were the adoption of a common tariff nomenclature,[72] the reduction in importance of specific tariffs, a tariff structure favouring imports of capital equipment over luxury consumer goods and a higher tariff *ceteris paribus* for competing imports.

One impact of these changes in industrial incentives was a substantial rise in imports of capital goods for industry (except in Nicaragua), although industrial performance was far from spectacular. Between 1954 and the end of the decade, the manufacturing sector's share of GDP was virtually unchanged, with a small decline recorded in Costa Rica and El Salvador (see Tables A.1 and A.8). Some of the increase in industrial production was of the import substituting kind, but much of it simply replaced artisan production with modern factory output, leading to a change in the capital–labour ratio rather than an increase in the relative importance of manufacturing.

Social infrastructure, benefiting from access to official international credits, received priority throughout the region. The supply of electricity, in particular, increased notably, with installed capacity more than doubling in all republics (except Honduras) between 1953 and 1960 and virtually all the increase coming from plants in the public sector. Between 1952 and 1961 the road network was nearly quadrupled in El Salvador; smaller increases were recorded elsewhere, but the increases were still substantial and a much higher proportion of roads were paved than ever before.[73]

The role of the state in providing social infrastructure and creating a legal framework of incentives generated the necessary conditions for a transfer of investible resources from export agriculture to the rest of the economy, and the results, although mixed, gave cause for moderate satisfaction. Between 1950 and 1960, the investment coefficent[74] rose in all republics although it had reached a plateau by the middle of the decade in Guatemala, Honduras and Nicaragua.

The investment performance in El Salvador and Nicaragua provided a study in contrasts. In El Salvador in the 1950s, real fixed capital formation more than doubled; at first, much of this investment was in agriculture in response to the opportunities for agricultural export diversification; imports of capital goods for agriculture peaked in 1958, however, with investment accelerating in other branches of the economy. In 1955, for example, a group of coffee producers collaborated with US capital to set up an instant coffee factory exporting to North America and in 1956 a group of cotton producers entered into a huge joint textile venture with Japanese interests.[75] Both were classic examples of forward linkages and showed the mechanisms by which a financial surplus in agriculture could be mobilised for non-agricultural investment. In Nicaragua, the rise in real fixed capital formation between 1950 and 1955 mirrored the Salvadorean experience, but was even more dramatic.[76] From 1955 to 1960, however, investment fell in real terms as the national bourgeoisie unallied to the Somoza family judged the conditions inappropriate for an expansion of investment into non-agricultural activities. *Continuismo* and capitalist modernisation proved to be in conflict, and the latent tensions within the Nicaraguan capitalist class were apparent.

While in general the investment performance gave grounds for modest satisfaction, the finance provided by domestic savings was unsatisfactory and pointed to a serious weakness in the model of capital accumulation.[77] Between 1955 and 1960, domestic savings even in nominal terms fell in Guatemala[78] and Nicaragua and were virtually stationary in Costa Rica so that (with the exception of Honduras) a growing proportion of investment was financed externally; the book value of US investments in Central America, for example, grew from $255 million in 1950 to $350 million in 1959, although less than 4% of this was in manufacturing.[79]

The objective of price stability was substantially successful in this period. In the second half of the 1950s, there was virtually no change in the cost of living index in any of the five republics (there was in fact a slight decline in Honduras and Nicaragua). This price stability was achieved despite tariff increases on many imported consumer goods, although the latter received little weight in the retail price index of each republic;[80] the key to price stability was provided by the exchange rate, which remained stable or even appreciated,[81] coupled with the high degree of openness in each republic.

There were some features of economic modernisation over which practice differed sharply among the republics, although publicly expressed opinions were often quite similar. The most important examples were provided by fiscal reform, labour questions and social expenditure (in the 1960s, but not the 1950s, agrarian reform was also an issue over which policy diverged sharply among the republics). Fiscal reform was a long-overdue area; capitalist modernisation required a substantial increase in public expenditure, which needed to be matched by a rise in revenue. The fiscal system in Central America relied almost exclusively on indirect taxes in the early 1950s with a heavy bias towards taxes on imports and exports. The former, being largely specific, did not rise in line with the value of imports, while the latter, being in many cases on a sliding scale, were vulnerable to a fall in world commodity prices.

The tariff reforms, described above, improved the elasticity of import taxes, but only Costa Rica and Honduras were able to increase the revenue from export taxes. El Salvador and Guatemala remained over-dependent on these trade taxes, the revenue from which declined sharply in the second half of the 1950s; in both these republics, coffee exporters were not subject to income tax, and the Guatemalan Congress resisted the introduction of a general income tax law until 1963.[82] Costa Rica and Honduras, on the other hand, raised the highest marginal tax rate to 30% in 1954 and 1955 respectively (Nicaragua followed suit in 1959) and foreign companies were made subject to income tax in both countries. Fiscal performance therefore differed sharply among the republics. All governments remained heavily dependent on indirect taxes, but by 1960 Costa Rica had increased the share of revenue from direct taxes to nearly 20% compared with some 10% in El Salvador and Guatemala. Total revenue did not increase at all in El Salvador between 1954 and 1960 and declined steeply in Guatemala after 1957.

The labour question revolved around the extent to which labour was to participate in the benefits of capitalist modernisation. Both El Salvador and Nicaragua kept labour participation to a minimum; social security programmes covered less than 5% of the labour force, minimum wage legislation was not extended to rural workers and trade union activity was heavily restricted and involved a small minority of urban workers. Costa Rica and Honduras (after Villeda Morales came to power) offered a very different answer to the labour question. The Honduran Labour Code of 1959 went a long way towards meeting workers' demands raised in the 1954 strike,[83] while in Costa Rica the non-communist trade union movement reaped its reward for support of Figueres in the civil war through government non-interference in labour disputes, the extension of Calderón's social security programme and a rise in minimum wages for both rural and urban workers.[84] Guatemala occupied a position mid-way between these two groups. Neither Castillo Armas nor Ydígoras Fuentes had much sympathy for labour, but the clock could not be reversed fully to the period before 1944. A compromise was therefore reached in which rural workers, outside the banana enclaves, were virtually excluded from the benefits of capitalist modernisation, while urban workers continued to enjoy some of the rights they had won under the revolutionary government.[85]

Government answers to the labour question were reflected in attitudes to education. All the republics increased expenditure on education in the 1950s in both absolute and relative terms, but in Guatemala, El Salvador and Nicaragua the resources were spent disproportionately in urban areas. Only in Costa Rica was the rural illiteracy rate in the early 1960s comparable with the urban rate, while in El Salvador, Guatemala and Honduras the rural illiteracy rate hovered around 60% and touched 70% in Nicaragua.

The intensification and diversification of export agriculture, the promotion of industry and the development of social infrastructure all contributed to a significant rise in real GDP between 1954 and 1960. When population growth is taken into account, however, the rise was more modest and in some countries was wiped out by terms of trade losses. The external shock implied by the deterioration in the net barter terms of trade after 1954 ultimately led to a serious balance of payments crisis. Initially, steps were taken to restrain imports, through the introduction of tariff surcharges, import licences and advanced deposit requirements. The current account deficit continued to grow, however, provoking a fall in international reserves everywhere after 1957/8.

One by one, the Central American republics therefore opened negotiations with the IMF for stand-by credits. IMF conditionality did not in general require that the recipient governments impose additional measures of restraint[86] and in some cases (e.g. Guatemala) the stand-by arrangements were never used, but the dealings with the IMF served two purposes. They contributed to balance of payments stability in the short run and they emphasised the need for a new model of development which would make the republics less vulnerable to external shocks in the long run.

### The formation of the Central American Common Market

The balance of payments difficulties faced by all Central American republics at the end of the 1950s was one of the factors which encouraged a more receptive attitude on behalf of policy-makers towards a change in economic strategy and the formation of the Central American Common Market (CACM). There were other factors involved, however, and the purpose of this section is to show how the CACM came into being and how resistance from various quarters was overcome.

The goal of Central American unity had never been abandoned since the collapse of the Federation in 1838 and a step in this direction had been taken in 1951 with the formation of the Organización de Estados Centroamericanos (ODECA). The latter was dominated by the Ministries of Foreign Affairs of the five republics and was a highly political organisation which temporarily fell apart over the issue of communism in Guatemala in 1953,[87] but recovered its cohesion following the victory of the counter-revolution in 1954. ODECA's efforts towards unification at the political level were complemented by a series of free trade treaties signed between 1950 and 1956 among different pairs of Central American republics. All countries signed at least one of these treaties, which involved free trade in a limited range of products, but El Salvador was the most heavily involved.[88] During the years of the bilateral trade treaties (1950–6), intra-regional imports rose from $8.6 million to $13.7 million (3% of all imports), but 65% of the increase was accounted for by Honduras and this consisted almost entirely of additional trade with El Salvador.

Both ODECA and the bilateral trade treaties, the first of which could be dated to 1918, represented somewhat old-fashioned attempts at Central American unity and both appeared doomed to the same fate as previous efforts. The situation was transformed, however, in the early 1950s by the efforts of the Economic Commission for Latin America (ECLA) to promote unity by means of an entirely novel approach. The ECLA approach took as its starting-point the Prebisch thesis regarding the shortcomings of an export-led model based on primary products and the need for inward-looking policies based on import-substituting industrialisation (ISI).[89] It was clear to ECLA, however, that in Central America the limitations of the national market would put an effective brake on ISI long before the traditional export-led growth model was superseded. Thus, industrialisation in general and ISI in particular had to be fostered within a regional context.

In view of the level of industrialisation in Central America in the 1950s, ECLA perceived industrialisation policy as consisting essentially of promoting new activities, which could be shared out on some equitable basis among the member states. In certain cases, the small size of the regional market might not be sufficient for more than one firm of optimal size, and ECLA responded to this problem by promoting the concept of an integration industry, which would be guaranteed monopoly status subject to various state controls. The ECLA approach has therefore been correctly described as 'limited integration with reciprocity'[90] and ECLA's institutional innovation was the creation of a Committee of Economic Cooperation which comprised the Ministers of Economic Affairs of each republic; it met regularly under ECLA's auspices beginning in August 1952.

ECLA's natural allies in each republic were the *tecnicos*, the young professionals (often trained abroad) who had moved into public administration in the wake of post-war capitalist modernisation. The *tecnicos*, however, lacked political influence and ECLA's success in promoting integration can be understood only in terms of the lack of opposition from the politically powerful. There were several sources of political opposition to ECLA. Governments in each country continued to rely heavily on trade taxes for public revenue, and a shift towards regional free trade might affect the fiscal position adversely; ECLA's original proposals, however, were of such a limited nature that the adjustment problem was likely to be small. The political opposition of the military in the four northern republics was avoided by making it clear that no supra-national organisation would challenge the authority of the nation state, while the *comerciantes* were disarmed by the knowledge that intra-regional trade would expand even if extra-regional trade declined. ECLA's ambitions, however, would surely have foundered if the agro-exporters had opposed the integration plan. The ECLA scheme neutralised the latter groups, because it explicitly avoided tampering with the vector of prices which determined profitability in the export sector. Thus, the export products themselves (e.g. cotton, coffee, sugar) and the wage goods which determined the cost of reproduction of the labour force (e.g. basic grains) were excluded from the integration scheme, while the tariff on commodity inputs was either to be left unchanged or even lowered. At the same time, the prospect of industrialisation at the regional level offered a new opportunity for capital accumulation and an alternative employment opportunity for labour displaced from the rural economy by the expansion of export agriculture.

ECLA's efforts came to fruition in June 1958 with the signing of the Multilateral Treaty on Free Trade and Central American Economic Integration (MT for short) and the Integration Industries Convention (IIC). This was followed by the Tariff Equalization Convention (TEC), signed in September 1959. The MT allowed for intra-regional free trade in 239 groups of Central American products with plans for expansion of the list to cover intra-regional free trade in all products of Central American origin within ten years. The IIC provided for the establishment of plants with 'integration industry' status in each republic on an equitable basis, and the TEC introduced immediate uniform import duties on some 270 products (in general the same products given free trade status under the MT) and presented an additional list of 200 products where tariff uniformity would be achieved within five years.[91]

It is probable that regional integration in Central America would have produced very modest results, if it had been conditioned entirely by these three treaties. Although the MT went into effect on 2 June 1959, it had still not been ratified by Honduras and Costa Rica, and implementation of the IIC was blocked by the requirement that all five republics must ratify. In any case, both treaties were rendered largely irrelevant by a change in US policy towards integration. The formation of ECLA in 1948 within the United Nations had been opposed by the United States, and the subsequent Prebisch thesis was greeted officially with a mixture of scepticism and hostility. The US administration did not undermine ECLA's efforts to promote regional integration in Central America, although nothing was done in support. The signing of the MT, however, focussed the attention of the Eisenhower régime on the integration scheme and signalled a change in policy.[92]

US support was conditional on a number of changes in the ECLA scheme; in particular the United States proposed intra-regional free trade as the norm, with any exceptions to be specifically listed (the opposite of the MT) and by implication an elimination of the monopoly status of designated integration industries. In return, the US administration would provide funds for the required panoply of regional institutions and increase its aid to the region. These ideas were canvassed among the three northern republics and resulted in the Tripartite Treaty (TT) of February 1960, which came into force in April. Neither Costa Rica nor Nicaragua were invited to participate (it was felt that they would have opposed the concept of intra-regional free trade as the norm)[93] and ECLA found the rug pulled from under its feet.

The signing of the TT provoked a strong reaction from ECLA and Nicaragua and a lesser one from Costa Rica. As a result, ECLA was invited to submit a new proposal incorporating the commitment of the TT to intra-regional free trade as the norm. The result was the General Treaty of Central American Economic Integration (GT for short), signed by all the republics except Costa Rica in December 1960, and which has provided the legal basis for the Central American Common Market (CACM) ever since.

The GT, which went into effect for Guatemala, El Salvador and Nicaragua in June 1961 and Honduras in April 1962, provided for intra-regional free trade within five years for all products originating in Central America with the exception of a small number of commodities; the latter tended to be of special interest either to governments for tax reasons (e.g. distilled spirits) or to agro-exporters (e.g. coffee, cotton, sugar). The GT incorporated the IIC (a victory for ECLA) and provided for the establishment of a permanent Secretariat (Secretaría Permanente del Tratado General de Integración Económica Centroamericana – SIECA) and a development bank (Banco Centroamericano de Integración Económica – BCIE). Later, a Central American Clearing House was established for settling regional trade transactions and US interest was confirmed by the opening in 1962 of a Regional Office for Central America and Panama (ROCAP) as a subdivision of the US Agency for International Development.

Costa Rican reluctance to sign the GT reflected the fear of the Echandi administration (and of Minister of Economy Jorge Borbón in particular) that the rapid transition towards intra-regional free trade would damage existing industry in Costa Rica without providing adequate safeguards or instruments for the introduction of new activities.[94] Membership of CACM became an electoral issue, however, and the victory of the opposition (PLN) candidate in the 1962 presidential elections paved the way for Costa Rica to join in 1963. By the beginning of the 1960s, therefore, all the republics were participating fully in the integration experiment.

# 9

## The illusion of a golden age, 1960–70

By conventional measures of economic progress the decade of the 1960s was a golden age for Central America. The Central American Common Market (CACM) took shape at the start of the decade and the Alliance for Progress, launched by President Kennedy in March 1961, increased the flows of external funds to each republic and to the new institutions of the CACM, contributing to a very respectable growth in GDP and GDP per head over the decade.[1]

The reality of the decade was somewhat different. Policy-makers failed to provide an adequate framework for ensuring that the net benefits from the CACM were distributed in an equitable fashion among the five republics, so that the industrialisation strategy was threatened at an early stage by inter-country differences. The failure, furthermore, to implement a common fiscal policy towards new industrial activities meant that Central America robbed itself of one of the major advantages (tax revenues) to be obtained from new foreign investment attracted by the CACM.

Even more serious was the response, or rather lack of response, provoked by the decline in import duties (the main source of government revenue) consequent upon the formation of the CACM. This crisis required a fiscal reform which would reduce the regressive nature of the tax system on the one hand and encourage domestic resources to shift into industry on the other. In fact, fiscal changes accentuated the regressive nature of the tax system, contributed to a worsening of income distribution and did little to reduce the relative profitability of export agriculture (EXA). In addition, the decision in 1968 to impose a surcharge on import duties (the San José Protocol) aggravated the bias of the structure of protection in favour of consumer goods and contributed substantially to the eventual stagnation of the industrialisation process.

The failure to tax EXA, coupled with an initial improvement in the external environment, produced a boom in traditional exports (now defined as coffee, bananas, cotton, sugar and beef). This relaxation of the foreign exchange constraint contributed to the rapid growth of industry during the decade, but it also imposed some heavy costs on the region. Domestic use agriculture

175

(DUA) came under pressure from the boom in EXA, while rural social and economic conditions deteriorated in several republics; the most serious case was El Salvador, where the deterioration led to an increase in migration to Honduras and therefore contributed to the 'guerra inutil' between the two republics in 1969.[2] Guerrilla groups, inspired by the Cuban revolution, appeared in Guatemala and Nicaragua, but their appeal to the peasantry was still very limited.[3]

The continuing attraction of EXA for local investors was a major reason for the dependence of industrial investment within CACM on external finance. Direct foreign investment (DFI) in the manufacturing sector soared in each republic and multinational enterprises (MNEs) acquired a dominant position in the leading industrial branches. Some local investors were also attracted by the industrial incentives under the CACM, but as a class they did not constitute a pressure group capable of matching the influence of the traditional oligarchy allied to EXA, and their influence on state policy in favour of new industrialisation strategies, when the CACM ran into crisis at the end of the decade, was limited.

The 1960s therefore gave only the *illusion* of a golden age. Certainly, intra-regional trade, GDP and income per head all rose rapidly, but the contribution of the CACM to the latter was relatively minor; the main engine of growth continued to be EXA and the pressure groups associated with it were as strong as ever.[4] The rapid growth of industry, however, reflected in a rising industrial share of GDP and a high rate of urbanisation, contributed to a sharp increase in the importance of an urban middle and working class whose political aspirations were blocked in several republics (El Salvador, Guatemala and Nicaragua) by the stranglehold on state power exercised by the traditional oligarchies and their military allies.[5]

As in the earlier period (1954–60), important differences emerged among the republics in policy and performance. El Salvador and Guatemala took the largest share of the additional benefits created by the CACM, but distributed them very unequally; neither republic rose to the challenge presented by the fiscal crisis (see below, pp. 180–5) and (at least in El Salvador) the narrow class interests of export agriculturalists remained paramount. Nicaragua, under Luis Somoza, softened the edge of class antagonisms through a series of minor social and economic reforms, although the interests of the state remained closely identified with those of the Somoza family. Only Costa Rica and Honduras showed sufficient flexibility in policy to avoid major class confrontation; Honduras responded to the fiscal crisis more positively than Costa Rica and slowly came to recognise the possibility of a partnership between capital and labour, while Costa Rica broadened the foundations of its welfare state through a massive extension of social security programmes.

## The Central American Common Market (CACM) and the strategy of industrialisation

Although Central American unity had been a constant preoccupation in the region since independence, the institutional framework for promoting it was almost non-existent when the General Treaty (see Chapter 8, pp. 173–4) was signed in December 1960. The progress of the integration movement, however, clearly depended on appropriate institutions and procedures for resolving the numerous problems and disputes which common market partners experience.

Mention has already been made of the Secretariat (SIECA) and the regional development bank (CABEI), both of which played a key role in the evolution of the CACM.[6] Neither institution, however, was appropriate for resolving the financial problems which arose in the settlement of intra-regional trade balances between pairs of countries, and this gap was filled in June 1961 with the formation of the Central American Clearing House. The purpose of the latter was to promote the use of local currencies in the settlement of trade deficits between pairs of countries, supported by a US dollar fund to guarantee the convertibility of accumulated balances and a local currency fund to extend temporary credits to deficit countries.[7]

The original aims of the Clearing House presupposed that deficits within Central American trade would be temporary rather than structural, i.e. each country's trade with its partners would be balanced over the medium term; in addition, the agreement assumed a fair degree of exchange rate stability, otherwise member countries holding local currencies of partners could be at risk from devaluation. A step was taken towards monetary union with the formation in 1964 of the Central American Monetary Council.[8] By then however, it was already clear that the balance of payments issue had been fudged, because the five republics agreed in 1963 to settle the balances among themselves in dollars twice yearly;[9] this was made possible by the improvement in the external terms of trade in the first half of the 1960s, which temporarily eased the foreign exchange constraint.

The institutional framework for monetary co-operation therefore assumed a degree of balanced development (absence of structural deficits) within the CACM which proved unjustified; furthermore, the framework took shape in an unusually favourable external environment, which avoided the question of what would happen when the latter turned hostile. The failure to resolve these questions became acute from the late 1960s onwards (see below, pp. 195–9) and it crippled the CACM in the 1980s (see Chapter 11).

The establishment of institutions to handle regional infrastructure was more successful. A Regional Highway Programme was adopted in 1963 which gave priority to twelve routes of 'regional interest', and steps were taken to standardise highway signs.[10] Regional communications, another precondition for regional industrial development, were promoted through the formation of a Regional Telecommunications Commission (COM-TELCA) in 1966[11] and air transport was developed by the Central American Corporation of Air Navigation Services (COCESNA); the latter leased to national governments its spare capacity on radio channels and helped to ease the constraint on communications between Central American capitals.[12]

The establishment of these and other regional institutions[13] took place during a phase of political upheaval in the first half of the 1960s, which brought governments dominated by the military to power everywhere except Costa Rica.[14] This did not threaten the integration process, because the latter in turn imposed very few limits on national sovereignty, but it did little to encourage the kind of political cooperation among the five republics which was a precondition for the formation of robust institutions capable of resolving major inter-country disputes. The only kind of cooperation it did actively foster was military, exemplified by the formation in December 1963 of the Council of Central American Defence (CONDECA) with Costa Rica as an observer.[15]

The external environment at the beginning of the 1960s was made favourable not just by changes in the terms of trade (see Table A.14), but also by US support for the CACM. The beginning of the latter coincided with the launching of the Alliance for Progress in March 1961, and the US commitment to Central America was underlined further by the meetings between Central American heads of state with President Kennedy in 1963 and President Johnson in 1967. US interest in Central America in the 1960s was stimulated by the potential threat to US security arising from the Cuban revolution and the emergence of guerrilla *foci* in Guatemala and Nicaragua. The CACM, however, was seen as a suitable vehicle for promoting both US strategic and economic interests, as well as being the kind of scheme favoured by the Alliance for Progress. Thus, US official development assistance to the region was increased sharply and the national governments were spared much of the financial burden arising from the need to fund the new regional institutions.

External finance, mainly from US official sources, was built into the budget of virtually all regional institutions, while the Central American contribution was in some cases zero.[16] The foreign assistance component of the road-building programme rose from 52% during 1955–63 to 75% during 1965–9; in order to stimulate the flow of foreign assistance, and at the same time comply with the Alliance for Progress conditions on borrowing, national plans were adopted in each republic despite their governments' preference for *laissez faire*, and a Joint Planning Mission for Central America was established with funds from outside sources.[17] External support, however, was bought at a price. Some of the regional institutions operated like foreign enclaves and the availability of foreign funds reduced the commitment of national governments to the integration effort; indeed, the lack of commitment was so severe that several regional institutions could not function properly because even the low level of expected Central American contributions was not forthcoming.[18]

Although monetary cooperation and regional infrastructure were important, the key problem faced by the CACM's institutions was the equitable distribution of net benefits among the member countries. As had been widely suspected, the CACM proved to be net trade diverting;[19] under conditions of foreign exchange scarcity, it has been demonstrated both generally,[20] and in particular for Central America,[21] that net trade diversion is not inconsistent with the creation of net benefits. Regional net trade diversion releases foreign exchange, which can be used to increase extra-regional purchases of capital and intermediate goods; these benefits accrue to the region as a whole, however, and the potential benefit to any one member will be lost if the latter runs a persistent trade deficit with its partners.

The ECLA emphasis in the 1950s on balanced development was therefore correct, although it had not developed a satisfactory approach to support its case. A key element in ECLA's strategy was the Integration Industries Convention (IIC) which was finally embodied in the General Treaty (see Chapter 8, pp. 173–4). The IIC, however, proved to be a blunt instrument and by the end of the 1960s only three firms had been given integration industry status.[22] The first of these was a tyre factory located in Guatemala; when a second tyre plant was established in Costa Rica a few years later, it effectively destroyed the IIC. The failure of the IIC has been blamed frequently on US hostility to the concept of a regional monopoly.[23] In fact the scheme was doomed by the signing of the General Treaty,[24] by flaws in the design of the scheme[25] and, above all, by inter-country rivalries over the location of plants. The latter was an example of the low level of commitment to the integration scheme by member governments and of a misunderstanding of how the potential benefits might best be exploited.

With the IIC unable to solve the problem of an equitable distribution of benefits, attention turned elsewhere.[26] In 1962, the four member states (Costa Rica had not yet joined) signed a fiscal incentives convention (FIC) designed to harmonise the tax advantages offered by each republic to new and existing industries. The FIC allowed Honduras and Nicaragua, the least developed members of the CACM, to offer tax exemptions for a longer period than the other countries, but the Honduran government would not ratify the convention until the other countries had recognised its need for greater temporary concessions. As the FIC could not go into force until it had been ratified by all members, Honduras was in a strong position to insist upon revisions. In March 1969, Honduras finally ratified the FIC after the other countries had agreed to pass a special protocol permitting her to offer more generous tax advantages to industrial firms than were allowed under the convention. Whether the compromise would have been sufficient to ensure an equitable distribution of benefits is academic: war broke out between Honduras and El Salvador a few months later and Honduras withdrew from the CACM in 1970.

With both the IIC and FIC in disarray, the task of promoting balanced development fell to the regional development bank. CABEI mainly financed investments in social infrastructure and its lending policy favoured Honduras and Nicaragua disproportionately;[27] it proved to be one of the most effective regional institutions (as well as being profitable),[28] but it could not be expected on its own to carry the burden of ensuring an equitable distribution of benefits among member countries. The institutional framework of the CACM was therefore insufficient to guarantee its survival, if the external (and internal) environment should turn hostile. Problems were recognised, but solutions were avoided wherever they imposed economic, social or political costs. This was also revealed quite clearly in the treatment of free trade in agricultural goods, an issue which naturally proved to be very sensitive with the powerful agricultural pressure groups.

The main export products (e.g., coffee, cotton, cattle) had been exempted from free trade permanently, but many other agricultural commodities (e.g., basic grains) had been given only a temporary reprieve (see Chapter 8, p. 174). As a result, the five republics signed in 1965 a special protocol on basic grains, which went into force on ratification by all members in February 1968. Although the protocol ostensibly promoted free intra-regional trade in basic grains, individual republics were still able to import from outside Central America subject to a tariff 'equal to the difference between the price of the imported grain and the support price paid by the government of the importing country to its local producers'.[29] The importing country was obliged only to 'consult' with the other members to ensure that regional grain supplies had been exhausted. Thus, no serious limitation was put on national farm policies and the cost of reproduction of the agricultural labour force remained under the control of the national authorities.

## The fiscal crisis

The formation of the CACM, coupled with the system of incentives adopted for new activities, created a potentially serious problem of shortfalls in public revenue. The search for new sources of revenue was largely thwarted by well-entrenched pressure groups and the resolution of the fiscal problem proved ultimately to be very unsatisfactory and extremely damaging to the region's chances of adopting an alternative model to export-led growth based on traditional primary goods.

The CACM involved tax exemptions for a variety of reasons. First, by the middle of the 1960s, intra-regional trade was almost entirely free of import duties;[30] this trade grew rapidly throughout the decade (see below, p. 195) and to a large extent replaced extra-regional trade in the same goods (which were still subject to tariffs). Secondly, the common external tariff (CET) adopted under the CACM increased nominal protection on consumer goods, while leaving unchanged or even reducing nominal tariffs on intermediate and capital goods;[31] calculations of the effective rate of protection (ERP)[32] showed that the bias towards consumer goods was even greater on this measure, so that intra-regional trade was shifted towards those goods which would have carried the highest tariff rates if imported from the rest of the world, while extra-regional trade was shifted in favour of commodities which carried the lowest duty rates. Not surprisingly, this also had a marked downward impact on revenue collected from import duties. Thirdly, all five republics adopted fiscal incentives for new activities, which involved generous exemptions not only from import duties on inputs, but also from direct taxes on profits.[33] The fiscal incentives available for existing activities were less generous (particularly in El Salvador and Guatemala), but all republics agreed to extend the same benefits to an existing firm as were enjoyed by any other competing firm in the CACM; thus, many existing enterprises ended up with the same liberal exemptions enjoyed by new firms.[34]

The impact of import duty exemptions on government revenue was particularly severe, because each republic relied so heavily on this form of taxation.[35] Throughout the 1960s, the Costa Rican authorities published a table in the annual Comercio Exterior showing duty collections foregone as a result of various exonerations. The figures are an exaggeration, because they imply zero substitution effects, but they are sufficiently dramatic to deserve comment. In 1968, for example, the amount 'exonerated' was 265% greater than the amount collected; nearly 50% of exonerations were accounted for by trade with the CACM under the integration treaty, 14% was explained by fiscal incentives to private firms under industrial promotion laws and 31% by tariff exemptions for firms operating under contract law (mainly the fruit companies).[36]

Pressure was also applied on the public sector from the expenditure side. Competition among the five republics in intra-regional trade was based on private enterprise, but investment was essentially foot-loose and depended to some extent on the quantity and quality of public expenditure on social infrastructure, human capital and public order. This pressure affected all republics, although Costa Rican expenditure (particularly on education) continued to stand out as exceptional. Throughout the region, autonomous or semi-autonomous institutions mushroomed in support of development programmes and by 1970 their expenditure accounted for nearly 10% of GDP in Costa Rica, El Salvador and Nicaragua; the figure was much lower in Guatemala and Honduras, but in all republics the proportion rose rapidly in the 1960s.[37]

Table 9.1 *The structure of taxation (as percentage of government revenue),*
*1960, 1965 and 1970*
(A) = Income tax   (B) = Property tax   (C) = Export tax

| | Costa Rica | | | El Salvador | | | Guatemala | | | Honduras | | | Nicaragua | | |
|---|---|---|---|---|---|---|---|---|---|---|---|---|---|---|---|
| | (A) | (B) | (C) | (A) | (B) | (C) | (A) | (B) | (C) | (A) | (B) | (C) | (A) | (B) | (C) |
| 1960 | 12.1 | 5.4 | 4.9 | 8.7 | 3.8 | 17.0 | 8.0 | 2.5 | 11.3 | 15.5 | 1.2 | 5.1 | 10.0 | 4.1 | 3.0 |
| 1965 | 17.3 | 6.5 | 1.5 | 16.0 | 3.5 | 17.4 | 12.2 | 3.1 | 7.8 | 16.9 | 1.7 | 5.4 | 13.1 | 7.5 | 1.9 |
| 1970 | 19.9 | 3.0 | 1.0 | 15.1 | 8.4 | 18.3 | 12.6 | 4.1 | 5.9 | 26.3 | 1.2 | 3.6 | 11.0 | 11.0 | 1.0 |

Source: SIECA/INTAL, 1973, Vol. 10

The combination of import duty exemptions coupled with a rapid rise in extra-regional trade produced stagnation in the nominal value of duties collected. When combined with the pressure on expenditure, each government faced the problem of additional sources of income to prevent a widening public sector deficit. The obvious candidate for fiscal reform was direct taxation, which consisted of income and property taxes. The yield from these taxes was very low, even by Latin American standards, and less than one per cent of the population (except in Costa Rica) in the early 1960s[38] was estimated to pay income tax, although by any reckoning income distribution was sufficiently unequal to have generated a large taxable surplus among the top deciles of income earners.[39] The prospects for increased revenue from direct taxation were not helped by the generous exemptions granted by each country to new and existing industries under national industrial promotion laws.[40] Nevertheless, several republics introduced legislation or revised existing legislation[41] with a view to increasing revenue from income, property and export taxes.[42]

The results of these endeavours varied from moderate to poor. Three of the republics (Guatemala, Honduras and Nicaragua) applied the same income tax law to businesses and individuals; this created excessive exemptions and deductions for wealthy individuals and encouraged the artificial division of firms in order to incur lower marginal tax rates.[43] The same three countries did not tax dividends, and Nicaragua did not even tax interest payments to nationals domiciled abroad.[44] The highest marginal tax rate varied from 30% in Nicaragua to 60% in El Salvador for individuals, but the yield from the tax depended more on administrative competence than on the rates themselves. Thus, Honduras – the poorest Central American country with the second lowest maximum marginal tax rate – increased the share of government revenue from income tax to 26.3% by 1970 compared with 15.5% in 1960. By contrast, the yield in Nicaragua as a proportion of government revenue was virtually unchanged (see Table 9.1).

Revisions to property tax laws were attempted in Guatemala by the Mendez Montenegro administration (1966–70). Although ostensibly committed to reform, this administration proved to be putty in the hands of the traditional oligarchy and the proposed changes were withdrawn.[45] Only Nicaragua succeeded in raising more than ten per cent of government revenue from property taxes (on the basis of laws passed in 1962), while in Costa Rica the proportion fell from 5.4% to 3.0% in 1970. The yield from export taxes (mainly on coffee) was equally disappointing. Guatemala lowered its export tax on coffee in 1967 and export taxes as a proportion of government declined everywhere except El Salvador during the decade; by 1970, the proportion had fallen to a pathetic one per cent in Costa Rica and Nicaragua, although in El Salvador the proportion remained just below 20% (see Table 9.1).

Administrative weakness, coupled with widespread tax evasion, made it clear that the yield from direct taxes was not going to rise sufficiently fast to compensate for the falls in import duties provoked by the formation of the CACM. The emphasis turned to indirect taxes other than import duties. At the beginning of the 1960s, none of the republics had a general sales or retail tax, so that consumption was taxed selectively in a highly regressive fashion. Honduras was the first to adopt a retail tax, which was set at three per cent and applied only to large retailers; sales to small retailers were taxable, however, because the tax was collected in this case by the wholesaler.[46] The tax was collected from just over 1,000 registered vendors and was copied by Costa Rica and Nicaragua.[47] An effort to raise consumer taxes during the Mendez Montenegro government was thwarted,[48] so that Guatemala (and El Salvador) continued to rely on the archaic stamp duty as the major source of indirect taxation (other than import duties). The stamp duty was extremely expensive to operate and provoked widespread evasion; it was inelastic and regressive and had an unpredictable effect on consumer prices, because it applied to all transactions.[49]

Fiscal reform was therefore insufficient to generate new sources of revenue, which could grow at a rate to match the increase in public expenditure. This provoked a series of responses from the republics which were ill-conceived and produced serious distortions in the allocation of resources. One such response was the San José Protocol signed by the five republics in 1968, which introduced a surcharge on import duties in an effort to salvage government revenues from this traditional source. The impact of the San José Protocol was threefold: first, it sought to avoid the painful question of fiscal reform by resorting to a traditional fiscal instrument; secondly, it increased the bias in favour of producing consumer goods in the CACM;[50] and, thirdly, it increased the bias against exports of the same goods. The Protocol was therefore very damaging to Central America's prospects of moving away from its traditional growth model, because it postponed the introduction of genuine tax reform and accentuated the risk of industrial stagnation.

Despite the San José Protocol, central government revenue as a proportion

Table 9.2  *Central government current revenue (as percentage of GDP),*
*1960, 1965 and 1970*

|      | Costa Rica | El Salvador | Guatemala | Honduras | Nicaragua |
|------|------------|-------------|-----------|----------|-----------|
| 1960 | 13.3       | 10.9[1]     | 7.6[1]    | 10.8     | 9.5       |
| 1965 | 13.3       | 11.2        | 8.9       | 10.5     | 10.3      |
| 1970 | 15.3       | 11.5        | 9.0       | 12.4     | 9.3       |

Source: SIECA/INTAL, 1973, Vol. 10, pp. 117–26
[1] The figure for 1960 is not given in the source, so current income (SIECA/INTAL, 1973, Vol. 10, pp. 134–5) has been divided by nominal GDP

of GDP hardly rose at all during the decade (see Table 9.2). In Nicaragua, the proportion actually fell, while the rise in Costa Rica was entirely due to the impact of higher import duties in 1970. The pressure to raise expenditure remained intense, and each republic was forced to address itself to the potential fiscal gap. The response was two-fold: in Guatemala, El Salvador and Nicaragua public capital expenditure programmes were cut back savagely after 1965, while Honduras and Costa Rica continued to press on with their development programmes. In these two republics, public capital expenditure as a proportion of GDP doubled during the decade, but the method of finance was very different. Costa Rica relied increasingly on internal (bank) credit while government savings on current account were negative for most of the decade.[51] Honduras, on the other hand, whose efforts at fiscal reform had been more successful than elsewhere, was able to finance some two-thirds of its capital expenditure through public sector savings on current account with the balance provided mainly by external finance.[52]

The fiscal crisis exposed many of the weaknesses of the Central American development model in the 1960s. Powerful pressure groups were able to cripple efforts at fiscal reform, while leaving traditional exports virtually untouched; this left the 'old' model of export-led growth based on primary products firmly in place, despite the appearance alongside it of a 'new' model based on industrialisation and balanced regional development. The unsatisfactory efforts to resolve the fiscal crisis produced distortions in the 'new' model (e.g., the San José Protocol), while doing little or nothing to reduce incentives in favour of the 'old' model.

The fiscal crisis did not affect all countries equally. Honduras and Costa Rica fared better than the others, although for different reasons: Honduras was able to reap advantages from the absence of powerful pressure groups (such as coffee growers)[53] to push through a modest fiscal reform capable of financing much of its capital spending programme. Costa Rican governments, on the other hand, suffered from the resistance of business pressure groups to fiscal reform and chose to borrow their way out of the problem;[54] this was a distinctly second-best solution, but even so it stands in contrast to the remaining three republics where resistance to tax reform, coupled with conservative fiscal and monetary policies, led to a reduction in the developmental role of the state at a time when social and political pressures demanded the opposite.

## The agricultural response to the CACM and the hybrid model

A model of industrialisation for Central America, designed to replace the traditional export-led model based on primary products, would have had revolutionary implications for the agricultural sector. The finance for new industrial investments would have had to come in large part from export agriculture (EXA), a growing proportion of the foreign exchange required for extra-regional imports of raw materials and capital goods would have had to be provided by extra-regional industrial exports, and agricultural diversification would have to be pursued at the expense of EXA in order to provide both the wage goods for the expanding urban labour force and the raw materials for industry to prevent the latter becoming too dependent on imported inputs. Such a model, if successfully executed, would have ended the economic, social and political dominance of the landowning oligarchy linked to EXA. The model was therefore ruled out as politically unrealistic by those who shaped the CACM; instead, the CACM was to be grafted on to the traditional export-led model without challenging the hegemony of the export agriculturalists.[55] In this way, it was assumed (correctly), the traditional pressure groups would not oppose the formation of the CACM.

This hybrid model of industrialisation had very different implications for the agricultural sector. In the first place, foreign exchange earnings to pay for extra-regional imports continued to be heavily (almost exclusively) dependent on EXA; in turn, this required the maintenance of incentives for investment in EXA, thus reducing the domestic financial surplus available for new industrial development; the strengthening of EXA, on the other hand, did little to promote agricultural diversification, so that the supply of wage goods and natural resources for industry were both at risk. Finally, the hybrid model (unless modified) could not be expected to challenge the dominance of the traditional oligarchy.

Throughout Central America, after the formation of the CACM, public policy continued to favour EXA. The new tariff schedules established under the common market yielded very low duties for imported intermediate and capital goods[56] and the Effective Rate of Protection for EXA, although negative, was so low that no bias was implied against agricultural exports.[57] Changes in export taxes (see previous section) favoured EXA and helped to offset the very mild real appreciation of the exchange rate.[58] The biggest boost to EXA, however, came from monetary and credit policies. Despite

Table 9.3  *Commercial bank credit to agriculture (including livestock) at*
*year-end ($ million), 1961, 1965 and 1970*
Figures in brackets are percentage of total lending

|      | Costa Rica | El Salvador | Guatemala | Honduras | Nicaragua |
|------|-----------|-------------|-----------|----------|-----------|
| 1961 | 67.8 (56.2) | 32.5 (26) | 52.9 (47.9) | 7.3 (20.0) | 34.9 (62.0) |
| 1965 | 95.1 (53.8) | 47.1 (28.3) | 63.4 (40.2) | 20.3 (31.3) | 57.2 (55.7) |
| 1970 | 144.0 (57.1) | 59.1 (26.7) | 84.2 (36.3) | 53.1 (31.6) | 99.4 (60.2) |

Source: Consejo Monetario Centroamericano, *Boletín Estadístico*, various years

the industrialisation programme, the share of commercial bank credit going
to agriculture (including livestock) tended to rise in all republics except
Guatemala[59] during the decade (see Table 9.3).[60] The increase in credit
extended was spectacular (particularly in Honduras and Nicaragua) and
by the end of 1970 commercial bank lending to agriculture was nearly three
times higher than to industry.[61]

Within total lending to agriculture, the traditional export crops (coffee,
bananas, cotton, sugar, beef) received priority. Livestock, in particular,
received special treatment; by 1970 lending for stock-raising purposes
accounted for over 40% of all new loans to agriculture in Costa Rica, Honduras and Nicaragua;[62] only in land-scarce El Salvador was lending for
livestock relatively unimportant, although even there the proportion rose
sharply during the decade.[63] Lending for agricultural crops was completely
dominated by coffee, cotton and sugar; these three export products
accounted for 85% of the total in Guatemala by the end of the decade
and 76% in El Salvador;[64] the proportions were not much lower elsewhere
and Costa Rica regularly channelled 50% of all credit to agriculture towards
coffee.[65] Interest rate policies also worked in favour of EXA. In no republic
were interest rates for agriculture higher than for other activities and in
some they were lower. (In Nicaragua, for example, commercial banks
charged a maximum 2% for financing cotton, coffee and the fattening of
livestock, while the maximum rate for general agricultural finance was 6%
(for other commercial bank credits it was 8%).)[66] Public policy, therefore,
continued to operate strongly in support of the traditional export products.

Public sector policy in favour of EXA was a necessary, but not sufficient,
condition for its success. The external environment (including climate) was
also very important and it became much more so in the 1960s. Coffee,
sugar and beef all became subject to export quotas over which the Central
American countries had no control; banana exports remained dominated
by the two multinationals Standard and United Fruit, so that among the
traditional exports only cotton was both subject to influence by public policy
and free from quota restraints. This no doubt helped to account for the
spectacular growth of value added in cotton in the first half of the decade

Table 9.4 *Net output at 1970 prices ($ million) for cotton, beef and sugar,*
*1960, 1965 and 1970*
(A) Cotton, (B) Beef, (C) Sugar

|      | Costa Rica | | | El Salvador | | | Guatemala | | | Honduras | | | Nicaragua | | |
|------|------|------|------|------|------|------|------|------|------|------|------|------|------|------|------|
|      | (A) | (B) | (C) | (A) | (B) | (C) | (A) | (B) | (C) | (A) | (B) | (C) | (A) | (B) | (C) |
| 1960 | 0.5 | 34.0 | 5.8 | 21.2 | 42.7 | 7.5 | 10.9 | 101.3 | 5.4 | 0.6 | 13.1 | 1.9 | 5.9 | 35.0 | 9.4 |
| 1965 | 2.2 | 40.8 | 9.8 | 42.5 | 45.8 | 11.3 | 49.2 | 115.4 | 3.4 | 3.4 | 25.6 | 3.4 | 45.7 | 47.4 | 5.4 |
| 1970 | 0.1 | 56.8 | 14.9 | 33.5 | 56.1 | 12.3 | 36.3 | 211.7 | 16.2 | 1.1 | 40.6 | 6.9 | 20.3 | 72.7 | 4.4 |

Source: See Methodological Appendix

(see Table 9.4). The techniques used, however, were applied in an irresponsible fashion[67] and throughout the region net output fell sharply in the second half of the decade; the rise and fall of cotton was most dramatic in Nicaragua, although only in Costa Rica did production fall below the levels achieved at the start of the decade.[68]

The cotton cycle in Central America took place against a background of relatively stable international prices. This was not true of coffee, however, where prices at first moved higher on the signing of the International Coffee Agreement (ICA) in 1963,[69] but slipped back in the second half of the decade as supply began to outstrip demand. The introduction of the ICA, however, meant that export earnings were determined by quotas as much as by prices; because of restraint by Brazil and Colombia, the quotas for Central American producers were not unreasonable (although El Salvador complained bitterly)[70] and net output rose substantially throughout the region during the decade.[71] The export of both beef and sugar relied heavily on import quotas provided unilaterally by the United States. Beef quotas were first introduced in 1964 in an effort to protect US domestic interests, but demand grew so rapidly that the quotas expanded steadily. The unit value of both beef and sugar exports rose almost without interruption during the decade,[72] and all republics registered big increases in net output, with the largest proportionate increases in Honduras (see Table 9.4).

The beginning of the 1960s coincided with the introduction of new techniques in banana production (see Chapter 8, pp. 151–3). The new disease-resistant varieties, however, were not introduced everywhere; the United Fruit Co. closed down its Tiquisate division on the Pacific side of Guatemala, with a disastrous impact on the country's banana exports, but the new techniques proved very effective when introduced on the Atlantic coast plantations, and net output rose rapidly after 1965. In Costa Rica and Honduras, both Standard and United Fruit increased their purchases from associate producers[73] and Costa Rica played host to two new banana export companies at the end of the 1960s; within a short time, however, one had been purchased by Del Monte (marking the latter's entry into Costa Rica), while the other was bought by United Fruit.[74]

Table 9.5  *Exports of traditional products as percentage of total extra-regional exports in 1970*

|         | Costa Rica | El Salvador | Guatemala | Honduras | Nicaragua |
|---------|-----------|-------------|-----------|----------|-----------|
| Coffee  | 39.5      | 72.0        | 53.5      | 17.0     | 24.2      |
| Bananas | 36.1      | —           | 7.2       | 47.0     | 0.2       |
| Cotton  | 0.2       | 14.6        | 14.1      | 0.7      | 25.8      |
| Beef    | 9.7       | —           | 6.8       | 6.4      | 20.3      |
| Sugar   | 5.5       | 4.5         | 4.9       | 0.8      | 7.4       |
| Total   | 91.0      | 91.1        | 86.5      | 71.9     | 77.9      |

Source: derived from SIECA, 1981

Emphasis on the five traditional exports was reflected in their high share of extra-regional exports (see Table 9.5). By 1970, these five products accounted for over 70% of the total from all republics and over 90% from Costa Rica and El Salvador; this commodity concentration of exports, although an improvement on the situation a decade earlier,[75] left the region vulnerable to the performance of a particular crop. Such vulnerability accounted for the sharp contrast between the first and second half of the decade. In the first half, net output per person for the four traditional export crops (excluding livestock) rose significantly everywhere except Costa Rica.[76] The decline in cotton production after 1965 was so abrupt, however, that net output per person was stagnant or falling for the same group of products in the second half of the decade, the exception again being Costa Rica where the boom in banana production was more than sufficient to offset the decline in cotton. This lack of dynamism in EXA contributed to the balance of payments crisis at the end of the decade, which in turn marked the end of the hybrid model of development described above.

The intensification of EXA, particularly in the first half of the 1960s, put enormous pressure on the rest of the agricultural sector. The demand for seasonal labour, an essential component in the production of coffee, cotton and sugar, rose throughout the region;[77] permanent migration to the export zones was less important than in the 1950s,[78] but the absorption of new lands into EXA contributed to a rapid rate of rural–urban migration in the 1960s and lowered the relative size of the rural labour force.[79] The pressure on domestic use agriculture (DUA) can be approximated by the net arable land/man ratio;[80] for all republics this ratio showed a significant deterioration during the 1960s, but the expected fall in the output of DUA per person did not occur in the first half of the decade except in El Salvador. Three republics (Guatemala, Honduras, Nicaragua) therefore recorded increases in both DUA and EXA per person,[81] a creditable performance, while in El Salvador (where EXA per person rose) and Costa Rica (where it fell) the two moved in opposite directions.

It was stated in Chapter 8 that the relationship between EXA and DUA is not deterministic, and this is supported by the above evidence. Several factors contributed to the rise in DUA per person everywhere except El Salvador in the first half of the 1960s; they included land reform, price support, credit policies and the growth of rural labour organisations.

Land reform was given high priority under the Alliance for Progress and funds were made available through various international agencies. All Central America, except significantly El Salvador, took advantage of this to revise or introduce legislation regarding land tenure;[82] the results were hardly spectacular, but in every republic where legislation was passed some landless families gained access to land, concentrating on the production of DUA.[83] In almost all cases, the new farms were created by colonisation rather than expropriation, which had the effect of making land reform complementary to EXA rather than competitive.

In 1960, Nicaragua became the last of the republics to create an institute (Instituto Nacional de Comercio Exterior y Interior – INCEI) to intervene in the market for basic grains. Each national institute set prices for basic grains, at which farmers could in theory sell; in practice, however, a shortage of public funds often prevented the institutions from fulfilling this function.[84] The price policy of these institutions could either harm or promote the production of basic grains and they came to represent a potentially powerful instrument of state policy towards the agricultural sector. Credit for DUA in general and basic grains in particular was limited by the preference of banks for lending to EXA. By the middle of the decade, however, the banking system had at least recognised the need for some credit to this sector, although only in Costa Rica with its network of nationalised Juntas Rurales de Crédito did the small farmer have much chance of access to bank lending.

Rural labour organisations in El Salvador, Guatemala and Nicaragua remained extremely weak during the decade, but important changes took place in Costa Rica and Honduras. In Costa Rica, the cooperative movement developed rapidly;[85] this benefited small farmers in DUA, although many cooperatives were also established among coffee growers.[86] The Costa Rican peasantry, subject to land pressure as elsewhere in Central America, also benefited from a relatively benign attitude of the state towards land invasions. The Instituto de Tierras y Colonización, established in 1961, had settled nearly 20,000 families by 1975.[87] In Honduras, the rural labour movement steadily consolidated the gains achieved in the 1954 strike. At the end of the decade, the Federación Nacional de Campesinos de Honduras (FENACH) was formed. Because of its Marxist orientation, FENACH was dissolved after the 1963 military coup and the main peasant organisation became the Asociación Nacional de Campesinos de Honduras (ANACH); the latter had been founded in 1962, as a non-communist rival to FENACH and it came to represent 80,000 peasants.[88] The organisation of the peasantry is one of the features which distinguishes Honduras from the rest of Central America, and the peasant movement proved sufficiently powerful even in the 1960s to extract a number of concessions from a reluctant state. These included a *de facto* acceptance of certain land invasions and a faster programme of land distribution than in some other republics.

Although these four factors contributed to the satisfactory performance of DUA in the first half of the 1960s (except in El Salvador), it was not sustained in the second half despite the lack of dynamism in EXA. Only El Salvador achieved a significant rise in cereals production per person between 1965 and 1970, while falls in Costa Rica, Honduras and Nicaragua were a matter for serious concern. The increases in El Salvador, a complete reversal of the earlier performance, again showed the importance of public policy. From 1965, the price support programme functioned efficiently and the resources devoted to the agricultural extension service increased significantly;[89] credit for basic grains rose from virtually zero to six per cent of the total and yields soared to levels far in excess of the rest of Central America.[90] By contrast, elsewhere in Central America, public policy towards DUA ran out of steam. The easy stage of land reform was soon exhausted and price support programmes began to favour urban consumers over rural producers with a corresponding increase in food imports.[91] Even in Costa Rica, credit to small farmers grew slowly[92] and throughout the region the huge increases in the area devoted to livestock threatened the small-farm sector producing for the home market.[93]

By the end of the decade, the net output of DUA per person had fallen in three republics (Costa Rica, El Salvador and Honduras); it had also fallen sharply since the middle of the decade in Nicaragua and had been stagnant in Guatemala since 1962/3. Public policy had demonstrated its ability to influence the outcome, but policy had been too often inconsistent, timid and poorly conceived. The overall performance of agriculture could not therefore be regarded as satisfactory, despite some successes in EXA. Landlessness had become a major problem by 1970[94] and rural wage policy could not provide a guarantee of fair or even minimum wages for many landless workers;[95] income distribution in agriculture[96] remained very unequal and the standard of nutrition among the rural population was very low.[97] The export products, despite the bias of state policy in their favour, could not prevent the re-emergence of a foreign exchange bottleneck, and the diversification of agriculture was far too limited so that industry became heavily dependent on imported inputs.

## Industrialisation and the CACM

The formation of a regional common market, coupled with exceptionally generous fiscal incentives for industry, could not fail to generate interest among Central American investors. The continuing attraction of investment in EXA, however, and the *de facto* support of the state for traditional export-led growth within the hybrid model of industrialisation implied that a large share of the finance for industrial investment would have to come from external sources. For the period 1962–9 (inclusive) nearly 30% of the total finance required for fixed and working capital in industry came from abroad, with the highest proportion in Nicaragua (37%) and the lowest in El Salvador and Honduras (20%).[98] Within this flow of external finance, direct foreign investment (DFI) accounted for 36%, reinvested earnings for 27% and external loans for the remainder. The extent of foreign participation was not, of course, measured very accurately by these figures, because firms with foreign equity were free to raise funds locally; the most careful study of DFI, however, suggested that by the end of the 1960s 30% of industrial output was produced by firms partially or fully financed by foreign capital,[99] although these same plants accounted for nearly half of all intra-regional industrial exports.

The new DFI changed the pattern of foreign investment in Central America. In 1959, the book value of manufacturing DFI was only $14.6 million; a decade later it was $233 million and its share of total DFI in the region had risen from 3.8% to 30.8% over the same period. The new manufacturing DFI showed a marked preference for Guatemala (over 40% of the increase in book value during the 1960s was located there)[100] and an aversion to Honduras; in some cases the new DFI represented a takeover of existing firms, but this was not the typical pattern.[101]

The role of multinational companies and their subsidiaries in Central America has been frequently studied[102] and there can be no doubt that they came to represent a pressure group of some importance, particularly in Guatemala. It is easy to lose sight of the fact, however, that by 1970 some 70% of industrial production was *not* controlled by foreigners and that this domestic branch of manufacturing had also grown rapidly during the 1960s. The domestic funding for industrial investment between 1962 and 1969 came from financial intermediaries (20%) and depreciation allowances (41%), the balance being provided by a residual category defined to include 're-invested earnings of local investors, local equity and loans from non-institutional sources'.[103] This residual category of finance was very important in El Salvador, Honduras and Costa Rica and represented a means by which small investors (without access to financial intermediaries) could enter the industrial sector.

Although studies of domestic investment in manufacturing are very scarce, the first decade of the CACM was marked by the survival of small firms (many of which used artisan techniques). In 1968, for example, 57% of resident-owned firms in Guatemala, Honduras and Costa Rica employed less than 20 workers and nearly 30% employed less than 10 workers.[104]

The traditional oligarchy also invested in industry, often as junior partners of foreign ventures, but the industrial experiment was not subject to their control and they did not play a leading role. The low industrial profile of the traditional wealth-holders during the 1960s was reflected in the character and importance of the Chambers of Industry in each republic. Although these joined together to form a regional Federation (FECAICA) in the early 1960s, neither this organisation nor its national counterparts exercised much influence; furthermore, foreign-owned subsidiaries were active in all these Chambers, so that the purely domestic industrial interests had no institutional representation.

It is true, of course, that state policy favoured the short-term interests of industrialists (but not the long-term objective of industrialisation) through tariff, exchange rate, fiscal and interest rate policies. This represented a public initiative, however, at the national and regional level to which domestic and foreign entrepreneurs responded positively (rather than the other way round). By the next decade, however, the industrialists in each country had become a more effective pressure group, partly as a result of industry's rapid growth in the 1960s. By merging their interests with the traditional pressure groups (EXA, commerce and finance) on specific issues, the industrialists were able to increase their influence and affect the new growth model favoured in the 1970s (see Chapter 10).

The structure of protection in CACM favoured the production of consumer goods at the expense of all other branches of industry (see above, pp. 183–4). The performance of the industrial sector over the decade reflected this bias. By the end of the decade, the food sector still accounted for 50% of gross industrial output[105] and the 'non-traditional' branches of industry were of very little importance. The dependence of industrial production on consumer goods was greater than might be expected from a comparison with other Latin American countries at similar income levels or at a comparable stage in their development.

The highly unequal distribution of income in Central America (see below, pp. 196–7) was bound to cause problems for an industrial system so heavily dependent on consumer goods production, once the 'easy' stage of ISI was completed. A more immediate problem, however, already visible in the 1960s, was the dependence of industry on imported inputs. This dependence was a direct consequence of the fact that tariff policy discriminated against the production of intermediate and capital goods, so that much of the demand for these commodities had to be met from outside the region. The extent of the problem by the end of the decade can be seen very clearly in Table 9.6. Although nearly one-quarter of industry's raw material requirements were met by the CACM, almost 100% of capital goods imports came from outside the region. Extra-regional imports for industry in 1970 accointed for nearly 60% of all extra-regional imports and used up nearly

Table 9.6 *Import intensity of industry in Central America in 1970 ($ million)*

|  | Costa Rica | El Salvador | Guatemala | Honduras | Nicaragua |
|---|---|---|---|---|---|
| (1) Total imports of raw materials for industry | 111.3 | 80.8 | 107.8 | 75.0 | 68.1 |
| (2) Percentage of (1) from outside CACM | 76.9 | 74.3 | 76.1 | 76.2 | 76.2 |
| (3) Total imports of capital goods for industry | 51.5 | 27.1 | 43.9 | 32.3 | 32.6 |
| (4) Percentage of (3) from outside CACM | 98.6 | 95.0 | 97.7 | 96.5 | 96.6 |
| (5) Extra-regional imports for industry as percentage of (a) total extra-regional imports | 55.0 | 56.0 | 57.0 | 53.3 | 56.1 |
| (b) Total extra-regional exports | 73.7 | 55.4 | 66.5 | 58.3 | 62.9 |

Source: derived from SIECA, 1981

two-thirds of earnings from extra-regional exports (almost none of which were industrial).

The demand for raw materials for industry was clearly linked to the current level of production, but the demand for capital goods was influenced by the exceedingly generous terms offered (e.g., accelerated depreciation allowances) under the system of fiscal incentives. Capital goods imports were therefore far in excess of what was required by short-term production targets and by the end of the decade capacity utilisation was less than 50% in many sectors.[106]

The capital-intensive bias of the 'rules of the game' under the CACM were responsible for the relatively small number of jobs whose creation could be attributed specifically to the formation of the CACM. One study estimated the total number of new manufacturing jobs created annually by the CACM between 1958 and 1968 at 3,000;[107] total employment, however, in manufacturing rose by nearly 200,000 between the beginning of the 1960s and 1970s, i.e., at an annual rate of some 20,000. The impact of the formationm of the CACM on job creation was therefore relatively minor, although employment in manufacturing performed reasonably well;

this paradox can only be understood by reference to the survival of the small-scale (often artisan) sector which continued to employ the bulk of the manufacturing labour force in the 1960s, was labour-intensive and was not as dependent on the CACM as the large-scale, capital-intensive firms. This symbiotic relationship between the small- and large-scale manufacturing sectors was not repeated in the 1970s (see Chapter 10); in the 1960s, the formation of large-scale industry was influenced by the opening up of the regional market. The growth of these firms therefore took place at the expense of extra-regional imports of consumer goods and was not at the expense of the small-scale industrial sector serving the national market; the latter, on the other hand, received a stimulus from the urbanisation associated with the growth of large-scale industry and the formation of the CACM.[108]

Given the incentives available, the strong participation of foreign firms, the additional processing of agricultural goods implied by the intensification of EXA and external support for infrastructure of direct benefit to industry, it was not surprising that the growth of manufacturing value added was rapid (see Table A.8). Two deviations from the overall trend, however, stood out; the first was the poor performance of Honduras in the first quinquennium and the marked deceleration in the rate of growth in El Salvador in the second. Honduras, as the poorest country with the least developed infrastructure, had failed to attract foreign investment into manufacturing on the same scale as other members of CACM. Honduran industrialists were unable to resist the penetration of their market by Salvadorean firms in particular, but by 1966 an unofficial boycott of Salvadorean goods had begun[109] and Honduran industry began to grow more rapidly. The same boycott contributed to the deceleration of industrial growth in El Salvador, but Salvadorean industrialists were also affected by the marked increase in trade unionism, urban labour unrest and the number of strikes after 1966 in their own country.[110]

After making due allowance for these deviations, it is reasonable to conclude that the response of industrialists during the 1960s to the incentives on offer was positive. It was not the fault of the industrialists that these incentives were excessive, produced a distorted allocation of resources and did not add up to a coherent growth model; that was a failure of state policy, over which the industrial pressure groups had little control in the 1960s, although this began to change in the next decade. Industrialists had shown in Central America, as elsewhere in Latin America, rational behaviour in the face of price signals, but the result was a distorted form of industrialisation: very capital-intensive, biassed towards consumer goods, heavily dependent on imports and offering little opportunity of backward linkages because of the preference built into the system for assembly of imported components over the manufacture and processing of local raw materials.

## Crisis in the hybrid model

The hybrid model outlined earlier (see above, pp. 185–90), under which industrialisation was to be grafted on to the traditional model of export-led growth, required for its successful operation balanced industrial growth among the CACM members and a steady rise in extra-regional exports. It was the failure to achieve these two goals, rather than the weakness of DUA, which led to the collapse of the hybrid model at the end of the 1960s.

Balanced industrial growth was needed to prevent trade diversion becoming unduly onerous for the weaker members of the CACM. Intra-regional exports grew rapidly, reaching 26% of total exports by 1970, although this concealed wide differences in the importance of intra-regional trade among the five republics.[111] More serious, however, was the tendency towards structural imbalances in intra-regional trade between the member countries. Nicaragua ran a deficit in every year from 1961 to 1970 and Honduras in every year from 1965 to 1970.[112] The Honduran deficit was particularly disturbing, because it increased in size every year after 1964; in the decade after the formation of the CACM, the accumulated Honduran deficit with CACM partners reached $85.4 million, virtually all of which was settled bilaterally in dollars. The accumulated Nicaraguan deficit was a similar amount, but it declined in size every year after 1967 and most of it was settled in dollars during the period when Nicaragua's extra-regional exports grew very rapidly.

Honduran dissatisfaction with the workings of the CACM was mollified to some extent by the willingness of the other countries not to apply the harmonisation of fiscal incentives to Honduras (see above, pp. 179–80). Such accommodation could do nothing, however, to resolve the plight of the estimated 150,000 Salvadoreans in Honduras, many of whom had migrated in the 1960s in response to the intensification of EXA in El Salvador.[113] The cowardly decision of the López Arellano administration in Honduras to implement a land reform programme at the expense of the Salvadoreans provoked a deterioration in relations between the two countries, the expulsion of the migrants in June 1969 and a brief, but bloody war in the following month, which left as its balance 2,000 dead and the repatriation of more than 100,000 Salvadoreans.

Although Honduras broke diplomatic and commercial relations with El Salvador and blocked Salvadorean exports in transit to the southern republics, she did not at first leave the CACM. This decision was taken only in December 1970, after the other republics (excluding El Salvador) had failed to reach agreement on a reform package proposed by Honduras.[114] On leaving the CACM, Honduras immediately signed bilateral trade treaties with Costa Rica, Guatemala and Nicaragua, which gave her duty-free access to those markets, but allowed her to charge tariffs on intra-regional imports.

She therefore became the first of the five republics to reject the hybrid model of industrialisation and her departure marked the end of the integration experiment. This was not widely realised at the time, because the exit of Honduras was only a symptom of the malaise of the CACM rather than the cause of it.

A second weakness in the hybrid model was the performance of extra-regional exports. In the first half of the decade, the growth of exports was very satisfactory; the major stimulus was the boom in cotton, but several republics also recorded favourable movements in the net barter terms of trade, and international reserves recovered from the low levels at the end of the 1950s. Indeed, export performance was so satisfactory that both Costa Rica and Nicaragua were able to agree to Article VIII of the IMF's Articles of Agreement (under which a country undertakes to perform the obligations of currency convertibility).[115] In the second half of the decade, however, it proved much more difficult to sustain exports. Coffee prices drifted lower (until the sharp rise in 1970) and cotton exports were adversely affected by domestic production problems. El Salvador, Guatemala and Nicaragua made frequent drawings from the IMF under the ordinary credit tranche, while Costa Rica was spared this humiliation only as a result of the boom in banana exports after 1965. The four northern republics were obliged to introduce various restrictions on imports, which were so severe in the case of El Salvador that import growth from 1965 to 1970 was only 6.5% even in nominal terms.

In an earlier period of its economic history, Central American import restraint would have implied cuts or postponement of purchases of foreign consumer goods with little damage to the production structure. Under the CACM, however, extra-regional imports came to be dominated by interme-diate and capital goods so that import restraint had more damaging conse-quences (this was one of the reasons for the slowdown in Salvadorean growth in the second half of the 1960s). Thus, the hybrid model increased rather than decreased the dependence of the economy on the external sector in general and EXA in particular.

The hybrid model also had a regressive impact on income distribution. The most careful study of wage profiles in Central America (see Table 9.7) suggested that between 1960 and 1971 the share of wages in national income declined in all republics except Nicaragua.[116] The most serious deterioration, however, took place in agriculture rather than industry, where the 'land-scarce' republics (Costa Rica, El Salvador and Guatemala) experienced a shift towards rental income as a consequence of export intensification.[117]

The decline in the wage share outside Nicaragua implied a deterioration in the size distribution of income; only Costa Rica and El Salvador were able to provide time-series evidence and in both countries the income share received by the bottom 10% fell, although there was a small increase in

Table 9.7 *Income distribution: wage shares (%), 1960 and 1971*

| | Costa Rica | | El Salvador | | Guatemala | | Honduras | | Nicaragua | |
|---|---|---|---|---|---|---|---|---|---|---|
| | 1960 | 1971 | 1960 | 1971 | 1960 | 1971 | 1960 | 1971 | 1960 | 1971 |
| Agriculture | 55.4 | 45.5 | NA | NA | 42.7 | 34.9 | NA | NA | 63.4 | 75.8 |
| Industry | 33.8 | 39.5 | 58.0 | 61.0 | 57.9 | 56.1 | 57.9 | 45.2 | 63.2 | 61.0 |
| National | 50.2 | 49.2 | 42.6 | 41.2 | 40.7 | 37.4 | 43.8 | 41.3 | 49.3 | 55.1 |

Source: Reynolds, 1978

the share of the bottom 50%.[118] Income distribution statistics are notoriously difficult to collect and even more difficult to interpret. The evidence for Central America, however, does not suggest that the hybrid model had made much impact on broadening the range of social classes who might be considered potential purchasers of consumer goods produced in the CACM. This is hardly surprising, but it helps to account for the reluctance of industrialists to throw their weight behind schemes to revive the CACM in the 1970s (see Chapter 10).

Many of those who helped to form the CACM and the hybrid model of industrialisation recognised that it would not reduce external dependence and that it could even increase the importance of traditional exports. These same *tecnicos*, however, justified the experiment not merely in terms of its ability to promote industrialisation without alienating the traditional pressure groups, but also because of its presumed impact on social and political modernisation.

The protagonists of political modernisation received a setback in the early 1960s, when the military intervened in El Salvador (January 1961), Guatemala (March 1963) and Honduras (October 1963). In each case, the motive for intervention was the fear by the traditional right and their military allies that a radical candidate might win the upcoming presidential elections.[119] In Nicaragua, the path towards political modernisation was blocked by the Somoza dynasty, which ruled through proxies from 1963[120] until Anastasio Somoza Debayle (brother of Luis Somza who died in 1967) was 'elected' president in February 1967.

Despite the lack of progress towards formal democracy outside Costa Rica, the pressures in favour of social and political modernisation identified by the *tecnicos* did indeed make themselves apparent. These pressures produced changes in the political party system, the labour movement and social security programmes. The increasing urbanisation associated with the formation of the CACM contributed to the growth of new political parties, whose support was drawn above all from the urban middle and working classes. The classic example was the Christian Democrat (CD) party in El Salvador, which won the election for mayor of San Salvador in 1964,[121] but CD successes were echoed in Guatemala, and even in Nicaragua the Social Christian Party, formed in 1957, was able to make some headway in the 1967 elections by forming an alliance with the older Independent Liberal Party. These CD parties formed the Christian Democratic Union of Central America in the 1960s, which was strengthened by the formation of a CD party in Honduras in the early 1970s, and they represented a centrist alternative which gave many voters (particularly in El Salvador) the expectation of peaceful political modernisation.

No CD party was formed in Costa Rica, but Dr Rafael Angel Calderón Guardia (the original standard-bearer of CD ideology in Central America) fought the 1962 elections as the presidential candidate of his Republican Party. His defeat, and that of Otilio Ulate, at the hands of the PLN's Francisco Orlich marked the end of *Calderonismo*, but social Christian ideas were strongly entrenched in both the PLN and the PUN, the latter narrowly winning the 1966 presidential elections through its candidate Professor José Joaquín Trejos Fernández.

The trade union movement also made some progress in the first decade of the CACM. Two countries (Costa Rica and Honduras) stood out from the rest; by 1973, nearly 11% of the labour force in Costa Rica was in trade unions while in Honduras the figure was nearly 9%.[122] In Honduras, however, nearly two-thirds of these workers were in agriculture, while in Costa Rica most were in the tertiary sector (including public administration).[123] In Guatemala and Nicaragua, trade unionism affected a negligible proportion of the labour force and the share in Nicaragua fell from 4.8% in 1969 to 2.0% in 1973. El Salvador, on the other hand, experienced a significant increase in the number of trade unions (nearly all urban) and their affiliates after 1966, although the proportion of the labour force affected was only 5% by the end of the decade.[124]

While trade union repression was widespread in Guatemala and Nicaragua, this did not rule out the spread of social security programmes. In Guatemala, 27% of the labour force was covered by the end of the decade, while in Nicaragua the proportion grew rapidly in the 1960s to cover 16% of the labour force by 1971.[125] Fiscal conservatism inhibited the spread of social security programmes even among urban workers in El Salvador and Honduras, but no such considerations restrained their growth in Costa Rica. The Echandi administration passed a law in 1961 promising to extend social security to all workers within ten years, but the revenue required to make this possible was never made available. The proportion of workers covered did indeed rise and with their families nearly 50% of the population benefited from social security by the end of the decade, but earmarked taxes covered only 22% of social security expenditure by the end of the decade compared with 81% in 1960 so that the cumulative state deficit grew from ¢3.8 million colones in 1960 to ¢287.5 million in 1970.[126]

The changes in political parties, trade unions and social security programmes benefited the urban population disproportionately. The rural population was seriously neglected and the extension of minimum wage laws to farm workers in El Salvador and Nicaragua was small compensation. The counter-insurgency programme in Guatemala during the 1960s weighed heavily against efforts at social or political modernisation in the countryside[127] and the formation of ORDEN in 1968 was hardly conducive to similar efforts in El Salvador.[128] The position in Costa Rica and Honduras, however, again formed a contrast. The development of the cooperative movement, backed by the Banco Nacional, took root in Costa Rica in the 1960s and the rural sector was the first to benefit from the extension of the social security programme in the 1960s. In Honduras, the rural labour movement developed strongly before the military coup of 1963, and the new López Arellano administration recognised the labour movement in general as one of the two 'new forces' in Honduran politics (the other being the military). The support which this administration received from labour during the war with El Salvador was one of the reasons for the greater political space enjoyed by the rural labour movement in Honduras compared with its counterparts elsewhere.

# 10

## External shocks and the challenge to the social order, 1970–9

The beginning of the 1970s coincided with a series of external shocks to Central America, not all of which were unfavourable; world commodity prices rose, increasing profitability in export agriculture (EXA), while the availability of new technologies (the Green Revolution) encouraged some large-scale farmers to try their hand at producing crops for the home market. The result was a squeeze on small-scale farmers and an acceleration of the marginalisation of the peasantry.

The decline of the CACM at the end of the 1960s proved irreversible despite the best efforts of the technocrats, and new industrial strategies began to emerge involving a partnership between the state and the private sector. At the same time, industry became subject to a profit squeeze, as the cost of inputs (mainly determined by world prices) rose faster than output prices. Industrial production began to be concentrated in large units, as firms looked to cut costs, and the artisan sector suffered a severe squeeze. Thus, in both agriculture and industry the shift towards proletarianisation of the labour force accelerated.

The squeeze on industrial profits was caused fundamentally by the sharp rise in world prices in the early 1970s, further aggravated by the oil crisis in 1973–4. Central American republics, among the most 'open' economies in the world, found themselves importing inflation, which reached levels unheard of for over two decades. A fiscal crisis ensued, provoking a policy of entrenchment in the more conservative republics and a cutback in social expenditure; only in Nicaragua did the embattled Somoza régime rely on external debt to fund a large central government deficit, but in all republics decentralised semi-autonomous institutions (e.g., public utilities) contracted external debt rapidly under seemingly favourable terms.

The acceleration of inflation coincided with a qualitative change in the nature of employers' organisations. Before the 1970s, the major private sector groups were associated with export agriculture; although the private sector in commerce, finance and industry had all established pressure groups, they were weak by comparison with those representing export agriculture and there was little common ground established between the private sector groups in each republic. In the 1970s, however, the pressure groups combined to form powerful associations capable of articulating their class as well as sectoral interests and confident of their ability to influence public policy in their favour. (Only in Nicaragua, where the Somoza family branched out into new economic activities after 1972 and broke the agreement on 'fair' competition between the rival capitalist groups, did the private sector fail to achieve institutional unity.) Thus, the capitalist class was in general well placed to influence in their own favour the region's adjustment to the upheavals in the world economy during the 1970s.

By contrast, the impact of rising inflation on labour groups – in a region where most of the workers' movements had not developed defence mechanisms – had a profound social impact. Real wages throughout Central America initially declined, but from the middle of the decade a sharp dichotomy appeared between the fortunes of the labour movement in Costa Rica and Honduras, on the one hand, and in the rest of Central America on the other. In the former republics, the new spirit of militancy shown by the labour movement was accommodated by the state with imaginative (if at times inconsistent) policies; elsewhere, the stirrings in the labour movement were met with almost blanket hostility.

This dichotomy had an important bearing on the drift towards civil war in El Salvador, Guatemala and Nicaragua, although other factors were also relevant. The collapse of the Somoza régime in July 1979 in Nicaragua, followed within a few months by the fall of General Romero in El Salvador, also presented the United States with an unprecedented challenge to its hegemony in the region and marked the end of the unwritten pact under which reactionary régimes had been given a free hand internally in return for unconditional support for US foreign policy postures.

### Agriculture and the marginalisation of the peasantry

The decline of the CACM at the end of the 1960s coincided with the end of the 'easy' stage of import-substituting industrialisation (ISI). By the close of the decade, the structure of extra-regional imports had shifted irreversibly towards intermediate and capital goods that could be replaced on a regional basis only; projects involving regional ISI, however, required a high degree of cooperation among the member states which was manifestly absent by 1970. Thus, ISI was not likely to be a reliable way of dealing with balance of payments (BOP) pressures in the 1970s.

It was unfortunate that the weakness of the CACM at the end of the 1960s should have been followed by an acceleration of world inflation at the start of the 1970s. The import price index began to rise sharply long before the first (1973–4) oil shock, bringing with it an acceleration of inflation (see Table 10.1), and the BOP came under pressure. Because of the

Table 10.1 *Annual average inflation rates (%) in Central America, 1950–79*

|           | Costa Rica | El Salvador | Guatemala | Honduras | Nicaragua |
|-----------|-----------|-------------|-----------|----------|-----------|
| 1950–60   | 1.8       | 3.0         | 0.9       | 2.0[1]   | 4.9       |
| 1960–70   | 2.0       | 0.8         | 0.7       | 2.2      | 1.9       |
| 1970–1    | 3.0       | 0.5         | −0.5      | 2.3      | 1.6       |
| 1971–2    | 4.6       | 1.5         | 0.6       | 5.3      | 1.1       |
| 1972–3    | 15.3      | 6.4         | 13.6      | 4.5      | 20.1      |
| 1973–4    | 30.1      | 16.9        | 16.6      | 13.4     | 23.3      |
| 1974–5    | 17.4      | 19.2        | 13.1      | 6.4      | 2.7       |
| 1975–6    | 3.5       | 7.0         | 10.7      | 4.8      | 2.8       |
| 1976–7    | 4.2       | 11.9        | 12.6      | 8.4      | 11.4      |
| 1977–8    | 6.0       | 13.2        | 7.9       | 6.2      | 4.6       |
| 1978–9    | 9.2       | 15.9        | 11.5      | 12.5     | 48.1      |

Source: World Bank, *World Tables*, Vol. 1 (third edition), 1984
[1] Derived from IMF, *International Financial Statistics Yearbook*, 1984

problems of saving foreign exchange through ISI, policy was concentrated on increasing earnings through extra-regional exports. Inevitably, because of their importance in the total, this meant heavy reliance on traditional agricultural exports; thus, at a time when long-run economic and social logic suggested a decline in the relative importance of agriculture for export (EXA), short-run policies were pushing each republic in the opposite direction.

Policy emphasis on EXA was encouraged by the movements in world prices for traditional exports. From 1971 to 1973, the overheating of the world economy pushed up commodity prices, leaving Central America's net barter terms of trade unchanged.[1] Inevitably, the sharp rise in oil prices after October 1973 produced a deterioration, but the explosion in coffee prices from 1975 (following the Brazilian frost) was reflected in an improvement in the terms of trade which did not fall back to their 1970 level until 1979.

Price increases for EXA were therefore sufficient on their own to absorb most of the first oil shock, but policy-makers could not have known this and they concentrated on measures to increase volumes. Their task was made easier by relatively high price elasticities of supply (both short- and long-run) for traditional exports[2] and by a shift in the internal terms of trade away from industry towards EXA (see next section). In addition, changes in world markets in the early 1970s reduced the importance of quotas for some products and thus removed an important constraint on increasing supply.

The absence of quota restraints, following the demise of the International Coffee Agreement (ICA),[3] provided an excellent opportunity for Central

American producers to increase exports; this was initially qualified by the rise in costs associated with the first oil crisis, which implied higher prices for fertilisers, insecticides, etc., and later by the discovery of coffee rust in Nicaragua, which spread slowly to other countries and required expensive regional measures to control and eradicate.[4] By the end of the 1970s, however, net output in coffee had doubled in Honduras, risen by 62% in Nicaragua and by 25% in Guatemala; in Costa Rica and El Salvador net output rose rapidly at first, but was plagued by technical difficulties after 1974/5 with yields falling sharply in El Salvador.[5]

The volume of banana exports, although controlled by the multinationals, also expanded significantly in the early 1970s. Standard Fruit re-entered Nicaragua, buying from independent producers, and exports grew rapidly after 1972; Del Monte purchased UFCO's plantations in Guatemala in the same year[6] and the programme of associate producers grew in importance with substantial state support in all republics. By 1973, net output in the four exporting countries was 32% higher than in 1970. In 1974, however, the expansion of the banana industry and the almost cordial relationship between multinationals and host governments went abruptly into reverse; the reason was the announcement in March of that year by the heads of state of Panama, Costa Rica and Honduras that their governments would impose a tax of one US dollar (equivalent to 50% of the f.o.b. price) on each box of bananas exported. The precipitate announcement caused a rift with Ecuador, the world's largest exporter, but Guatemala and Colombia were persuaded to join in discussions with the other three countries which ended in the formation of the Unión de Países Exportadores de Banano (UPEB) in September.[7]

The inspiration behind UPEB was the success of the Organisation of Petroleum Exporting Countries (OPEC) in raising world oil prices, but other factors were also at work. Associate producers, who were large-scale farmers and had formed politically influental cooperatives, sold their bananas to the multinationals under fixed prices on long-term contracts. The acceleration of their input costs in the early 1970s squeezed their profit margins, forcing them to seek a revision of their contracts and a rise in the prices agreed with the fruit companies.

Initially, the fruit companies were unimpressed by the arguments in favour of a fifty-fold increase in the banana tax and they fought its introduction with a ferocity not seen since the late 1940s. In this they had some success, but the discovery in 1975 that United Brands (formerly UFCO) had bribed the President of Honduras (leading to his resignation and the suicide of United Brands' chairman) turned public opinion strongly against the multinationals and by 1976 the new banana tax was in force among the UPEB members. The tax varied from 0.35 dollars per box in Honduras to 0.45 in Guatemala[8] and was therefore lower than originally intended, but it represented a huge rise on previous revenues from bananas and it increased the retained value from banana exports whose c.i.f. price almost doubled between 1973 and 1974.[9] The introduction of the new banana tax represented a victory for the host governments over the multinationals, but like all such victories it was bought at a price. Banana exports, already hurt by damage to plantations in 1974 by Hurricane Fifi,[10] slumped and the main beneficiaries were countries outside UPEB where the banana tax did not apply. The value of exports, however, rose steadily after 1974 in response to much higher world prices.

Sugar prices, which had been rising rapidly since 1970, soared to their all-time peak in 1974; at the end of the same year, the US Sugar Act expired[11] and US imports ceased to be subject to quotas. Within a few years, protectionist sentiment in the USA had gained the upper hand, but in the meantime Central America was well placed to take advantage of the opportunities; net output doubled in three republics in the 1970s (El Salvador, Guatemala, Honduras) and rose substantially elsewhere. With the exception of Guatemala, yields increased sharply so that the increase in area harvested was much less than the rise in production.

The opposite was true of cotton production, which recovered quickly from its demise in the second half of the 1960s. Stimulated by a three-fold increase in world prices in the 1970s, the net output from cotton trebled in Guatemala and Honduras, doubled in Nicaragua and rose 40% in El Salvador, with Costa Rica reviving production after 1971 with state support.[12] Most of the increase, however, came from the area harvested, reversing the gains made by basic grains in the late 1960s, and yields declined significantly in El Salvador and Nicaragua after 1972.[13]

Although still subject to export quotas in the US market, cattle production was stimulated by higher world prices and the opening of non-traditional export markets (e.g., Japan).[14] As a consequence, the net output from livestock in the 1970s rose by two-thirds in El Salvador and by more than 50% in Guatemala. The increases elsewhere were more modest, although in Costa Rica this did not prevent a further erosion in the forest cover as the land frontier was sacrificed for the development of the cattle industry.

While some success was achieved in export diversification, notably cardamom in Guatemala[15] and African palm oil in Costa Rica,[16] the pre-eminence of the five traditional exports was not disturbed; their contribution to Central America's extra-regional exports in 1979 (82%) was virtually the same as it had been in 1970 (84%), while their contribution to total exports (including the CACM) actually increased.[17] Even at constant prices the performance of these five products was remarkable; net output per person rose everywhere except Honduras between 1970 and 1978 (the last 'normal' year) despite the rapid population growth rate.[18] The production of EXA therefore intensified in the 1970s, but the major stimulus was higher world prices. State policies towards EXA were more concerned with capturing a higher share of the economic rent through taxation than with increasing production, although government support for the introduction of new export crops was important. The state was therefore in principle free to devote some of its limited resources towards encouraging domestic use agriculture (DUA), which had come under pressure from a number of different directions.

Some of this pressure is familiar territory; the intensification of EXA, cet. par., reduced land available for DUA (most notably in the case of cotton) and attracted seasonal labour in large quantities as well as some permanent labour; in addition, high world prices for EXA pushed up land rents for all agricultural tenants and even DUA was not immune to cost pressures from increased prices for intermediate inputs. Furthermore, the closure of trade between El Salvador and Honduras lost an export market in basic grains for the latter and rendered import substitution in agriculture (ISA) even more urgent for the former. Finally the high population growth rates, stimulated by the decline in infant mortality,[19] increased the number of young dependents requiring access to food at a disproportionately rapid rate.

The precarious nature of DUA in the 1970s was emphasised by the growing number of land invasions throughout Central America,[20] which forced the problem to the attention of the authorities; all responded, although in different ways, and the results were very uneven. Only Costa Rica achieved a significant increase in food security (see below) and throughout the region policy towards DUA concentrated on increasing production – if necessary, through the large-scale farm sector. The precarious nature of DUA was most apparent in El Salvador, where the absence of a land frontier presented the authorities with the starkest of choices: application of the new technology (Green Revolution) in favour of medium- to large-scale farmers in an effort to increase yields or land redistribution to the probable detriment of EXA.

Land reform had been a taboo subject in El Salvador since the peasant uprising of 1932, but the humiliation in the war with Honduras and the return of the Salvadorean migrants compelled the government to open the question for debate in 1970.[21] Land reform legislation was finally passed in 1975 with the first district for its application designated in 1976.[22] Coffee estates were explicitly excluded from any redistributive measures, but private sector opposition was so violent that the government soon abandoned the legislation.[23]

The Salvadorean strategy for DUA therefore reverted to more conventional 'modernisation' policies. The Instituto Regulador de Abastecimientos (IRA) was reorganised in 1972 with increased purchase and storage capacity, and a state Agricultural Development Bank was formed in 1973; together with the Central Bank and the private commercial banks, this enabled the state to channel an increasing volume of credit towards basic grains production,

Table 10.2  *Basic grains*[1] *net output per person (1970 dollars), 1970–9*

|        | Costa Rica | El Salvador | Guatemala | Honduras | Nicaragua |
|--------|------------|-------------|-----------|----------|-----------|
| 1970   | 9.7        | 18.0        | 16.2      | 15.7     | 21.0      |
| 1971   | 10.1       | 18.6        | 16.7      | 17.2     | 20.1      |
| 1972   | 11.2       | 12.7        | 16.7      | 16.8     | 24.8      |
| 1973   | 11.8       | 17.8        | 16.4      | 15.0     | 26.8      |
| 1974   | 9.8        | 15.0        | 15.6      | 15.7     | 29.3      |
| 1975   | 14.7       | 18.9        | 17.4      | 14.7     | 21.8      |
| 1976   | 15.7       | 14.7        | 15.5      | 15.3     | 19.9      |
| 1977   | 16.6       | 14.7        | 15.1      | 14.3     | 25.6      |
| 1978   | 16.6       | 18.7        | 16.0      | 15.3     | 18.2      |
| 1979   | 17.5       | 19.1        | 16.7      | 13.8     | 19.9      |

Source: See Methodological Appendix
[1] Defined as maize, beans, rice and sorghum for El Salvador, Honduras and Nicaragua. Defined as maize, beans and rice for Costa Rica and Guatemala

with the major beneficiaries being large- and medium-size farms. Finally, two large-scale public sector irrigation projects were launched in the 1970s which stimulated the production of DUA, but concentrated the benefits in the hands of large-scale farms.[24]

Other republics did not face such a stark choice in their policies towards DUA, but the results were nonetheless similar to the Salvadorean case. Guatemala, for example, decreed in 1970 the formation of an agricultural development zone in the previously undeveloped Franja Transversal del Norte,[25] creating at the same time a state agricultural development bank and signing a $13 million loan with USAID for the support of small farmers. A substantial volume of credit was channelled towards basic grain production in the 1970s and yields rose rapidly, but by the end of the decade it was clear that the increment in production had been achieved mainly at the expense of small farmers whose share of total output declined,[26] and net output per person was stagnant (see Table 10.2).

Like Guatemala, Costa Rica was able to secure substantial increases in yields, but in her case *per caput* net output of basic grains also rose rapidly (see Table 10.2); the two *Liberacionista* governments in power from 1970 to 1978 adopted a series of programmes towards agriculture, which made available the complementary inputs required to obtain the most from the new high-yield varieties of seeds. Honduras and Nicaragua, on the other hand, suffered a serious reverse in *per caput* basic grain production; Honduras in particular was unable to recover from the loss of agricultural export markets in El Salvador (she also suffered from droughts) and by 1975 had become a net importer of basic grains,[27] while Nicaragua's efforts to stimulate basic grain output in the wake of huge increases in EXA were wholly inadequate.[28]

The performance of DUA, heavily influenced by basic grain production, was therefore unsatisfactory outside Costa Rica. Production *per caput* declined in Honduras and Nicaragua, remaining unchanged in El Salvador until after 1977. Only in Costa Rica did basic grain production (the most important component of DUA) increase significantly on a *per caput* basis, while the share of DUA in total agricultural value added (even at constant prices) also declined everywhere except Costa Rica. This relative decline of DUA outside Costa Rica was a serious matter, but it was made even worse by the shift within DUA in favour of production by the larger farms. This is a frequently observed consequence of the application of the Green Revolution, and it had the effect in Central America (even in Costa Rica) of accelerating the marginalisation of the peasantry; by the end of the decade, some 40% of the rural labour force in El Salvador and Nicaragua was estimated to be without access to land,[29] while Costa Rica and Guatemala had both experienced a sharp increase in the inequality of land distribution.[30] Only in Honduras, where the coffee boom had benefited small farmers and where land invasions often went unchallenged (see below, pp. 218–24), had agricultural development brought a reduction in the concentration of land holdings.[31]

## The decline of CACM and industrial strategy

High world commodity prices during most of the 1970s were sufficient to stave off BOP pressures, but the intensification of EXA was neither a desirable nor feasible long-term strategy. Each government, with increasingly influential pressure from private industrialists, recognised the need for industrial promotion and some sort of industrial strategy; the main problem was to choose the right strategy and find the resources to underpin it. The Central American Common Market (CACM) seemed at first to be the obvious candidate, despite the withdrawal of Honduras in late 1970, and the region's governments empowered SIECA in 1971 to consider a new formula for the CACM appropriate to the 1970s. SIECA presented its proposal for a Central American Economic Community in October 1972; it was approved in principle by the ministers of finance and economy together with Central Bank presidents in December 1972 and a Comité de Alto Nivel (CAN) was set up to construct a draft treaty.

The technocrats were therefore in broad agreement on the restructuring of CACM; the SIECA proposal would have made CACM into a real common market with new institutions (such as a Council of Ministers and a Permanent Committee) similar to those in the European Economic Community (EEC) and with the harmonisation of tariff, industrial, agricultural, tax and investment policy.[32] As such, it would have imposed certain restrictions on the private sector's freedom of manoeuvre and the state's national sovereignty. As a consequence, the private sector and the non-technocratic branches of the state resisted the SIECA proposal. The CAN's draft treaty was not presented until March 1976, when it met with considerable opposition from business groups; discussions continued, but by 1978 the tension created within Central America by the struggle for power in Nicaragua effectively ruled out any possibility of a radical restructuring of the CACM.[33]

The ground rules for the CACM therefore remained as they had been in the 1960s. This provided established industries with a regional market, but it could not sustain the growth of intra-regional trade observed in the 1960s; the CACM share of Central America's total exports declined from the 1970 peak of 26.1% to 20.3% in 1979, with each republic recording a declining share over the same period,[34] although the total value of trade expanded in all years except 1971.[35] The decline of the CACM in the 1970s was therefore only relative, but this was sufficient to imply the need for alternative industrial strategies. Two separate strands can be identified; first, there was a recognition by the state that the next generation of industrial projects would require new sources of finance and, secondly, a move was made in the direction of promoting exports outside the CACM. The first strategy allowed for the possibility of new developments in mining as well as ISI in intermediate and capital goods at the national or regional level, while the second was a response to the new orthodoxy regarding industrialisation in developing countries.

The 'financial strategy' was pursued with some vigour in Costa Rica, Guatemala and Honduras, less so in El Salvador and Nicaragua.[36] The former republics created state corporations for channelling finance to new industries with a majority local shareholding; in the Costa Rican case, the Corporación Costarricense de Desarrollo (CODESA) frequently took an equity stake, giving the state for the first time an important share of industrial output.[37] The Corporación Financiera Nacional (CORFINA) in Guatemala and the Corporación Nacional de Inversiones (CONADI) in Honduras preferred loans to equity, but in all three republics the state became closely and actively involved with the private sector in new projects.[38] The traditional sources of funding for industry continued to be commercial banks and private *financieras*. All republics increased the share of commercial bank lending going to industry in the 1970s, but Costa Rica and Guatemala stand out as the republics with the highest increase;[39] by contrast, El Salvador remained the republic with the lowest ratio of commercial bank credit devoted to industry and with total lending in the mid-1970s lower even than in industrially backward Honduras.[40] Thus, the shift of scarce financial resources towards industry, implying painful adjustments elsewhere, was not given the same priority in all republics.

The same imbalance between words and deeds can be observed in the case of export promotion. Four republics (the exception is Costa Rica) set up industrial free zones in the 1970s for promoting exports outside CACM, but the incentives offered in support of these activities were modest. Costa Rica, on the other hand, on the basis of its 1972 export promotion law, steadily increased the incentives available for such activities (which could be located anywhere); a special fund was set up to promote non-traditional exports, and tax payment certificates (CATs), equivalent to 10% of f.o.b. value, were made available for such goods.[41]

The beginning of the 1970s was a difficult time for industry. Heavy reliance on imported inputs made manufacturing firms very vulnerable to cost pressures emanating from the acceleration of world inflation,[42] while price increases had to be restrained for two reasons: first, several republics imposed price controls in 1974 following the rise in oil prices and, secondly, continuing heavy reliance on specific tariffs meant that local prices had to be kept below dollar price rises in order to remain competitive with imports.[43]

This squeeze on industrial profits[44] had very serious consequences for Central America. In the first place, it reduced the opportunities for funding investment through self-finance and made access to outside sources of finance much more important; those states (Costa Rica, Guatemala), where the development of industrial finance was taken most seriously, were clearly in the strongest position to rise to the challenge presented by the profit squeeze. In the second place, the profit squeeze increased the vulnerability of the small-scale industrial sector, which had survived the previous decade with some success. These small firms were also dependent on imported inputs, but lacked the resources or access to outside finance to ensure their survival. In all republics, the process of industrial concentration accelerated rapidly in the 1970s; the average firm size (see Table 10.3) increased sharply, the number of firms declined in several republics and the largest firms raised their share of total output to such an extent that even medium-sized firms were eclipsed. Nor did the artisan sector[45] escape these pressures; in Costa Rica, it was virtually destroyed, although the rapid growth of industrial jobs in the 'modern' sector was some compensation.[46] In Guatemala, as the first ever artisan census showed, the sector survived, but its contribution to the gross value of industrial production was small and average earnings were very low.[47]

The difficulties faced by industry were in general reflected in the sector's performance in the 1970s. In three republics (El Salvador, Honduras and Guatemala), the annual average rate of growth of manufacturing was virtually the same as GDP, leaving the sectoral share unchanged. In Nicaragua the sectoral share steadily increased, but this was only because the GDP growth rate fell even faster than the manufacturing growth rate. Only Costa Rica — the republic where state policies in support of industry had been applied most vigorously — secured a substantial increase in the level of

Table 10.3 *Modern industrial sector*[1] *concentration, 1961–5 and 1975–9*

| | Costa Rica | | El Salvador | | Guatemala | | Honduras | | Nicaragua | |
|---|---|---|---|---|---|---|---|---|---|---|
| | 1964 | 1975 | 1961 | 1978 | 1958 | 1975 | 1962 | 1975 | 1965 | 1979 |
| (1) No. of establishments | 1051 | 1912 | 2670 | 1128 | 2140[2] | 1999 | 510 | 849 | 999 | 696 |
| (2) Average size (employees per establishment) | 21.5 | 29.1 | 20.4 | 51.7 | 13.0[2] | 34.2 | 31.0 | 43.3 | 24.3 | 48.1 |
| (3) % age of firms with >50 employees | 7.7 | | | | 17.5 | | | | 20.1 | |
| (4) % age of total value of production from firms with >50 employees | 79.3 | | | | 81.3 | | | | 87.6 | |

Sources: Rows (1) and (2) from SIECA, 1967, and SIECA, 1981, except final column for Nicaragua (for which see Instituto Nacional de Estadísticas y Censos, *Anuario Estadístico*, 1982). Rows (3) and (4) from the industrial census for each country
[1] Defined as firms with five or more employees
[2] Establishments with more than three workers, but excluding rural establishments and coffee beneficios

manufacturing output *per caput* and a significant increase in the sector's share of GDP, although even Costa Rica suffered a fall in the manufacturing growth rate by comparison with the 1960s.

This lack of dynamism in manufacturing meant that the sectoral distribution of activity remained virtually unchanged in the 1970s (see Table 10.4). The traditional branches of food, drink and tobacco continued to dominate the generation of value-added, and the fastest-growing branch was chemicals and petroleum derivatives, where each republic fostered its own refining capacity on a national rather than regional basis. Sales of manufactures outside the CACM, except from Costa Rica, continued to make a negligible impact on foreign exchange earnings; indeed, the sector 'textiles, clothing and footwear', conventionally a candidate for export promotion from LDCs, even saw its share of manufacturing value added decline (see Table 10.4) except in Honduras.

Mining developments in Guatemala, but not elsewhere, offered some compensation for poor industrial performance, although it proved a false dawn. Both nickel and oil production came on stream in the late 1970s: the former involved a joint venture between the government and foreign investment,[48] while the latter gave the state a large share of revenues.[49] By the end of the decade, however, nickel production had been suspended as a result

Table 10.4 *Sectoral distribution of industrial value added (%), 1969 and 1978–9*

| | Costa Rica | | El Salvador | | Guatemala | | Honduras | | Nicaragua | |
|---|---|---|---|---|---|---|---|---|---|---|
| | 1969 | 1979 | 1969 | 1978 | 1969 | 1979 | 1969 | 1978 | 1969 | 1979 |
| Food, drink & tobacco | 44.3 | 42.2 | 41.9 | 42.7 | 43.4 | 46.6 | 35.7 | 37.8 | 52.4 | 57.5 |
| Textiles, clothing & shoes | 11.4 | 10.0 | 23.7 | 19.2 | 23.8 | 18.6 | 8.9 | 9.7 | 13.3 | 7.4 |
| Wood, cork, furniture | 7.7 | 6.5 | 2.4 | 2.4 | 4.1 | 3.5 | 10.3 | 9.3 | 4.9 | 3.3 |
| Paper, paper products, printing | 4.0 | 3.9 | 3.1 | 3.5 | 3.1 | 3.2 | 4.0 | 3.6 | 3.5 | 2.8 |
| Leather, skins, rubber products | 3.0 | 2.6 | 1.5 | 2.2 | 2.8 | 2.1 | 2.6 | 2.9 | 2.0 | 1.4 |
| Chemicals & oil refining | 7.5 | 9.6 | 11.5 | 14.2 | 3.6 | 2.7 | 7.0 | 6.4 | 10.4 | 17.2 |
| Others | 22.1 | 25.2 | 15.9 | 15.8 | 19.2 | 23.3 | 31.5 | 30.3 | 13.5 | 10.4 |

Source: Inforpress, 1983a, pp. 61–4

of low world prices and oil production never fulfilled its expectations.

Industrial performance in the 1970s, except in Costa Rica, was therefore very disappointing: the sector enjoyed state support in all republics and industrial pressure groups had come of age, but this was not sufficient to enable industry to surmount the limitations on its growth imposed by the difficulties of the CACM, the small size of the national market, and the highly skewed income distribution. Indeed the share of the market for manufactures met by extra-regional imports rose in all the republics except Costa Rica, implying negative ISI.[50]

The Costa Rican industrial performance, by contrast, showed what could be done when long-term industrial strategies were matched by consistent state policies. The administrations of Presidents Figueres (1970–4) and Oduber (1974–8) gave a high priority to industrial development with the CACM expected to play a supportive, but not exclusive, role.[51] Industry was seen as the key to the long-term diversification of the economy, making it less vulnerable to external shocks and less dependent on EXA, and the Costa Rican government was not seduced away from this objective by temporarily high world prices for traditional agricultural exports. Instead, Costa Rica provided new sources of finance (including a Stock Exchange), increased traditional sources and introduced a broad range of incentives for extra-regional exports.[52] Shortages of skilled manpower were reduced through the state's accelerated training programme and, more controversially, the public sector increased substantially its share of the output of manufacturing activities. It was these measures, rather than the alleged superior income distribution,[53] which pulled Costa Rican industry through the 1970s at a respectable rate despite being subject to many of the same problems as elsewhere in Central America.

## Inflation, debt and the public sector

Central America inherited from the 1960s a fiscal problem (see Chapter 9, pp. 180–5), which was initially aggravated in the 1970s by a series of external shocks; in the second half of the decade, however, the fiscal problem was concealed by two favourable developments (high world commodity prices and increased availability of external finance), so that fundamental fiscal reform could be (and was) avoided. By the following decade, therefore, when both these favourable developments went into reverse, the weakness of the fiscal position was revealed and a crisis could not be averted.

The first external shock was the acceleration of world inflation, which was imported into Central America through high dollar prices for imports. This imported inflation, by general consent, explains most of the rise in the regional price indexes[54] and after nearly two decades of almost stable prices each republic began to suffer double digit inflation (see Table 10.1, p. 202). Some of the impact of imported inflation was repressed through price control, but the recorded price increases were still very severe by comparison with the earlier period.

The acceleration of inflation exposed the unsatisfactory nature of the central government's revenue structure. The reliance on import duties, much of which was obtained from specific tariffs, meant that collections did not keep pace with inflation and the ratio of import taxes to nominal GDP fell sharply (see Table 10.5) until emergency measures in the form of import tariff surcharges were introduced. The yield from property taxes (see Table 10.5) also failed to maintain its share of GDP, until painful and politically awkward property revaluations were carried out. With progressive marginal income tax rates, the Central American republics might at least have expected to see the income tax share of GDP rising from its initially low proportion (see Table 10.5). This did in general occur, although the unfulfilled potential of the income tax was revealed by the fact that Honduras, the poorest republic, had the highest share.

The second external shock was the oil crisis beginning in October 1973. The quadrupling of dollar oil prices not only had an impact on inflation,[55] but also disrupted the balance of payments current account. The share of oil in total imports leapt from 2.7% in 1970 to 10.2% in 1974; international reserves throughout the region came under pressure in that year and adjustment programmes went into effect in 1974/5. These measures, designed to reduce imports, had the effect of lowering import tax receipts and

Table 10.5  *Tax revenue as percentage of nominal GDP, 1970, 1975 and 1979*

|  | Import taxes | Property taxes | Income taxes | Central government revenue (1) | Central government revenue (2) |
|---|---|---|---|---|---|
| Costa Rica |  |  |  |  |  |
| 1970 | 3.7 | 0.08 | 2.6 | 13.5 | 13.4 |
| 1975 | 2.0 | 0.03 | 2.6 | 13.6 | 12.6 |
| 1979 | 2.2 | 0.16 | 2.7 | 12.6 | 11.7 |
| El Salvador |  |  |  |  |  |
| 1970 | 2.5 | 0.9 | 1.5 | 11.3 | 9.4 |
| 1975 | 2.1 | 0.7 | 2.7 | 12.9 | 10.4 |
| 1979 | 2.0 | 0.8 | 2.2 | 13.9 | 9.4 |
| Guatemala |  |  |  |  |  |
| 1970 | 2.0 | 0.3 | 1.0 | 8.5 | 8.1 |
| 1975 | 1.5 | 0.2 | 1.5 | 9.0 | 8.3 |
| 1979 | 1.7 | 0.1 | 1.3 | 10.7 | 8.0 |
| Honduras |  |  |  |  |  |
| 1970 | 3.1 | 0.1 | 2.9 | 12.1 | 11.7 |
| 1975 | 2.8 | 0.1 | 3.4 | 13.5 | 13.0 |
| 1979 | 3.4 | 0.1 | 3.4 | 14.8 | 13.4 |
| Nicaragua |  |  |  |  |  |
| 1970 | 2.9 | 0.9 | 1.0 | 10.5 | 10.4 |
| 1975 | 3.1 | 0.8 | 1.6 | 11.8 | 11.7 |
| 1977* | 3.1 | 0.8 | 1.9 | 12.1 | 11.8 |

Source: derived from SIECA, 1981, and IMF, 1984
(1) All revenues   (2) Exclusive of all export taxes (except banana tax)
* The years 1978 and 1979 were seriously affected by civil war in Nicaragua. 1977 has therefore been chosen as the last 'normal' year of the decade

aggravating the fiscal problem; the adjustment programmes were dropped, however, as the coffee price began to soar and international reserves rose again after 1975.

The third shock was a set of natural disasters, which afflicted three of the five republics. In December 1972, Managua was virtually destroyed by earthquake, Hurricane Fifi ravaged the north coast of Honduras in September 1974 and Guatemala was hit by earthquakes in February 1976. All these disasters had serious fiscal repercussions, because they reduced the yields from many taxes at the same time as damage-related expenditure soared; access to foreign emergency relief funds provided considerable support, but could not offset completely the fiscal implications.

In view of these shocks to the fiscal system, it might seem at first sight cause for congratulation that in every republic the ratio of revenue to nominal

GDP actually rose in the 1970s (see Table 10.5). This ratio is a misleading indicator of fiscal performance, however, because it includes the impact of progressive export tax rates on coffee and sugar whose prices reached previously unthinkable levels in the 1970s. These prices could not be expected to last, so that the 'improvement' in fiscal performance was due to windfall gains which could not be regarded as a substitute for fiscal reform.[56] This evaluation of export duties must be qualified by recognising that the new specific tax on bananas (see above, pp. 203–4) was a genuine element of fiscal reform; the yield from this tax did not depend on high world prices (although the latter made it easier for the fruit companies to pay it). The banana tax represented a correction of an old distortion and the duty collected was a permanent addition to fiscal revenues.[57] When fiscal performance is therefore calculated exclusive of export duties (but inclusive of the new tax on bananas), the results are much less impressive (see Table 10.5). Only Honduras was able to raise the fiscal ratio significantly with the yield from the banana tax accounting for two-thirds of the increase; by contrast, the ratio in Guatemala was unchanged despite a big increase in real GDP and in Costa Rica the ratio actually fell.

The poor performance should not be taken as evidence that no efforts were made in favour of fiscal reform. Costa Rica, for example, introduced new taxes on net wealth in 1976 and social security contributions almost doubled in 1978; in all republics, however, the windfall gains from export taxes and the increased availability of external finance qualified these efforts, leaving the fiscal structure largely unchanged and postponing fundamental reform.

The increase in central government current revenue was generally insufficient to justify a major increase in current expenditures. This created difficulties, because current expenditure was dominated by the wages and salaries of public employees whose goodwill was essential for all the region's governments. The dilemma was resolved in two different fashions: Costa Rica and Honduras allowed the ratio of current expenditure to nominal GDP to rise, while the other republics restrained it to the 1970 level. This difference in response was reflected in several social indicators. While real expenditure per person on public education and health soared in Costa Rica and Honduras, it was almost unchanged elsewhere (see Table 10.6). Indeed, the latter republics saw the share of government spending on health and education decline, partly in response to a rise in the defence share as military spending rose to counter the guerrilla threat (see below, pp. 225–9).

The expansion of current expenditure in Honduras was justified by the improvements in fiscal performance, and current savings remained positive throughout the decade; in Costa Rica, on the other hand, no such justification existed and current savings were negative in 1972 and 1978. Thus, the whole of the capital account and part of the current account in those years

Table 10.6 *Real public expenditure per person (1970 dollars) on health (H) and education (E), 1970, 1975 and 1979*

|  | Costa Rica | | El Salvador | | Guatemala | | Honduras | | Nicaragua | |
|---|---|---|---|---|---|---|---|---|---|---|
|  | H | E | H | E | H | E | H | E | H | E |
| 1970 | 2.2 | 20.6 | 4.3 | 8.3 | 3.6 | 5.8 | 3.9 | 8.6 | 5.9 | 9.2 |
| 1975 | 5.7 | 26.6 | 4.7 | 9.3 | 3.5 | 5.6 | 5.4 | 9.3 | 4.4 | 10.1 |
| 1979 | 8.1 | 35.1 | 4.2 | 9.6 | 4.3 | 7.0 | 6.4 | 10.1 | 3.3 | 10.2 |

Source: derived from SIECA, 1981, using change in cost-of-living index

had to be financed by borrowing. The fiscal situation in Costa Rica was therefore far from healthy and it rapidly became the Achilles heel of the republic's social democratic model. At the root of the problem was a ten-fold rise in current transfers between 1970 and 1978 unmatched by revenue increases. These transfers were extremely varied in character[58] and contributed greatly to the quality of life in Costa Rica, but the state failed to raise revenue in line with the increase in transfers. The problem was not the welfare state as such; Costa Rican current expenditure as a ratio of GDP was much the same as in Honduras, a much poorer republic, but successive Costa Rican governments had shown a reluctance to raise taxes and implement fiscal reform.[59]

While the problem of current expenditure was resolved in different ways, all republics increased central government capital expenditure at a very rapid rate. The principal beneficiary was the road system (a central government responsibility) with the paved distance increasing by 50% between 1970 and 1977,[60] but capital expenditure in the health and educational fields also increased substantially: this brought an improvement in key social indicators (notably the secondary school enrolment ratio),[61] but the quality of education and health suffered in those republics (El Salvador, Guatemala and Nicaragua) where capital spending was not matched by current resources.[62] In Guatemala and Nicaragua, much of the increase in central government capital expenditure was due to reconstruction after earthquake damage. In Guatemala in particular, capital transfers from the central government quadrupled in 1976 over the previous year; in Nicaragua allegations of corruption in the use of such transfers were widespread.[63]

The increase in central government capital expenditure pushed total expenditure as a proportion of GDP to exceptionally high rates. This expansion affected the ultra-conservative republics (El Salvador and Guatemala) as well as the others, although only in Honduras and Nicaragua did the proportion exceed 20%; the increase was in general greater than could be justified even by the windfall gain from export duties, and the budget deficit as a proportion of GDP rose steadily.[64]

It might be expected that all republics would have relied on cheap foreign credits to finance these increases in the central government deficits. This was not true, however, of Costa Rica and El Salvador; in these two cases, the deficit was funded in the main internally through the bank system, although the level of borrowing did not carry very serious inflationary implications during the 1970s. Furthermore, the Guatemalan deficit (although largely funded externally) was very small for most of the 1970s; thus, central government performance alone was not sufficient to account for the rapid increase in public sector external debt during the 1970s (see Figure 10.1).

The missing ingredient was provided by the decentralised, autonomous institutions (DAI) which form part of the public sector in each republic, but which are largely independent. These included public utilities and development banks in all republics together with the new financial corporations in Costa Rica, Guatemala and Honduras channelling funds to industry (see above, p. 208), while in Costa Rica the list of DAIs had been expanded rapidly in the 1970s to include many manufacturing activities. These DAIs were in general sufficiently autonomous to take advantage of the new availability of foreign finance, much of it channelled through CABEI and the Venezuelan Investment Fund, and their borrowing soared. In Costa Rica, for example, over three-quarters of the ten-fold increase in public external debt between 1970 and 1979 is explained by the DAIs. Elsewhere, neither the increase in debt nor the DAIs share was so spectacular, but in all republics except Nicaragua the DAI share of the debt was 40% or more by the end of the decade.

The fact that Nicaragua was the exception reflected that republic's slide into civil war. At the beginning of the decade, the central government share of the debt was only one-third, but the Somoza family found itself depending increasingly on foreign loans (much of it official) for its survival. Between the end of 1970 and 1978 (six months before its fall), the external debt of the Somoza government had risen nearly thirteen-fold and this accounted for three-quarters of the increase in all public external indebtedness.

In view of subsequent criticisms regarding the explosion of debt in the 1970s, it is worth stressing that in Central America at least the increase in indebtedness was associated with a spectacular rise in the rate of capital formation. The ratio of investment to GDP – often taken as a crude indicator of development effort – exceeded 25% by the end of the 1970s in Costa Rica and Honduras; even in El Salvador and Nicaragua the ratio rose above 20% before collapsing under the impact of civil war and social unrest.[65]

This association does not prove that the external finance was used wisely, yet the 'case against' is not strong; in all republics except Honduras public investment rose much more rapidly than private[66] and helped to compensate for the relatively slow growth of direct foreign investment.[67] The share of

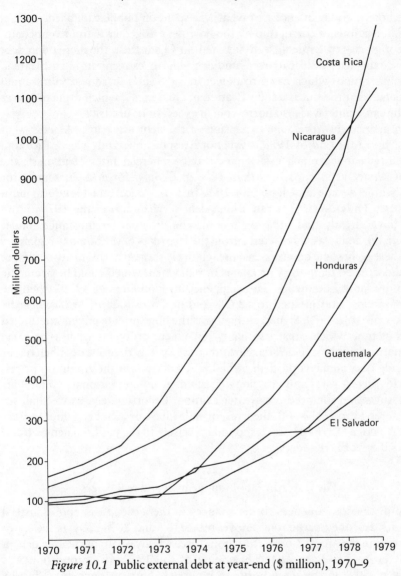

*Figure 10.1* Public external debt at year-end ($ million), 1970–9

public investment 'accounted for' by annual increases in public external debt steadily increased, without in general exceeding 100%,[68] and public capital expenditure on many highly desirable projects, such as hydro-electric schemes, accelerated.[69]

There were, of course, some clear cases of waste. From 1972 to 1975 inclusive, and again in 1979, the public sector in Nicaragua under Somoza's rule borrowed far in excess of what was spent on public capital formation, and allegations of corruption by the borrower (together with incompetence or complicity by lenders) seem justified. In Costa Rica, the increase in debt came dangerously close to over-funding public investment during the Carazo administration, which came to power in 1978, and there is circumstantial evidence that the Lucas administration in Guatemala, which came to power at the same time, was also borrowing in excess of its needs.[70]

In general, however, the expansion of the debt in Central America – at least up to the end of 1978 – was not irresponsible. Only Costa Rica and Nicaragua made much use of credit at commercial rates of interest; the debt service ratio[71] was less than 10% in El Salvador and Guatemala for the whole decade and less than 10% in Costa Rica and Honduras until 1978/9. Only Nicaragua ran a high debt service ratio in the 1970s[72] and we have already had occasion to note the different circumstances under which the debt was contracted during the last years of the Somoza régime.

There were some danger signs; the relatively short-term maturity of private credits created temporary problems of repayment which could be overcome only by more borrowing. This happened in Honduras in 1979, when the debt service ratio jumped to 12.6% and in Costa Rica in 1978 when the ratio leapt to 23.3%. Significantly, it was the huge private credits contracted at that time which caused so many repayment problems when they came to maturity in the mid-1980s. Nevertheless, we may describe debt behaviour outside Nicaragua as prudent until 1978, after which the rise in oil prices, world interest rates and growing uncertainties in international capital markets suggested the need for greater caution. Unfortunately, as we shall see (Chapter 11, pp. 237–44), the irresponsible phase of debt behaviour in Central America (1979–81) corresponded precisely to the period when restraint needed to be exercised.

### The state, the labour movement and real wages

One of the consequences of the changes in the agricultural and industrial sectors described earlier (see above, pp. 201–7 and 207–12) was the sharp increase in the proportion of the labour force wholly or almost wholly dependent on wages. Even at the beginning of the 1970s the proportion was close to 50% in the three northern republics (higher elsewhere),[73] but by the end of the decade the impact of the squeeze on the artisan sector, the increase in landlessness and the rise in the proportion of *microfincas*[74] had transformed the situation.

The formation of a rural and urban proletariat was a logical (and inevitable) consequence of capitalist modernisation, but in Central America the process accelerated at almost the same moment that inflation started to rise. At the beginning of the 1970s, the labour movement was still very

Table 10.7  *Real wages in Central America (1970 = 100)*

|  | Costa Rica | | El Salvador | | Guatemala | | Honduras | | Nicaragua | |
|---|---|---|---|---|---|---|---|---|---|---|
|  | Urban | Rural | Urban | Rural | Urban | Rural | Urban[1] | Urban[2] | Urban | Rural |
| 1970 | 100 | 100 | 100 | 100 | 100 | NA | 100 | — | 100 | — |
| 1971 | 104 | NA | 99 | NA | 101 | NA | 101 | — | 99 | — |
| 1972 | 107 | 111 | 103 | 94 | 97 | 100 | 100 | 100 | 99 | — |
| 1973 | 106 | 97 | 101 | 108 | 95 | 91 | 100 | 104 | 84 | — |
| 1974 | 96 | 105 | 94 | 101 | 82 | 81 | 95 | 74 | 85 | 100 |
| 1975 | 97 | 99 | 80 | 87 | 76 | 76 | 79 | 85 | 88 | 100 |
| 1976 | 106 | 114 | 95 | 98 | 75 | 73 | 88 | 98 | 93 | 100 |
| 1977 | 116 | 124 | 92 | 88 | 70 | 65 | 82 | 92 | 88 | 106 |
| 1978 | 124 | 137 | 87 | 88 | 74 | 60 | 86 | 107 | 87 | 109 |
| 1979 | 130 | 143 | 88 | 103 | 74 | 54 | 128 | — | 77 | — |

Sources: The urban series are based on industrial market wage rates and are taken from McCarthy, 1984. The rural series are based on minimum agricultural wage rates and have been derived by the author using the annual change in the Cost of Living index (see Table 10.1). The sources for the rural series are: (a) Wilkie, 1983, for Costa Rica and El Salvador; (b) Orellana and Cancino, 1981, for Guatemala; (c) PREALC, 1980, for Nicaragua
[1] The first urban series is from the source described above
[2] The second urban series (based on manufacturing and construction) is taken from Booth, 1982b

weak and workers' organisations had not in general developed defence mechanisms capable of protecting nominal wages against the rise in the cost of living. Inevitably, therefore, real wages (see Table 10.7) started to fall after the acceleration of price increases in 1972.

The evidence on real wages is derived in general from wage rates. Consequently, an increase in hours worked (decrease in under-employment) would act as a cushion against a decline in real wages; there is little evidence in favour of this hypothesis, however, since both un- and under-employment rates remained high over the decade.[75] It is safer to conclude, therefore, that the initial fall after 1971/2 in real wage rates (see Table 10.7) also represented a fall in real wages.

The proletarianisation of the labour force coupled with a decline in real wages provoked two inter-related responses from the labour movement. The first response was pressure on the state to ameliorate the critical situation faced by wage-earners, while the second was formation of new labour organisations to cope with the more hostile economic environment. As we shall see, the impact of these efforts in Costa Rica and Honduras was sufficient to push real wages above their level at the beginning of the decade, giving workers in those two republics a share in the increase in real GDP per head during the 1970s; elsewhere the losses in real wages were not recouped and the pressure on living standards created a further breeding ground for the revolutionary left (see below, pp. 225–9).

The state's contribution to the fortunes of the labour movement in the 1970s had four main features: the formation of cooperatives, the setting of minimum wages, social security programmes and land reform. By contrast, the formation of new trade unions and umbrella organisations by the labour movement was largely independent of the state.

The cooperative movement gained in importance during the 1970s, as the government in all republics used state banks to channel resources towards the agricultural sector in particular. The Federación de Cooperativas de la Reforma Agraria de Honduras (FECORAH), founded in 1970 with eleven cooperatives, was given legal recognition by the Honduran government in 1974 and ended the decade with 132 affiliated organisations;[76] even in Guatemala, where rural labour organisations had virtually collapsed after 1954, the number of cooperatives jumped from 145 in 1967 to 510 in 1976 with a total membership of 132,000.[77] In Costa Rica agricultural cooperatives were mainly confined to coffee growers, with membership of some 10,000,[78] but the cooperative principle spread rapidly to other branches of the economy, leading to the formation of an influential Consejo Nacional de Cooperativas (CONACOOP).

The setting of minimum wages, particularly for agricultural workers, proved much more controversial. While the Costa Rican government altered its laws in 1974 to allow annual changes in minimum agricultural wage rates (as a compensation for accelerating inflation)[79] minimum urban wage rates in Guatemala were unchanged from 1973 (rural rates from 1976) until 1980.[80] In El Salvador, minimum rural wage rates changed more frequently, but the decline in the real rate was still substantial until the sharp reverse after the revolution in October 1979 (see below, pp. 225–9). In Nicaragua, real minimum wage rates improved after 1976, but these changes appear suspect on closer examination.[81] The importance of minimum wage rates varied from country to country, depending on the extent to which they determined or were determined by market wage rates. In those republics (El Salvador, Guatemala) with very high rates of under-employment in the 1970s we may assume that the setting of minimum wage rates acted as a crucial determinant of living standards; significantly, in both republics real minimum wage rates fell throughout most of the decade.

Living standards for rural and urban workers are not determined exclusively by real market wages. On the contrary, the social wage (i.e. those goods and services to which workers are entitled without additional payment) also has an important bearing on living standards; by increasing its social security programme, the state was therefore in a position to counter any tendency for the real wage to decline. Both Costa Rica and Honduras expanded the coverage of the programmes rapidly in the 1970s. In the latter case, the expansion was not consistent and the number insured dropped in absolute terms in 1977 and 1979; nonetheless, by 1978 the Honduran social security programme covered over 30% of the labour force, a creditable achievement for a poor country, and the programme itself was financially sound.[82] In Costa Rica, the breakthrough in coverage came after the decision in 1971 to eliminate the salary ceiling for beneficiaries;[83] by 1977 over sixty per cent of the labour force had minimum insurance, but the programme had become ruinously expensive and the Carazo administration (1978–82) felt obliged to raise contributions sharply and reduce social security expenditure.[84]

The social security programme in Guatemala, one of the few legacies of the revolutionary period (1944–54), also expanded and at its peak in 1978 covered 30% of the labour force; unlike the rest of the region, a majority of affiliates were agricultural workers, owing to the legal provision that all employers with three workers or more must participate. In 1979, however, the number of workers affiliated started falling (mainly in agriculture) and this fall became a precipitate decline after minimum wage rates were doubled in 1980. Elsewhere in Central America, the expansion of the social security programme was very modest. In Nicaragua, the Somoza government extended the coverage of urban workers in a vain attempt to defuse the opposition, but rural workers were virtually excluded and only one per cent of beneficiaries worked in agriculture. A similar situation prevailed in El Salvador, where even urban coverage was very low.

All the republics except El Salvador had made modest steps in the direction of land reform in the 1960s (see Chapter 9, pp. 189–90). With the demise of the Alliance for Progress, however, the programme of land distribution was quietly shelved in Nicaragua, while Guatemala prosecuted land reform in the Franja Transversal del Norte mainly in the interests of government officials; El Salvador (see above, pp. 205–6) failed miserably to address the problem seriously, but governments in Costa Rica and Honduras gave land distribution a high priority. The number of land invasions during the two *Liberacionista* governments (1970–8) rose sharply as a direct consequence of the marginalisation of the Costa Rican peasantry. The administration responded with a programme to create peasant enterprises (1970–5),[85] followed by a programme for zones of agricultural development (1975–8) in different parts of the country. The land invasions continued, however, and in 1975 the Instituto de Tierras y Colonización (ITCO) claimed to have settled 19,359 families. In the next few years, ITCO purchased with public funds large areas of land in order to settle many of those who had invaded private farms elsewhere.[86]

The use of land distribution by the state in Costa Rica to ameliorate rural labour conditions was unremarkable. The PLN was much more closely associated with the industrial bourgeoisie than large landowners, and land reform was an accepted instrument of state policy, although both the PLN and the opposition were careful to employ it in a way which did not prejudice export agriculture. Much more remarkable was the commitment, albeit at times inconsistent, of the Honduran military to land redistribution. Land reform laws had been passed under the presidency of Villeda Morales in 1962, but the military coup led by López Arellano in 1963 reduced the scope of the programme, which was carried out frequently at the expense of migrant Salvadorean landowners.

The López Arellano administration did not, however, eliminate the programme, and the support of the workers' movement for the government during the war with El Salvador led to a reappraisal. The government of national unity, elected in 1971 and backed by both business and labour federations, paid lip-service to land reform, but President Ramón Ernesto Cruz gave it very low priority; the rural labour movement's disquiet culminated in a planned hunger march on 6 December 1972, which provoked a military coup two days earlier. Once again the coup was led by General López Arellano, but this time any ambiguities he may have felt regarding collaboration with the labour movement had disappeared; labour, along with the military, was one of the two new social forces in Honduras[87] and within a few days of the coup the new administration had passed a new land reform law (Decree Law No. 8): this provided for the temporary surrender of land to peasants for periods of up to two years and virtually instituted a system of forced rents for large landowners on terms favourable to tenants.[88] The reaction of the large landowners, organised in the Federación Nacional de Agricultores y Ganaderos (FENAGH), was understandably hostile and their opposition succeeded in reducing the proportion of land distributions made from private estates;[89] nevertheless, by the time Decree Law No. 8 expired in January 1975 23,627 families had been settled on over 100,000 manzanas of land.

By this time, the military government had passed new land reform legislation (Decree Law No. 170), which ANACH (the main peasant organisation) characterised as 'conventional'. It is certainly true that Decree Law No. 170 was designed to accelerate the modernisation of capitalist agriculture and was wholly consistent with an emphasis on export agriculture,[90] but it did not enjoy consistent support from the military governments after 1974. The administration of General Juan Alberto Melgar Castro (1975–8), which replaced that of López Arellano after his resignation following the banana bribes scandal (see above, p. 203), was less enthusiastic towards land reform, particularly towards the close of 1976, and the military triumvirate led by General Policarpo Paz García (which succeeded Melgar Castro) was preoccupied with a return to civilian rule. Nevertheless, the land reform programme continued and by the beginning of 1978 29,901 had become beneficiaries on 163,083 hectares of redistributed land (an average of nearly six hectares each). Many of these families contained workers who had lost their jobs in the banana industry following the convulsions of 1974 (see above, pp. 203–4). Only ten per cent of the peasantry therefore benefited directly from land reform, but the numbers were sufficiently large and state support for the programme sufficiently serious to give others a realistic prospect of access to land in the future. The Honduran peasantry and its representative pressure groups therefore had a legitimate target for their efforts and a reason to eschew revolutionary alternatives.[91]

Throughout Central America at the start of the 1970s, only a small proportion of the labour force was organised in trade unions and in each country the organised labour movement was dominated by federations affiliated to the Organización Regional Interamericana de Trabajadores (ORIT) and subject to the influence of the United States AFL-CIO labour organisation (which channelled funds to these organisations through its affiliate American Institute for Free Labor Development – AIFLD). In some republics (El Salvador, Guatemala and Honduras) these US-sponsored labour federations enjoyed the support of the ruling parties,[92] while in Costa Rica and Honduras they exercised a certain independence.[93] The semi-independent character of these federations reduced their ability to respond to the crisis affecting the labour movement at the beginning of the 1970s and created opportunities for rural organisations. The first to emerge were the social Christian labour federations founded in the 1960s throughout Central America; these were subject to the influence of the Catholic church, affiliated to the Christian Democrat parties (or their equivalent) and linked internationally to the Confederación Latinoamericana de Trabajadores (CLAT).

These labour federations of social Christian persuasion often had their greatest influence among rural workers, including the peasantry, and the proletarianisation of the rural labour force allowed them to make important inroads into this (largely unorganised) section of the labour force.[94] The depth of the crisis, however, was such that the major inroads were made by more radical labour organisations. Thus, for example, the Marxist Confederación General de Trabajadores (CGT) in Costa Rica recovered much of the ground it had lost after the 1948 civil war,[95] the key banana workers' unions in Honduras split from ORIT in 1975,[96] the defunct peasant league Federación Cristiana de Campesinos de El Salvador (FECCAS) re-emerged in the early 1970s with a militant leadership,[97] the moderate Federación Autónoma Sindical de Guatemala (FASGUA) moved sharply to the left[98] and the Asociación de Trabajadores del Campo (ATC), with close links to the Frente Sandinista de Liberación Nacional (FSLN), was formed in Nicaragua.[99]

The radicalisation of the organised labour movement, reflected in a decline in the importance of federations affiliated to ORIT,[100] also produced new labour federations with a more political outlook. One of the most important of these was the Frente de Unidad Campesina (FUNC) in Honduras, which brought together the main peasant organisations irrespective of their (different) international affiliations.[101] Also important were the new federations formed in Guatemala; the Comité Nacional de Unidad Sindical (CNUS) became the spearhead for virtually all labour groups following the infamous Coca Cola strike in March 1976[102] and the clandestine Comité de Unidad Campesina (CUC) provided an umbrella organisation for all the peasantry from 1978.[103]

The new radicalism among workers' organisations produced significant gains for the labour movement in Costa Rica and Honduras. In both republics, the number of unions and their membership accelerated rapidly: in the former case the gains were concentrated in services (above all in the public sector),[104] but in the latter the single most important group was the small peasantry with ANACH as the leading organisation. In both republics, the new radicalism brought a rapid recovery in real wages after the initial fall so that by the end of the decade they registered a notable increase compared with 1970 (see Table 10.7, p. 219). In the other republics, the new militancy brought few gains: in Nicaragua, construction workers affiliated to the 'independent' Confederación General de Trabajo (it was in fact linked to the Partido Socialista Nicaragüense)[105] carried out a successful strike in 1973, but this was due to the unprecedented increase in their bargaining position caused by the earthquake in December 1972; militancy in Guatemala reached its peak in 1978 with 229 industrial disputes and in El Salvador in 1979, but the 'success rate' for strikes was poor[106] and real wages at the end of the decade remained well below the level at the beginning (see Table 10.7).

The difference between the two groups of countries is therefore very striking. The state did not go out of its way to foster the labour movement in any of the republics, but in Costa Rica and Honduras the new labour militancy led to a policy of accommodation with occasional periods of repression. In the other republics the new militancy was greeted with extreme hostility and repression, although there was a period of ambiguity in Guatemala during the presidency of Kjell Laugerud (1974–8).[107] The hostility of the state towards the labour movement in El Salvador, Guatemala and Nicaragua inevitably pushed the workers' organisations in a leftward direction, forcing some of them to make common cause with the small revolutionary groups which emerged in the 1970s (see below, pp. 225–9). This alliance increased enormously the influence of the revolutionary movements in El Salvador and Nicaragua, although in Guatemala it was countered by the ferocity of the repression unleashed by the Lucas García administration (1978–82).

## The fall of Somoza and the challenge to US hegemony

In the three republics (El Salvador, Guatemala and Nicaragua) where the new mood of militancy in the labour movement was met with hostility and repression, the political situation deteriorated rapidly during the 1970s; this process culminated in 1979 with the falls of Somoza in Nicaragua and General Romero in El Salvador, while in Guatemala repression was sufficiently brutal to avert a similar chain of events. The breakdown of social and political order and the emergence of a revolutionary government in Nicaragua presented the United States with a grave challenge to its hegemony in the region.

There were three key elements in the breakdown of the established order. In the first place, part of the labour movement in the three affected republics came to identify with the small revolutionary groups in existence since the 1960s or early 1970s, giving the latter an important social base for the first time; secondly, the widespread use of electoral fraud persuaded a segment of the followers (mainly urban middle-class) of the centrist parties that extra-parliamentary tactics were legitimate in the pursuit of political change; thirdly, divisions within the armed forces and the main private sector pressure groups contributed to the loss of authority by the ruling administrations.

The blanket hostility faced by the labour movement in El Salvador persuaded some of the most militant workers' organisations to form in 1974 the Frente de Acción Popular Unificada (FAPU);[108] FAPU laid stress on securing partial reforms within the system and proved insufficiently radical for two of its component groups (FECCAS and ANDES).[109] These two organisations combined with the Unión de Trabajadores del Campo (UTC), a peasant group born out of the failures of the land invasions in San Vicente, and other labour groups to form the Bloque Popular Revolucionario (BPR) in 1975. The BPR later established links with the Fuerzas Populares de Liberación (FPL), the oldest guerrilla group in El Salvador formed in 1970 by Cayetano Carpio as a breakaway from the Salvadorean Communist Party; it played a leading role in mobilising popular opposition to the Romero administration, which came to power in 1977, and claimed 60,000 members within two years of its formation.[110]

In Guatemala the CNUS, which came to prominence after the Coca Cola strike in 1976 (see above), remained independent of the four small guerrilla groups[111] and identified more closely with the social democratic Frente Unido de la Revolución (FUR). The revolutionary groups therefore did not acquire an important urban social base (CNUS was strongest in Guatemala's cities), but they achieved a breakthrough in rural areas when the CUC joined forces with the guerrillas after a reign of terror was unleashed by the Lucas García régime (1978–82).[112] As in El Salvador, the consequence of state repression was therefore to deliver the revolutionary left a constituency out of all proportion to its original influence.

The identification of the revolutionary left with the labour movement was more complete in Nicaragua, because Somoza's tactics had left workers' organisation relatively weak and fragmented. There were no powerful workers' federations in Nicaragua in the mid-1970s and the FSLN often took the initiative in establishing labour groups (for example, the ATC – see above). The inability of the Partido Socialista Nicaragüense (PSN) to capitalise on its long established links with the labour movement[113] made it easier for the FSLN to play a vanguard role[114] and by the time of Somoza's fall (July 1979) it had acquired a dominant position.

The centrist alternative to the revolutionary left, represented in the main by Christian Democrat (CD) parties in El Salvador and Guatemala and in Nicaragua by the Partido Socialcristiano (PSC) and the Partido Liberal Independiente (PLI), had made some progress in the 1960s through electoral strategies.[115] Confidence in the parliamentary road to power was rudely shattered, however, by a series of electoral frauds perpetrated in the early 1970s. The most extreme case was in El Salvador in 1972, where the Unión Nacional Opositora (UNO) – a coalition between Christian and Social Democrats – was robbed of victory in the presidential elections by blatant fraud; the CD candidate in the 1977 presidential elections, although a retired army colonel, was also cheated of victory by fraud. The same was true in Guatemala in 1974, where the CD party had chosen General Ríos Montt as their candidate, while in Nicaragua the pact in 1971 between President Somoza and the leader of the Conservative Party (Fernando Agüero), whereby the latter would lead a triumvirate until Somoza's 're-election' in 1974, finally convinced the centrist parties that parliamentary struggle alone was not sufficient.

The reaction of the centrist parties to electoral fraud was to form broad alliances which could play an extra-parliamentary role. The most important of these was the Unión Democrática de Liberación (UDEL) in Nicaragua, led by the charismatic Pedro Joaquín Chamorro and formed in 1974. By 1978 UDEL had merged with the Frente Amplio Opositor (FAO), another broad alliance including the PSC and the group of intellectuals ('los doce') who played a leading role in winning international support for the anti-Somoza cause; negotiations between Somoza and the FAO in late 1978, however, split the latter and left the anti-Somoza initiative with the broad coalition dominated by the FSLN. Electoral fraud was crucial in shifting the centrist parties and many of their supporters away from a strictly parliamentary opposition role. Indeed, such was the reaction to electoral fraud that the rate of abstention steadily accelerated and there is plenty of circumstantial evidence to suggest that this lack of confidence in the ballot box was translated into growing support for revolutionary methods of political change. The centrist parties drew their main support from the urban middle classes, and the alienation of a part of these groups from electoral strategies was further evidence of a breakdown of the established order.

The third element in the breakdown was divisions within the dominant political groups themselves. In Nicaragua the private sector, organised through the Consejo Superior de la Empresa Privada (COSEP), had for years had an uneasy relationship with the Somoza family over the division of business opportunities and the question of 'fair' competition; this relationship broke down after the earthquake in December 1972, however, as Somoza ruthlessly exploited his dominant position to enhance his business interests, and many private sector groups openly joined the anti-Somoza coalition. In Guatemala and El Salvador the private sector remained united, with the business pressure groups playing a leading role in resisting any attempt at economic reforms. The armed forces, however, began to reflect some of the divisions increasingly apparent in civilian society; this was most obvious in El Salvador, where junior officers master-minded the successful coup against General Romero in October 1979 and brought to power a reform-minded junta supported (until the end of the year) by many of the most radical elements in the country. In Guatemala, divisions within the armed forces did not surface until March 1982, when General Ríos Montt (the 1974 CD presidential candidate) seized power with the support of junior officers following a further round of electoral fraud.

While Nicaragua, El Salvador and Guatemala were drifting towards civil war, Costa Rica and Honduras succeeded in avoiding an upsurge of revolutionary violence. The crucial difference in both cases was a policy of accommodation towards the labour movement, despite occasional periods of repression, and the granting of at least some of the demands of the workers' organisations. Only Costa Rica could claim to operate a fully democratic political system,[116] with the opposition candidate winning the 1978 presidential elections, but Honduras did take important steps in the direction of formal democracy and averted the alienation among centre party supporters so apparent in the neighbouring republics. In 1980, the Liberal Party won a surprise victory in the Constituent Assembly elections in which a massive 81% of the electorate voted and in the following year Roberto Suazo Córdova was elected president as candidate of the Liberal Party in elections fought by the Christian Democrats for the first time.[117]

The establishment of a revolutionary government in Nicaragua and a reformist junta in El Salvador, both integrated and supported by Marxists, presented the United States with an unprecedented challenge to its authority in the region. Since 1954, when it engineered the overthrow of the Arbenz régime, successive US administrations had enjoyed cordial relations with the governments of all five republics and the greatest threat to US hegemony (from the Guatemalan guerrillas in the 1960s) had been crushed by the

Guatemalan armed forces with US counter-insurgency experts playing a purely supportive role. AIFLD had been encouraged to 'tame' the emergence of organised labour in Honduras after 1954 and to counter the influence of Marxist labour groups in Costa Rica, although AIFLD initiatives in El Salvador among the peasantry were largely stifled by government hostility.[118]

The result was a sense of false confidence among officials at the US State Department, who – as late as the mid-1970s – were contemplating an end to official aid to Central America.[119] The quality of ambassadorial postings in the region left much to be desired[120] and this had a predictable impact on the accuracy of information flowing back to the United States. The Soviet Union appeared to be interested only in establishing normal commercial and diplomatic relations with the region[121] and Cuba appeared to have lost interest following the demise of the Guatemalan guerrillas in the early 1970s. This sense of false confidence led the USA to overestimate its influence over Central American governments. The appearance of cordial relations was in any case somewhat misleading; in return for unquestioning support of the United States in foreign policy matters, repressive régimes in Central America had gained a largely free hand in their own internal affairs. Well documented abuses of civil rights in Guatemala, El Salvador and Nicaragua (and occasionally Honduras) escaped critical comment from the State Department and little pressure was brought to bear in favour of change.

The situation changed dramatically with the election of President Carter in 1976. Carter's foreign policy claimed to draw its moral authority from human rights questions, and military assistance was linked to progress in eliminating human rights abuse. The repressive régimes in El Salvador and Guatemala, however, voluntarily denied themselves access to such assistance in 1977 rather than risk US interference in their own internal affairs[122] and the cutoff of military aid to Somoza in 1978 had no effect whatever on the dictator's campaign of terror against the opposition. The Carter administration therefore found that its ability to dictate the course of events in the region was very modest and this unexpected impotence was emphasised even further by its failure to make any headway in its anti-Sandinista project in favour of Somocismo without Somoza. The Carter administration was therefore reluctantly forced to support the broad coalition led by the FSLN which took power in July 1979.

Within weeks of the fall of Somoza, President Carter's foreign policy in Central America was subject to major revision and El Salvador had become the centre of attention. The precise role of the administration in the fall of Romero is still unclear,[123] but the new sense of urgency and 'Realpolitik' was readily apparent. Spurred on by the humiliation of the Iranian hostages, President Carter's foreign policy gave priority to the defeat of the revolutionary left in El Salvador – a policy that was inherited and refined by President Reagan after his inauguration in January 1981.

The success of the counter-revolution in Guatemala in 1954 showed that a US administration could still dictate events where its perceived security interests were at risk. A quarter of a century later, the Salvadorean revolution tested US ability and influence even more severely; this time, however, the existence of a revolutionary government in Nicaragua made the final outcome less certain.

# 11

## The descent into regional crisis

The fall of Somoza in July 1979 was greeted with enthusiasm by the progressive forces in Central America and with a feeling of inevitability by others; while the Carazo administration in Costa Rica actively supported the Sandinistas, the military governments elsewhere did nothing to save Somoza[1] and normal relations were established immediately with the Junta de Gobierno de Reconstrucción Nacional (JGRN).

Some of the factors contributing to Somoza's downfall, however, were present in other republics. Within a few months the Romero administration had fallen in El Salvador and a revolutionary junta had been formed, but the new government failed to establish its authority over the armed forces and civil war broke out in January 1980. The guerrilla challenge in Guatemala was met with state terror by the Lucas García régime (1978–82) and Central America began to experience a major refugee problem as innocent families fled to neighbouring republics to avoid the effects of war.

Meanwhile, the consolidation of Sandinismo in Nicaragua began to destroy the broad alliance which had brought down Somoza; by the end of 1981, a counter-revolutionary army based on former National Guardsmen had been created (with CIA assistance) in Honduras, and Nicaragua began an irreversible descent into crisis before the country had even had time to recover from the war against Somoza. Nicaraguan refugees joined families from El Salvador and Guatemala seeking a safe haven elsewhere.

As if the social dislocations associated with three civil wars were not sufficient, Central America began to feel after 1979 the impact of the world recession; the terms of trade deteriorated, while higher world interest rates increased the cost of both new and past external borrowing. Efforts to avoid the need for external adjustment through additional borrowing simply compounded the problem and made the eventual economic crisis even more severe. The fall in living standards resulting from this combination of shocks was the most severe since the 1930s and in some republics was even more severe.

The fall of Somoza in 1979 emphasised the need for social and political reform elsewhere in Central America, a severe task at the best of times;

the subsequent regional crisis, however, increased even further the need for such changes, while making their implementation more difficult. Furthermore, the Marxist guerrilla challenge in El Salvador, the consolidation of a pro-Soviet régime in Nicaragua and the US efforts to destabilise it added an East–West dimension to the regional crisis and contributed to the difficulty of carrying out social and political change.

The regional crisis provoked national and international responses. The United States – its hegemony under threat – answered the Marxist challenge not only with military assistance to its regional allies, but also with a variety of economic programmes. These included increased economic aid, pressure on multinational institutions for favourable credit treatment and even discreet influence over the conditions imposed by the International Monetary Fund (IMF) for standby loans; the novel feature of the US response, however, was the Caribbean Basin Initiative (CBI) with its duty-free access for most commodities exported to the US market. Mexico and Venezuela responded with the San José oil facility (first begun in 1980) under which countries of the region could purchase oil on favourable terms; both countries also joined forces with Colombia and Panama in January 1983 to form the Contadora group in a Latin American initiative to resolve the regional crisis. Finally, the European Economic Community (EEC) signed a Cooperation Agreement with all of the countries of the region (including Panama) in November 1985, which provided for a substantial increase in multilateral aid and pledged EEC support for efforts to achieve a peaceful resolution of the regional crisis by the Contadora group; the latter's initiative was boosted at the end of 1985 by the formation of a support group composed of four South American democracies (Argentina, Brazil, Peru, Uruguay).

While the international responses were motivated primarily by geopolitical and security considerations, each Central American republic was forced by domestic considerations to address the issues of social and political change. Agrarian and fiscal reform were tackled with varying convictions and differing results, but the formation of a stronger and more independent labour movement received a very low priority as the requirements of short-term economic recovery took precedence. Not surprisingly, progress towards democracy outside Costa Rica was painfully slow and fraught with difficulties, although between 1984 and 1986 elections occurred in all five republics.

By the end of 1986, the regional crisis had sharpened the differences between the Central American republics. Costa Rica and Honduras had adjusted their economies most effectively to the hostile external environment and faced the best prospects for limited economic recovery; both republics had also weathered the political storm better than elsewhere and Honduras' fragile democracy survived a major constitutional crisis in April 1985. Elsewhere, the economic and political prospects were mixed. The armed forces had gained the upper hand in the Salvadorean civil war, but the reform programme had been essentially frozen and organised labour continued to be treated more as a threat to security than as a partner in development. Guatemala inched towards a fragile civilian rule, but the limitations of fiscal reform thwarted efforts at economic stabilisation, and economic recovery remained a distant goal; finally, Nicaragua remained afflicted by a ruined economy, the victim of a combination of external aggression and horrendous policy errors, while the prospects of a rapprochement with the USA were as remote as ever.

## The challenge of Sandinismo

The victory of the anti-Somocista forces in Nicaragua and the establishment of a five-member junta with non-Sandinista membership[2] suggested that the JGRN's programme would conform to that agreed before the fall of Somoza[3] and preserve the broad alliance which had contributed to the defeat of the dictator. The new government's economic measures commanded considerable support. The expropriation of property owned by Somoza and his supporters became the basis of the Area de Propriedad del Pueblo (APP), giving the state a substantial interest in many sectors,[4] but it was not at first opposed by Nicaragua's business groups. Even the nationalisation of mining, the banks and foreign trade were measures which commanded broad support.[5]

The broad alliance began to break up, however, as the Sandinistas sought to consolidate their political and ideological grip over the Nicaraguan revolution. Sandinista membership of the legislative Council of State was increased, the new Nicaraguan army (to replace Somoza's National Guard) was closely linked to the Sandinista leadership,[6] popular organisations – such as the Comités de Defensa Sandinista (CDS) – began to spring up with strong ideological overtones[7] and the Sandinista nine-member National Directorate emerged as the real power in the land. By April 1980, the two moderates on the junta had resigned, while many influential groups and individuals began to register their disapproval of the Sandinista hegemony within the government. The trickle of defections speeded up in 1981, when the Sandinistas began to trample on the traditional autonomy of the Atlantic coast communities; by March 1982, a state of emergency had been declared following the first serious counter-revolutionary offensive against the government.

Despite the growing opposition of leading moderates, the Sandinistas still commanded widespread support. The literacy campaign, the priority given to health and educational services and the reduction in human rights abuse by comparison with the Somoza period were measures which benefited virtually all Nicaraguans. At the same time, the labour and other popular organisations created by the Sandinistas (to fill the vacuum left by the dictatorship) provided the new régime with a fairly broad social base.

The march of events in Nicaragua was observed with a great deal of concern in Washington. The Sandinista refusal to condemn the Soviet invasion of Afghanistan in late 1979[8] had been noted, but the Carter administration pressed ahead with direct and indirect financial support for the new government. A reluctant Congress was pressured into a $75 million aid package for Nicaragua in 1980, but any political benefits the Carter administration might have hoped to reap were undermined by the numerous conditions attached to the aid by Congress.[9]

When the Reagan administration came to power in January 1981, the attitude towards the Sandinistas had turned sour; in March a $10 million credit for wheat purchases was suspended and in the following month the remaining $15 million of the $75 million aid package was cancelled, the Reagan administration announcing that it would make no more bilateral agreements with Nicaragua. By the end of the year, multinational institutions with strong US participation were under immense pressure to reduce their commitments to Nicaragua and the CIA had begun its covert operations in support of the counter-revolutionaries ('contras') to destabilise the Sandinista régime. The ostensible reason for these US decisions was Sandinista support for the guerrillas in El Salvador's civil war. How much of this support was military (rather than political) has never been satisfactorily determined, but the prospect of a guerrilla victory in El Salvador was something which not even the Carter administration was prepared to stomach and the defeat of the guerrilla threat was made one of the highest foreign policy priorities of the Reagan administration.

The revolutionary junta which came to power in El Salvador in October 1979, following the successful coup against General Romero, promised a peaceful resolution of the country's main social and political problems; the proclamation announced on 15 October included the right of all workers to form trade unions, political freedom for all parties, the promise of free elections and agrarian reform and a general amnesty for all political prisoners and exiles.[10] The junta was widely supported[11] and its original membership included two members of the armed forces, two representatives of the Foro Popular (a broad-based group representing the middle ground of politics and organised labour)[12] and one representative of the business community.

The government formed by the junta, however, discovered very quickly the limitations of its power. The traditional military élite remained firmly in control of the armed forces and the reform programme was frustrated at every turn. By the end of 1979, the Foro Popular members of the junta and government had resigned and later joined forces with the guerrilla groups which had never supported the first junta; the organisational expression of this alliance became in 1980 the Frente Democrático Revolucionario (FDR) – Frente Farabundo Martí para la Liberación Nacional (FMLN), with the FMLN representing the guerrilla groups and the FDR representing the left-of-centre political parties and the mass organisations.

The departure of the two Foro Popular members led to the inclusion of two Christian Democrats (CD) in the junta; by March 1980 the leader of the CD party, José Napoleon Duarte, had been installed on the junta and El Salvador began a reform programme under the most inauspicious circumstances; the government lacked the support of the mass organisations, a civil war was under way and the armed forces remained under the control of their traditional leaders. Even the CD party itself was split, with many of its leaders and supporters joining the FDR–FMLN.[13]

The reform programme covered many features observed in Sandinista Nicaragua, such as nationalisation of the banks and state control over the export of the main commodities. Representatives of the private sector, however, strongly opposed these measures and their opposition became explosive when the details of a land reform programme were announced on 6 March 1980; Phase I involved expropriation of all properties over 500 hectares (and therefore struck at the heart of the traditional oligarchy), Phase II affected estates larger than 100 hectares and Phase III concerned claims to freehold title by small-scale cultivators.[14]

A weak junta, with little social or political base and facing an intransigent private sector, could not under normal circumstances in El Salvador have expected to carry out a mild, let alone radical, reform programme. The consolidation of Sandinismo in Nicaragua, however, and the revolutionary threat from the FDR–FMLN meant that these were far from normal circumstances and the US administration (under both Presidents Carter and Reagan) gave its very considerable support to the implementation of the formal structure of the reform programmes. In particular, Phase I of the land reform programme went ahead, with the US government footing much of the bill and exercising enormous pressure on the Salvadorean armed forces to prevent a successful coup.

The reform programme did not reverse the drift into civil war and the FDR–FMLN scored not only military victories, but also diplomatic successes; France and Mexico jointly recognised the FDR–FMLN as a 'representative political force' in 1981 and its leaders were warmly received in the chancelleries of many Western countries. The Duarte-led government was accused of presiding over a hollow reform programme, massive human rights abuse and an unreformed army with no stomach for a prolonged guerrilla war. Faced with this challenge, Duarte offered elections for a Constituent Assembly in March 1982 and received strong support from the Reagan administration. The elections, which were opposed by the FDR–FMLN, produced a 40% vote for the Christian Democrats, but an overall majority for the right-wing parties.[15] The Assembly chose Alvaro Magaña as provisional President and the reform programme, including Phase II of the land reform, was effectively suspended. The civil war raged on, but by mid-1982 the armed forces and the private sector pressure groups had begun to regain some of their composure and self-confidence.

The impact of the Sandinista revolution in Nicaragua and the descent into civil war in El Salvador inevitably had repercussions elsewhere in Central America. The most directly affected was Honduras; the rump of Somoza's defeated National Guard had fled into Nicaragua's northern neighbour and the civil war in El Salvador threatened to aggravate the still unresolved border dispute with Honduras because of the potential security offered to the guerrillas by the *bolsones* (small pockets of disputed territory).[16] The government of General Policarpo Paz García in Honduras reacted with uncharacteristic speed. A peace treaty was signed with El Salvador in October 1980, which ended eleven years of hostility and paved the way for the renewal of commercial trade. The military build-up in Nicaragua under the Sandinistas was matched by an increase in US military aid to Honduras and an emphasis on the quality rather than quantity of the armed forces. In February 1983, the first of a continuous series of joint military manoeuvres with the United States took place close to the Nicaraguan border.

The military triumvirate led by General Policarpo Paz García, which came to power in August 1978, accelerated its plans for the democratisation of the country. Constituent Assembly elections went ahead in April 1980 with the Christian Democrat (CD) party excluded, but the military's 'ally' — the Partido Nacional (PN) – performed badly and the Partido Liberal (PL) returned to share power with the military after its long exclusion from office. In the presidential elections of November 1981, in which the CD party was allowed to participate, the PL candidate Roberto Suazo Córdova scored an impressive victory.[17]

The return to civilian rule and democracy in Honduras, however, took place under most inauspicious circumstances. The distrust of the Sandinista revolution in Washington was mirrored in Honduras by a fear among the military and the civilian élite of the implications of the growing militarisation in Nicaragua. Nothing was done to restrain the 'contras' operating against Nicaragua from Honduran bases and the rapid rise in US military aid, together with the joint military manoeuvres, increased the authority of the Honduran armed forces at a time when the new civilian administration was still struggling to assert its independence. General Alvarez Martínez, an officer noted for his hostility to organised labour,[18] emerged as the strong man in the Honduran military and played a leading part in the formation of the Asociación para el Progreso de Honduras (APROH), a semi-fascist organisation which threatened to perpetuate military rule in Honduras.[19]

The impact of the Sandinista revolution in Nicaragua also affected Guatemala, where the régime of General Romeo Lucas García came to power at the head of a right-wing coalition determined to destroy the small guerrilla groups which had resurfaced during the presidency of General Kjell Laugerud

(1974–8); these groups had enjoyed some success in establishing links with the organised labour movement and its left-wing political representatives, so that all three became targets for the reign of terror unleashed by the Lucas administration. International condemnation of human rights abuse and pressure from the Carter administration left the Lucas régime unmoved,[20] so that Guatemala rapidly acquired international pariah status.

The fall of Somoza accelerated Guatemala's descent into crisis. The military élite and its civilian allies interpreted any opposition to the régime as a threat to national security and the small parties of the Guatemalan political centre became a target for political attack. Alberto Fuentes Mohr, leader of the small Social Democratic Party, and Manuel Colom Argueta, founder of the centrist Frente Unido de la Revolución, were both murdered, many Roman Catholic priests were killed or arrested and the main labour organisations (other than those controlled by the state) moved to semi-clandestine operations.

While the repression was at its height, the illegal Comité de Unidad Campesina (CUC) led a strike early in 1980 among day labourers on the south coast plantations. The widespread support for the strike threatened the harvest and the government was forced to agree to a massive increase in the daily minimum wage from Q1.20 to Q3.20. This victory for organised labour produced a ferocious response from the private sector and the number of agricultural workers reported to the Social Security Institute dropped from 374,609 in 1979 to 225,688 in 1981 (a fall of 40%), while their nominal earnings over the same period rose by a mere seven per cent despite the huge increase in legal minimum wages.[21]

The blatant use of fraud in favour of the 'official' candidate in the March 1982 presidential elections precipitated the crisis among Guatemala's ruling groups which had been brewing for several years. A successful military coup led by General Efrain Ríos Montt, an evangelical Protestant and former Christian Democrat presidential candidate, emphasised just how deep were the divisions within even the military élite over the appropriate response to Guatemala's social and political crisis. The new head of state, however, while making some progress against corruption and reducing the scale of state terror, was unable to resolve the differences within the ruling military circles and another coup in August 1983 brought General Mejía Victores to power in place of Ríos Montt.

Among Nicaragua's neighbours, the only one whose government greeted Somoza's fall with real enthusiasm was Costa Rica. President Carazo (1978–82), along with General Torrijos in Panama, had aided and abetted the Sandinistas and their allies in the crucial months before July 1979; diplomatic relations with Somoza's government had been severed in 1978 and Costa Rican territory was used to launch the decisive military blow against the dictator. Enthusiasm for the new régime, however, rapidly waned. Costa

Rica, with no standing army, viewed with concern the consolidation of Sandinista rule and the rapid military build-up. Many former Sandinista supporters, notably Eden Pastora ('Comandante Zero'), took refuge in Costa Rica and by 1981 the Nicaraguan government was being blamed in the Costa Rican press for every strike, land invasion or disturbance of the social peace.[22] By 1982, Pastora had organised his own counter-revolutionary force, which attacked Nicaragua from bases in Costa Rica. President Carazo, and his PLN successor President Luis Alberto Monge (1982–6), found themselves sucked into the Central American maelstrom, while Costa Rica's traditional sense of superiority towards regional political strife looked increasingly flimsy.

## The balance of payments crisis

While Central America was sliding into political crisis, a process accelerated by the fall of Somoza, the region began to be affected by the upheavals in the world economy following the second round of massive oil price increases in 1979. World interest rates soared, pushing up the burden of external debt service, while the slowdown in the world economy (and eventual recession) produced a predictable deterioration in the external terms of trade. The result was a very severe balance of payments (BOP) crisis, which – when coupled with the political problems – justifies the term 'regional crisis'.

The outward and visible sign of the BOP crisis was the massive loss of gross international reserves in the years after 1978, although significantly this decline began earlier in Nicaragua. Deterioration in the current account BOP deficit is often taken as an indicator of reserve loss, but this is not appropriate where (as in Central America) the current account is traditionally in deficit and financed 'autonomously' through long-term capital flows. A more appropriate indicator is the basic balance, i.e., the current account deficit adjusted for long-term capital flows. We may therefore ask what proportion of the reserve loss was due to a deterioration in the basic balance and what proportion was due to changes in short-term capital flows (including net errors and omissions). The answer is provided by Table 11.1, which shows that during the period of heavy reserve loss the major cause of disequilibrium was changes in short-term capital flows in El Salvador, Guatemala and Nicaragua, while in Costa Rica changes in such flows accounted for nearly 30% of the deterioration.

The key element in short-term capital flows has been 'other short-term capital of other sectors'. This includes changes in the US bank accounts of Central American residents, the other important entry being trade credits. The drying-up of trade credits after 1978 was clearly related to developments in the international financial system and could therefore be optimistically

Table 11.1.  *Balance of payments contributions to cumulative reserve losses (inclusive of exceptional financing), 1978–82*

| | Period (end-year) | (1) (%) | (2) (%) | (3) Total Loss (million SDR) |
|---|---|---|---|---|
| Costa Rica | 1978–81 | +72.7 | +27.3 | 774.2 |
| El Salvador | 1978–81 | −8.5 | +108.5 | 399.6 |
| Guatemala | 1978–81 | +21.2 | +78.8 | 492.6 |
| Honduras | 1979–82 | +113.6 | −13.6 | 194.8 |
| Nicaragua | 1977–80 | −67.9 | +167.9 | 288.7 |

(1) Percentage contribution of current account deficit net of long-term capital flows to cumulative reserve loss
(2) Percentage contribution of short-term capital flows (inclusive of net errors and omissions, but exclusive of exceptional financing) to cumulative reserve loss
(3) Reserve loss defined to include exceptional financing, e.g. payments arrears, rescheduling of debt in arrears, loans from Central American Stabilization Fund

Source: IMF, *Balance of Payments Yearbook*, 1984

construed as 'temporary', but the outflow of private capital to US bank accounts requires a more sophisticated explanation.

The two conventional explanations of such outflows are interest rate differentials and the expectation of exchange rate depreciation. Neither carries much weight in an understanding of Central America's capital flight problem. It is true that US interest rates rose sharply in 1979, but this was matched to some extent in Central America. Indeed, Costa Rica launched its ill-fated 'financial liberalisation' programme (with a sharp increase in interest rates) in October 1978,[23] but this could not prevent an increase in 1979 of SDR 62.3 million ($80.5 million) in claims on US banks.

Expectation of exchange rate depreciation is also unconvincing as an explanation of private capital flows. It is true that Nicaragua devalued in 1979 shortly before the fall of Somoza, but the outflow of private capital began in 1977; similarly, the Costa Rican currency was floated in December 1980, but the outflow began much earlier. Meanwhile, capital outflows were of great importance from Guatemala and El Salvador, two countries with a very long history of exchange rate stability.[24]

Both interest rate differentials and exchange rate expectations no doubt provide part of the explanation for the private capital outflow. More convincing, however, is the concept of political uncertainty as a cause of capital flight; thus, Nicaraguan investors, aware as early as 1977 that the future of the Somoza government was not secure, began to withdraw capital. By the time of Somoza's fall, Nicaraguan capital flight was more or less complete (at least in its first stage), but the Sandinista victory provoked capital flight elsewhere.[25] This was reinforced by the fall of General Romero in October

1979 in El Salvador and by the sequel of events throughout the region (see above, pp. 232–7).[26]

Much of this capital flight was clearly not of a temporary nature. In the Nicaraguan case, capital outflow (much of it belonging to the Somoza family) was lost forever and the probability of capital repatriation in El Salvador, following the reform programme of early 1980, could only be considered low. Both Guatemala and Costa Rica, on the other hand, could reasonably have expected a reversal of the capital outflow if the regional political environment should improve. As the environment steadily deteriorated, however, it was clear that a reversal of capital flight could not be expected in the short term.

Despite the problems created by capital flight, virtually nothing was done to correct it. During 1980, Guatemala and Honduras introduced exchange control, but it was very mild and largely ineffective; El Salvador legalised dollar deposit accounts towards the end of 1980 in an effort to reverse capital outflows, but the result was unimpressive. Nicaragua and El Salvador nationalised their banking systems in 1979 and 1980 respectively, but by then the bulk of the capital outflows had already taken place. In effect, a decision was taken in each republic to finance the outflows by running down reserves accumulated during the years of high coffee prices in the second half of the 1970s.

The other element in the balance of payments crisis was the deterioration in some republics of the basic balance (see Table 11.1). In this context, it *is* relevant to ask what happened to the current account deficit, since the cause of the widening basic balance deficit was not a decline in long-term capital outflows, but an increase in the current account deficit not financed by additional long-term flows. Several factors contributed to the widening of current account deficits in the three republics (Costa Rica, Guatemala, Honduras) where a deterioration of the basic balance was a factor in reserve loss. One was the rise in the price of oil, while another was a fall in the price of coffee from its all-time peak in 1977. Between 1978 and 1981, the terms of trade (TOT) for the region fell by 29.7%.[27]

The change in the TOT was by no means the whole story, however, as world interest rate rises also added to the cost of servicing international debt. As Table 11.2 shows, this additional interest charge accounted for a substantial part of the deterioration in the current account deficit in the cases of Costa Rica and Honduras. The table shows that coffee, oil and interest costs are sufficient to account for most of the change in the current account during the period when the deficit was increasing. In addition, Guatemala suffered badly because of a sharp fall in tourist earnings as a result of the adverse publicity surrounding the country during the Lucas García régime (1978–82). One should also note that the contribution of the 'other' column in Table 11.2 to BOP deterioration was negative or zero. This column

Table 11.2. *Contributions to deterioration in current account deficit, 1978–81*

| | Period | Increase in deficit (million SDR) | (1) (%) | (2) (%) | (3) (%) | (4) (%) |
|---|---|---|---|---|---|---|
| Costa Rica | 1978–80 | +219.3 | +27.3 | +33.4 | +39.3 | +0.1 |
| Guatemala | 1978–81 | +281.0 | +38.6 | +64.9 | +19.8 | −23.3 |
| Honduras | 1978–81 | +131.1 | +16.7 | +59.0 | +48.2 | −23.9 |

(1) Fall in value of coffee exports as percentage of increase in deficit
(2) Increase in value of oil imports as percentage of increase in deficit
(3) Increase in debt service interest payments as percentage of increase in deficit
(4) Deterioration in current account other than items (1) to (3) as percentage of increase in deficit (a minus sign denotes an improvement)

Source: IMF, *Balance of Payments Yearbook*, 1983

is roughly equivalent to movements in the non-oil, non-coffee trade account and a negative sign means an improvement; much of this was due to favourable movements in the prices of traditional exports (e.g. sugar, bananas, cotton, beef) together with a small decline in the volume of imports.[28]

Following the first oil crisis of 1973–4, the need for BOP adjustment was largely averted through a sharp increase in coffee prices. This time, however, coffee prices could only be expected to fall, so that the deterioration of TOT from 1979 onwards could not be regarded as temporary; in addition, uncertainties about the world economy and the revival of monetarism suggested that the rise in interest rates might not be temporary either. Thus, prudent policy-making would have counselled at least a modest adjustment programme following the balance of payments deterioration in 1979.

El Salvador and Nicaragua did indeed 'adjust', although policy-making played little part in the programme of adjustment. Both countries ran a trade and current account surplus in 1979, as imports fell even in value terms in response to lower levels of economic activity. In Nicaragua, the value of imports was halved between 1977 and 1979 and the case for financing in response to balance of payments pressure after 1979 was very strong; the same could be said for El Salvador, where imports continued to decline in 1980. Elsewhere, however, the failure to adopt adjustment programmes in response to a BOP crisis, which could not be construed as temporary, was a serious error. The irresponsible resort to finance, particularly in Guatemala and Costa Rica, inevitably increased the burden when adjustment programmes were finally adopted.

Any division between a financing and adjustment phase in response to a BOP crisis is to some extent arbitrary, because there will usually be elements of both in any policy mix. Central America is no exception, yet in each

Table 11.3. *Responses to balance of payments crisis*

|  | Costa Rica | El Salvador | Guatemala | Honduras | Nicaragua |
|---|---|---|---|---|---|
| Financing (FN) phase | Up to September 1980 | Up to November 1980 | Up to mid-1982 | Up to April 1981 | Up to September 1981 |
| Adjustment without conditionality (AWOC) phase | Up to December 1982 | Up to July 1982 | Up to September 1983 | Up to November 1982 | Up to end 1982 |
| Adjustment with conditionality (AWIC) phase | Up to January 1984 | Up to August 1983 | Up to July 1984 | Up to January 1984 | NA |
| Post-Adjustment phase | In progress | In progress | In progress | In progress | NA |

republic there is a clear contrast between the first response to the crisis, when financing was dominant, and the second, when adjustment prevailed. As Table 11.3 shows, the financing (FN) phase came to a halt at the end of 1980 in Costa Rica and El Salvador; it had ended in Honduras and Nicaragua by the close of 1981, while in Guatemala the adjustment phase was delayed until 1982. In each case the transition was marked by a package of emergency measures.

Although the initial response to BOP difficulties in each republic was a resort to finance, this was not sufficient to prevent a slowdown in the rate of growth of real GDP. On the contrary, the massive capital outflow documented above (pp. 237–40) had as its corollary a collapse of private investment; by 1979, private investment had peaked in all republics except Honduras (where it peaked in 1980) and by 1981 it had fallen to nearly half its peak level in Costa Rica and Guatemala, 33% of its peak level in El Salvador and 91% in Honduras.[29]

Two factors helped to offset the rapid decline in aggregate demand implied by the private investment figures. In turn, this made possible positive growth throughout the region, although at a much lower rate than in 1978 and 1979 (except in Nicaragua, where post-war reconstruction lifted the economy by over 10% in 1980). The first stimulus to aggregate demand was provided by the Central American Common Market (CACM) with intra-regional trade in 1980 growing by 31% and lifting its value above one billion US dollars for the first (and only) time in its history. Nearly 70%, however, of the increase in trade between 1979 and 1980 was accounted for by increased Nicaraguan purchases. This rate of increase could not be sustained and Nicaragua soon found itself unable to pay its debts arising from the imbalance in intra-regional trade. Between 1980 and 1982, Nicaragua's cumulative deficit with Central America on intra-regional trade reached some $425 million and the failure of the Sandinista government to service this debt was one of the factors behind the decline of CACM after 1980.

The second stimulus to real aggregate demand came from public investments. While private investment was falling, public capital expenditure rose rapidly between 1978 and 1980 in Costa Rica and Honduras. Expansion continued until 1981 in Guatemala and Nicaragua (where the increase began after 1979)[30] and even in El Salvador a sharp fall in public investment was prevented until 1982. The increase in public capital expenditure was much faster than the rise in revenue. Indeed, by 1980 (Costa Rica, El Salvador, Nicaragua) or by 1981 (Guatemala, Honduras), government revenue was not even sufficient to cover *current* expenditure and the whole of the capital budget had to be financed by borrowing. The budget deficit as a percentage of GDP rose sharply, reaching over 8% in Costa Rica and over 7% elsewhere in 1981.[31]

During 1978 (i.e., before the BOP crisis), there was very roughly a one to one ratio between the stock of bank credit and the flow of imports.[32] After 1978, this ratio rose sharply in all republics, as domestic credit expansion (DCE) outpaced the rise in imports even in value terms, suggesting an increase in liquidity with the public forced to hold unwanted cash balances leading to a rise in inflation. This did not happen, however, and indeed the money stock expanded in line with nominal GDP after 1978 leaving velocity more or less unchanged.[33]

What happened, instead, is that the public sucessfully converted its excess money holdings into foreign currency, draining international reserves out of the banking system and forcing the Central Banks in particular to borrow massively in the international capital market. By the end of the FN phase, net foreign assets had turned or were about to turn negative in each republic and the inflationary pressures usually accompanying excessive DCE were avoided only by converting the excess into capital flight. This reduced the stock of money of external origin and contributed to a lowering of overall monetary expansion.[34]

The price paid for this *largesse* on the part of the authorities was a massive rise in external public indebtedness. It was argued in the previous chapter (see pp. 212–18) that outside Somoza's Nicaragua the increase in external debt up to the end of 1978 was not irresponsible, and service payments were manageable. In the three years, however, after the end of 1978 (see Table 11.4) the disbursed public external debt doubled or more than doubled in all republics; credit from official sources rose the most rapidly in 'war-torn' republics, while elsewhere private credit was the most buoyant. Because of the relatively low starting base for private credit, however, only Costa

Table 11.4. *Disbursed public external debt: increase from end-1978 to end-1981 ($ million)*

|  | Total increase | % | Official | % | Private | % | % Increase due to private sources |
|---|---|---|---|---|---|---|---|
| Costa Rica | 1302.5 | 137 | 424.2 | 82 | 878.3 | 203 | 67.4 |
| El Salvador | 329.1 | 99 | 339.1 | 108 | −9.9 | −47 | Negative |
| Guatemala | 505.5 | 166 | 444.9 | 150 | 60.6 | 904 | 12.0 |
| Honduras | 639.1 | 107 | 381.8 | 79 | 257.0 | 227 | 40.0 |
| Nicaragua | 1126.3 | 116 | 713.0 | 130 | 413.0 | 98 | 37.0 |

Source: World Bank, *World Debt Tables*, 1983–4

Rica funded more than 50% of its increase in public external indebtedness from private sources.

The rise in debt during the FN phase was so large that it is not unreasonable to blame much of the later debt problems on the increases incurred in this phase. A considerable share, for example, of the commercial debt (the rescheduling of which has caused such problems for Costa Rica, Honduras and Nicaragua) was contracted during the financing stage. While adjustment, as we shall see, has its problems, failure to adjust imposes costs and an increase in debt burden is one of them.

During the FN phase, several governments paid lip-service to the need for adjustment programmes and some (Costa Rica, Honduras, Guatemala) even reached agreement with the IMF on stand-by credits.[35] In all cases except one these credits were suspended and the exception (Guatemala in November 1981) hardly counts, as the stand-by was a first credit tranche which is *de facto* free of conditions and is wholly disbursed at the start of the programme; thus, it cannot later be suspended if the borrowing country fails to meet the 'conditions'.

Why did the adjustment programmes in Costa Rica, Guatemala and Honduras fail? In the Guatemalan case, there is no mystery: the Fund's conditions included a rise in interest rates and a reduction in the public sector borrowing requirement (PSBR); interest rates were raised in late 1981, but significantly they were lowered immediately the programme expired[36] and no action was taken to lower the PSBR other than a cut in capital expenditure. In other words, the adjustment programme in Guatemala was not taken seriously.

In the Honduran case, the three-year Extended Fund Facility (EFF) of February 1980 was suspended because the authorities failed to meet PSBR targets. During 1980, Honduras introduced new and raised existing taxes (mainly direct) and government revenue rose sharply by 20%. Government expenditure, however, rose even more rapidly on both current and capital account and the PSBR doubled over its 1979 level. The Honduran failure cannot be attributed to the indexed nature of expenditure. Only half the rise in current expenditure was due to wages and salaries, the remainder being due to the increase in purchases of goods and services. The Honduran public sector is highly decentralised and the armed forces in particular, in anticipation of the return to civilian rule, appear to have increased their share of the government budget and contributed in no small measure to the failure of the agreement with the IMF.

While the outgoing military administration of General Policarpo Paz García faced few problems in raising public revenue in Honduras, the incoming civilian administration of President Carazo in Costa Rica (1978–82) found itself in the opposite position. Carazo and his economic team were committed to a strategy of financial liberalisation on taking office and looked with favour on a reduced public sector and a shrunken PSBR. Minister of Finance Hernan Saenz recognised early in 1980 that an adjustment programme was needed to solve the BOP crisis and the Carazo administration welcomed the one-year stand-by credit agreed with the IMF in March 1980. The relationship with the Fund, therefore, could not have been more cordial, with both sides taking a similar view on policy. By November, however, the credit had been suspended and a year later Carazo expelled an IMF mission from the country.[37] What went wrong?

The Fund's conditions for the March loan were conventional,[38] but the stumbling block proved to be raising additional tax revenue. While monetary policy (particularly interest rates) was firmly under the control of the authorities, fiscal policy required the support of a national assembly in which the government enjoyed only a paper majority. Time and again, efforts to introduce tax reform packages failed, so that the government could not meet the end-March, -June, -September quarterly targets set by the Fund for fiscal and credit performance.

### Stabilisation programmes and the burden of adjustment

The balance of payments crisis, with which the FN phase began, did not prove temporary and was reflected in a collapse of net foreign assets. The finance strategy therefore came to a halt, when emergency measures were introduced in support of the BOP. This can be dated to September 1980 in Costa Rica, November 1980 in El Salvador, April 1981 in Honduras, September 1981 in Nicaragua and mid-1982 in Guatemala. Each republic then entered on an adjustment phase which ended with the approval of a non-suspended IMF credit subject to conditions. This 'adjustment without conditionality' (AWOC) phase-therefore runs until July 1982 in El Salvador, November 1982 in Honduras, December 1982 in Costa Rica and September 1983 in Guatemala.[39] In Nicaragua, this stage ended in a different way, as no agreement was reached with the IMF (see below, pp. 252–8).

As in the FN stage, efforts were made to reach agreement with the IMF; both Costa Rica and Honduras received three-year EFF's in 1981, in June and August respectively, but the Fund suspended both within six months. In the Honduran case the size of the budget deficit proved the stumbling block, while in Costa Rica the Fund took exception to the introduction of new restrictions on imports and the accumulation of debt arrears. Adjustment programmes were in force, however, despite the problems with the Fund and we may therefore observe how the five Central American republics approached the adjustment problem when not subject to IMF conditionality. Unfortunately, this cannot be viewed as a 'controlled experiment', because policy-making operated under the shadow of conditionality, but one can still observe a difference of emphasis in policy between adjustment with and without IMF conditions.

The preferred method of adjustment in this stage was without doubt the increased use of import controls. Indeed, because such an increase is anathema to the Fund, it is not surprising that relations with the IMF were so strained. The increase in import controls consisted of changes in prior deposits, import licences, quotas, increased taxes and outright prohibition. In effect, the authorities graded imports according to their 'importance' and rationed foreign exchange accordingly.

In most republics, this rationing was carried out with the help of multiple exchange rates. in El Salvador, a parallel market was authorised in late 1981,[40] and dealings were brought within the purlieu of the nationalised banking system in August 1982. Nicaragua legalised a parallel market in January 1982, also at a substantial discount, and in both republics a black or free market also operated, without government approval, although in El Salvador the black and parallel markets never drifted too far apart.[41] Guatemala and Honduras, the two republics with the oldest history of exchange rate stability, did not introduce a parallel market in this phase. A black market existed in both republics, however, with the home currency trading at around 25% below the official rate.

The republic which relied most heavily on the exchange rate as an instrument of policy was Costa Rica. In September 1980, 50% of trade was channelled through a free market and in December the colón (¢) was allowed to float freely. By the end of 1981, there were three exchange rates in force, all of which can be compared with the rate of ¢8.60 per US dollar in August 1980: an official rate of ¢20, which was used for about 1% of transactions, an inter-bank rate of ¢36 (which applied to virtually all trade items) and a parallel rate of ¢39 for tourism in particular. By the end of 1982, when the adjustment without conditionality phase finished, the interbank rate was ¢40.50 and the parallel rate ¢45.

While measures to control imports were adopted vigorously and comprehensively, the same enthusiasm was not displayed in promoting exports.

Nicaragua introduced new export incentives for agricultural products in the first quarter of 1982, followed by further incentives in the first quarter of 1983, but neither set of measures came close to compensating exporters for an effective *appreciation* of the real exchange rate. Guatemala also adopted an export incentives law in September 1982, and Costa Rica in December 1981 reduced the exchange taxes on export proceeds (introduced to enable the public sector to benefit from the windfall gains associated with devaluation). Nevertheless, the emphasis on export promotion was very slight during the period of adjustment without conditionality.

The combination of import restrictions coupled with some export incentives had a devastating effect on taxes on external trade. The revenue from these taxes fell sharply during the AWOC stage, although the decline began during the FN phase. With taxes on trade accounting for nearly one-third of government revenue in 1978, this sharp decline inevitably provoked a fiscal crisis. During the AWOC phase, little attention was given to replacing lost income from trade taxes with other revenue sources so that government revenue declined in real terms (except in Nicaragua) and in three cases (El Salvador, Guatemala, Honduras) was stagnant even in money terms. Nicaragua, on the other hand, succeeded in increasing revenue five-fold between 1979 and 1983 partly through the introduction of new taxes (e.g., a levy on the net worth of private assets), partly through increasing existing taxes (e.g., a 10% surcharge on income tax), but above all through improvements in administration, tax evasion having been such a noticeable feature of the pre-revolutionary period.

Fiscal policy, therefore, tended to focus on expenditure cuts rather than revenue increases. A key element in several republics was wage restraint, with an outright freeze in El Salvador, strict control in Nicaragua and indexing to a basic wage basket in Costa Rica.[42] Some efforts were made to raise the price of public services, but price control continued to be widespread (making an increase in government transfers inevitable) and food subsidies were common. Even these efforts to lower expenditure, however, tended to be dwarfed by the pressure to raise expenditure in support of increased defence spending.

Under these circumstances, it is scarcely surprising that the size of the budget deficit continued to be a severe problem during the AWOC phase. Only Costa Rica and Guatemala managed to lower the deficit as a percentage of GDP in this phase, while in Nicaragua it reached 12.1% in 1982. Even in Costa Rica and Guatemala, the value of bank credit to the public sector increased sharply, as the opportunities for funding the deficit externally became more and more restricted.

With private credit also increasing, although at a slower rate than public credit, the credit–import ratio continued to rise. As in the FN phase, however, this excess credit creation was not monetised; velocity remained stable and the inflation rate declined throughout the AWOC phase (except in Costa Rica where the rise to 90% in 1982 was clearly caused by the collapse of the exchange rate).[43] There were several reasons why excess credit creation did not result in monetary instability during the AWOC phase. First, all republics except Guatemala raised interest rates, thereby increasing the attraction of non-monetary assets; secondly, the use of advanced import deposit schemes encouraged the growth of quasi-money, which was also promoted by interest rate changes. Thirdly, capital flight continued during the AWOC phase, so that the decline in net foreign assets (and therefore money of external origin) was not reversed. Finally, exchange rate depreciation (whether *de facto* or *de jure*) soaked up a large proportion of any excess liquidity.

Policy during the AWOC phase relied most heavily on import controls, devaluation (often *de facto*) and exchange restrictions. This was reflected in a sharp fall in imports (see Table 11.5) and an improvement in the current account balance of payments deficit. This might be seen as a justification for AWOC phase policy and, indeed, one should not ignore the impact that a direct assault on the balance of payments can have. Nevertheless, several important *caveats* are in order.

First, the fall in imports was indiscriminate and affected trade within the Central American Common Market (CACM) as much as imports from outside the region.[44] To some extent the fall in the value of CACM trade after 1980 (see Table 11.5) was inevitable, since much of this trade consisted of consumer goods, which were the most obvious candidates for import suppression; yet one country's CACM imports are another's exports, so that the effect of import restrictions was to increase the burden of adjustment above what was strictly necessary.

Secondly, the improvement in the balance of payments position was achieved partly through accumulation of debt service arrears. Costa Rica suspended all service payments in 1981 and resumed interest payments only at a token level in July 1982. By the end of 1982, Guatemalan arrears were estimated at $344 million[45] and Honduras went into arrears in October 1982. Nicaragua, which had reached agreement with its creditors on debt rescheduling in August 1982,[46] narrowly avoided default in December and was again accumulating arrears in 1983.[47] By the close of the AWOC phase, the external debt problem and the difficulty of obtaining new credits had acquired major significance everywhere except El Salvador and, indeed, was the main reason why Costa Rica, Guatemala and Honduras were prepared to try to honour the IMF agreements which marked the end of the AWOC phase.

Thirdly, the weak fiscal position during the AWOC phase was not very satisfactory. The means by which excessive DCE had not been monetised could only be regarded as temporary and the rapid growth of quasi-money

Table 11.5.  *Imports in nominal and real terms ($ million), 1978–83*

| | Real imports at 1982 prices (including service imports) | | | | | |
| | 1978 | 1979 | 1980 | 1981 | 1982 | 1983 |
|---|---|---|---|---|---|---|
| **Costa Rica** | | | | | | |
| 1 Imports (c.i.f.) | 1166 | 1397 | 1540 | 1209 | 889 | 988 |
| 2 Imports (CACM) | 203 | 212 | 220 | 152 | 112 | 120 |
| 3 Service Imports | 355 | 425 | 522 | 545 | 672 | 665 |
| 4 Real Imports | 1708 | 1757 | 1609 | 1185 | 806 | 840 |
| **El Salvador** | | | | | | |
| 1 Imports (c.i.f.) | 1027 | 1039 | 962 | 985 | 857 | 891 |
| 2 Imports (CACM) | 240 | 257 | 320 | 305 | 261 | 223 |
| 3 Service Imports | 346 | 431 | 392 | 383 | 370 | 386 |
| 4 Real Imports | 1514 | 1320 | 1031 | 922 | 768 | 721 |
| **Guatemala** | | | | | | |
| 1 Imports (c.i.f.) | 1286 | 1504 | 1598 | 1674 | 1388 | 1135 |
| 2 Imports (CACM) | 208 | 207 | 155 | 186 | 219 | 225 |
| 3 Service Imports | 451 | 483 | 635 | 650 | 490 | 404 |
| 4 Real Imports | 1640 | 1518 | 1387 | 1330 | 1054 | 838 |
| **Honduras** | | | | | | |
| 1 Imports (c.i.f.) | 699 | 826 | 1039 | 975 | 739 | 823 |
| 2 Imports (CACM) | 92 | 98 | 104 | 118 | 87 | 83 |
| 3 Service Imports | 227 | 288 | 352 | 335 | 361 | 320 |
| 4 Real Imports | 928 | 1025 | 1108 | 972 | 671 | 627 |
| **Nicaragua** | | | | | | |
| 1 Imports (c.i.f.) | 596 | 360 | 887 | 999 | 776 | 772 |
| 2 Imports (CACM) | 139 | 111 | 301 | 211 | 117 | 110 |
| 3 Service Imports | 213 | 206 | 214 | 235 | 254 | 214 |
| 4 Real Imports | 581 | 472 | 1058 | 1025 | 764 | 710 |

Sources: Row (1), Table A.11; row (2), Consejo Monetario Centroamericano, *Boletín Estadístico, 1983*, San José, 1984; row (3) IMF, *International Financial Statistics Yearbook, 1984*. Row (4) Inter-American Development Bank, *Economic and Social Progress in Latin America*, 1984 Report

posed a potential threat to financial stability. In this respect, as we shall see, the IMF proved to be more imaginative (and flexible) than is often realised.

The adjustment with conditionality (AWIC) phase began with the approval by the IMF of stand-by credits in support of adjustment programmes which were substantially completed. The dates were July 1982 for El Salvador, November 1982 for Honduras, December 1982 for Costa Rica and September 1983 for Guatemala. No agreement was reached with Nicaragua, which failed to come to any accommodation with the Fund after the revolution; the exact reasons for this have never been stated publicly, but it is assumed to be due to US leverage over the IMF on the one side and Sandinista reluctance to submit to conditionality on the other (see below, pp. 252–8). The AWIC phase therefore excluded Nicaragua.

The central policy element in the AWIC phase was a reduction in the budget deficit. Although the Fund (as we shall see) proved flexible in other respects, it clung to orthodoxy as far as the budget deficit was concerned; targets were set for the deficit as a proportion of GDP (except for El Salvador)[48] and each letter of intent committed the signatories to raising revenue as well as cutting expenditure. The revenue raising target took place against a background of falling or stagnant trade taxes; thus, any rise in revenue could be achieved only through disproportionately large increases in non-trade taxes. In each republic the executive was able to secure congressional support, but faced serious public unrest in consequence; in several cases, this led to a reversal or partial reversal of the original tax increases.

The most serious case of reversal occurred in Guatemala, the least democratic of the four republics concerned. The Ríos Montt government introduced a Value Added Tax (VAT) at 10% in July 1983 as a precondition for IMF support; the new tax, however, is widely conceded to have been one reason for the fall of Ríos Montt in August; the new military government, led by General Mejía Victores, agreed a standby credit with the IMF in September, but promptly lowered VAT to 7% in October. The failure by the Fund to secure a reimposition of VAT at 10% finally provoked suspension in July 1984.

The pressure to raise revenue also affected the price of public services controlled by decentralised public sector agencies. These increases in several cases were cancelled,[49] but the Fund remained unyielding in its determination to root out loss-making activities in the public sector. The justification for the Fund's concern was the fact that a large share of the increase in public external indebtedness was accounted for by the operations of these agencies. The latter included the investment corporations, which had become holding companies for a number of private sector lame ducks.[50]

It was argued previously that the growth of quasi-money in the AWOC phase created a potentially dangerous situation for the preservation of financial stability. In El Salvador and Guatemala, the Fund was credited with pioneering the use of dollar-denominated bonds with a medium-term maturity which served a dual purpose; first, they could be used to soak up the quasi-money overhang and, secondly, they could be used to pay for imports without the need for current dollars.[51] It is possible that this unorthodox measure, which proved moderately successful, was approved by the Fund in El Salvador and Guatemala, because of their relatively low levels of public external indebtedness to private creditors. In any case, such bonds were not issued by Costa Rica and Honduras.

More emphasis was put on export promotion during the AWIC than the AWOC phase. This was partly due to the opportunities created by the Caribbean Basin Initiative (CBI), formally launched in January 1984 (see below, p. 260), but whose probable implementation was known about well in advance.[52] It was also due to the Fund's 'export optimism' and preference for export-increasing over import-decreasing measures. A key element in export promotion was the use of tax credit certificates (CATs), which were increased particularly for non-traditional exports outside the region. Other measures included reductions in export taxes and the use of Free Zones.

The Fund insisted on orthodox credit policies, with targets set for DCE, but relied merely on exhortation in the case of interest rates. In fact, interest rate policy was extremely inactive during the AWIC phase; nominal interest rates hardly varied at all despite a big fall in inflation,[53] which left real interest rates positive for most types of non-monetary assets. The Fund, perhaps surprisingly, did not give much priority to the exchange rate in establishing preconditions for Fund support. In the case of Costa Rica, the IMF insisted on a narrowing of the spread between the inter-bank rate and the free market rate to no more than 2%; this was achieved in November 1983, one month before the expiry of the agreement. Elsewhere, the Fund called for the phasing out of exchange restrictions, but nothing substantial was done; the best that could be said is that restrictions were not actually increased.

The IMF gave considerable prominence to questions of external indebtedness. In Costa Rica and Honduras, the agreements were explicitly linked to debt reschedulings; the Fund's approval, however, turned out to be a necessary but not sufficient condition for debt rescheduling. Costa Rica, it is true, came to an arrangement with its official creditors quickly (in January 1983), but agreement with private creditors on debt falling due in 1983–4 was reached only in January 1984 (i.e. after the Fund programme had expired). The Honduran debt problem proved even more stubborn; an agreement in principle was reached in late 1983 covering $230 million of arrears, but was not implemented until 1985. In the case of Guatemala, the IMF agreement was not explicitly linked to debt rescheduling, but the letter of intent stated that commercial arrears should be reduced by $50 million in 1983 and $100 million in 1984; in the agreement with El Salvador, however, the question of external debt does not appear to have entered at all.

Despite the attention given by the Fund to debt problems, the burden of external debt service remained acute.[54] In return for submitting to IMF conditionality the republics of Central America expected not only to reschedule their debts on favourable terms, but also to qualify for new credits from the international banking system. The need for such a response from lenders became more and more important as export earnings declined sharply and world interest rates soared after 1979–80.

On both counts, the Central American republics subject to Fund condition-

Table 11.6.  *Indicators of burden of adjustment, 1980–3*

|  | (1) | (2) | (3) | (4) |
|---|---|---|---|---|
| Costa Rica | −13.1 | −33.6 | +53 | −26 |
| El Salvador | −21.9 | −31.2 | +85 | −39 |
| Guatemala | −13.4 | +19.2 | +264 | −9 |
| Honduras | −10.8 | −4.5 | +98 | −19 |
| Nicaragua | −3.7 | −34.1 | −4 | −39 |

(1) Percentage change in real GDP per head
(2) Percentage change in real wages
(3) Percentage increase in unemployment rate (a minus sign indicates a fall). (The unemployment rate in 1980 for the five republics was 5.9%, 16.2%, 2.3%, 10.7% and 18.3% in the country order listed above)
(4) Percentage change in real private consumption per head

Sources: col. (1) from Table A.3; cols. (2) to (3) from Inforpress, *Centro America 1984–6*, Guatemala, 1984, p. 6; col. (4) derived from Consejo Monetario Centroamericano, *Boletín Estadístico, 1983*, San José, 1984

ality received disappointments. Debt rescheduling was limited to two years at a time and new commercial lending was pitifully small.[55] International banks made it clear that they wished to reduce, not increase, their exposure to Central America, so that IMF conditionality proved to be only a necessary but not a sufficient condition for favourable treatment by commercial banks.

Where external debts must be serviced, but new commercial lending is not available, a BOP trade surplus is usually required to achieve the necessary transfer of resources to the rest of the world. An increase in *official* lending, however, as a consequence of the regional crisis acquiring an East–West dimension, enabled the Central American republics to avoid running large trade surpluses.[56] This additional official lending (see below, pp. 258–63) did not eliminate the region's debt problems, but it did (outside Nicaragua) help to make them more manageable.[57]

Adjustment programmes carry costs, which raises the question of who bears the burden of adjustment. The period of adjustment (AWOC and AWIC) corresponded roughly to the period 1981 to 1983. Taking 1980 as the base, one can, therefore, look at the changes in a number of indicators over the period 1980–3 which are relevant to the question of the burden of adjustment (see Table 11.6). The first indicator refers to the fall in real GDP per head. As the table makes clear, this has been particularly severe in El Salvador (where the decline actually began in 1978); indeed, the fall in real GDP per head from 1978 to 1984 in El Salvador was 36.7% and from 1977 to 1984 in Nicaragua it was 42.5% (see Table A.3). The second column of Table 11.6 refers to the change in real wages, which fell particularly heavily in Costa Rica, El Salvador and Nicaragua, but are estimated to have risen in Guatemala because of the sharp increase in minimum wages in 1980–1 from their very low base.[58] The third column of Table 11.6 refers to the percentage increase in the estimated rate of unemployment; only Nicaragua was able to prevent a sharp rise in the unemployment rate, although it should be remembered that the unemployment rate in Nicaragua in 1980 was already very high (18.3%).

Data on unemployment and wages (both real and nominal) are notoriously unreliable in Central America; in any case, wage labour accounts for only a part of total labour supply.[59] Consequently, a better indicator of the burden of adjustment (see column 4) is the change in real consumption per head. As Table 11.6 shows, all the republics have been badly affected on this score with the worst sufferers being El Salvador and Nicaragua. The fall in real consumption per head has indeed been so severe that the crisis of the early 1980s can be compared in magnitude with the crisis in the early 1930s, fifty years earlier. Thus, Central America – in addition to its accumulated problems inherited from before 1979 – must now face the task of rebuilding living standards back to the level of the late 1970s in a world and regional environment which has become far more hostile.

Not all the burden of adjustment can be attributed to the stabilisation programmes and even less to the IMF-inspired programmes during the AWIC phase. War-related adjustment was very important in El Salvador and Nicaragua and was the main reason why those two republics carried a heavier burden than the others; similarly, once the effects of the war are taken into account, it seems safe to assume that most of the burden of adjustment was carried during the AWOC rather than AWIC phase. It would be impossible, however, to quantify the distribution of the burden; in any case it would be inappropriate, as the external environment was much more hostile in the AWOC than AWIC phase.

One final question should be raised, although it cannot be fully answered: what additional costs of adjustment were incurred as a result of delaying adjustment during the FN stage? The answer again cannot be quantitative, but it can be assumed that the additional costs were substantial. Costa Rica in particular would have been able to incur a much smaller burden, if adjustment had begun in 1979 while all republics paid a heavy price for their failure to stem capital flight at an earlier stage.

## Growth and adjustment in Nicaragua

Although Nicaragua maintained correct relations with the IMF after the revolution, even settling all its outstanding debts in May 1985 and playing host to a Fund mission the following month, the Sandinista government did not follow the rest of Central America into the AWIC phase; instead, a public sector boom was engineered from early 1983 (marking the close of the AWOC phase) which lasted until the adjustment programme of February 1985.

Since 1983, therefore, the performance of the Nicaraguan economy has been *sui generis*, and many factors account for this. The most obvious is that it is highly unlikely that the Fund and the Sandinista government could have reached agreement on an adjustment programme, given US influence over the IMF on the one hand and internal Nicaraguan political realities on the other. It was also the case, however, that debt problems (which were forcing other Central American republics into the arms of the Fund) did not have the same significance in Nicaragua; it was clear, for example, by early 1983 that the revolutionary government could not expect any new money from foreign commercial banks or multinational institutions with strong US participation (above all, the World Bank and the InterAmerican Development Bank),[60] while on the other hand its anticipated credits from other sources were not conditional on an agreement with the Fund.

The necessary conditions for avoiding an agreement with the Fund might therefore be said to have existed in 1983, but the external environment deteriorated sharply in that year and the consequent BOP disequilibrium required the continuation and even intensification of adjustment programmes; under these circumstances, the choice of a public sector boom as the engine of growth of the economy (GDP rose by nearly 5% in 1983) proved to be most unfortunate.[61]

Several factors accounted for the deterioration of the external environment in 1983. Virtually no new loans were forthcoming from multilateral official creditors (although some disbursements continued because of previous commitments) and the increasing intensity of the war against the 'contras' distorted the allocation of scarce foreign exchange away from the export sector towards the military. The unit value of all major export products (except seafoods) fell in 1983 and gold exports ceased altogether.[62] Finally, Nicaragua lost virtually all its sugar quota to the US market, although this was subsequently picked up by Iran and Algeria at comparable prices.

The public sector boom in 1983 was the consequence of a 75% rise in central government nominal expenditure unmatched by revenue increases.[63] The central government deficit soared to 24.4% of nominal GDP with most of it financed internally through the banking system; between the end of 1982 and 1983, the money supply $(M_1)$ rose by 67% and the ratio of $M_1$ to nominal GDP rose from around 20% to 30% – a sure sign of short-run, unwanted accumulation of money balances on the part of the public. The huge rise in government expenditure occurred despite a fall in interest payments. Debt repayment problems (see below) led to a virtual 'passive default' and central government interest payments accounted for only 2.5% of expenditure in 1983. By contrast, central government current expenditure on salaries, goods and services rose by around 50% in 1983 compared to 1982, with much of the increase accounted for by additional outlays on defence.

The main reason for the deterioration of the fiscal situation was the 213% rise in 1983 in transfers and subsidies. These reached nearly 20% of total expenditure compared with 7% in 1982 and the change was explained by the increasing gap between the producer and consumer prices of controlled goods and services. These included basic foodstuffs (e.g., rice, beans, maize, sugar, milk), as well as the services of public utilities.

The rise in producers' prices for foodstuffs was part of the effort by the state National Foodstuffs Enterprise, ENABAS, to achieve self-sufficiency in food supply.[64] The impact on production of agricultural goods for internal consumption was not unsuccessful,[65] but the state proved incapable of matching supplies through controlled distribution channels to demand (particularly in urban areas). A two-tier market developed for most foodstuffs with prices in the black market far in excess of official guidelines, although the latter continued to be used in the calculation of the official cost of living index.

The Sandinista government denounced speculators and hoarders for the breakdown in the distribution system, but it was clear that the fiscal expansion played a major part in generating an effective demand for foodstuffs which could not be matched by official channels of distribution. Once the two-tier market was in place, moreover, it created a vicious circle; private producers by-passed ENABAS in a search for higher prices, and farmers in the export sector abandoned the production of foodstuffs for their workers since the same commodities could be purchased much more cheaply through official channels. Finally, high prices in the black market attracted migrants to urban areas (particularly Managua) and the informal urban sector mushroomed through the expansion of petty commerce.

The scarcity of foreign exchange, coupled with strict import controls, prevented the excess money creation from spilling over into imports, so that financial instability was reflected in domestic inflationary pressures. The rise in inflation (31% in 1983 and 36% in 1984) was not a correct measure of these pressures, because the index relied on official, controlled prices. A proxy for inflationary pressures, however, was provided by the black market exchange rate; this fell from 70 córdobas to the dollar at the end of 1983 to nearly 500 by the end of 1984.

While the black market exchange rate was rapidly depreciating in 1983 and 1984, the official exchange rate was unchanged at ten córdobas to the dollar. Since foreign trade had been nationalised by the revolutionary government, the exchange rate that mattered for exporters was the one used by the authorities to convert dollar earnings into actual producer receipts; this varied from product to product and the authorities adjusted the rates for the main export crops to reflect (at least partly) the rise in domestic prices. As a result of these efforts, the volume of exports of the main products (coffee, cotton, sugar, bananas) rose in 1983 and there was also an increase in the dollar value of export earnings from these crops (except sugar) despite the fall in world prices. Nonetheless, total export earnings were stagnant in 1983, reaching only 63.6% of the pre-revolution level.

The problem of exports continued to be the decline in non-traditional products (including sales to CACM). Only one-third of the fall in the value of exports from 1978 to 1983 could be explained by the performance of traditional exports,[66] although they accounted for 70% of exports in 1978 and nearly 90% in 1983. The non-traditional products came mainly from the industrial sector, where the unrealistic exchange rate and foreign exchange shortages for the purchase of inputs, spare parts, etc. were the major problems rather than demand factors.

The weakness of exports continued in 1984, aggravated by external aggression,[67] and earnings fell below $400 million for the first time since 1975. This was virtually the same as projected service payments on the public external debt, so that the external disequilibrium became unmanageable; the 'passive default' begun in 1983 was continued into 1984 with no payments even of interest on the commercial debt owed to private, external creditors. By the middle of 1984, it was quite clear that the Sandinista attempt to circumvent the external disequilibrium through internal demand expansion had failed. Not only had the external environment deteriorated, but real GDP also fell in 1984 by 1.4%; the need for a further round of adjustment was recognised, but electoral considerations (see below, p. 261) postponed a decision until early 1985.

The adjustment programme announced in February 1985 was intended to reduce the fiscal deficit, curb inflationary pressure and at the same time remove some of the worst distortions in the Nicaraguan economy (the authorities correctly noted that all these were linked). The core of the programme was the raising of official consumer prices in an effort to end transfers and subsidies and reduce the fiscal deficit, while operating under a very tight constraint in which security considerations meant that defence would take 50% of the budget. Government investment and other expenditure were cut and new taxes were introduced (particularly on petty commerce in the urban informal sector).

Salaries were reorganised into twenty-eight groups and were increased in nominal, but not real terms. This inevitable element of the adjustment programme was largely nullified in April, when a further round of salary increases was announced to 'compensate' a further round of consumer price increases; the whole package therefore ran the risk of simply creating the same set of problems at a higher level of prices, and this was confirmed in June when the authorities announced new consumer prices for basic food-stuffs and an 'iron fist' offensive against speculation, hoarding, overcharging and contraband. By the end of the year, inflation had reached 334% and continued to accelerate throughout 1986, while the budget deficit remained above 20% of GDP in both years.

The increase in nominal salaries was designed to benefit workers in the formal sector and reverse the drift into the informal sector, which was responsible for the explosion of Managua's population. The acceleration of inflation, however, throughout 1985 and 1986 undermined real wages and salaries so that the latter fell to half their 1977 level by mid-1986; the attractions of petty commerce and the informal sector remained as great as ever and the government launched a series of programmes in 1986 designed to control the distribution and prices of articles of basic necessity, ensure the availability of such articles through official channels and penalise those profiting from unofficial prices in the black market. None of these measures proved particularly successful, as more and more urban Nicaraguans came to rely on the black market to satisfy a part of their basic requirements.

The adjustment programme legalised a parallel exchange rate (which settled temporarily at around 650 córdobas to the dollar) and introduced an official multiple exchange rate; the new rates, however, varied from 10 to 50 córdobas to the dollar, so that the devaluation came nowhere near eliminating the gap between the free and official rates and did not compensate exporters (particularly of industrial goods) for the rise in production costs. The currency was devalued again at the start of 1986 with the exchange rate unified at 70 córdobas to the dollar, and incentives increased for farmers to retain part of their export earnings in foreign exchange. With the parallel market at 1,200 córdobas to the dollar by the end of the year (and a black market rate close to 2,500) this was an important concession, but the enormous gap between the official and other exchange rates continued to encourage contraband, petty commerce and black market activities in the informal sector.

While the adjustment programme was being implemented, the external environment was subject to a number of important changes not all of which were unfavourable. In June 1985, an agreement (renewed in 1986) was reached with the creditor banks to postpone all debt service payments for one year, and the Soviet Union replaced Mexico as the country's source of oil supplies; Nicaragua even received a $44 million loan from the Central American Monetary Council to help her industrial exports to CACM. The most dramatic event, however, was the US embargo on trade with Nicaragua in May, which had in fact been anticipated by the authorities for several years and whose impact was therefore less damaging than at first was believed.[68]

The fall in exports in 1985 – they dropped below $300 million — was far more severe than could be justified by the change in the external environment alone. For the first time since the disruption caused by the revolution, exports of several traditional products fell sharply in volume terms. The previous decline of exports had been attributed to the poor performance of non-traditional products and falling terms of trade, but the sharp volume decline for cotton, cotton-seed, sugar cane and sesame was a new phenomenon. Only coffee exports recorded an increase in volume terms, although this still did not bring production back to the level before the 'contra' offensive of 1984.

The authorities attributed the collapse in exports to drought, economic sabotage and shortages of inputs. Equally important, however, was the impact of the land reform programme, which entered a new, more radical phase after 1984. One of the major concerns of the Sandinistas since 1979 had been to implement land reform in a way which safeguarded earnings from traditional exports and kept the support of farmers in the export sector. The expropriation of Somocista properties in 1979 (some 20% of the country's arable land) and their operation as state farms mainly producing export crops was consistent with these goals, as was the original agrarian reform law of 1981 which safeguarded from expropriation farms below 500 manzanas (350 hectares) in the Pacific area and below 1,000 manzanas (700 hectares) elsewhere.[69]

The agrarian reform law of August 1981 allowed the government to expropriate, usually with compensation, large farms either abandoned, underutilised or subject to illegal rental and share-cropping arrangements. Between October 1981 and the end of 1985, 2,523,388 manzanas were distributed to 83,322 families, figures which suggest a very radical programme; only 20% of these distributions, however, were achieved through expropriations under the agrarian reform law and most of the expropriations occurred in the first year of the programme. The distributions consisted mainly (56%) of giving title to peasants with insecure property rights, while the government reduced the size of the state sector (Area Propriedad del Pueblo) to encourage the formation of cooperatives.[70]

The large- and medium-size farmers producing traditional export crops were therefore largely unaffected by the agrarian reform and output rose steadily from its 1980 base. The landless workers and peasants without adequate access to land, however, were virtually ignored despite the fact that the Sandinista government claimed to represent these groups. By the end of 1984, only 1,009 families had received *new* lands with individual title, with nearly 30,000 given title to lands they already worked.[71] Impatient at the slow pace of progress, the landless peasantry in over-populated central Nicaragua launched a series of land invasions in 1985, which involved some of the most productive export farms and forced the Sandinistas to reconsider their agrarian reform programme.

The result was a revision of the law, introduced in January 1986, which abolished the limits on the size of farms subject to expropriation, eliminated compensation for expropriation and gave the state the right to expropriate any rural property 'under the right of public domain'. The latter was a catch-all phrase, which gave the authorities the right to seize land which was otherwise not subject to the agrarian reform law. The new law marked an end to the state's efforts to reach an accommodation with the rural bourgeoisie and gave legal backing to the process of distributing new land to individuals with the right of inheritance (but not of sale). In 1985, even before the new law came into effect, 6,204 families received title to 142,680 manzanas and the process accelerated in 1986. Not surprisingly, production of crops for the home market began to boom, while export crops languished.

Several lessons can be drawn from the Nicaraguan experience since the end of the AWOC phase. First, external aggression (however unjustified) is not unlike other external shocks in terms of its macroeconomic impact and should not prevent the adoption of adjustment programmes (however painful). Secondly, revolutionary governments ignore the need for internal as well as external balance at their peril, because the eventual costs of adjustment may be so severe as to rob the revolutionary government of its social and political base. Thirdly, the adjustment package begun in February 1985 was not unlike an IMF-inspired programme, although its impact was softened by subsequent, inconsistent policies which threatened to cancel the effectiveness of the original package. Fourthly, the combination of external aggression and internal policy errors produced a situation where the external debt could not be serviced; in the Nicaraguan case, passive default was the only 'solution'. Finally, the Sandinista agrarian reform programme – until it entered its radical phase in 1985 – showed that it was possible to combine land reform with the preservation, and even intensification, of EXA. The latest phase has shown, however, that when land reform is adopted for purely political reasons it is likely to be very damaging to agricultural exports.

## National and international response to the crisis

As it became clear that Central America was engulfed in a regional crisis, the external powers with an interest in Central America began to fashion their responses. Since these international responses reflected the (different) perceived interests of the external powers, the result was a bewildering array of proposals and measures which frequently contradicted one another and which circumscribed the room for manoeuvre of individual Central American republics.

Flushed with the wealth produced by the latest round of oil price increases, the two major oil exporters in the region (Mexico and Venezuela) joined forces in August 1980 to offer Caribbean Basin countries a comprehensive energy package under the San José oil facility. The latter, renewed every year, provided countries of the region with guarantees of oil supplies and long-term loans up to 30% of the value of purchases on concessionary terms, with the most favourable interest rates reserved for energy-saving projects.[72] Both Mexico and Venezuela also supplied substantial bilateral aid to individual Central American republics (Mexico in particular became Nicaragua's single most important source of concessionary aid after the revolution),[73] and the Venezuelan Investment Fund (VIF) became an important source of BOP support for several republics during the worst years of the BOP crisis.

As the major regional powers, Mexico and Venezuela also had a strong interest in regional stability, and it became clear after 1980 that the San José facility alone could not prevent an increase in instability and a descent into regional crisis. The two powers therefore joined forces with Colombia and Panama to form the Contadora group[74] in January 1983; the stated purpose of Contadora was to find a peaceful solution to the regional crisis and, in particular, to promote peaceful coexistence between Sandinista Nicaragua on the one hand and the United States with its Central American allies on the other.[75]

The Contadora group's emphasis on peaceful coexistence with Nicaragua ran counter to the increasingly hard-line anti-Sandinista posture emanating from Washington. This contradiction came to a head in late 1984, when the US administration put pressure on its regional allies (Costa Rica, El Salvador and Honduras) to reject Contadora's draft peace treaty without substantial modifications;[76] the rejection marked a near-mortal blow to Contadora's pretensions, although the group continued to command widespread international support. Indeed, a European Economic Community aid package for Central America (including Nicaragua) was agreed in 1985 in support of Contadora's regional initiative.[77]

Cuba had responded enthusiastically to the Sandinista-led victory and thousands of Cubans were soon active in Nicaragua as teachers in the literacy campaign,[78] as health and construction workers and, more controversially, as military advisers. The Soviet Union, and its East European allies, responded more cautiously at first, but trade with and aid (including military) from the Soviet bloc accelerated as the survival of the Sandinista régime began to be called into question by the operations of the 'contras' and the US trade and aid embargo. By 1984, Comecon countries accounted for nearly 30% of imports (compared with 1% in 1980) and by 1985 90% of oil was supplied by the Soviet Union. Together with bilateral aid these measures were sufficient to prevent total economic collapse in Nicaragua, but insufficient to provide the resources needed for sustained growth.

Despite all these initiatives, the major external power in the region remained the United States and, indeed, many of the initiatives described above were adopted in response to US policies. The latter have frequently been described as 'two-track' in reference to the combination of militaristic measures designed to defeat left-wing insurgents and destabilise the Sandinista revolution together with socio-economic measures designed to reduce regional instability and promote economic growth.[79] The two tracks sometimes crossed each other, however, and were the outcome of the many conflicting pressures to which the US administration was subject rather than a consistent response to the regional crisis.[80]

The militaristic measures were designed in response to the perceived threat to US security interests in the region arising from the consolidation of Sandinismo in Nicaragua and left-wing insurgency in El Salvador and Guatemala. In addition to a huge increase in military assistance to El Salvador and Honduras, the Reagan administration secured Congressional approval for a reversal of the ban on military aid to Guatemala; Costa Rica, despite the absence of a standing army, was also involved in these measures, with US military assistance being used to increase the quality and quantity of its Civil Guard.

The Reagan administration increasingly blamed Cuba and the Soviet Union for fomenting regional instability, but recognised that socio-economic conditions had provided a fertile seedbed for political unrest. The initial response from both the Carter and Reagan administrations was an increase in US economic aid, but the depth of the regional crisis made it clear that this alone was not sufficient. Increased aid was therefore supplemented with trade measures under the Caribbean Basin Initiative (CBI), giving the countries of the region (except Nicaragua) duty-free access to the US market for most products for a period of twelve years from 1 January 1984.

The US trade and aid measures conformed to a view of the development process in Central America which was exemplified by the Kissinger Report.[81] This view emphasised the need for less state intervention in Central America, a more receptive attitude to direct foreign investment, the reduction or elimination of price controls and the dismantling of high-cost, inefficient import-substituting industries. It stressed the need for an emphasis on outward-looking growth through export promotion, thereby reinforcing policies promoted by the IMF and the World Bank, but it recognised that some social and political reforms were an essential companion to these economic measures; in particular, great importance was attached to land reform and democratisation.

This view of the development process was widely criticised for its contradictions with other aspects of US policy and for failing to recognise the realities of development in Central America.[82] Much of this criticism was of the 'knee-jerk' variety and proved to be misplaced (as we shall see), but the US administration's vision of the development process was seriously distorted by the failure to attach any real importance to the revival of CACM, the development of the organised labour movement, the need for greater food security, an easing of the external debt problem and the difficulties faced by the dependence of exports (and the rest of the economy) on a handful of primary commodities with uncertain prospects.

Increased official development assistance, from whatever source, reduced the burden of adjustment below what it would otherwise have been and eased the short-term economic problems. All the Central American republics, however, entered the 1980s with a variety of long-term problems inherited from the past. The regional crisis made the need for a solution to these problems even more acute, but the internationalisation of the crisis and the perceptions of the external powers imposed limits on which problems could be tackled and what methods could be employed.

The struggle for democracy illustrated this dilemma. The Reagan adminis-tration emphasised the need for a process of democratisation, but US security interests emphasised the need to defend and promote the armed forces in the three northern republics. The result was limited progress towards formal democracy together with an enhancement of the authority of the military. This increase in military presitge was not necessarily inconsistent with pro-gress towards democracy. In Honduras, for example, leaders of the armed forces removed (in March 1984) the authoritarian and anti-democratic General Alvarez and then intervened (in April 1985) in a dispute between the civilian politicians which was threatening to disrupt the electoral process. As a result, Honduras averted a constitutional crisis and the fledgling democ-racy survived. In El Salvador, on the other hand, the traditional right-wing political parties have fallen into disarray and the Christian Democrats (CD) have become the main beneficiary from the electoral cycle imposed since 1982,[83] but the growing prestige of the armed forces has put severe limi-tations on what even a CD administration can achieve and left unresolved the problem of how to reduce military influence over the Salvadorean politi-cal process.

The Sandinistas responded to the US emphasis on democratisation with elections of their own in November 1984. Outside observers in general con-cluded that these elections (won handsomely by the FSLN)[84] were no less fair or representative than those which had recently been held in El Salvador and Guatemala,[85] although by the more demanding standards of Costa Rica they fell a long way short of being fully competitive.[86] The whole episode emphasised, however, how fragile was the progress towards democracy in Central America, so that by the beginning of 1986, it was still only in Costa Rica that the future of democracy could be forecast with confidence.[87]

The development of the organised labour movement was similarly afflicted by the contradiction between the demands for social reform on the one hand and security restrictions on the other. In El Salvador, Guatemala and Honduras (during the 'reign' of General Alvarez),[88] organised labour con-tinued to be viewed with suspicion; the latter's efforts to reverse the sharp decline in real wages brought about by the stabilisation programmes were often treated as a threat to national security, and the labour movement in those republics faced some of the worst repression in its history.[89] Even in Costa Rica, the organised labour movement was not exempt from these trends; land invasions, strikes and demands for higher wages were frequently denounced in the national press as part of a Sandinista plan to destabilise the government, and the authorities began to restrict some of labour's traditional freedoms.

The development of an organised labour movement in Sandinista Nicaragua was made a high priority and trade unionism flourished as never before. The vast majority, however, belonged either to the Central Sandinista de Trabajadores (CST) or to the Asociación de Trabajadores del Campo (ATC), both controlled by the FSLN, so that the creation of an independent organised labour movement in Nicaragua remained a distant goal.[90] Furthermore, the introduction of the state of emergency in March 1982 ended the right to strike, so that even the threat of industrial action became a threat to national security. After the fall of General Alvarez, the Honduran labour movement began to recover some of the ground lost between 1982 and 1984, and labour organisations played an honourable role in the resolution of the constitutional crisis in April 1985; in Costa Rica the labour movement maintained its independence despite the occasional hostility of the authorities, and organised labour in Guatemala received a stimulus from its long struggle to reopen the Coca Cola plant in the capital.[91]

These achievements of organised labour should not be ignored, but outside Nicaragua only a small proportion of the labour force has been brought into trade unions and the ability of the labour movement to promote a fairer distribution of the benefits from future economic growth remains in doubt. The omens are perhaps more favourable in Costa Rica and Honduras, but a vigorous, independent labour movement elsewhere in Central America remains a remote objective.

The emphasis given by the US administration to the promotion of non-traditional exports outside the area coincided with the preferences of the IMF and the World Bank and gave a stimulus to such policies. Despite the regional crisis, the combination of incentives provided by the CBI and local tax authorities did produce a response; Costa Rica, in particular, benefited from the rapid growth of the US economy in 1984 and recorded a 14% increase in non-traditional exports outside the CACM. These efforts were praiseworthy, but the low starting base meant that exports continued to be dominated by earnings from traditional primary products and from sales to the CACM. Both these were neglected by the external powers, and the loss of earnings occasioned by the impact of the world recession on primary products and by the impact of the regional crisis on the CACM far outweighed any increase from non-traditional exports outside the area.

The US administration appeared to recognise the problems caused by dependence on primary product exports. When the Nicaraguan US sugar quota was cut in 1983 to 10% of its previous level, the beneficiaries were other Central American sugar exporters; the US sugar import quota in 1985–6 was set higher than implied by US sugar consumption in order to avoid a sharp cut in imports from Latin American sugar exporters, and US influence was used to secure a higher coffee quota for Honduras under the International Coffee Agreement (ICA). Yet these positive steps were cancelled by other features of US policy; the protectionist measures in favour of US sugar producers promoted high domestic prices, a substitution effect by consumers in favour of cheaper alternatives and a slump in world prices. Similarly, US insistence (in common with other major consumers) in favour of a big increase in the global coffee export quota in 1984–5 pushed world prices down and undermined the price range defended by the ICA.[92]

While the problems facing commodity exports were at least recognised, the difficulties confronting the CACM were almost entirely ignored by the US administration and other external actors seeking to influence economic policy in Central America. Following the boom in the CACM in 1980 (see above, pp. 241–2), the level of intra-regional trade declined sharply in the following years despite the reopening of commerce between Honduras and El Salvador. Some of the decline in intra-regional trade was simply a reflection of the fall in real income in Central America after 1980. Intra-regional trade was further complicated by exchange rate instability, import restrictions and the regional political crisis; part of the decline, however, was due to the accumulation of unpaid debts between pairs of countries, with Nicaragua the main (but not the only) offender. Agreements with the IMF and negotiations with creditors on debt rescheduling ignored these inter-CACM debts which became an increasing threat to intra-regional trade.

The failure to include these inter-CACM debts in general debt renegotiations was one reason for the crisis in the CACM. Another reason was the perception by the US administration (reflected in the Kissinger Report) that a revival of the CACM would benefit all Central American countries including Nicaragua and would therefore contradict US efforts to destabilise the Sandinista régime. Finally, the emphasis on import-substituting industrialisation in the CACM did not appeal to the IMF, the World Bank, the Inter-American Development Bank and the US Agency for International Development, all of whom were pressing their clients in Central America to adopt more outward-looking strategies.

The neglect of the CACM restricted the degrees of freedom available to Central American countries for promoting economic recovery. While far from perfect and in need of far-reaching reform, the CACM remained an important component of each country's total trade and manufacturing output; its neglect made the task of economic recovery significantly harder and robbed industrialists of a market which could provide a convenient stepping-stone between the protected domestic market and the full rigours of international trade.

The interests of the external powers, as we have seen, did not necessarily coincide with Central America's inherited needs for reform; the main casualties were the development of a strong and independent labour movement and the revival of the CACM. There were at least three areas, however, where the interests of the two groups of countries sometimes coincided.

The first was projects to save on imported energy. This area was explicitly supported by the San José facility and was viewed with favour by multilateral lending institutions; the huge hydroelectric schemes begun in the 1970s were brought to completion and new schemes were started. Nicaragua, with Italian support, exploited the geothermal resources of the Momotombo volcano, and several republics used Brazilian technology to produce alcohol from sugar. In all republics the proportion of electricity generated by non-thermal means increased and the heavy burden of oil imports began to decline.[93]

The second area was fiscal reform. Although the conditions for implementing reform were scarcely ideal, governments in Central America were under intense pressure to raise tax revenues; the pressure came not only from the IMF, but also from the impact of depression on the budget deficit and the authorities' fears of the consequences of financial instability. The initial efforts to raise revenue from fiscal reform were frequently defeated, but by the end of 1984 four of the five republics had been able to increase the ratio of tax revenue to nominal GDP; the exception was Guatemala, where all efforts at fiscal reform and increasing tax revenues were defeated by the powerful private-sector organisation Cámara de Agricultura, Comercio, Industria y Finanza (CACIF).

The third area was agrarian reform. By the end of the 1970s (see Chapter 10, pp. 201–7) the land question was still far from resolved in Central America, although both Costa Rica and Honduras had established effective institutional procedures for implementing land redistribution. The fall of Romero, however, prompted US policymakers to raise agrarian reform to one of its highest priorities in El Salvador, and Sandinista Nicaragua introduced a comprehensive agrarian reform package in 1981. Even Guatemala made some modifications to its land reform legislation.[94]

The achievements of these land reform programmes, however, were very questionable: land distributions in Guatemala left the rural landless largely untouched; the Salvadorean programme was suspended as soon as the right-wing parties gained a majority in the National Assembly in 1982, and the suspension was not lifted when the Christian Democrats won an outright victory in 1985. In Costa Rica land invasions, aggravated by the decision of UFCO to pull out,[95] received much less sympathy from the Monge administration (1982–6) than from its predecessors, and shortage of funds compelled the authorities to slow down the rate of land redistribution.

The Nicaraguan land reform decree was announced in August 1981 and allowed for the expropriation of uncultivated or insufficiently cultivated holdings as well as land not cultivated by the owner.[96] The decree identified the beneficiaries as those currently working the land, landless workers and participants in the struggle against Somoza; the law provided for compensation through payment in government bonds based on the land's fiscal (not market) value, and the new beneficiaries were denied the right to sell their holdings, which could be transferred only through inheritance.

The Nicaraguan approach to the land question was the most radical in Central America since the agrarian reform during the Arbenz régime in Guatemala. Despite this, it was at first implemented cautiously and did not provoke major resistance from the private sector. From 1983 onwards, the pace of agrarian reform accelerated as the government used land distribution as a deliberate counter-insurgency strategy, and by mid-1984 the total affected area (including holdings expropriated from the Somoza family) represented 37% of the area in farms.[97] The acceleration of land reform provoked resistance from the private sector, led by the Consejo Superior de la Empresa Privada (COSEP) and in 1985 the government expropriated lands from the leader of COSEP, although his estates were not a candidate for takeover under the provisions of the 1981 decree.[98] Land reform in Nicaragua therefore became highly political, and the Sandinista claim to operate a mixed economy was threatened by private sector opposition, although efficient private landowners continued to produce much of the export crops.

In Honduras the policy of land redistribution, which had virtually lapsed during the years of direct military rule,[99] was revived during the Suazo Córdova administration. During its first three years (1982–4), the administration distributed 58,770 hectares; this was only half the area distributed in 1975 (when the present law went into effect) and progress towards agrarian reform was constantly denounced by the peasant leaders. Nevertheless, some progress was made, the private sector cooperated with the government, and the prospect of future land distributions was sufficient to keep the influential peasant unions on the reformist path.

By the end of 1986 the prospects for resolving the regional crisis were still very poor. Neither the US administration nor its Central American allies were much nearer to peaceful coexistence with the Sandinista government, whose ties with the Soviet bloc were becoming closer. Adjustment to external disequilibrium produced a BOP improvement outside Nicaragua and some republics, aided by the expansion of the US economy, returned to positive rates of economic growth after 1983; in no republic, however, were the medium-term growth prospects favourable. Guatemala failed to adjust fully to the external disequilibrium, El Salvador was still engaged in civil war, and both Honduras and Costa Rica were obliged by their debt problems to moderate the expansion of internal demand. Finally, the Nicaraguan economy was in a state of crisis provoked by the severity of the adjustment programme on the one hand and external aggression on the other.[100]

# 12

## Conclusions

This chapter brings together the analysis of the previous chapters to summarise the main findings and provide certain conclusions. It will be apparent that some periods lend themselves more easily to conclusions at the regional level than others; in particular the period since 1979 has vastly complicated the Central American reality, shifting the balance between conformity and diversity in the region significantly in favour of the latter. While diversity has always been a feature of Central America – both between countries and within countries – conformity has been generated by the existence (at least until the 1980s) of an economic model which imposed similar options, opportunities and constraints for each republic.

A dominant theme of this chapter is macroeconomic performance, making use of the statistical appendix for the period 1920 to 1984. External conditions have heavily influenced each country's performance, but inter-country differences in growth rates still remain and require explanation. The ranking of the five republics in terms of real Gross Domestic Product (GDP) per head has altered over time and performance has clearly been affected by the policy-mix. 'Getting policies right', however, is not just a technical question, but also a political problem requiring the establishment of a minimum consensus.

Central America has pursued since 1920 (and even earlier) an export-led model, but the latter has passed through five phases each of which has carried different implications for economic and social relations. The theory of export-led growth is based on a number of assumptions, which have not been generally applicable to Central America; thus the non-export economy has failed to match the sometimes spectacular performance of the export sector, leaving the region with an overemphasis on external trade and very vulnerable to fluctuations in world commodity and capital markets. In addition, the weakness of the non-export sector has left the pressure groups associated with the export sector in a dominant position and capable of affecting policies in a way which reinforces the export-led model.

The evolution of the export-led model has demanded reforms, but the

267

pace and character of reform has been heavily influenced by the needs of the export sector. Fiscal, agrarian and labour reforms have proved the most difficult to implement, although governments in Costa Rica and Honduras before 1979 were notably more successful in combating vested interests. Since 1979, in the wake of the most severe economic and political crisis perhaps this century, real progress has been made in fiscal and agrarian reform in all republics except Guatemala, although improved labour relations and the emergence of a strong, independent labour movement have proved elusive goals.

The period since 1920 permits an examination of external actors in Central America, their influence over economic policy and their impact on political change. Before 1979, the main actors were foreign creditors, foreign companies and the US government, but since 1979 international financial agencies and many other governments must be added to the list. In general, there has been a tendency for a variety of motives to exaggerate external influence in Central America, and Central American governments have had a not inconsiderable room for manoeuvre in internal affairs, although the postures and preferences of external actors have always formed a backcloth against which decisions must be taken.

The final section of the chapter considers the 1979 crisis in historical perspective. The year 1979 has proved to be a watershed, leading to the worst economic crisis since the early 1930s and monumental political upheavals. The 1979 crisis has dramatically affected macroeconomic performance, undermined financial and exchange-rate stability and forced the region into a new phase of the export-led model. The consolidation of Sandinismo in Nicaragua has brought new external actors into the region, forcing the United States to lower its hegemonic pretensions and increasing the international character of the crisis.

## Macroeconomic performance over the long run

The macroeconomic performance of the Central American economies since 1920 has been subject to marked cycles around a rising trend. In terms of real GDP (see Table A.1), the increase from the lowest point in the 1920s to the highest point in the late 1970s/early 1980s has varied from a factor of seven (Honduras) to a factor of seventeen (Costa Rica). In terms of real GDP per head (see Table A.3), the rise has ranged from a factor of 1.6 (Honduras) to a factor of 3.4 (Costa Rica) with El Salvador and Nicaragua close to the Costa Rican performance and Guatemala in the middle of the range. With the exception of Honduras (about which more will be said below), the long-run increases in real GDP and real GDP per head therefore suggest a relatively dynamic performance in which growth rather than stagnation has been the rule.

Table 12.1  *Central America: trade coefficients (%),*[1]
1920–84
(Three-year averages)

| Year | Costa Rica | El Salvador | Guatemala | Honduras | Nicaragua |
|---|---|---|---|---|---|
| 1920[2] | 78.8 | 42.1 | 35.3 | 52.7 | 39.9 |
| 1929 | 80.9 | 52.6 | 36.3 | 64.1 | 46.2 |
| 1939 | 57.4 | 37.0 | 19.7 | 38.2 | 32.1 |
| 1949 | 51.0 | 37.0 | 24.9 | 46.0 | 34.6 |
| 1959 | 47.6 | 46.6 | 27.5 | 40.2 | 42.2 |
| 1969 | 59.3 | 51.4 | 31.9 | 60.1 | 53.2 |
| 1979 | 56.6 | 46.0 | 32.9 | 62.8 | 61.4 |
| 1984[2] | 45.4 | 41.4 | 26.6 | 54.2 | 55.2 |

[1] Defined as $(x + m/y)$ where 'x' is real exports at 1970 prices (see Table A.12), 'm' is real imports at 1970 prices (see Table A.13) and 'y' is real GDP at 1970 prices (see Table A.1)
[2] Two-year average

The picture is complicated substantially when the cycles are considered in addition to the trend. The most recent cyclical downswing (since 1978/9), for example, has wiped out nearly three decades of increases in real GDP per head in El Salvador and Nicaragua, two decades in Honduras, one and one-half in Guatemala and one decade in Costa Rica. These declines are clearly comparable with those in the 1930s during the cyclical downswing after 1929, from which Central American economies took many years to recover. Indeed, in terms of real GDP per head, recovery in Honduras and Nicaragua had not been fully completed when the Second World War broke out, so that a second cyclical downswing was added to the first and real GDP per head did not surpass its 1920s peak in Nicaragua until 1952 and in Honduras until 1965.

The combination of cycles and trends shows how vulnerable these economies are to adverse shocks. Under favourable circumstances (e.g., improving net barter terms of trade) substantial progress is achieved, but the gains can be wiped out rapidly when the environment turns hostile. Thus, it is not realistic to expect the 1970s peak in real GDP per head to be regained before the 1990s in Costa Rica, Guatemala and Honduras, while El Salvador and Nicaragua must expect to wait until after the year 2000.[1]

The strongest influence over the long run on both the trend and the cycle has been the openness of the economy. The trade coefficient (defined as the sum of exports and imports divided by GDP) has been and remains high (see Table 12.1),[2] so that the region's macroeconomic performance has been strongly conditioned by both favourable and adverse external shocks. The most important of these shocks has been movements in the net barter terms of trade (see Table A.14), which have shown a modest upward trend subject to an asymmetrical cycle. Thus, a short period of rapid improvement (e.g., 1921–6, 1949–54) has been followed by a long period of steady decline (e.g., 1928–44, 1956–70). Since the period 1975–9 was one of rapid improvement, the fear that the consequent decline will continue until the mid-1990s cannot be dismissed as groundless.

Although macroeconomic performance has been influenced by the net barter terms of trade, it has not been dictated by it. Thus, the secular decline in the barter terms of trade from the mid-1950s to early 1970s was offset by a spectacular increase in the quantum of exports, so that the income terms of trade improved. This increased rather than decreased the openness of the economy, however, so that the vulnerability to external shocks remained high. Indeed, export quotas for traditional products (e.g., coffee, sugar, beef) have become an important determinant of macroeconomic performance as well as world commodity prices and the net barter terms of trade. In addition, during the Second World War, disruptions to international shipping and loss of traditional markets (both external shocks) were more important determinants of the relatively poor macroeconomic performance than movements in the net barter terms of trade.

While external conditions have remained dominant explanatory variables of economic trends and cycles since 1920, three internal factors have been influential during specific periods. The first is import substitution in agriculture (ISA), which was particularly important in Costa Rica, El Salvador and Guatemala during the 1930s and was an important recovery mechanism from the Great Depression; following the Second World War, and the relaxation of the foreign exchange constraint, it ceased to be of much importance (indeed, negative ISA frequently occurred) until after the 1979 crisis, although it has still not been powerful enough to produce recovery in the most recent period. The second factor has been import substitution in industry (ISI), which – together with the improvement in the income terms of trade – contributed to the high growth rate of real GDP during the 1960s (the golden age of the CACM); ISI, however, because it operated in a regional context under the shadow of a dominant export-led growth model, never came close to cancelling out the impact of external conditions on macroeconomic performance.

The third factor has been civil unrest and, while the first two have acted to raise real GDP per head, the third has lowered it. The civil war in Nicaragua (1978–9) stands out as a period in which real GDP per head fell by 37%, while external conditions remained favourable; armed conflicts (e.g. El Salvador in 1932 and after 1980, Nicaragua after 1981 and during the Sandino episode) have occurred when external conditions have been unfavourable, so that both adverse shocks have occurred simultaneously and the impact of violence cannot be isolated. There can be little doubt that in El Salvador since 1980 and in Nicaragua since 1981 civil war has taken

Table 12.2  *Agriculture's share of GDP (%), 1920–84*
(Export agriculture share in brackets (%), three-year average)

|  | Costa Rica | El Salvador | Guatemala | Honduras | Nicaragua |
|---|---|---|---|---|---|
| 1920[1] | 46.9 (28.0) | 45.6 (19.0) | 41.8 (22.1) | 49.8 (24.4) | 56.5 (13.1) |
| 1929 | 42.1 (25.4) | 45.9 (23.4) | 36.2 (18.0) | 56.0 (39.2) | 66.0 (17.3) |
| 1939 | 35.1 (16.2) | 47.6 (21.9) | 44.9 (11.6) | 49.9 (22.9) | 53.1 (14.6) |
| 1949 | 39.0 (20.8) | 43.2 (17.6) | 37.7 (11.3) | 45.8 (19.6) | 35.3  (7.3) |
| 1959 | 30.3 (12.6) | 37.1 (18.4) | 33.1 (11.3) | 36.3 (12.7) | 30.7 (12.1) |
| 1969 | 25.8 (11.6) | 29.9 (15.3) | 30.3  (9.7) | 35.6 (15.1) | 28.4 (14.7) |
| 1979 | 19.6  (8.6) | 28.9 (14.5) | 28.2  (9.5) | 24.9 (12.0) | 29.6 (16.2) |
| 1984[1] | 21.5 (10.3) | 30.3 (14.7) | 28.4  (8.5) | 26.8 (12.8) | 27.8 (15.6) |

Source: derived from Tables A.1, A.4 and A.5
[1] Two-year averages

a heavy toll on the economy; on the other hand, Costa Rica's macroeconomic performance was barely affected by the 1948 civil war and the armed conflict between El Salvador and Honduras in 1969 was only one factor causing stagnation in both economies between 1968 and 1970. Clearly, both the scale and duration of civil unrest are relevant in this context; the Guatemalan counter-revolution of 1954, for example, involved very few people, but the civil unrest which preceded it had lasted for several years, leading to a sharp reduction in private investment and a decline in real GDP per head despite exceptionally favourable external conditions.

The period since 1920 has witnessed not only the macroeconomic trends and cycles referred to above, but also significant shifts in the sectoral composition of output. As would be expected,[3] the proportion of real GDP generated by agriculture has declined from around 50% in 1920 to around 25% in 1984 (see Table 12.2), but there have been important exceptions to the law of agriculture's declining share. Some of these are straightforward; for example, the rise in the share of agriculture from 1979 to 1984 (everywhere except Nicaragua) is a reflection of the decline in real GDP per head, i.e. just as agriculture's share is expected to fall with increases in real GDP per head, so the share should increase when real GDP per head declines. Other changes are not so straightforward; e.g. the increase in Costa Rica between 1939 and 1949, in El Salvador, Nicaragua and Honduras between 1920 and 1929 and in Guatemala between 1929 and 1939. In addition, the virtually unchanged agricultural share in all republics (except Costa Rica) for part of the post-1949 period is at first sight puzzling.

With one exception,[4] all these paradoxical results can be explained by reference to the performance of export agriculture (EXA). The law of agriculture's declining relative share is most commonly explained by the inelastic nature of income demand for agricultural products, but a small country can circumvent this constraint through an increase in its world market share of agricultural exports. Thus, EXA[5] has frequently grown so rapidly that it has raised its share of GDP sufficiently to counteract the 'law' of agriculture's relative decline. A good example is provided by the expansion of banana production for export in Honduras in the 1920s; while domestic use agriculture declined from 25.4% of GDP in 1920 to 16.8% in 1929, EXA (mainly bananas) rose from 24.4% to 39.2% so that agriculture's share increased by six points to 56.0% (see Table 12.2).

Specialisation in export agriculture reveals both the strengths and weaknesses of the export-led model. In the 1920s, Honduras took specialisation to its extreme limit: nearly 40% of real GDP was accounted for by one product (bananas) on the eve of the Great Depression, and Honduran real GDP per head (see Table A.3) was second only to Costa Rica's. By 1942, following the impact of the depression, disease and the outbreak of war, Honduran real GDP per head was the lowest in Central America. By contrast, Nicaragua in 1920 generated only 13% of GDP from EXA (see Table 12.2) and had the lowest real GDP per head for most of the 1920s, while the dramatic increase in real income after 1949 coincided with an increase in EXA's share to the highest level in Central America. These two examples suggest that there is an optimal level of export specialisation: high enough to reap economies of scale and to participate in the international division of labour, low enough to isolate the economy from too sharp a shock during the downswing of the international trade cycle. The recent performance of the Central American economies suggests that EXA's share of real GDP (over 10% in 1984 everywhere except Guatemala) is still too high, although the share has declined significantly since 1929 (see Table 12.2).

The decline in the agricultural share of GDP has been offset by increases in the other sectors. In the case of the manufacturing sector, the major leap forward was in the 1960s during the golden age of the CACM, but there were significant changes (see Table 12.3) in the 1930s (Costa Rica and Nicaragua), the 1940s (El Salvador and Guatemala), the 1950s (Honduras) and the 1970s (Costa Rica and Nicaragua). In no republic (see Table 12.3) has the share exceeded that of agriculture, reinforcing the conclusion that the Central American economies remain fundamentally based on primary products with the engine of growth provided by natural resource-based exports. ISI has contributed to the above proportionate growth of the manufacturing sector, but has not been the only factor: intra-regional exports and the processing of agricultural products for extra-regional exports, as well as traditional income elasticity effects, have also been important. Since industrial production has been, and remains, very dependent on imported intermediate goods, spare parts and capital equipment, it has not yet advanced to a point where it might benefit from adverse external shocks to the economy. Thus, with rare exceptions,[6] industrial dynamism has not

Table 12.3  *Manufacturing share of GDP (%), 1920–84*
(General government share in brackets (%); three-year averages)

|  | Costa Rica | El Salvador | Guatemala | Honduras | Nicaragua |
|---|---|---|---|---|---|
| 1920[1] | 7.5 (3.0) | 10.0 (5.6) | 13.7 (3.9) | 6.5 (4.6) | 9.2 (0.6) |
| 1929 | 8.7 (4.7) | 11.7 (6.3) | 13.7 (9.2) | 5.0 (3.3) | 5.0 (0.7) |
| 1939 | 12.6 (4.7) | 10.3 (5.9) | 8.3 (3.3) | 6.9 (3.8) | 9.3 (2.1) |
| 1949 | 11.0 (6.1) | 12.5 (6.4) | 11.7 (8.4) | 8.4 (3.9) | 11.3 (10.9) |
| 1959 | 12.4 (10.7) | 13.6 (9.1) | 11.8 (8.8) | 13.3 (5.8) | 13.0 (10.9) |
| 1969 | 14.9 (11.9) | 17.7 (8.2) | 14.7 (6.9) | 13.6 (3.6) | 18.2 (8.0) |
| 1979 | 17.1 (11.0) | 17.6 (9.8) | 15.3 (7.2) | 14.8 (5.0) | 22.1 (11.1) |
| 1984[1] | 16.6 (11.4) | 16.2 (13.1) | 14.8 (9.2) | 13.8 (5.7) | 23.2 (14.0) |

Source: derived from Tables A.1, A.8 and A.9
[1] Two-year averages

been a marked feature of either the 1930s depression or the Second World War, nor of the period since 1979.

The other sector, whose share of GDP has increased sharply since 1920, is general government or public administration (see Table 12.3). This activity measures the government wage and salary bill at constant prices, i.e. it represents employment in public administration. An increased share therefore means that government employment has grown more rapidly than the economy as a whole. This is a reflection partly of the growing complexity of government functions, partly of a swelling bureaucracy and partly of different perceptions of what constitutes the appropriate arena for public administration. Thus, the leap in the share in Costa Rica in the 1950s was due above all to the social democratic tendencies of Figueres' second administration (1953–8), while the decline in the share in the 1960s everywhere except Costa Rica was a response to the conservative fiscal and monetary policies preferred by the military governments in the four northern republics.

An outstanding feature of Table 12.3 is the low share of public administration in GDP before the Second World War in all republics. This reflected not only the relatively simple character of each economy, but also the preference for balanced budgets together with orthodox fiscal and monetary policies. The most remarkable case is Nicaragua during its semi-colonial phase under US marine occupation (up to 1933); the assumption of the presidency by the founder of the Somoza dynasty in 1937 was marked by a rapid increase in general government employment (which included the National Guard), while the consolidation of Sandinista rule since 1979 has pushed the share to the highest in Central America. Following the Second World War, Costa Rican performance diverged from the rest of Central America until the 1970s, when the northern republics increased government employment both for security reasons (larger armed forces) and under the stimulus of the availability of cheap external finance.

While macroeconomic performace has been conditioned by external factors, which have been roughly the same for all republics, individual country performances have still diverged substantially. A league table based on real GDP per head would show that Costa Rica not only held on to first position for virtually the whole period (see Table A.3),[7] but also increased its margin over its nearest rival in absolute and relative terms; Costa Rican real GDP per head in 1984 was nearly twice that of its nearest rival (Guatemala) and three times that of the bottom republic (Honduras). By contrast, Honduras slipped from second place during the second half of the 1920s to bottom place in 1942 – a position she still occupied in 1984.[8] Nicaragua, on the other hand, leapt from bottom place in the early 1920s to second position in the second half of the 1960s, only to collapse to the bottom of the table in 1979.

Several factors account for differences in country performance despite the similarity of external conditions. The first is differences in commodity-mix; a fall in coffee prices may affect all coffee producers equally, but coffee is not equally important in all republics. The performance of Honduras, for example, before the mid-1950s was determined fundamentally by world market conditions for bananas; because Honduras remained far more dependent on bananas than any other republic, world market conditions for this commodity did not affect other countries in Central America in like fashion. By the mid-1950s, however, coffee in Honduras had come of age and macroeconomic performance from then until the present does not compare so unfavourably with the rest of Central America.

The second factor has been internal policies. As has been frequently pointed out in this book, the influence of external conditions does not prevent each republic from following an active state policy, despite the fact that it has had to operate a small, open economy. The superior performance of Costa Rica since 1920 owes much to this factor and has included the introduction with state support throughout the period of non-traditional exports, a more active exchange rate policy, more aggressive fiscal (and counter-cyclical) policies, incentives for small farmers and domestic use agriculture, industrial promotion, selective nationalisation etc. Few, if any, of these state policies have been unique to Costa Rica, but Costa Rica (with its enviable democratic traditions) has enjoyed much greater consistency in policy-making, backed by a broader consensus and implemented by a state bureaucracy with a high level of training and competence.

The third factor has been political upheaval and geopolitical considerations. The latter have not affected all republics equally; Nicaragua, for example, paid dearly for its strategic location in the 1920s and is again paying a heavy price, although the Somoza dynasty mastered the technique of exploiting geopolitical considerations to serve Nicaraguan (or their own) interests. Similarly, Costa Rica since 1979 has exploited its sensitive position, wedged between Sandinista Nicaragua and the Panama canal, to extract a very high level of official aid and other development assistance, thereby avoiding the need for adjustment programmes as severe as those in other parts of Latin America. The impact of political upheaval, on the other hand, speaks for itself and has already been referred to above.

## The export-led model

Although the period since 1920 can be characterised as one of export-led growth, the nature of the export-led model has changed. One can in fact identify five models, each of which carries different implications for the non-export economy and for social relations within each republic. The openness of the economy has remained a constant throughout the variations in the export-led model, and the non-export economy has not yet acquired a business cycle independent of external conditions. Indeed, the conditions under which export expansion leads to growth and diversification of the non-export economy have frequently not been fulfilled, so that the region in general remains overdependent on exports and external market conditions. This feature of Central American development has been ignored by most of the policy recommendations put forward for the region in recent years,[9] so that Central America is still very far from resolving its fundamental economic problems.

The first phase of the export-led model, which survived until the late 1940s, focussed almost exclusively on coffee and bananas; indeed, in the case of El Salvador (coffee) and Honduras (bananas) it emphasised only one commodity. These products dominated exports and exports in turn determined investment, credit and imports; the latter heavily influenced commerce and many branches of industry, while foreign trade (imports and exports) determined government revenue. It was a very simple model, which performed quite well under favourable circumstances (e.g., the first half of the 1920s) and which survived the 1930s depression and the Second World War because of active state policies in support of the export (mainly coffee) sector. The second phase of the model ran from the late 1940s to the early 1960s and was based on agricultural export diversification; exports were now dominated by five products (coffee, bananas, cotton, sugar and beef). This second phase had many features in common with the first, but the reduction in commodity concentration lowered the vulnerability of the economy to adverse shocks in one commodity market, while increasing the vulnerability to adverse shocks in all commodity markets.[10] The new export products were also mainly in national hands, so that the extent of foreign control of exports (through the banana companies) was reduced.

The third phase occurred in the 1960s and was marked by the grafting of regional ISI through the CACM onto the traditional export-led growth. Because regional ISI involved the export of manufactured goods (to the regional market), the whole experiment can be considered a variation on export-led growth, which has been called the hybrid model (see Chapter 9, pp. 185–90). The third phase differed in many ways from the first two: first, the new export activities were urban rather than rural; secondly, the goods were sold in protected, rather than unprotected, markets so that resistance to wage claims on the part of employers was less marked; and thirdly, Central American businesses were selling in each other's national markets for virtually the first time in Central American history. Commercial competition between Central American countries therefore became important in a way that had never occurred in the first two phases of the export-led model.

The fourth phase occurred in the 1970s, as each republic sought to emphasise non-traditional exports outside the region as well as regional (manufactured) exports and traditional (agricultural) exports. This phase, marked by changes in industrial legislation, new incentives and free trade zones, was in fact overwhelmed by the upheavals in the world economy and changes in the fortunes of extra-regional commodity exports. The final phase, still not fully in place, has begun since the demise of the CACM after 1981 and involves a shift of attention away from the regional market in favour of traditional and non-traditional exports to the rest of the world. The policy changes demanded by this phase (and favoured by international agencies)[11] involve flexible exchange rates, dismantling of protective structures, increased direct foreign investment and real wage discipline.

The first phase generated two interest groups centred round coffee on the one hand and bananas on the other. Since the coffee sector had developed in the nineteenth century in response to state initiatives, relations between coffee interests and the government were extremely cordial; only during the 1930s depression did coffee interests feel obliged to establish formal associations to press the government for policy changes in their favour. The banana industry, on the other hand, had developed under the control of foreign companies, whose success depended from the beginning on extracting favourable concessions from governments. These concessions were more likely to be extracted from a government made weak by adverse external conditions or by internal political rivalries, so that the foreign-owned fruit companies felt a certain ambivalence towards the emergence of a strong state.

Both interest groups were important sources of demand for rural labour. The coffee sector's demand, however, was fundamentally seasonal and depended on a large part of the rural labour force being not only available for work at harvest time, but also prepared to undertake it. Since a free market in labour might produce a real wage rate which could undermine the profitability of goods sold in world markets, an adequate supply of labour was assumed by coffee interests to depend on coercion (debt peonage, vagrancy laws etc.) and this conclusion was reinforced in the early 1920s when exchange rate flexibility was abandoned in favour of the gold standard.

The combination of labour coercion and seasonal demand for rural labour had serious implications for much of Central America, and these were reinforced when cotton and sugar (both seasonal employers) were added to the export list. The expansion of EXA posed a threat to domestic use agriculture (DUA), which – if not countered by active state policies – could produce a marginalisation of the peasantry without transforming it into a fully employed rural proletariat. Although labour coercion became more sophisticated after the Second World War, export interests backed by a sympathetic state could shift the labour supply curve to the right by restricting access to land. These practices, common in Guatemala, El Salvador and Nicaragua, gave the political élite little interest in rural education, without which the development of formal and meaningful democracy was impossible. Only Costa Rica and Honduras, where coffee remained in small- to medium-sized family farms making less use of hired labour, escaped the worst effects of export agricultural specialisation, although Costa Rican governments after 1940 had to rely on very active policies in favour of DUA to avoid a damaging conflict between the two branches of agriculture.

The banana industry, completely foreign-controlled during the first two phases of the export-led model, did not depend on labour coercion for its labour supply. Foreign competition involved exports to third countries from divisions of the same multinational companies in other countries, so that wage rates could be set on a global basis and increases forced on the companies by local militancy (e.g. Honduras in 1954) could be met either by world price manipulation (reduction in global supply) or by relocation of production to other divisions. The policy of maintaining vast reverses of idle land or abandoning disease-stricken plantations, however, restricted the scope for counter-cyclical policies based on DUA, while the development of the railway system to favour banana production (particularly in Guatemala and Honduras) involved the misuse of a key resource.

The major problem of banana production, however, particularly during the first phase of export-led growth, was the failure to convert a capitalist surplus into capital accumulation. In the case of the nationally controlled export products, the capitalist surplus was more susceptible to taxation and more likely to be reinvested either directly (in EXA) or indirectly (in the non-export economy). The banana industry, because of the concessions extracted from a weak state, was not subject to significant direct taxation until 1949 at the earliest, while the industry itself was incapable of absorbing the capitalist surplus through increased investment in almost all years. The cumulative loss of productive resources through profit repatriation was therefore very substantial.

The second, third and fourth phases of the export-led model have added influential pressure groups to the coffee and banana interests of the first phase. Furthermore, the influence of the multinational fruit companies responsible for banana exports has declined since the 1950s, as independent producers have grown in importance, and the companies have ceased to be the lender of last resort for regional governments. In addition, the expansion of financial institutions complementary to the second, third and fourth phases of the export-led model created powerful banking circles, although they lost their influence after 1979 in El Salvador and Nicaragua following bank nationalisation.[12] These pressure groups for many years acted independently, although all shared a common interest in the success of the export-led model; in addition, the EXA interests and industrialists found monetary and exchange rate stability an acceptable régime, because it guaranteed access to complementary imports on favourable terms, avoided the need for exchange controls and provided for the possibility of capital exports ('capital flight').

The independent pressure groups began to fuse into a single private sector voice in the 1970s, as the world economic situation became more volatile and as internal political conditions became less stable. The new umbrella organisations representing the private sector have provided and still provide a vigorous defence of capitalism and sectional interests; even in Sandinista Nicaragua, the umbrella organisation (COSEP) has maintained a strong presence, although its real influence is minor compared with equivalent organisations elsewhere in the region. Indeed, a major problem in Central America has been the inability of the government (especially in Guatemala) or the labour movement (especially in El Salvador) to match the organisation, ideological conviction and technical training of the private sector representatives.

The justification for an export-led model stems from the belief that emphasis on exports, according to comparative advantage, will stimulate the non-export economy to the point where the latter will ultimately achieve rapid self-sustained growth. Indeed, under certain circumstances, the non-export economy may grow so rapidly under the stimulus of the export-led model that the openness of the economy declines and it becomes less vulnerable to adverse external shocks. This process was observed in Argentina, in Brazil and in other major Latin American countries during their period of export-led growth before 1929. The stimulus to the non-export economy comes from backward linkages (demand for intermediate goods), forward linkages (supply of raw materials) and other indirect linkages based on the complementary nature of many branches of the non-export economy (e.g. internal transport, financial institutions and the provision of taxation for the expansion of government services).

This virtuous circle has not been achieved as yet in any part of Central America. As the post-1979 crisis shows, the non-export economy remains intensely vulnerable to adverse external conditions and is far from achieving self-sustained growth. It is important to establish the reasons for this, because the region (other than Sandinista Nicaragua) is being pushed towards a new (fifth) phase in the export-led model without sufficient consideration of whether the necessary preconditions for successful export-led growth have been met. If they have not been met, there can be little confidence that the fifth phase will be more successful than the previous phases.

Several factors account for the weakness of the export-led model in Central America. Until the formation of the CACM, the small size of the (national) market was a barrier to backward linkages, while the design of the CACM discriminated against backward linkages by favouring consumer goods. Forward linkages have worked better: cotton exports, for example, have stimulated textile and clothing production, sugar cane production has given rise to sugar milling and an expansion of food-processing, but several exportable commodities (e.g. bananas, assembled consumer goods) do not lend themselves easily to forward linkages. Unequal income distribution within the agricultural export sector has weakened the effective demand for goods sold in the national (and regional) market, while export interests have monopolised financial resources (credit). The export sector has postponed increases in taxation, often for many years, and government efforts to raise revenue from other sources have distorted the allocation of resources. Agricultural export interests have frequently squeezed the small-farm sector, leading to pressure on domestic use agriculture (DUA) and a reduction in the range of agricultural commodities available for industrial processing.

It would be wrong to conclude from this that the export-led model should be abandoned. On the contrary, export specialisation and export-led growth during certain periods have brought substantial benefits. Most of the defects listed above are capable of correction through various kinds of reform, although some are easier to achieve than others. Reform and attempts at reform have been a feature of many periods since 1920, as will now be examined, but they have not yet fully succeeded in creating the necessary conditions for successful export-led growth.

## Reform and the labour movement

The success of economic and social reform in Central America has been heavily influenced by the implication of the proposed change for the dominant export-led model. Where the change has been favoured by export pressure groups, or marginal to their interests, reform has been feasible. Where it has run counter to their perceived short-term interests, it has proved much more difficult and sometimes impossible. Because of the evolution of the export-led model itself, however, the need for economic and social reform has been an almost constant feature of the period since 1920.

The first major reform was financial (see Chapter 2, pp. 28–33), establishing the long period of exchange-rate stability which began in the 1920s and finally ended only in the 1980s.[13] These reforms, inspired in several cases by Kemmerer,[14] were intended primarily to serve the interests of the government rather than export interests, although the latter's fears were assuaged by the knowledge that the reforms would be accompanied by the abolition of exchange controls and real wage discipline.[15] Exchange-rate stability was temporarily shaken during the 1930s (except in Guatemala and Honduras) and exchange controls were reimposed, but the financial system survived due to banking reforms which continued until the late 1940s. By then, the conditions had been created for again abolishing exchange control, and the combination of freedom of exchange with exchange-rate stability continued until the 1980s, when it abruptly came to a halt.

While the financial system adapted admirably to the needs of the export sector, it did not serve the interests of the non-export economy so well. This was one of the reasons for the nationalisation of the banks in Costa Rica in 1948, as well as for bank nationalisation in El Salvador and Nicaragua after 1979. After the civil war in Costa Rica, the state banks did indeed play an important part in the development of the small-farm sector and the cooperative movement, although the process had in fact begun as early as the 1930s. Since the banks were very closely linked to export interests, it was unrealistic to expect 'moral suasion' by the government on its own to achieve the necessary reforms in bank lending, so that nationalisation was a not unreasonable response. Honduran banks are a possible exception to this rule, because the expansion of banking after 1950 occurred with state participation and without such strong ties to export interests.

Although governments have generally supported the export-led model and export interests, fiscal questions have frequently been a bone of contention. Since the export sector has generated the largest taxable surplus, it has been a prime candidate for increased taxation. An increase in the fiscal burden has, however, been bitterly resisted – often with considerable success. Thus, Guatemalan and Salvadorean export interests resisted for years the application of income taxes to their earnings, while Nicaraguan export interests under Somoza enjoyed very modest levels of export taxes. Property tax rates have remained very low and have frequently been evaded, if not avoided, through undervaluation. None of this is unique to Central America – nobody likes to pay taxes – but an inability or reluctance to tax the most profitable sector carries two opportunity costs: first, alternative (less efficient or equitable) taxes must be introduced, and, secondly, many government services will be left underfunded or neglected.

An example of the first problem was the introduction of the San José protocol in 1968, raising average nominal tariffs by 30% and giving a further twist to the distorted allocation of resources in the CACM; the San José protocol was a panic response to the fiscal crisis caused by the reduction in import duties after the formation of the CACM, which should have been met by a shift in the structure of government revenue towards progressive direct taxation. An example of the second kind of problem has been the neglect of rural health and education in many parts of Central America due to a shortage of government current revenue. The long-term consequences of the fiscal problem have therefore been very serious.

The economic and political crisis since 1979 has, paradoxically, done much to resolve the fiscal problem and ensure that in future the elasticity of tax receipts with respect to nominal GDP will be significantly greater than one. No one, for example, could now claim that Nicaraguans are under-taxed, but this is not an isolated example: Costa Rica, El Salvador and Honduras have all overhauled their tax systems in the direction of greater equity and efficiency, while all Central America agreed to phase out from the beginning of 1986 the tax privileges enjoyed by firms under the CACM.[16] By the end of 1985, only Guatemala had failed to make much progress on fiscal reform, with government efforts consistently blocked by private sector opposition, but the Christian Democrat government which came to power in January 1986 in Guatemala made it clear that fiscal reform would be a high priority. Thus, there are grounds for cautious optimism regarding the fiscal question in the sense that economic reactivation within an export-led model should contribute to a much more satisfactory flow of government revenue than in previous periods.[17]

Phase one of the export-led model (based on coffee and bananas) brought with it only partial capitalist modernisation. Even within the coffee sector (particularly in Nicaragua), there were pre-capitalist remnants. Parts of the non-export economy remained relatively unaffected by capitalism or hindered by anti-capitalist legislation (e.g. laws banning imports of modern machinery). Later phases of the export-led model demanded a much greater extension of capitalist modernisation and sweeping reform of existing laws. This process began in a small way in the 1930s,[18] but gained real momentum only in the late 1940s and early 1950s; during this period (approximately the first decade after 1945), legislation affecting industry[19] and finance was overhauled, the tariff system was refined to produce appropriate incentives and labour relations were subject to legal revision, with rural labour (even in revolutionary Guatemala) much less favourably treated than its small (relatively privileged) urban counterpart. The success of capitalist modernisation was reflected in the rapid rise in the investment rate (ratio of fixed capital formation to real GDP) and the process of capitalist modernisation continued in the 1960s with new legislation applied at the regional level to stimulate intra-regional trade within the CACM.

The process of capitalist modernisation was complicated in Guatemala and Nicaragua by the local political situation. The Guatemalan revolution began as a relatively straightforward exercise in political and economic modernisation, but by the time Arbenz assumed the presidency in 1950 it had acquired an anti-imperialist character with socialist tendencies; Guatemala's land reform programme and the labour bias of its Labour Courts drove a wedge between the local capitalist élite and the government, so that the institutions and legislation of capitalist modernisation were created without the support of the capitalist class. In Nicaragua, Somoza faced a similar problem for different reasons until 1950: the local capitalist élite (other than the Somoza family) remained profoundly suspicious (even hostile) towards the dynasty until the famous 1950 pact buried their political differences. From then on, capitalist modernisation proceeded rapidly, giving Nicaragua the fastest rate of growth in Central America during the 1950s and 1960s.

Initially (at least outside Guatemala), capitalist modernisation was not interpreted by the local élite to include land reform. The latter was pushed on to the political agenda by the Alliance for Progress in the early 1960s and, not surprisingly, was implemented either not at all (as in El Salvador) or only in a very mild form. The acceleration in the investment rate and the GDP growth rate was seen by the élite as evidence that land reform was not necessary for capitalist modernisation; consequently, it could be justified only on social and political grounds and it therefore acquired radical, even revolutionary, overtones.

The economic case for land reform was dismissed too hastily. Specialisation in EXA not only brought pressure on DUA, but also narrowed the range of commodities offered by agriculture to the detriment of agro-industrial diversification and growth. These economic targets could be achieved by other means (as was shown by several republics' performance in the 1970s), but land reform was also a legitimate means to achieve these goals. Given the resistance of export interests, however, to land expropriation, agrarian reform programmes acquired a political dimension so that the programme could be implemented only by a strong and determined state. These conditions have now been met in several republics; Honduran land reform was given real significance during military rule in the early 1970s, while Phase I of the land reform programme in El Salvador in 1980 (expropriating estates in excess of 500 hectares) has meant that land distribution in that republic has ceased to be the most critical factor in political debate. The Nicaraguan land reform programme has turned more radical in each year since the revolution, and Costa Rica, through its practice of tolerating land invasions and promoting small-scale agriculture, has lowered the tensions associated with unequal land distribution and export specialisation. In Guatemala, however, the question of land reform remains critical; either it must be implemented or the government must adopt policies (as in Costa Rica) which will prevent a further erosion of the small-scale sector and further increases in social tension.

While the post-1979 crisis has coincided with some progress towards resolving the land question,[20] the same cannot be said of reform in labour relations. The export-led model depended on a degree of social control over rural labour, which in several republics was inconsistent with a functioning democracy. This coercion obviously carried implications for urban labour, although the latter never suffered from the same degree of repression because of its protected status (most urban labour is employed either in non-traded activities or in the production of protected tradeable goods). The right to form unions, minimum wage legislation, social security programmes and the promotion of cooperatives were extended first to urban workers and only later, with great reluctance in some cases, to rural labour. As a result, the labour movement remains very weak and has been unable to protect the real wages of its members from drastic declines since 1979; this is true even of Sandinista Nicaragua, where a majority of the labour force is in pro-government trade unions and real wages in the formal sector have plummeted since revolution.

The existence of a weak labour movement has had several adverse consequences, which have been mitigated to some extent in Costa Rica and Honduras. Although it has helped the profitability of EXA, the weakness of the labour movement has contributed to marked income inequality and lowered wage profiles, and has made it very difficult for future entrepreneurs to emerge from the ranks of the working class. Weak unions, covering only a small fraction of the labour force, have often depended on external funding and training and workers' representatives have played little part in national politics. Workers' parties have remained small and dominated by communists, so that they have become objects of fear to the ruling élite out of all proportion to their size and influence.

This dismal picture, still relevant in the case of Guatemala and El Salvador, requires some modification in the case of Sandinista Nicaragua, Costa Rica and Honduras. In Nicaragua, the welfare of workers and peasants has become the stated objective of the Sandinista state, but deeds have lagged behind words. The labour movement, although marshalled in unions and now enjoying a high literacy rate, is still far from independent or free; the right to strike has been withdrawn for much of the period since 1979, real wages have declined and labour representation within the FSLN is weak. While labour's position is superior to that prevailing before 1979, it cannot realistically be claimed that Sandinista Nicaragua has solved the labour question.

In Costa Rica, the proportion of the labour force in unions is still very low and one of the main labour federations is communist-led, making it an object of concern for the ruling élite, but rural labour achieved important gains as early as the 1930s,[21] the non-communist wing of the labour movement supported the victorious side in the 1948 civil war and the cooperative movement has made important strides since the 1960s. As a result, although the labour movement is still weak, labour demands have frequently been accommodated without bloodshed or political upheaval; labour relations became severely strained during the post-1979 recession, but a flexible response by sympathetic governments averted a major crisis. In Honduras, the responsible behaviour of the labour movement during and after the 1954 strike together with its patriotic responses to the 1969 war, convinced sections of the military that labour relations need not be based on confrontation; labour unions, including peasant unions, have become relatively strong in Honduras and non-communist labour organisations remain important. Both military and (since 1982) civilian administrations have been able to accommodate labour's demands without much use of force[22] and labour again demonstrated its 'patriotic' character during the constitutional crisis of April 1985.[23]

### External influence, economic policy and political change

External influence has always been important in Central America; it has frequently been exaggerated, however, so that the true relationship between internal forces and external agents has often been misunderstood. Many internal actors, as well as external powers, have had a vested interest in overemphasising external influence so that a powerful mythology has been created. The purpose of this section is to try and put the relationship in historical perspective.

From the 1920s to the 1979 crisis, external influence came in three significant forms: foreign bondholders, foreign-owned companies and the US government (the latter's claim that revolutionary Mexico was extending its influence over Nicaragua in the 1920s can be dismissed, although Mexico did support the Nicaraguan Liberals in the 1926/7 civil war and for historical reasons was regarded with suspicion in many parts of Central America). Dollar diplomacy had been used by the US administration to isolate the influence of European bondholders in Nicaragua and El Salvador, but had failed elsewhere; European bondholders therefore retained a certain influence in the 1920s and occasionally secured the active support of their government.[24] North American (individual) bondholders were relatively unimportant, but US banks by the end of the 1920s had acquired considerable influence in Nicaragua, El Salvador and Honduras.

In order to guarantee payment, foreign creditors of Central America (bondholders and banks) constantly pressed for control over part of government revenue. By the end of the 1920s, all Central American republics had been compelled to make concessions in this direction. In El Salvador 70% of customs revenue (the major source of government income) were committed to repayment of bonds issued in 1923 as part of a debt rescheduling package; Honduras, under a 1926 debt agreement, authorised the National City Bank of New York to collect the revenues of consulates of Honduras out of which bondholders were to be paid; Guatemala committed its coffee export tax under a 1929 debt agreement to provide service payments on a new bond issue, while foreign bondholders were able to secure a first lien in Costa Rica in 1926 and 1927 on both customs and railway revenues for debt service payments. The most extreme case was Nicaragua, where customs duties were placed under the supervision of a US Collector-General 'nominated by the (US) Bankers, approved by the Secretary of State of the United States, and appointed by the Republic'.[25] Under the agreement with the US authorities, Nicaragua 'agreed not to alter the import and export duties or make any changes that would affect the value of the customs revenue without agreement with the Bankers'.[26]

As far as economic policy is concerned, it should be clear that the leverage of foreign creditors reduced the prospects for an independent, and active, fiscal policy. Indeed, since the first beneficiary of an increase in government revenue was often the bondholders, treasury officials and government ministers could be said to have a certain disinterest in fiscal reform, while prompt payment of taxes could hardly be described as patriotic if foreigners were the first beneficiaries. Thus, it is not unreasonable to claim that one of the reasons for the weak and unreformed fiscal system inherited from the 1920s was the influence exerted by foreign creditors; short-term interests prevailed to the detriment of a long-term policy, which could have protected the interests of the creditors and debtors with greater success. This became clear in the 1930s, when all republics except Honduras defaulted on their external obligations. Debt default effectively crippled the influence of foreign creditors: the US Collector-General of Customs remained in Nicaragua until the 1940s, but even this could not prevent partial suspension of external debt service payments after 1932.

Foreign companies, mainly of US origin, were present in railway transportation, public utilities, banking, mining and agriculture, while foreign immigrants played an important part in the development of coffee and the embryonic manufacturing sector. Foreign companies dominated railway transportation by the beginning of the 1920s[27] and acquired a decisive position in electricity supply by the end of the decade;[28] mining exports in Honduras and Nicaragua were also largely controlled by foreign companies. The most extreme case of domination, however, was in the banana industry, where by 1929 two firms (UFCO and Standard Fruit) controlled all banana exports and most banana production. The power of these two fruit companies was enhanced still further by their control of much of the railway system through subsidiaries.

There can be no doubt that concessions to foreign firms, including the fruit companies, have been exceedingly generous in Central America, robbing the host country of many of the potential benefits from foreign direct investment; the companies have also used dubious tactics to extract or extend these concessions and have on occasions broken the law with impunity by violating the terms of their concessions.[29] The relationship between host government and foreign company was therefore very unequal and reflected the desperation at times of the former for the investment and fiscal support which it was felt only the latter could provide.

The tax concessions offered to foreign companies had a very damaging cumulative effect on fiscal policy. In republics where import taxes were for many years the principal source of government revenue, a zero tariff for foreign company imports implied higher tariffs for other importers and a reduction in real income not necessarily offset by higher real income generated by foreign company operations. Contracts explicitly exempting foreign firms from income taxes made it much more difficult to introduce or increase direct taxation on the remainder of the corporate population, while negligible export taxes for foreign companies were used by coffee and other exporters to justify low rates of tax on all exportable commodities.

Relationships between foreign (particularly banana) companies and organised labour limited the state's ability to improve labour relations. Somoza's advanced 1945 Labour Code, cynical though it may have been,[30] would not have been possible without the absence from Nicaragua of the two giant fruit companies at that time; Guatemala's efforts during the revolutionary period to improve the status of labour ran into fierce opposition from UFCO, while the progressive Labour Codes in both Costa Rica (1943) and Honduras (1957) occurred after organised labour in the banana industry had won important concessions from the fruit companies through strikes.

Foreign companies have also influenced the nature and extent of social security programmes. As the largest single employer in Costa Rica, Guatemala and Honduras, the fruit companies had a strong interest in controlling the pace of national social security programmes to a rate consistent with their own practices. This is one reason why compensation laws were adopted before the Second World War in some republics which did not apply to agricultural workers.[31] These problems have diminished since the 1940s, as the companies have come to recognise the necessity of accepting national laws and have become more sensitive to their public image.

Fiscal, labour and social security questions have been the policy areas most affected by foreign companies. While the latter's influence on these areas has at times been considerable, it should not be forgotten that neither

El Salvador nor Nicaragua (both of whom have received relatively little direct foreign investment)[32] have pursued since 1920 policies in these areas which could be described as very different from those adopted in Guatemala and Honduras (where foreign company operations have been important). Similarly, Costa Rica has not been prevented from pursuing (at least since the 1940s) relatively enlightened socio-economic policies despite the continued presence of foreign companies.

By the late 1940s, alternative sources of finance for both investment and government purposes were available, and the relationship between host governments and foreign companies has become less unequal. By the 1970s, foreign direct investment had been largely forced out of railways and public utilities, leaving a strong foreign presence only in bananas, mining and (since the formation of the CACM) manufacturing. The fiscal contribution of foreign companies has also increased notably in recent years, although the memory of the unequal relationship has left a bitter taste in many Central American mouths.

The rise of a more equal relationship between host government and foreign company, particularly since the mid-1950s, has reduced the latter's overt political influence. How great such influence was even before the mid-1950s is hard to determine; it must be remembered that foreign companies were in general pressing for concessions which host governments were often ready to provide even without political influence. Concessions to foreign companies in El Salvador, a country without banana exports, were little different from concessions in Honduras, where the giant fruit companies were dominant. Both the liberal oligarchic state before the depression and authoritarian *causillismo* after it accepted the need for foreign direct investment, but were in a weak position to dictate terms: Costa Rican efforts, for example, to extract more favourable terms from UFCO in the late 1920s collapsed from the consequences of the 1929 crisis rather than political legerdemain by the fruit company.

The foreign companies, particularly UFCO, have been accused of making and breaking governments. With one exception, which occurred before 1920,[33] this was not the case;[34] the foreign companies were not responsible for the changes of government at the start of the 1930s nor for the *continuismo* practised under *caudillo* rule. Tiburcio Carías Andino, caudillo of Honduras from 1932 to 1949, was often said to be within UFCO's sphere of influence, but Honduran *continuismo* did not differ significantly from *continuismo* in El Salvador, where UFCO had no banana interests. Even in Guatemala in 1954, UFCO's resistance to land expropriations under Arbenz was not the crucial factor in persuading the US administration to adopt covert operations, nor were UFCO's manoeuvres critical in bringing down the revolutionary government. The worst charge that could be laid against the companies – and it was a very serious one – concerned their irresponsible behaviour in border areas, bringing two countries close to war on three occasions.[35]

The third, and most important, source of external influence in the 1920s was the US government. United States interest in Central America was primarily strategic, although this was often confused in the public mind with its economic and political interests (the latter being initially conceived as reducing or removing European and Mexican influence in the region). US strategic interest originated in the mid-nineteenth century, when the United States became a continental power that could be bridged most easily through the Central American isthmus. Later, this interest focussed heavily on Nicaragua as the site of a possible inter-oceanic canal, but after the Panama Canal was constructed the proximity of the whole region to the Canal Zone made it an area of major strategic concern.

Because US interest was primarily strategic, US influence over economic policy was usually indirect. The major exception was Nicaragua during its semi-colonial phase, when US officials and US bankers played a dominant role in the execution of even day-to-day decisions. US efforts to apply dollar diplomacy in Guatemala and Honduras before 1920 had failed and the two Kemmerer missions to Guatemala were a Guatemalan rather than US initiative. US official loans to Central America did not exist before the Second World War, and the State Department was generally wary of being dragged into disputes involving US companies and host governments. External trade with the United States, however, was increasingly important for each Central American republic, so that indirectly US influence over economic policy was considerable; no government wished to put at risk its major external market by adopting economic policies which might have provoked a hostile response.

US government influence over economic policy remained slight during the 1930s. Even in Nicaragua, where a US economic and financial presence continued after the marines had been withdrawn, direct influence declined and Somoza gradually asserted his authority over economic policy (e.g. the massive devaluations after 1937). The US government could not prevent or reverse default on external debt obligations, and the State Department's main concern was to press for reciprocal bilateral trade treaties involving tariff concessions, which were largely symbolic; these treaties did, however, make it more difficult for Central American countries to raise tariffs on commodities supplied by US exporters.

The US administration's influence over economic policy increased considerably during the Second World War. The United States became virtually the only market for exports and the US quota under the Pan-American Coffee Agreement was a powerful bargaining counter. US official lending began for the first time and Central American governments adapted their economies to serve the needs of the US war effort. The first decade after the war, however, witnessed a boom in the main commodity markets affecting Central American exports, and US influence over economic policy during this period was slight. This influence revived in the late 1950s, as the detailed discussions began on the shape of the CACM, and the final outcome was a compromise between the original ECLA plan, US government preferences and Central American interests. Funds supplied under the Alliance for Progress in the 1960s, however, did not produce the intended reforms, and US influence over economic policy had declined to a low point by the time of the 1979 crisis, after which (in common with that of international financial agencies) it increased sharply (see below).

US influence over economic policy has therefore fluctuated sharply, but Central American political stability has been a much more constant source of concern to successive US administrations. In the 1920s, US attitudes were shaped by the Washington Conferences (1907 and 1922), under which Central American governments would not receive recognition if they came to power through unconstitutional methods. This still gave considerable leeway for undemocratic procedures, as was demonstrated when the non-recognition policy was used by the US administration as an argument in favour of ousting Emiliano Chamorro from the Nicaraguan presidency in 1926 in favour of the pliant Adolfo Díaz.[36] The non-recognition policy was also used by the US administration in 1924 to deny Tiburcio Carías the presidency in Honduras, although Carías was known to have the support of UFCO.[37]

The non-recognition policy came under pressure after the 1929 crisis in the wake of presidential changes of a dubious constitutional character in Guatemala and El Salvador. Ubico's rule in Guatemala was accepted, but Martínez' assumption of power in El Salvador in 1931 was deemed to be unconstitutional, and the Hoover administration denied recognition. This policy proved ineffective, however, and ran counter to the anti-interventionist sentiment among Latin American countries which was so apparent at the 1928 Pan-American conference in Havana. In addition, Roosevelt's Good Neighbor Policy – adopted in March 1933 – appeared to contradict the non-recognition policy, and the Roosevelt administration was forced to recognise Martínez in 1934.[38] This change of policy paved the way for the practice of *continuismo* under *caudillo* rule in the northern Central American republics. It also had important implications for US policy towards Nicaragua, where the US minister Arthur Bliss Lane witnessed with impotence Somoza's bid to remove President Sacasa from power. Lane pressed the US State Department for a public declaration of the non-recognition policy, but was told it would be inadvisable and was transferred to Lithuania for his pains. The switch from non-recognition to non-interference played into Somoza's hands and the head of the 'non-political' National Guard (created by the US administration in 1928) assumed the presidency on 1 January 1937. It was a supreme example of the impossibility of neutrality by a hegemonic power that had convinced the Nicaraguan élite for nearly two generations that its wishes must always be paramount.

The period of *caudillo* rule during the Good Neighbor Policy established the unwritten rule under which authoritarian governments in Central America would be left in peace provided their support could be counted on in external affairs. These 'rules of the game' deprived the United States of an excellent opportunity to promote democracy in 1944, when *caudillismo* came under attack from broad-based reformist alliances, so that the system collapsed only in Guatemala. The post-war confrontation with the Soviet Union, however, and the rise of the Cold War produced a more interventionist US foreign policy and a revival of the non-recognition policy. As a result, the puppet régime installed by Somoza in 1947 was not recognised until March 1948, when the Costa Rican civil war and Somoza's intervention on behalf of the *Calderon-comunistas* forced the State Department to put the interests of the global struggle against communism above that of Central American democracy. The revolutionary junta led by the anti-communist Figueres was immediately recognised despite the fact that its route to power was clearly unconstitutional.

Cold war politics dominated US perceptions of the Guatemalan revolution. President Arévalo's support for Figueres in the Costa Rican civil war passed without comment, but the growing influence of communists after 1947 and the challenge to US economic interests finally provoked President Eisenhower to authorise covert operations against the Arbenz régime. The success of the counter-revolution, which incidentally provoked enormous over-confidence in the Central Intelligence Agency to its cost in the Cuban Bay of Pigs fiasco, removed the last traces of communist influence from Central American governments. When they re-emerged in 1960 (in El Salvador), the local anti-communist élite acted so swiftly that US intervention proved unnecessary. Only during the bitter guerrilla war in Guatemala during the 1960s was US intervention necessary and even then it was confined to an advisory role.

The US administration in the early 1970s therefore viewed the political situation in Central America with considerable satisfaction. The local élite in the four northern republics made up in anti-communist virulence what it lacked in democratic procedures, and the US government appeared to have won staunch anti-communist allies in return for a very small financial and political investment. The overweening confidence of the Carter administration was made clear by its decision to link US military aid to human rights questions. This decision, which weakened the dictatorship in Nicaragua severely and in El Salvador and in Guatemala modestly, contributed to the fall of Somoza and the consolidation of Sandinista rule. Carter administration officials could be forgiven for concluding with the benefit of hindsight that no good deed goes unpunished.

## The 1979 crisis in historical perspective

In the history of Central America since independence, four moments stand out for their special significance. The first was 1870–1, ushering in the period of liberal revolutions and the dominance of coffee in the economy; the second was 1930–1, marking the beginning of the depression and the demise of the liberal oligarchic state; the third was 1944, when the democratic reform movement shook the foundations of authoritarian *caudillismo* to its roots. The fourth was 1979, which – it is now clear – marked a watershed in the region's development: the fall of Somoza in Nicaragua, the collapse of General Romero's régime in El Salvador, and the beginning of the worst economic crisis since 1929 (if not before) mark out 1979 as a year of very special significance.

The economic crisis experienced since 1979 in all republics of Central America has not only been exceptionally severe in terms of macroeconomic performance (see above, pp. 268–75); it has also undermined the financial and exchange rate stability established over sixty years. Inflation rates have reached three-digit levels in Costa Rica (1982) and Nicaragua (1985/6) and regularly exceeded two-digit levels in all republics of a region which prided itself on virtually stationary prices in the 1950s and 1960s. Exchange rate devaluation has become accepted in countries, such as Guatemala and El Salvador where a few years ago the fixed peg to the US dollar had acquired quasi-religious significance. Only Honduras has clung doggedly to its pre-1979 exchange rate,[39] although even in Honduras the black market exchange rate slipped to a substantial discount during the mid-1980s.

Exchange rate problems have been exacerbated by capital flight and public external indebtedness. Capital flight is not new in Central America, but the region has been transformed since 1979 into one of the most heavily indebted in the world in *per caput* terms. While this burden has fallen with particular severity on Costa Rica and Nicaragua, none of the five republics has escaped and the region has lost its reputation (acquired slowly since the 1920s) for fiscal conservatism and prudent debt accumulation. Debt default (or the more tactful declaration of a moratorium) is now more costly than in the 1930s because of the cartelisation of international capital[40] and only Nicaragua, where payment proved impossible,[41] has adopted it as a medium-term strategy. By any reasonable projections,[42] service payments on the public external debt will therefore impose a severe strain on both the balance of payments and the government budget until well into the 1990s.

The 1979 crisis has also forced a revision of the export-led model. The combination of exports to (unprotected) third markets and sales to (protected) regional markets has been undermined by the demise of the CACM. Between 1980 and 1985 the nominal value of intra-regional trade fell by nearly 50%, while prices were rising steadily. An expansion of trade has been blocked not only by the fall in regional living standards, but also by the beggar-my-neighbour non-tariff barriers erected in response to balance of payments deterioration and non-payment of intra-regional debt arrears. The crisis of the CACM, coupled with the difficulties faced since 1979 by traditional exports, has led to a tentative experiment in export substitution[43] designed to promote non-traditional sales outside the region.

The driving force behind the latest phase in the export-led model has been the US administration in alliance with various international financial agencies (notably the IMF and the World Bank). The carrot has been provided by the Reagan administration's Caribbean Basin Initiative (CBI), giving duty-free access to the US market for twelve years in a wide range of non-traditional products.[44] The stick has come from the conditions attached to lending by the US Agency for International Development, the World Bank and the IMF. The stick, however, has been more effective than the carrot (neither have been applied to Sandinista Nicaragua); [45] Costa Rica, El Salvador and Guatemala (Honduras only to a lesser extent) have been cajoled and bullied into shaping their economic institutions to favour the new phase of the export-led model, but the results have been disappointing. The base of the new model (non-traditional exports to third markets) has been so small that even spectacular rates of growth would not have major macroeconomic impact for many years, while actual rates of growth of the exports in question have been far from spectacular. There is no evidence to suggest that the new phase of the export-led model will succeed where the others (see above, pp. 275–9) failed.

The 1979 crisis has had important implications for the pace of reform in Central America. While the loss of exchange rate stability has been traumatic, exchange rate realignment had become necessary by the early 1980s; fixed rates served the region well before 1979, but in the uncertain post-1979 environment exchange rate flexibility can achieve many given objectives (e.g. balance of payments improvement) at much lower costs than the alternatives (Nicaragua, for example, has paid a heavy price in terms of real output foregone as a result of its post-1979 preference for quantitative controls over exchange rate devaluation to solve the balance of payments problem). Exchange rate flexibility has been achieved fully only in Costa Rica, which – as so often since 1920 – has taken the initiative in adopting new policies, but both El Salvador and Guatemala moved in 1985/6 towards realistic and flexible exchange rates.

Agrarian reform has also advanced significantly since 1979, to the point where only in Guatemala does it remain an explosive (and potentially revolutionary) issue. While the Salvadorean agrarian reform programme has invited harsh criticisms from various quarters,[46] it has undoubtedly altered the nature of the land question since its inception in 1980. Phase I of the pro-

gramme, expropriating the largest farms, has broken the back of the traditional oligarchy (the so-called 'fourteen families') and is now irreversible.
The Nicaraguan agrarian reform programme, surprisingly timid until 1983,
turned radical in 1984 as the landless peasantry began to acquire individual
plots and a reversal to the pre-1979 situation is also extremely unlikely
irrespective of the future of Sandinismo. Costa Rica and Honduras have
continued with their more modest programmes for land reform. A more
rational use of Central America's land resources is now possible, although
it will still take many years for the correct balance to be struck between
efficiency, equity and social justice.

Fiscal reform has been adopted, in many cases unwillingly, throughout
Central America in response to budgetary crises. Direct taxation has
increased in importance, while tariff rates generally declined with the new
*Arancel de Aduanas* adopted by the CACM members on 1 January 1986.
Export taxes have increased in line with devaluation in El Salvador and
Guatemala, while the practice of granting excessive tax holidays to firms
in Central America (a zero-sum game) has been phased out. Greater central
government control (in response to IMF, World Bank and USAID pressure)
has been exerted over autonomous and semi-autonomous public sector institutions, and budget deficits outside Nicaragua have been reduced to manageable proportions. While fiscal reform is far from complete, tax evasion and
avoidance is still high and public sector waste remains a problem, it would
be unreasonable to deny the progress that has been made in all these areas
since 1979.

While the progress on exchange rate, agrarian and fiscal reform has been
encouraging, there have been several areas in need of reform which have
been left virtually untouched; in addition, some of the key social issues
in Central America (such as the Indian question in Guatemala) have been
left unresolved, while other matters (e.g. human rights violations) have been
seriously aggravated by the 1979 crisis. These deficiencies suggest the utmost
caution in interpreting the recent situation in Central America, since an
acceleration in the pace of reform may not be sufficient if the underlying
problems have deteriorated.

One of the key areas still in need of reform is labour relations, for the
region still lacks a strong, responsible independent labour movement. This
objective, the need for which has been emphasised repeatedly in this book,
remains a distant goal in Guatemala, El Salvador and even Nicaragua –
the three republics which stood in greatest need before 1979. The inability
of the state to remain neutral in the struggle between labour and capital
for income shares undermines political stability and weakens the prospects
for genuine democracy. Costa Rica and Honduras had both achieved more
success before 1979 than the rest of Central America in this area, but neutrality came close to being abandoned in Honduras between 1982 and 1984

and President Monge in Costa Rica (1982–6) had some difficulty in restraining a revanchist capitalist class from reversing the pre-1979 progress in labour relations.

While the economic crisis since 1979 has played a large part in shaping national political struggle, regional and international relations have been increasingly dominated by the consolidation of Sandinismo and the growing isolation from the western world of Nicaragua. The rise of Sandinismo has had major repercussions on the political economy of Central America. The presence of a Marxist régime in Nicaragua and the search for a solution to the political crises provoked by the tension between Nicaragua and the United States on the one hand and Nicaragua and her neighbours on the other has brought new external actors onto the Central American stage: these include Cuba and the Soviet Union as allies of Nicaragua, eight Latin American republics as members of the Contadora group together with its support group, and the EEC as a US partner concerned by the implications for international security of a new source of East–West conflict. Irrespective of the outcome in Central America in general and Nicaragua in particular, the United States has lost forever its hegemony among the external countries and must now share external influence with other regional and international powers. This will require a considerable adjustment by the United States from its traditional perspective towards the region, although it effectively has no choice: its inability to establish in Managua, after many years of intense effort, a régime more acceptable to perceived US interests is living witness of the limitations on US foreign policy imposed by domestic political considerations on the one hand and the intricacy of international relations on the other.

The Sandinista régime will therefore survive, but the balkanisation of Central America will continue. Neither the CACM nor other forms of regional cooperation can counter the suspicion and hostility engendered by the gulf between a Soviet-backed Nicaragua and a US-backed rest of Central America. Both superpowers have the resources to guarantee the survival of their allies, but neither has the authority to impose its will throughout the region. Each Central American republic will therefore come under strong pressure to look beyond the region for economic stimulus and political support. This process will maintain the long tradition of export-led growth, but it will leave each republic very vulnerable to cycles in world commodity and capital markets and postpone still further the establishment of a dynamic non-export sector with its own business cycle capable of self-sustained growth.

# Methodological Appendix

The preparation of national accounts for the Central American republics since 1920 was a necessary prerequisite for the writing of this book. The purpose of this appendix is to explain the methodology underlying these national accounts estimates and to provide for the benefit of scholars working in this field the detailed statistics on which much of the book's analysis has been based.[1]

First, however, some consideration needs to be given to the question of whether such an exercise is justified. Although all scholars are in broad agreement that it is desirable to have statistical series of good quality, it is worth remembering that an unreliable series can do more harm than good. The problem is not only lack of information in certain areas of economic activity, but also published figures in which the authorities themselves place little confidence. For example, the director of the Dirección General de Estadísticas y Censos in Costa Rica complained in 1930 that the statistics on agriculture and commerce were valueless because of 'the anarchy that reigns in the reports sent to this office by the political authorities.'[2] The director then published a table on the area cultivated with various agricultural products with a note stating: 'The object of the above table is to demonstrate the inefficiency of the data collection system in current use, in view of the differences in the figures from one year to the next.'[3] Similarly, a survey on Guatemalan statistics (published in 1946) had the following to say about agriculture: 'Each year the Ministry of Agriculture sends questionnaires asking for information with regard to agricultural products, livestock and the number of acres planted and harvested. About 10,000 large and small farms are surveyed to obtain information regarding agricultural production on those farms. The results of these surveys are published annually in the *Memoria* of the Ministry of Agriculture. The information is wrongly presented as estimates of total production, which is not the case since only those farms which return the questionnaires are included in the summary tables' (author's translation).[4]

There are therefore formidable obstacles in the way of preparing reliable national accounts estimates for the years before the official series became available. I am convinced, however, that the exercise is still worthwhile for the following reasons: first, the openness of the Central American

295

economies means that a great deal of economic activity is either captured or approximated by international trade statistics; secondly, the quality of international trade statistics for each republic is comparatively high; thirdly, the trade statistics provide a check or control on the accuracy of production data for traded commodities; and, fourthly, the smallness of each republic (in the physical sense) and the geographical concentration of the population (e.g. the Meseta Central in Costa Rica) reduce the problems associated with collecting data from remote regions.

Before outlining the methodology used in my national accounts estimates, it is appropriate to mention other estimates for the years before 1950 (after which an official series is available for all republics). The Central Bank of Guatemala published in 1955 a series starting in 1923,[5] but it uses nominal prices and is based on expenditure rather than net output by sector; a quasi-official estimate of net output by sector at constant prices for the period 1936/7 to 1947/8 has also been published[6] and this series proved very useful. El Salvador's Gross Domestic Product (GDP) and its breakdown by sector were estimated from 1945 by a United Nations team,[7] but the results were heavily criticised and a rival series for the years since 1945 was produced by Joseph Mooney.[8] The University of Costa Rica published very detailed estimates of the national accounts for Costa Rica from 1946[9] and the Central Bank of Nicaragua published a similar series for Nicaragua from 1945.[10] W. W. Cumberland published an estimate of Nicaraguan national income in 1928,[11] and his methodology was subsequently used by two authors for the early 1940s,[12] but these estimates are too crude to be of any value.[13]

The most important estimate for the years before 1950 is for Honduras and was prepared by Paul Vinelli and Manuel Tosco. The series begins in 1925 and was given official status when published by the Central Bank.[14] It is generally considered a reliable series and I was relieved to find that my own methodology, when applied to Honduras, gave very similar results.[15] This is an additional reason for believing that the preparation of national accounts estimates for all the Central American republics since 1920 is a worthwhile exercise.

The origin of my own estimates is derived from my contribution to a research project on the impact of the 1930s depression on Latin America.[16] The absence of national accounts was a severe handicap for the study of Central America between 1920 and 1940 and the preparation of GDP series for those years became my first task. Subsequently, it was a relatively simple matter to extend the series for each republic up to the year in which official national accounts statistics start.[17]

At the time my research began on the national accounts (in 1981), I was unaware of the existence of the work by the Economic Commission for Latin America (CEPAL) on a time-series for GDP for all Latin American countries.[18] The CEPAL study estimates GDP at net factor cost using 1970 as the base year with inter-country comparisons based on purchasing power parity exchange rates; my original research estimated GDP at market prices using 1950 as the base year with inter-country comparisons based on official exchange rates. It is not in the interests of scholars to have to work with rival estimates so that I felt it appropriate to reconcile my original series with the figures published by CEPAL.

The remainder of this Appendix will proceed as follows: I shall first outline the methodology used in the original series (1950 base); I will then explain how the original series was reconciled with the CEPAL series (1970 base). Finally, the most important statistics are presented as a series of tables (from 1920 to 1984) at the end of the Methodological Appendix.

The base year chosen for the original series was 1950 and its choice was dictated by several factors. It was the first year for which official GDP figures covering the whole of Central America are available; the figures, estimated from the net output side at market prices, are roughly comparable and are presented in the original sources in considerable detail. The official estimates for 1950 are in the currency of the country in question. These were converted to US dollars (Central American pesos) at the official exchange rate; this is unlikely to have introduced serious distortions, as the official domestic currency–US dollar rate would not have differed from the purchasing-power parity rate significantly in 1950 in each republic and because, within Central America, official exchange rates were not under pressure in 1950 (with the possible exception of Costa Rica).

The national accounts estimates are based on value added (net output) by sector. An expenditure-based series was rejected on the grounds that it would prove impossible to estimate private consumption in real terms. The factor shares approach was ruled out by the absence of suitable data on labour income.

The sectors for which an estimate of net output proved possible for all republics were (a) agriculture, (b) mining, (c) manufacturing, (d) commerce and (e) general government. Between them, these sectors represented 70–80% of GDP in each republic in 1950. It was assumed that the sectors for which estimates were not in general possible (construction, public utilities, transport and services) represented in aggregate the same proportion of GDP as in 1950 for those years when no official estimate existed. In effect, therefore, net output for the five sectors listed above was added together for each republic in each year and 'grossed-up' to produce an estimate of GDP.

Estimation of net output in agriculture (including livestock, forestry and fishing) proceeded as follows: agricultural value added in 1950 was first broken down by product in the most detailed manner possible. In Costa Rica, for example, the original sources[19] contained 33 products or product groups; each republic provided a detailed listing of products, although in some cases net output was provided at the aggregate level (i.e. for all agriculture) and the information on individual products referred to the gross value of production. In this case, I had to estimate intermediate consumption (the difference between the gross value of production and net output) on a product by product basis; this required a disaggregation of intermediate consumption at the aggregate level and it was necessary to assume that each product made the same proportionate contribution to total intermediate consumption as it made to total gross value of production.

For each republic, the product list was then divided into those products where exports were very important and those products where supply was mainly directed to the home market; the two lists varied from country to country, although the first list included coffee in all republics and the second list included basic grains (maize, beans, rice and sorghum) throughout the region.

For each product or product group for which information could be obtained, an index (1950 = 100) based on the volume of output was prepared. In the case of products for which foreign demand was dominant, the index was compiled using international trade statistics in those cases where production data were unavailable or unreliable. In the case of other agricultural products, data on the volume of output were obtained from figures supplied by each country to the International Institute of Agriculture, a League of Nations organisation, and in later years to the Food and Agriculture Organisation, a United Nations dependency. Where these production figures were incomplete or inconsistent, the data were supplemented by information on imports, inventories and estimated consumption per head.[20] In the case of livestock (*ganado vacuno* and *ganado porcino*), the index was compiled from information on slaughterings (less imports) where available and from information on the stocks of cattle/pigs where data on slaughterings were not available.

In principle, the data for each product include auto-consumption. The reason is that the production figures are typically based on an estimate of total area devoted to a particular crop which is then multiplied by an estimate of yield per hectare: the area estimate is supposed to include information on each product irrespective of its end use and should therefore include products for consumption on the farm; this was no doubt not always the case, but it would not be appropriate (or possible) to make a separate estimate.

For each republic it was possible to construct indexes for between ten and fifteen products. Each index was then used to project backwards net outputs for the relevant product from 1950 to 1920; this assumes that the ratio of net output to gross output was constant during this time period. This is a strong assumption and is more realistic for some products (e.g. basic grains) than for others (e.g. bananas). The net outputs for each product were then added together and 'grossed-up' to give value added in agriculture in each year. The grossing-up factor was the inverse of the ratio of the sum of the net output for the given products to total agricultural net output in 1950; this assumes that the unidentified products (i.e. products for which no index could be constructed) carried the same weight in total agricultural value added in each year, but this was not a serious problem because the unidentified products were only of minor importance. In Costa Rica, for example, the identified products represented 82% of agricultural net output in 1950.

The estimate of industrial value added in each republic was made as follows: industrial net output in 1950 was broken down, using the official sources, into (a) mining, (b) food-processing, (c) drinks, (d) tobacco products and (e) other manufacturing industries. In the case of (a) mining and (b) food-processing, a further subdivision was carried out by product or product groups.

For each mining product (e.g. gold, silver) for which information could be obtained, an index (1950 = 100) based on the volume of output was constructed. The index was obtained from either production or international trade data. The identified products were then summed together and 'grossed-up' to give mining value added; the technique was very similar to that used for agriculture and therefore no further comment is required. Only in Honduras and Nicaragua did mining value added account for more than one per cent of GDP in 1950.

The technique used to estimate value added in food-processing proceeded as follows: those agricultural products requiring some sort of industrial processing before marketing were identified (e.g. cattle, sugar-cane and rice); the division of food-processing net output in 1950 was carried out in such a way as to include all these products and an index (1950 = 100) for each product was constructed using the equivalent series for agriculture. Thus, for example, the index for rice-milling was assumed to be the same as the index for rice. The indexes were then applied to value added in 1950 and net output for each product was then added together; the sum of these net outputs was then 'grossed-up' to give value added by food-processing in each year from 1920 to 1950 and the 'grossing-up' technique was the same as for agriculture and mining. The technique for estimating value added by drink and tobacco products was similar, although the construction of the indexes of volume of production was sometimes more difficult. Where there was no series of physical output, I used information on excise taxes (both products were heavily taxed) and on complementrary imports (e.g. imports of malt to make beer, imports of tobacco leaf to make tobacco products). In general, the quantity and quality of the data on physical output for these two sub-sectors improve as one moves closer to 1950.

The procedure for the sub-sector 'other manufacturing industries' was different to that used for the rest of industry. First, it was sometimes possible to identify new industries (e.g. cement) which had begun after 1920 and for which information on the volume of production was available; this information was used to construct an index (1950 = 100), from which value added before 1950 could then be obtained. For the rest of the sub-sector, it was assumed that value added was proportional to complementary imports. As a proxy for the latter, I used Class III of the Brussels nomenclature defined as 'materials, raw or partially manufactured'. This information was published in volume form for all republics except Nicaragua, and it was used to form an index (1950 = 100) from which value added by other manufacturing industries could be obtained.[21]

The sum of value added for mining, food-processing and drink products, tobacco products and other manufacturing industries then gave industrial value added at 1950 prices from 1920 to 1950. The estimation of industrial net output was a difficult exercise and the difficulty reflected the paucity of data on the volume of output for individual industries. Scattered information was available from a variety of sources,[22] but this could be used only as a check on the value added estimates; it could not provide a direct estimate, because the information was not available for all the relevant years.

Once agricultural and industrial net output had been calculated, it was a relatively simple matter to calculate value added by commerce. I assumed that the following were subject to distributive margins: (a) all agricultural output other than the products for which foreign demand was dominant, (b) industrial output and (c) all imports. The division of agriculture into export agriculture (EXA) and domestic use agriculture (DUA) was the same as the division already used to estimate agricultural net output (see above). I therefore had time-series for both DUA and industrial net output at 1950 prices.

Time-series for nominal imports were easily available for all republics, but these had to be converted into real imports at 1950 prices. I assumed that the price deflator was the same for all republics and was therefore able to use the information published by the Central Bank of Honduras[23] to construct the price deflator for the years from 1925 to 1950. For the years 1920–5 I constructed my own price deflator using information on the volume and value of imports in each of the five groups identified by the Brussels nomenclature and used by the League of Nations to classify international trade flows.

The next step was to add together for each republic (a) net outputs from DUA, (b) industrial value added and (c) real imports for the years from 1920 to 1950. All three series were now at 1950 prices so that the summation was feasible. The sum of the three series was then used to construct an index (1950 = 100) which was applied to value added from commerce in 1950. The result was net output from commerce at 1950 prices from 1920 to 1950 for all five republics.

The estimation of value added from commerce involved several strong assumptions which require further comment. First, the assumption that EXA was not subject to distributive margins is not strictly accurate; coffee, for example, was typically sold to export houses which earned a distributive margin before selling it abroad, although no such margin arose in the case of bananas. Secondly, the net output from DUA includes auto-consumption, which was not subject to commercialisation by definition. These two errors to some extent cancelled each other out and I did not feel that I could justify a more detailed treatment of which agricultural goods were subject to commercial margins. Thirdly, the structure of imports was not the same for all republics, so that the price deflator for imports could vary from country to country, but it remains the case that the structure of imports was broadly similar, so that a more detailed treatment was not justified. Fourthly, it is the *gross* value of production which is subject to commercial margins, whereas my series referred to *net* output in the case of DUA and industry; there was nothing I could do about this, so that in the construction of the index for commerce too much weight was given to real imports.

The final sector where I made an estimate of value added was general government (public administration). I first constructed an index for each republic from 1920 to 1950 on government expenditure in nominal terms.[24] Wherever possible, this referred to current expenditure, but in the earlier years the fiscal authorities often did not distinguish current from capital expenditure. The index was then adjusted to constant (1950) prices using a price deflator for government (current) expenditure. I used the price deflator for Honduras for the years 1925 to 1950, because the Central Bank of Honduras published for these years value added by public administration in both nominal and constant terms (this was the same procedure as I used to construct the price deflator for imports – see above). For the years from 1920 to 1925, I assumed no change in prices.[25] The index was then used to estimate value added by general government at 1950 prices for the years 1920 to 1950 for all republics.

The use of the Honduran price deflator to estimate general government net output in all republics was far from ideal. It assumes that the annual change in the prices of goods and services consumed by the government in Honduras was the same in the other four republics; the main item of expenditure was the wages and salaries of public employees (including the armed forces) and for some periods from 1920 to 1950 it is reasonable to assume that Honduran wage inflation (deflation) was the same as in other republics; unfortunately, it is not true for all periods.[26]

The next step was to add together value added in the five identified sectors (agriculture, mining, manufacturing, commerce, general government). The inverse of the ratio of this sum to GDP in 1950 was then used for each republic as the 'grossing-up' factor to give GDP from 1920 to 1950 at 1950 prices. The 'missing' sectors included transport and public utilities, where incomplete information was sometimes available, and personal services, where virtually no information was available. The 'grossing-up' technique assumes that the contribution of these 'missing' sectors to GDP was the same in each year before 1950 as it was in 1950 itself.

I have already explained that I did not become aware of the CEPAL series for Latin America (see CEPAL, 1978) until I had completed much of this work. The CEPAL series is now widely respected and frequently used and I resolved to revise my own series to make the two consistent. The procedure I used was very simple: CEPAL provided information at constant (1970) prices for net output by the five sectors for which I had constructed independent estimates.[27] In whatever year the CEPAL series started (e.g. 1946 for Costa Rica), I constructed an index (e.g. 1946 = 100 for Costa Rica) from my own net output estimates;[28] this was applied to the first year of the CEPAL series[29] to give a time series from 1920 to 1970 (the last year of the CEPAL series which I considered was not likely to be subject to revision). Then, I extended the CEPAL series forward to the present using the relevant national sources;[30] this gave a time-series at constant 1970 dollars (using purchasing power parity exchange rates)[31] from 1920 to 1984 for GDP at net factor cost. This appears in the Statistical appendix as Table A.1.

Population figures for the period since 1920 are conveniently summarised in the Statistical Abstract for Latin America (see Wilkie, 1983). For the years since 1970 (1956 for Honduras and 1966 in the case of Guatemala) I used national sources that provide consistency with the earlier years. The population series covers the years 1920 to 1984 and is presented in Table A.2. Figures for the last five years are clearly subject to revision; the national sources do not take account of refugees who have fled the country nor those living illegally in a country. The Salvadorean population, for example, is estimated to have increased by 21 per cent between 1979 and 1984, although circumstantial evidence concerning Salvadorean emigration to other parts of Central America, Mexico and the United States suggests that the population may actually have fallen; this is an important point, because it suggests that estimates of GDP per head (see Table A.3) may be biased downward in recent years for those countries with an estimated net outflow of refugees (El Salvador, Guatemala, Nicaragua).

The series for value added in agriculture, forestry and fishing at 1970 prices for 1920 to 1984 (see Table A.4) was obtained as follows: the CEPAL series (see CEPAL, 1978) was used from 1970 to the beginning of the period chosen by CEPAL (e.g. 1946 for Costa Rica). For the earlier years, I constructed an index of agricultural net output at 1950 prices from my original estimates (see above) and spliced this to the earliest years of the CEPAL series. For the years since 1970, I constructed an index from national sources at constant prices (conveniently summarised in SIECA, 1981, and SIECA, 1985) and spliced this to the CEPAL data for 1970.

The series for value added in agriculture, forestry and fishing (1920–84) is given in Table A.4. The breakdown of this series between export agriculture (see Table A.5) and domestic use agriculture (see Table A.6) was achieved by defining export agriculture (EXA) as coffee, bananas, sugar and cotton,[32] so that domestic use agriculture (DUA) becomes the residual. This definition of EXA was chosen because it represents the lowest common denominator for all five republics: all four commodities are important export products with only two exceptions (bananas in El Salvador and cotton in Costa Rica) and exports account for the majority of sales. National definitions of EXA vary: in Guatemala, for example, the Central Bank includes cotton-seed, chicle and cardamom, while in Nicaragua the Central Bank includes cotton-seed, sesame and Havana tobacco, but I have chosen to work with the narrower definition in order to achieve consistency and comparability between the five republics.

The preparation of Table A.5 required knowledge of net output for each of the four export products. Using 1970 as the base and adjusting for purchasing-power parity exchange rates to achieve consistency with Table A.4, I used unpublished sources provided by the Central Banks of each republic; this information is constructed (but not in general published) as part of the preparation for the national accounts. These unpublished sources go back to 1950 in El Salvador and Honduras, 1957 in Costa Rica, 1958 in Guatemala and 1960 in Nicaragua. In the latter three cases, the series was extended back to 1950 using production data available from a variety of sources (see, for example, FAO, Production Yearbook). From 1950 back to 1920, I then constructed indices for the net output of each export product from my earlier estimates of agricultural value added at 1950 prices (see above). These indices were then spliced to the 1950 data at 1970 prices to gave the complete series for EXA from 1920 to 1984 (see Table A.5). DUA (see Table A.6) was then obtained by subtraction from Table A.4.

The series for value added by mining and quarrying (Table A.7), value added by manufacturing (Table A.8) and value added by general government (Table A.9) were obtained as follows: the CEPAL series (CEPAL, 1978) was used from 1970 to the beginning of the period chosen by CEPAL. For the earlier years, I constructed an index of net output for the three series from my original estimates at 1950 prices (see above) and spliced this to the earliest years of the CEPAL series. For the years after 1970, I constructed an index from national sources at constant prices (see national accounts tables in SIECA, 1981, and SIECA, 1985) and spliced this to the CEPAL data for 1970. This then gave the three series from 1920 to 1984 at 1970 dollars (calculated at purchasing power parity exchange rates) and at net factor cost.

The nominal value of exports from 1920 to 1984 is given in Table A.10. The general procedure was as follows: for the years 1955 to 1984, I used the IMF's *Yearbook of International Financial Statistics*. For 1930 to 1955, I used the United Nations *Yearbook of International Trade Statistics*, while for 1920 to 1930 I used the League of Nations *International Trade Statistics*. The aim was to achieve a consistent series, valued f.o.b., at nominal dollars, converted, where appropriate, at *official* exchange rates. There are a few exceptions to the above procedures. The Costa Rican data for 1920 to 1934 are valued c.i.f. (not f.o.b.), the Salvadorean data from 1920 to 1955 are based on the series published in the Anuario Estadístico (converted from colones at the official exchange rate). From 1947 onwards, the series for all republics incorporate the revaluation of banana exports carried out at the suggestion of the IMF to reflect the movement in world market prices (before 1947, prices used for bananas are administered prices which reflect local currency costs by the multinational fruit companies). The nominal value of exports includes gold, which is of some importance for Honduras and of great importance for Nicaragua for much of the period.

The nominal value of imports (valued c.i.f.) is given in Table A.11. The general procedure was as follows: the IMF's *Yearbook of International Financial Statistics* was used for 1955 to 1984 with the information taken from line 71 giving imports valued c.i.f. in the local currency; this was then converted to dollars at the official exchange rate. From 1930 to 1955, I used the United Nations *Yearbook of International Trade Statistics*, while for 1920 to 1930 the League of Nations publication *International Trade Statistics* was used. This gave a consistent series from 1920 to 1984 valued c.i.f. at nominal dollars converted (where appropriate) at the official exchange rate.

The exceptions to this procedure are as follows: for Guatemala, imports before 1942 are valued free alongside ship (f.a.s.), although an adjustment has been made to a c.i.f. basis for 1935 to 1942. In the case of Honduras, imports before 1950 are valued f.o.b.; calendar year estimates have been presented since 1950 in Honduras with a fiscal year basis in earlier years (1 August to 31 July from 1920 and 1 July to 30 June from 1939) so that before 1950 in Honduras the calendar year (t) estimate refers to the fiscal year (t−1/t). In Nicaragua, imports before 1950 are valued f.o.b.

The real value of exports at 1970 prices are presented in Table A.12. The series has been calculated at purchasing-power parity exchange rates to make it consistent with Table A.1. Thus, the 1970 data in Table A.10 are first multiplied by the official exchange rate and then divided by the purchasing-power parity exchange rate (see CEPAL, 1978, p. 8). I then proceeded as follows: I used the export quantum index in the historical terms of trade series prepared for each country by CEPAL (see CEPAL,

1976) to construct the real value of exports from 1970 back to 1937 (1928 in the case of El Salvador). For the years 1920 to 1937 (1928 for El Salvador) I constructed a weighted index for each republic from the constant price data on export agriculture (Table A.5), together with mining and quarrying (Table A.7), although the latter received a zero weight for Costa Rica, El Salvador and Guatemala. This index was assumed to be a good proxy for the real value of exports and was then spliced to the year 1937 (1928 in El Salvador). For the years from 1970 to 1983 I used the export quantum index published by CEPAL in its Anuario Estadístico de América Latina, while for 1983/4 I constructed the index from national sources on the real value of exports (see the tables on national accounts in SIECA, 1985).[33] The only exception was provided by El Salvador, where the index for 1970 to 1983 was provided by the IMF's *Yearbook of International Financial Statistics* on the volume of exports (line 72). These indices were then spliced to the 1970 data to give the series on the real value of exports from 1920 to 1984 (see Table A.12).

The series for the real value of imports is given in Table A.13. This series has also been calculated at purchasing-power parity exchange rates to make it consistent with Table A.1, and the procedure was the same as for Table A.12. I then used CEPAL's import quantum index (see CEPAL, 1976) to construct the real value of imports from 1970 back to 1937 (1928 in the case of El Salvador). For the years from 1920 to 1937 (1928 for El Salvador) I constructed an index from the series for real imports used to prepare estimates of value added by commerce (see above). This index was then spliced to the year 1937 (1928 in El Salvador) to complete the series from 1920 to 1970. For the years from 1970 to 1983, I used the import quantum index published by CEPAL in its Anuario Estadístico de América Latina and for 1983/4 I constructed the index from national sources on the real value of imports (see the constant price tables on national accounts in SIECA, 1985). The only exception was provided by Guatemala, where the index from 1970 was constructed from the real value of imports in the national accounts (see SIECA, 1981, and SIECA, 1985). Finally, these indices were spliced to the 1970 data to give the series on the real value of imports from 1920 to 1984 (see Table A.13).

The net barter terms of trade series from 1920 to 1984 (see Table A.14) was derived from Tables A.10 to A.13. The first step was to adjust Tables A.11 and A.13 to constant prices at official exchange rates (in order that the 1970 data in Tables A.10 and A.12 on the one hand and A.11 and A.13 on the other should be equal). A price index for exports (Px) was then obtained by dividing the nominal by the real value of exports, and a similar procedure produced a price index for imports (Pm). The net barter terms of trade is defined as (Px/Pm × 100) and is given in Table A.14 (1970 = 100). An index was then formed for the real value of exports in Table

A.12 (1970 = 100) and multiplied by (Px/Pm) to give the purchasing power of exports (Table A.15).

I began working on these statistical series in 1981 and finally completed the work, with the help of various research assistants, in 1986. I believe that the estimates represent the best that can be achieved under the circumstances, but it is important to emphasise that the estimates can be no better than the quality of the primary data from which they are drawn; there is, for example, a quantum leap in the statistics for agriculture in Guatemala in 1936 which was not 'corrected' until 1943. This introduces a distortion to the national accounts estimates for Guatemala in those years, but I have taken a deliberate decision not to 'smooth' the data. Fortunately, this example is the most serious one I have found of clear errors in the primary data.

The tables in the Statistical Appendix are intended both to act as a reference for readers of this book and to assist scholars in future research on Central America. For too long the study of Central America has been thwarted by inadequate statistics or by conclusions drawn without reference to the quantitative evidence. I hope that the tables in the Statistical Appendix will contribute to a better understanding of the Central American reality and act as a guide to future research.

# Statistical Appendix

*Table A.1*  Gross Domestic Product, 1920–84. 1970 prices (thousand dollars calculated at purchasing-power parity exchange rates). Net factor cost

*Table A.2*  Population, 1920–84 (in thousands)

*Table A.3*  Gross Domestic Product per head, 1920–84. 1970 prices (in dollars calculated at purchasing-power parity exchange rates). Net factor cost

*Table A.4*  Value added in agriculture, forestry and fishing, 1920–84. 1970 prices (thousand dollars calculated at purchasing-power parity exchange rates). Net factor cost

*Table A.5*  Value added by export agriculture, 1920–84. 1970 prices (thousand dollars calculated at purchasing-power parity exchange rates). Net factor cost

*Table A.6*  Value added by domestic use agriculture, 1920–84. 1970 prices (thousand dollars calculated at purchasing-power parity exchange rates). Net factor cost

*Table A.7*  Value added in mining and quarrying, 1920–84. 1970 prices (thousand dollars calculated at purchasing-power parity exchange rates). Net factor cost

*Table A.8*  Value added in manufacturing, 1920–84. 1970 prices (thousand dollars calculated at purchasing-power parity exchange rates). Net factor cost

*Table A.9*  Value added by general government, 1920–84. 1970 prices (thousand dollars calculated at purchasing-power parity exchange rates). Net factor cost

*Table A.10*  Nominal value of exports (f.o.b.), 1920–84. Thousand dollars at official exchange rates

*Table A.11*  Nominal value of imports (c.i.f.), 1920–84. Thousand dollars at official exchange rates

*Table A.12*  Real value of exports (f.o.b.), 1920–84. 1970 prices (thousand dollars calculated at purchasing-power parity exchange rates)

*Table A.13*  Real value of imports (c.i.f.), 1920–84. 1970 prices (thousand dollars calculated at purchasing-power parity exchange rates)

*Table A.14*  Net barter terms of trade, 1920–84 (1970 = 100)

*Table A.15*  Purchasing power of exports, 1920–84 (1970 = 100)

Table A.1 *Gross Domestic Product, 1920–84*
1970 prices (thousand dollars).[1] Net factor cost

|  | Costa Rica | El Salvador | Guatemala | Honduras | Nicaragua |
|---|---|---|---|---|---|
| 1920 | 119,208 | 193,521 | 290,407 | 157,477 | 108,806 |
| 1921 | 116,717 | 193,930 | 318,958 | 159,091 | 112,926 |
| 1922 | 127,144 | 205,450 | 300,983 | 172,966 | 103,435 |
| 1923 | 117,539 | 214,173 | 331,001 | 171,999 | 110,669 |
| 1924 | 134,379 | 229,118 | 357,909 | 160,704 | 117,328 |
| 1925 | 133,939 | 213,315 | 351,099 | 193,943 | 129,517 |
| 1926 | 148,066 | 252,080 | 354,466 | 195,714 | 112,603 |
| 1927 | 134,378 | 221,653 | 377,747 | 214,914 | 113,086 |
| 1928 | 141,375 | 259,947 | 386,277 | 241,714 | 143,306 |
| 1929 | 135,563 | 260,228 | 431,065 | 239,314 | 160,074 |
| 1930 | 142,154 | 266,891 | 449,595 | 254,857 | 129,452 |
| 1931 | 140,360 | 239,118 | 419,222 | 260,400 | 121,005 |
| 1932 | 129,122 | 214,598 | 366,919 | 233,257 | 108,936 |
| 1933 | 153,814 | 243,578 | 370,676 | 218,800 | 137,051 |
| 1934 | 135,596 | 251,592 | 419,296 | 211,943 | 124,464 |
| 1935 | 146,910 | 276,855 | 484,637 | 202,514 | 126,461 |
| 1936 | 156,676 | 270,659 | 665,639 | 206,229 | 100,622 |
| 1937 | 182,660 | 296,365 | 652,826 | 197,143 | 109,096 |
| 1938 | 193,630 | 275,560 | 670,863 | 208,571 | 112,832 |
| 1939 | 199,245 | 295,591 | 754,982 | 214,343 | 140,112 |
| 1940 | 191,138 | 321,027 | 862,410 | 229,086 | 153,216 |
| 1941 | 213,966 | 314,234 | 908,491 | 228,457 | 167,637 |
| 1942 | 191,838 | 341,220 | 920,326 | 208,914 | 161,388 |
| 1943 | 191,517 | 369,934 | 613,709 | 209,257 | 176,982 |
| 1944 | 173,479 | 351,053 | 594.863 | 214,143 | 175,300 |
| 1945 | 197,619 | 336,400 | 604,038 | 263,771 | 176,000 |
| 1946 | 218,400 | 341,800 | 715,610 | 283,829 | 191,200 |
| 1947 | 259,900 | 429,900 | 725,603 | 302,114 | 191,800 |
| 1948 | 274,700 | 547,800 | 750,147 | 308,571 | 208,500 |
| 1949 | 285,800 | 497,500 | 820,640 | 312,800 | 204,700 |
| 1950 | 297,600 | 512,000 | 884,800 | 322,743 | 238,600 |
| 1951 | 305,500 | 522,100 | 897,300 | 340,286 | 254,900 |
| 1952 | 342,500 | 561,200 | 915,900 | 353,314 | 298,000 |
| 1953 | 394,600 | 601,300 | 949,700 | 381,029 | 305,200 |
| 1954 | 397,900 | 608,300 | 967,300 | 359,486 | 333,600 |
| 1955 | 443,900 | 639,600 | 991,100 | 368,914 | 356,100 |
| 1956 | 431,200 | 689,800 | 1,081,300 | 398,629 | 355,800 |
| 1957 | 467,900 | 726,500 | 1,142,300 | 416,914 | 385,900 |
| 1958 | 525,900 | 742,300 | 1,195,700 | 430,171 | 387,100 |
| 1959 | 545,200 | 775,600 | 1,254,700 | 440,914 | 392,900 |
| 1960 | 592,700 | 807,100 | 1,285,300 | 468,229 | 398,300 |
| 1961 | 617,300 | 835,500 | 1,340,400 | 480,229 | 428,100 |
| 1962 | 655,100 | 935,400 | 1,387,900 | 507,886 | 474,800 |
| 1963 | 711,300 | 975,700 | 1,520,300 | 526,857 | 526,400 |
| 1964 | 745,900 | 1,066,700 | 1,590,700 | 554,286 | 587,900 |
| 1965 | 813,500 | 1,123,900 | 1,660,000 | 602,229 | 643,900 |

Table A.1 (*cont.*)

|      | Costa Rica | El Salvador | Guatemala | Honduras  | Nicaragua |
|------|-----------|-------------|-----------|-----------|-----------|
| 1966 | 876,800   | 1,204,400   | 1,751,700 | 637,257   | 665,200   |
| 1967 | 930,500   | 1,269,900   | 1,823,500 | 673,143   | 711,600   |
| 1968 | 1,002,100 | 1,311,000   | 1,983,500 | 713,029   | 721,100   |
| 1969 | 1,068,800 | 1,356,700   | 2,077,300 | 718,743   | 769,100   |
| 1970 | 1,139,400 | 1,397,100   | 2,196,200 | 737,486   | 776,500   |
| 1971 | 1,214,500 | 1,461,600   | 2,318,900 | 780,905   | 802,161   |
| 1972 | 1,321,400 | 1,544,400   | 2,488,900 | 814,255   | 819,975   |
| 1973 | 1,424,500 | 1,610,300   | 2,657,700 | 860,820   | 872,593   |
| 1974 | 1,502,900 | 1,706,300   | 2,827,208 | 855,157   | 996,435   |
| 1975 | 1,534,460 | 1,777,830   | 2,848,020 | 826,211   | 994,908   |
| 1976 | 1,619,130 | 1,862,050   | 3,079,260 | 881,585   | 1,046,740 |
| 1977 | 1,763,300 | 1,988,950   | 3,306,490 | 965,276   | 1,134,730 |
| 1978 | 1,873,906 | 2,116,589   | 3,471,705 | 1,036,900 | 1,045,701 |
| 1979 | 1,966,418 | 2.080,204   | 3,635,342 | 1,107,423 | 769,373   |
| 1980 | 1,981,247 | 1,899,718   | 3,771,545 | 1,137,725 | 846,302   |
| 1981 | 1,936,351 | 1,742,335   | 3,796,673 | 1,150,948 | 891,146   |
| 1982 | 1,795,271 | 1,644,728   | 3,661,927 | 1,130,563 | 880,592   |
| 1983 | 1,837,445 | 1,633,321   | 3,568,455 | 1,125,053 | 912,833   |
| 1984 | 1,953,493 | 1,657,723   | 3,591,034 | 1,156,458 | 883,839   |

[1] Calculated at purchasing-power parity exchange rates

Table A.2 *Population, 1920–84 (in thousands)*

|  | Costa Rica | El Salvador | Guatemala | Honduras | Nicaragua |
|---|---|---|---|---|---|
| 1920 | 420 | 1,170 | 1,270 | 720 | 640 |
| 1921 | 430 | 1,190 | 1,320 | 740 | 640 |
| 1922 | 430 | 1,220 | 1,370 | 770 | 650 |
| 1923 | 440 | 1,240 | 1,420 | 800 | 650 |
| 1924 | 450 | 1,270 | 1,470 | 820 | 660 |
| 1925 | 460 | 1,300 | 1,510 | 850 | 660 |
| 1926 | 470 | 1,330 | 1,560 | 880 | 670 |
| 1927 | 470 | 1,350 | 1,600 | 890 | 670 |
| 1928 | 480 | 1,390 | 1,660 | 910 | 670 |
| 1929 | 490 | 1,410 | 1,710 | 930 | 680 |
| 1930 | 500 | 1,440 | 1,760 | 950 | 680 |
| 1931 | 510 | 1,460 | 1,810 | 970 | 690 |
| 1932 | 520 | 1,470 | 1,860 | 990 | 690 |
| 1933 | 530 | 1,490 | 1,910 | 1,010 | 700 |
| 1934 | 540 | 1,510 | 1,940 | 1,020 | 710 |
| 1935 | 550 | 1,530 | 1,980 | 1,040 | 730 |
| 1936 | 560 | 1,550 | 2,020 | 1,060 | 750 |
| 1937 | 580 | 1,570 | 2,070 | 1,080 | 770 |
| 1938 | 590 | 1,590 | 2,110 | 1,100 | 780 |
| 1939 | 610 | 1,610 | 2,150 | 1,120 | 810 |
| 1940 | 620 | 1,630 | 2,200 | 1,150 | 830 |
| 1941 | 630 | 1,650 | 2,250 | 1,170 | 840 |
| 1942 | 650 | 1,680 | 2,300 | 1,200 | 860 |
| 1943 | 660 | 1,690 | 2,340 | 1,210 | 880 |
| 1944 | 680 | 1,720 | 2,390 | 1,240 | 900 |
| 1945 | 700 | 1,740 | 2,440 | 1,260 | 920 |
| 1946 | 710 | 1,760 | 2,500 | 1,290 | 950 |
| 1947 | 730 | 1,780 | 2,570 | 1,320 | 980 |
| 1948 | 750 | 1,810 | 2,640 | 1,350 | 1,000 |
| 1949 | 770 | 1,840 | 2,720 | 1,390 | 1,030 |
| 1950 | 800 | 1,860 | 2,810 | 1,430 | 1,060 |
| 1951 | 830 | 1,900 | 2,890 | 1,470 | 1,090 |
| 1952 | 920 | 1,970 | 2,980 | 1,530 | 1,120 |
| 1953 | 950 | 2,020 | 3,070 | 1,570 | 1,150 |
| 1954 | 990 | 2,080 | 3,180 | 1,620 | 1,180 |
| 1955 | 1,030 | 2,140 | 3,290 | 1,650 | 1,220 |
| 1956 | 1,070 | 2,200 | 3,390 | 1,710 | 1,260 |
| 1957 | 1,110 | 2,260 | 3,490 | 1,770 | 1,290 |
| 1958 | 1,150 | 2,320 | 3,610 | 1,830 | 1,330 |
| 1959 | 1,190 | 2,390 | 3,720 | 1,890 | 1,370 |
| 1960 | 1,250 | 2,450 | 3,830 | 1,950 | 1,410 |
| 1961 | 1,300 | 2,510 | 3,950 | 2,025 | 1,450 |
| 1962 | 1,350 | 2,630 | 4,060 | 2,089 | 1,500 |
| 1963 | 1,390 | 2,720 | 4,190 | 2,153 | 1,540 |
| 1964 | 1,440 | 2,820 | 4,310 | 2,238 | 1,580 |
| 1965 | 1,490 | 2,930 | 4,410 | 2,304 | 1,620 |
| 1966 | 1,540 | 3,040 | 4,500 | 2,384 | 1,660 |

Table A.2 *(cont.)*

|      | Costa Rica | El Salvador | Guatemala | Honduras | Nicaragua |
|------|-----------|-------------|-----------|----------|-----------|
| 1967 | 1,590 | 3,150 | 4,700 | 2,466 | 1,710 |
| 1968 | 1,630 | 3,270 | 4,840 | 2,552 | 1,740 |
| 1969 | 1,690 | 3,360 | 5,020 | 2,638 | 1,790 |
| 1970 | 1,730 | 3,440 | 5,270 | 2,639 | 1,830 |
| 1971 | 1,800 | 3,550 | 5,420 | 2,720 | 1,890 |
| 1972 | 1,840 | 3,670 | 5,580 | 2,805 | 1,950 |
| 1973 | 1,870 | 3,770 | 5,740 | 2,895 | 2,010 |
| 1974 | 1,920 | 3,890 | 6,050 | 2,991 | 2,080 |
| 1975 | 1,970 | 4,010 | 6,240 | 3,093 | 2,160 |
| 1976 | 2,020 | 4,120 | 6,430 | 3,202 | 2,230 |
| 1977 | 2,070 | 4,240 | 6,630 | 3,318 | 2,300 |
| 1978 | 2,120 | 4,350 | 6,840 | 3,439 | 2,370 |
| 1979 | 2,170 | 4,440 | 7,050 | 3,564 | 2,478 |
| 1980 | 2,220 | 4,750 | 7,260 | 3,691 | 2,693 |
| 1981 | 2,270 | 4,870 | 7,480 | 3,821 | 2,800 |
| 1982 | 2,320 | 5,000 | 7,700 | 3,955 | 2,909 |
| 1983 | 2,370 | 5,230 | 7,930 | 4,092 | 3,017 |
| 1984 | 2,425 | 5,386 | 8,160 | 4,231 | 3,117 |

Table A.3  *Goss Domestic Product, per head, 1920–84*
1970 prices.[1] Net factor cost

| | Costa Rica | El Salvador | Guatemala | Honduras | Nicaragua |
|---|---|---|---|---|---|
| 1920 | 283.8 | 165.4 | 228.6 | 218.7 | 170.0 |
| 1921 | 271.4 | 162.9 | 241.9 | 214.9 | 176.4 |
| 1922 | 295.6 | 168.4 | 219.6 | 224.6 | 159.1 |
| 1923 | 267.1 | 172.7 | 233.0 | 214.8 | 170.2 |
| 1924 | 298.6 | 180.4 | 243.4 | 195.9 | 177.7 |
| 1925 | 291.1 | 164.0 | 232.5 | 228.1 | 196.2 |
| 1926 | 315.0 | 189.5 | 227.2 | 222.4 | 168.0 |
| 1927 | 285.9 | 164.1 | 236.0 | 241.4 | 168.7 |
| 1928 | 294.5 | 187.0 | 232.6 | 265.2 | 213.8 |
| 1929 | 276.6 | 184.5 | 252.0 | 257.3 | 235.4 |
| 1930 | 284.3 | 185.3 | 255.4 | 268.2 | 190.0 |
| 1931 | 275.2 | 163.7 | 231.6 | 268.4 | 175.3 |
| 1932 | 248.3 | 145.9 | 197.2 | 235.6 | 157.8 |
| 1933 | 290.2 | 163.4 | 194.0 | 216.6 | 195.7 |
| 1934 | 251.1 | 166.6 | 216.0 | 207.7 | 175.3 |
| 1935 | 267.1 | 180.9 | 244.7 | 194.7 | 173.2 |
| 1936 | 279.7 | 174.6 | 329.5 | 194.5 | 134.1 |
| 1937 | 314.9 | 188.7 | 315.3 | 182.5 | 141.6 |
| 1938 | 328.1 | 173.3 | 317.9 | 189.6 | 144.6 |
| 1939 | 326.6 | 183.5 | 351.1 | 191.3 | 172.9 |
| 1940 | 308.2 | 196.9 | 392.0 | 199.2 | 184.5 |
| 1941 | 339.6 | 190.4 | 403.7 | 195.2 | 199.5 |
| 1942 | 295.1 | 203.1 | 400.1 | 174.0 | 187.6 |
| 1943 | 290.1 | 218.8 | 262.2 | 172.9 | 201.1 |
| 1944 | 255.1 | 204.1 | 249.0 | 194.4 | 194.7 |
| 1945 | 282.3 | 193.3 | 247.5 | 209.3 | 191.3 |
| 1946 | 307.6 | 194.2 | 286.2 | 220.0 | 201.2 |
| 1947 | 356.0 | 241.5 | 282.3 | 228.8 | 195.7 |
| 1948 | 366.2 | 302.6 | 284.1 | 228.5 | 208.5 |
| 1949 | 371.1 | 270.3 | 301.7 | 225.0 | 198.7 |
| 1950 | 372.0 | 275.2 | 314.8 | 225.6 | 225.0 |
| 1951 | 368.0 | 274.7 | 310.4 | 231.4 | 233.8 |
| 1952 | 372.2 | 284.8 | 307.3 | 230.9 | 266.0 |
| 1953 | 415.3 | 297.6 | 309.3 | 242.6 | 265.3 |
| 1954 | 401.9 | 292.4 | 304.1 | 221.9 | 282.7 |
| 1955 | 430.9 | 298.8 | 301.2 | 223.5 | 291.8 |
| 1956 | 402.9 | 313.5 | 318.9 | 233.1 | 282.3 |
| 1957 | 421.5 | 321.4 | 327.3 | 235.5 | 299.1 |
| 1958 | 457.3 | 319.9 | 331.2 | 235.1 | 291.0 |
| 1959 | 458.1 | 324.5 | 337.2 | 233.3 | 286.7 |
| 1960 | 474.1 | 329.4 | 335.5 | 240.1 | 282.4 |
| 1961 | 474.8 | 332.8 | 339.3 | 237.2 | 295.2 |
| 1962 | 485.2 | 355.6 | 341.8 | 243.1 | 316.5 |
| 1963 | 511.7 | 358.7 | 362.8 | 244.7 | 341.8 |
| 1964 | 517.9 | 378.2 | 369.0 | 247.7 | 372.0 |
| 1965 | 545.9 | 383.5 | 376.4 | 261.4 | 397.4 |

## Table A.3 (*cont.*)

|      | Costa Rica | El Salvador | Guatemala | Honduras | Nicaragua |
|------|------------|-------------|-----------|----------|-----------|
| 1966 | 569.3      | 396.1       | 389.2     | 267.3    | 400.7     |
| 1967 | 585.2      | 403.1       | 388.0     | 273.0    | 416.1     |
| 1968 | 614.7      | 400.9       | 409.8     | 279.4    | 414.4     |
| 1969 | 632.4      | 403.7       | 413.8     | 272.5    | 429.6     |
| 1970 | 658.6      | 406.1       | 416.7     | 279.5    | 424.3     |
| 1971 | 674.7      | 411.7       | 427.8     | 287.1    | 424.4     |
| 1972 | 718.1      | 420.8       | 446.0     | 290.3    | 420.5     |
| 1973 | 761.7      | 427.1       | 463.0     | 297.3    | 434.1     |
| 1974 | 782.8      | 438.6       | 467.3     | 285.9    | 479.0     |
| 1975 | 778.9      | 443.3       | 456.4     | 267.1    | 460.6     |
| 1976 | 801.5      | 451.9       | 478.9     | 275.3    | 469.4     |
| 1977 | 851.8      | 469.0       | 498.7     | 290.9    | 493.3     |
| 1978 | 883.8      | 486.6       | 507.6     | 301.5    | 441.2     |
| 1979 | 906.1      | 468.5       | 515.7     | 310.7    | 310.4     |
| 1980 | 892.4      | 399.9       | 519.5     | 308.2    | 314.2     |
| 1981 | 853.0      | 357.8       | 507.6     | 301.2    | 318.2     |
| 1982 | 773.8      | 328.9       | 475.6     | 285.9    | 303.0     |
| 1983 | 775.2      | 312.3       | 450.0     | 274.9    | 302.6     |
| 1984 | 805.6      | 307.8       | 440.1     | 273.3    | 283.6     |

[1] Calculated at purchasing-power parity exchange rates

Table A.4 *Value added in agriculture, forestry and fishing, 1920–84*
1970 prices (thousand dollars).[1] Net factor cost

|  | Costa Rica | El Salvador | Guatemala | Honduras | Nicaragua |
|---|---|---|---|---|---|
| 1920 | 56,476 | 94,370 | 121,933 | 77,887 | 60,690 |
| 1921 | 54,243 | 82,176 | 132,611 | 79,770 | 64,500 |
| 1922 | 58,295 | 103,301 | 130,638 | 87,732 | 62,512 |
| 1923 | 52,058 | 108,520 | 131,176 | 85,850 | 70,923 |
| 1924 | 59,704 | 114,022 | 143,209 | 80,059 | 74,240 |
| 1925 | 58,444 | 90,556 | 132,905 | 99,314 | 80,134 |
| 1926 | 65,216 | 115,383 | 127,234 | 104,857 | 69,879 |
| 1927 | 58,934 | 95,275 | 141,895 | 118,686 | 69,629 |
| 1928 | 59,790 | 119,211 | 135,775 | 136,571 | 93,998 |
| 1929 | 55,296 | 112,723 | 153,803 | 134,857 | 105,808 |
| 1930 | 61,494 | 128,983 | 168,611 | 140,686 | 85,682 |
| 1931 | 59,540 | 117,659 | 147,013 | 151,829 | 78,442 |
| 1932 | 54,246 | 93,800 | 148,525 | 138,914 | 71,531 |
| 1933 | 65,303 | 121,089 | 147,341 | 125,429 | 92,247 |
| 1934 | 53,303 | 119,597 | 161,656 | 118,457 | 81,859 |
| 1935 | 58,877 | 133,043 | 183,975 | 104,000 | 84,313 |
| 1936 | 61,370 | 127,941 | 260,469 | 107,829 | 63,464 |
| 1937 | 73,106 | 145,169 | 265,713 | 96,514 | 69,293 |
| 1938 | 73,059 | 131,562 | 292,022 | 101,943 | 67,431 |
| 1939 | 67,963 | 141,116 | 345,199 | 107,714 | 76,614 |
| 1940 | 64,108 | 152,276 | 390,767 | 115,943 | 71,589 |
| 1941 | 75,835 | 141,600 | 411,232 | 113,200 | 70,545 |
| 1942 | 67,100 | 161,014 | 414,970 | 97,829 | 68,070 |
| 1943 | 68,163 | 170,675 | 240,164 | 95,257 | 73,934 |
| 1944 | 60,351 | 164,512 | 236,812 | 124,343 | 69,923 |
| 1945 | 67,188 | 153,200 | 238,884 | 124,343 | 65,500 |
| 1946 | 76,600 | 147,700 | 286,681 | 132,571 | 69,600 |
| 1947 | 91,700 | 189,500 | 282,428 | 141,200 | 66,600 |
| 1948 | 111,000 | 247,730 | 306,876 | 146,286 | 73,200 |
| 1949 | 109,200 | 215,400 | 295,212 | 141,714 | 69,600 |
| 1950 | 114,700 | 209,700 | 323,400 | 144,686 | 87,300 |
| 1951 | 121,200 | 209,800 | 319,300 | 149,143 | 87,500 |
| 1952 | 135,200 | 211,700 | 327,500 | 146,229 | 106,200 |
| 1953 | 141,400 | 230,700 | 339,700 | 151,771 | 102,200 |
| 1954 | 140,000 | 228,200 | 341,500 | 137,943 | 106,300 |
| 1955 | 142,500 | 246,100 | 335,800 | 140,000 | 116,200 |
| 1956 | 128,900 | 255,500 | 357,800 | 159,086 | 113,200 |
| 1957 | 145,700 | 267,800 | 363,800 | 163,200 | 124,000 |
| 1958 | 160,500 | 283,700 | 387,000 | 165,257 | 119,100 |
| 1959 | 167,800 | 289,000 | 418,600 | 167,829 | 125,700 |
| 1960 | 175,800 | 290,700 | 429,700 | 153,714 | 117,500 |
| 1961 | 187,600 | 307,700 | 437,100 | 163,771 | 127,900 |
| 1962 | 190,800 | 366,400 | 452,500 | 171,543 | 140,600 |
| 1963 | 201,900 | 353,700 | 518,000 | 177,771 | 160,500 |
| 1964 | 200,000 | 368,400 | 519,700 | 188,914 | 187,400 |
| 1965 | 222,900 | 352,800 | 526,000 | 218,629 | 204,700 |

Table A.4 (*cont.*)

|  | Costa Rica | El Salvador | Guatemala | Honduras | Nicaragua |
|---|---|---|---|---|---|
| 1966 | 234,100 | 359,700 | 550,800 | 236,457 | 198,100 |
| 1967 | 245,700 | 380,500 | 551,400 | 245,657 | 213,000 |
| 1968 | 262,500 | 387,300 | 610,900 | 263,314 | 202,600 |
| 1969 | 279,700 | 401,500 | 625,300 | 253,029 | 231,500 |
| 1970 | 285,300 | 427,800 | 661,500 | 255,257 | 209,700 |
| 1971 | 302,100 | 443,900 | 708,300 | 278,462 | 226,690 |
| 1972 | 320,800 | 450,400 | 776,300 | 281,598 | 221,528 |
| 1973 | 337,900 | 458,400 | 817,400 | 294,769 | 249,108 |
| 1974 | 336,200 | 505,400 | 869,600 | 238,172 | 285,776 |
| 1975 | 346,402 | 538,138 | 891,372 | 200,542 | 275,868 |
| 1976 | 348,128 | 494,487 | 931,556 | 223,120 | 281,476 |
| 1977 | 355,976 | 512,221 | 967,916 | 238,172 | 290,190 |
| 1978 | 379,428 | 584,154 | 998,446 | 257,268 | 307,986 |
| 1979 | 381,310 | 604,949 | 1,026,680 | 274,773 | 260,854 |
| 1980 | 379,428 | 573,415 | 1,042,891 | 285,912 | 217,907 |
| 1981 | 398,537 | 536,937 | 1,055,589 | 290,686 | 240,019 |
| 1982 | 380,007 | 511,710 | 1,023,843 | 292,808 | 246,935 |
| 1983 | 394,773 | 495,516 | 1,006,146 | 300,765 | 262,572 |
| 1984 | 421,554 | 501,482 | 1,026,410 | 309,783 | 236,099 |

[1] Calculated at purchasing-power parity exchange rates

Table A.5 *Value added by export agriculture,*[1] *1920–84*
1970 prices (thousand dollars).[2] Net factor cost

| | Costa Rica | El Salvador | Guatemala | Honduras | Nicaragua |
|---|---|---|---|---|---|
| 1920 | 33,836 | 41,829 | 65,948 | 35,445 | 10,827 |
| 1921 | 32,278 | 31,872 | 68,801 | 41,781 | 18,111 |
| 1922 | 35,779 | 48,157 | 70,990 | 48,922 | 16,542 |
| 1923 | 27,613 | 47,896 | 74,023 | 45,101 | 22,595 |
| 1924 | 37,455 | 55,763 | 76,822 | 44,550 | 24,184 |
| 1925 | 34,708 | 37,119 | 71,766 | 58,214 | 20,400 |
| 1926 | 33,599 | 56,374 | 68,687 | 62,892 | 21,273 |
| 1927 | 34,548 | 40,503 | 79,934 | 77,731 | 17,248 |
| 1928 | 33,489 | 59,129 | 70,920 | 95,299 | 24,126 |
| 1929 | 34,623 | 52,281 | 73,230 | 93,079 | 25,013 |
| 1930 | 38,480 | 72,248 | 83,902 | 99,877 | 25,616 |
| 1931 | 36,179 | 61,040 | 62,523 | 112,721 | 22,728 |
| 1932 | 27,129 | 45,015 | 71,578 | 94,781 | 18,611 |
| 1933 | 40,055 | 63,251 | 60,211 | 78,314 | 23,475 |
| 1934 | 27,341 | 56,792 | 74,801 | 70,838 | 20,742 |
| 1935 | 32,784 | 58,262 | 66,667 | 53,041 | 24,676 |
| 1936 | 31,718 | 58,765 | 84,937 | 52,100 | 17,534 |
| 1937 | 41,691 | 78,113 | 90,235 | 43,031 | 22,702 |
| 1938 | 38,855 | 62,565 | 91,831 | 44,494 | 19,894 |
| 1939 | 27,836 | 65,492 | 91,059 | 48,044 | 21,329 |
| 1940 | 28,055 | 67,411 | 83,616 | 56,649 | 17,891 |
| 1941 | 33,344 | 51,395 | 76,381 | 51,932 | 14,227 |
| 1942 | 29,038 | 64,905 | 70,476 | 31,039 | 13,428 |
| 1943 | 33,285 | 69,729 | 65,096 | 29,504 | 12,148 |
| 1944 | 25,550 | 76,688 | 79,826 | 45,434 | 10,794 |
| 1945 | 33,646 | 72,294 | 94,293 | 56,246 | 10,712 |
| 1946 | 30,276 | 63,292 | 99,791 | 59,089 | 11,661 |
| 1947 | 44,029 | 78,683 | 108,790 | 64,950 | 11,151 |
| 1948 | 60,872 | 80,149 | 102,431 | 65,332 | 14,175 |
| 1949 | 55,431 | 99,519 | 80,824 | 60,414 | 9,821 |
| 1950 | 62,051 | 94,190 | 93,740 | 58,994 | 23,541 |
| 1951 | 57,698 | 91,690 | 96,961 | 60,082 | 24,265 |
| 1952 | 67,774 | 96,769 | 86,467 | 55,301 | 23,665 |
| 1953 | 75,396 | 101,701 | 106,690 | 56,643 | 29,182 |
| 1954 | 65,641 | 94,724 | 109,462 | 47,540 | 52,084 |
| 1955 | 72,619 | 116,290 | 108,922 | 44,819 | 44,167 |
| 1956 | 54,073 | 120,992 | 109,238 | 46,469 | 47,508 |
| 1957 | 71,444 | 134,827 | 128,305 | 48,175 | 48,044 |
| 1958 | 78,741 | 146,962 | 125,053 | 57,429 | 49,900 |
| 1959 | 62,561 | 147,050 | 143,857 | 57,288 | 52,128 |
| 1960 | 68,985 | 133,055 | 152,130 | 55,625 | 40,838 |
| 1961 | 73,029 | 153,995 | 149,725 | 60,905 | 47,552 |
| 1962 | 75,751 | 200,577 | 156,235 | 61,074 | 68,152 |
| 1963 | 75,156 | 192,180 | 195,299 | 63,253 | 91,142 |
| 1964 | 73,274 | 212,571 | 193,012 | 71,684 | 128,959 |
| 1965 | 77,770 | 197,763 | 196,540 | 86,938 | 163,620 |

Table A.5 *(cont.)*

|      | Costa Rica | El Salvador | Guatemala | Honduras | Nicaragua |
|------|-----------|-------------|-----------|----------|-----------|
| 1966 | 91,539    | 182,459     | 203,115   | 98,046   | 134,945   |
| 1967 | 97,378    | 199,922     | 177,905   | 103,642  | 141,545   |
| 1968 | 111,314   | 197,259     | 198,404   | 114,727  | 103,862   |
| 1969 | 125,016   | 204,033     | 201,130   | 104,743  | 128,346   |
| 1970 | 134,889   | 219,803     | 206,240   | 105,700  | 100,000   |
| 1971 | 144,801   | 233,430     | 215,127   | 116,906  | 113,639   |
| 1972 | 157,524   | 247,114     | 256,289   | 114,045  | 127,738   |
| 1973 | 167,478   | 222,701     | 278,770   | 124,461  | 143,900   |
| 1974 | 158,870   | 270,843     | 317,724   | 102,162  | 186,737   |
| 1975 | 156,827   | 279,361     | 307,428   | 83,147   | 171,669   |
| 1976 | 152,301   | 243,883     | 314,389   | 95,142   | 169,792   |
| 1977 | 156,420   | 256,281     | 330,625   | 103,983  | 179,791   |
| 1978 | 167,287   | 281,530     | 334,087   | 118,561  | 183,590   |
| 1979 | 164,717   | 306,328     | 345,003   | 135,215  | 153,099   |
| 1980 | 166,594   | 296,923     | 355,907   | 139,349  | 93,411    |
| 1981 | 173,934   | 267,698     | 349,016   | 140,750  | 135,714   |
| 1982 | 180,092   | 264,722     | 322,596   | 139,412  | 134,168   |
| 1983 | 188,324   | 249,243     | 298,621   | 143,579  | 148,237   |
| 1984 | 201,711   | 233,511     | 309,416   | 148,554  | 131,434   |

[1] Defined as coffee, bananas, cotton and sugar
[2] Calculated at purchasing-power parity exchange rates

Table A.6 *Value added by domestic use agriculture[1], 1920–84*
1970 prices (thousand dollars).[2] Net factor cost

|  | Costa Rica | El Salvador | Guatemala | Honduras | Nicaragua |
|---|---|---|---|---|---|
| 1920 | 22,640 | 52,541 | 55,985 | 42,442 | 49,863 |
| 1921 | 21,965 | 50,304 | 63,810 | 37,989 | 46,389 |
| 1922 | 22,516 | 55,144 | 59,648 | 38,810 | 45,970 |
| 1923 | 24,445 | 60,624 | 57,153 | 40,749 | 48,328 |
| 1924 | 22,249 | 58,259 | 66,387 | 35,509 | 50,056 |
| 1925 | 23,736 | 53,437 | 61,139 | 41,100 | 59,734 |
| 1926 | 31,617 | 59,009 | 58,547 | 41,965 | 48,606 |
| 1927 | 24,386 | 54,772 | 61,961 | 40,955 | 52,381 |
| 1928 | 26,301 | 60,082 | 64,855 | 41,272 | 69,872 |
| 1929 | 20,673 | 60,442 | 80,573 | 41,778 | 80,795 |
| 1930 | 23,014 | 56,735 | 84,709 | 40,809 | 60,066 |
| 1931 | 23,361 | 56,619 | 84,490 | 39,108 | 55,714 |
| 1932 | 27,117 | 48,785 | 76,947 | 44,133 | 52,920 |
| 1933 | 25,248 | 57,838 | 87,130 | 47,115 | 68,772 |
| 1934 | 25,962 | 62,805 | 86,855 | 47,619 | 61,117 |
| 1935 | 26,093 | 74,781 | 117,308 | 50,959 | 59,637 |
| 1936 | 29,652 | 69,176 | 175,532 | 55,729 | 45,930 |
| 1937 | 31,415 | 67,056 | 175,478 | 53,483 | 46,591 |
| 1938 | 34,204 | 68,997 | 200,191 | 57,449 | 47,537 |
| 1939 | 40,127 | 75,624 | 254,140 | 59,670 | 55,285 |
| 1940 | 36,053 | 84,865 | 307,151 | 59,294 | 53,698 |
| 1941 | 42,491 | 90,205 | 334,851 | 61,268 | 56,318 |
| 1942 | 38,062 | 96,109 | 344,494 | 66,790 | 54,642 |
| 1943 | 34,878 | 100,946 | 175,068 | 65,753 | 61,786 |
| 1944 | 34,801 | 87,824 | 156,986 | 78,909 | 59,129 |
| 1945 | 33,542 | 80,906 | 144,591 | 68,097 | 54,788 |
| 1946 | 46,324 | 84,408 | 186,890 | 73,482 | 57,939 |
| 1947 | 47,671 | 110,817 | 173,638 | 76,250 | 55,449 |
| 1948 | 50,128 | 167,581 | 204,445 | 80,954 | 59,025 |
| 1949 | 53,769 | 115,881 | 214,388 | 81,300 | 59,779 |
| 1950 | 52,649 | 115,510 | 229,660 | 85,692 | 63,759 |
| 1951 | 63,502 | 118,110 | 222,339 | 89,061 | 63,235 |
| 1952 | 67,426 | 114,931 | 241,033 | 90,928 | 82,535 |
| 1953 | 66,004 | 128,999 | 233,010 | 95,128 | 73,018 |
| 1954 | 74,359 | 133,476 | 232,038 | 90,403 | 54,216 |
| 1955 | 69,881 | 129,810 | 226,878 | 95,181 | 72,033 |
| 1956 | 74,827 | 134,508 | 248,562 | 112,617 | 65,692 |
| 1957 | 74,256 | 132,973 | 235,495 | 115,025 | 75,956 |
| 1958 | 81,759 | 136,738 | 261,947 | 107,828 | 69,200 |
| 1959 | 105,239 | 141,950 | 274,743 | 110,541 | 73,572 |
| 1960 | 106,815 | 157,645 | 277,570 | 98,089 | 76,662 |
| 1961 | 114,571 | 153,705 | 287,735 | 102,866 | 80,348 |
| 1962 | 115,049 | 165,823 | 296,265 | 110,469 | 72,448 |
| 1963 | 126,744 | 161,520 | 322,701 | 114,518 | 69,358 |
| 1964 | 126,726 | 155,829 | 326,688 | 117,230 | 58,441 |
| 1965 | 145,130 | 155,037 | 329,460 | 131,691 | 41,080 |

Table A.6 (*cont.*)

|  | Costa Rica | El Salvador | Guatemala | Honduras | Nicaragua |
|------|------------|-------------|-----------|----------|-----------|
| 1966 | 142,561 | 177,241 | 347,685 | 138,411 | 63,155 |
| 1967 | 148,322 | 180,578 | 373,495 | 142,015 | 71,455 |
| 1968 | 151,186 | 190,041 | 412,496 | 148,587 | 98,738 |
| 1969 | 154,684 | 197,467 | 424,170 | 145,286 | 103,154 |
| 1970 | 150,411 | 207,997 | 455,260 | 149,557 | 109,700 |
| 1971 | 157,299 | 210,470 | 493,173 | 161,556 | 113,051 |
| 1972 | 163,276 | 203,286 | 520,011 | 167,553 | 93,790 |
| 1973 | 170,422 | 235,699 | 538,630 | 170,308 | 105,208 |
| 1974 | 177,330 | 234,557 | 551,876 | 136,010 | 99,039 |
| 1975 | 189,575 | 258,777 | 583,944 | 117,395 | 104,199 |
| 1976 | 195,827 | 250,604 | 617,167 | 127,978 | 111,684 |
| 1977 | 199,556 | 255,940 | 637,291 | 134,189 | 110,401 |
| 1978 | 212,141 | 302,624 | 664,359 | 138,707 | 124,396 |
| 1979 | 216,593 | 298,621 | 681,677 | 139,558 | 107,755 |
| 1980 | 212,834 | 276,492 | 686,984 | 146,563 | 124,496 |
| 1981 | 224,603 | 269,239 | 706,573 | 149,936 | 104,305 |
| 1982 | 199,915 | 246,988 | 701,247 | 153,396 | 112,767 |
| 1983 | 206,449 | 246,273 | 707,525 | 157,186 | 114,335 |
| 1984 | 219,843 | 267,971 | 716,994 | 161,229 | 104,665 |

[1] Defined as agriculture, forestry and fishing less coffee, cotton, bananas and sugar
[2] Calculated at purchasing-power parity exchange rates

Table A.7 *Value added in mining and quarrying,*[1] *1920–84*
1970 prices (thousand dollars).[2] Net factor cost

|  | El Salvador | Guatemala | Honduras | Nicaragua |
|---|---|---|---|---|
| 1920 | 69 | 838 | 2,047 | 1,493 |
| 1921 | 69 | 862 | 1,941 | 1,654 |
| 1922 | 69 | 758 | 2,354 | 1,673 |
| 1923 | 69 | 1,012 | 2,785 | 1,631 |
| 1924 | 69 | 1,066 | 2,915 | 1,674 |
| 1925 | 69 | 1,034 | 3,200 | 1,653 |
| 1926 | 69 | 1,098 | 3,371 | 1,619 |
| 1927 | 69 | 1,106 | 3,371 | 1,601 |
| 1928 | 69 | 1,098 | 3,486 | 1,635 |
| 1929 | 69 | 1,160 | 4,057 | 1,641 |
| 1930 | 69 | 1,276 | 5,200 | 1,674 |
| 1931 | 69 | 1,334 | 5,543 | 1,598 |
| 1932 | 226 | 956 | 5,543 | 1,580 |
| 1933 | 337 | 1,002 | 4,914 | 1,510 |
| 1934 | 1,614 | 1,230 | 4,229 | 1,562 |
| 1935 | 1,923 | 1,420 | 4,914 | 1,504 |
| 1936 | 2,104 | 1,834 | 5,829 | 1,553 |
| 1937 | 2,022 | 1,627 | 6,057 | 1,675 |
| 1938 | 2,407 | 1,381 | 6,229 | 1,784 |
| 1939 | 1,999 | 1,219 | 6,514 | 1,946 |
| 1940 | 2,215 | 1,282 | 7,143 | 2,828 |
| 1941 | 1,988 | 1,370 | 6,857 | 3,613 |
| 1942 | 5,760 | 1,448 | 3,886 | 4,081 |
| 1943 | 5,492 | 1,448 | 4,457 | 3,685 |
| 1944 | 4,559 | 1,426 | 6,114 | 3,717 |
| 1945 | 2,600 | 1,581 | 6,229 | 3,472 |
| 1946 | 3,600 | 1,726 | 5,829 | 3,472 |
| 1947 | 2,600 | 1,838 | 5,200 | 3,364 |
| 1948 | 3,700 | 1,893 | 6,514 | 3,472 |
| 1949 | 4,400 | 1,960 | 7,543 | 3,436 |
| 1950 | 5,100 | 2,000 | 7,543 | 3,600 |
| 1951 | 4,500 | 2,200 | 7,657 | 3,900 |
| 1952 | 4,700 | 2,200 | 9,257 | 4,000 |
| 1953 | 4,000 | 1,700 | 12,114 | 4,200 |
| 1954 | 2,300 | 1,400 | 11,600 | 3,800 |
| 1955 | 1,600 | 2,400 | 6,800 | 3,800 |
| 1956 | 2,000 | 3,000 | 5,086 | 3,400 |
| 1957 | 2,100 | 3,300 | 5,829 | 3,800 |
| 1958 | 2,000 | 2,800 | 6,686 | 3,600 |
| 1959 | 1,900 | 2,200 | 7,486 | 3,800 |
| 1960 | 1,800 | 2,400 | 8,743 | 4,600 |
| 1961 | 1,700 | 3,000 | 9,314 | 5,200 |
| 1962 | 1,600 | 1,800 | 10,343 | 7,600 |
| 1963 | 1,600 | 2,000 | 10,800 | 7,200 |
| 1964 | 1,600 | 2,000 | 10,857 | 7,100 |
| 1965 | 2,000 | 2,000 | 12,571 | 7,100 |

Table A.7 *(cont.)*

|      | El Salvador | Guatemala | Honduras | Nicaragua |
|------|-------------|-----------|----------|-----------|
| 1966 | 2,200 | 2,000  | 12,800 | 7,700 |
| 1967 | 2,300 | 2,200  | 15,943 | 8,000 |
| 1968 | 2,000 | 1,600  | 18,000 | 7,000 |
| 1969 | 2,200 | 1,700  | 16,971 | 5,900 |
| 1970 | 2,500 | 2,100  | 16,629 | 5,200 |
| 1971 | 2,400 | 2,100  | 16,571 | 5,013 |
| 1972 | 2,700 | 1,800  | 16,629 | 4,262 |
| 1973 | 2,900 | 2,000  | 21,746 | 4,748 |
| 1974 | 3,000 | 2,500  | 28,781 | 5,955 |
| 1975 | 3,000 | 2,625  | 21,106 | 4,133 |
| 1976 | 2,400 | 3,375  | 17,908 | 2,872 |
| 1977 | 2,400 | 3,875  | 17,850 | 7,651 |
| 1978 | 2,400 | 6,000  | 22,015 | 4,668 |
| 1979 | 2,400 | 10,875 | 25,585 | 1,962 |
| 1980 | 2,560 | 18,500 | 22,610 | 1,940 |
| 1981 | 2,400 | 11,875 | 21,420 | 2,057 |
| 1982 | 2,400 | 13,375 | 23,205 | 1,911 |
| 1983 | 2,400 | 11,750 | 23,205 | 1,947 |
| 1984 | 2,400 | 9,750  | 24,990 | 1,532 |

[1] Figures for Costa Rica are included in Manufacturing (see Table A.8)
[2] Calculated at purchasing-power parity exchange rates

Table A.8 *Value added in manufacturing, 1920–84*
1970 prices (thousand dollars).[1] Net factor cost

| | Costa Rica[2] | El Salvador | Guatemala | Honduras | Nicaragua |
|---|---|---|---|---|---|
| 1920 | 8,667 | 19,785 | 41,146 | 10,541 | 9,859 |
| 1921 | 9,058 | 19,124 | 42,324 | 10,055 | 10,547 |
| 1922 | 10,711 | 20,207 | 37,218 | 9,974 | 7,995 |
| 1923 | 9,576 | 20,823 | 49,689 | 9,766 | 7,682 |
| 1924 | 11,710 | 23,377 | 52,341 | 9,562 | 8,296 |
| 1925 | 11,168 | 26,786 | 50,769 | 9,943 | 9,040 |
| 1926 | 13,194 | 29,947 | 53,911 | 10,343 | 7,667 |
| 1927 | 11,133 | 28,488 | 54,304 | 11,029 | 7,385 |
| 1928 | 12,700 | 30,896 | 53,911 | 11,886 | 7,199 |
| 1929 | 11,547 | 33,225 | 56,957 | 12,971 | 7,792 |
| 1930 | 12,379 | 28,350 | 62,651 | 12,229 | 6,692 |
| 1931 | 13,138 | 24,234 | 65,499 | 10,686 | 6,620 |
| 1932 | 12,585 | 21,666 | 46,939 | 10,629 | 5,202 |
| 1933 | 15,268 | 26,410 | 49,199 | 11,257 | 6,400 |
| 1934 | 14,480 | 26,529 | 60,393 | 11,600 | 6,303 |
| 1935 | 15,342 | 27,079 | 69,722 | 13,086 | 6,576 |
| 1936 | 16,693 | 27,820 | 90,049 | 13,714 | 5,722 |
| 1937 | 19,480 | 31,182 | 79,866 | 13,943 | 6,431 |
| 1938 | 22,854 | 27,995 | 67,807 | 14,743 | 7,987 |
| 1939 | 25,604 | 30,356 | 59,873 | 14,914 | 12,755 |
| 1940 | 25,235 | 33,129 | 62,937 | 15,600 | 16,888 |
| 1941 | 26,523 | 35,116 | 67,277 | 16,914 | 20,171 |
| 1942 | 24,406 | 32,663 | 71,077 | 16,057 | 18,277 |
| 1943 | 21,809 | 40,106 | 71,077 | 16,457 | 20,410 |
| 1944 | 18,469 | 36,447 | 70,016 | 17,714 | 19,884 |
| 1945 | 20,839 | 38,200 | 77,637 | 19,657 | 20,100 |
| 1946 | 24,700 | 39,900 | 84,727 | 21,257 | 21,100 |
| 1947 | 28,700 | 52,500 | 90,236 | 22,229 | 21,736 |
| 1948 | 28,200 | 67,400 | 92,946 | 23,257 | 24,128 |
| 1949 | 31,600 | 61,900 | 96,237 | 26,971 | 23,464 |
| 1950 | 34,400 | 66,000 | 98,200 | 29,314 | 25,800 |
| 1951 | 37,600 | 63,600 | 101,300 | 32,800 | 28,700 |
| 1952 | 41,300 | 73,900 | 103,900 | 36,743 | 32,700 |
| 1953 | 45,600 | 78,500 | 105,800 | 42,400 | 34,100 |
| 1954 | 50,300 | 85,000 | 112,200 | 38,914 | 39,000 |
| 1955 | 54,500 | 88,100 | 111,400 | 43,714 | 41,100 |
| 1956 | 56,700 | 97,800 | 121,000 | 47,314 | 42,100 |
| 1957 | 60,300 | 101,200 | 132,400 | 49,543 | 46,600 |
| 1958 | 64,500 | 101,500 | 140,500 | 52,171 | 50,400 |
| 1959 | 67,000 | 102,000 | 147,300 | 54,457 | 50,300 |
| 1960 | 74,100 | 112,500 | 153,600 | 71,543 | 52,000 |
| 1961 | 75,700 | 122,600 | 162,900 | 70,971 | 57,700 |
| 1962 | 81,900 | 135,400 | 171,300 | 73,600 | 67,500 |
| 1963 | 93,400 | 147,200 | 188,100 | 75,943 | 80,400 |
| 1964 | 102,100 | 165,800 | 199,900 | 79,257 | 90,200 |
| 1965 | 109,700 | 186,700 | 216,400 | 82,057 | 101,100 |

Table A.8 (*cont.*)

|  | Costa Rica[2] | El Salvador | Guatemala | Honduras | Nicaragua |
|---|---|---|---|---|---|
| 1966 | 122,300 | 208,000 | 238,900 | 85,371 | 106,100 |
| 1967 | 134,400 | 225,400 | 259,000 | 90,171 | 120,900 |
| 1968 | 147,100 | 235,200 | 288,800 | 94,857 | 126,800 |
| 1969 | 159,200 | 237,000 | 309,800 | 97,714 | 136,100 |
| 1970 | 172,600 | 245,900 | 320,700 | 103,143 | 148,900 |
| 1971 | 189,700 | 263,000 | 343,700 | 107,997 | 156,000 |
| 1972 | 206,200 | 273,100 | 362,600 | 112,244 | 163,200 |
| 1973 | 221,400 | 291,500 | 392,100 | 116,491 | 171,302 |
| 1974 | 243,500 | 306,000 | 410,400 | 115,278 | 193,606 |
| 1975 | 251,208 | 313,761 | 404,385 | 118,312 | 198,153 |
| 1976 | 265,786 | 348,685 | 446,605 | 124,379 | 206,337 |
| 1977 | 299,627 | 367,533 | 494,413 | 137,120 | 227,278 |
| 1978 | 324,273 | 384,201 | 526,307 | 150,483 | 227,385 |
| 1979 | 332,872 | 364,894 | 555,704 | 162,685 | 165,183 |
| 1980 | 335,494 | 325,724 | 587,144 | 171,400 | 195,094 |
| 1981 | 333,921 | 291,693 | 568,870 | 171,981 | 200,636 |
| 1982 | 295,747 | 267,246 | 539,246 | 162,104 | 197,225 |
| 1983 | 299,312 | 264,607 | 529,031 | 155,713 | 208,309 |
| 1984 | 329,307 | 269,469 | 531,642 | 159,199 | 207,705 |

[1] Calculated at purchasing-power parity exchange rates
[2] Includes mining and quarrying

Table A.9 *Value added by general government, 1920–84*
1970 prices (thousand dollars).[1] Net factor cost

| | Costa Rica | El Salvador | Guatemala | Honduras | Nicaragua |
|---|---|---|---|---|---|
| 1920 | 3,475 | 10,914 | 8,060 | 7,595 | 801 |
| 1921 | 3,657 | 10,989 | 15,890 | 7,109 | 504 |
| 1922 | 3,850 | 10,147 | 14,272 | 7,360 | 480 |
| 1923 | 4,049 | 10,072 | 16,269 | 5,519 | 683 |
| 1924 | 4,348 | 10,989 | 19,893 | 7,518 | 718 |
| 1925 | 5,391 | 12,904 | 22,036 | 8,057 | 797 |
| 1926 | 4,750 | 13,212 | 28,693 | 8,057 | 757 |
| 1927 | 4,736 | 13,977 | 30,098 | 7,257 | 810 |
| 1928 | 5,589 | 15,395 | 37,124 | 7,429 | 985 |
| 1929 | 7,333 | 16,312 | 41,560 | 8,286 | 1,059 |
| 1930 | 6,757 | 17,462 | 37,494 | 8,286 | 734 |
| 1931 | 6,022 | 16,580 | 33,351 | 8,743 | 857 |
| 1932 | 5,626 | 13,992 | 26,548 | 6,971 | 822 |
| 1933 | 5,607 | 13,325 | 20,115 | 7,429 | 838 |
| 1934 | 5,914 | 13,633 | 20,189 | 7,714 | 889 |
| 1935 | 6,740 | 14,092 | 22,554 | 7,714 | 851 |
| 1936 | 7,369 | 15,969 | 23,221 | 7,886 | 1,002 |
| 1937 | 7,819 | 16,773 | 23,960 | 8,057 | 1,818 |
| 1938 | 8,860 | 17,806 | 23,886 | 8,743 | 1,919 |
| 1939 | 9,005 | 17,462 | 23,960 | 8,114 | 2,608 |
| 1940 | 9,706 | 17,653 | 25,660 | 7,886 | 4,187 |
| 1941 | 10,173 | 15,240 | 25,660 | 8,057 | 4,782 |
| 1942 | 11,629 | 15,891 | 26,105 | 8,286 | 6,279 |
| 1943 | 14,361 | 15,776 | 29,211 | 8,057 | 6,704 |
| 1944 | 13,642 | 19,530 | 28,767 | 8,571 | 10,280 |
| 1945 | 15,924 | 21,941 | 31,946 | 9,257 | 14,072 |
| 1946 | 14,774 | 24,529 | 40,155 | 9,657 | 18,331 |
| 1947 | 15,029 | 24,235 | 49,842 | 10,171 | 19,002 |
| 1948 | 16,346 | 29,588 | 62,489 | 11,486 | 20,452 |
| 1949 | 18,369 | 31,765 | 69,293 | 12,629 | 24,945 |
| 1950 | 17,622 | 37,529 | 73,951 | 13,086 | 25,491 |
| 1951 | 18,153 | 42,824 | 78,272 | 15,429 | 28,003 |
| 1952 | 21,179 | 54,588 | 86,790 | 15,829 | 31,591 |
| 1953 | 28,546 | 56,706 | 89,630 | 18,229 | 34,228 |
| 1954 | 30,806 | 60,000 | 83,704 | 19,429 | 36,147 |
| 1955 | 38,841 | 60,000 | 78,148 | 19,886 | 35,008 |
| 1956 | 41,120 | 63,706 | 91,728 | 22,229 | 37,301 |
| 1957 | 43,065 | 69,588 | 92,963 | 26,914 | 40,421 |
| 1958 | 53,261 | 69,353 | 100,617 | 26,914 | 42,871 |
| 1959 | 57,348 | 70,059 | 115,062 | 28,286 | 42,371 |
| 1960 | 63,635 | 72,000 | 113,086 | 22,229 | 43,541 |
| 1961 | 67,446 | 78,176 | 126,790 | 20,400 | 46,240 |
| 1962 | 73,065 | 84,941 | 107,407 | 21,257 | 49,610 |
| 1963 | 79,843 | 84,471 | 108,519 | 20,857 | 47,270 |
| 1964 | 86,974 | 84,176 | 112,099 | 22,514 | 50,827 |
| 1965 | 93,458 | 88,294 | 115,556 | 22,743 | 52,402 |

Table A.9 (*cont.*)

| | Costa Rica | El Salvador | Guatemala | Honduras | Nicaragua |
|------|-----------|-------------|-----------|----------|-----------|
| 1966 | 106,326 | 97,412 | 118,519 | 24,400 | 51,763 |
| 1967 | 111,768 | 103,647 | 128,272 | 26,286 | 58,908 |
| 1968 | 118,585 | 102,647 | 130,123 | 25,771 | 58,393 |
| 1969 | 127,505 | 115,235 | 146,667 | 26,114 | 63,588 |
| 1970 | 136,189 | 117,765 | 154,321 | 26,743 | 58,471 |
| 1971 | 139,057 | 128,471 | 156,420 | 29,417 | 58,982 |
| 1972 | 149,627 | 137,706 | 173,086 | 36,103 | 62,117 |
| 1973 | 155,914 | 144,000 | 177,160 | 32,092 | 59,315 |
| 1974 | 171,493 | 145,765 | 188,889 | 30,086 | 68,994 |
| 1975 | 176,941 | 146,365 | 208,536 | 30,086 | 79,396 |
| 1976 | 183,675 | 163,761 | 232,238 | 36,103 | 87,599 |
| 1977 | 192,869 | 172,759 | 229,975 | 41,452 | 91,474 |
| 1978 | 202,459 | 191,938 | 242,430 | 46,979 | 100,202 |
| 1979 | 214,333 | 199,130 | 258,568 | 57,342 | 93,886 |
| 1980 | 222,096 | 204,824 | 285,934 | 59,415 | 100,949 |
| 1981 | 226,358 | 207,371 | 298,389 | 62,178 | 106,059 |
| 1982 | 219,661 | 213,514 | 309,966 | 64,251 | 110,711 |
| 1983 | 216,159 | 212,765 | 324,702 | 64,251 | 127,248 |
| 1984 | 217,225 | 218,458 | 333,823 | 64,941 | 125,066 |

[1] Calculated at purchasing-power parity exchange rates

Table A.10 *Nominal value of exports (f.o.b.), 1920–84*
(thousand dollars)

|      | Costa Rica | El Salvador | Guatemala | Honduras | Nicaragua |
|------|-----------|-------------|-----------|----------|-----------|
| 1920 | 12,456 | 18,210 | 18,100 | 15,785 | 10,790 |
| 1921 | 11,900 | 8,900 | 12,130 | 12,330 | 8,070 |
| 1922 | 14,200 | 16,290 | 11,650 | 12,240 | 7,900 |
| 1923 | 12,800 | 17,310 | 14,730 | 22,755 | 11,030 |
| 1924 | 16,565 | 24,370 | 24,460 | 17,920 | 13,000 |
| 1925 | 16,416 | 16,880 | 29,650 | 27,210 | 12,360 |
| 1926 | 18,962 | 24,640 | 28,970 | 30,570 | 13,030 |
| 1927 | 18,058 | 14,150 | 33,920 | 33,040 | 9,030 |
| 1928 | 19,636 | 24,460 | 28,210 | 42,245 | 11,690 |
| 1929 | 18,198 | 18,420 | 24,930 | 37,420 | 10,870 |
| 1930 | 16,330 | 13,660 | 23,570 | 38,250 | 8,340 |
| 1931 | 14,280 | 11,030 | 15,170 | 38,895 | 6,570 |
| 1932 | 8,530 | 5,500 | 10,670 | 38,795 | 4,540 |
| 1933 | 10,680 | 6,910 | 9,330 | 41,865 | 4,870 |
| 1934 | 8,700 | 9,250 | 14,800 | 40,485 | 5,230 |
| 1935 | 8,250 | 10,840 | 12,470 | 30,130 | 5,660 |
| 1936 | 8,820 | 10,100 | 16,930 | 22,355 | 4,650 |
| 1937 | 11,510 | 15,520 | 17,900 | 24,280 | 7,040 |
| 1938 | 10,140 | 10,940 | 18,230 | 16,590 | 5,880 |
| 1939 | 9,080 | 12,740 | 18,780 | 23,230 | 8,300 |
| 1940 | 7,480 | 12,228 | 12,040 | 23,135 | 9,500 |
| 1941 | 10,230 | 11,208 | 14,500 | 22,195 | 11,930 |
| 1942 | 10,570 | 18,464 | 20,440 | 21,225 | 14,330 |
| 1943 | 12,430 | 22,524 | 20,140 | 9,280 | 15,440 |
| 1944 | 10,530 | 22,984 | 23,850 | 19,910 | 15,410 |
| 1945 | 11,610 | 21,332 | 30,430 | 28,340 | 13,970 |
| 1946 | 14,340 | 26,148 | 36,680 | 30,605 | 18,080 |
| 1947 | 31,060 | 40,056 | 68,030 | 42,935 | 20,980 |
| 1948 | 45,960 | 45,396 | 69,160 | 49,690 | 26,680 |
| 1949 | 48,190 | 54,960 | 62,420 | 57,675 | 23,660 |
| 1950 | 55,580 | 69,496 | 78,900 | 66,530 | 34,640 |
| 1951 | 63,410 | 85,528 | 84,300 | 65,375 | 45,520 |
| 1952 | 73,350 | 88,284 | 94,700 | 63,100 | 51,250 |
| 1953 | 80,150 | 89,608 | 99,600 | 69,255 | 54,550 |
| 1954 | 84,700 | 105,232 | 104,900 | 56,615 | 62,770 |
| 1955 | 80,900 | 106,500 | 106,300 | 53,700 | 80,020 |
| 1956 | 67,450 | 123,000 | 122,500 | 72,900 | 65,500 |
| 1957 | 83,360 | 127,100 | 115,900 | 64,800 | 70,600 |
| 1958 | 91,900 | 118,000 | 107,900 | 69,500 | 70,400 |
| 1959 | 76,680 | 111,800 | 103,700 | 68,500 | 75,000 |
| 1960 | 85,830 | 102,600 | 115,900 | 63,100 | 63,900 |
| 1961 | 84,150 | 118,800 | 114,000 | 73,000 | 69,900 |
| 1962 | 92,970 | 138,900 | 119,000 | 81,500 | 90,400 |
| 1963 | 95,020 | 150,200 | 153,400 | 84,400 | 106,600 |
| 1964 | 113,900 | 175,500 | 174,300 | 95,100 | 125,500 |
| 1965 | 111,820 | 190,000 | 192,100 | 128,200 | 149,200 |

Table A.10  (*cont.*)

|      | Costa Rica | El Salvador | Guatemala | Honduras | Nicaragua |
|------|-----------|------------|-----------|----------|-----------|
| 1966 | 135,510   | 189,500    | 231,900   | 144,400  | 142,500   |
| 1967 | 143,780   | 207,900    | 203,900   | 155,900  | 147,900   |
| 1968 | 170,820   | 211,700    | 233,500   | 181,000  | 162,300   |
| 1969 | 189,710   | 202,100    | 262,500   | 170,900  | 158,700   |
| 1970 | 231,160   | 236,100    | 297,100   | 178,200  | 178,600   |
| 1971 | 225,300   | 243,900    | 286,900   | 194,600  | 187,300   |
| 1972 | 278,800   | 301,700    | 335,900   | 212,100  | 249,400   |
| 1973 | 344,800   | 358,400    | 442,000   | 266,600  | 278,400   |
| 1974 | 440,200   | 464,500    | 582,300   | 300,300  | 381,000   |
| 1975 | 493,100   | 533,000    | 640,900   | 309,700  | 374,900   |
| 1976 | 592,400   | 744,600    | 760,400   | 411,700  | 541,800   |
| 1977 | 827,800   | 973,500    | 1,160,200 | 529,900  | 636,200   |
| 1978 | 863,900   | 801,600    | 1,092,400 | 626,200  | 646,000   |
| 1979 | 942,100   | 1,132,300  | 1,221,400 | 756,500  | 615,900   |
| 1980 | 1,000,900 | 1,075,300  | 1,519,800 | 850,300  | 450,400   |
| 1981 | 1,002,600 | 798,000    | 1,291,300 | 783,800  | 508,200   |
| 1982 | 869,000   | 704,100    | 1,170,400 | 676,500  | 406,000   |
| 1983 | 852,500   | 735,400    | 1,091,700 | 694,200  | 428,400   |
| 1984 | 955,900   | 725,400    | 1,132,200 | 765,800  | 394,540   |

Table A.11 *Nominal value of imports (c.i.f.), 1920–84*
(thousand dollars)

|      | Costa Rica | El Salvador | Guatemala | Honduras | Nicaragua |
|------|-----------|-------------|-----------|----------|-----------|
| 1920 | 17,800    | 12,820      | 18,340    | 12,860   | 13,860    |
| 1921 | 9,200     | 8,910       | 13,620    | 16,720   | 5,310     |
| 1922 | 8,300     | 7,470       | 10,750    | 12,800   | 5,120     |
| 1923 | 9,800     | 8,900       | 13,760    | 14,340   | 7,270     |
| 1924 | 12,000    | 14,010      | 18,270    | 11,140   | 8,810     |
| 1925 | 13,821    | 19,390      | 25,000    | 12,750   | 10,380    |
| 1926 | 13,826    | 25,760      | 28,530    | 9,900    | 10,250    |
| 1927 | 16,311    | 14,870      | 25,730    | 10,630   | 10,210    |
| 1928 | 17,893    | 19,190      | 30,790    | 12,570   | 13,350    |
| 1929 | 20,164    | 17,860      | 30,400    | 14,860   | 11,800    |
| 1930 | 10,847    | 11,960      | 16,480    | 15,900   | 8,170     |
| 1931 | 8,681     | 7,240       | 12,970    | 10,200   | 6,020     |
| 1932 | 5,453     | 5,140       | 7,450     | 7,500    | 3,480     |
| 1933 | 6,346     | 5,550       | 7,560     | 6,100    | 3,810     |
| 1934 | 8,720     | 8,270       | 9,970     | 8,300    | 4,610     |
| 1935 | 7,975     | 9,060       | 12,000    | 9,500    | 5,070     |
| 1936 | 9,388     | 8,430       | 14,360    | 8,200    | 5,580     |
| 1937 | 11,879    | 10,420      | 20,900    | 9,900    | 5,620     |
| 1938 | 12,621    | 9,150       | 20,860    | 9,450    | 5,120     |
| 1939 | 16,885    | 8,850       | 19,020    | 9,700    | 6,360     |
| 1940 | 16,840    | 8,096       | 15,790    | 10,100   | 7,050     |
| 1941 | 17,798    | 8,304       | 16,090    | 10,250   | 10,440    |
| 1942 | 12,287    | 8,544       | 13,650    | 11,150   | 6,770     |
| 1943 | 20,387    | 11,804      | 17,780    | 10,250   | 13,530    |
| 1944 | 21,539    | 12,256      | 20,680    | 13,350   | 10,150    |
| 1945 | 26,949    | 13,516      | 23,350    | 15,200   | 11,960    |
| 1946 | 33,041    | 21,108      | 36,200    | 19,555   | 14,990    |
| 1947 | 48,079    | 36,928      | 57,320    | 29,455   | 21,090    |
| 1948 | 42,344    | 41,460      | 68,350    | 35,605   | 24,130    |
| 1949 | 43,352    | 40,788      | 67,980    | 33,960   | 21,330    |
| 1950 | 46,020    | 48,672      | 71,220    | 39,400   | 24,700    |
| 1951 | 55,730    | 62,904      | 80,800    | 53,600   | 29,970    |
| 1952 | 67,860    | 69,316      | 75,700    | 66,300   | 39,710    |
| 1953 | 73,660    | 72,356      | 79,500    | 59,050   | 43,550    |
| 1954 | 80,020    | 86,776      | 86,300    | 56,650   | 58,310    |
| 1955 | 87,470    | 91,880      | 104,300   | 59,900   | 69,550    |
| 1956 | 91,230    | 104,728     | 137,700   | 66,100   | 68,670    |
| 1957 | 102,780   | 115,152     | 134,200   | 77,900   | 80,780    |
| 1958 | 99,320    | 108,396     | 132,900   | 74,200   | 77,940    |
| 1959 | 102,660   | 99,764      | 117,900   | 69,450   | 66,850    |
| 1960 | 110,390   | 122,624     | 121,200   | 71,800   | 71,700    |
| 1961 | 107,160   | 109,048     | 120,600   | 72,000   | 74,350    |
| 1962 | 113,350   | 125,220     | 119,900   | 79,800   | 98,230    |
| 1963 | 123,850   | 151,748     | 171,100   | 95,100   | 110,790   |
| 1964 | 138,600   | 191,124     | 202,100   | 101,650  | 137,030   |
| 1965 | 178,230   | 201,224     | 229,300   | 121,950  | 160,290   |

Table A.11 (*cont.*)

|      | Costa Rica | El Salvador | Guatemala | Honduras | Nicaragua |
|------|-----------|-------------|-----------|----------|-----------|
| 1966 | 178,450   | 220,740     | 206,900   | 149,050  | 181,920   |
| 1967 | 190,700   | 224,512     | 247,300   | 164,750  | 203,910   |
| 1968 | 213,940   | 214,144     | 249,400   | 184,700  | 184,657   |
| 1969 | 245,140   | 209,772     | 250,200   | 184,250  | 176,986   |
| 1970 | 316,202   | 213,581     | 284,273   | 220,668  | 198,748   |
| 1971 | 349,209   | 247,440     | 303,000   | 193,400  | 209,664   |
| 1972 | 372,871   | 278,080     | 324,000   | 192,800  | 217,677   |
| 1973 | 455,243   | 373,760     | 431,000   | 262,250  | 325,776   |
| 1974 | 717,050   | 563,400     | 700,500   | 380,100  | 560,660   |
| 1975 | 694,049   | 598,040     | 732,700   | 404,300  | 516,880   |
| 1976 | 770,362   | 734,680     | 838,900   | 453,100  | 532,166   |
| 1977 | 1,021,354 | 929,080     | 1,052,500 | 579,400  | 762,041   |
| 1978 | 1,165,694 | 1,027,360   | 1,285,600 | 699,200  | 596,029   |
| 1979 | 1,396,850 | 1,039,080   | 1,503,900 | 825,800  | 360,216   |
| 1980 | 1,540,373 | 961,720     | 1,598,200 | 1,039,500| 887,214   |
| 1981 | 1,208,519 | 984,600     | 1,673,500 | 975,450  | 999,443   |
| 1982 | 889,005   | 856,760     | 1,388,000 | 738,700  | 775,582   |
| 1983 | 987,808   | 891,480     | 1,135,000 | 822,650  | 771,811   |
| 1984 | 1,086,992 | 977,440     | 1,277,400 | 953,650  | 807,532   |

Table A.12 *Real value of exports (f.o.b.), 1920–84*
1970 prices (thousand dollars)[1]

| | Costa Rica | El Salvador | Guatemala | Honduras | Nicaragua |
|---|---|---|---|---|---|
| 1920 | 58,742 | 60,861 | 66,210 | 41,641 | 15,552 |
| 1921 | 56,037 | 46,374 | 69,074 | 48,764 | 24,976 |
| 1922 | 62,115 | 70,069 | 71,272 | 56,983 | 23,005 |
| 1923 | 47,938 | 69,689 | 74,317 | 53,695 | 30,611 |
| 1924 | 65,025 | 81,135 | 77,127 | 53,147 | 32,675 |
| 1925 | 60,256 | 54,008 | 72,051 | 68,489 | 27,870 |
| 1926 | 58,331 | 82,024 | 68,960 | 73,968 | 28,917 |
| 1927 | 59,978 | 58,932 | 80,251 | 90,405 | 23,805 |
| 1928 | 58,140 | 86,033 | 71,201 | 110,130 | 32,551 |
| 1929 | 60,108 | 76,815 | 73,521 | 108,486 | 33,660 |
| 1930 | 66,804 | 95,251 | 84,235 | 117,253 | 34,461 |
| 1931 | 62,810 | 92,179 | 62,771 | 132,046 | 30,734 |
| 1932 | 47,098 | 64,525 | 71,862 | 111,774 | 25,499 |
| 1933 | 69,539 | 92,179 | 60,450 | 92,597 | 31,566 |
| 1934 | 47,466 | 76,815 | 75,098 | 83,830 | 28,178 |
| 1935 | 56,916 | 73,743 | 66,931 | 64,653 | 33,075 |
| 1936 | 55,065 | 86,033 | 85,274 | 64,653 | 24,113 |
| 1937 | 72,379 | 113,687 | 90,593 | 54,791 | 30,796 |
| 1938 | 66,703 | 86,033 | 95,012 | 40,318 | 24,380 |
| 1939 | 59,607 | 101,396 | 90,593 | 55,825 | 25,663 |
| 1940 | 49,672 | 46,089 | 81,754 | 53,757 | 20,530 |
| 1941 | 61,026 | 73,743 | 81,754 | 54,791 | 17,964 |
| 1942 | 55,349 | 92,179 | 92,802 | 51,690 | 17,964 |
| 1943 | 59,607 | 101,396 | 90,593 | 25,845 | 21,814 |
| 1944 | 49,672 | 107,542 | 90,593 | 50,656 | 23,097 |
| 1945 | 52,511 | 95,251 | 112,688 | 63,061 | 19,247 |
| 1946 | 51,091 | 82,961 | 103,850 | 66,163 | 23,097 |
| 1947 | 68,122 | 110,614 | 123,736 | 81,670 | 21,814 |
| 1948 | 87,991 | 113,687 | 112,688 | 92,007 | 41,061 |
| 1949 | 82,314 | 129,050 | 99,431 | 86,839 | 33,362 |
| 1950 | 78,056 | 122,905 | 97,221 | 85,805 | 47,477 |
| 1951 | 79,475 | 116,760 | 90,593 | 85,805 | 44,910 |
| 1952 | 96,506 | 122,905 | 97,221 | 77,534 | 55,176 |
| 1953 | 96,506 | 122,905 | 101,641 | 79,602 | 60,308 |
| 1954 | 87,991 | 116,760 | 95,012 | 58,926 | 57,742 |
| 1955 | 92,248 | 132,123 | 103,850 | 53,757 | 79,555 |
| 1956 | 70,960 | 135,195 | 110,479 | 80,636 | 62,874 |
| 1957 | 93,667 | 172,067 | 112,688 | 75,467 | 73,140 |
| 1958 | 120,632 | 172,067 | 123,736 | 85,805 | 79,555 |
| 1959 | 110,698 | 196,648 | 145,832 | 89,939 | 98,803 |
| 1960 | 129,147 | 205,866 | 150,251 | 90,974 | 76,989 |
| 1961 | 127,728 | 221,229 | 156,880 | 98,210 | 83,405 |
| 1962 | 143,339 | 267,318 | 165,718 | 100,278 | 109,068 |
| 1963 | 141,920 | 307,262 | 220,958 | 103,379 | 128,315 |
| 1964 | 157,532 | 334,916 | 218,748 | 109,582 | 153,978 |
| 1965 | 160,370 | 337,988 | 243,054 | 148,866 | 183,491 |

Table A.12 (cont)

|      | Costa Rica | El Salvador | Guatemala | Honduras | Nicaragua |
|------|-----------|-------------|-----------|----------|-----------|
| 1966 | 195,850 | 341,061 | 304,922 | 174,711 | 175,792 |
| 1967 | 217,138 | 384,077 | 262,940 | 189,184 | 191,190 |
| 1968 | 263,972 | 399,441 | 307,131 | 210,894 | 192,473 |
| 1969 | 288,098 | 384,077 | 344,694 | 199,522 | 184,774 |
| 1970 | 300,871 | 347,206 | 366,790 | 203,657 | 195,039 |
| 1971 | 317,720 | 327,917 | 384,029 | 215,673 | 207,326 |
| 1972 | 376,991 | 366,495 | 437,214 | 229,318 | 243,409 |
| 1973 | 387,823 | 388,999 | 477,927 | 248,869 | 240,483 |
| 1974 | 430,246 | 289,338 | 529,645 | 218,117 | 260,962 |
| 1975 | 413,397 | 440,437 | 525,243 | 210,378 | 276,370 |
| 1976 | 436,263 | 379,355 | 546,884 | 238,890 | 316,938 |
| 1977 | 426,936 | 347,206 | 594,200 | 240,315 | 301,335 |
| 1978 | 457,023 | 247,545 | 552,386 | 271,678 | 322,595 |
| 1979 | 473,571 | 437,222 | 620,609 | 336,441 | 319,279 |
| 1980 | 445,891 | 321,487 | 672,693 | 314,243 | 202,450 |
| 1981 | 496,136 | 231,471 | 598,601 | 314,650 | 248,285 |
| 1982 | 455,218 | 205,752 | 598,969 | 283,083 | 211,032 |
| 1983 | 466,651 | 289,338 | 625,377 | 296,525 | 246,334 |
| 1984 | 486,221 | 286,439 | 618,500 | 314,464 | 200,898 |

[1] Calculated at purchasing-power parity exchange rates

Table A.13  *Real value of imports (c.i.f.), 1920–84*
1970 prices (thousand dollars)[1]

|      | Costa Rica | El Salvador | Guatemala | Honduras | Nicaragua |
|------|-----------|-------------|-----------|----------|-----------|
| 1920 | 46,884    | 32,908      | 45,720    | 33,216   | 34,466    |
| 1921 | 24,232    | 22,871      | 33,955    | 43,185   | 13,204    |
| 1922 | 21,862    | 19,175      | 26,800    | 33,061   | 12,732    |
| 1923 | 25,811    | 22,846      | 34,303    | 37,038   | 18,079    |
| 1924 | 31,607    | 35,963      | 45,546    | 28,772   | 21,908    |
| 1925 | 36,403    | 49,773      | 62,325    | 32,932   | 25,812    |
| 1926 | 38,236    | 69,431      | 80,425    | 26,849   | 26,764    |
| 1927 | 48,579    | 43,162      | 72,533    | 31,047   | 28,711    |
| 1928 | 54,635    | 57,107      | 88,987    | 37,638   | 38,488    |
| 1929 | 62,456    | 63,697      | 89,125    | 45,137   | 34,509    |
| 1930 | 36,970    | 35,143      | 53,163    | 53,142   | 26,291    |
| 1931 | 34,438    | 28,554      | 48,700    | 39,681   | 22,548    |
| 1932 | 24,102    | 26,357      | 31,166    | 32,506   | 14,522    |
| 1933 | 27,858    | 30,750      | 31,412    | 26,259   | 15,790    |
| 1934 | 34,382    | 39,536      | 37,205    | 32,091   | 17,161    |
| 1935 | 30,694    | 32,947      | 43,714    | 35,855   | 18,424    |
| 1936 | 35,290    | 32,947      | 51,091    | 30,226   | 19,804    |
| 1937 | 41,889    | 37,339      | 69,755    | 34,234   | 18,711    |
| 1938 | 46,916    | 30,750      | 65,395    | 31,952   | 18,711    |
| 1939 | 60,321    | 35,143      | 65,395    | 34,234   | 21,205    |
| 1940 | 51,943    | 30,750      | 52,316    | 33,093   | 19,958    |
| 1941 | 50,267    | 35,143      | 50,136    | 33,093   | 27,442    |
| 1942 | 33,511    | 32,947      | 39,237    | 20,541   | 16,216    |
| 1943 | 43,565    | 35,143      | 41,417    | 26,246   | 28,689    |
| 1944 | 46,916    | 35,143      | 50,136    | 28,529   | 19,958    |
| 1945 | 51,943    | 39,536      | 54,496    | 34,234   | 21,205    |
| 1946 | 60,321    | 41,732      | 71,935    | 45,646   | 23,700    |
| 1947 | 73,725    | 61,500      | 71,935    | 55,916   | 29,937    |
| 1948 | 56,969    | 63,697      | 104,632   | 59,339   | 31,184    |
| 1949 | 61,996    | 63,697      | 113,352   | 55,916   | 33,679    |
| 1950 | 70,374    | 83,464      | 119,891   | 54,775   | 38,668    |
| 1951 | 78,752    | 98,840      | 115,531   | 62,763   | 53,637    |
| 1952 | 90,481    | 105,429     | 106,812   | 82,162   | 63,616    |
| 1953 | 107,237   | 112,018     | 113,352   | 81,021   | 74,842    |
| 1954 | 112,263   | 136,179     | 124,251   | 71,892   | 92,305    |
| 1955 | 120,641   | 142,768     | 150,409   | 75,315   | 92,305    |
| 1956 | 123,992   | 160,340     | 191,826   | 86,727   | 79,832    |
| 1957 | 137,397   | 173,518     | 215,804   | 96,997   | 86,068    |
| 1958 | 137,397   | 162,536     | 211,444   | 92,432   | 87,316    |
| 1959 | 140,748   | 155,947     | 209,265   | 90,150   | 74,842    |
| 1960 | 154,153   | 191,090     | 185,286   | 89,009   | 79,832    |
| 1961 | 147,450   | 164,733     | 170,027   | 90,150   | 82,326    |
| 1962 | 155,828   | 188,893     | 176,567   | 100,420  | 113,510   |
| 1963 | 167,557   | 219,643     | 217,984   | 114,114  | 124,737   |
| 1964 | 194,366   | 276,751     | 259,401   | 127,808  | 152,179   |
| 1965 | 249,660   | 303,109     | 285,559   | 149,489  | 184,610   |

Table A.13 (*cont.*)

|  | Costa Rica | El Salvador | Guatemala | Honduras | Nicaragua |
|---|---|---|---|---|---|
| 1966 | 251,336 | 333,858 | 259,401 | 182,582 | 215,795 |
| 1967 | 258,038 | 331,661 | 300,818 | 201,982 | 225,774 |
| 1968 | 289,874 | 327,269 | 313,897 | 236,216 | 213,300 |
| 1969 | 325,061 | 318,483 | 311,717 | 221,381 | 203,321 |
| 1970 | 411,249 | 314,090 | 350,954 | 252,192 | 217,042 |
| 1971 | 441,869 | 357,120 | 373,450 | 216,885 | 227,026 |
| 1972 | 442,281 | 385,388 | 352,659 | 199,736 | 242,002 |
| 1973 | 460,830 | 449,777 | 387,928 | 236,556 | 323,176 |
| 1974 | 501,636 | 457,943 | 443,569 | 294,812 | 405,652 |
| 1975 | 476,905 | 477,103 | 421,312 | 250,174 | 313,192 |
| 1976 | 531,726 | 581,067 | 546,952 | 268,080 | 305,161 |
| 1977 | 639,308 | 705,760 | 598,046 | 306,413 | 416,938 |
| 1978 | 604,272 | 704,190 | 624,131 | 347,773 | 296,913 |
| 1979 | 679,703 | 618,443 | 577,704 | 388,628 | 182,098 |
| 1980 | 633,538 | 489,038 | 527,927 | 400,985 | 311,889 |
| 1981 | 478,554 | 467,052 | 506,269 | 357,104 | 345,314 |
| 1982 | 334,287 | 406,432 | 400,014 | 267,828 | 257,195 |
| 1983 | 360,667 | 388,215 | 320,561 | 302,378 | 266,528 |
| 1984 | 408,954 | 398,234 | 340,783 | 322,500 | 277,385 |

[1] Calculated at purchasing-power parity exchange rates

Table A.14 *Net barter terms of trade, 1920–1984 (1970 = 100)*

|  | Costa Rica | El Salvador | Guatemala | Honduras | Nicaragua |
|------|-----------|-------------|-----------|----------|-----------|
| 1920 | 55.9 | 76.8 | 68.2 | 98.0 | 172.5 |
| 1921 | 56.0 | 49.2 | 44.5 | 65.4 | 80.4 |
| 1922 | 60.2 | 59.7 | 40.8 | 55.5 | 85.4 |
| 1923 | 70.4 | 63.7 | 49.4 | 109.6 | 89.6 |
| 1924 | 67.1 | 77.1 | 79.1 | 87.2 | 99.0 |
| 1925 | 71.8 | 80.2 | 102.6 | 102.7 | 110.3 |
| 1926 | 89.8 | 80.9 | 118.4 | 112.2 | 117.7 |
| 1927 | 89.7 | 69.6 | 119.1 | 106.8 | 106.8 |
| 1928 | 103.2 | 84.6 | 114.6 | 114.8 | 103.5 |
| 1929 | 93.8 | 85.6 | 99.4 | 104.8 | 94.5 |
| 1930 | 83.2 | 42.2 | 90.2 | 109.0 | 78.0 |
| 1931 | 90.2 | 47.2 | 90.7 | 114.5 | 79.9 |
| 1932 | 80.2 | 43.7 | 62.1 | 150.3 | 74.2 |
| 1933 | 67.5 | 41.6 | 64.2 | 195.0 | 63.8 |
| 1934 | 72.3 | 57.5 | 73.5 | 186.5 | 69.2 |
| 1935 | 55.8 | 53.5 | 67.9 | 175.8 | 62.1 |
| 1936 | 60.3 | 45.9 | 70.6 | 127.5 | 68.4 |
| 1937 | 56.0 | 49.0 | 65.9 | 153.5 | 76.1 |
| 1938 | 56.5 | 42.7 | 60.1 | 139.1 | 88.1 |
| 1939 | 54.5 | 49.9 | 71.3 | 146.8 | 107.7 |
| 1940 | 46.4 | 100.8 | 48.7 | 140.9 | 130.9 |
| 1941 | 47.4 | 64.4 | 55.3 | 130.8 | 174.8 |
| 1942 | 52.1 | 77.3 | 63.4 | 75.7 | 191.0 |
| 1943 | 44.6 | 66.1 | 51.8 | 92.0 | 150.1 |
| 1944 | 46.2 | 61.3 | 63.9 | 84.0 | 131.3 |
| 1945 | 42.6 | 65.5 | 63.0 | 101.3 | 128.7 |
| 1946 | 51.3 | 62.3 | 70.2 | 107.9 | 123.7 |
| 1947 | 70.0 | 60.3 | 69.0 | 99.8 | 136.6 |
| 1948 | 70.3 | 61.4 | 94.0 | 89.9 | 84.0 |
| 1949 | 83.8 | 66.5 | 104.7 | 109.4 | 111.9 |
| 1950 | 108.9 | 96.9 | 136.7 | 107.8 | 114.2 |
| 1951 | 112.9 | 115.1 | 133.1 | 89.2 | 181.5 |
| 1952 | 101.5 | 109.2 | 137.4 | 100.9 | 148.7 |
| 1953 | 121.1 | 112.9 | 139.7 | 119.4 | 155.6 |
| 1954 | 135.2 | 141.5 | 159.0 | 121.9 | 172.1 |
| 1955 | 121.0 | 125.3 | 147.6 | 125.6 | 133.5 |
| 1956 | 129.3 | 139.2 | 154.5 | 118.6 | 121.2 |
| 1957 | 119.0 | 111.3 | 165.3 | 106.9 | 102.8 |
| 1958 | 105.5 | 102.8 | 138.7 | 100.9 | 99.0 |
| 1959 | 95.0 | 88.8 | 126.1 | 98.9 | 85.0 |
| 1960 | 92.9 | 77.6 | 117.9 | 86.0 | 92.4 |
| 1961 | 90.7 | 81.2 | 102.4 | 93.0 | 92.8 |
| 1962 | 89.2 | 78.4 | 105.8 | 102.3 | 95.8 |
| 1963 | 90.7 | 70.8 | 88.5 | 98.0 | 93.5 |
| 1964 | 101.5 | 75.9 | 102.3 | 109.1 | 90.5 |
| 1965 | 97.8 | 84.7 | 98.5 | 105.6 | 93.7 |
| 1966 | 97.6 | 84.1 | 95.3 | 101.2 | 96.1 |

Table A.14 (*cont.*)

|      | Costa Rica | El Salvador | Guatemala | Honduras | Nicaragua |
|------|-----------|-------------|-----------|----------|-----------|
| 1967 | 82.8      | 80.0        | 94.3      | 101.1    | 85.7      |
| 1968 | 87.8      | 81.0        | 95.7      | 109.7    | 97.4      |
| 1969 | 87.4      | 79.9        | 94.8      | 102.9    | 98.6      |
| 1970 | 100.0     | 100.0       | 100.0     | 100.0    | 100.0     |
| 1971 | 89.7      | 107.3       | 92.0      | 101.2    | 97.8      |
| 1972 | 87.8      | 114.1       | 83.6      | 95.8     | 113.9     |
| 1973 | 90.0      | 110.9       | 83.2      | 96.6     | 114.8     |
| 1974 | 72.0      | 130.5       | 69.6      | 106.8    | 105.7     |
| 1975 | 82.0      | 96.6        | 70.2      | 91.1     | 82.2      |
| 1976 | 93.6      | 155.3       | 90.6      | 101.9    | 98.0      |
| 1977 | 121.4     | 213.0       | 110.9     | 116.6    | 115.5     |
| 1978 | 98.0      | 222.0       | 96.0      | 114.6    | 99.8      |
| 1979 | 96.8      | 154.2       | 75.6      | 105.8    | 97.5      |
| 1980 | 92.3      | 170.2       | 74.6      | 104.4    | 78.2      |
| 1981 | 80.0      | 163.5       | 65.3      | 91.2     | 70.7      |
| 1982 | 71.8      | 162.3       | 56.3      | 86.6     | 63.8      |
| 1983 | 66.7      | 110.7       | 49.3      | 86.1     | 60.1      |
| 1984 | 74.0      | 103.2       | 48.8      | 82.4     | 67.5      |

*Statistical appendix*

Table A.15 *Purchasing power of exports, 1920–84 (1970 = 100)*

|      | Costa Rica | El Salvador | Guatemala | Honduras | Nicaragua |
|------|------------|-------------|-----------|----------|-----------|
| 1920 | 10.9 | 13.4 | 12.3 | 20.0 | 13.8 |
| 1921 | 10.4 | 6.6  | 8.4  | 15.6 | 10.3 |
| 1922 | 12.4 | 12.1 | 7.9  | 15.5 | 10.1 |
| 1923 | 11.2 | 12.8 | 10.0 | 28.9 | 14.1 |
| 1924 | 14.5 | 18.0 | 16.6 | 22.8 | 16.6 |
| 1925 | 14.4 | 12.5 | 20.1 | 34.5 | 15.8 |
| 1926 | 17.4 | 19.1 | 22.3 | 40.7 | 17.4 |
| 1927 | 17.8 | 11.8 | 26.1 | 47.4 | 13.0 |
| 1928 | 19.9 | 21.0 | 22.2 | 62.1 | 17.3 |
| 1929 | 18.7 | 18.9 | 19.9 | 55.9 | 16.4 |
| 1930 | 18.5 | 11.6 | 20.7 | 62.8 | 13.8 |
| 1931 | 18.9 | 12.5 | 15.5 | 74.2 | 12.6 |
| 1932 | 12.6 | 8.1  | 12.2 | 82.5 | 9.7  |
| 1933 | 15.6 | 11.0 | 10.6 | 88.7 | 10.3 |
| 1934 | 11.4 | 12.7 | 15.1 | 76.8 | 10.0 |
| 1935 | 10.5 | 11.3 | 12.3 | 55.7 | 10.5 |
| 1936 | 11.0 | 11.4 | 16.4 | 40.4 | 8.5  |
| 1937 | 13.5 | 16.0 | 16.3 | 41.3 | 12.0 |
| 1938 | 12.6 | 10.6 | 15.6 | 27.5 | 11.0 |
| 1939 | 10.8 | 14.6 | 17.6 | 40.2 | 14.2 |
| 1940 | 7.7  | 13.4 | 10.9 | 37.2 | 13.7 |
| 1941 | 9.6  | 13.7 | 12.3 | 35.2 | 16.1 |
| 1942 | 9.6  | 20.5 | 16.0 | 19.2 | 17.6 |
| 1943 | 8.8  | 19.3 | 12.8 | 11.7 | 16.8 |
| 1944 | 7.6  | 19.0 | 15.8 | 20.9 | 15.5 |
| 1945 | 7.5  | 17.9 | 19.3 | 31.4 | 12.7 |
| 1946 | 8.7  | 14.9 | 19.9 | 35.1 | 14.6 |
| 1947 | 15.8 | 19.2 | 23.2 | 40.0 | 15.3 |
| 1948 | 20.5 | 20.1 | 28.9 | 40.7 | 17.7 |
| 1949 | 23.0 | 24.7 | 28.4 | 46.6 | 19.1 |
| 1950 | 28.2 | 34.3 | 36.2 | 45.4 | 27.7 |
| 1951 | 29.8 | 38.7 | 32.9 | 37.6 | 41.7 |
| 1952 | 32.6 | 38.7 | 36.4 | 38.4 | 42.1 |
| 1953 | 38.9 | 40.0 | 38.7 | 46.7 | 48.1 |
| 1954 | 39.5 | 47.5 | 41.2 | 35.2 | 50.9 |
| 1955 | 37.2 | 47.7 | 41.8 | 33.2 | 54.5 |
| 1956 | 30.5 | 54.2 | 46.5 | 47.0 | 39.0 |
| 1957 | 37.0 | 55.2 | 50.8 | 39.7 | 38.6 |
| 1958 | 42.3 | 51.0 | 46.8 | 42.5 | 40.4 |
| 1959 | 35.0 | 50.3 | 50.2 | 43.7 | 43.1 |
| 1960 | 38.9 | 46.0 | 48.3 | 38.4 | 36.5 |
| 1961 | 38.6 | 51.7 | 43.8 | 44.8 | 39.7 |
| 1962 | 42.5 | 60.9 | 47.8 | 50.3 | 53.5 |
| 1963 | 42.8 | 62.6 | 53.2 | 49.7 | 61.5 |
| 1964 | 53.2 | 73.2 | 60.9 | 58.7 | 71.4 |
| 1965 | 52.1 | 82.4 | 65.3 | 77.2 | 88.1 |
| 1966 | 63.5 | 82.5 | 79.2 | 86.9 | 86.6 |

Table A.15 (*cont.*)

|      | Costa Rica | El Salvador | Guatemala | Honduras | Nicaragua |
|------|-----------|-------------|-----------|----------|-----------|
| 1967 | 59.8  | 88.5  | 67.6  | 93.9  | 84.0  |
| 1968 | 77.0  | 93.2  | 80.1  | 113.7 | 96.2  |
| 1969 | 83.7  | 88.3  | 89.1  | 100.8 | 93.4  |
| 1970 | 100.0 | 100.0 | 100.0 | 100.0 | 100.0 |
| 1971 | 94.7  | 101.3 | 96.4  | 107.2 | 103.9 |
| 1972 | 110.0 | 120.5 | 99.7  | 107.9 | 142.2 |
| 1973 | 116.0 | 124.2 | 108.4 | 118.1 | 141.6 |
| 1974 | 103.0 | 108.7 | 100.5 | 114.4 | 141.4 |
| 1975 | 112.7 | 122.5 | 100.5 | 94.1  | 116.5 |
| 1976 | 135.7 | 169.7 | 135.1 | 119.6 | 159.3 |
| 1977 | 172.3 | 213.0 | 179.7 | 137.6 | 178.5 |
| 1978 | 148.9 | 158.3 | 144.6 | 152.9 | 165.0 |
| 1979 | 152.4 | 194.1 | 127.9 | 174.8 | 159.7 |
| 1980 | 136.8 | 157.6 | 136.9 | 161.0 | 81.2  |
| 1981 | 131.9 | 109.1 | 106.5 | 140.9 | 90.0  |
| 1982 | 108.6 | 96.3  | 91.9  | 120.4 | 69.0  |
| 1983 | 103.5 | 92.2  | 84.1  | 125.3 | 75.9  |
| 1984 | 119.6 | 85.1  | 82.3  | 128.0 | 69.5  |

# Notes

## 1 A century of independence

1 Central America obtained its independence from Spain in 1821. This was immediately followed by annexation to Mexico, which ended in 1823. From then Central America was ruled as one country until the Central American Federation broke up in 1838. In the years following, each of the five Central American republics declared its independence as a separate republic (see Karnes (1961)).

2 Costa Rica's early entry into the coffee trade is not particularly surprising. In the colonial period it was, by all accounts, desperately poor and almost entirely self-sufficient. Independence provided the republic with an incentive to establish foreign trade, but there were no 'traditional' exports to exploit; hence the interest in new commodities. Costa Rica's success, however, after the 1840s was an inspiration to the rest of Central America to try their hand at coffee.

3 In recent years, there has been a revival of interest in German coffee growers in Guatemala and the extent of their influence. See, for example, Cambranes (1985), which draws on archives in Germany to support his research. In 1913, Germans owned 8.2% of the 2079 coffee fincas, but produced 34% of the total output. See Mosk (1955), p. 13 and Munro (1918), p. 267, n. 1.

4 This stake was later repurchased by the Nicaraguan government in 1924.

5 The best example is provided by the Mosquito Coast in Nicaragua, which was a British protectorate until 1860 and a separate 'kingdom' until 1894. The British also controlled the Bay Islands off the North coast of Honduras until 1859.

6 The choice of the Atlantic coast (which ruled out El Salvador) was dictated by soil conditions and proximity to the principal markets on the east coast of North America and in Western Europe. The development of plantations on the Pacific coast was not seriously attempted until the 1930s.

7 UFCO's monopoly in Costa Rica was obtained automatically through incorporation of Minor Keith's Tropical Trading and Transport Co. Its monopoly in Guatemala was obtained soon after its entry to that country in 1906.

8 The book value of US direct foreign investment (DFI) in Central America in 1919 has been estimated (Rosenthal (1973), p. 74) at $112.5 million, of which the main components were agriculture ($36 million), railroads ($43.3 million), mining ($13.5 million). Public utilities represented only $0.5 million. British direct investment has been estimated (Rippy (1954)) at £15 million, all of which was in railways. Even this low figure, however, involves substantial double counting with the US DFI (see Rosenthal (1973), p. 73).

9 Anti-vagrancy laws were most important in Guatemala and are well discussed in Jones (1940), ch. 12. They were also applied in El Salvador (see Burns

338

(1984)) and Nicaragua, where they were however abolished in 1912. They do not appear to have played as much of a role in Costa Rica and Honduras.

10 After the First World War, the daily wage rate on coffee fincas varied from 16 US cents to 50 US cents (see Thompson (1926), pp. 29, 97 and 137). In the same period, banana workers in Honduras, following a successful strike in 1919, obtained $1.75 per day with double pay for overtime (see Karnes (1978), p. 68). Even after allowance is made for free food on coffee farms, the difference is striking.

11 See Kepner (1936), pp. 168–79.

12 See Young (1925), chs. 6 and 9. All the republics were at first on the silver standard, but only El Salvador and Honduras retained it after the First World War.

13 In Guatemala the note issue went from 10.7 million pesos in 1897 (when the régime of inconvertible paper money was started) to 274.8 million in 1920 (it reached 402.4 million in 1923). In Nicaragua, the paper currency rose from 5.3 million pesos in 1901 to 48.6 million in 1911 – the year before the US occupation and the imposition of monetary reform. See Young (1925), chs. 4 and 12.

14 The problems of switching to the gold from a silver standard, during a period when the gold price of silver was falling, were considerable. The main danger was that newly minted gold coins would be driven out of circulation in accordance with Gresham's law. Costa Rica circumnavigated this problem by minting gold coins from 1896 which were deposited in the Banco de Costa Rica and issuing gold certificates against them which could not be redeemed in the new currency until after 1900. This gave the government a breathing space for retiring the old paper notes and building up a sufficient stock of new gold currency (see Young (1925), pp. 195–6).

15 El Salvador tried to switch to the gold standard in 1892, but the rate of exchange adopted for gold into silver (the mint ratio) seriously undervalued gold and the few gold coins minted soon disappeared from circulation (*ibid.*, pp. 65–6).

16 Wage costs, and other local expenditures, were proportionately less important for banana companies than coffee growers.

17 Except in Honduras, where arrears of payment had multiplied many times the face value of the loans contracted between 1867 and 1871 (see Council of Foreign Bondholders, 1922).

18 Most coffee exports went to Europe, while most banana exports went to North America.

19 Pessimism concerning the prospects for industrialisation was also derived from the lack of raw materials and energy supplies.

20 See, for example, Munro (1964), pp. 225–7.

21 The reasons why Honduras did not benefit to the same extent as the rest of Central America from the introduction of coffee are discussed in Pérez Brignoli (1973).

22 See Munro (1964), pp. 530–8. In these few pages, Munro offers a much more satisfactory assessment of US–Central America relations than is provided in whole chapters of recent books (e.g., Pearce (1981), Part i, and Lafeber (1983), ch. 1).

23 These efforts were defeated in Guatemala and Honduras; they were more successful in Nicaragua, where 'dollar diplomacy' was supported by a US military presence after 1912.

24 See, for example, Denny (1929).

25 Scc Posas (1981), pp. 70–4.

26 See Posas (1983), pp. 17–21.

27 There are several excellent studies of labour coercion in this period of Guatemalan history. See, for example, McCreery (1983).

28 See Frassinetti (1981), pp. 51–2.

29 The main attempts during the rule of the conservative aristocracy to increase the supply of labour available for EXA are listed in Wheelock (1980), pp. 76–8.

30 Efforts at coercion, such as laws against vagrancy and begging, were made, but were ineffectual. See Cardoso (1977), p. 194.

31 Labour was better paid in Costa Rica than the other republics, but all contemporary reports continued to suggest that labour was in scarce supply. See Cardoso (1977), pp. 177–8.

32 *Ibid.,* pp. 192–3.

33 See Frassinetti (1981), pp. 67–74.

34 See Taracena (1984), p. 82.

35 See Figueroa Ibarra (1979), pp. 13–17.

36 In fact, it was some sixty families, rather than fourteen, which dominated economic, social and political life in El Salvador, but the degree of concentration was still remakable.

37 See, for example, his interesting essay on the need for protecting the livestock industry: Jiménez Oreamuno (1980), pp. 72–81.

38 See Seligson (1980), pp. 42–7.

39 See Stone (1975), pp. 265–9.

## 2 Central America in the 1920s

1 Federico Tinoco, Minister of War in the administration of Alfredo González Flores, seized power in 1917 (see Oconitrillo García, 1982). His government was not recognised by the United States and this, together with the assassination of his brother, forced his resignation in 1919. See Munro (1964), pp. 427–42.

2 The United Strates did not favour the overthrow of Cabrera, but was obliged to recognise his successor, Carlos Herrera, despite the unconstitutional nature of his accession to the Presidency. See Munro (1964), pp. 463–5.

3 *Ibid.,* pp. 452–6.

4 See Viteri Bertrand (1976), pp. 59–65.

5 See Munro (1964), pp. 465–8.

6 The non-recognition clauses can be found in Denny (1929) pp. 187–8. Applied strictly, very few changes of government in Central America could be considered legitimate in the 1920s, since relatives or close associates were not supposed to succeed each other (as happened in El Salvador). The Treaty of Peace and Amity is discussed in detail in Grieb (1967).

7 See Swerling (1949), p. 29.

8 The term 'unit values' is used here in preference to 'price', because it has been obtained by dividing export values by export quantities.

9 Fortunately for Nicaragua, the volume of coffee sales almost doubled in the same period.

10 In Honduras, imports actually increased in 1921, but this was due to the expansion of the investment programme in the banana industry.

11 The valuation of coffee exports differed between republics in the 1920s. Most countries used declared values, which reflect rather imperfectly changes in market conditions. Guatemala, however, used an official valuation, which took no account of the recovery in market prices in 1922.

12 The government imposed a freeze on rents and exonerated new housing from all taxation. See Soley Güell (1975), p. 88.

13 This interest was expressed most forcefully in the so-called Roosevelt Corollary to the Monroe Doctrine. See Denny (1929), pp. 44–5.

14 The gold exchange standard, unlike the gold standard, did not require that Nicaragua actually hold gold stocks herself. It was sufficient to sell on demand drafts on New York, where dollars were freely exchangeable into gold. See Cumberland (1928), p. 141.

15 Details of the plan can be found in Appendix F to his brother's book. See Young (1925).

16 An attempt had been made in 1926 (when the lempira was first created) to put Honduras on the gold standard, but it failed. See Castillo Flores (1974), pp. 187–98.

17 See Young (1925), p. 206.

18 *Ibid.*, p. 56.

19 This bias is well described in several essays in Sobral (1925).

20 See Kepner (1936), p. 67.

21 *Ibid.*, pp. 114–15.

22 See Karnes (1978), pp. 127–37.

23 The contract is summarised and criticised in detail in Bauer Paíz (1956).

24 An excellent account of this dispute can be found in Rodriguez Beteta (1980).

25 The yield fell to 125 bunches per acre compared with an average of 200 on virgin lands. See Kepner (1936), p. 94.

26 See Kepner and Soothill (1935), pp. 70–6.

27 *Ibid.*, p. 213.

28 See Kepner (1936), pp. 95–8.

29 Purchases from private planters increased in relative importance as soil fatigue set in (e.g. Costa Rica in the 1920s). Elsewhere, they were of minor importance, except on the Pacific coast of Guatemala where the industry was just being established. See Kepner and Soothill (1935), ch. 10.

30 *Ibid.*, chapter VI.

31 See Wickizer (1943), p. 142.

32 Except in Guatemala (see note 11).

33 See Montero Umaña (1972), p. 246.

34 See League of Nations (1936), p. 102.

35 See Kepner and Soothill (1935), pp. 212–13.

36 A notable exception is provided by the Costa Rican economist Rodrigo Facio, whose graduation thesis, completed in 1941, provides a clear statement of the tension between EXA and the rest of the economy. See Facio (1972), pp. 27–183.

37 The *colono* usually received a plot of land and accommodation on the coffee finca in return for which he was expected to work at the going daily rate whenever required. The *jornalero*, as the name implies, was a casual worker hired on a daily basis.

38 Except in the case of Salvadorean labour used on Honduran banana plantations, which clearly affected DUA in El Salvador. See Durham (1979), p. 124.

39 See Edel (1969), ch. 2.

40 The value of food imports into El Salvador, for example, rose by 250% between 1920 and 1929.

41 See Kepner (1936), p. 134.

42 The most important development in producers' associations, particularly for coffee, were not however realised until after the decline of commodity prices at the end of the 1920s. See Monfils (1938).

43 The drying and shelling of coffee in *beneficios* and the crushing of sugar cane in *ingenios* are both industrial activities and the value added is accordingly allocated to food-processing. Inconsistently, the national accounts do not give the same treatment to *panela*, the unrefined sugar used widely in local consumption and obtained by boiling the juice from cane sugar crushed in *trapiches* and allowed to crystallise.

44 The problems of starting large-scale industries in countries where wood and charcoal were the main sources of energy can easily be forgotten. Some hydroelectric plants were established by the end of the 1920s, but their scale was small.

45 The banks often accepted payment of loans in the form of coffee, thus obtaining a share of the opportunities presented by flexible commodity prices.

46 Despite this, imports of textiles and clothing remained very important. The local industry tended to provide the more basic articles of clothing, while imports were relied on for articles not related to the needs of the work-place.

47 There were also disappointments: the proposed line connecting Nicaragua's Pacific with Atlantic coastlines was never constructed and in Guatemala the electrified Los Altos line, linking the capital with Guatemala City, proved to be a financial disaster. See Jones (1940), pp. 254–5.

48 The contract is presented and criticised in Bauer Paíz (1956).

49 See Menjívar (1980), p. 69.

50 Direct taxes were, however, introduced in Costa Rica in the 1920s, although their yield was still negligible by the end of the decade.

51 The problems of the banana sector in Costa Rica, for example, produced a fall in real GDP per head after 1926.

52 A possible exception is the 1924 election, in which Jorge Volio's Partido Reformista participated (see Volio (1973)). The Party was formed through the dissolution of the Confederación General de Trabajadores (Rojas Bolaños, 1978), and, unlike its rivals, had an identifiable political programme.

53 See Monge (1974), pp. 278–92.

54 See Dalton (1972), ch. 3.

55 The origins and history of these organisations is discussed in Taracena (1984), pp. 81–93.

56 See Obando Sanchez (1980), pp. 45–7.

57 See Grieb (1979), pp. 2–3.

58 See Posas (1981), pp. 72–4.

59 See Karnes (1978), pp. 60–70.

60 See Posas and Del Cid (1982), p. 75.

61 Although the Nicaraguan government purchased from US banks in 1924 a controlling interest, the bank was still managed by US interests although it now had 100% state ownership. See Cumberland (1928), pp. 135–40.

62 By the late 1920s, three Claims Commissions were in existence dealing with (a) concessions signed during Zelaya's régime, (b) guaranteed bonds, (c) civil war losses. US interests were prominently represented on all these commissions. See Hill (1933), pp. 88–92.

63 See Kamman (1968), pp. 97–117.

64 El Salvador was particularly hostile and joined Mexico at the Havana Pan-American Conference of 1928 in trying to table motions opposing the US intervention. These efforts were outmanoeuvred by the US delegates and shortly afterwards the Salvadorean Foreign Minister was replaced by someone more acceptable to US interests. See White (1973), p. 97.

### 3 The 1929 depression

1 The absence of regular price statistics in this period of Central American economic history makes it impossible to measure accurately the change in the cost of living. The unit value of imports did fall, however, and so did the prices of locally produced foods.

2 Brazilian production rose from 15.8 million bags in 1926/7 to 27.1 million bags in 1927/8. By the end of 1928, world stocks had risen to 18.7 million bags, equivalent to 80% of world consumption. (See Wickizer (1943), table 6, pp. 248–9.)

3 In 1932, out of total banana exports from Brazil, Mexico and the main Caribbean areas of 87.9 million bunches, UFCO exported 51.6 million and Standard Fruit 15.6 million (see Kepner (1936), Table 5, p. 67).

4 Imports of bananas into the United States (the leading market) fell from 65.1 million bunches in 1929 to 39.6 million in 1933 (Kepner and Soothill (1935), p. 264). Banana prices, however, in 1933 fell to only 85.7% of their level in 1926 compared to 65.9% for all commodities and 51.4% for farm products (see Kepner and Soothill (1935), pp. 264–5 and p. 383, n. 10).

5 The dividend from UFCO $100 par value stock was $4.00 in 1929, 1930 and 1931, £2.50 in 1932 and $2.00 in 1933 (see Kepner (1936), p. 24). UFCO's share price did, however, fall sharply and was one of the reasons why Sam Zemurray forced his way onto the board in 1932, when he became chairman.

6 Renewal of the contract had been debated as early as 1926 by Congress and in 1929 a sliding-scale export tax law, allowing for a maximum tax of 5 cents US gold per bunch of bananas, had been approved This was later abandoned, however, and the new twenty-year contract agreed in 1930 provided for an increase in the banana tax from only one cent to two cents US gold. See Kepner and Soothill (1935), pp. 77–82.

7 In addition to the decline in economic activity brought on by the depression, there were restrictions on the migration of black workers to the highlands in search of alternative opportunities. These restrictions do not appear to have been legal (Seligson (1980), pp. 68–70), but were none the less real.

8 The contracts themselves, however, gave the companies considerable flexibility over such matters as rejections, quality, etc. By sticking to the small print of the contract, the companies could effectively lower the price paid in bad years.

9 A banana stem with nine hands was entitled to the full count-bunch price. If the stem had eight hands, it received only 75% of the full count-bunch price, while seven hands brought 50% and six hands 25% of the nine-hand count-bunch price.

10 See Swerling (1949), pp. 42–4.

11 In Nicaragua, for example, despite its status as a virtual US protectorate, sugar exports fell from 8.6 million kg in 1928 to 1.3 million kg in 1933.

12 Honduras had no need to run a deficit in the first years of the depression, because the value of exports started to fall sharply only after 1934 (see Table A.10).

13 The only source for import prices in Central America in the inter-war period is unit values constructed from trade data. In Honduras, however, official estimates of real imports (see Banco Central de Honduras, 1956) have been obtained from *weighted* unit values, using as weights the five classes in the Brussels trade nomenclature, and the implicit price deflator, obtained by comparing the real and money values of Honduran imports, is therefore the best guide to import prices in Central America. For that reason, I have used Honduran import prices in constructing the barter terms of trade indices in Figure 3.2.

14 The terms of trade indices in Figure 3.2 are theoretical. They represent the cases of a republic which obtains all its export revenue from either coffee or bananas. In practice, the indices reflect closely the reality in Central America, because Honduras obtained 75% of export earnings from bananas while in 1928 Costa Rica, Guatemala, Nicaragua and El Salvador obtained 62%, 82%, 58% and 93% of export earnings from coffee respectively. For each republic's terms of trade index, see Table A.14.

15 In general, the reserve requirement for banks was 40% gold against outstanding notes, although only rarely did banks go close to the legal minimum ratio. In El Salvador, for example, the three banks of issue had gold reserves in 1929 of 9.57 million colones (2 colones = $1) with a note circulation of 14.5 million colones. This gave a gold reserve ratio of 65.9%, which had fallen to 51.7% by 1932 when the note circulation was 12.2 million colones. See Moody's (1934), p. 2739.

16 Except Honduras, of course, which was never on the gold standard (see above, pp. 29–31). Honduras did make a futile attempt to switch from the silver to the gold standard in November 1931, but throughout the worst years of the depression the reserve backing for the note circulation was either silver (Banco de Honduras) or US dollars (Banco de Atlántida).

17 The Costa Rican colón depreciated sharply again in 1935, averaging 5.94 to the US dollar, and in 1936, when it averaged 6.13 to the US dollar. In 1937 it was pegged at 5.6 to the dollar.

18 The one exception was Honduras, which met its external debt service payments promptly, although the internal debt went into default in 1932. Nicaragua also met its interest payments promptly on the external debt, but defaulted on bond redemption.

19 In El Salvador, for example, the gross receipts of the railway system fell from £272,268 in 1927/8 to £73,154 in 1933/4. See Council of Foreign Bondholders, *Annual Report* (1939).

20 The workers' demands (see Seligson (1980), p. 71) included a six-hour work day, an increase in salary to six colones a day, payment in cash instead of in scrip and union recognition. After three weeks, an agreement was signed in which it was agreed to increase the salary to 4.20 colones a day (it had been 4.00 colones) and which met the workers' other demands. UFCO, however, did not honour the agreement and the strikers were eventually defeated after serious confrontation with the police.

21 Wages were lowered to 20 US cents per hour rather than 18. See Posas (1981), p. 79.

22 *Ibid.*, p. 81.

23 See White (1973), pp. 97–8, and Monfils (1938).

24 See Seligson (1980), p. 36.

25 In El Salvador, the resistance of coffee workers to wage cuts contributed to the rise in influence of the newly formed Communist Party in the two years

before the peasant uprising of January 1932. Salvadorean employers frequently responded, however, by laying off workers and rural unemployment became very severe. See Marroquín (1977), pp. 121–2.

26 For an interesting attempt to measure agricultural *money* wages in Guatemala (mainly derived from coffee), see McCreery (1983), pp. 748–9. McCreery's series shows money wage rates falling sharply after 1929, but the same article (p. 751) also provides evidence for an even steeper fall in corn prices.

27 See Anderson (1971), pp. 55–6.

28 See Soley Güell (1975), p. 107.

29 See Grieb (1979), p. 55.

30 See Costa Rica, Dirección Gral. de Estadística y Censos, Censo de Desempleo, 1932.

31 Unfortunately, the labour force in 1932 is not known with precision. The employment rate is therefore an estimate based on a comparison of the Census of Unemployment with the 1927 Census of Population. See Rojas Bolaños (1978).

32 See Grieb (1979), p. 3.

33 One of those shot was Juan Pablo Wainwright, a Honduran by birth who played a very active role in establishing the communist movement throughout Central America. See Obando Sanchez (1978), pp. 102–4.

34 Martí was not in fact present at the founding meeting of the Salvadorean Communist Party in 1930 (he was with Sandino in Mexico – see Macaulay (1967)) and he did not have an official position in the Party. He was, however, director of the Salvadorean branch of the Socorro Rojo Internacional (SRI) and the two organisations had very close ties. In any case, Martí was acknowledged by all as the pre-eminent communist leader. See Gómez (1972).

35 This doctrine, which Masferrer expounded in numerous articles and books, was based on ideas of class reconciliation and a peaceful redistribution of income and wealth. See Masferrer (1950), pp. 179–210.

36 It should be pointed out that, although the 1931 election has earned a reputation for being free and fair, the vote (as in Costa Rica) was not extended to women.

37 General Martínez had been initially a candidate in the 1930 presidential elections, but abandoned his campaign in return for a promise of the vice-presidency if Araujo won. The marriage of the two seems to have been based on convenience alone. Martínez knew he could never win in a fair contest, but Araujo needed to be sure of military support for his régime in case of victory.

38 Anderson, in his book on the uprising, makes much of the racial tension between Indians and Ladinos in Western El Salvador, where the uprising occurred. See Anderson (1971), pp. 69–71.

39 See Posas (1981), p. 88.

40 Although the presidential elections had been held regularly every four years since the 1880s (with the exception of the Tinoco dictatorship), the vote was not extended to women (whom liberals believed would be subject to undue influence by the Church) and presidential campaigns continued to be fought on a highly personalistic note.

41 This peculiar method of solving problems in Costa Rica is stressed in Biesanz (1982) and Ameringer (1982). 'Tico' is the adjective applied by Costa Ricans to themselves.

42 See Soley Güell (1975), p. 107, and Rojas Bolaños (1978), p. 17.

43 See Seligson (1980), p. 66.

44 The rise of the Communist Party was helped by the decline of Jorge Volio's Partido Reformista; the latter had been somewhat discredited in its claim to

represent workers, when Volio accepted the vice-presidency in Ricardo Jiménez's second administration (1924–8). See Rojas Bolaños (1978), p. 17.

45 *Ibid.*, p. 17.

46 See Ameringer (1982), p. 27.

47 Martí and the international communist movement broke with Sandinismo in 1930. Nevertheless, Martí had a high opinion of Sandino as a man and a patriot and paid tribute to him shortly before his death. For an excellent account of the break between Sandino and international communism, see Cerdas (1984), pp. 90–130.

48 See Selser (1981), ch. 11.

49 See Diederich (1982), pp. 14–15.

50 Somoza was clearly implicated in the assassination of Sandino; he endeavoured to clear his name, and blacken Sandino's reputation, in a book published soon afterwards (see Somoza (1936)).

## 4 Economic recovery and political reaction in the 1930s

1 Ubico's government in Guatemala was the first to extend diplomatic recognition to General Franco's régime following the outbreak of the Spanish civil war in 1936. This action was soon followed by Presidents Martínez of El Salvador and Somoza of Nicaragua. President Carías' Honduran government followed suit in March 1939. See Grieb (1979), p. 203 and p. 325, n. 70.

2 This action provoked the resignation of the entire Electoral Council, but to no avail. See Bell (1971), p. 13.

3 See, for example, Torres Rivas (1973), pp. 154–66.

4 The urban economy, because of its role as a commercial trading centre, was much more dependent on imports than the rural economy.

5 Interest payments on the 3% National Bonds and Customs House notes were resumed in 1934/5 and redemption on the latter also began in 1934. The floating debt, consisting mainly of arrears of expenditure, was not, however, serviced.

6 The word 'peso' is used as short-hand for the domestic currency unit of each republic.

7 The amounts paid out on public debt service (on both internal and external debt) declined as follows:

| Country | Period | Decline |
| --- | --- | --- |
| Costa Rica | 1932–4 | 54% |
| El Salvador | 1929–35 | 69% |
| Guatemala | 1929–35 | 61% |
| Honduras | 1929–36 | 4% |
| Nicaragua | 1929–35 | 62% |

8 A Provisional Claims Commission was appointed in Nicaragua to consider claims against the government arising out of the 1926/7 civil war and subsequent civil disturbances. 19.1 million córdobas had been claimed (of which 18 million had been added to the internal debt), but only 0.9 million córdobas were awarded after the Commission completed its work in September 1934. See League of Nations (1938), pp. 5–6 (Nicaraguan section).

9 At the end of 1932, Costa Rica's external public debt was estimated at 77.5 million colones ($17.6 million), equivalent to $32 per person. In the same year, the external public debt per head was $10 in El Salvador, $8 in Guatemala, $5 in Honduras and $3.5 in Nicaragua.

10 This included service on the internal debt, the latter representing some 30% of total debt in 1932.

11 In Salvador, for example, national defence expenditure rose from 3.2 million colones in 1931/2 to 3.7 million colones in 1936/7. As a proportion of government expenditure, this represented a modest decline.

12 Costa Rica's achievements by the 1930s in the education sphere were, however, substantial. The 'Olympians' (Cleto González Víquez and Ricardo Jiménez Oreamuno) had both attached enormous importance to education in the half century before the 1930s (during which time they dominated public policy), and in the 1927 census the literacy rate was estimated at 76%. The highest figure elsewhere in Central America was 40% (in El Salvador) and the lowest was 20% (in Guatemala).

13 In 1936/7, the road tax yielded some 400,000 quetzales (i.e. payment had been made by 200,000 adults). As the tax was levied on all males between 18 and 60 years of age (i.e. about half the male population) and as the male population of Guatemala was nearly one million in 1936/7, this gives a maximum of 300,000 male adults who worked off the tax in kind.

14 Between February 1935 and January 1937, the purchase and sale of foreign exchange between private parties was permitted on condition of declaration of such transactions to the Exchange Control Board.

15 See Facio (1973), p. 130.

16 In March 1937, Somoza had appointed a US expert, James Edwards, to draw up a financial plan. The Edwards plan called for parity between the córdoba and the dollar (see Cuadra Cea (1963), pp. 115–16), but this aspect of the plan was not implemented.

17 Not surprisingly, this rapid depreciation of the exchange rate provoked a huge rise in prices. Between 1937 and 1939, retail food prices rose by 124% (see IMF, *International Financial Statistics*, June 1950). In the rest of Central America during the same period, prices either fell (El Salvador, Guatemala) or were unchanged (Costa Rica). Figures for Honduras are unavailable.

18 Unlike Costa Rica and El Salvador, Guatemala lacked a private association for the defence of coffee. Instead, it had a government service (Oficina Central de Café) which had many of the same functions as the private associations in El Salvador and Costa Rica, but which was firmly under state control (see Monfils (1938), p. 38).

19 In El Salvador, for example, the three banks empowered to issue notes held a gold reserve ratio in the 1920s against the note circulation ranging from a low of 57% to a high of 66%. The legal minimum ratio was 40%.

20 The Banco Internacional, although not in public ownership, had a monopoly of note issue at this time and acted in many respects like a monetary authority.

21 It was reduced from $2.57 per 100 kg bag to $0.82.

22 For Martínez, whose régime did not obtain US recognition until 1934, this alliance represented a high political priority.

23 Anderson (1971), pp. 8–9, however, has found evidence to suggest that coffee holdings became more concentrated during the depression (presumably as a result of forced sales by small producers) and Rodrigo Facio (1972, pp. 102–3) reproduced a table published by the Instituto de Defensa del Café in 1940 to demonstrate the unexpectedly high degree of concentration in Costa Rican coffee holdings. (While 55.74% of all coffee farms had less than 1,000 coffee bushes, 0.86% had more than 50,000 bushes and there were seven estates each with more than 400,000 bushes.) Perhaps it is safest to conclude that

land distribution among coffee growers would have been even more uneqeual without debt moratoria.

24 Wage rates in El Salvador are estimated to have fallen from 25 to 20 US cents per day for *jornaleros* (day-workers on coffee plantations receiving subsistence).

25 In Guatemala, the impact of Ubico's Vagrancy Law (see above, p. 81) was at first to raise wages (see Jones (1940), p. 165). In Costa Rica, President Jiménez's 1933 minimum wage law was extended to rural workers in 1935 (see Chapter 3, p. 65).

26 See Posas (1982), p. 106.

27 Sigatoka disease was first encountered in 1913 in the Fiji islands' Sigatoka Valley. It reached Surinam and Trinidad in 1933, coming to Central America in 1935 (see Karnes (1978), p. 186).

28 This was the concession, according to some commentators, which was responsible for UFCO agreeing to a doubling of the tax on bananas from one to two cents per stem (see Woodbridge (1972), pp. 149–50).

29 The details can be found in Grieb (1979), p. 185.

30 See May and Plazo (1958), pp. 166–7.

31 Changes in the fortunes of the banana industry are the principal determinants of changes in the book value of US direct foreign investment in Central America in the 1930s. In Costa Rica, the book value fell from $22 million in 1929 to $13 million in 1936, rising to $24 million in 1940. A similar pattern was observed in Guatemala, while in Honduras the book value was reduced by nearly 50% in a decade. See Torres Rivas (1973), table 7, p. 295.

32 In both cases, the mines were owned by subsidiaries of US companies.

33 Only Costa Rica signed a bilateral trade agreement with Nazi Germany (see Facio (1973), pp. 150–1), but the Aski system affected all Central American countries in varying degrees.

34 The discount on Aski marks in El Salvador was never less than 20% (see Hill (1938), p. 2).

35 The rate of growth of DUA in Guatemala between 1932 and 1938 (see Table 4.2) is distorted by the upward revision to the crop series adopted by the Ministerio de Agricultura in 1936. Even allowing for this, however, the expansion of DUA was still very rapid.

36 With the possible exception of Costa Rica (see Soley Güell (1949), Vol. 2, pp. 329–32).

37 In Nicaragua, for example, the ratio of the value of tariffs collected to the value of imports rose from 34% in 1928 to 50% in 1933. It should also be remembered that most import duties were specific, not *ad valorem*, and in a period of declining world prices the *ad valorem* equivalent of such taxes would have been rising.

38 President Ubico of Guatemala held a Central American Conference in 1934, which was intended to establish Central American unity (economic as well as political). The other governments of the region, however, regarded the Guatemalan proposal with suspicion and the plan collapsed. See Grieb (1979), pp. 97–113.

39 Agricultural workers cultivating 'with their personal work' three manzanas of corn in a hot zone, four manzanas in a cold zone, or four manzanas of wheat, potatoes, vegetables or other products in any zone were exempted from the provisions of the anti-vagrancy law. If Wagley's (1941) study of Chimaltenango is representative, a significant minority of the rural population would have

had access to farms of this size and the incentive to increase production of domestic crops would have risen accordingly. This incentive was reinforced in 1937, when rural workeres cultivating at least one and five-sixteenth manzanas of land on their own account were required to work for others a minimum of 100 days per year rather than the 150 days applied to landless labourers.

40 A notable exception is provided by Rodrigo Facio, Rector of the University of Costa Rica. See Facio (1972), pp. 97–126.

41 The 'active/passive' distinction is employed by Díaz-Alejandro (1984) in his overview of Latin America in the 1930s.

42 The High Commission had been established to reorganise Nicaragua's finances. It supervised debt service payments throughout the 1930s. Under the Financial Plan of 1917, the first claim on the government's revenues was that of the collector of customs (a US appointee) for the service of the external debt (see Cox (1927), pp. 841–58).

43 See Council of Foreign Bondholders, *Annual Report* (1940), p. 358.

44 This opinion is not shared by a well-known biography of Carías (see Díaz-Chávez, 1982). The latter argues that Carías was totally subordinate to fruit company interests and was responsible for turning Honduras into a neo-colony. The book's main criticism, however, hinges on Carías' failure to apply legislation to the banana companies to which they were not subject in any other part of the Caribbean basin. This seems an unfair criticism; Carías' presidency ended the cycle of civil wars in Honduras, which had left the Honduran state a weak prey for unscrupulous foreign companies. The authority of the state increased notably during his presidency, so that in the late 1940s (see Chapter 6, p. 123) it was possible to strike a much fairer bargain with the fruit companies.

45 Honduras did have its own liberal reform period in the 1870s (see Reina Valenzuela and Argueta (1978)), but the state saw its role as providing the basic infrastructure needed to attract foreign capital rather than promoting a nationally owned coffee sector. See Pérez Brignoli (1973).

46 In the 'elections' in December 1936 Somoza received 107,201 votes. His opponent, Leonardo Argüello, received 169 votes (see Black (1981), p. 29).

47 This organisation, supported at first by communists, helped to establish other workers' organisations in the last years of the Martínez dictatorship.

48 This illegal communist party became the legalised Partido Socialista Nicaragüense (PSN) in 1944, publishing its own newspaper 'Hoy'. See Sanchez (1967), p. 47.

49 See Ameringer (1982), p. 27.

50 See Stone (1975), p. 279.

51 See Stokes (1950), p. 261.

52 It has usually been assumed that the successful movement to overthrow Arias as Panamanian President in 1941 had US support. See Humphreys (1981), p. 104.

## 5 Central America and the Second World War

1 See Humphreys (1981), pp. 43–45.

2 Even before Pearl Harbor, Costa Rica had offered the United States bases on the Cocos Islands and Nicaragua had invited the United States to establish coastal bases (see Mecham (1961), p. 197).

3 A special provision, approved March 1941, made the Lend-Lease Act applicable to Latin American countries for buying weapons of any kind. Nicaragua was

one of the first republics to benefit (see Mecham (1961), pp. 199–200).

4  *Ibid.*, p. 216.

5  The story of how Somoza secured for 380,000 córdobas the properties of the German Julio Bahlke, valued at 5 million dollars, is told in Alegría and Flakoll (1982), pp. 120–1.

6  The properties were not finally nationalised until June 1944 (just before the fall of Ubico), although the German owners' operations were severely restricted before then. These coffee *fincas* were to resurface frequently as a political issue in post-war governments. See Melville and Melville (1971), pp. 128–31.

7  By 1945, the Inter-American Highway (3,334 miles in length) was 46.7% paved with a further 27.9% in all-weather roads and 8.4% in dry-weather roads. Much of the 17% consisting of trails was in Costa Rica. See James (1945), p. 618.

8  In Brazil, for example, Congress refused to allow US troops to be based on Brazilian territory, which meant that the strategic Atlantic bulge was vulnerable to an Axis invasion (see Humphreys (1981), pp. 139–40).

9  Honduras did not provide bases, because she was not asked to do so. The Carías government contributed to the war effort, however, in many other ways.

10  See *Bulletin of the Pan American Union*, July 1943, p. 404.

11  See Torres Rivas (1973), table 7, p. 295.

12  See Montero Umaña (1972), p. 245.

13  The first conference was held in 1936 with the participation of all Central American Republics except Honduras. The second was held in Havana in 1937 (this time with Honduras as an observer) and established agreement in principle on export quotas; the failure to take any action, however, led to a sharp price fall. See Wickizer (1943), ch. 11.

14  The text of the agreement is contained in Wickizer (1943), pp. 233–9.

15  Each country was awarded a basic quota (in 60 kg bags) which was subsequently increased as follows:

| Country | Basic Quota | April 1944 | June 1945 |
|---|---|---|---|
| Costa Rica | 200,000 | 220,000 | 382,652 |
| El Salvador | 600,000 | 660,000 | 1,147,956 |
| Guatemala | 535,000 | 588,500 | 1,023,594 |
| Honduras | 20,000 | 21,997 | 38,265 |
| Nicaragua | 195,000 | 214,500 | 373,086 |

16  El Salvador, for example, more than doubled the value of her merchandise exports between 1941 and 1943.

17  See Karnes (1978), p. 208.

18  The dividend paid on the two companies' stocks during the war years was as follows (in US dollars):

|  | UFCO | Standard Fruit |
|---|---|---|
| 1939 | 4.00 | 2.25 |
| 1940 | 4.00 | 3.00 |
| 1941 | 4.00 | 4.50 |
| 1942 | 3.75 | 2.25 |
| 1943 | 2.25 | 2.25 |
| 1944 | 3.25 | 3.00 |
| 1945 | 4.00 | 9.00 |

See Moody's (1945), pp. 1243 and 1378.

19 In 1945, coffee still accounted for 88% of the value of exports.
20 The increase in gold's value was, however, due more to prices than quantity changes.
21 This is not true of Nicaragua, because of the sharp increase in the value of gold exports. The figures for exports ($ million) are:

| | Merchandise exports | Gold exports | Total exports |
|---|---|---|---|
| 1939 | 4.8 | 3.5 | 8.3 |
| 1940 | 3.7 | 5.8 | 9.5 |
| 1941 | 4.6 | 7.3 | 11.9 |
| 1941 | 5.9 | 8.4 | 14.3 |
| 1943 | 7.7 | 7.7 | 15.4 |
| 1944 | 7.8 | 7.6 | 15.4 |
| 1945 | 6.9 | 7.1 | 14.0 |

See United Nations (1955).

22 The modest increase in the unit value of imports for Guatemala (see CEPAL (1976), p. 45) can be assumed to be an underestimate. For example, the price-index for raw materials for construction in Guatemala rose by 46% between 1939 and 1945 and the unweighted unit value of imports (i.e. the value of imports divided by the weight of all imports) rose by 68%. Thus, it seems safe to assume that the increase in Guatemala was in line with the increase in the rest of Central America.
23 Between 1939 and 1945, the barter terms of trade for all Latin America improved by 12.1%, while the purchasing power of exports increased by 16% (*ibid.*, p. 25).
24 The Juntas Rurales de Crédito Agrícola, organised by the Banco Nacional de Costa Rica (BNCR), channelled funds to small farmers (see BNCR (1949), p. 188).
25 Small-scale credit for farmers in El Salvador was organised through the Cajas de Crédito. The latter were subsidiaries of the Banco Hipotecario de El Salvador, established in 1934 with finance provided by coffee growers. In 1944 there were 42 Cajas. See Banco Hipotecario de El Salvador (1944), pp. 39–42.
26 The CNP started operations in 1943 under the control of the BNCR.
27 Nicaragua ran a trade surplus in most years when merchandise exports are defined to include gold.
28 Devaluation of the córdoba after 1936 in Nicaragua produced a serious infla-tionary problem, so that revenue rose rapidly in nominal terms.
29 The main exception was the salary bill of the armed forces. In Nicaragua, for example, the National Guard received wage increases above the rate of inflation, whereas real wages in general fell by 44% between 1941 and 1945 (see Castro Silva (1947), tables 9 and 20).
30 See Backer (1974), pp. 71–75.
31 Calderón's social programme has been discussed by many authors. See, for example, Rosenberg (1983), ch. 3.
32 See Rodríguez (1981), p. 88.
33 See May et al. (1952), p. 282, table 49.
34 The mission's recommendations are contained in Bernstein et al. (1943). The Central Bank was finally established in 1950.

35 The establishment of the National Bank as a Central Bank was a consequence of the Monetary Law, passed in 1940, which replaced the 1912 Monetary Law introduced during the US occupation. See Cuadra Cea (1963), pp. 122–3.

36 See Triffin (1944), pp. 102–3.

37 El Salvador's Banco de Reserva was also permitted to sell participation certificates in these same investments (bonds and cedulas) to the commercial banks or the public (see Triffin (1944) p. 99). This facility was used as an anti-inflation device in 1944. See Banco Central de El Salvador (1944), p. 21.

38 The free rate in Costa Rica fell from ¢5.85 per US dollar in 1941 to ¢5.68 in 1945 (the official rate remained ¢5.62). The free rate in Nicaragua fell from ¢6.36 in 1940 to ¢5.16 in 1943 (the official rate remained ¢5.0). Against all expectations, the free rate in Nicaragua then rose against the dollar to reach ¢7.2 in May 1945; this is usually attributed (see Krehm (1984), pp. 116–17) to capital flight by the Somoza family.

39 Calderón abolished export duties on coffee in one of his first acts as President.

40 By the end of the war, Somoza's business interests were vast and included a wide range of enterprises, which sold to local as well as overseas markets (*ibid.*, pp. 112–15).

41 See Torres Rivas (1973), p. 307.

42 By the early 1940s, a fall in the death rate had pushed population growth above 2% per annum in all republics.

43 See Cantarero (1949), p. 61, table 6.

44 Population censuses were produced in Guatemala in 1921 and 1940.

45 The rural economy was not altogether exempt. Banana production declined sharply after 1941 and this produced considerable hardship. In Costa Rica the Communist Party (with strong representation among banana workers) secured 16% of the popular vote in elections for deputies in 1942.

46 See Humphreys (1982), pp. 11–13.

47 See Ameringer (1974), pp. 61–2.

48 See White (1973), p. 103.

49 See Posas (1983), pp. 112–13.

50 See Alegría and Flakoll (1982), pp. 128–9.

51 In Nicaragua, Somoza's refusal to hold elections led to the formation in 1944 of the Partido Liberal Independiente (PLI). In the same year, the Communist Party (Partido Socialista Nicaragüense) also acquired legal existence. See Gould (1985).

52 See Grieb (1979), ch. 18.

53 In Costa Rica, the US commander of the military mission participated in anti-fascist demonstrations with Mora in 1942. See Bell (1971), p. 43, n. 1.

54 *Ibid.*, p. 43.

55 See Ameringer (1978), pp. 13–16.

56 The year 1943 also saw a serious split in the labour movement as Archbishop Sanabria set up a Catholic labour confederation (Confederación Costarricense de Trabajadores Rerum Novarum) to counter the influence of communism in the workers' organisations. See Backer (1974), pp. 99–107.

57 Calderón had reopened the National University in 1940 (closed for over fifty years), but this still did not bring him the support of the students.

58 Somoza's flirtation with the labour movement in 1944–5 is ably discussed in Gould (1985).

59 He had helped to suppress the 1932 uprising and to organise the reprisals. See White (1973), p. 104.

60 See Cardoza y Aragón (1955), p. 48.

## 6 Post-war economic recovery

1 In the aftermath of the Second World War, several Central American governments commissioned studies on investment opportunities by international bodies (e.g. International Bank for Reconstruction and Development (IBRD) (1953)). A recurring theme in these reports was the possibility that labour shortages might impede economic development; a notable exception, however, was a US study on El Salvador (Feuerlein (1954)), which recognised the possibility of a growing labour surplus.
2 See Ellis (1983), p. 176.
3 See Torres Rivas (1973), p. 295, table 7, and p. 296, table 8.
4 See Ellis (1983), p. 402, table C3.
5 Starting in 1947, a first attempt was made to value banana exports at market prices rather than at the administered prices adopted by the fruit companies and used by each republic in its trade returns. In the words of the IMF (Balance of Payments Yearbook, 1955, p. 100): 'The value of the companies' exports from each country is calculated at a unit price designed to apportion, in a uniform manner, their profits or losses between their local production operations and their selling operations abroad.' Consequently, statistics on the value of banana exports since 1947 are not strictly comparable with those for earlier years.
6 Table 6.2 begins in 1947 for the reason given in note 5, i.e. the switch in the valuation of exports. The new valuation apportions 'profits' on banana operations to each republic, much of which is then treated as a current account debit (income payments on direct foreign investment). Table 6.2 refers to all direct foreign investment, but in Costa Rica, Guatemala and Honduras nearly all the entries refer to the fruit companies, while in El Salvador and Nicaragua the entries (which refer to mining, railway companies and public utilities) are relatively unimportant.
7 See Posas and Del Cid (1982), pp. 129–30.
8 See Araya Pochet (1975), pp. 48–50.
9 See Labarge (1960), p. 36, n. 4.
10 As in 1975, for example, when the Honduran president (General López Arellano) was forced to resign following disclosures that he had received bribes from United Brands (formerly UFCO) in an effort to dissuade him from applying the proposed banana export tax of one US dollar per box (see McCann (1976)).
11 Representatives of the fourteen Latin American coffee-producing countries (including all five Central American republics) met in September 1945 at the Fourth Pan American Coffee Conference. A major demand was the elimination of US price controls on imported coffee (see *Bulletin of the Pan American Union* (1945), pp. 720–1).
12 The Inter-American Coffee Agreement was extended for one year from 1 October 1945, but export quota restrictions were suspended even before the expiry date (see *Bulletin of the Pan American Union* (1946), pp. 412–13).
13 The traditional coffee grown in Central America was *café arábigo*. After the war, however, new varieties were introduced, which enjoyed superior genetic properties and were thus one way in which yields could be increased. See, for example, Hall (1982), pp. 158–60.
14 Experiments carried out in Costa Rica, for example, showed that the application

of fertilisers could raise yields substantially. See Universidad de Costa Rica (1959), p. 60, table V.3, and p. 61, table V.4.

15  *Ibid.*, pp. 57–8.

16  *Ibid.*, p. 58.

17  In the same period, the number of coffee *fincas* increased in Costa Rica by 44% to 21,987. The average yield for the period 1953–5 was 576.5 kg per hectare, a 30% increase on the average yield in 1950–2, and Costa Rican coffee producers were now much closer to the high Salvadorean yield of 660 kg per hectare. See *ibid.*, pp. 56–7.

18  The most extreme cases of concentration were El Salvador and Guatemala. In both countries, the small number of large-scale coffee estates (those in excess of 50 hectares) accounted for some 60% of the harvested area. Only in Honduras, where the industry expanded rapidly after 1945, was production concentrated in medium-sized farms (five to fifty hectares). See Checchi (1959), pp. 57–8.

19  See Reuben Soto (1982), p. 210, table 6, and p. 215, table 11.

20  In Nicaragua, for example, the export of coffee in the late 1940s was mainly in the hands of two firms: Calley-Dagnall (with a virtual monopoly in the north central zone) and Cía Mercantil de Ultramar, a subsidiary of the Banco Nacional, with a dominant position in the south-west. In the early 1950s, two new export houses were established with private Nicaraguan capital, but coffee exporting remained a highly concentrated activity. See Wheelock (1980), pp. 144–5. A similar process of concentration was observed among *beneficiadores*, since only one-third of coffee farms owned their own *beneficio*. See Gariazzo (1984), p. 15, table 1.

21  The exact figures for 1954 (as a % of total exports) were:

| | Costa Rica | El Salvador | Guatemala | Honduras | Nicaragua |
|---|---|---|---|---|---|
| Coffee | 43.2 | 87.6 | 67.3 | 25.9 | 45.9 |
| Bananas | 40.5 | — | 23.5 | 51.7 | 0.9 |
| Total | 83.7 | 87.6 | 90.8 | 77.6 | 46.8 |

22  In addition, UFCO established in 1946 a Department of New Crops 'to promote agricultural research on tropical products with some prospect of profitable commercial cultivation in Middle America' (see Labarge (1960), p. 40).

23  Between 1952 and 1954, abacá production fell by 39% in Guatemala (Labarge (1960), p. 29) and by 46% in Costa Rica (see Universidad de Costa Rica (1959a), p. 67).

24  In Costa Rica, however, production of rubber continued to rise rapidly in the early 1950s, although an increasing proportion of the crop was required by domestic users and exports fell (see *ibid.*, p. 67).

25  See May et al. (1952), p. 66.

26  The commissioned studies (see n. 1) were all agreed on this. In addition, an unofficial study of Costa Rica (May et al. (1952)), commissioned by the US 20th Century Fund, came to similar conclusions.

27  This conviction was almost certainly erroneous (see next chapter), but it was frequently made the basis for policy recommendations. For example, the World Bank study on Nicaragua stated: 'During the harvests of 1952 there were local shortages of unskilled labour. The growing labour shortage on the west coast will necessitate increased mechanization in agriculture and more efficient techniques in industry' (IBRD (1953), p. xxv).

28  In Costa Rica, for example, the nationalised banking system financed over 80% of the coffee crop in the 1953–4 season (see Universidad de Costa Rica (1959), p. 58).

29  Although the Pacific lowlands represented a land frontier, much of it was already in private hands; thus, access to the uncultivated lands would require payment of rent in cash or kind.

30  The most powerful were in El Salvador, where the Asociación Cafetalera had created in the Cía Salvadoreña de Café in 1942 to wrest control of coffee exports from the foreign-owned houses.

31  In 1954, Nicaraguan earnings from cotton reached 26.7% of all exports. In Guatemala, they reached 3.8% and in El Salvador 6.2%.

32  All growers belonged to it by law. See Browning (1971), pp. 230–1.

33  The construction of this highway began in 1951. See Dada (1983), p. 97, n. 19, and Williams (1986), p. 23.

34  See Baumeister et al. (1983), p. 5, table 1.

35  These figures should be compared with exports of 513,360 kg in 1945 valued at $12,000.

36  See IBRD (1951), pp. 51–2.

37  The cooperative was named Oficina Controladora de Aceites Esenciales. See IBRD (1951), p. 51.

38  Food balance sheets are available for both Costa Rica and Honduras for part of this period. See Universidad de Costa Rica (1959), pp. 36–55 for Costa Rica, and FAO, *Production Yearbook* (1958), p. 242 for Honduras.

39  With the highest income per head, Costa Rica can be assumed to have had the highest consumption of meat and dairy products per head.

40  See Universidad de Costa Rica (1959), p. 50.

41  In the 1950 agricultural census, 81% of farms were recorded as owner-occupied in Costa Rica. See Monteforte Toledo (1972), Vol. 1, p. 190, table 12. Of these owner-occupied farms, 77.9% were smaller than 50 manzanas or 34.4 hectares (see Riismandel (1972), p. 131).

42  Between 1944 and 1954, the population growth rate accelerated from around 2% to nearly 3%. The acceleration in the rate of growth of population was due in almost equal proportions to the rise in the Crude Birth Rate on the one hand and the fall in the Crude Death Rate (CDR) on the other, except in Nicaragua where the fall in CDR was of greater importance.

43  In Costa Rica, for example, several laws were passed in the 1930s giving unemployed males access to public lands; these were land grants and they helped to promote production of DUA, albeit with very low yields (see Saenz (1969), pp. 53–8).

44  A study by the Economic Commission for Latin America in the 1950s showed not only how low were yields in basic grain production, but also what huge increases could be achieved through the use of improved techniques. See CEPAL, *El Abastecimiento de Granos en Centroamerica y Panama*, quoted in Universidad de Costa Rica (1959), pp. 75–8.

45  *Ibid.*, p. 77.

46  See Browning (1971), pp. 274–80.

47  See Fletcher *et al.* (1970), p. 136.

48  See, for example, Dean (1969) for the case of coffee in Brazil.

49  See, for example, Levin (1960) for the case of Peruvian guano.

50  In El Salvador, for example, the Martínez administration had passed laws res-

tricting the import of capital goods for industry in an effort to protect artisan firms. See Dada (1983), pp. 62–3.

51 In the period 1944–54, the first studies were made of the distribution of income. Although allowance must be made for the poor quality of the data, lack of coverage, etc., all the studies agree on the highly unequal nature of income distribution. The UN study of El Salvador (Feuerlein (1954), pp. 10–11) estimated that the top 7.9% of families received 51.3% of GNP. The World Bank study of Nicaragua (IBRD (1953), p. 75) estimated that the top 1% controlled 25% of national income, while a study of Guatemala (Adler et al. (1952), p. 217, table 57) estimated that the top 1.2% of families received 19.6% of national income.

52 See Dada (1983), p. 47.

53 See Feuerlein (1954), p. 24.

54 See IBRD (1951), p. 116.

55 See Universidad de Costa Rica (1959a) p. 30. The law, however, was modified in 1946. See *Bulletin of the Pan American Union* (1946), pp. 107–8.

56 See Universidad de Costa Rica (1959b), p. 57.

57 El Salvador, for example, signed commercial treaties with Honduras, Nicaragua and Guatemala which provided for free trade in a limited range of goods. See Feurelein (1954), p. 61.

58 The introduction of Labour Codes in Costa Rica and Nicaragua has already been mentioned (see Chapter 5). Guatemala passed a Labour Code in 1947, finally burying the vagrancy laws inherited from Ubico, with disputes between workers and employers to be settled by labour courts. Labour legislation in El Salvador remained very rudimentary until the revolution of December 1948, when unions became legal again, but even after 1948 the provision of labour legislation did not apply to rural workers.

59 Import-substituting industrialisation (ISI) does not appear to have been particularly important in this period. In Costa Rica, for example, the fraction of total industrial supply accounted for by imports hovered around 60% between 1946 and 1954. There was, however, a significant reduction in import penetration in the case of intermediate goods destined for agriculture. See Universidad de Costa Rica (1959b), p. 108.

60 In 1951, for example, some 25% of all commercial bank loans in Guatemala were given to real estate.

61 Many of these were capital goods, such as trucks and buses, which provided evidence of the opportunities for private investment. In particular, the number of trucks imported between 1950 and 1954 rose by a factor of 2.5 in most republics. See United Nations (1957), p. 46.

62 See Wheelock (1980), pp. 199–200.

63 The most heavily taxed items included tobacco, sugar, drink and imported clothing, all items which bulked large in the consumption pattern of the poor. The World Bank study of Nicaragua (IBRD (1953)) made much of the fact that the very rich paid hardly any tax at all.

64 Costa Rica, for example, in the 1940s was still using the system of nomenclature and classification borrowed from Spain in 1885. See Watkins (1967), p. 443.

65 Guatemala, however, had taxed business profits at progressive rates since 1934 and income from invested capital since 1944 (*ibid.*, pp. 150–1).

66 This was raised to 30% in 1955 (*ibid.*, p. 334).

67 During the revolutionary period in Guatemala, UFCO's tax liability was broadly determined by the 1936 contract agreed with the Ubico government. The Arbenz government in particular pressed for a revision of the contract, but its efforts failed. A new contract was signed, on 27 December 1954, with the Castillo Armas government in which UFCO agreed to pay a tax of 30% on its profits and hand over 100,000 acres of (previously expropriated) land. The whole of the contract is reproduced in Bauer-Paíz (1956), pp. 398–403.

68 See Posas and Del Cid (1982), p. 130. By 1954, however, national firms contributed 88% of receipts under this tax heading.

69 See CEPAL (1956), p. 123.

70 See Feuerlein (1954), p. 46.

71 Coffee exports in Honduras were not subject to export taxes until 1955, but coffee exports on a large scale were a new venture and special considerations therefore applied.

72 One should also mention in Guatemala the special case of the Fincas Nacionales, taken over from their German proprietors in the Second World War and mainly devoted to coffee exports. Until 1949, the Fincas operated as a government department and their profits accrued directly to the government; in 1949, the Fincas were given a measure of autonomy but their operating profits contributed substantially to government revenue (some 10% of tax receipts in 1950).

73 Figures are not available on the breakdown of investment in Nicaragua in this period between the public and private sectors.

74 Both were translated into Spanish and made available to the public. See Banco Central de Honduras (1951).

75 i.e. the inflexibility of commercial banks and their preference for lending to export agriculture and commerce.

76 See Gil Pacheco (1974), p. 248.

77 See Council of Foreign Bondholders (1955).

78 In 1950, the official exchange (buying) rate was devalued from 5.0 to 6.6 córdobas per dollar.

79 As part of its efforts to finance the work of reconstruction after the civil war, the revolutionary junta in Costa Rica introduced a large import surcharge (included in the free exchange rate) in 1948–9.

80 In particular, the prolonged strike and poor weather in the banana sector (see Chapter 7).

81 Coffee growers were not subject to the business profits tax, because income from coffee was treated as accruing to individuals.

82 A 'surplus' sector in this context means a net financial surplus, i.e. profits in excess of investment within the sector itself. A 'deficit' sector is one which must borrow from outside to finance that part of its investment requirements which cannot be met by retained profits.

83 One must distinguish, however, between the *growing* of coffee and its preparation in *beneficios* for sale. The latter did give rise to the possibility of labour-saving technical progress and this proved important at a later date.

84 The figures for capital outflow should be interpreted as minima, because of the probability that some outflows were not recorded.

85 It is noticeable, for example, in the Guatemalan case, that huge outflows were recorded in 1949 and 1952. The former was the year of an army revolt, following the assassination of Colonel Arana, which was put down only after the government distributed arms to the urban workers. The latter was the year in which land reform was launched.

## 7 The struggle for democracy

1 The origins, and eventual collapse, of the PTN are dealt with in great detail in Pérez Bermudez and Guevara (1985), pp. 99–159.

2 See James (1954), p. 110.

3 See Alexander (1957), p. 369.

4 See Gould (1985).

5 See Posas (1984), pp. 239–43.

6 See James (1954), p. 69.

7 The PSN never formally allied with Somoza, but they refused to join the other opposition parties in the critical 1944–5 period; this prevented the formation of a broad-based anti-Somoza alliance and contributed indirectly to the survival of the dictatorship. See Gould (1985).

8 James (1954), p. 48, gives a list of leading Guatemalan communists who were given overseas appointments during Arévalo's presidency. James' purpose is to show Arévalo as a willing tool of international communism, but a more realistic interpretation is that Arévalo felt ambivalent towards the Guatemalan communists and wished to minimise their influence domestically. The Guatemalan Communist Party was never legalised under Arévalo.

9 Arévalo, for example, shut down the communist school (Escuela Claridad) for the study and propagation of Marxism. See Schlesinger and Kinzer (1982), p. 56.

10 See Gould (1985).

11 See Schifter (1981), p. 66.

12 There was a split in the communist-led CTG as early as 1945 (see Chapter 7, pp. 138–9).

13 See *Bulletin of the Pan American Union* (1945), pp. 228–30. The new labour law of January 1946, however, was distinctly unsympathetic to labour, with many kinds of work stoppages declared illegal. See *Bulletin of the Pan American Union* (1946), p. 54.

14 See James (1954), p. 155.

15 The ballot was not secret, with Aguado's supporters obliged to form a highly visible queue outside each polling station. Despite this, the National Guard – confronted by long queues of Aguado supporters – closed the polls before the official time and carried off the ballots for counting. The margin of Argüello's 'victory' was almost as dramatic as his 'defeat' in 1936. See Crawley (1979), p. 106.

16 Somoza had been able to undermine US opposition towards his régime in 1945–6 only by promising not to run for re-election. See Millett (1979), ch. 9.

17 The Picado administration had been the first to recognise the Nicaraguan puppet régime in late 1947; Somoza and Picado were also close personal friends, with the latter allegedly aiding and abetting the former in cattle smuggling across the border between the two countries. Somoza, however, is most unlikely to have acted out of personal loyalty, and the motives behind his invasion have a more sophisticated interpretation. In particular, Somoza had no wish to see Figueres (his sworn enemy) triumph.

18 This is the interpretation, almost certainly correct, of Schifter (1982), p. 169. Jacobo Schifter's book is based on a thorough sifting of State Department documents.

19 *Ibid.*, p. 170.

20 There are therefore parallels with 1944–5. This time, however, it was the traditional parties rather than organised labour which had no interest in a broad alliance.

21 In 1943 a coup had been launched against Calderón, with the director of the Banco Nacional de Costa Rica as its civilian head, but it had failed.

22 Figueres later broke with the PSD and rejoined the Cortesista Democratic Party; subsequently, he again left the Democratic Party and formed the Partido Cortesista Auténtico with Cortés' son, Otto. Finally, in February 1947 he joined the broad opposition movement being formed to challenge Calderonismo. See Ameringer (1978), pp. 32–3.

23 The unification was achieved just in time for the 1946 congressional elections; the opposition coalition obtained 41,821 votes to 57,154 for Calderonismo. See Schifter (1981), pp. 75–6.

24 León Cortés died in 1946 (otherwise he would almost certainly have led the coalition). Ulate was a Cortesista, although he was nominally independent of the Democratic Party and operated politically through his own Partido Unión Nacional (PUN). See Ameringer (1978), p. 28.

25 The work of the junta is competently discussed in Ameringer (1978), ch. 4.

26 See Schifter (1981), pp. 112–13.

27 *Ibid.*, p. 112.

28 See Rojas Bolaños (1978), p. 25. Nuñez was minister of labour and social welfare in the revolutionary junta and one of its most radical members, but he was replaced by a much more conservative figure during the presidency of Otilio Ulate.

29 Colonel Edgar Cardona, Minister of Public Security, attempted a coup (the 'Cardonazo') in April 1949. Cardona had been one of Figueres' closest allies in the civil war, but disapproved of the junta's radical measures. The Cardonazo was the last attempted coup in Costa Rica.

30 Although the PLN has cultivated the urban labour vote, it has not always been very successful; urban labour remains lukewarm towards a party which challenged its strong position before 1948. See the intriguing analysis of voting patterns since 1953 in Schifter (1981), ch. 4.

31 See Menjívar (1979), p. 129.

32 See Dunkerley (1982), p. 35.

33 The opposition parties, notably the liberals, withdrew on the grounds that the election results were a foregone conclusion. See Posas (1984), p. 244.

34 Although Gálvez was no friend of organised labour, his régime did introduce a number of measures designed to improve working conditions (*ibid.*, p. 249).

35 The responsibility for the killing of Arana remains a mystery, but the finger of guilt has been pointed frequently at Jacobo Arbenz; certainly, the latter stood to gain most from Arana's death.

36 See Leonard (1984), p. 103.

37 The FSG, whose most important member was the railway workers' union, had been formed following the split in the CGT in 1945. It was opposed to communist influence in the Guatemalan labour movement, but the events of 1949 convinced the FSG that labour unity must be the highest priority of the workers' movement.

38 See Woodward (1962), pp. 363–74.

39 See Leonard (1984), p. 104.

40 See Geiger (1953), p. 39.

41 See Immerman (1982), ch. 5.

42 See Schlesinger and Kinzer (1982), pp. 99–101.

43 See Melville and Melville (1971), pp. 100–1.
44 See Schlesinger and Kinzer (1982), p. 219.
45 See McClintock (1985), p. 128.
46 Ydígoras Fuentes served in the Arévalo government as Ambassador to Great Britain, but (as he himself makes clear – Ydígoras Fuentes (1963), p. 38) this was a ruse to get him out of the country.
47 See González (1978), pp. 605–6.
48 See Posas (1984), p. 338.
49 See Checchi (1959), p. 140.
50 See Morris (1984), pp. 37–8, and Natalini de Castro et al. (1985), pp. 88–9.
51 See Connell-Smith (1966), pp. 125–6.
52 See Mecham (1961), p. 429.
53 See Poblete-Troncoso and Burnett (1960), pp. 142–3.
54 The overthrow of Arbenz was the culmination of a big campaign by the United States in Latin America and elsewhere in support of its position; at the Tenth International Conference of American States in Caracas in March 1954, for example, the US Secretary of State John Foster Dulles pushed through an anti-communist resolution designed to isolate Guatemala diplomatically; Dulles obtained the support of all the Latin American republics (except Mexico and Argentina who abstained and Guatemala who opposed the resolution) but the episode created a great deal of bad feeling towards the United States. See Mecham (1961), pp. 440–5.
55 See Ameringer (1974), p. 74.
56 During the forty-day civil war, the small airforce controlled by the Figueristas made nineteen trips to Guatemala, bringing back arms, ammunition and men. See Bell (1971), p. 136.
57 This, the so-called Rio Treaty, had been introduced in 1947 and entered into full effect at the end of 1948. Ironically, it was Costa Rica's ratification of the Treaty (on 3 December 1948), the fourteenth state to do so, which brought it into force, and Costa Rica was the first republic (eight days later) to invoke the Treaty. See Mecham (1961), pp. 392–3.
58 In 1949, following the incidents in December 1948, Costa Rica and Nicaragua signed a Pact of Amity. This did not, however, eliminate the hostility between Somoza and Figueres, and the latter was implicated in an assassination attempt against the former in 1954; in January 1955, as if by way of retaliation, Teodoro Picado, Jr, led an army into Costa Rica from Nicaragua in an unsuccessful attempt to overthrow Figueres. The Picado forces received support from Somoza, but the US administration intervened quickly on behalf of Figueres and a year later Costa Rica and Nicaragua signed two further bilateral agreements, designed to put an end to hostilities. See Ameringer (1978), pp. 119–24, and Mecham (1961), pp. 402–5.
59 These accusations reached a climax at the Conference of American States in Caracas in March 1954.
60 See Schlesinger (1982), ch. 10.
61 This is the phrase used by Baloyra (1983), in an illuminating article.
62 The professionalisation of the Honduran armed forces had begun in 1954 with the signing of a US–Honduran military treaty, and the Honduran military extracted sufficient concessions from Villeda Morales to ensure themselves a fair degree of autonomy. Their lack of antagonism to the liberal president was therefore based on self-interest rather than altruism. See Natalini de Castro et al. (1985), pp. 120–4.

## 8 The foundations of modern export-led growth, 1954–60

1 US *per caput* consumption of bananas was 10.5 kg in the period 1934–8, falling steadily to 7.8 kg in the period 1965–6. See Grunwald and Musgrove (1970), p. 371, table 13.1.
2 See Wall (1968), pp. 46–50.
3 See Ellis (1983), p. 130.
4 Export prices from Costa Rica fell by 32.8% between 1956 and 1960, while in Honduras the decline between 1957 and 1960 was 22%. See Grunwald and Musgrove (1970), p. 373, table 13.3.
5 The law was introduced in July 1956. See Ellis (1983), p. 118.
6 The division of purchases in Guatemala between fruit company plantations and independent producers is given in Ellis (1983), p. 412, table C.13 (see also p. 129, table 13).
7 By 1961, the value of banana exports from Nicaragua had fallen to $55,000, equivalent to 0.1% of all exports.
8 Figures on average labour productivity (APL) for the major banana-producing divisions can be found in Ellis (1983), p. 409, table C.10, which records an average increase in APL of 63% between 1954 and 1960. Figures on yield per hectare can be found in Ellis (1983), p. 410, table C.11; the average annual increase (1954–60) was 3.7%.
9 See Ellis (1983), p. 408, table C.9.
10 The capital–labour ratio on the Lima division of UFCO in Honduras is estimated to have risen by 168% between 1953 and 1960. See Ellis (1983), p. 185, table 25.
11 The FAO estimated for Brazil that the interval between a maximum or minimum price and the corresponding maximum or minimum production averaged 4–7 years between 1870 and 1953; a similar lag is plausible for Central America. See Grunwald and Musgrove (1970), p. 311.
12 The quotas averaged 90% of previous exports. See IMF, *International Financial News Survey*, 16 October 1959.
13 US *per caput* consumption peaked in 1950–2 at 8.0 kg, falling to 6.8 kg by 1964–6. See Grunwald and Musgrove (1970), p. 323, table 10.5.
14 The new varieties had higher yields and made it possible to increase density per hectare. See Hall (1982), pp. 160–1.
15 The government did not, however, agree to this request (*ibid.*, p. 162).
16 An exhaustive study on coffee in this period in El Salvador showed that 58% of total cash outlays consisted of labour costs. See FAO (1958), p. 105.
17 Farms over fifty hectares accounted for the bulk of the land area in coffee in these three republics (see Grunwald and Musgrove (1970), p. 325, table 10.8). These large farms also had the highest yields and were the most dependent on hired labour.
18 Between 1950 and 1963, Costa Rica increased the area planted to coffee by 66%, with 53% of the new bushes located in the crowded Valle Central, the traditional epicentre of Costa Rican coffee production. See Hall (1982), p. 156.
19 In Costa Rica, costs of production do not vary enormously by size of coffee farm (see Hall (1982), p. 163); this is both cause and effect of non-discrimination by banks.
20 By the early 1960s, the largest 4% of farms accounted for some 60% of coffee production in El Salvador and over 70% of the area in coffee in Guatemala. See Grunwald and Musgrove (1970), p. 326, table 10.8.

21 The key months are October to January; these months accounted for 60% of annual labour inputs in El Salvador. See FAO (1958), p. 111, table 5.

22 The trade coefficient is the sum of exports and imports divided by GDP. By 1960, the figures for Central America ranged from 40% to 50%, except in Guatemala where it only reached 27%.

23 The exception is gold exports from Nicaragua, which reached an important position in the 1940s (see Chapter 6).

24 In the case of Nicaraguan sesame, the substitute was Nicaraguan cotton-seed (a byproduct of increased cotton production).

25 In Nicaragua, from 1954 onwards, credit for cotton was limited to growers with relatively high yields, thus favouring the larger estates. See CEPAL (1966), p. 98, n. 11.

26 See CEPAL (1959), p. 21, table 18.

27 By the period 1964–7, yields in Central America were twice the world average and at very similar levels in the four northern republics (slightly lower in Costa Rica). See Grunwald and Musgrove (1970), p. 437, table 16.1.

28 In June 1954, Costa Rican authorities authorised the sale of 65% of cotton exports in the free market; the proportion was increased to 99% for a limited quantity in March 1959. In Nicaragua, advance deposit requirements were dropped in 1954 for imports of cotton picking and ginning machinery, and the dual exchange rate was used to favour cotton exports from December 1957.

29 See CEPAL (1966), p. 98.

30 Restrictions, were, however, introduced in 1964. See Grunwald and Musgrove (1970), p. 416.

31 In the early 1960s, less than 20% of the cattle stock was under the control of the largest farm size in El Salvador; in Honduras, the comparable figure was 7%. See CEPAL et al. (1980), p. 186.

32 In Costa Rica, credit for livestock had reached 16.6% of total bank lending by the end of 1960 (see Bulmer-Thomas (1976), p. 9, table 4).

33 In Nicaragua, for example, the Instituto de Fomento Nacional concentrated 80% of its lending to agriculture on livestock. See CEPAL (1966), p. 122, table 120.

34 See Parsons (1964), pp. 155–6, and Williams (1986), pp. 102–5.

35 See CEPAL (1960), pp. 80–1.

36 See Grunwald and Musgrove (1970), p. 357, table 12.5.

37 See Dubois et al. (1983), pp. 47–8.

38 See CEPAL et al. (1980), tables A.3, A.7, A.8.

39 The ratio by 1960 had fallen below 80% in Costa Rica and Guatemala, below 70% in El Salvador and Honduras, and was 30% in Nicaragua.

40 The proportion of the population classified as rural in Central America fell from 68.9% in 1950 to 66.4% in 1960. The 1960 figures for each republic (1950 in brackets) were: Costa Rica 65.8% (66.5%); El Salvador 61.6% (63.5%); Guatemala 66.6% (69.2%); Honduras 77.3% (80.4%) and Nicaragua 60.5% (64.8%). See CEPAL et al. (1980), p. 192, table C-13.

41 The zones of expulsion in El Salvador between 1950 and 1961 included those northern provinces (Santa Ana, Chalatenango, Cabañas and Morazán) where labour was migrating towards Honduras as well as central El Salvador; they also included, however, several Pacific coast provinces (Usulután, San Vicente, La Unión) where cotton production was being established. See CSUCA (1978), p. 72 and compare with Browning (1971), p. 233, map 23.

42 For the case of Nicaragua, see CSUCA (1978), p. 386. The DUA calendar is described in Pearce (1986), pp. 72–6.

43 The Costa Rican figure for the proportion of the agricultural labour force without land (42%) is even higher than for Nicaragua, but this is explained by the greater importance of banana production in the former republic.

44 The coffee boom in Honduras was the main reason for this change.

45 The big change in El Salvador was the increase in the importance of mixed forms ('formas mixtas') of tenancy (not shown in Table 8.6). This was a response by landowners to the opportunities created by the cotton boom.

46 By the 1950s, the absence of a land frontier in El Salvador was driving significant numbers of Salvadoreans into Honduras. See Durham (1979), p. 61, table 2.6.

47 See CSUCA (1978), pp. 156–7.

48 See CEPAL (1966), p. 103, table 97.

49 The Castillo Armas régime repealed the controversial 1952 agrarian reform law, setting up in its place a National Institute for Agrarian Transformation (INTA) which virtually limited land reform to colonisation. By 1961, some 21,700 families had benefited from the programme. See Monteforte Toledo (1972), Vol. 1, p. 266.

50 See Reuben Soto (1982), p. 53.

51 In 1950, it is estimated that only 3% of cereal production costs in El Salvador were financed by bank credits. See Aquino et al. (1950), p. 55.

52 See Banco Central de Costa Rica (1961), pp. 237 and 239.

53 See CEPAL (1960), p. 77.

54 See CEPAL (1966), p. 93.

55 Sorghum (outside Honduras) is used mainly as a cattle feed and is therefore an indirect component of the cost of reproduction of the labour force.

56 An Instituto Regulador de Abastecimientos (IRA) was set up in El Salvador in the 1950s to guarantee the supply of basic grains at stable prices (see Dada, 1983, p. 90). The IRA, however, interpreted stable prices to mean those consistent with free trade, and resisted demands for an increase in the local price above levels prevailing in world markets.

57 Between 1954 and 1960, the net barter terms of trade fell by an average of 33.6% in Central America. The worst hit were Nicaragua and El Salvador (see Table A.14) with falls of nearly 40 per cent.

58 These events are described in more detail in Chapter 7.

59 For a brief review of this period in Guatemalan history, see Whetten (1961), pp. 336–41.

60 The main focus of right-wing discontent was the junta's acceptance of the Partido Revolucionario Abril y Mayo (PRAM) as a contender in the elections. PRAM, founded in 1959, included some communists (the Communist Party itself was not legalised). See White (1973), pp. 107 and 213.

61 In addition, Somoza purchased 25 fighter aircraft from Sweden, making the Nicaraguan air force the most powerful in Central America. See Millett (1979), p. 284.

62 Led by the irrepressible Emiliano Chamorro. See Alegría and Flakoll (1982), pp. 137–8.

63 Anastasio Somoza had taken steps to ensure the survival of the Somoza dynasty before his own death. His eldest son Luis had been named President of Congress in 1956 and First Designate for the Presidency. See Alegría and Flakoll (1982), pp. 144–5.

64 *Ibid.*, pp. 153–4.

65 The role of Villeda Morales in the antidictatorial struggle in the Caribbean is described in Ameringer (1974).

66 See Baciu (1970), pp. 28–9.

67 See Ameringer (1978), pp. 135–7.

68 See Jiménez Castro (1977), p. 26.

69 Echandi was the candidate of the Partido Unión Nacional (PUN), which had been founded by Otilio Ulate in the 1940s (see Ameringer (1978), p. 28).

70 A good example is provided by the Costa Rican Instituto Nacional de Vivienda y Urbanismo (INVU), founded by the Figueres administration in 1954. INVU's task was the promotion of low-cost housing, but it did this through encouragement of the private sector rather than through direct building operations.

71 See Watkins (1967).

72 Called Nomenclatura Arancelaria Uniforme Centroamericana (NAUCA). This was prepared by ECLA and replaced tariff classifications going back, in some cases, to the nineteenth century.

73 Nearly one-quarter of all roads were paved by 1961 in Central America (see SIECA (1967), p. 61). The proportion was lowest in Honduras (14.8%) and highest in Costa Rica (32.2%).

74 Defined as the ratio of gross fixed capital formation to GDP.

75 See Dada (1983), p. 75.

76 The investment coefficient rose from 9.5% in 1950 to 15.7% in 1955.

77 Domestic private savings were buoyant in Honduras in the second half of the 1950s and reflected the success of a small number of newly established financial institutions specialising in the promotion of savings. The most important was Capitalizadora Hondureña. See Checchi (1959), p. 125.

78 Following the triumph of the counter-revolution in Guatemala in 1954, the government received substantial official transfer payments from the US administration. These rose from zero in 1953 to a peak of $20.7 million in 1957, although they were still running at nearly $15 million in 1960. Between 1955 and 1960, these transfers financed 46% of the accumulated current account deficit and help to explain the relatively poor performance of domestic savings.

79 The *locus classicus* for analysis of foreign investment in Central America is Rosenthal (1973).

80 The cost of living indices in Central America are mainly based on surveys of households with low or medium incomes. Imported consumer goods in the 1950s were not a very important component of these groups' expenditure.

81 Only Nicaragua officially devalued during this period, the par value of the córdoba falling from ¢5 to ¢7 per US dollar. In fact, this effectively represented an *appreciation* because many imports had previously been traded at rates higher than ¢7. See IMF, *Annual Report* (1954), pp. 243–5, and (1955), p. 241.

82 President Ydígoras Fuentes, in his autobiography, described the resistance of Congress to the tax change. He also described how the government of Flores Avendaño (1957–8) implemented the cut in coffee production consistent with Guatemala's exportable quota entirely at the expense of the state farms, leaving private growers unaffected. See Ydígoras Fuentes (1963), pp. 75–6.

83 Honduras had already passed in 1955 La Carta Constitutiva de Garantías del Trabajo. This charter, drafted with the assistance of the ILO, guaranteed freedom of organisation and collective bargaining to trade unions and labour's gains were extended further in the 1957 Constitution. See Posas (1981), pp. 203–7.

84 Between 1956 and 1960, for example, minimum hourly rates of pay in Costa Rica for coffee workers rose by 12.8%; for other farm workers they rose by 7.1%.

85 See Whetten (1961), pp. 104–5.

86 The republic which experienced the greatest difficulty in its dealings with the IMF was Costa Rica, whose balance of payments problems were attributed by the Fund to 'excessive' public spending. Fund pressure in 1961 is thought to have contributed to Costa Rica's decision to unify its dual exchange rate in September at the higher rate (¢6.625 colones per US dollar).

87 See Zeledón (1966), pp. 72–6.

88 See Dada (1983), pp. 105–6.

89 The Prebisch thesis is outlined in Prebisch (1959).

90 See Cohen Orantes (1972), ch. 2.

91 See Watkins (1967).

92 The change was signalled during the visit to Washington in 1959 of Salvadorean President Lemus. See Bodenheimer (1981), pp. 32–3.

93 Another reason may have been Nicaragua's border dispute with Honduras, finally resolved by arbitration in 1960. Whatever the reasons, however, both countries reacted angrily and the Nicaraguan government said that it would regard US assistance to the three northern participants as an act of economic aggression (see Cochrane (1969), p. 66).

94 See Staley (1962).

## 9 The illusion of a golden age, 1960–70

1 The measurement of the contribution of the CACM to the regional growth rate in the 1960s has been a source of endless speculation. Suffice it to say that the quantitative impact was seriously overestimated in early studies and has subsequently been downgraded substantially. See Lizano and Willmore (1975) and Cline and Delgado (1978), Appendix B, pp. 459–64.

2 The orgins of this war are well discussed in Durham (1979). The details of the war itself are given in Rowles (1980).

3 The Guatemalan guerrilla movement of the 1960s, and its failure to appeal to the peasantry, is discussed in Debray (1978). In Nicaragua, the Frente Sandinista de Liberación Nacional (FSLN) was formed in 1961 and there is a competent, if uncritical, account of its operations in the 1960s in Alegría and Flakoll (1982), ch. 7.

4 See Cochrane (1969), p. 100.

5 There was much greater space for the new aspirants in Costa Rica and Honduras, although for very different reasons. Modern democracy was consolidated in Costa Rica in the 1960s with the main parties competing fiercely for the new urban vote; in Honduras, on the other hand, the military after the coup in 1963 had no traditional oligarchy to rely on and slowly came to perceive the labour movement as a possible ally.

6 See Chapter 8, p. 174

7 See Cochrane (1969), pp. 140–2.

8 See Gonzalez Del Valle (1966), pp. 13–25.

9 See Cohen Orantes (1972), p. 57.

10 See Cochrane (1969), p. 142.

11 See Cohen Orantes (1972), p. 54.

12 *Ibid.*, pp. 51–2.

13 A listing of the main institutions can be found in Inforpress (1983), p. 40.

14 Military coups occurred in Guatemala and Honduras in 1963. A similar intervention had already taken place in El Salvador in 1961, and the Somoza family continued to rule in Nicaragua with the support of the National Guard despite the use of presidential 'nominees' from 1963 to 1967.

15 CONDECA could not survive the war between two of its members in 1969, but it was temporarily revived again in 1983 (without Nicaraguan or Costa Rican participation) in a US-inspired move to exert pressure on the Sandinista government.

16 See Joseph S. Nye, Jr, 'Central American Regional Integration', *International Conciliation* No. 562, March 1967, p. 35. Quoted in Cochrane (1969), p. 181.

17 The hollow nature of this planning exercise is discussed in Cohen Orantes (1972), p. 62.

18 This was the fate of the Central American School of Public Administration (ESAPAC) and the Central American Institute of Industrial Technology (ICAITI). See Cohen Orantes (1972), pp. 62–3.

19 See Bulmer-Thomas (1982), pp. 243–9.

20 See Fishlow (1984), pp. 238–43.

21 See Cline (1978), pp. 63–76.

22 See Watkins (1967), pp. 45–8.

23 See, for example, Vaitsos (1978), pp. 728–9.

24 The General Treaty established free trade on a *product* basis, leaving little room for protection by *plant*. See Bulmer-Thomas (1982), p. 242.

25 See Ramsett (1969), pp. 63–74.

26 The first protocol to the IIC implicitly recognised the weakness of the scheme by offering an alternative Special System for the Promotion of Industrial Activities (see Watkins (1967), p. 47). This did not, however, represent an instrument for balanced development.

27 In its first twenty years of existence, CABEI authorised loans valued at $1.57 billion to Central America. Over 40% went to Honduras and Nicaragua (the least developed) compared with 35% for the more developed and more heavily populated El Salvador and Guatemala. See SIECA (1981), pp. 546–7.

28 By 1970, CABEI's rate of return on capital was 7.7%. See Inforpress (1983), p. 126.

29 See Watkins (1967), pp. 53–4.

30 The main exceptions were coffee, cotton, sugar, tobacco, petroleum products and wheat flour. For a complete list, see Watkins (1967), pp. 81–90.

31 See Hansen (1967), p. 27. See also Table C.5 (p. 510) in Appendix C of Cline and Delgado (1978).

32 The ERP measures the percentage change in value added as a result of the tariff system. It is therefore a superior measure of resource allocation than the nominal rate of protection. For measures of the ERP, see Bulmer-Thomas (1976a) and Appendix K of Cline and Delgado (1978).

33 See Joel (1971).

34 The ratification of the FIC (see above, pp. 179–80) in 1969 did not make much difference. New industries continued to be very generously treated, although the concessions to existing industries were made more modest (*ibid.*, pp. 233–4).

35 In 1960, at the start of the CACM, the proportion of government revenue obtained from import duties varied from 32% in Guatemala to 54% in Costa Rica. See SIECA (1967), p. 99.

36 The remainder was accounted for by tariffs foregone on public sector imports. See DGEC, *Comercio Exterior de Costa Rica* (1968), p. xvii. For estimates of tariffs foregone as a result of industrial promotion laws for other republics, see SIECA/INTAL (1973), Vol. 10, p. 147.

37 See SIECA/INTAL (1973), Vol. 10, pp. 115–25.

38 See Watkins (1967). The figures varied from 2.5% in Costa Rica (p. 468) to 0.2% in Nicaragua (p. 405).

39 See Best (1976).

40 See Joel (1971).

41 Guatemala passed legislation at the end of 1962, after a long delay, introducing a personal income tax for the first time (see Watkins (1967), p. 175). The passage of a new income tax law in El Salvador in December 1963 was also strongly resisted and the income from coffee and cotton growing continued to be exempt (see Watkins (1967), pp. 251–3).

42 In view of the world market conditions facing Central America's traditional exports, there is a case for treating export taxes as direct taxation. See Hinrichs (1974), p. 93, n. 17.

43 *Ibid.*, p. 109.

44 See SIECA/INTAL (1973), Vol. 10, p. 210.

45 See NACLA (1974), pp. 6–7. Mendez Montenegro, the reformist presidential candidate of the Partido Revolucionario (PR), had won the 1966 elections; the latter were untainted by fraud and brought to an end three years of direct military rule, but the new president had already reached a written agreement with the military which reduced considerably his room for manoeuvre. See McClintock (1985), p. 78.

46 See Due (1966), p. 59.

47 The sales tax as applied at 5% in Costa Rica and Nicaragua. See SIECA/INTAL (1973), Vol. 10, p. 189.

48 See NACLA (1974), p. 6.

49 This unpredictability arises from the 'cascading' effect of the stamp duty, which applied to each transaction and therefore had an uncertain impact on the actual tax rate applicable to a commodity by the time it reached the retail stage. See Hinrichs (1974), p. 101, although it should be noted that the same author (p. 102) makes a brave, if unconvincing, statement of the case for stamp duties.

50 See Bulmer-Thomas (1976a), p. 20, table 3, where an estimate is made for Costa Rica of the impact of the San José Protocol on the ERP.

51 Government current savings were negative in all but three of the eleven years from 1960 to 1970. The budget deficit widened from $4.6 million in 1960 to $28.7 million in 1970 with 89% of the accumulated deficit from 1960 to 1970 financed internally. See SIECA/INTAL (1973), Vol. 10, p. 132.

52 *Ibid.*, p. 130.

53 Coffee growers in Honduras, it must be remembered, were a relatively new social force and were mainly represented by small- and medium-sized farmers.

54 This was true during the presidencies of both Francisco Orlich (1962–6) of the PLN and José Joaquín Trejos (1966–70) of the Partido Unificación Nacional (PUN). Both parties, despite the rhetoric, shared similar views on the role of the state and were subject to much the same pressures from business and labour groups.

55 As a result, the regional economy became *more*, not less, dependent on EXA. See Castillo (1966), p. 97.

56 The multinational fruit companies in the banana industry continued to enjoy zero duties for most imports under their special contracts.

57 Since EXA is sold in world markets, it cannot benefit from tariff protection in the home market; the ERP must therefore be zero or negative. In the case of Costa Rica, the ERP for EXA has been estimated at −2.1% (a negligible figure). See Bulmer-Thomas (1976a), p. 19, table 2.

58 Nominal exchange rate stability coupled with very modest inflation produced a mild real appreciation.

59 In Guatemala, bank lending for industrial and real estate purposes grew very rapidly, squeezing the agricultural share.

60 Table 9.3 excludes lending to agriculture by the Central Bank (very important in El Salvador) and the Development Banks.

61 The regional total at the end of 1970 was $160 million for industry compared with $440 million for agriculture. See Consejo Monetario Centroamericano (1972), p. 28.

62 The source for this is the Memoria of the Central Bank in each republic.

63 It had reached 5% of total credit to agriculture by 1969/70 compared with 0.9% in 1960/1. See Cabarrus (1983), p. 68, table 6.

64 See SIECA/INTAL (1973), Vol. 4, pp. 109–10.

65 *Ibid.*

66 See *Area Handbook for Nicaragua* (1970), p. 316.

67 Insects developed immunity to the constant spraying with insecticides and yields fell sharply. For the case of El Salvador, see White (1973), pp. 129–30.

68 Production in Costa Rica declined after 1965 and collapsed after 1968. Most of the textile industry's requirements have since been met by imports.

69 See Grunwald and Musgrove (1970), pp. 314–18.

70 See White (1973), pp. 125–6.

71 The growth of coffee production in Costa Rica was interrupted in the early 1960s by volcanic eruptions, but it grew rapidly from 1965 onwards.

72 The rise in the unit value for sugar occurred despite the fall in the free market price, thus emphasising the dependence of sugar exports on the US market.

73 See Ellis (1983), pp. 139–50, table C.16 (pp. 415–16), and table C.18 (p. 418).

74 See Ellis (1983), pp. 123–6.

75 At that time, coffee and bananas alone accounted for the bulk of exports.

76 In Costa Rica, the rise of EXA was interrupted by volcanic eruptions. See n. 71.

77 The classic study of seasonal migration is Lester Schmid's work on Guatemala (see Schmid, 1973). There is also a useful survey for all Central America in CSUCA (1978), Anexo No. 3.

78 The export zones had been poles of attraction for permanent rural–rural migration in the 1950s everywhere except El Salvador. See Chapter 8, pp. 161–2.

79 The proportion of the labour force classified as in agriculture was as follows:

| | Census Year | % | Census Year | % |
|---|---|---|---|---|
| Costa Rica | 1973 | 36.4 | 1963 | 49.1 |
| El Salvador | 1971 | 46.7 | 1961 | 60.3 |
| Guatemala | 1973 | 57.2 | 1964 | 64.7 |
| Honduras | 1974 | 60.4 | 1961 | 66.8 |
| Nicaragua | 1971 | 47.0 | 1963 | 59.7 |

80 The net arable land/man ratio is the arable land and permanent crop area (net of EXA) divided by the agricultural labour force. This ratio deteriorated

for all republics in the 1960s, the deterioration being most severe in El Salvador. See Bulmer-Thomas (1983), p. 290, table 5.

81 During the 1960s, it is legitimate to treat livestock as an export product. DUA is therefore defined as value added in agriculture exclusive of coffee, bananas, cotton, sugar and livestock.

82 Land reform legislation and implementation are reviewed in Monteforte Toledo (1972), Vol. 1, pp. 255–72.

83 In El Salvador, where land reform legislation was not passed, the Instituto de Colonización Rural was established to settle landless families on small plots of (vacant) land. This was not unlike the practice of land reform in other republics, although the progress in El Salvador was even slower (*ibid.*, p. 272).

84 See SIECA/INTAL (1973), Vol. 4, pp. 102–6.

85 Between 1962 and 1969, the number of cooperatives in Costa Rica grew from 54 to 240 and the membership from 13,200 to 54,547. Cooperative membership therefore exceeded 20% of the agricultural labour force by the end of the decade. See Wilkie (1982), table 1409.

86 See Hall (1982), pp. 164–5.

87 See Villarreal (1983), p. 86.

88 See Meza (1981), p. 120.

89 See SIECA/INTAL (1973), Vol. 4, p. 102, table 39.

90 The yield (output per hectare) rose by 68% in El Salvador for maize from 1965 to 1970 and at the end of the decade exceeded the average in the rest of Central America by 64%. The yield for rice and beans also rose rapidly in contrast to the general performance elsewhere in Central America.

91 See SIECA/INTAL (1973), Vol. 4, ch. 2.

92 See Banco Central de Costa Rica (1970), p. 49.

93 By 1970, 43.2% of all farm lands were devoted to pasture. The figure was lowest in Guatemala (29.8%) and highest in Nicaragua (51.8%). See SIECA (1981), p. 114, table 72.

94 The proportion of the agricultural labour force without land by 1970 averaged 27.7% for all Central America without much variation among the republics. When, however, one adds those with farms of less than 0.7 hectares (the *microfincas*) the figure rises to over 50% in Costa Rica and El Salvador and over 40% in Guatemala and Honduras (*ibid.*, p. 115).

95 Minimum wage legislation was finally extended to rural labour in El Salvador in 1965. See White (1973), pp. 118–20, who argues that women and children may in fact have been seriously disadvantaged by the law. Nicaragua amended its labour code in 1962 and set up a National Minimum Wage Commission (see *Area Handbook for Nicaragua* (1970), p. 252).

96 The Gini coefficient for agricultural income has been estimated for 1970. The highest (i.e., the most unequal) was for El Salvador, closely followed by Guatemala, with coefficients suggesting an extremely skewed distribution of income. The lowest figure was for Nicaragua, with Honduras and Costa Rica in the middle. See SIECA/INTAL (1973), Vol. 4, p. 82, table 34.

97 There is an excellent study of nutritional trends in *ibid.*, ch. 3.

98 See Willmore (1976), p. 501.

99 See Rosenthal (1973).

100 There is a good study of foreign investment in manufacturing in Guatemala in Poitevin (1977), ch. 3.

101 See Bulmer-Thomas (1982), p. 255.

102 See, for example, Bodenheimer (1981).

103 See Willmore (1976), p. 501.
104 See SIECA/INTAL (1973), Vol. 9, p. 102, quoted in Willmore (1976), p. 502, table 4.
105 See Weeks (1985), p. 136.
106 *Ibid.*, p. 138.
107 See Frank (1978), p. 158.
108 There is a useful study of the small-scale industrial sector in Costa Rica in Santos and Herrera (1979).
109 See Inforpress (1983a), p. 48 and p. 56, n. 5.
110 The number of trade unions and the total membership almost doubled between 1965 and 1970 (see Menjívar (1982), p. 137). In 1968, the first of the teachers' strikes took place in El Salvador, giving rise to the organisation ANDES 21 de junio and marking a sharp increase in the politicisation of the middle class.
111 Intra-regional exports exceeded 30% of all exports by the end of the decade in El Salvador and Guatemala compared with only 10% in Honduras. See Bulmer-Thomas (1982), p. 244, table 12.2.
112 See Inforpress (1983), p. 65.
113 See Durham (1979), p. 61
114 See Inforpress (1983), p. 50.
115 The other republics had already agreed to these obligations.
116 The Somoza dynasty came under considerable political pressure in the 1960s, but responded with economic concessions. Wage policy was fairly lax and urban real wages rose significantly (see Banco Central de Nicaragua (1970), p. 307).
117 Table 9.7 does not provide figures for agriculture in El Salvador in 1960, but related evidence (reviewed on pp. 180–90) strongly suggests a deterioration in the wage share.
118 See Reynolds (1978), p. 243, table 25.
119 For the case of El Salvador, see White (1973), pp. 106–7. In Guatemala, the military intervened when it became clear that President Ydígoras Fuentes planned to allow ex-President Arévalo to return and stand for election. In Honduras, the prospect of a victory by the Liberal Party presidential candidate Modesto Rodas Alvarado, a populist and demagogue, provoked military intervention ten days before the elections.
120 The proxies as president were René Schick from 1963 until his death in 1966 and Lorenzo Guerrero from 1966 to 1967. See Millett (1979), pp. 301–4.
121 See Webre (1979), pp. 77–81. The successful candidate for mayor was José Napoleon Duarte.
122 In Honduras, however, much of the increase took place after the war with El Salvador. López Arellano, following the coup in 1963, had described the labour movement as one of the two 'new forces' in Honduran politics (the other being the military), but it was the support of the labour movement for the government in the war which convinced the military that trade unionism need not represent a subversive force. See Meza (1981), ch. 6.
123 See Reynolds (1978), pp. 188–9.
124 See Menjívar (1982), p. 137.
125 See Rosenberg (1983), p. 210, table 6.
126 *Ibid.*, p. 207, table 3.
127 Counter-insurgency in Guatemala in the 1960s, heavily influenced by a US Military Assistance Programme, saw the defeat of guerrilla activity as a purely military matter. See McClintock (1985), pp. 54–75.

128 The Organización Democrática Nacionalista (ORDEN) was created by President Rivera and General José Alberto ('Chele') Medrano in the middle 1960s; it was a counter-revolutionary organisation, which recruited heavily from the peasantry and in return granted small favours (e.g., access to health services). See Cabarrus (1983), p. 43.

## 10 External shocks and the challenge to the social order, 1970–9

1 See table 9.1 in Bulmer-Thomas (1985), p. 132.
2 See table 3 in Siri (1982), p. 310.
3 A new International Coffee Agreement was signed in 1968, but the Brazilian frost led to the suspension of export quotas.
4 See Economist Intelligence Unit, *Quarterly Economic Review of Guatemala, El Salvador and Honduras*, No. 2, 1978, p. 8.
5 Production was affected by drought in Costa Rica (see Banco de Costa Rica, *Memoria*, 1977, p. 47). Yields were still high, however, and had overtaken El Salvador's as the highest in Central America by 1977.
6 See Burbach and Flynn (1983), pp. 177–86.
7 See Ellis (1983), pp. 331–8.
8 Nicaragua was not a member of UPEB and did not apply the tax.
9 See Ellis (1983), p. 343.
10 The main victim of Hurricane Fifi was Honduras, but Guatemala also suffered.
11 See Díaz-Franjul (1982), p. 169.
12 Production in Costa Rica was stimulated by the establishment of a state cotton ginning plant (Algodones de Costa Rica S.A.). See Vega (1982), pp. 75–6.
13 An important factor in the decline in yields was the increase in costs of fertilisers after the first oil crisis.
14 There is an excellent case study of the beef industry in Honduras in Slutsky (1979), pp. 101–204.
15 Cardamom had been exported from Guatemala for years, but production accelerated rapidly after 1970 and it had become the third most valuable export (after coffee and cotton) by 1978. See Guerra Borges (1981) pp. 256–8.
16 African palm cultivation was expanded on abandoned banana lands in the early 1970s. See Villarreal (1983), pp. 73–4.
17 From 62% in 1970 to 65% in 1979.
18 Population growth rates (annual averages) are estimated as follows:

| | Costa Rica | El Salvador | Guatemala | Honduras | Nicaragua |
|---|---|---|---|---|---|
| 1950–60 | 3.7 | 2.8 | 2.8 | 3.3 | 2.9 |
| 1960–70 | 3.4 | 3.5 | 2.8 | 3.1 | 3.0 |
| 1970–7 | 2.5 | 3.1 | 2.9 | 3.3 | 3.3 |

(See World Bank, *World Tables*, 1980, 2nd edition.) By the mid-1970s, Costa Rica had entered the 'demographic transition', with the Crude Death Rate (CDR) down to a floor of five per thousand and the Crude Birth Rate (CBR) still falling. Elsewhere, falls in the two rates tended to be equal leaving population growth rates roughly the same.

19 Infant mortality, which had been running at a high rate in the 1960s everywhere except Costa Rica, dropped rapidly in the 1970s. The infant mortality rate (per thousand) was as follows:

| | Costa Rica | El Salvador | Guatemala | Honduras | Nicaragua |
|---|---|---|---|---|---|
| 1960 | 83.1 | 135.5 | 91.9 | 144.7 | 144.0 |
| 1970 | 58.3 | 106.5 | 87.1 | 117.4 | 115.6 |
| 1975 | 40.1 | 92.9 | 81.1 | 103.1 | 102.7 |
| 1980 | 27.5 | 77.9 | 65.9 | 88.5 | 90.5 |

(See World Bank, *World Tables*, Vol. 2, 1984, 3rd edition.)

20 The most careful study of land invasions in this period is for Costa Rica (see Villarreal (1983)). They occurred throughout the region, however, and new rural labour organisations were born as a result (see pp. 223–4).

21 See North (1981), pp. 68–9.

22 Significantly the new institution set up to oversee the process (Instituto Salvadoreño de Transformación Agraria – ISTA) did not carry the word 'reform'.

23 The private landowners of eastern El Salvador created a new lobby (Frente de Agricultores de la Región Oriental – FARO) and joined forces with the rest of the private sector, organised in the Asociación Nacional de Empresas Privadas – ANEP, to defeat the land reform legislation. ANEP included industrialists, merchants and financiers, as well as landlords, all of whom interpreted land reform as an attack on the whole institution of private property. See Dunkerley (1982), p. 65.

24 See Downing (1978), pp. 27–8.

25 The Franja Transversal runs from Lake Izabal in the east almost to the western extremity of the country with only the Petén district to the north. It therefore represents the area linking the over-populated Indian highlands with the under-populated lowlands. See Instituto Nacional de Transformacion Agraria (1984).

26 The 1979 Agricultural Census revealed that over half the production of basic grains came from medium- and large-scale farms. See Dirección General de Estadística, *III Censo Nacional Agropecuario*, Vol. 2, Tomo 1, 1983, tables 1 to 10, Guatemala.

27 See Serna (1982), p. 2.

28 The construction boom after the earthquake in December 1972 attracted rural migrants to Managua, putting additional obstacles in the path of increasing basic grains production.

29 See Programa Regional Del Empleo para America Latina y El Caribe (PREALC) (1979), pp. ii.9 and v.7.

30 See Bulmer-Thomas (1983), p. 290.

31 The 1974 agricultural census showed that the largest class of farms (greater than 500 hectares) contained 22.1% of the farm area. See Instituto Hondureño de Desarrollo Rural (IHDER) (1981), p. 72. In the previous census (1965/6), the proportion had been 27.5%.

32 The SIECA proposals, sometimes known as the Rosenthal Report after the distinguished Guatemalan economist who headed the team of experts, are contained in SIECA/INTAL/IDB, *El Desarrollo Integrado de Centroamerica en la Presente Década: Bases y Propuestas para el Perfeccionamiento y la Reestructuración del Mercado Común Centroamericano*, 13 vols., Buenos Aires, 1973/4. A good critique of the proposals is contained in Lizano (1975).

33 In 1978, Nicaragua threatened to impose a 30% tariff on imports from CACM (subsequently the proposal was dropped), and Costa Rica closed its border with Nicaragua in an attempt to force the resignation of Somoza. The only hopeful sign for the CACM was the appointment of a former Peruvian president,

Sr José Luis Bustamente y Rivero, as a mediator in the dispute between El Salvador and Honduras. He began his work in January 1978.

34  The sharpest fall was recorded by El Salvador. CACM exports were 40.1% of total exports in 1968 and fell to 21.8% in 1977. See SIECA (1981), p. 326.

35  The recession in 1975, provoked by adjustment programmes in several republics (see pp. 212–13), also produced a virtual stagnation in CACM trade in that year.

36  The main state institution promoting industrialisation in El Salvador was the Instituto Salvadoreño de Fomento Industrial (INSAFI), while in Nicaragua it was the Instituto de Fomento Nacional (INFONAL). Both pre-dated the 1970s (INSAFI was founded in 1961, INFONAL in 1950).

37  See Vega (1982). By 1977, the public sector's share of industrial value added was 5.5% compared with 2.9% in 1973. See Banco Central de Costa Rica, *Cuentas Nacionales de Costa Rica 1973–82*, tables 18 and 34, San José, 1983.

38  The state's involvement in production activities in Honduras also included forestry, and the Corporación Hondureña de Desarrollo Forestal (COHDEFOR) was set up in 1974 (see Montes (1982), p. 46). Both Honduras and Guatemala also founded new state financial institutions to promote industry: the Fondo Nacional de Desarrollo Industrial (FONDEI) in Honduras and the Banco Industrial (privately owned, but government sponsored) in Guatemala.

39  Both Costa Rica and Guatemala had raised the share of commercial bank credit allocated to industry to 25% by 1979. In both republics, the value of industrial credit increased by nearly 500% between 1970 and 1979. See SIECA (1981), pp. 536–9.

40  Central bank lending to industry (not included in commercial bank figures) was, however, more important in El Salvador than elsewhere.

41  Costa Rica was also the republic which made the greatest effort to raise the skill level of its labour force. The number of workers graduating from the state Instituto Nacional de Aprendizaje (INA) rose from 3,539 in 1970 to 55,008 in 1977. Honduras also made a substantial effort in the same field, although starting much later than Costa Rica; the Instituto Hondureño de Formación Professional (INFOP) was created by law at the end of 1972 and in 1979 nearly 22,000 workers graduated.

42  Input–output tables for the 1970s yield the following information on the importance of imported inputs for industry:

| | Costa Rica (1972) | Nicaragua (1974) | Honduras (1975) | Guatemala (1978) |
|---|---|---|---|---|
| Imported inputs as % of gross output | 24.7 | 19.4 | 36.9 | 21.5 |
| Imported inputs as % of total intermediate inputs | 39.9 | 29.1 | 49.3 | 38.6 |

(See SIECA (1982), pp. 207, 179, 176. For Costa Rica, see CEPAL (1983), p. 167.)

43  The ratio of import taxes to extra-regional imports for all Central America fell from 15.6% in 1970 to 9.3% in 1979.

44  As implied, for example, by the slower growth of domestic manufacturing prices compared with the price of imported inputs. See Weeks (1985), p. 149.

45  Defined conventionally, if inaccurately, as firms with less than five employees.

46 See Santos and Herrera (1979), Part II. In 1975, the artisan sector represented a mere 1.6% of the total value of industrial production.

47 The census revealed 42,192 firms with employment of 66,232 workers. The value of total production was 5% of national industrial output. See Dirección General de Estadística, *I Censo Artesanal 1978*, Guatemala, 1982.

48 The contract signed by the Guatemalan government with EXMIBAL, the foreign mining company, stirred up a host of nationalist passions. See Instituto de Investigaciones Económicas y Sociales (1979).

49 In 1975, Guatemala passed a new petroleum law giving the government a 55–60% share of revenues. See Economist Intelligence Unit (1981), pp. 41–3.

50 See Weeks (1985), p. 149.

51 See Oficina de Planificación (1974), pp. 90–6.

52 These included devaluation in 1974, when the colón was unified at the higher rate (¢8.6 per US dollar).

53 The percentage of income received by the lowest 20% of households fell from 5.7% in 1961 to 3.3% in 1971. This was scarcely different from the rest of Central America (see World Bank, *World Tables*, Vol. II, Social Data, 1984 (3rd ed.).

54 See, for example, Siri and Dominguez (1981).

55 See Bulmer-Thomas (1977).

56 In Nicaragua, the windfall gains occurred only in 1973 and 1974; export duties were subsequently lowered and the yield from 1975 onwards was negligible.

57 The yield from the banana tax was not unimpressive. Figures in $million (as a percentage of nominal GDP in brackets) were as follows for the three Central American members of UPEB:

| | Costa Rica | Guatemala | Honduras |
|------|------------|-----------|----------|
| 1974 | 8.0 (0.5) | 0.28 (–) | 4.1 (0.4) |
| 1975 | 22.3 (1.1) | 0.43 (–) | 6.0 (0.5) |
| 1976 | 24.0 (1.0) | 6.23 (0.1) | 11.1 (0.9) |
| 1977 | 23.7 (0.8) | 6.66 (0.1) | 17.2 (1.1) |
| 1978 | 23.0 (0.7) | 7.57 (0.1) | 15.2 (0.8) |
| 1979 | 24.2 (0.6) | 6.50 (0.1) | 24.2 (1.1) |

(See IMF, *Government Financial Statistics Yearbook*, 1984.)

58 A complete list of these transfers occupies nearly 200 pages in the 300-page annual report on fiscal expenditure. See, for example, Controloría General de la Republica (1974).

59 The Carazo administration (1978–82) initially tackled monetary and fiscal reform boldly. Social security expenditure was cut, contributions were increased and interest rates were liberalised. The experiment soon turned sour, however, and the fiscal gap reached critical levels. See Chapter 11, pp. 237–44.

60 The greatest proportionate and absolute increase was in Honduras, where the road network nearly trebled from 4,940 kilometres in 1970 to 12,316 kilometres in 1979. See SIECA (1981), p. 445.

61 This ratio, defined as the proportion of those of secondary school age enrolled in secondary school, doubled or nearly doubled everywhere except El Salvador in the 1970s. In 1979, the ratio was 48% in Costa Rica, 16% in Guatemala and around 30% elsewhere. See World Bank, *World Tables*, Vol. 2, 1984 (3rd ed.).

62 This is borne out by Table 10.6, giving real public expenditure per person on education and health.

63 See, for example, Booth (1982), p. 81.

64 The rise in the budget deficit as a proportion of GDP in Guatemala, however, was restrained until 1979 by traditional conservative fiscal policies.

65 In El Salvador the rate of capital formation (ratio of gross fixed capital formation to GDP) dropped from 22.4% in 1978 to 18.6% in 1979. In Nicaragua it collapsed from 24.3% in 1977 to 7.7% in 1979.

66 Honduras, furthermore, cannot be considered an exception, as public investment rose very rapidly and private investment (which grew even more rapidly) was stimulated by the public sector (e.g., loans from CONADI).

67 Net DFI did increase in the 1970s, but it was not a very dynamic factor and its share of total investment tended to decline; net DFI turned negative in El Salvador and Nicaragua in 1979.

68 A share in excess of 100% suggests over-funding, which in turn implies waste and/or corruption.

69 There is a very detailed study for Guatemala of public capital expenditure in this period, which was dominated (as elsewhere in Central America) by electrification programmes. See Instituto de Investigaciones Económicas y Sociales (1978).

70 There is no doubt that the Lucas administration was highly corrupt. This does not necessarily imply, however, that foreign credits were misused.

71 Defined as the ratio of interest and amortization payments on the public external debt to merchandise exports.

72 It exceeded double figures in every year from 1970 to 1979 and reached 22% in 1973.

73 The proportions in Nicaragua and Costa Rica were 61.4% and 76.5% respectively. See Dierckxsens and Campanario (1983), p. 8.

74 Almost by definition, families operating *microfincas* were obliged to hire out their labour services off-farm for much of the year. The proportion of farmers in *microfincas* rose sharply from the 1960s to 1970s. The most dramatic case was Guatemala, where a comparison of the 1964 with the 1979 agricultural census shows an increase from 20.4% to 41.1%.

75 Only Honduras (after 1974) recorded a significant increase in registered unemployment and this was due mainly to lay-offs in the banana industry (see above, pp. 203–4). PREALC has estimated un- and under-employment rates at the end of the decade as follows:

| | Costa Rica | El Salvador | Guatemala | Honduras | Nicaragua |
|---|---|---|---|---|---|
| Unemployment rate | 5.9 | 7.4 | 3.2 | 14.3 | 11.8 |
| Underemployment rate (unemployed equivalent) | 7.5 | 25.5 | 31.4 | 27.4 | 10.9 |

(See PREALC (1983), table 2.) The PREALC method of estimating underemployment is very crude, but the figures above hardly suggest an improvement in labour market conditions over the 1970s.

76 See Posas (1981), pp. 18–19.

77 See Berryman (1984), p. 175.

78  See Seligson (1980), pp. 37–8.
79  See Lizano (1981), p. 367.
80  See Orellana and Cancino (1981), pp. 20–2.
81  In three out of four years (from 1974/5 to 1977/8) Nicaragua had the lowest recorded annual rate of inflation (see Table 10.1) in Central America. These rates look suspiciously low, so that the 'improvement' in rural real wages may be artificial.
82  Social security contributions exceeded expenditure in several years during the 1970s in Honduras.
83  See Rosenberg (1983), ch. 7.
84  The incoming Carazo administration turned a 'loss' of $55 million on social security in 1977 into a 'profit' of $90 million in 1978 and $137 million in 1979.
85  The programme was called Formación de las Empresas Campesinas; see Villarreal (1983), p. 96.
86  The province where land invasions were most frequent was Guanacaste; the latter had been the centre of the beef industry expansion.
87  See Meza (1981), p. 147.
88  *Ibid.*, p. 148.
89  See Posas (1981), p. 31.
90  *Ibid.*, p. 32.
91  For a useful review of the land reform programme in Honduras, see Ruhl (1984), pp. 49–56.
92  The Confederación General de Sindicatos (CGS) in El Salvador, for example, had been established with the approval of President Lemus in 1958 and received funds from AIFLD.
93  The Costa Rican labour federation eventually supported by AIFLD, the Confederación Costarricense de Trabajadores Democráticos (CCTD), had originally been founded in 1943 by Father Benjamin Nuñez as an anti-communist organisation without any US support.
94  The Catholic church played an important part in this organisational work (see Berryman, 1984), since even highly authoritarian states felt that labour organisations controlled by the Catholic church would be 'safe'. The success and independence of Social Christian labour groups, however, eventually produced a clash between the state and sections of the Catholic church (notably in El Salvador, Guatemala and Nicaragua) and radical Catholic priests became a target for right-wing death squads.
95  The communist Confederación de Trabajadores de Costa Rica (CTCR) had been banned after the 1948 civil war (see Chapter 7, pp. 136–7) and only re-emerged (as the CGT) in the late 1950s.
96  Ever since the strike in the Honduran banana industry in 1954, the vanguard of the labour movement had been represented by the Sindicato de Trabajadores de la Tela Railroad Co. (SITRATERCO), the union representing banana workers in UFCO. The equivalent organisation for Standard Fruit was the Sindicato Unificado de Trabajadores de la Standard Fruit Co. (SUTRASFCO). The labour movement in Honduras, and banana workers in particular, had been a principal target for ORIT and AIFLD in the 1950s and 1960s, but changes in the leadership of SITRATERCO in 1975 brought to an end ORIT's dominance. See Meza (1981), pp. 155–60.
97  See Berryman (1984), p. 109.
98  See McClintock (1985), p. 128.

99 See Black (1981), p. 101.
100 In El Salvador, for example, the proportion of unionised workers affiliated to the CGS (the labour federation linked to ORIT) declined from 42% in 1971 to 19% in 1976. See Dunkerley (1982), p. 59.
101 See Posas (1981), p. 34.
102 See Frundt (1985).
103 The Confederación Unificada de Trabajadores Salvadoreños (CUTS), formed by dissident urban labour unions in El Salvador, posed a real threat to the CGS by the mid-1970s. See Dunkerley (1982), p. 59.
104 Between 1963 and 1976 over 60% of the increase in union membership was in services, 30% in agriculture and only 9% in industry. See Rojas Bolaños (1981), p. 27.
105 See Booth (1982), p. 122.
106 Of the fifteen main strikes in El Salvador between 1974 and 1977, seven ended in defeat. See Menjívar (1982), p. 159.
107 Laugerud, for example, met with the unofficial CNUS, thereby giving it semi-legal status.
108 See Dunkerley (1982), p. 99.
109 ANDES, the teachers' organisation, had led a major strike in 1968 with political overtones.
110 See Dunkerley (1982), p. 101.
111 See McClintock (1985), p. 155.
112 For an autobiographical account of how one CUC member came to join the guerrillas, see Burgos-Debray (1984).
113 The pro-Moscow PSN split in the early 1970s, one splinter becoming the Partido Comunista de Nicaragua, and the PSN gradually lost influence over those labour groups, such as construction workers, whose loyalty it had traditionally enjoyed.
114 The FSLN was subject to its own internal difficulties, being split three ways from 1975 until March 1979, but the military success of each group proved a powerful attraction for the weak labour movement.
115 Even in Nicaragua. See Chapter 9, pp. 197–8.
116 The Communist Party (Partido Vanguardia Popular) was not legalised until 1970 (it had been banned after the 1948 civil war). Its leader, Manuel Mora, was elected to parliament in 1970 under the banner of the Partido Acción Socialista.
117 The Christian Democrats had not been allowed to participate in the 1980 elections on 'technical' grounds.
118 See Dunkerley (1982), p. 98.
119 Personal information from a former US Assistant Secretary of State for Inter-American Affairs.
120 Turner Shelton, appointed ambassador to Nicaragua in 1970, seems to have been a particularly inappropriate choice. See Black (1981), pp. 57–8.
121 As it did with Costa Rica in the early 1970s.
122 President Molina actually expelled AIFLD from El Salvador in 1976. See Dunkerley (1982), p. 111.
123 It is examined in detail in Keogh (1984), pp. 153–83.

## 11 The descent into regional crisis

1 Honduras, Guatemala and El Salvador abstained on the crucial vote in the OAS on 22 June 1979, which proposed the immediate resignation of Somoza.

The latter also requested the intervention of CONDECA to give military support to the National Guard, but the three northern republics again refused to intervene. See Black (1981), pp. 177–8.

2 The first junta included a leading industrialist and representative of the private sector, Alfonso Robelo, together with Violeta Barrios de Chamorro (widow of the murdered Pedro Joaquín Chamorro). The remaining three members were all supporters of the FSLN, although that was not fully appreciated at the time. See Payne (1985), p. 17.

3 The published programme of the FSLN stressed three features: a mixed economy, political pluralism and a nonaligned foreign policy. See Booth (1982), p. 147.

4 The APP within a short period represented around 20% of net output in the agricultural sector, 30% in the manufacturing sector and some 50% in the tertiary sector, giving the APP an overall weight of 40% in GDP. See Vilas (1986), table 4.1, p. 156.

5 Arturo Cruz, the first president of the Central Bank after the fall of Somoza, wrote: 'These measures were predicated on the fact that it was necessary to reassure depositors, preserve Nicaragua's international credit, guarantee a more effective collection of foreign exchange revenues and taxes, and provide higher prices to producers'. Cruz wrote these words *after* he had joined the opposition to the Sandinistas. See Cruz (1983), p. 1035.

6 There had been a clear understanding among the non-Sandinistas in the broad alliance before the fall of Somoza that the National Guard would be abolished and replaced with an apolitical army.

7 The CDS were clearly based on the neighbourhood defence committees in Cuba and their administrative functions became increasingly important after rationing was introduced.

8 They abstained on the vote in the United Nations.

9 Congress provided for the suspension of the aid if labour or press freedoms were seen to be infringed, if the funds were spent in schools or other institutions employing Cubans or if Nicaragua were to finance insurgency movements elsewhere. See Economist Intelligence Unit (1980), pp. 11–12.

10 See Keogh (1984), pp. 173–4.

11 Only the Ejercito Revolucionario del Pueblo (ERP), a guerrilla group founded in 1972 by dissident Christian Democrats, responded to the coup on 15 October with a call to arms.

12 See Dunkerley (1982), pp. 137–44.

13 The most important defection was that of Rubén Zamora, Minister of the Presidency in the first junta, who became a leading spokesman for the FDR.

14 See Browning (1983), pp. 419–23.

15 The election results have been carefully analysed in Baloyra (1982), ch. 8.

16 The *bolsones* were disputed pockets of territories claimed by both countries.

17 See Morris (1984), p. 37.

18 Alvarez led the military intervention in February 1977 against the Empresa Asociativa Campesina 'Isletas', a cooperative formed on lands expropriated from Standard Fruit. The leadership of the cooperative was imprisoned for two years on charges that were never proved. See Posas (1981), p. 44.

19 APROH brought together the main representatives of the private sector under the presidency of Alvarez Martínez. See Centro de Documentación de Honduras (CEDOH) (1984).

20 The Carter administration had already cut off military aid to Guatemala even before the Lucas régime took office.

21 See Instituto Guatemalteco de Seguridad Social (1983), tables 1 and 2.
22 For the most part, the campaign appears to have been quite unjustified.
23 The programme is described in Ministerio de Hacienda (1980). It is discussed more critically in Rivera Urrutia (1982), pp. 77–91.
24 The Guatemalan quetzal had been at par with the US dollar since 1925 and the official rate of exchange in El Salvador had not changed since 1934. Both countries finally devalued at the beginning of 1986.
25 The Sandinistas in 1979 were very successful in convincing North Americans and Western Europeans that they were representatives of a broad-based government which would not interfere with capitalist relations of production. The capitalist class in Central America was suspicious from the start and capital flight was one way of hedging their bets.
26 Table 11.1 suggests that capital flight was not a problem in Honduras. This contradicts a number of contemporary reports (including those provided by the US embassy) and suggests that capital flight from Honduras was concealed. Perhaps it is no accident that the BOP entry 'net errors and omissions' was strongly negative in 1979 and 1980.
27 See Bulmer-Thomas (1985), table 9.1.
28 The small decline was not enough, however, to justify calling this period one of adjustment.
29 Figures are not available on private investment in Nicaragua after the revolution, but it is generally agreed that it also fell to very low levels.
30 It is assumed that virtually all of the increase in investment in Nicaragua can be attributed to the public sector.
31 See table 9.3 in Bulmer-Thomas (1985).
32 In Nicaragua, however, this ratio was nearer 2:1. See Bulmer-Thomas (1987), table 5.
33 The only sharp changes in velocity were in Costa Rica in 1981 (which can be explained by the conversion of both nominal GDP and the money stock into dollars at the rapidly depreciating exchange rates) and Nicaragua in 1983, when excess money creation was a very serious problem (*ibid.*).
34 We should therefore distinguish between the initial capital flight from Central America, which was accommodated by a (passive) financial system, and a later stage of capital flight which was fuelled by the financial system as a result of irresponsible fiscal policies during the FN stage.
35 For details of these agreements, see Bulmer-Thomas (1987), table 7.
36 At the start of the IMF programme, the maximum ceiling for interest rates on commercial bank credits was raised from 11% to 15%; at the end of the programme it was lowered to 12%.
37 See Rivera Urrutia (1982), pp. 154–5.
38 See Bulmer-Thomas (1987), table 7.
39 The Guatemalan standby credit of 1983 was in fact suspended in July 1984 due to the government's failure to meet performance criteria; it is still correct, however, to think of adjustment in Guatemala in two stages: one without and one with conditionality.
40 By December 1981, the parallel market rate was 3.50 colones per US dollar compared with 2.50 in the official market.
41 In Nicaragua, on the other hand, the gap grew progressively wider. While the parallel market remained at 28.50 córdobas per US dollar, the black market rate stood at 70 by the end of 1983.
42 See Rivera Urrutia (1982), p. 165.

43 The inflation rate reached 9.2% in 1979, 18.2% in 1980, 37% in 1981 and 90.1% in 1982. By 1984, it had fallen back to 12% with changes in the inflation rate determined primarily by exchange rate movements. For a fuller discussion of recent inflation in Central America, see Bulmer-Thomas (1987).

44 Some efforts were made to discriminate in favour of CACM, but they were not sufficient to cancel the forces working in the opposite direction.

45 Between mid-1981 and mid-1983, Guatemala received no major credits from private sources.

46 Agreement had also been reached by Nicaragua with its creditors on part of its debts in the FN phase. See Weinert (1981), pp. 187–94.

47 See Maxfield and Stahler-Sholk (1985), p. 261.

48 The Salvadorean programme was extremely flexible, so that the risk of suspension was minimal. The charge that the agreement was politically motivated has been made by several observers; see, for example, Arias Peñate (1983).

49 Costa Rican electricity price increases, for example, were suspended in July 1983 as a result of public opposition.

50 The most notorious are the Corporación Costarricense de Desarrollo in Costa Rica and the Corporación Nacional de Inversiones in Honduras; the Corporación Financiera Nacional was also a heavy loss-maker in Guatemala (see Chapter 10, pp. 208–9).

51 There is a good description of the scheme in Gonzalez (1984), pp. 157–65.

52 The CBI offered duty-free entry to the US markets for almost all commodities for a twelve-year period. The scheme applied to all countries of the Caribbean Basin except Cuba, Nicaragua and Guyana. See Feinberg (1984).

53 Inflation rates outside Costa Rica started to decline after 1980 in response to the impact of the world recession on imported dollar prices. This favourable trend was cancelled by rapid exchange rate depreciation in Costa Rica from 1980 to 1982 and by monetary instability in Nicaragua after 1982.

54 Recorded debt service ratios can be misleading, because they exclude payments of interest or principal due but not paid. Nevertheless, the Costa Rican debt service ratio reached 50.6% in 1983 and it rose to 35.8% in Nicaragua in 1982. See World Bank, *World Debt Tables*, 1984/5.

55 In the arrangements for rescheduling Costa Rica's debts for 1985/6, the commercial banks agreed to lend $75 million in new loans, but made it clear that no new funds would be forthcoming in future reschedulings.

56 Costa Rica ran a trade surplus in 1982 and Guatemala in 1983, but both were small and the experience was not repeated.

57 Thus Costa Rica, with its massive debt (roughly $2,000 per person at the end of 1985), was still able to maintain debt service payments despite the unwillingness of commercial banks to extend new loans.

58 It can safely be assumed that not all employers respected the new minimum wage rules, particularly in rural areas. Nevertheless, many employers responded by cutting employment (see col. (3) of Table 11.6), so that an increase in real wages for Guatemala during the period 1980–3 is not improbable.

59 See PREALC (1983), table 5. Furthermore, a significant proportion of wage labour is employed in the informal sector, where wage rates are often hard to determine. One recent study estimates that about one-third of the capital city labour force in 1982 was employed in the informal sector. See Haan (1985), p. 16.

60 Credit from the World Bank was frozen in 1982; the Inter-American Development Bank (IDB) approved its last loan for Nicaragua in 1982, although it

was not disbursed until 1984. A $58 million IDB loan was blocked in April 1985, when the USA threatened to reduce its financial commitments to the Bank if the loan was approved.

61 In an interview with the *Financial Times* (9 July 1985), the vice-president of the Central Bank justified the policy as follows: 'At first [1980 and 1981] our expansionist policy brought high levels of growth.... However, external finance began to fall sharply and we were faced with the choice of either stopping growth, or trying to continue with internal finance.'

62 See Banco Interamericano de Desarrollo (1984), table 12.

63 Revenue did rise (by 41.2%) with income tax receipts up by 64.9%, but these efforts were dwarfed by the rise in expenditure (*ibid.*, table 7).

64 See Austin (1985), pp. 15–40, and Colburn (1986), pp. 94–5.

65 By the 1983/4 season, production of rice, beans and sorghum had surpassed pre-revolutionary (1978/9) levels. The growth of maize production was disappointing, however, and the expansion of meat and dairy products was very poor. See Banco Interamericano de Desarrollo (1984), table 17, and Austin et al. (1985), p. 25, table 1.

66 Defined as cotton, coffee, sugar, beef, bananas, shrimps and gold.

67 The crop most seriously affected was coffee. Earnings plunged by 20% despite a rise of 22.8% in its unit value. See IMF, International Financial Statistics, July 1985.

68 Exports to the USA (mainly bananas, meat and shellfish) had been reduced to $57 million by 1984 and new markets were found fairly quickly. Imports from the USA (almost double the value of exports in 1984) proved more difficult to replace, because Nicaraguan machinery (particularly within the private sector) is dependent on US spare parts.

69 See Thome and Kaimonowitz (1985), pp. 303–4.

70 See Luciak (1986), table 1.

71 *Ibid.*, table 3.

72 See Grayson (1985).

73 In the first five years after the revolution, Mexico supplied an estimated $500 million in bilateral aid. This was exceeded by total Soviet bloc aid, but not by the aid of any single Soviet bloc country.

74 Named after the Panamanian island, where they first met.

75 An excellent analysis of the motivation behind the Contadora group can be found in Farer (1985).

76 The crisis was caused by Nicaragua's indication in September 1984 that it was willing to sign the draft treaty in its existing form.

77 The EEC foreign ministers had met in San José in September 1984 with their counterparts from Central America and the Contadora group. The United States was not invited to the meeting.

78 The literacy campaign was launched in 1980 and, according to official figures, reduced the country's illiteracy rate from 50% to 13%.

79 A critical commentary on the 'two-track policy' can be found in Baloyra (1985), pp. 35–62.

80 See Whitehead (1983).

81 Henry Kissinger chaired the National Bipartisan Commission on Central America set up by President Reagan in 1983. The Kissinger Report (1984) endorsed much of the administration's policies towards Central America.

82 See, for example, Romero (1985), pp. 116–29.

83 Following the constituent assembly elections in March 1982, presidential elections (won by José Napoleon Duarte) were held in 1984 and a further election for a legislative assembly was held in 1985, in which the CD gained a majority.

84 A comprehensive treatment of the Nicaraguan elections can be found in Latin American Studies Association (1984).

85 Guatemala held elections for a constituent assembly in 1984. The party securing the largest number of votes was the Christian Democrats, but none of the left-wing parties participated.

86 The Coordinadora Demócrata, a grouping of several moderate political parties and independent trade unions, boycotted the Nicaraguan elections, in which the Sandinista virtual monopoly over the means of communication and its control over the armed forces were clearly important factors.

87 Presidential elections were held in Costa Rica in February 1986 and resulted in victory for Oscar Arias Sanchez, candidate of the PLN.

88 The dominant position of Alvarez lasted from the time he was elected as Head of the Armed Forces in 1982 by the national assembly to the moment he was sent into exile by his fellow officers in March 1984. See CEDOH (1985).

89 This was still true in El Salvador after the Christian Democrat Duarte became president in 1984, although the confidence of the labour movement revived in 1985–6.

90 See Vilas (1985), pp. 128–30.

91 See Frundt (1985). The revival of an independent labour movement continued with the election as president of the Christian Democrat Vinicio Cerezo.

92 Fortunately for Central America, a drought in Brazil in 1985 reduced world supply so that coffee prices soared to record levels at the beginning of 1986.

93 By 1984, for example, oil represented 8.6% of all imports in Costa Rica compared with 13.1% in 1980. The fall in oil prices in 1986 accelerated this decline.

94 The civilian government of President Vinicio Cerezo, who assumed power in January 1986, made it clear, however, that radical land reform was not on his agenda and that his administration would pursue reforms through a tax on idle land.

95 A crippling strike among banana workers on United Brands (formerly UFCO) plantations in 1984 provoked the company into abandoning banana production in Costa Rica after virtually a century of unbroken activity. Subsequent unemployment among former banana workers was a powerful factor behind an increase in land invasions.

96 See Luciak (1986).

97 The Nicaraguan land reform, which at first favoured state farms and cooperatives, came increasingly to favour individual peasant farmers after 1984. This shift in the character of the land reform programme provoked considerable debate. See, for example, Deere (1985).

98 See Envío (1985), pp. 1c–19c.

99 See Robleda (1982), pp. 5–34.

100 For a similar assessment of the gloomy prospects for a political settlement, see Whitehead (1986).

## 12 Conclusions

1 Assuming an annual increase in real GDP per head of two per cent (a strong assumption), it would take 23 years for El Salvador and 28 years for Nicaragua to recover the 1970s peak starting from the 1984 base.

2 The recent decline in the trade coefficient (see Table 12.1) is clearly linked to the depression since 1981 and does not reflect an increase in economic maturity.

3 See, for example, Chenery and Syrquin (1975) on sectoral shares and the causes of their change.

4 The exception is Guatemala from 1929 to 1939, when ISA rather than EXA was the dynamic factor. (The agricultural share for Guatemala in 1939 is, however, biassed upwards by distortions in the underlying statistics – see Methodological Appendix.)

5 EXA is defined here (as in Table A.5) to include coffee, bananas, cotton and sugar. It therefore excludes beef, because domestic demand has always been very important in the case of the latter.

6 The most important exception is Costa Rica in the 1930s (see Table 12.3).

7 Costa Rica was temporarily replaced by Guatemala from 1936 to 1942. This, however, corresponds to the period when the Guatemalan figures are distorted upwards (see Methodological Appendix).

8 Preliminary figures for 1985 suggest that bottom place has now been taken by Nicaragua.

9 See, for example, the National Bipartisan Commission on Central America (Kissinger Report, 1984), pp. 55–7.

10 This was so, because of the increase in the openness of the economy during the second phase. See Table 12.1.

11 The main agencies promoting the policy changes are the World Bank and the US Agency for International Development, with the International Monetary Fund playing a supportive role and the Inter-American Development Bank a neutral one.

12 Costa Rica nationalised the banks in 1948, so that private financial interests (confined to secondary financial institutions) never acquired the same influence as in the northern republics.

13 Remnants of this long period of exchange-rate stability remain, e.g. the continued peg of the Honduran currency to the US dollar at its 1918 rate, but exchange rate flexibility (devaluation) is now the rule rather than the exception.

14 Kemmerer was a North American academic whose missions to Latin America acquired much the same significance as an IMF mission today. Kemmerer himself visited Guatemala only twice, but his former students were responsible for financial reform in Honduras and Nicaragua. See Kemmerer (1983), p. 26.

15 Exchange-rate stability, coupled with abolition of exchange controls, meant that the foodstuffs required by the labour force for its reproduction could be obtained, if necessary, cheaply from abroad. This tended to produce real wage discipline.

16 This was part of the agreement on a new tariff system (Arancel de Aduanas) adopted by the CACM on 1 January 1986, which revised the tariff rates and applied *ad valorem* rates universally.

17 Regional governments (particularly in Costa Rica, Guatemala and Honduras) remained under intense external pressure in 1986 to raise additional government revenue. This pressure, however, stemmed from short-term balance of payments considerations rather than from long-term analysis of the workings of the export-led model.

18 The switch under Ubico in Guatemala from a system of debt peonage to anti-vagrancy laws in 1934 is sometimes cited as an example of a change in

social legislation designed to favour the interests of capitalists (see McCreery (1983), p. 757).

19 There is a very useful summary of this early period of industrial legislation in SIECA (1977), pp. 1–10.

20 It has still not been solved in any republic, but land reform (outside Guatemala) has ceased to have revolutionary significance and is now merely radical. A future political solution is therefore more feasible.

21 The banana strike of 1934 extracted some concessions, and minimum wage legislation was extended to rural labour in 1935.

22 The labour movement temporarily passed through a very difficult phase in the early 1980s, until General Alvarez was dismissed from his post as head of the armed forces in April 1984.

23 Labour joined forces with the military to demand a peaceful end to the constitutional crisis provoked by President Suazo Córdova's attempt to name his successor.

24 The British government, for example, played an important role in renegotiating the Honduran debt owed to bondholders in 1926.

25 See Young (1925), p. 141.

26 *Ibid.*, pp. 141–2.

27 The most important company was International Railways of Central America, a subsidiary of UFCO, which had a virtual monopoly in Guatemala and El Salvador and owned much of the railway system in Costa Rica and Honduras.

28 The US Electric Bond and Share Company, through subsidiaries, dominated production of electricity in Guatemala and Costa Rica. A Canadian company occupied a similar position in El Salvador. See Rosenthal (1973), pp. 68–72.

29 Such accusations are still made. The operations in Guatemala, for example, of the Canadian subsidiary, EXMIBAL, which produces nickel, have provoked a great deal of nationalistic resentment. See IIES (1979).

30 This Labour Code, unlike virtually all other Somocista legislation, was not repealed by the Sandinistas after 1979. See Huembes (1984), pp. 225–6.

31 See Kepner (1936), pp. 147–51.

32 In 1959, for example, only 4.9 per cent of the estimated book value of Central American foreign investments was in Nicaragua. The figure for El Salvador was 11%. See Rosenthal (1973), p. 86.

33 Sam Zemurray, head of the Cuyamel Fruit Co., played a leading role in overthrowing President Davila in 1911. Curiously, the US State Department opposed Zemurray, but was outmanoeuvred. See Deutsch (1931), pp. 110–13.

34 When UFCO, now called United Brands, did try to influence Honduran policy in 1974–5 through bribery, the end result was the resignation of President Arellano – the opposite of what was intended.

35 See Rosenthal (1973), p. 63.

36 See Kamman (1968), pp. 62–8.

37 See Lafeber (1983), p. 62. Carías launched a civil war on being denied the presidency and provoked, not for the first time, a clash of interests between the State Department and UFCO.

38 See Leonard (1985), pp. 11–12.

39 Guatemala still maintains the fiction of an official exchange rate at par with the US dollar, but this is used only for external debt servicing.

40 See Díaz-Alejandro (1987).

41 By 1985, payments due on the public external debt exceeded the value of all exports.

42  See, for example, World Bank (1985).
43  This is the phrase coined by Gustav Ranis to describe the export policies adopted so successfully by the super-exporters of South East Asia. See Ranis (1981).
44  For details of the CBI, see Feinberg (1984).
45  Membership of the CBI was not extended to Nicaragua, which has ceased since 1981 to receive multilateral loans from financial agencies such as the World Bank.
46  Critics emphasise the suspension of Phase II of the programme in 1982 and the limited impact of Phase III (the land-to-the-tiller programme). See, for example, Pearce (1986), pp. 292–302.

## Methodological appendix

1  Some of these statistics have already been published. See Bulmer-Thomas (1986).
2  See Jones (1941), p. 79.
3  See Dirección General de Estadística y Censos (1930), p. 59.
4  See Corcoran (1946), p. 92.
5  See Banco Central de Guatemala (1955).
6  See Adler et al. (1952).
7  See United Nations (1959).
8  See Mooney (1968).
9  See Universidad de Costa Rica (1959b).
10  See Banco Central de Nicaragua (1961).
11  See Cumberland (1928).
12  See Hennessey (1946) and Cantarero (1949).
13  The method assumed that national income was equal to 25 per cent of an estimated 'net national wealth', which in turn was equal to gross national wealth of the country less the Government funded debt. See Cantarero (1949), p. 84 note 2.
14  See Banco Central de Honduras (1956).
15  See Bulmer-Thomas (1984), p. 306.
16  See Thorp (1984).
17  This series provided the basis for an article on long-run development. See Bulmer-Thomas (1983).
18  See CEPAL (1978).
19  See Banco Central de Costa Rica (1956), p. 87, table 42.
20  Consumption per head (c) does not in general change sharply from one year to the next. If 'q' is production per head. 'e' is export per head, 'm' is import per head and '$\Delta s$' is stock change per head, the formula

$$q = c + e - m + \Delta s$$

can be used to estimate production per head in the years when production data are unavailable.
21  For Nicaragua, I was forced to construct the index from information on the volume of imports of machinery, petroleum and iron and steel products.
22  See, for example, the Sección Agrícola Industrial in the Anuario Estadístico produced by the Dirección General de Estadísticas y Censos in Costa Rica in the 1920s.
23  See Banco Central de Honduras (1956). The Banco Central de Honduras published data on imports in nominal terms and at constant (1948) prices from 1925. It was a simple matter to adjust the series to constant (1950) prices and to obtain from this the price deflator for imports.

24 The published statistics on government expenditure are affected by frequent changes in methodology. The use of an index number to construct a consistent series avoids many of these problems provided there are two estimates of government expenditure in years when the methodology changes; this was always the case.

25 This was clearly inaccurate for Guatemala, which experienced rapid inflation from 1920 to 1924.

26 Nicaragua, for example, devalued the córdoba sharply in the late 1930s and experienced wage and price inflation at a time when wages and prices in the rest of Central America were more or less unchanged.

27 In the case of commerce, the CEPAL series aggregates this sector with finance. It is therefore not strictly comparable to my pre-1950 estimates of commerce, which is why there is no series for commerce in the Statistical Appendix.

28 The CEPAL series starts in 1950 for Guatemala, 1946 for Costa Rica, 1945 for El Salvador and Nicaragua and 1925 for Honduras.

29 The CEPAL series are at net factor cost; my index numbers were based on market prices. This introduces a small distortion to the extent that the ratio of net indirect taxes to net output varies from one year to the next.

30 These sources are conveniently summarised in the national accounts tables at constant prices in various SIECA publications. See, for example, SIECA (1981), (1982a) and (1985).

31 The purchasing-power parity exchange rates used by CEPAL for 1970 in terms of national currency per US dollar were as follows (official exchange rates in 1970 in brackets): Costa Rica 5.09 (6.62); El Salvador 1.70 (2.50); Guatemala 0.81 (1.0); Honduras 1.75 (2.0); Nicaragua 6.41 (7.0).

32 I considered extending the definition of EXA to include livestock, but rejected it for the following reasons: beef exports have increased enormously in importance since 1960, but the bulk of output is still sold in the domestic market; livestock is also defined to include raising pigs and chickens, neither of which are important export products. For some purposes it is appropriate to link livestock with the other four export products, but for a series covering the whole period from 1920 to 1984 it seemed more sensible to exclude it.

33 This was necessary, because at the time the work was done the CEPAL quantum index ended in 1983.

# Bibliography

Adams, F. U. (1914), *Conquest of the Tropics*. New York: Doubleday, Page and Co.

Adler, J. H., Schlesinger, E. R. and Olson, E. C. (1952), *Public Finance and Economic Development in Guatemala*. Stanford: Stanford University Press.

Alegría, C. and Flakoll, D. J. (1982), *Nicaragua: La Revolución Sandinista. Una Crónica Política/1855–1979*. Mexico: Ediciones Era.

Alexander, R. J. (1957), *Communism in Latin America*. New Brunswick, New York: Rutgers.

Ameringer, C. D. (1974), *The Democratic Left in Exile: The Anti-dictatorial Struggle in the Caribbean, 1945–1959*. Coral Gables: University of Miami Press.

(1978), *Don Pepe: A Political Biography of José Figueres of Costa Rica*. Albuquerque: University of New Mexico Press.

(1982), *Democracy in Costa Rica*. New York: Praeger.

Anderson, T. P. (1971), *Matanza – El Salvador's Communist Revolt of 1932*. Lincoln: University of Nebraska Press.

Aquino, F., et al. (1950), 'El Crédito Agrícola Salvadoreño', *Revista de Economía de El Salvador*, Tomo I. San Salvador.

Araya Pochet, C. (1975), *Historia Económica de Costa Rica, 1950–1970*. San José, Costa Rica: Editorial Fernandez-Arce.

*Area Handbook for Nicaragua* (1970), Washington: US Government Printing Office.

Arias Peñate, E. (1983), *El F.M.I. y La Politica Contrainsurgente en El Salvador*. Cuadernos de Pensamiento Propio I. Managua: INIES/CRIES.

Austin, J., Fox, J. and Kruger, W. (1985), 'The Role of the Revolutionary State in the Nicaraguan Food System', *World Development*, January, pp. 15–40.

Baciu, S. (1970), *Ramón Villeda Morales, Ciudadano de América*. San José, Costa Rica: Lehmann.

Backer, J. (1974), *La Iglesia y El Sindicalismo en Costa Rica*. San José, Costa Rica: Editorial Costa Rica.

Baloyra, E. (1982), *El Salvador in Transition*. Chapel Hill: The University of North Carolina Press.

(1983), 'Reactionary Despotism in Central America', *Journal of Latin American Studies*, Vol. 15, part 2, pp. 295–319.

(1985), 'Central America on the Reagan Watch: Rhetoric and Reality', *Journal of Interamerican Studies and World Affairs*, February, pp. 35–62.

Banco Central de Costa Rica (1956), *Ingreso y Productos Nacionales de Costa Rica*. San José, Costa Rica.

(1961), *Memoria Anual – La Economía Nacional*. San José, Costa Rica.

(1970), *Memoria Anual – La Economía Nacional*. San José, Costa Rica.

388 *Bibliography*

Banco Central de Guatemala (1955), *Memoria*. Guatemala.

Banco Central de Honduras (1951), 'El Sistema Monetaria en Honduras hasta 1950', in *Primera Memoria del Banco Central de Honduras*. Tegucipalpa, Honduras, pp. 26–35.

(1956), *Cuentas Nacionales: 1925–1955*. Tegucipalpa, Honduras.

Banco Central de Nicaragua (1961), *Primer Informe Anual*. Managua.

(1970), *Informe Anual*. Managua.

Banco Central de El Salvador (1944), *Memoria 1943/4*. San Salvador.

Banco Hipotecario de El Salvador (1944), *Memoria*. San Salvador.

Banco Interamericano de Desarrollo (1984), *Informe Economico – Nicaragua*. Washington.

Banco Nacional de Costa Rica (1949), *Memoria Anual 1945*. San José, Costa Rica.

Bauer-Paíz, A. (1956), *Cómo opera el capital Yanqui en Centroamérica (El Caso de Guatemala)*. Mexico: Editorial Ibero–Mexicana.

Baumeister, E., et al. (1983), 'El Subsistema del Algodón en Nicaragua', paper given to II Seminario Centroamérica y el Caribe, En Busca de Una Alternativa Regional, February. Managua: INIES/CRIES.

Bell, J. P. (1971), *Crisis in Costa Rica: the Revolution of 1948*. Austin, Texas: University of Texas Press.

Bernstein, E. M., et al. (1943), *Informe de la Misión Tecnica y Financiera*. Tegucipalpa, Honduras.

Berryman, P. (1984), *The Religious Roots of Rebellion*. London: SCM Press.

Best, M. H. (1976), 'Political Power and Tax Revenues in Central America', *Journal of Development Economics*, Vol. 3, pp. 49–82.

Biesanz, R., Biesanz, K. Z. and Biesanz, M. H. (1982), *The Costa Ricans*. Englewood Cliffs, New Jersey: Prentice-Hall.

Black, G. (1981), *Triumph of the People – The Sandinista Revolution in Nicaragua*. London: Zed Press.

Bodenheimer, S. J. (1981), 'El Mercomún y la Ayuda Nortamericana', in Menjívar, R. (ed.), *La Inversión Extranjera en Centroamérica*, 3rd edition. San José, Costa Rica: EDUCA.

Booth, J. A. (1982), *The End and the Beginning – The Nicaraguan Revolution*. Boulder, Colorado: Westview Press.

(1982a), 'Towards Explaining Regional Crisis in Central America: The Socio-economic and Political Roots of Rebellion', paper given to 44th International Congress of Americanists, University of Manchester, September.

Browning, D. (1971), *El Salvador: Landscape and Society*. Oxford: Oxford University Press.

(1983), 'Agrarian Reform in El Salvador', *Journal of Latin American Studies*, Vol. 15, Part 2, pp. 399–426.

Bulletin of the Pan American Union (BPAU), *Monthly Report*, Washington.

Bulmer-Thomas, V. (1976), 'An Input–Output Planning Model for Costa Rica'. Unpublished DPhil thesis, Oxford University.

(1976a), 'The Structure of Protection in Costa Rica – a New Approach to Calculating the Effective Rate of Protection', *Journal of Economic Studies*, Vol. 3, pp. 13–28.

(1977), 'A Model of Inflation for Central America', *Bulletin of the Oxford Institute of Economics and Statistics*, Vol. 39, pp. 319–32.

(1982), 'The Central American Common Market', in El-Agraa, A. (ed.), *International Economic Integration*. London: Macmillan.

(1983), 'Economic Development over the Long Run – Central America Since 1920', *Journal of Latin American Studies*, Vol. 15, Part 2, pp. 269–94.

(1984), 'Central America in the Interwar Period', in Thorp, R. (ed.), *Latin America in the 1930s*. London: Macmillan; New York: St Martin's Press.

(1985), 'World Recession and Central American Depression: Lessons from the 1930s for the 1980s', in Durán, E., *Latin America and the World Depression*. Cambridge: Cambridge University Press.

(1986), 'Cuentas Nacionales de Centroamérica desde 1920: Fuentes y Métodos', *Anuario de Estudios Centroamericanos*, Vol. 12, No. 1.

(1987), 'The Balance of Payments Crisis and Adjustment Programmes in Central America', in Thorp, R. and Whitehead, L. (eds.), *Latin American Debt and the Adjustment Crisis*. London: Macmillan; Pittsburg: University of Pittsburg Press.

Burbach, R. and Flynn, P. (1983), 'A New "banana republic": Del Monte in Guatemala', in Stanford Central American Action Network (ed.), *Revolution in Central America*. Boulder, Colorado: Westview Press.

Burgos-Debray, E. (ed.) (1984), *I, Rigoberta Menchú. An Indian Woman in Guatemala*. London: Verso Editions.

Burns, E. B. (1984), 'The Modernisation of Underdevelopment in El Salvador', *Journal of Developing Areas*, April, pp. 293–316.

Cabarrús, C. R. (1983), *Génesis de Una Revolución*. Mexico: Ediciones de la Casa Chata.

Cambranes, J. C. (1985), *Coffee and Peasants*. Stockholm: Institute of Latin American Studies.

Cantarero, L. A. (1949), 'The Economic Development of Nicaragua, 1920–1947'. Unpublished PhD thesis, University of Iowa.

Cardoso, C. (1977), 'The Formation of the Coffee Estate in Nineteenth-century Costa Rica', in Duncan, K. and Rutledge, I., *Land and Labour in Latin America*. Cambridge: Cambridge University Press.

Cardoza y Aragón, L. (1955), *La Revolución Guatemalteca*. Mexico: Ediciones Cuadernos Americanos.

Castillo, C. (1966), *Growth and Integration in Central America*. New York: Praeger.

Castillo Flores, A. (1974), *Historia de la Moneda de Honduras*. Tegucigalpa: Banco Central de Honduras.

Castro Silva, J. M. (1947), *Barómetros Económicos de Nicaragua*. Managua: Banco Nacional de Nicaragua.

CEDOH (1984), 'APROH: Orígenes, Desarrollo y Perspectivas', *Boletín Informativo*, Especial 9, March. Tegucigalpa.

(1985), 'Militarismo en Honduras: El Reinado de Gustavo Alvarez 1982–4', *Serie: Cronologias*, No. 2, August. Tegucigalpa.

CEPAL (1956), *La Política Tributaria y el Desarrollo Económico en Centro América*. *Mexico: United Nations*.

(1959), *El Desarrollo Económico de El Salvador*. Mexico: United Nations.

(1960), *El Desarrollo Económico de Honduras*. Mexico: United Nations.

(1966), *El Desarrollo Económico de Nicaragua*. Mexico: United Nations.

(1976), *América Latina: Relación de Precios del Intercambio*. Cuadernos Estadísticos de la CEPAL. Santiago.

(1978), *Series Históricas del Crecimiento de América Latina*. Cuadernos Estadísticos de la CEPAL. Santiago.

(1983), *Tablas de Insumo-Producto en América Latina*. Cuadernos Estadísticos de la CEPAL. Santiago.

CEPAL, et al. (1980), *Tenencia de la Tierra y Desarrollo Rural en Centroamérica*. San José, Costa Rica: EDUCA (3rd edition).

Cerdas, R. (1984), *Sandino, EL APRA y la Internacional Comunista*. Lima: Editor 'EDIMSSA'.

Checchi, V. (1959), *Honduras: A Problem in Economic Development*. New York: Twentieth Century Fund.

Chenery, H. and Syrquin, M. (1975), *Patterns of Development, 1950–1970*. Oxford: Oxford University Press.

Cline, W. R. (1978), 'Benefits and Costs of Economic Integration in Central America', in Cline, W. and Delgado, E. (eds.), *Economic Integration in Central America*. Washington: Brookings Institution.

Cline, W. R. and Rapoport, A. I. (1978), 'A Survey of Literature on Economic Development in the Central American Common Market', in Cline, W. R. and Delgado, E. (eds.), *Economic Integration in Central America*. Washington: Brookings Institution.

Cochrane, J. D. (1969), *The Politics of Regional Integration: The Central American Case*. The Hague: Martinus Nijhoff.

Cohen Orantes, I. (1972), *Regional Integration in Central America*. Lexington, Massachusetts: Lexington Books.

Colburn, F. D. (1986), *Post-Revolutionary Nicaragua – State, Class, and the Dilemmas of Agrarian Policy*. Berkeley: University of California Press.

Connell-Smith, G. (1966), *The Inter-American System*. Oxford: Oxford University Press.

Consejo Monetario Centroamericano, *Boletín Estadístico*. San José, Costa Rica.

Controloría General de la Republica (1974), *Liquidación Detallada de los Presupuestos de Gastos Ordinarios y Extraordinarios 1973*. San José, Costa Rica.

Corcoran, T. F. (1946), 'La Estadística en Guatemala', *Revista de Economía*, May–August. Guatemala.

Council of Foreign Bondholders (1940), *Annual Report*. London.

(1955), *Annual Report*. London.

Crawley, E. (1979), *Dictators Never Die*. London: C. Hurst & Co.

Cruz, A. (1983), 'Nicaragua's Imperiled Revolution', *Foreign Affairs*, Summer, Washington.

CSUCA (1978), *Estructura Demográfica y Migraciones Internas en Centroamérica*. San José, Costa Rica: EDUCA.

Cuadra Cea, L. (1963), *Aspectos históricos de la Moneda en Nicaragua*. Managua: Edición Banco Central.

Cumberland, W. W. (1928), *Nicaragua: An Economic and Financial Survey*. Washington: Government Printing Office.

Cunningham, E. (1922), *Gypsying Through Central America*. New York: E. P. Dutton & Co.

Cox, I. J. (1927), *Nicaragua and the United States*. Boston: World Peace Foundation Pamphlets. Vol. 10, No. 7.

Dada, H. (1983), *La Economía de El Salvador y la Integración Centroamericana 1954–1960*. San José, Costa Rica: EDUCA.

Dalton, R. (1972), *Miguel Marmol – Los Sucesos de 1932 en El Salvador*. San José, Costa Rica: EDUCA.

Dean, W. (1969), *The Industrialization of São Paulo, 1880–1945*. Austin, Texas: University of Texas Press.

Debray, R. (1978), *The Revolution on Trial. A Critique of Arms*, Vol. 2. London: Penguin Books.

Deere, C., Marchetti, P. and Reinhardt, N. (1985), 'The Peasantry and the Development of Sandinista Agrarian Policy, 1979–84', *Latin American Research Review*, Vol. 20, No. 3.

Denny, H. N. (1929), *Dollars for Bullets – The Story of American Rule in Nicaragua*. New York: Dial Press.

Deutsch, H. B. (1931), *The Incredible Yanqui – The Career of Lee Christmas*. London: Longmans, Green & Co.

Díaz-Alejandro, C. (1984), 'Latin America in the 1930s', in Thorp, R. (ed.), *Latin America in the 1930s*. London: Macmillan; New York: St. Martin's Press.

(1987), 'Some Aspects of the Development Crisis in Latin America', in Thorp, R. and Whitehead, L. (eds.), *Latin American Debt and the Adjustment Crisis*. London: Macmillan; Pittsburg: University of Pittsburg Press.

Díaz-Chavez, F. (1982), *Carías – el Ultimo Caudillo Frutero*. Tegucigalpa: Editorial Guaymuras.

Díaz-Franjul, M. (1982), 'The World Sugar Market', in IDB/INTAL, *Terms of Trade and the Optimum Tariff in Latin America*. Washington.

Diederich, B. (1982), *Somoza and the Legacy of US Involvement in Central America*. London: Junction Books.

Dierckxsens, W. and Campanario, P. (1983), *Economía y Trabajo en Honduras*. Tegucigalpa: Editorial Guaymuras.

Direccíon General de Estadística y Censos (DGEC) (1930), *Anuario Estadístico 1929*. San José, Costa Rica.

Downing, T. (1978), *Agricultural Modernisation in El Salvador*. Cambridge University, Centre of Latin American Studies, Working Paper No. 32.

Dubois, A., et al. (1983), 'El Subsistema del Azúcar en Nicaragua'. Paper given to II Seminario Centroamérica y el Caribe, February. Managua, Nicaragua: INIES/CRIES.

Due, J. F. (1966), 'The Retail Sales Tax in Honduras', *Inter-American Economic Affairs*, Winter, Vol. 20, No. 3, pp. 55–67.

Dunkerley, J. (1982), *The Long War – Dictatorship and Revolution in El Salvador*. London: Junction Books.

Durham, W. H. (1979), *Scarcity and Survival in Central America*. Stanford: Stanford University Press.

Economist Intelligence Unit (1980), *Quarterly Economic Report for Nicaragua, Costa Rica and Panama*, 2nd Quarter.

(1981), *Quarterly Economic Review: Latin America and the Caribbean*, Annual Supplement.

Edel, M. (1969), *Food Supply and Inflation in Latin America*. New York: Praeger.

Ellis, F. (1983), *Las Transnacionales del Banano en Centroamérica*. San José, Costa Rica: EDUCA.

*Envío* (1985), 'The Nicaraguan Peasantry Gives New Direction to Agrarian Reform', September, Vol. 4, Issue 51, pp. 1c–19c.

Facio, R. (1972), *Estudio Sobre Economía Costarricense*. San José, Costa Rica: Editorial Costa Rica.

(1973), *La Moneda y la Banca Central en Costa Rica*. San José, Costa Rica: Editorial Costa Rica.

FAO, Various years, *Production Yearbook*. Rome.

(1958), *Coffee in Latin America. Productivity Problems and Future Prospects.* I Colombia and El Salvador. New York: United Nations.

Farer, T. (1985), 'Contadora: The Hidden Agenda', *Foreign Policy*, Summer, pp. 59–72.

Feinberg, R. and Newfarmer, R. (1984), 'The Caribbean Basin Initiative: Bold Plan or Empty Promise?', in Newfarmer, R. (ed.), *From Gunboats to Diplomacy – New U.S. Policies for Latin America*. Baltimore: Johns Hopkins University Press.

Feuerlein, W. (1954), *Proposals for the Further Economic Development of El Salvador*. New York: United Nations.

Figueroa Ibarra, C. (1979), *Contenido de Clase y Participación Obrera en el Movimiento Antidictatorial de 1920*. Guatemala: Universidad de San Carlos.

Fishlow, A. (1984), 'Reciprocal Trade Growth: The Latin American Integration Experience', in Syrquin, M., Taylor, L. and Westphal, E. (eds.), *Economic Structure and Performance*. New York: Academic Press.

Fletcher, L., Graber, C., Merrill, W. and Thorbecke, E. (1970), *Guatemala's Economic Development: The Role of Agriculture*. Ames, Iowa: The Iowa State University Press.

Frank, C., Soto, M. and Sevilla, C. (1978), 'The Demand for Labour in Manufacturing Industry in Central America', in Cline, W. and Delgado, E. (eds.), *Economic Integration in Central America*. Washington: The Brookings Institution.

Frassinetti, A. (1981), 'Economía Primaria Exportadora y Formación del Proletariado. El Caso Centroamericano'. *Economía Política*, No. 19, pp. 40–78. Tegucigalpa.

Frundt, H. (1985), 'To Buy the World a Coke: Trade Union Redevelopment in Guatemala', Paper presented at LASA Conference, April. Albuquerque.

Gariazzo, A., et al. (1984), 'El Café en Nicaragua: Los Pequeños Productores de Matagalpa y Carazo'. Managua: Cuadernos de Pensamiento Propio, INIES.

Geiger, T. (1953), *Communism Versus Progress in Guatemala*. Washington: National Planning Association.

Gil Pacheco, R. (1974), *Ciento Cinco Años de Vida Bancaria en Costa Rica*. San José, Costa Rica: Editorial Costa Rica.

Gómez, J. A. (1972), *Farabundo Martí, Esbozo Biográfico*. San José, Costa Rica: EDUCA.

Gonzalez, C. H. (1984), 'Experiencia de Guatemala con el Proceso de Ajuste en 1982–3'. Centro de Estudios Monetarios Latino-americanos (CEMLA), *Boletín*, Mayo–Junio, Vol. 30, No. 3, pp. 157–165.

Gonzalez, V. (1978), 'La Insurrección Salvadoreña de 1932 y la Gran Huelga Hondureña de 1954'. *Revista Mexicana de Sociología*, April–June, pp. 560–606.

Gonzalez Del Valle, J. (1966), 'Monetary Integration in Central America: Achievements and Expectations'. *Journal of Common Market Studies*, Vol. 5, No. 1, pp. 13–25.

Gould, J. (1985), 'Dangerous Friends: Somoza and the Labour Movement', April: Managua (mimeo).

Grayson, G. (1985), 'The San José Oil Facility', *Third World Quarterly*, April.

Grieb, K. (1967), 'The United States and the Central American Federation', *The Americas*, Vol. 24, No. 2, pp. 107–21.

(1979), *Guatemalan Caudillo. The Régime of Jorge Ubico*. Athens, Ohio: Ohio University Press.

Grunwald, J. and Musgrove, P. (1970), *Natural Resources in Latin American Development*. Baltimore: Johns Hopkins University Press.

Guerra Borges, A. (1981), *Compendio de Geografía Económica y Humana de Guatemala*, Tomo II. Guatemala: Instituto de Investigaciones Económicas y Sociales.

Haan, H. (1985), *El Sector Informal en Centroamérica*. PREALC, Investigaciones sobre Empleo. Santiago: Organización Internacional del Trabajo.

Hall, C. (1982), *El Café y el Desarrollo Histórico-Geográfico de Costa Rica*. San José, Costa Rica: Editorial Costa Rica (3rd edition).

Hansen, R. D. (1967), *Central America: Regional Integration and Economic Development*. National Planning Association, Studies in Development Progress, No. 1, Washington.

Harris, R. and Vilas, C. (eds.) (1985), *Nicaragua – a Revolution Under Siege*. London: Zed Books.

Hennessey, J. F. (1946), 'The National Economy of Nicaragua', *Commercial Panamerica*, Vol. 15, No. 2.

Henry, O. (1917), *Cabbages and Kings*. New York: Doubleday, Page & Co.

Hill, A. J. (1938), *Report on Economic and Social Conditions in the Republic of El Salvador*. London: Department of Overseas Trade.

Hill, R. R. (1933), *Fiscal Intervention in Nicaragua*. New York.

Hinrichs, H. (1974), 'Tax Reform Constrained by Fiscal Harmonization Within Common Markets – Growth Without Development in Guatemala', in Geithman, D. (ed.), *Fiscal Policy for Industrialization and Development in Latin America*. Gainesville: University of Florida Press.

Huembes, C. (1984), 'Situación Laboral y Sindical', in *Nicaragua 1984*. San José, Costa Rica: Libro Libre.

Humphreys, R. (1981), *Latin America and the Second World War. Vol. 1, 1939–1942*. London: Athlone Press.

(1982), *Latin America and the Second World War. Vol. 2, 1942–1945*. London: Athlone Press.

IBRD (1951), *The Economic Development of Guatemala*. Baltimore: Johns Hopkins University Press.

(1953), *The Economic Development of Nicaragua*. Baltimore: Johns Hopkins University Press.

Immerman, R. (1982), *The CIA in Guatemala. The Foreign Policy of Intervention*. Austin, Texas: University of Texas Press.

Inforpress (1983), *El Futuro Del Mercado Común Centroamericano*. Guatemala: Inforpress.

(1983a), *Centro América 1983 – Análisis Económicos y Políticos Sobre la Región*. Guatemala: Inforpress.

(1984), *Centro América 1984–6 – Orígenes, Alcances y Perspectivas de la Crisis en los Países de la Región*. Guatemala: Inforpress.

Instituto Guatemalteco de Seguridad Social (IGSS) (1983), *Trabajadores y Salarios. Período: 1974–1982*. Guatemala.

Instituto Hondureño de Desarrollo Rural (IHDER) (1981), *La Tenencia de la Tierra en Honduras*. Tegucigalpa: Colección Siembra.

Instituto de Investigaciones Económicas y Sociales (IIES) (1978), *Endeudamiento Externo Del Sector Público de Guatemala 1955–1976*. Guatemala: IIES.

(1979), *EXMIBAL Contra Nicaragua* (2nd edition). Guatemala: IIES.

Instituto Nacional de Transformación Agraria (INTA) (1984), *Creación, Organización y Funcionamiento del INTA*. Guatemala (mimeo).

Inter-American Development Bank (IDB), *Economic and Social Progress in Latin America*. Washington: IDB.

International Monetary Fund (IMF), *Balance of Payments Yearbook*. Washington: IMF.

*Yearbook of International Financial Statistics*. Washington: IMF.

(1950), *International Financial Statistics*, Vol. 3, No. 6, June.

(1984), *Government Financial Statistics Yearbook*. Washington.

James, D. (1954), *Red Design for the Americas*. New York: John Day.

James, E. W. (1945), 'A Quarter Century of Road Building in the Americas'. *Bulletin of the Pan American Union*, November, Vol. 79, No. 11, pp. 609–18.

Jiménez Castro, W. (1977), *Análisis Electoral de Una Democracia, Estudio Del Comportamiento Político Costarricense Durante El Periodo 1953–1974*. San José, Costa Rica: Editorial Costa Rica.

Jiménez Oreamuno, R. (1980), *Su Pensamiento*, Biblioteca Patria No. 17. San José, Costa Rica: Editorial Costa Rica.

Joel, C. (1971), 'Tax Incentives in Central American Development', *Economic Development and Cultural Change*, Vol. 19, No. 1, January, pp. 229–52.

Jones, C. L. (1940), *Guatemala – Past and Present*. Minneapolis: The University of Minnesota Press.

Kamman, W. (1968), *A Search for Stability: United States Diplomacy Towards Nicaragua, 1925–1933*. Notre Dame, Indiana: University of Notre Dame Press.

Karnes, T. L. (1961), *The Failure of Union: Central America: 1824–1960*. Chapel Hill: University of North Carolina Press.

(1978), *Tropical Enterprises: Standard Fruit and Steamship Company in Latin America*. Baton Rouge: Louisiana State University Press.

Kemmerer, D. and Dalgaard, B. (1983), 'Inflation, Intrigue and Monetary Reform in Guatemala, 1919–1926', *The Historian*, Vol. 5, Part 46(1).

Keogh, D. (1984), 'The Myth of the Liberal Coup: The United States and the 15th October Coup in El Salvador'. *Millennium: Journal of International Studies*, Vol. 13, No. 2, pp. 153–83.

Kepner, C. (1936), *Social Aspects of the Banana Industry*. New York: Columbia University Press.

Kepner, C. and Soothill, J. (1935), *The Banana Empire: A Case Study in Economic Imperialism*. New York: The Vanguard Press.

Kissinger Report (1984), *Report of the National Bipartisan Commission on Central America*. Washington: Government Printing Office.

Krehm, W. (1984), *Democracies and Tyrannies of the Caribbean*. Westport, Connecticut: Lawrence Hill & Co.

Labarge, R. A. (1960), *Impact of the United Fruit Company on the Economic Development of Guatemala 1946–1954*. New Orleans: Tulane University.

Lafeber, W. (1983), *Inevitable Revolutions – The United States in Central America*. New York: W. W. Norton & Co.

Latin American Studies Association (LASA) (1984), *The Electoral Process in Nicaragua: Domestic and International Influences*. Austin, Texas.

League of Nations, *International Trade Statistics*. Geneva.

(1936), *Public Finance 1928–1935*. Geneva.

(1938), *Public Finance 1928–1937*. Geneva.

León Gómez, A. (1978), *El Escándalo Ferrocarril*. Tegucigalpa, Honduras: Soto.

Leonard, T. (1984), *The United States and Central America 1944–1949*. Alabama: University of Alabama Press.

(1985), *The Decline of the Recognition Policy in United States–Central American Relations, 1933–1945*, Latin American and Caribbean Centre, Florida International University, Occasional Paper Series, No. 49.

Levin, J. (1960), *The Export Economies: their Pattern of Development in Historical Perspective*. Harvard: Harvard University Press.

Lizano, E. (1981), 'Towards a National Employment Policy: the Case of Costa Rica', *International Labour Review*, Vol. 120, No. 3, May–June.

Lizano, E. and Willmore, L. (1975), 'Second Thoughts on Central America: The Rosenthal Report', *Journal of Common Market Studies*, Vol. 13.

Luciak, I. (1986), 'Popular Hegemony or National Unity – An Analysis of the 1986 Reform of the Sandinista Agrarian Reform Law', Ohio: Ohio State University (mimeo).

McCann, T. (1976), *An American Company – the Tragedy of United Fruit*. New York: Crown Books.

McCarthy, P. (1984), *Consumer Prices, Real Wages, the Long-Run Structures of Wages, Inter-Industry Wage Differentials and the Long-Run Equalisation of Wages in 19 Latin American Countries*. Social Science Working Paper No. 64, Paisley College of Technology, Scotland.

McClintock, M. (1985), *The American Connection. Vol. 2: State Terror and Popular Resistance in Guatemala*. London: Zed Books.

McCreery, D. (1983), 'Debt Servitude in Rural Guatemala, 1876–1936', *Hispanic American Historical Review*, Vol. 63, Part 4, pp. 735–59.

McLeod, M. (1973), *Spanish Central America – A Socioeconomic History 1520–1720*. Berkeley: University of California Press.

Macaulay, N. (1967), *The Sandino Affair*. Chicago: Quadrangle Books.

Marroquín, A. (1977), 'Estudio sobre la Crisis de los Años Treinta en El Salvador', in González Casanova, P. (ed.), *América Latina en los Años Treinta*. Mexico: Universidad Nacional Autónoma de Mexico.

Masferrer, A. (1950), *El Minimum Vital y Otras Obras de Carácter Sociológico*. Guatemala: Ediciones del Gobierno de Guatemala.

Maxfield, S. and Stahler-Sholk, R. (1985), 'External Constraints', in Walker, T. W. (ed.), *Nicaragua. The First Five Years*. New York: Praeger.

May, S., et al. (1952), *Costa Rica – A Study in Economic Development*. New York: The Twentieth Century Fund.

May, S. and Plazo, G. (1958), *The United Fruit Company in Latin America*. Washington: National Planning Association.

Mecham, J. L. (1961), *The United States and Inter-American Security, 1889–1960*. Austin, Texas: University of Texas Press.

Melville, T. and Melville, M. (1971), *Guatemala – The Politics of Land Ownership*. New York: The Free Press.

Menjívar, R. (1980), *Acumulación Originaria y Desarrollo del Capitalismo en El Salvador*. San José, Costa Rica: EDUCA.

    (1982), *Formación y Lucha del Proletariado Industrial Salvadoreño*. San José, Costa Rica: EDUCA (2nd edition).

Meza, V. (1981), *Historia del Movimiento Obrera Hondureño*. Tegucigalpa, Honduras: Editorial Guaymuras.

Millet, E. (1979), *Guardianes de la Dinastía*. San José, Costa Rica: EDUCA.

Ministerio de Hacienda (1980), 'La Reforma Financiera en Costa Rica'. Banco Central de Costa Rica: Serie 'Comentarios Sobre Asuntos Económicos', No. 37. San José, Costa Rica: Banco Central de Costa Rica.

Molina Chacón, G. (1982), *Estado Liberal y Desarrollo Capitalista en Honduras*. Tegucigalpa, Honduras: Editorial Universitaria.

Monfils, M. (1938), *Le Café au Salvador et au Guatemala*. Service National de la Production Agricole et de l'Enseignement Rural, Bulletin No. 12. Port-au-Prince, Haiti: Imprimerie de l'Etat.

Monge Alfaro, C. (1974), *Nuestra Historia y Los Seguros*. San José, Costa Rica: Editorial Costa Rica.

Monteforte Toledo, M. (1972), *Centro América – Subdesarrollo y Dependencia*, 2 vols. Mexico: Universidad Nacional Autónoma de Mexico.

Montero Umaña, L. (1972), *Resumen de la Legislación Tributaria Costarricense 1900–1970*. San José, Costa Rica: Escuela de Ciencias Económicas y Sociales, Instituto de Investigaciones.

Montes, M. (1982), *La Crisis Económica de Honduras y la Situación de los Trabajadores*. Tegucigalpa: Ediciones Sitraunah.

Moody's (1934), *Manual of Investments – America and Foreign*. New York.
(1945), *Manual of Investments – American and Foreign*. New York.

Mooney, J. P. (1968), 'Gross Domestic Product, Gross National Product and Capital Formation in El Salvador, 1945–1965', *Estadística*, No. 100, September, pp. 491–517.

Morris, J. (1984), *Honduras – Caudillo Politics and Military Rulers*. Boulder, Colorado: Westview Press.

Mosk, S. (1955), 'The Coffee Economy of Guatemala, 1850–1918: Development and Signs of Instability', *Inter-American Economic Affairs*, Vol. 9, No. 3, pp. 6–20.

Munro, D. (1918), *The Five Republics of Central America*. New York: Oxford University Press.
(1964), *Intervention and Dollar Diplomacy in the Caribbean 1900–1921*. Princeton, New Jersey: Princeton University Press.

NACLA (1974), 'Pushing Counterrevolution in Guatemala', in NACLA's *Latin American and Empire Report*, Vol. 8, No. 3, March.

Natalini de Castro, S., De Los Angeles Mendoza Saborío, M. and Pagán Solórzano, J. (1985), *Significado Histórico del Gobierno del Dr. Ramón Villeda Morales*. Tegucigalpa, Honduras: Editorial Universitaria.

North, L. (1981), *Bitter Grounds: Roots of Revolt in El Salvador*. Toronto: Between the Lines.

Nye, J. (1967), 'Central American Regional Integration', *International Conciliation*, No. 562, March.

Obando Sanchez, A. (1980), *Memorias – la Historia del Movimiento Obrero en Guatemala en Este Siglo*. Guatemala: Editorial Universitaria.

Oconitrillo García, E. (1982), *Los Tinoco (1917–1919)*. San José, Costa Rica: Editorial Costa Rica (2nd edition).

Oficina de Planificación (OFIPLAN) (1974), *Plan Nacional de Desarrollo, Estrategia y Plan Global*. San José, Costa Rica.

Orellana, R. A. and Cancino, J. R. (1981), *La Inflación en Centroamérica – El Caso de Guatemala*. Guatemala: Instituto de Investigaciones Económicas y Sociales.

Pan American Union (1927), *Guatemala*. American Nation Series. No. 10. Washington.

Parsons, J. (1964), 'Cotton and Cattle in the Pacific Lowlands of Central America', *Journal of Inter-American Studies*, Vol. 8, No. 2, pp. 149–59.

Payne, D. (1985), 'The "Mantos" of Sandinista Deception', *Strategic Review*, Spring, pp. 9–20.

Pearce, J. (1981), *Under the Eagle: U.S. Intervention in Central America and the Caribbean*. London: Latin American Bureau.
(1986), *Promised Land: Peasant Rebellion in Chalatenango, El Salvador*. London: Latin American Bureau.

Pérez Bermudez, C. and Guevara, O. (1985), *El Movimiento Obrero en Nicaragua*. Managua: Editorial 'El Amanecer'.

Pérez Brignoli, H. (1973), 'La Reforma Liberal en Honduras', *Cuaderno de Ciencias Sociales*, No. 2, Tegucigalpa, pp. 1–19.

Poblete Troncoso, M. and Burnett, B. (1960), *The Rise of the Latin American Labour Movement*. New Haven, Connecticut: College and University Press.

Poitevin, R. (1977), *El Proceso de Industrialización en Guatemala*. San José, Costa Rica: EDUCA.

Posas, M. (1981), *Luchas Del Movimiento Obrero Hondureño*. San José, Costa Rica: EDUCA.

(1983), 'El Surgimiento de la Clase Obrera en Honduras', *Anuario de Estudios Centroamericanos*, Vol. 9, pp. 17–35.

(1984), *El Movimiento Obrero Hondureño (1880–1964)*. Tegucigalpa (mimeo).

Posas, M. and Del Cid, R. (1982), *La Construcción del Sector Público y del Estado Nacional en Honduras 1876–1979*. San José, Costa Rica: EDUCA.

PREALC (1979), *Diagnóstico de las Estadísticas y Bibliografía sobre el Empleo en Centroamérica y Panama*. Santiago.

(1980), *Empleo y Salarios en Nicaragua*. Santiago.

(1983), *Producción de Alimentos Basicos y Empleo en el Istmo Centroamericano*. Santiago.

Prebisch, R. (1959), 'Commercial Politics in Underdeveloped Countries', *American Economic Review*, Vol. 49, pp. 251–73.

Ramsett, D. (1969), *Regional Industrial Development in Central America: A Case Study of the Integration Industries Scheme*. New York: Praeger.

Ranis, G. (1981), 'Challenges and Opportunities Posed by Asia's Superexporters: Implications for Manufactured Exports from Latin America', in Baer, W. and Gillis, M., *Export Diversification and the New Protectionism*. Champaign, Illinois: University of Illinois.

Reina Valenzuela, J. and Argueta, M. (1978), *Marco Aurelio Soto, Reforma Liberal de 1876*. Tegucigalpa: Banco Central de Honduras.

Reuben Soto, S. (1982), *Capitalismo y Crisis Económica en Costa Rica – Treinte Años de Desarrollo*. San José, Costa Rica: Editorial Porvenir.

Reynolds, C. (1978), 'Employment Problems of Export Economies in a Common Market: The Case of Central America', in Cline, W. and Delgado, E. (eds.), *Economic Integration in Central America*. Washington: The Brookings Institution.

Riismandel, J. N. (1972), 'Costa Rica: Self-Image, Land Tenure and Agrarian Reform, 1940–1965'. Unpublished PhD thesis, University of Maryland.

Rippy, J. F. (1954), 'British Investments in Central America, the Dominican Republic and Cuba: A story of Meager Returns'. *Inter-American Economic Affairs*, Vol. 8, pp. 89–98.

Rivera Urrutia, E. (1982), *El Fondo Monetario Internacional y Costa Rica 1976–1982*. San José, Costa Rica: Colección Centroamérica.

Robleda, R. (1982), 'Latifundio, Reforma Agraria y Modernización', *Economía Política*, No. 21, Enero–Diciembre, pp. 5–34. Tegucigalpa.

Rodriguez, E. (1981), *De Calderón a Figueres*. San José, Costa Rica: Editorial Estatal a Distancia.

Rodriguez Beteta, V. (1980), *No es Guerra de Hermanos sino de Bananos*. Guatemala: Editorial 'José de Pineda Ibarra' (2nd edition).

Rojas Bolaños, M. (1978), 'El Desarrollo del Movimiento Obrero en Costa Rica, un Intento de Periodización', *Revista de Ciencias Sociales*, Marzo–Octubre, No. 15–16, pp. 13–31. San José, Costa Rica.

Romero, A. (1985), 'The Kissinger Report and the Restoration of US Hegemony'. *Millennium*, pp. 116–129.

Rosenberg, M. (1983), *Las Luchas por El Seguro Social en Costa Rica*. San José, Costa Rica: Editorial Costa Rica.

Rosenthal, G. (1973), *The Role of Private Foreign Investment in the Development of the Central American Common*. Guatemala (mimeo).

Rossbach, L. and Wunderich, V. (1985), 'Derechos Indígenas y Estado Nacional en Nicaragua: La Convención Mosquita de 1894', *Encuentro, Revista de la Universidad Centroamericana en Nicaragua*, Abril–Septiembre, No. 24–5, pp. 29–53. Managua.

Rowles, J. (1980), *El Conflicto Honduras–El Salvador y El Orden Jurídico Internacional (1969)*. San José, Costa Rica: EDUCA.

Ruhl, M. (1984), 'Agrarian Structure and Political Stability in Honduras', *Journal of Interamerican Studies and World Affairs*, Vol. 26, No. 1, February, pp. 33–68.

Saenz, C. J. (1969), 'Population growth, Economic Progress and Opportunities on the Land: the Case of Costa Rica'. Unpublished PhD thesis, University of Wisconsin.

Sanchez, M. (1967), *Nicaragua. Colección Nuestros Países, Centro de Documentación*. Habana, Cuba: Casa de las Americas.

Santos, R. and Herrera, L. (1979), *Del Artisano al Obrero Fabril*. San José, Costa Rica: Editorial Porvenir.

Schifter, J. (1981), *La Fase Oculta de la Guerra Civil en Costa Rica*. San José, Costa Rica: EDUCA (2nd edition).

(1982), *Costa Rica 1948*. San José, Costa Rica: EDUCA.

Schlesinger, S. and Kinzer, S. (1982), *Bitter Fruit – The Untold Story of the American Coup in Guatemala*. London: Sinclair Browne.

Schmid, L. (1973), *El Papel de la Mano de Obra Migratoria en el Desarrollo Económico de Guatemala*. Guatemala: Universidad de San Carlos.

Seligson, M. (1980), *Peasants of Costa Rica and the Development of Agrarian Capitalism*. Madison, Wisconsin: University of Wisconsin Press.

Selser, G. (1981), *Sandino*. New York: Monthly Review Press.

Serna, R. (1982), 'La Situación Actual de los Campesinos Pequeños Productores de Granos Basicos en Honduras', *Magister Latinoamericano de Trabajo Social*, Universidad Nacional Autónoma de Honduras, Cuaderno No. 9, Tegucigalpa.

SIECA (1967), *Quinto Compendio Estadístico Centroaméricano*. Guatemala: SIECA.

(1977), *Análisis de la Legislación de Fomento Industrial en Centroamérica*. Guatemala: SIECA.

(1981), *VII Compendio Estadístico Centroamericano*. Guatemala: SIECA.

(1982), *Memoria de Seminario Sobre Matrices de Insumo Producto en Centroamérica*. Guatemala: SIECA.

(1982a), *Estadísticas Macroeconómicas de Centroamérica 1971–1981*. Guatemala: SIECA.

(1985), *Series Estadísticas Seleccionadas de Centroamérica*, No. 20. Guatemala: SIECA.

SIECA/INTAL (1973), *El Desarrollo Integrado de Centroamérica en la Presente Década: Bases y Propuestas para el Perfeccionamiento y la Reestructuración del Mercado Común Centroamericano*, 13 vols. Buenos Aires: INTAL.

Siri, G. (1982), 'Import Tariffs, Export Taxes and Trade Policy Options for Central

America', in IDB/INTAL, Terms of Trade and the Optimum Tariff in Central America. Washington.

Siri, G. and Dominguez, R. (1981), 'Central American Accommodation to External Disruptions', in Cline, W. (ed.), World Inflation and the Developing Countries. Washington: Brookings Institution.

Slutsky, D. (1979), 'La Agroindustria de la Carne en Honduras', Estudios Sociales Centroamericanos, Enero–Abril, pp. 101–204. San José, Costa Rica.

Sobral, E. M. (1925), Artículos Relativos a la Reforma Monetaria de Guatemala. Guatemala: Secretaria de Hacienda y Crédito Público.

Soley Güell, T. (1949), Compendio de la Historia Económica y Hacendaria de Costa Rica, 2 vols. San José, Costa Rica: Editorial Universitaria.

(1975), Compendio de Historia Económica y Hacendaria de Costa Rica. Biblioteca Patria No. 12. San José, Costa Rica: Editorial Costa Rica.

Somoza, A. (1936), El Verdadero Sandino o el Calvario de las Segovias. Managua.

South American Handbook (1924), The South American Handbook 1924, including Central America, Mexico and Cuba. London: South American Publications Ltd.

Stahler-Sholk, R. (1985), 'Debt and Stabilization in Revolutionary Nicaragua', paper presented at XII Conference of the Latin American Studies Association, Albuquerque, New Mexico, April.

Staley, C. (1962), 'Costa Rica and the Central American Common Market', Economía Internazionale, pp. 117–30.

Stokes, W. (1950), Honduras: An Area Study in Government. Madison, Wisconsin: University of Wisconsin Press.

Stone, S. (1975), La Dinastía de los Conquistadores. San José, Costa Rica: EDUCA.

Swerling, B. (1949), International Control of Sugar, 1918–1941. Stanford: Stanford University Press.

Taracena, A. (1984), 'La Confederación Obrera en Centroamérica (1921–1928)', Anuario de Estudios Centroamericanos, Vol. 10, pp. 81–93. San José, Costʻ Rica.

Thome, J. R. and Kaimonowitz, D. (1985), 'Agrarian Reform', in Walker, T. (ed.), Nicaragua – The First Five Years. New York: Praeger.

Thompson, W. (1926), Rainbow Countries of Central America. New York: E. P. Dutton & Co.

Thorp, R. (ed.) (1984), Latin America in the 1930s: The Role of the Periphery in World Crisis. London: Macmillan; New York: St Martin's Press.

Torres Rivas, E. (1973), Interpretación del Desarrollo Social Centroamericano. San José, Costa Rica: EDUCA (3rd edition).

Triffin, R. (1944), 'Central Banking and Monetary Management in Latin America', in Harris, S. E., Economic Problems of Latin America. New York: McGraw Hill.

United Nations (1955), Yearbook of International Trade Statistics. New York.

(1957), Compendio Estadístico Centroamericano. Mexico.

(1959), El Desarrollo Económico de El Salvador. Mexico.

Universidad de Costa Rica (1959), El Desarrollo Económico de Costa Rica. No. 3, Estudio del Sector Agropecuario. San José, Costa Rica: Universidad de Costa Rica.

(1959a), El Desarrollo Económico de Costa Rica. No. 2, Estudio del Sector Industrial. San José, Costa Rica: Universidad de Costa Rica.

Vaitsos, C. (1978), 'Crisis in Regional Economic Cooperation (Integration) among Developing Countries: a Survey', World Development, Vol. 6, No. 6, pp. 719–77.

Vega, M. (1982), *CODESA y la Fracción Industrial*. San José, Costa Rica: Editorial Hoy.

Vilas, C. (1985), 'The Workers' Movement in the Sandinista Revolution', in Harris, R. and Vilas, C. (eds.), *Nicaragua – A Revolution under Siege*. London: Zed Books.

(1986), *Sandinista Revolution – National Liberation and Social Transformation in Central America*. New York: Monthly Review Press.

Villareal, B. (1983), *El Precarismo Rural en Costa Rica 1960–1980. Orígenes y Evolución*. San José, Costa Rica: Editorial Papiro.

Viteri Bertrand, E. (1976), *El Pacto de Unión de 1921. Sus Antecedentes, Vicisitudes y la Cesación de sus Efectos*. Guatemala: Editorial Apolo.

Volio, M. (1973), *Jorge Volio y El Partido Reformista*. San José, Costa Rica: Editorial Costa Rica.

Wagley, C. (1941), 'Economics of a Guatemalan Village', *Memoirs of the American Anthropological Association*, No. 58, pp. 51–81.

Walker, T. (ed.) (1985), *Nicaragua: The First Five Years*. New York: Praeger.

Wall, D. (1968), 'The International Banana Market', *Journal of Economic Studies*, Vol. 3, No. 3/4, December, pp. 45–61.

Watkins, V. (1967), *Taxes and Tax Harmonisation in Central America*. Harvard: Harvard University Press.

Webre, S. (1979), *José Napoleon Duarte and the Christian Democratic Party in Salvadorean Politics 1960–1972*. Baton Rouge: Louisiana State University Press.

Weeks, J. (1985), *The Economics of Central America*. New York: Holmes and Meier.

Weinert, R. (1981), 'Nicaragua's Debt Renegotiation', *Cambridge Journal of Economics*, Vol. 5, pp. 187–94.

Wheelock, J. (1980), *Nicaragua: Imperialismo y Dictadura*. Habana, Cuba: Editorial de Ciencias Sociales.

Whetten, N. (1961), *Guatemala: The Land and the People*. New Haven: Yale University Press.

White, A. (1973), *El Salvador*. London: Ernest Benn Ltd.

Whitehead, L. (1983), 'Explaining Washington's Central American Policies', *Journal of Latin American Studies*, Vol. 15, Part 2, November, pp. 321–63.

(1986), 'The Prospects for a Political Settlement: Most Options have been Foreclosed', in Di Palma, E. and Whitehead, L. (eds.), *The Central American Impasse*. London: Croom Helm.

Wickizer, C. (1943), *The World Coffee Economy With Special Reference to Control Schemes*. Stanford: Stanford University Press.

Wilkie, J. (ed.) (1982), *Statistical Abstract of Latin America*, Vol. 21. Los Angeles: University of California.

(1983), *Statistical Abstract of Central America*, Vol. 22. Los Angeles: University of California.

Williams, R. E. (1986), *Export Agriculture and the Crisis in Central America*. Chapel Hill: University of North Carolina Press.

Willmore, L. (1976), 'Direct Foreign Investment in Central American Manufacturing', *World Development*, Vol. 4, No. 6, pp. 419–517.

Wilson, C. (1947), *Empire in Green and Gold – the Story of the American Banana Trade*. New York: Henry Holt.

Woodbridge, P. (1972), *El Contrato Ley*. San José, Costa Rica: Editorial Costa Rica.

Woodward, E. L. (1962), 'Octubre: Communist Appeal to the Urban Labor Force of Guatemala, 1950–1953', *Journal of Inter-American Studies and World Affairs*, July, pp. 363–74.

World Bank (1980), *World Tables* (2nd edition). Washington.

(1984), *World Tables* (3rd edition). Washington.

(1985), *World Debt Tables 1984/5*. Washington.

(1986), *World Debt Tables 1985/6*. Washington.

Ydígoras Fuentes, M. (1963), *My War With Communism*. Englewood Cliffs, New Jersey: Prentice-Hall.

Young, J. P. (1925), *Central American Currency and Finance*. Princeton: Princeton University Press.

Zeledón, M. T. (1966), *La ODECA, Sus Antecedentes Históricos y Su Aporte al Derecho Internacional Público*. San José, Costa Rica: Colegio de Abogados de Costa Rica.

# Author index

Bracketed numbers refer to notes

Adams, F., 10
Adler, J., 385(6)
Alegría, C., 350(5), 352(50), 363(62), 363(63), 363(64), 363(3)
Alexander, R., 358(3)
Ameringer, C., 345(41), 346(46), 349(49), 352(47), 352(57), 359(22), 359(24), 359(25), 360(55), 360(58), 364(65), 364(67), 364(69)
Anderson, T., 345(27), 345(38), 347(23)
Aquino, R., 363(51)
Araya Pochet, C., 353(8)
*Area Handbook for Nicaragua*, 368(66), 369(95)
Argueta, M., 349(45)
Arias Peñate, E., 380(48)
Austin, J., 381(64), 381(65)

Baciu, S., 364(66)
Backer, J., 351(30), 352(56)
Baloyra, E., 360(61), 378(15), 381(79)
Banco Central de Costa Rica, 363(52), 369(92), 385(19)
Banco Central de Guatemala, 385(5)
Banco Central de Honduras, 344(13), 357(74), 385(14), 385(23)
Banco Central de Nicaragua, 370(116), 385(10)
Banco Central de El Salvador, 352(37)
Banco Hipotecario de El Salvador, 351(25)
Banco Interamericano de Desarrollo, 381(62), 381(63), 381(65)
Banco Nacional de Costa Rica, 351(24)
Bauer-Paíz, A., 341(23), 342(48), 357(67)
Baumeister, E., 355(34)
Bell, J., 346(2), 352(53), 352(54), 360(56)
Bernstein, E., 351(34)
Berryman, P., 375(77), 376(94), 376(97)
Best, M., 367(39)
Biesanz, R., 345(41)
Black, G., 349(46), 377(99), 377(120), 378(1)

Bodenheimer, S., 365(92), 369(102)
Booth, J., 219(table), 375(63), 377(105), 378(3)
Browning, D., 355(32), 355(46), 362(41), 378(14)
Bulletin of the Pan American Union, 92(table), 350(10), 353(11), 353(12), 356(55), 358(13)
Bulmer-Thomas, V., 362(32), 366(19), 366(24), 366(32), 367(50), 368(57), 369(80), 369(101), 370(111), 371(1), 372(30), 374(55), 379(25), 379(31), 379(32), 379(33), 379(35), 379(38), 380(43), 385(1), 385(15), 385(17)
Burbach, R., 371(6)
Burgos-Debray, E., 377(112)
Burnett, B., 360(53)
Burns, E. B., 338(9)

Cabarrús, C., 368(63), 371(128)
Cambranes, J., 338(3)
Campanario, P., 375(73)
Cantarero, L., 352(43), 385(12), 385(13)
Cardoso, C., 340(30), 340(31), 340(32)
Cardoza y Aragón, L., 353(60)
Castillo, C., 367(55)
Castillo Flores, A., 341(16)
Castro Silva, J., 351(29)
CEDOH, 378(19), 382(88)
CEPAL, 162(table), 351(22), 355(44), 357(69), 362(25), 362(26), 362(29), 362(31), 362(35), 362(38), 362(40), 363(48), 363(53), 363(54), 373(42), 385(18)
Cerdas, R., 346(47)
Checchi, V., 354(18), 360(49), 364(77)
Chenery, H., 383(3)
Cline, W., 365(1), 366(21), 366(31)
Cochrane, J., 365(93), 365(4), 365(7), 365(10), 366(16), 366(32)
Cohen Orantes, I., 365(90), 365(9), 365(11), 365(12), 366(17), 366(18)

403

Colburn, F., 381(64)
Connell-Smith, G., 360(51)
Consejo Monetario Centroamericano, 186(table), 368(61)
Controloría General de la República, 374(58)
Corcoran, T., 385(4)
Council of Foreign Bondholders, 14(table), 339(17), 344(19), 349(43), 357(77)
Cox, J., 349(42)
Crawley, E., 358(15)
Cruz, A., 378(5)
CSUCA, 362(41), 363(42), 363(47), 368(77)
Cuadra Cea, L., 347(16), 352(35)
Cumberland, W., 341(14), 342(60), 385(11)
Cunningham, E., 1

Dada, H., 355(33), 356(50), 356(52), 363(56), 364(75), 365(88)
Dalton, R., 342(54)
Dean, W., 355(48)
Debray, R., 365(3)
Deere, C., 382(97)
Del Cid, R., 342(60), 353(7), 357(68)
Delgado, E., 365(1), 366(31), 366(32)
Denny, H., 339(24), 340(6), 341(13)
Deutsch, H., 384(33)
Díaz-Alejandro, C., 349(41), 384(80)
Díaz-Chavez, F., 349(44)
Díaz-Franjul, M., 371(11)
Diederich, B., 346(49)
Dierckxsens, W., 375(73)
Domínguez, R., 374(54)
Downing, T., 372(24)
Dubois, A., 362(37)
Dunkerley, J., 359(32), 372(23), 377(100), 377(103), 377(108), 377(110), 377(118), 377(122), 378(12)
Due, J., 367(46)
Durham, W., 341(38), 363(46), 365(2)

Economist Intelligence Unit, 371(41), 374(49), 378(9)
Edel, M., 341(39)
Ellis, F., 353(2), 353(4), 361(3), 361(5), 361(6), 361(8), 361(9), 361(10), 368(73), 368(74), 371(7), 371(9)
Envío, 382(98)

Facio, R., 341(36), 347(15), 347(23), 348(33), 349(40)
FAO, 164(table), 355(38), 361(16), 362(21)
Farer, T., 381(75)
Feinberg, R., 380(52), 385(43)
Feuerlein, W., 353(1), 356(51), 356(53), 356(57), 357(70)
Figueroa Ibarra, C., 340(35)
Fishlow, A., 366(20)

Flakoll, D., 350(5), 352(50), 363(62), 363(63), 363(64), 365(3)
Fletcher, L., 355(47)
Flynn, P., 371(6)
Frank, C., 370(107)
Frassinetti, A., 340(28), 340(33)
Frundt, H., 377(102), 382(91)

Gariazzo, A., 354(20)
Geiger, T., 359(40)
Gil Pacheco, R., 357(76)
Gómez, J., 345(34)
González, C., 380(51)
González, V., 360(47)
González del Valle, J., 365(8)
Gould, J., 352(51), 352(58), 358(4), 358(7), 358(10)
Grayson, G., 381(72)
Grieb, K., 340(6), 342(57), 345(29), 345(32), 346(1), 348(29) 348(38), 352(52)
Grunwald, J., 154(table), 155(table), 157(table), 158(table), 361(1), 361(4), 361(11), 361(13), 361(17), 361(20), 362(27), 362(30), 362(36), 368(69), 371(15)
Guevara, O., 358(1)

Haan, H., 380(59)
Hall, C., 353(13), 361(14), 361(15), 361(18), 361(19), 369(86)
Hansen, R., 366(31)
Hennessey, S., 385(12)
Henry, O., 1
Herrera, L., 370(108), 374(46)
Hill, R., 342(62), 348(34)
Hinrichs, H., 367(42), 367(43), 367(49)
Huembes, C., 384(30)
Humphreys, R., 349(52), 349(1), 350(8), 352(46)

IBRD, 355(36), 355(37), 356(63)
Immerman, R., 359(41)
Inforpress, 211(table), 365(13), 366(28), 370(109), 370(112), 370(114)
Instituto Guatemalteco de Seguridad Social, 379(21)
Instituto Hondureño de Desarrollo Rural, 372(31)
Instituto de Investigaciones Económicas y Sociales, 374(48), 375(69), 384(29)
Instituto Nacional de Transformación Agraria, 372(25)
Inter-American Development Bank, 248(table)
International Monetary Fund, 361(12), 364(81), 374(57)

James, D., 358(2), 358(6), 358(8), 358(14)
James, E., 350(7)
Jiménez Castro, W., 364(68)
Jiménez Oreamuno, R., 340(37)
Joel, C., 366(33), 366(34), 367(40)
Jones, C., 338(9), 342(47), 348(25)

Kamman, W., 343(63), 384(36)
Karnes, T., 338(1), 339(10), 341(22), 342(59), 348(27), 350(17)
Kemmerer, D., 383(14)
Keogh, D., 377(123), 378(10)
Kepner, C., 15, 339(11), 341(20), 341(21), 341(25), 341(26), 341(27), 341(28), 341(29), 341(30), 341(35), 342(41), 343(3), 343(4), 343(5), 343(6), 384(31)
Kinzer, S., 358(9), 359(42), 360(44)
Kissinger Report, 381(18), 383(9)
Krehm, W., 352(38), 352(40)

Labarge, R., 353(9), 354(22), 354(23)
Lafeber, W., 339(22), 384(37)
Latin American Studies Association, 382(84)
League of Nations, 9(table), 34(table), 55(table), 56(table), 79(table), 341(34), 346(8)
León Gómez, A., 5
Leonard, T., 359(36), 359(39), 384(38)
Levin, J., 355(49)
Lizano, E., 365(1), 376(79)
Luciak, I., 381(70), 381(71), 382(96)

McCann, T., 353(10)
McCarthy, P., 219(table)
McClintock, M., 360(45), 367(45), 370(127), 376(98), 377(111)
McCreery, D., 340(27), 345(26), 384(18)
McLeod, M., 1
Macaulay, N., 345(34)
Marroquín, A., 345(25)
Masferrer, A., 345(35)
Maxfield, S., 380(47)
May, S., 348(30), 351(33), 354(25), 354(26)
Mecham, J., 349(2), 350(3), 360(52), 360(54), 360(57), 360(58)
Melville, T., 350(6), 360(43)
Menjívar, R., 342(49), 359(31), 370(110), 370(124), 377(106)
Meza, V., 369(88), 370(122), 376(87), 376(88), 376(96)
Millet, R., 358(16), 363(61), 370(120)
Ministerio de Hacienda, 379(23)
Monfils, M., 342(42), 344(23), 347(18)
Monge Alfaro, C., 342(53)
Monteforte Toledo, M., 163(table), 355(41), 363(49), 369(82), 369(83)
Montero Umaña, L., 341(33), 350(12)

Montes, M., 373(38)
Moody's, 344(15), 350(18)
Mooney, J., 385(8)
Morris, J., 360(50), 378(17)
Mosk, S., 338(3)
Munro, D., 8(table), 9(table), 338(3), 339(20), 340(1), 340(2), 340(3), 340(5)
Musgrove, P., 154(table), 155(table), 157(table), 158(table), 361(1), 361(4), 361(11), 361(13), 361(17), 361(20), 362(27), 362(30), 362(36), 368(69), 371(15)

NACLA, 367(45), 367(48)
Natalini de Castro, S., 360(50), 360(62)
North, L., 372(21)
Nye, J., 366(16)

Obando Sánchez, A., 342(56), 345(33)
Oconitrillo García, E., 340(1)
Oficina de Planificación, 374(51)
Orellana, R., 219(table), 376(80)

Pan American Union, 23(table)
Parsons, J., 362(34)
Payne, D., 378(2)
Pearce, J., 339(22), 363(42), 385(46)
Pérez Bermudez, C., 358(1)
Pérez Brignoli, H., 339(22), 349(45)
Plazo, G., 348(30)
Poblete Troncoso, M., 360(53)
Poitevin, R., 369(100)
Posas, M., 340(25), 340(26), 342(58), 342(60), 344(21), 344(22), 345(39), 348(26), 352(49), 353(7), 357(68), 358(5), 359(33), 359(34), 360(48), 364(83), 375(76), 376(89), 376(90), 377(101), 378(18)
PREALC, 219(table), 372(29), 380(59), 375(75)
Prebisch, R., 365(89)

Ramsett, D., 366(25)
Ranis, G., 385(43)
Reina Valenzuela, J., 349(45)
Reuben Soto, S., 354(19), 363(50)
Reynolds, C., 197(table), 370(118), 370(123)
Riismandel, J., 355(41)
Rivera Urrutia, E., 379(23), 379(37), 379(42)
Robleda, R., 382(99)
Rodriguez Beteta, V., 341(24)
Rojas Bolaños, 342(52), 345(31), 345(42), 346(44), 346(45), 359(28), 377(104)
Romero, A., 381(82)
Rosenberg, M., 351(31), 370(125), 370(126), 376(83)

Rosenthal, G., 338(8), 364(79), 369(99), 384(28), 384(32), 384(35)
Rossbach, L., 3
Rowles, J., 365(2)
Ruhl, M., 376(91)

Sánchez, M., 349(48)
Santos, R., 370(108), 374(46)
Schifter, J., 358(11), 358(18), 358(19), 359(23), 359(26), 359(27), 359(30)
Schlesinger, S., 358(9), 359(42), 360(44), 360(60)
Schmid, L., 368(77)
Seligson, M., 340(38), 343(7), 344(20), 344(24), 345(43), 376(78)
Selser, G., 346(48)
Serna, R., 372(27)
SIECA, 182(table), 184(table), 188(table), 193(table), 210(table), 213(table), 215(table), 366(27), 366(35), 367(36), 367(37), 367(44), 367(47), 367(51), 367(52), 368(64), 369(84), 369(89), 369(91), 369(93), 369(94), 369(96), 369(97), 370(104), 372(32), 373(34), 373(39), 373(42), 374(60), 384(19), 386(30)
Siri, G., 371(2), 374(54)
Slutsky, D., 371(14)
Sobral, E., 341(19)
Soley Güell, T., 341(12), 345(28), 345(43), 348(36)
Somoza, A., 346(50)
Soothill, J., 15, 341(26), 341(27), 341(29), 341(30), 341(35), 343(4), 343(6)
South American Handbook, 23 (table)
Stahler-Sholk, R., 380(47)
Staley, C., 365(94)
Stokes, W., 349(50)
Stone, S., 340(39), 349(50)
Swerling, B., 340(7), 343(10)

Taracena, A., 340(34), 342(55)
Thome, J., 381(69)
Thompson, W., 10, 23(table)
Thorp, R., 385(16)
Torres Rivas, E., 50(table), 346(3), 348(31), 350(11), 352(41), 353(3)

Triffin, R., 352(36), 352(37)

United Nations, 351(21), 356(61), 385(7)
Universidad de Costa Rica, 354(14), 354(15), 354(16), 354(17), 354(23), 354(24), 355(28), 355(38), 355(44), 355(45), 356(55), 356(56), 356(59), 385(9)

Vaitsos, C., 366(23)
Vega, M., 371(12), 373(37)
Vilas, C., 378(4), 382(90)
Villareal, B., 369(87), 371(16), 372(19), 376(85)
Viteri Bertrand, E., 340(4)
Volio, M., 342(52)

Wagley, C., 348(39)
Wall, D., 361(2)
Watkins, V., 356(64), 356(65), 356(66), 364(71), 365(91), 366(22), 366(26), 366(29), 366(30), 367(38), 367(41)
Webre, S., 370(121)
Weeks, J., 370(105), 370(106), 373(44), 374(50)
Weinert, R., 380(46)
Wheelock, J., 340(29), 354(20), 356(62)
Whetten, N., 363(59), 365(85)
White, A., 343(64), 344(23), 352(48), 352(59), 363(60), 368(67), 368(70), 369(95)
Whitehead, L., 381(80), 382(100)
Wickizer, C., 341(31), 343(2), 350(13), 350(14)
Wilkie, J., 219(table), 302, 369(85)
Williams, R., 355(33)
Willmore, L., 365(1), 369(98), 370(103), 370(104)
Woodbridge, P., 348(28)
Woodward, E., 359(38)
World Bank, 202(table), 371(18), 372(19), 374(53), 374(61), 380(54), 385(42)

Ydígoras Fuentes, M., 360(46), 364(82)
Young, J., 339(12), 339(13), 339(14), 339(15), 341(15), 341(17), 341(18), 384(25), 384(26)

Zeledón, M., 365(87)

# General index

Abacá, 94, 111–12
Acosta García, Julio, 28, 31, 43
Adjustment programmes, 240–1, 243–58
AFL-CIO, 137, 142, 143, 145–6, 149, 223
African palm oil, 204
Aguado, Enoc, 134
Agriculture, 271–2, 297–9, 302–3 (see also
    Export Agriculture and Domestic Use
    Agriculture)
Agüero, Fernando, 226
Aguirre y Salinas, Colonel Osmin, 104
AIFLD, 228
Alliance for Progress, 178, 189, 221, 282,
    289
Alvarez Martínez, General, 235, 261, 262
ANDES, 225
Antivagrancy laws, 10, 81, 127
Arana, Francisco Javier, 139
Araujo, Arturo, 62–3
Arbenz, Jacobo, 108, 109, 119, 124, 139,
    140, 141–2, 143, 148, 282
Area Propiedad del Pueblo, see Nicaragua
Arévalo, Juan José, 104, 132, 138–9, 140,
    141, 147
Argentina, 144–5, 278
Argüello, Leonardo, 134
Aski-marks, 78–9
Artisan Sector, 191, 209, 218
Asociación Cafetalera de El Salvador, 59
Asociación Nacional de Campesinos de
    Honduras (ANACH), 189, 222, 224
Asociación para el Progreso de Honduras
    (APROH), 235
Asociación Nacional de Productores de Café,
    59
Asociación Revolucionaria Cultura Obrera,
    64
Asociación de Trabajadores del Campo
    (ATC), 262
Atlantic Charter, 101
Atlantic Coast, 20, 232
Atlantic Fruit Co., 35
ATLAS, 148

Balance of payments, 69–70, 237–44
Bananas
    Concessions, 76
    Discriminatory tariffs, 151
    Disease, 37, 76, 107–8, 151–3, 187
    Expansion, 33–7, 107–9, 203
    Export tax, 35–6, 123, 203, 214
    Foreign companies' political influence, 15,
        109, 278
    Hurricane Fifi, 203, 213
    Independent planters, 59, 187, 203
    Labour relations, 12, 20–1, 277
    Origins, 5–8, 16
    Pacific coast production, 76–7
    Per caput consumption, 151
    Prices, 27, 36, 50–1, 108, 152
    Strikes, 44–5, 59, 109, 143–4
    Taxes, 109, 123
    Unemployment, 59
    Varieties, 152, 187
    Vertical integration, 15
    Wages, 36–7, 59, 143
    Yields, 152–3
Banco Agrícola Comercial, 120
Banco de América (BANAMER), 120, 159
Banco Atlántida, 11, 30
Banco Central de Costa Rica, 123
Banco Central de Guatemala, 32
Banco Central de Honduras, 301
Banco Central de Nicaragua, 296
Banco Central de Reserva (El Salvador), 54,
    99
Banco de Comercio, 120
Banco de Fomento de Honduras, 163–4
Banco de Guatemala, 123
Banco Internacional de Costa Rica, 32, 73
Banco Nacional de Costa Rica, 73, 97, 113
Banco Nacional de Nicaragua, 3, 29, 45, 99,
    112
Banco Nacional Nicaragüense, 159
Banco Nicaragüense (BANIC), 120, 159
Banks, 3, 7–8, 11, 40, 73–4, 119, 123–4,
    127, 158, 208, 280

407

Banks (*contd*)
  Credit, 98, 114, 163–4, 184, 186, 205
  Nationalisation, 118, 119, 124, 136, 232,
    234, 239, 245, 278, 280
Barrios, Justo Rufino, 18
Barter Terms of Trade, 42, 53, 171, 196, 202,
  239, 270, 305
Basic balance, 237, 239
Basic grains, 180, 189, 205, 206
Beef, 158, 186–7, 204
Belgium, 97
*Beneficios, see* Coffee
Bernstein mission, 123
Bertrand, Francisco, 25
Bloque Popular Revolucionario (BPR), 225
Bondholders, 284–5
Bonds, 74, 99, 249
Borbón, Jorge, 174
Bragman's Bluff Lumber Co., 34
Brazil, 37, 49, 278
Budget deficit, 28, 56–7, 70–1, 96, 122, 124,
  216, 246, 249, 253, 255
Burden of adjustment, 251–2

Cacao, 78, 113
Calderón, Rafael Angel, 84, 91, 95, 96, 100,
  101, 102, 104, 135–6, 198
Cámara de Agricultura, Comercio y Finanza
  (CACIF), 264
Capital outflows, 238–9, 241, 291
Capitalist modernisation, 122, 123–4, 125–
  9, 166–7, 170, 281
Capitalist surplus, 42–3, 159, 277–8
Carazo, Rodrigo, 218, 236, 237, 244
Cardamom, 204
Cardonazo, 137
Carías Andino, Tiburcio, 45, 64, 76, 83–4,
  99, 103, 132, 133, 138
Caribbean Basin Initiative (CBI), 250, 260,
  262, 292
Caribbean Legion, 141–2, 144, 147–8
Carter, President J., 228, 233, 236, 290
Castañeda Castro, General Salvador, 104,
  133, 137, 145
Castillo Armas, Carlos, 109, 126, 128, 142–
  3, 146–7, 165–6, 170
Castle and Cooke, *see* Standard Fruit and
  Steamship Co.
Catholic Church, 132, 223
Cattle, 77, 157–8, 204
*Caudillismo*, 60, 61–7, 74, 84, 85, 100–4,
  287
Cement, 40, 95, 119
Central America
  Bilateral trade treaties, 118, 172
  Clearing House, 177
  Common Market (CACM), 171–4, 177–

    80, 181, 183, 185, 191, 192–4, 195–7,
    200, 204, 207–12, 241–2, 247, 255,
    260, 263, 270, 279, 287, 289, 291
  Court of Justice, 20
  Declaration of war on axis powers, 89
  Economic integration, 118
  Elections, 17
  Expansion of coffee, 18
  Federation of Labour, 44
  Introduction of bananas, 5–8
  Introduction of coffee, 2
  Introduction of railways, 3
  Monetary Council, 177, 256
  Reformist political parties, 85
  Trade with Germany, 78–9
  Trade with USA, 9, 78–9
  Treaty of Peace and Amity, 20, 25
  Treaty of Union, 25
Central American Bank for Economic
  Integration (CABEI), 177, 180, 216
Central Bank and Trust Co. of New Orleans,
  76
Central Banking, 74, 118
Central Intelligence Agency (CIA), 142, 290
Central Sandinista de Trabajadores (CST),
  262
Chadbourne Committee, 51
Chambers of Industry, 192
Chamorro, Emiliano, 25, 45–6, 134–5
Chicle, 156
Christmas, Lee, 1
Cinchona bark, 90
Coca Cola, 224, 225, 262
Coffee
  *Beneficios*, 21, 40
  Brazilian valorisation scheme, 37, 49
  Concentration, 110
  Debt moratoria, 75
  Expansion, 18
  Export tax, 24, 37, 75, 91, 123, 127
  German growers, 3, 78
  Inter-American Coffee Agreement, 91–2,
    109
  International Coffee Agreement, 153, 187,
    263
  Labour, 58
  Oligarchy, 22
  Pan-American Conference, 91
  *Per caput* consumption, 153
  Prices, 26–7, 37, 49, 58, 91, 109–10, 153,
    196, 202, 239–40, 274
  Producers' Associations, 59, 154
  Quotas, 153, 186–7, 202–3, 263, 288
  Return on Capital, 75
  Rust, 203
  State support, 13–14, 75, 154
  Tariff discrimination, 153

Wages, 37, 58–9, 60, 75
Yields, 109–10, 154–5
Cold war, 104, 141, 144–5, 290
Colombia, 203, 259
*Colonos*, 39
Comité de Alto Nivel (CAN), 207–8
Comités de Defensa Sandinista, *see*
  Nicaragua
Comité Nacional de Unidad Sindical (CNUS),
  224, 225
Comité Organizador de la Confederación de
  Trabajadores Nicaragüenses (COCTN),
  132
Comité de Reorganización Obrero Sindical
  (CROS), 137
Comité de Unidad Campesina (CUC), 224,
  225, 236
Commerce, 57, 119, 254, 300
Commercial banks, *see* Banks
Common External Tariff (CET), 181
Communal lands, 11, 22
Confederación General de Trabajadores
  (CGT), 223, 224
Confederación General de Trabajadores de
  Guatemala (CGTG), 139, 142
Confederación Nacional Campesina de
  Guatemala (CNCG), 133, 139, 142
Confederación Latinoamericana de
  Trabajadores (CLAT), 132, 138, 144,
  223
Confederación de Trabajadores
  Costarricenses (CTCR), 103, 135, 136
Confederación de Trabajadores de
  Guatemala (CTG), 131, 138
Confederación de Trabajadores de Nicaragua
  (CTN), 132, 133–4
Confederación de Trabajadores Rerum
  Novarum (CCTRN), 132, 146
Conservatives, 17
Contadora group, 259
*Continuismo*, 61, 63, 67, 83, 287
Contras, *see* Nicaragua
Cooperativa Algodonera Salvadoreña, 112
Cooperativa Bananera Costarricense, 35
Cooperatives, 189, 199, 220
Corporación Costarricense de Desarrollo
  (CODESA), 208
Corporación Financiera Nacional
  (CORFINA), 208
Corporación Nacional de Inversiones
  (CONADI), 208
Cortés, León, 65, 66, 84, 85, 96, 102, 103
Costa Rica
  Abolition of army, 136
  Acción Democrática, 135
  Bananas, 5, 11, 35–6, 50–1, 77, 108, 109,
  187

Bloque de Obreros y Campesinos, 65, 85
Board of Control, 72
Caja de Conversión, 32, 54
Catholic Church, 132
Centre for the Study of National Problems,
  102, 135
Civil war, 110, 134
Coffee, 2, 10, 24, 75, 100, 109–10, 154
Communist Party, 59, 64, 65, 85, 102, 132
Consejo Nacional de Producción (CNP),
  95, 99, 113, 164
Currency reform, 31–2
Democratic Party, 102, 103, 135
Education, 18
Gold standard, 13
Labour, 44, 60, 189, 198
Labour Code, 97, 103, 133
Land reform, 221, 264
Meseta Central, 64
Minimum wage law, 65
Oficina de Café, 154
Partido Liberación Nacional (PLN), 136,
  167, 174, 198, 221–2
Partido Republicano Nacional, 101, 102,
  133, 198
Partido Social Demócrata, 135, 136
Partido Unión Nacional (PUN), 198
Political stability, 18, 43–4
Social security programme, 97, 198
Taxes, 55
Vanguardia Popular, 102, 132, 135, 136,
  137
Welfare state, 97, 215
Cotton, 78, 80, 94, 112–13, 116, 156–7,
  186–7, 204, 277
Cotton-seed, 112
Council of Central American Defence
  (CONDECA), 178
Council of State, *see* Nicaragua
Crédito Hipotecario Nacional (Guatemala),
  114
Cruz, President Ramón Ernesto, 222
Cuba, 228, 259, 260
Cuban revolution, 166, 178
Cuban sugar quota, 158
Customs revenues, 41, 95–6, 246
Cuyamel Fruit Co., 7, 33, 35, 45, 50, 75

Debt, 14, 27, 28–9, 41, 55–6, 70–1, 79, 83,
  95, 103, 124, 217–18, 237, 242–3, 247,
  249–50, 253, 255, 291
  peonage, 21, 81
Decentralised autonomous institutions, 216
De León, General Mauro, 61
Del Monte, 187, 203
Depression, 25–6, 26–8, 70, 125
Devaluation, *see* exchange rates

Díaz, Adolfo, 45–6, 66
Distribution of income, 117, 196–7, 279
Dollar diplomacy, 288
Domestic Use Agriculture (DUA), 9, 20, 38–
    9, 57, 80–1, 113–16, 161–5, 188–90,
    205–7, 277, 300, 303
Duarte, José Napoleon, 234

Echandi, Mario, 167, 174, 198
Economic Commission for Latin America
    (ECLA), 115, 118, 172–4, 179, 289,
    296–7, 302
Ecuador, 152–3, 203
Education, 170, 214
Effective Rate of Protection (ERP), 181, 185
Effinger, Max, 85
Eisenhower administration, 173
Electric Bond and Share Co., 40, 141
Electricity, 81, 123, 168
El Salvador
    Alianza Nacional de Zapateros, 85
    Armed forces, 60
    Christian Democrat Party, 197–8, 226,
        234, 261, 264
    Civil war, 201, 233–4, 270
    Coffee, 2, 75, 94, 112, 154–5, 205
    Communist Party, 44, 132, 225
    Cotton, 94, 156–7
    Currency reform, 31
    Frente Democrático Revolucionario
        (FDR)–Frente Farabundo Martí para la
        Liberación Nacional (FMLN), 233–4
    Industrial promotion, 118
    Instituto de Colonización Rural, 116
    Labour, 44
    Land reform, 82, 116, 205, 234, 264
    La Matanza, 63
    Meléndez-Quiñónez dynasty, 18, 22, 44
    Partido de Conciliación Nacional (PCN),
        166
    Partido Laborista, 62, 85
    Partido Revolucionario de Unificación
        Democrático (PRUD), 137
    Partido Unión Democrática, 132
    Political instability, 60
    Pro-Patria Party, 84
    Social Improvement Fund, 82, 116–17
    Sugar, 94
    War with Honduras, 180, 205
Energy, 81
Estrada Cabrera, Manuel, 19, 22, 25, 28
Exchange control, 239
Exchange rates, 12, 27, 28–33, 53–4, 72, 80,
    83, 100, 125, 127, 238, 245, 254–5,
    280, 291, 297
Exportadora Comercial Internacional
    (CISA), 119

Export Agriculture (EXA), 9, 20, 38, 114,
    117, 160, 185–9, 200, 202–3, 271–2,
    277, 300, 303
Export diversification, 94–5, 111–14, 128,
    156–60, 275
Export-led growth, 11, 33–8, 57, 66–7, 267,
    272, 275–9
Export promotion, 209, 211, 246, 249–50,
    262
Export specialisation, 42–3, 57, 82, 262, 279
Extended Fund Facility (EFF), 243–4
Extra-regional exports, 202, 211, 276
European Economic Community (EEC), 259

Facio, Rodrigo, 82
Farabundo Martí, Augustín, 62
Fascism, 85
Federación Autónoma Sindical de Guatemala
    (FASGUA), 142, 223
Federación Cristiana de Campesinos de El
    Salvador (FECCAS), 223, 225
Federación Nacional de Agricultores y
    Ganaderos (FENAGH), 222
Federación Nacional de Campesinos de
    Honduras (FENACH), 189
Federación Regional Obrera de Guatemala,
    44
Federación Sindical de Guatemala (FSG), 138
Ferrocarril al Pacífico, 40
Figueres, José, 102, 109, 119, 135–7, 147,
    152, 166, 167, 211, 273
Financial Institutions, *see* Banks
Fiscal Incentives Convention (FIC), 179
Fiscal reform, 169, 180–5, 212–18, 264,
    280–1, 293
Food security, 205
Foreign borrowing, 123, 127
Foreign companies, 285–7
Foro Popular, 233–4
Fortuny, José Manuel, 139–40
Franco, General, 85
Frente de Acción Popular Unificada (FAPU),
    225
Frente Democrático Revolucionario (FDR)–
    Frente Farabundo Martí para la
    Liberación Nacional (FMLN), *see* El
    Salvador
Frente Sandinista de Liberación Nacional
    (FSLN), *see* Nicaragua
Frente de Unidad Campesina (FUNC), 224
Fuerzas Populares de Liberación (FPL), 225

Gálvez, Manuel, 109, 133, 138, 142, 143
Germany, 78, 88–9, 91
Gold, 38, 53, 77–8, 94, 253
Gold exchange standard, 29
Gold standard, 13, 53–4, 58, 72

González Víquez, Cleto, 24, 43
Goodyear Rubber Co., 112
Government revenue, 15, 96–7, 124, 214,
   273
Gutiérrez, Víctor Manuel, 140
Great Britain, *see* United Kingdom
Green Revolution, 200, 207
Guardia, Tomás, 18
Guatemala
   Bananas, 5, 35, 50, 76–7, 108–9, 126
   Caja reguladora, 32
   Christian Democrat Party, 226
   Civil war, 201
   Coffee, 2, 10, 110, 154–5
   Communist Party, 44, 85, 132, 140
   Cotton, 112–13
   Currency reform, 32–3
   Franja Transversal del Norte, 206, 221
   Frente Unido de la Revolución (FUR), 225,
      236
   Industrial promotion, 118
   Labour, 44, 80, 142
   Labour Code, 133, 138, 142
   Land reform, 109, 116, 128, 141–2, 162,
      166
   Law of Probity, 62
   Movimiento de Liberación Nacional
      (MLN) 142, 166
   Partido Acción Revolucionaria (PAR), 132
   Partido Guatemalteco de Trabajadores
      (PGT), 140
   Progressive Liberal Party, 84
   Revolución Nacional (RN), 132
   Road-building programme, 80
   Social Democratic Party, 236
   Social Security Programme, 138, 166, 198
   Vanguardia Democrática, 132

Havana Conference, 90
Health, 214
Henequen, 80
Herrera, Carlos, 28, 32
Honduras
   Bananas, 5, 7, 33–4, 44, 50, 76, 94, 109
   Christian Democrat Party, 227, 235
   Coffee, 2–3, 24, 110, 154–5
   Communist Party, 138
   Currency reform, 29–31
   Government revenue, 15
   Labour, 45, 143–4, 149, 189–90, 198–9
   Labour Code, 143
   Land reform, 195, 222–3, 265
   Liberal Party, 84, 138, 143, 167, 227, 235
   National Party, 45, 64, 84, 143, 235
   Partido Democrático Revolucionario
      Hondureño (PDRH), 132, 138
   Partido Reformista, 143

Political unrest, 17, 45
Railway scandal, 3–4
Social Security Programme, 198
Sugar, 159
Unions, 45
U.S. intervention, 45
War with El Salvador, 180, 195
Hoover, President H., 65
Hydro-electricity, 81, 264

Import controls, 245–7
Import Substitution in Agriculture (ISA), 79–
   82, 94, 270
Import Substitution in Industry (ISI), 79–82,
   95, 172, 201, 263, 270
Industrial promotion, 118, 167, 190–1
Infant mortality, 205
Inflation, 13, 28, 94, 97–100, 122, 124–5,
   200, 201–2, 212–18, 255–6, 291
*Ingenios, see* Sugar
Instituto de Fomento de Producción
   (Guatemala), 112–13, 114, 164
Instituto Nacional de Seguros, 43
Instituto Regulador de Abastecimientos
   (IRA), 205
Instituto de Tierras y Colonización (ITCO),
   189, 221
Inter-American Development Bank (IDB),
   253, 263
Inter-American Development Commission, 90
Inter-American Financial and Economic
   Advisory Committee, 90
Inter-American Highway, 89, 91, 95
Inter-American Institute of Agricultural
   Sciences, 90
Inter-American Treaty of Reciprocal
   Assistance, 147
Interest rates, 186, 237–8, 250
Integration Industries Convention (IIC), 179
International Coffee Agreement, *see* Coffee
International Monetary Fund (IMF), 123,
   171, 196, 243–4, 245–52, 260, 262,
   264, 292
International Railways of Central America
   (IRCA), 40, 77, 141
International reserves, 237
International Sugar Agreement, 159
Investment
   Direct Foreign Investment, 10, 40, 95, 108,
      119, 191, 194, 216, 287
   in Industry, 191, 194
   Net financial surplus, 116–17, 120–1
   Portfolio, 238
   Private, 117, 119–20, 121, 241
   Public, 242
   Ratio, 216
   Real fixed capital formation, 168–9

Irrigation, 206
Italy, 89

Japan, 89
Jiménez Oreamuno, Ricardo, 24, 43, 64
Johnson, President L., 178
*Jornaleros*, 39
Junta de Gobierno de Reconstrucción
  Nacional, *see* Nicaragua

Keith, Minor, 5, 40
Kemmerer, E. W., 32, 280, 288
Kennedy, President J., 178
Kissinger Report, 260, 263

Labour
  Antivagrancy laws, 11, 277
  Codes, 118, 127, 133
  Courts, 139, 282
  Federations, 22, 131–3, 135, 145–6, 283
  Landlessness, 161, 218
  Proletarianisation, 219, 277
  Real wages, 218–19, 246, 251–2, 255,
    261–2
  Rural, 20–1, 128, 189, 190, 218, 276–7,
    283
  Seasonal, 20, 160
  Supply, 11, 12, 276–7
  Unemployment, 60, 252
  Wage rates, 12, 117, 127, 160, 190, 218,
    246, 255
  Unions, 127–8, 132–3, 198, 283
  Unrest, 46
Ladinos, 2
Land frontier, 162
Land ownership, 162, 207
Land reform, 189–90, 195, 205, 221–3, 264,
  282–3, 292–3
Laugerud, Kjell, 224, 235
Lázaro Chacón, General, 44, 61
Lemongrass oil, 113
Ley Vialidad, 72
Liberals, 17
Liberal oligarchic state, 46–7, 57
Liberal revolutions, 11, 17
Literacy rates, 114, 127, 171, 283
Livestock, *see* Beef
Lombardo Toledano, Vicente, 132, 144
López Arellano, General, 199, 222
López Gutierrez, General, 25, 34, 44
Los Altos Railway, 41
Lozano, Julio, 143–4, 167
Lucas García, General, 218, 224, 235, 236,
  239

Macroeconomic performance, 267, 268–75
*Mandamientos*, 21

Manufacturing, 9, 40, 79–80, 117–18, 193–
  4, 209–11, 272–3, 299–300
Marginalisation of the peasantry, 201, 207,
  277
Marmol, Miguel, 44, 140
Martínez, Bartolomé, 45
Martínez, General Maximiliano Hernández,
  63, 66, 67, 72, 84, 85, 101, 103
Masferrer, Alberto, 62
Max, Hermán, 99
Mejía Colindres, Vicente, 45, 64
Mejía Victores, General, 236
Meléndez family, *see* El Salvador
Melgar Castro, Juan Alberto, 222
Méndez Montenegro, President, 183
Meseta Central, *see* Costa Rica
Mexico, 19, 256, 258–9
Migration, 20, 161, 195
Minimum wages, 65, 128, 170, 199, 220,
  236
*Minifundistas*, 114
Mining, 119, 126, 156, 208, 210, 272, 299,
  303
Moncada, José María, 46
Money supply, 73, 97, 242, 253
Monge, Luis Alberto, 237, 264–5
Monroe Doctrine, *see* United States of
  America
Mooney, Joseph, 296
Mora Valverde, Manuel, 65, 102, 103, 136
Muñoz P., Plutarco, 76
Multinational companies, *see* Direct Foreign
  Investment

National City Bank of New York, 55
National Directorate, *see* Nicaragua
National Guard, *see* Nicaragua
Nicaragua
  Area Propiedad del Pueblo (APP), 232
  Bananas, 5, 11, 34–5, 50, 76
  Beef, 158
  Board of Control, 73
  Board of Price and Trade Control, 99
  *Camisas Azules*, 85
  Civil war, 201, 270
  Claims Commissions, 45
  Coffee, 2, 10, 24, 75, 109–10, 127, 154–5
  Comités de Defensa Sandinista (CDS), 232
  Communisty Party, 85
  Conservative Party, 84, 120, 134, 226
  Contras, 233
  COSEP, 227, 265, 278
  Cotton, 112, 157
  Council of State, 232
  Currency reform, 29
  ENABAS, 254
  Frente Amplio Opositor (FAO), 226

Frente Sandinista de Liberación Nacional
(FSLN), 223, 226, 228, 238, 253, 261,
265, 294
Gold exchange standard, 29
High Commission, 83
Junta de Gobierno de Reconstrucción
Nacional (JGRN), 230, 232
Labour Code, 103, 133
Land reform, 257–8, 265
Lend-Lease agreement, 89
Liberal Party, 84, 120
*Los Doce*, 226
National Directorate, 232
National Guard, 65–6, 232, 235
Occupation by USA, 1, 20, 45–6
Partido Liberal Independiente (PLI), 226
Partido Socialista Nicaragüense (PSN),
132, 133–4, 224
Partido Trabajador Nicaragüense, 131
Social Christian Party, 198, 226
Sugar, 159
Unión Democrática de Liberación (UDEL),
226
U.S. Collector-General of Customs, 29, 54,
73, 83
Nickel, 210

Oduber, Daniel, 211
Oil production, 210–11
Oil shocks, 201–2, 209, 212, 239
OPEC, 203
ORDEN, 199
Orellana, José M., 28, 32, 44, 62
Organización de Estados Centroamericanos
(ODECA), 171–2
Organización Regional Interamericana de
Trabajadores (ORIT), 145–6, 223
Orlich, Francisco, 198
Osorio, Major Oscar, 137, 166

Pact of Amapala, 45
Panama, 85, 236, 259
Panama Canal, 19, 20, 89, 90, 91, 112, 275,
288
Pan-American Federation of Labour, 22, 44
Pan-American Highway, *see* Inter-American
Highway
Pan-American Conference (Ninth), 134, 145
Pastora, Eden, 237
Paz Baraona, Miguel, 45
Paz García, Policarpo, 222, 235, 244
Pearl Harbor, 89, 90, 93
Pellecer, Carlos Manuel, 140
Perón, Juan, 148
Picado, Teodoro, 103, 124, 134, 135, 136
Political Parties, *see* individual countries
Ponce, General Federico, 104

Population growth, 114, 171, 302
Public Utilities, 119, 127
Purchasing power of exports, 42, 306
Purchasing power parity exchange rates, 297

Quinine, 90

Railways, 3–4, 40, 41, 119, 127
Reagan, President R., 228–9
Real Gross Domestic Product per head, 268–
9
Regional Federation of Workers of El
Salvador, 44
Regional Integration, *see* Central America –
Common Market
Regional Office for Central America and
Panama (ROCAP), 174
Ríos Montt, General, 226, 236, 249
Rivera, Colonel Julio, 166
Roads, 71, 81, 215
Román y Reyes, Victor, 134
Romero, Arturo, 103–4, 132, 141
Romero, General Carlos H., 225, 233, 238
Romero, Bosque, Pío, 44, 62
Roosevelt, President F., 85, 91
Roosevelt, President T., 19
Roosevelt, Corollary, 19
Rubber, 90, 111–2, 119

Sacasa, Juan Bautista, 45–6, 66
Sanabria, Archbishop Victor Manuel, 97, 102
Sandinistas, *see* Nicaragua – Frente
Sandinista de Liberación Nacional
Sandino, A. C., 34–5, 46, 65–6, 89
San José Oil Facility, 258–9, 264
San José Protocol, 183, 281
Savings, 169, 184
School of Pan-American Agriculture, 90
Secretaría Permanente del Tratado General
de Integración Centroamericana
(SIECA), 174, 177, 207, 208
Sesame, 94, 113, 156
Short-term capital flows, 237
Sigatoka, *see* Bananas-disease
Silver, 12–13, 27, 30, 38, 77
Silver standard, 12–13
Social Improvement Fund, *see* El Salvador
Social Infrastructure, 127, 168
Social Security Programmes, 97, 133, 170,
198, 214, 220–1, 286
Solórzano, Carlos, 45
Somoza Debayle, Anastasio, 197, 225, 230,
232, 238
Somoza Debayle, Luis, 166–7, 176, 197
Somoza García, Anastasio, 66, 67, 73, 84,
89, 91, 95, 100, 103, 120, 132, 133,
134–5, 141, 147, 166

Stabilisation, *see* Adjustment Programmes
Standard Fruit and Steamship Co., 7, 33, 76, 93, 126, 143, 152, 186–7, 203
Stimson, Henry, 46, 65
Suazo Córdova, Roberto, 235, 265
Sugar, 40, 45, 51, 77, 94, 158–9, 186, 204, 253, 263, 277
Swedish Match Co., 55–6

Tariffs, 55, 80, 122, 168, 212, 246
Taxes
   Direct, 122–3, 127, 182–3
   Export, 183, 185, 214, 215, 246
   Indirect, 121, 183
   Property, 182–3, 214
   Sales, 183
Tela Railroad Co., 33, 59, 143
Telecommunications, 40
Textiles, 40, 119
Third Reich, 78
Timber, 38, 77
Tinoco, Federico, 25, 28, 31
Torrijos, General Omar, 236
Tosco, Manuel, 296
Tosta, General Vicente, 45
Tourism, 239
Trade coefficient, 269–70
Trade diversion, 179
Trade Unions, *see* Labour
Treaty of Peace and Amity, *see* Central America
Trejos Fernandez, José Joaquín, 198
Truman, President H., 145
Triffin, R., 99
Trujillo, President Rafael, 147
Truxillo Railroad Co., 33, 59

Ubico, Jorge, 61–2, 67, 73, 80, 104
Ulate, Otilio, 136, 137, 198
Unemployment, *see* Labour
Unión Nacional de Trabajadores (UNT), 131
Unión Nacional Opositora (UNO), 226
Union of Soviet Socialist Republics (USSR), 90, 132, 140–1, 148, 256, 259, 260, 265, 290
Unión de Trabajadores del Campo (UTC), 225
Unión de Países Exportadores de Banano (UPEB), 203
United Brands, *see* United Fruit Co.
United Fruit Co. (UFCO), 7, 33, 35–6, 40,

57, 70, 75, 76, 90, 93, 95, 102, 108, 109, 112, 113, 126, 136, 141–3, 152, 186–7, 203, 287
United Kingdom, 78–9, 88
United States of America (USA)
   Agency of International Development, 174, 292
   Alliance with USSR, 132
   Challenge to hegemony, 225–9
   Constitution, 17
   Export–Import Bank, 95
   Good Neighbor Policy, 85–6, 289
   Intervention in Guatemala, 141–3, 146–7
   Lend-Lease Agreement, 89, 95
   Military aid, 235, 260
   Military missions, 89
   Monroe Doctrine, 19, 29
   Non-recognition policy, 63, 85, 289
   Occupation of Nicaragua, 1, 20, 273
   Official Development Assistance, 178, 233
   Strategic interests, 88–90, 288
   Trade embargo against Nicaragua, 256
   Trade with Central America, 9
   Washington Peace Conference, 19, 289
   Washington Treaties, 25, 61, 63
University of Costa Rica, 296

Vaccaro Bros., 7, 33
Value Added Tax, 249
Venezuela, 258–9
Venezuela Investment Fund, 216, 259
Villeda Morales, Ramón, 138, 143, 148–9, 167, 222
Vinelli, Paul, 296

Washington Peace Conference, *see* United States of America
Washington Treaties, *see* United States of America
Williams, Abraham, 143
Wilson, President W., 3
World Bank, 123, 253, 260, 262, 292
World Federation of Trade Unions (WFTU), 138, 144

Ydígoras Fuentes, Miguel, 139, 143, 165, 170
Young, Arthur, 30

Zaldívar, Rafael, 18
Zelaya, José Santos, 18, 19, 20, 21, 29
Zemurray, S., 7, 33, 75

# CAMBRIDGE LATIN AMERICAN STUDIES

3 Peter Calvert. *The Mexican Revolution 1910–1914: The Diplomacy of Anglo-American Conflict*

7 David Barkin and Timothy King. *Regional Economic Development: The River Basin Approach in Mexico*

8 Celso Furtado. *Economic Development of Latin America: Historical Background and Contemporary Problems* (second edition)

10 D. A. Brading. *Miners and Merchants in Bourbon Mexico, 1763–1810*

15 P. J. Bakewell. *Silver Mining and Society in Colonial Mexico, Zacatecas 1564–1700*

22 James Lockhart and Enrique Otte. *Letters and People of the Spanish Indies: The Sixteenth Century*

24 Jean A. Meyer. *The Cristero Rebellion: The Mexican People between Church and State 1926–1929*

25 Stefan de Vylder. *Allende's Chile: The Political Economy of the Rise and Fall of the Unidad Popular*

31 Charles F. Nunn. *Foreign Immigrants in Early Bourbon Mexico, 1700–1760*

32 D. A. Brading. *Haciendas and Ranchos in the Mexican Bajio*

34 David Nicholls. *From Dessalines to Duvalier: Race, Colour and National Independence in Haiti*

35 Jonathan C. Brown. *A Socioeconomic History of Argentina, 1776–1860*

36 Marco Palacius. *Coffee in Columbia, 1850–1970: An Economic, Social and Political History*

37 David Murray. *Odious Commerce: Britain, Spain and the Abolition of the Cuban Slave Trade*

38 D. A. Brading. *Caudillo and Peasant in the Mexican Revolution*

39 Joe Foweraker. *The Struggle for Land: A Political Economy of the Pioneer Frontier in Brazil from 1930 to the Present Day*

40 George Philip. *Oil and Politics in Latin America: Nationalist Movements and State Companies*

41 Noble David Cook. *Demographic Collapse: Indian Peru, 1520–1620*

42 Gilbert Joseph. *Revolution from Without: Yucatan, and the United States, 1880–1924*

43 B. S. McBeth. *Juan Vicente Gomez and the Oil Companies in Venezuela, 1908–1935*

44 J. A. Offner. *Law and Politics in Aztec Texcoco*

45 Thomas J. Trebat. *Brazil's State-Owned Enterprises: A Case Study of the State as Entrepreneur*

46 James Lockhart and Stuart B. Schwartz. *Early Latin American: A History of Colonial Spanish America and Brazil*

47 Adolfo Figueroa. *Capitalist Development and the Peasant Economy in Peru*

48 Norman Long and Bryan Roberts. *Miners, Peasants and Entrepreneurs: Regional Development in the Central Highlands of Peru*

49 Ian Roxborough. *Unions and Politics in Mexico: The Case of the Automobile Industry*

50 Alan Gilbert and Peter Ward. *Housing, the State and the Poor: Policy and Practice in Three Latin American Cities*

51 Jean Stubbs. *Tobacco on the Periphery: A Case Study in Cuban Labour History, 1860–1958*

52 Stuart B. Schwartz. *Sugar Planatations in the Formation of Brazilian Society: Bahia, 1550–1835*

53 Richard J. Walter. *The Province of Buenos Aires and Argentine Politics, 1912–1945*

54 Alan Knight. *The Mexican Revolution, vol. 1: Porfirians, Liberals and Peasants*

55 Alan Knight. *The Mexican Revolution, vol. 2: Counter-revolution and Reconstruction*

56 P. Michael McKinley. *Pre-revolutionary Caracas: Politics, Economy and Society, 1777–1811*

57 Adriaan C. van Oss. *Catholic Colonialism: A Parish History of Guatemala, 1524–1821*

58 Leon Zamosc. *The Agrarian Question and the Peasant Movement in Colombia: Struggles of the National Peasant Association, 1967–1981*

59 Brian R. Hamnett. *Roots of Insurgency: Mexican Regions 1750–1824*

60 Manuel Caballero. *Latin America and the Comintern, 1919–1943*

61 Inga Clendinnen. *Ambivalent Conquests: Maya and Spaniard in Yucatan, 1517–1570*

62 Jeffrey D. Needell. *A Tropical Belle Epoque: Elite Culture and Society in Turn-of-the-century Rio de Janeiro*

6192